The Legacy of a Collector:
The **Panza** di Biumo Collection at The Museum of Contemporary Art, Los Angeles

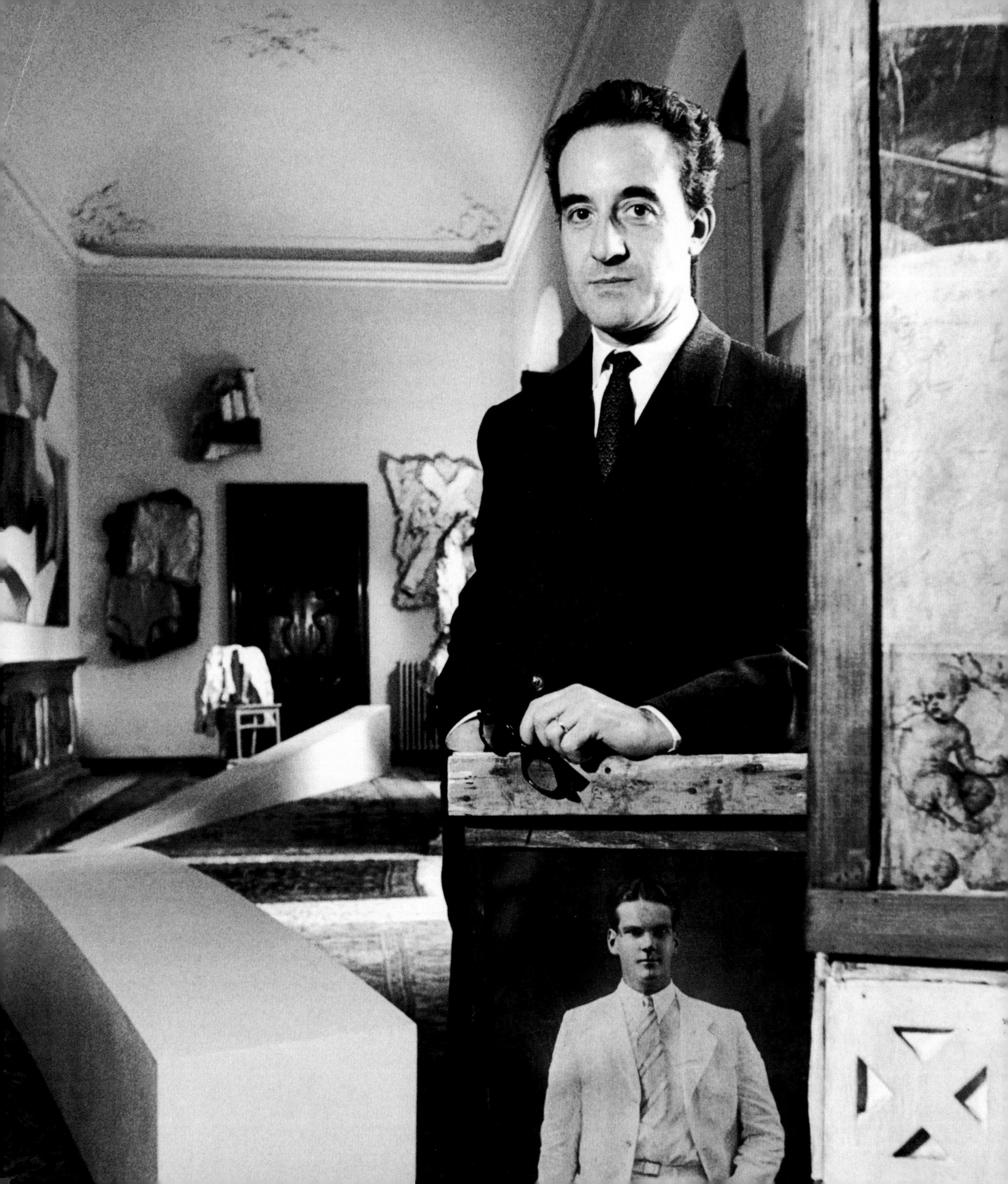

Panza

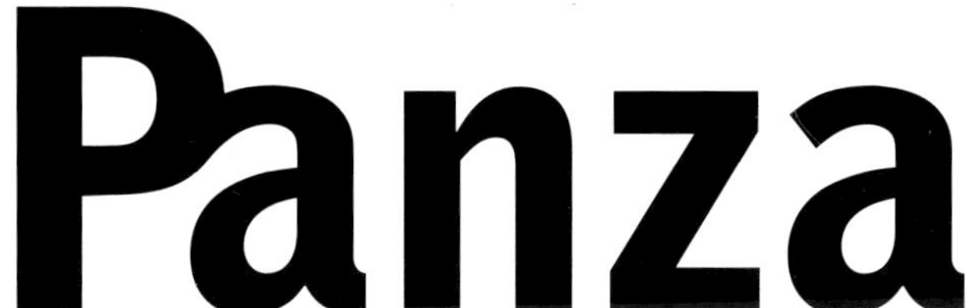

1943 TO 1969   1982 TO 1993

The Museum of Contemporary Art, Los Angeles

"Panza: The Legacy of a Collector" is made possible in part by generous support from Betye Monell Burton.

This publication accompanies the exhibition "Panza: The Legacy of a Collector" organized by Cornelia H. Butler and presented at The Museum of Contemporary Art, Los Angeles, December 12, 1999—April 30, 2000.

Editor: Stephanie Emerson
Assistant Editor: Jane Hyun
Publication Design: Tracey Shiffman
Assistant Designer: Hillary Sunenshine
Printer: Cantz, Ostfildern, Germany

Printed in Germany

Library of Congress Cataloging-in-Publication Data

Museum of Contemporary Art (Los Angeles, Calif.).Giuseppe Panza di Biumo Collection.
    Panza: the legacy of a collector: the Giuseppe Panza di Biumo
Collection at the Museum of Contemporary Art, Los Angeles / Cornelia H. Butler.
    p. cm.
    Catalog of an exhibition held at the Museum of Contemporary Art, Los Angeles, Dec. 12, 1999–Apr. 30, 2000.
    Includes bibliographical references.
    ISBN 0-914357-73-5 (alk. paper)
    1. Museum of Contemporary Art (Los Angeles, Calif.). Giuseppe Panza di Biumo Collection—Exhibitions. 2. Panza, Giuseppe—Art collections—Exhibitions. 3. Panza di Biumo, Giovanna—Art collections—Exhibitions. 4. Art, Modern—20th century—Exhibitions. I. Title.

N648.L67 M886 1999
709'.04'007479494—dc21

99-047687

frontispiece:
Giuseppe Panza di Biumo photographed
by Ugo Mulas with
Robert Rauschenberg's
Untitled (Man with White Shoes), 1955
at the Villa Menafoglio Litta Panza,
Varese, Italy, 1966

Foreword, Richard Koshalek — 7

Acknowledgments, Jeremy Strick — 8

The Panza Collection and Art in Los Angeles, Giuseppe Panza di Biumo — 11

Picturing the Collection, Cornelia H. Butler — 17

Coca-Cola Plan *or, How New York Stole the Soul of Giuseppe Panza,* Caroline A. Jones — 22

The Panza Collection, 1943–1969 — 50
Artist entries by Rebecca Morse and Jane Hyun

End of the Century Art: Production in Los Angeles, Kenneth Baker — 130

The Panza Gift, 1982–1993 — 140
Artist entries by Rebecca Morse

Selected Exhibition Chronologies and Bibliographies — 217

CONTENTS

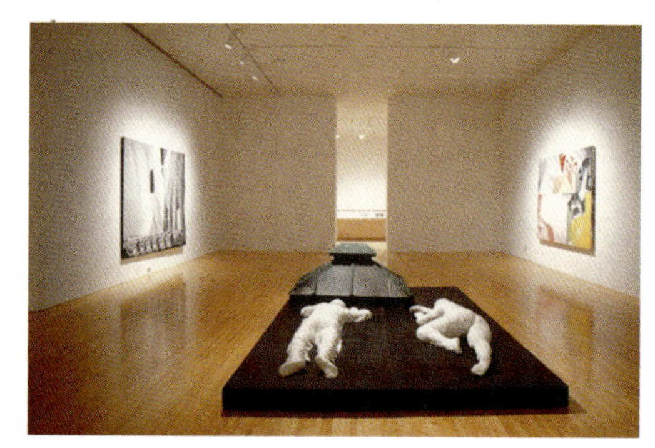
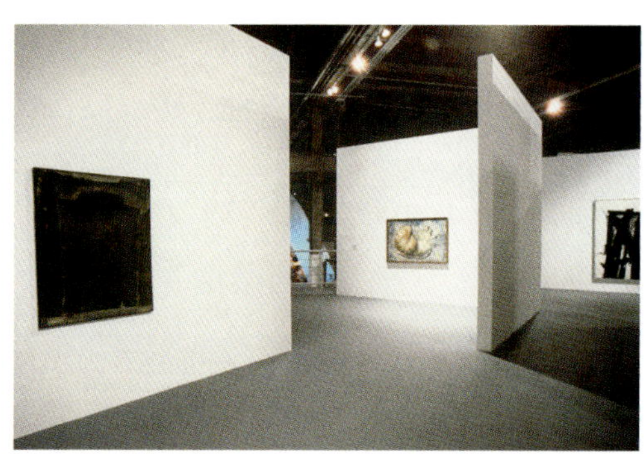
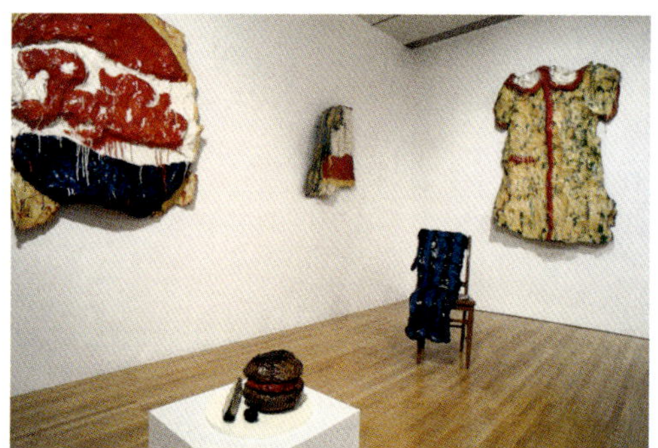
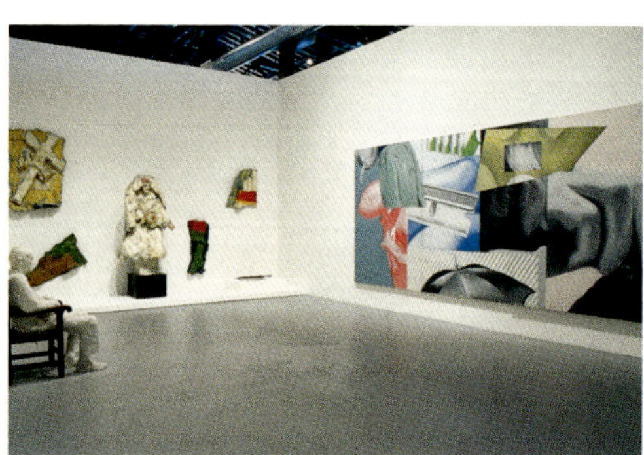
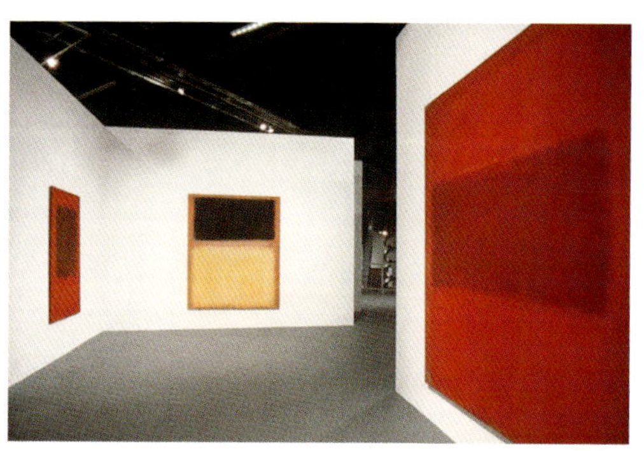

FOREWORD In 1984, the Museum's inaugural year and four years after Dr. Panza was elected to the Board of Trustees, the museum purchased eighty works from the collection of Dr. Giuseppe and Mrs. Giovanna Panza di Biumo of Milan, Italy. Hailed at the time as one of the world's most important acquisitions of contemporary art, this purchase became the core of MOCA's permanent collection, then consisting of approximately one hundred objects.

The artist Robert Irwin introduced Dr. Panza to MOCA. Panza had championed the work of California artists since his first visit to Los Angeles in 1973. From the beginning he collected environmental works by seminal figures such as Irwin and others, representing the history of Minimalism, Light and Space, and Conceptual art in his growing collection. Panza's leading patronage of Southern California art, which he has continued to the present with the artists represented in this exhibition, has greatly increased international awareness and appreciation of the region's rich art history. His support of California artists continues in the form of the recent gift to MOCA of seventy works collected during the eighties and early ninties by artists for whom he remains a committed patron.

I came to know Dr. and Mrs. Panza over the course of my tenure as Director at the Fort Worth Art Museum in Texas, and later as Director at MOCA, and value them both as thinkers in the world of contemporary art and as dear friends. Their wonderful family have all been part of the growth of this institution in one way or another, and most recently, it has been my pleasure to work with their daughter Giuseppina, who shares the Panzas' passion for contemporary art and is committed to her parents' legacy as collectors. Dr. and Mrs. Panza share a love of art, and their seemingly infinite desire to learn more about the art of our time is an inspiration. Their courage as early collectors of postwar American art is exemplary within our field. Most especially, the Panzas' commitment to the Museum from its inception has encouraged other collectors and benefactors to contribute valuable works to MOCA's collection and to support the ongoing evolution of one of the country's premier collections of contemporary art. I look forward to continued years of friendship.

Richard Koshalek, President, Art Center College of Design

Installation views of works
in the Panza Collection
at The Museum of Contemporary Art,
Los Angeles, 1988–1998

ACKNOWLEDGMENTS Since The Museum of Contemporary Art's inception, the acquisition of focused, international collections of contemporary art has been the driving force of the institution. As a relatively young museum, MOCA has been the beneficiary of extraordinary collections of postwar art. Certainly the works of painting and sculpture acquired from Count Giuseppe Panza and his wife Giovanna are among the most outstanding in the museum's collection. Spanning the periods 1943–1969 in Europe and America, and 1982–1993 in California, the works in the exhibition illustrate major international and regional tendencies in postwar art as well as Dr. Panza's unique sensibility which has always existed outside of the trends of the art market.

The Panza Collection is characterized by its commitment in depth to nine of the most highly regarded artists of the postwar period who are now represented in MOCA's collection by works from a key period within their careers. Most of the works by Mark Rothko, Franz Kline, Robert Rauschenberg, Roy Lichtenstein, James Rosenquist, Jean Fautrier, Antonio Tàpies, Claes Oldenburg, and George Segal, were acquired by Panza shortly after their creation, often from visits to the artists' studios and through ongoing relationships with internationally regarded critics and curators. The Collection represents the first of several historically significant collections amassed by the Panzas.

Their deeply felt passion for the creative process and the relationship with work gained through the intimate experience in the artist's studio is something that has continued as Dr. and Mrs. Panza have collected the work of more recently emerging contemporary artists. Their passion for the work they have collected is legendary and is reflected in the care and interpretation they bring to each installation. In 1994, MOCA was the beneficiary of another astounding acquisition—the gift of seventy works by ten Los Angeles-based artists. Lawrence Carroll, Jeff Colson, Greg Colson, Ron Griffin, Mark Lere, Gregory Mahoney, Ross Rudel, Peter Shelton, Robert Therrien, and Roy Thurston are among the most significant figures to emerge in California during the last decade. Lere and Therrien received exhibitions at MOCA early in their careers and early in the history of the Museum.

It is my great pleasure to acknowledge the many members of MOCA's staff and Board of Trustees whose foresight and commitment to this important project throughout the museum's history have contributed to a milestone for the institution. I can think of no more distinguished an occasion to honor the museum's twentieth-anniversary year than the exhibition, in its entirety, of the remarkable Panza Collection at MOCA.

Five years in the making, this ambitious exhibition would not have been possible without the leadership and commitment of a few individuals. First I would like to acknowledge my predecessor, Richard Koshalek, who built MOCA's impressive permanent collection based on the foundation of such important and early acquisitions as the Panza Collection. It is a tribute to Richard's close relationship to the art of our time and his ability to recognize the achievement of great collectors like Dr. and Mrs. Panza, that MOCA's collection is internationally regarded and has been able to attract other such significant gifts over the years.

Former Curator Kerry Brougher, now Director of the Museum of Modern Art in Oxford, England, initiated the project and saw it through its early stages. He worked closely with Curator of Special Exhibitions Julia Brown and Curatorial Assistant Susan Cross of the Solomon R. Guggenheim Museum when a collaboration bringing together the holdings of both great institutions was discussed. Kerry and Julia's personal relationships with Dr. Panza and his collection made the first years of planning productive and fruitful. Assistant Director Kathleen S. Bartels and Chief Curator Paul Schimmel shepherded the gift of the California works to MOCA's collection and were instrumental in facilitating this important exhibition. Associate Curator Connie Butler coordinated the exhibition and worked closely with Dr. Panza to realize the exhibition and its publication. Exhibitions Production Manager John Bowsher collaborated with Dr. Panza to design and realize the beautiful and sensitive installation. This publication which accompanies the exhibition would not have been possible without Senior Editor Stephanie Emerson, who expertly oversaw all aspects of the catalogue. Assistant Editor Jane Hyun efficiently contributed to all stages of the catalogue and wrote a number of the individual artists' entries.

We are grateful to essayists Caroline A. Jones and Kenneth Baker whose insightful texts make an important contribution to scholarship in the field of postwar art. For their invaluable research assistance we gratefully acknowledge Charles Merewether and Lynda Bunting at The Getty Research Institute. We also thank the Ugo Mulas Foundation for allowing us to reproduce several of the late photographer's images. Tracey Shiffman, as always, created a sensitive and handsome design for this publication and was a pleasure to work with. Our deepest gratitude and respect is also extended to Mrs. Giuseppina Caccia Dominioni, whose assistance on this project was crucial. We also thank Ace Gallery, Angles Gallery, Griffin Fine Art, Hosfelt Gallery, L.A. Louver, Maureen Mahoney, and Pace Wildenstein for their assistance.

Other members of MOCA's dedicated staff who contributed in invaluable and myriad ways to this project include Curatorial Secretary Rebecca Morse, who provided critical administrative assistance at all stages of the project and authored many of the catalogue entries and compiled much of the bibliographic material. First as Kerry Brougher's assistant and now as Exhibitions Coordinator, Stacia Payne has provided crucial administrative support for the exhibition and has been committed to its successful realization. Assistant Registrar Liz Bradley and Chief Exhibition Technician Jang Park oversaw the installation and handling of these valuable works.

MOCA's respected exhibition program is supported by the generosity of the Trustees of The Museum of Contemporary Art. I extend particular thanks to Audrey M. Irmas as Chairman and Gilbert B. Friesen as President, as well as Vice Chairs Ruth Bloom, Robert C. Davidson, Jr., and Clifford J. Einstein for their dedication to the museum. We also give special thanks to Lenore S. Greenberg whose commitment and leadership as Program Liaison to the Board of Trustees is longstanding and exemplary. I am grateful to Betye Burton for her generous support of the exhibition. It is because of the vision of MOCA's Trustees and the commitment of resources that the acquisition of The Panza Collection, and the later acquisition of The Panza Gift were possible.

Finally, I extend my deepest admiration and thanks to Dr. Giuseppe and Mrs. Giovanna Panza and the wonderful artists whose work they have championed. The Panza's contribution as great patrons of late twentieth-century art is unparalleled, and we are grateful that, because of their foresight and generosity, MOCA's galleries are now the proud home of a seminal collection of contemporary art.

Jeremy Strick, Director, The Museum of Contemporary Art, Los Angeles

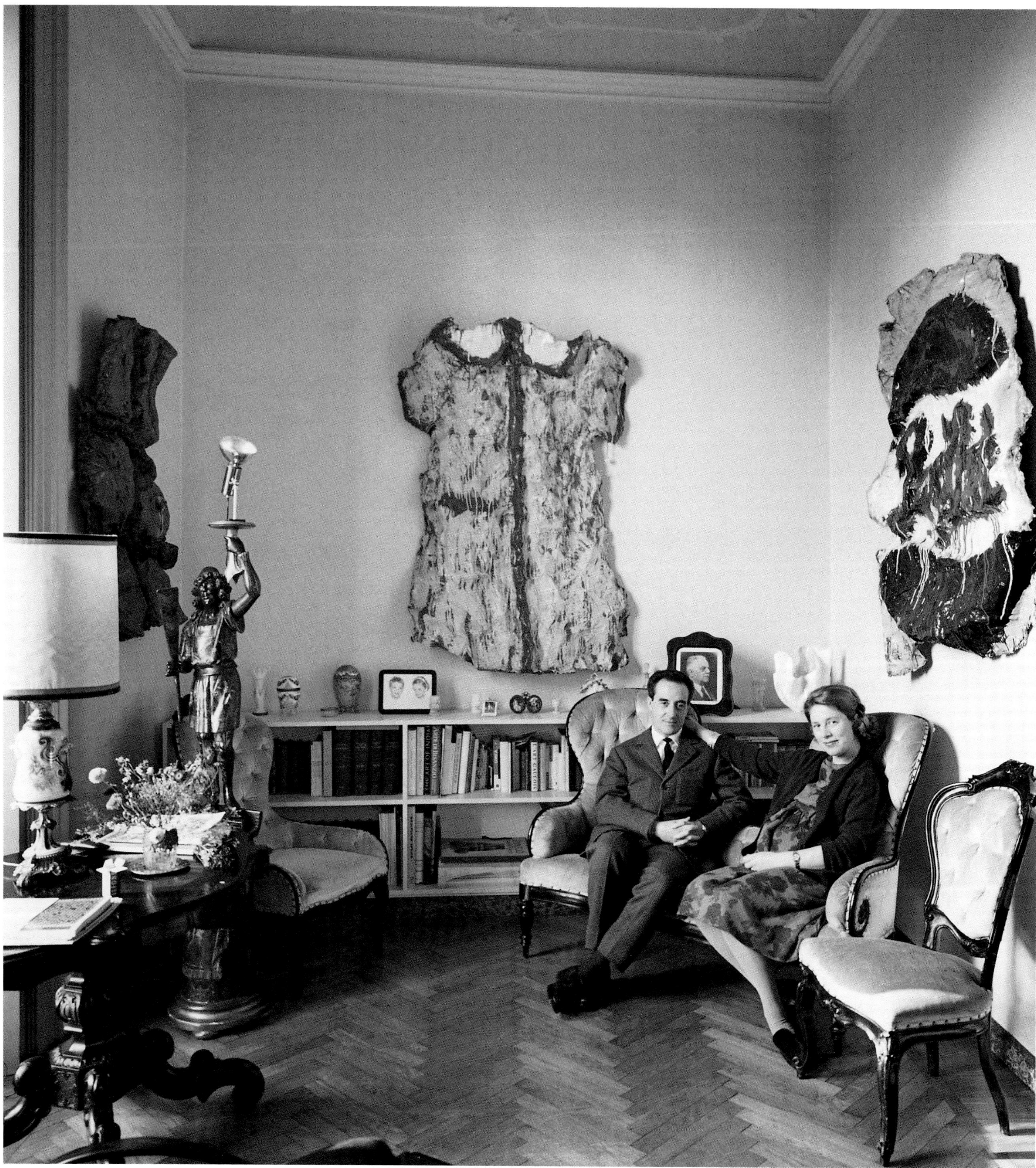

THE PANZA COLLECTION AND ART IN LOS ANGELES

by Giuseppe Panza di Biumo *Translated by Murtha Baca*

The Panza Collection, begun in 1956 and still evolving today, sheds light on many events of the second half of the twentieth century. The collection is composed of three parts, for a total of some 2,500 works of art. The first part of the collection is made up of eighty works acquired between 1956 and 1962, all of which are at MOCA. The second part is made up of works of Minimal, Conceptual, and Environmental art, most of which now belong to the Solomon R. Guggenheim Museum of Art. The third part is made up of art purchased between 1987 and 1999; this is the largest part of the collection, built up during a particularly favorable period.

During this period, the interest of the public—and of the media—focused on a dominant trend that followed the prejudices of a postmodern way of thinking. In reality it would be more accurate to define this trend as "anti-modern," since it rejected all of the values of modernism that made this century a great one artistically. This trend marginalized the best artists who did not share the philosophy of rejection; their vision of life was different. Contrary to popular belief, the last twenty-five years have been particularly rich in original artistic personalities—indeed, probably superior to preceding periods. But the public did not realize this, believing that they were following an art that was new because it was different from Minimal art and Conceptual art. We marvel at the fact that van Gogh died at the age of thirty-seven without ever having sold a painting, but this is a phenomenon that still occurs today. We think that the society and culture of our time are very liberal in their judgments, and that things that are different are accepted, but this isn't really the case. Things that are different are not always rejected—something worse happens: they aren't even seen, because people lack the mental preparation to see them. People understand and value what they want to understand and see; otherwise, they look without seeing. Unfortunately, consciousness-raising takes time; we can't foretell when it will occur. I have always purchased art that was rejected, derided, and even ignored, but thirty years later entered museums. Good ideas are assimilated slowly.

Dr. Giuseppe and Mrs. Giovanna Panza
photographed by Ugo Mulas
at the Villa Menafoglio Litta Panza,
Varese, Italy, 1966

I am immensely grateful to the staff and Board of Trustees of MOCA, and particularly to former Trustee president Eli Broad, who in 1984 decided to purchase the first part of my collection—with works by Fautrier, Tàpies, Kline, Rothko, Rauschenberg, Lichtenstein, Rosenquist, Oldenburg, and Segal. Today the total price that MOCA paid in 1984 for those eighty pictures would pay for two Rothkos. At the time of the MOCA purchase, my wife and I turned down several more lucrative cash offers. We wanted the collection to be in a museum, and that museum was MOCA, where I had been a trustee since the time of its founding. Someone who truly loves art is concerned about its future. Someone who believes he has made choices that represent ideal, lasting values of a certain historical period wants to prevent their dispersion, and is anguished at the thought of that possibility. For someone who loves art, avoiding that danger is a necessity, even at the cost of a financial sacrifice. The ultimate objective is to participate in one of the greatest gifts that life can offer: beauty. To see works that had been ignored, disdained, and rejected become part of the common cultural patrimony after many years is the dream of every good collector.

In forty-four years of activity and continual growth, the Panza Collection has arrived at a total of around 2,500 works of art. A considerable number of these works are now in museums, including the 150 at MOCA (we donated seventy works to MOCA, and sold eighty). Three hundred-fifty works from the 1960s and 1970s went to the Guggenheim, 150 of which we donated; these works represent Minimal art, Conceptual art, and Environmental art by Southern California artists. Other works are on long-term loan. We have donated our home in Biumo in the province of Varese in Lombardy, which contains 132 works of art, twenty-three African sculptures, and 300 decorative arts pieces from the fifteenth to the mid-nineteenth century, to the F.A.I. (Fondo per l'Ambiente Italiano). The works of art in our home date from the 1960s, '70s, '80s, and '90s. It will open to the public as a museum in the spring of 2000, occupying about 50,000 square feet. We donated 200 works of art from the 1980s and 1990s to the Museo Cantonale d'Arte in Lugano, Switzerland, in anticipation of a major enlargement of the building, which is currently quite small. Fifty works from the 1980s and 1990s are on long-term loan to the Ducal Palace in the Umbrian town of Gubbio; this *palazzo,* built in 1476, is a masterpiece of the Italian Renaissance. Seventy works from the same period will be loaned for a period of several years to the new museum in Rovereto on the Adige River in the Tridentine Alps designed by architect Mario Botta, which will open to the public at the end of 2001. We have had requests from other museums, and I hope that in the future a large part of the available works in our collections can be exhibited to the public in a permanent way.

When we began collecting in 1956, my wife and I were among the first European collectors to discover American art, and certainly the first with a deep commitment to a new kind of art—new even to Americans, it seemed, and not yet comparable to the art being created in Paris during the same period. Before many others did, we discovered the great contribution made to world culture by the United States during the second half of the twentieth century.

Since the late 1960s, the Panza Collection has been strongly committed to art created in Los Angeles; about half of the artists whose works I purchased after that time came from Southern California. This proportion remained unchanged during the 1980s and 1990s as well, with the addition of works by a few artists from Northern California. The first Southern California artists in the Collection, whose works I purchased in 1968, were Larry Bell and Robert Irwin, both of whom represented a dramatic shift in the way that art was conceived: the discovery of light. In their work, art becomes "de-materialized" in order to express a reality hidden within our consciousness, capable of an instinctive relationship with something essential and primordial. This was the culmination of an evolution that began 500 years ago with the Italian Renaissance, when the search began for the most effective way to render light on the flat surface of a painting. Light is life, it is vision, it is knowledge; it is a beautiful gift given to us by Nature. Our days differ depending upon whether they are filled with light, or deprived of it. One of the hallmarks of great artists, from da Vinci to Caravaggio to Vermeer to the Impressionists, is their depiction of light.

This shift in the way that art was conceived—when light, along with space, became the fundamental element of artistic representation—was bound to happen in Los Angeles due to a series of favorable circumstances. During the 1960s, Minimalist and Conceptual art in New York had opened the door with the works of Dan Flavin, who used artificial light from a mass-produced product to express all of our emotions and instincts through color. To get to Los Angeles on the other side of the continent, you have to cross the deserts of the Far West where light, in all of its beauty and splendor, is the dominant element. One discovers a new vision of the world and a different dimension of life. Time stands still, and there appears an immutable, unattainable, yet at the same time totally present, sense of reality. Los Angeles is just the opposite of the desert—everything is in motion, nothing stands still. We don't know how long anything we see will last—it has no past to give it certainty. This situation can provoke an acute sense of instability. When the wind from the desert blows away the smog, the light in Los Angeles is beautiful as in no other city. This is the situation that some artists wished to express. Fifty years from now, when the true history of the art of this century is written, we shall see that the art of light created in Los Angeles between 1965 and 1975 was one of the most important artistic developments of the twentieth century—a culminating moment in the long evolution of art over the centuries. Ignorance, and the difficulty that audiences had in understanding their best works, discouraged many of these artists, who were forced to stop working because of lack of interest on the part of institutions. Eric Orr, one of the best of this group of artists, died recently without ever having an exhibition that showed his work in any breadth.

Starting in 1987, my wife and I again began actively collecting art by the recent generation of Los Angeles artists. This city always offers new creativity to anyone who approaches it without preconceived notions; this is how authentic new trends are discovered. Unfortunately, they usually receive a tepid welcome. This is an art that develops in the shadows, supported by a handful of galleries and collectors. The fate of the best of these artists is that they are understood only after many years. When I was collecting Tàpies, Kline, Rothko, Rauschenberg, Oldenburg, and Lichtenstein, I could choose the best pictures at modest prices because I had no competition; I was almost alone in my enthusiasm for the work of these artists. A similar situation is recurring today, as artists whom I reject because they are alien to my idea of what art is, but above all because they represent a way of living and thinking contrary to my own, have enjoyed great success.

Having purchased many works by several Southern California artists working after 1987, I felt it would be good for MOCA to have some examples of the works my wife and I had acquired. I saw this as a complement to the works from the Panza Collection that MOCA has had in its possession for a decade and a half, but in which the art of Los Angeles was not represented. So I decided to donate seven works each by ten artists in order to give a good idea of their work. Since I made this selection in 1995, some important artists were left out, including Patricia Moisan, Linda Stark, Carter Potter, and several others whom I would have liked to include—also other West Coast artists, such as David Simpson, Ann Appleby, and Peter Wegner. Strangely enough, it wasn't easy for me to donate these seventy works. I owe the fact that the obstacles were overcome to the support of an influential trustee, Fred Nicholas, with the help of MOCA's then-director Richard Koshalek and Chief Curator Paul Schimmel.

The third part of the Panza Collection, which contains the seventy works we donated to MOCA, includes works by artists of the generation following the Minimalists and the Conceptual artists. Every artistic period evolves from a point of departure in the preceding period, at times following a completely different line of experimentation, or else inserting new experiences upon the foundation of preceding ones. Of the ten artists whose works I donated to MOCA, only two share affinities with Minimalism: Roy Thurston and Mark Lere. Peter Shelton and Ross Rudel instead experiment with organic forms reminiscent of the shapes of living bodies, constructed from nature on the basis of a functionality dictated by laws that differ from those of human logic; this was an interesting new trend begun by a great African-American sculptor, Martin Puryear. Lawrence Carroll also developed a body of work very different from Minimalism: an idealization of the realities of life in its simplest, most humble, most real aspects, which has an affinity with Rauschenberg's experiments, though the results are quite different. Gregory Mahoney uses rusted sheet metal that has undergone the ravages of natural events in Death Valley; time has transformed a manufactured material into an element of nature. Mahoney's work revisits the phenomenon of the existence of all things within a life of which we know neither the beginning nor the end. Ron Griffin transforms into art such humble objects as writing paper, envelopes, and crushed cigarette boxes—the little universe of our daily life, which we use up and discard without considering the possibility of a hidden aesthetic quality. In Griffin's work, generally disregarded objects are invested with artistic dignity; he re-crafts them with tiny, almost imperceptible modifications. This is an operation similar to Lichtenstein's, which was related to American social life during the years of the economic boom. If the subject of Pop art was society, the subject of Griffin's art is the humble objects all around us. With loving care, Griffin re-fashions small, mass-produced objects so that they are almost identical to their original form, magically transforming paper into art. This is very different from the work of Oldenburg, who re-created ordinary objects in order to exalt their dignity, adding a human personality to neutral things; Oldenburg's colors are strong, bright—very different from an object's true colors. Griffin, instead, respects the true nature of objects; he simply makes their invisible qualities shine.

Robert Therrien utilizes forms that are rich in allusions and metaphors for fundamental aspects of our existence. In an almost unidentifiable way, he transforms objects, constructing a series of allusions to their possible meanings. These can be the keystone of the arch that supports the thrust of two opposing forces, or the round shapes of a snowman from our childhood, souvenir of a distant, happy past, or even the shape of the coffin where our bodies will lie for the last time, the inevitability of the end. The past, hope, death—these are the subjects of Therrien's art, in which the eternal themes that accompany our existence, divested of all descriptive realism, assume a universal significance.

The brothers Greg and Jeff Colson are an interesting example of two different artistic conceptions. Greg Colson is concerned with a relationship to reality—basic, apparently very simple questions that can be answered in an intuitive way. Experience teaches us how to solve the inevitable problems with which reality presents us. If we analyze what knowledge consists of, many doubts arise; it is an occurrence that logic can only partly explain. Intuition—an undefinable entity—resolves it. Greg Colson dismantles this operation in order to reconstruct it. Jeff Colson goes beyond the relationship with reality. In his works, images are the projection of a condition of the psyche; they depart from within the artist's consciousness.

Mark Lere and Roy Thurston are two artists who have some relationship with the Minimalist experience. Minimalism is based on the "Less is more" principle. This idea was developed during the 1960s by several New York artists, but it has always existed; indeed, prehistoric Chinese and Egyptian art apply this very same principle. The most intensely expressive art is an art that uses the maximum economy of forms to obtain the maximum emotional intensity and richness of context. This is the most difficult art; it doesn't allow for errors or approximations. It cannot use narrative or decoration to conceal its own defects and limitations.

The work of Mark Lere is at the crossroads of the quest for minimalism and an exploration of the possibilities of an organic art that creates forms with affinities to the processes that shape living beings, the possibility of developing forms that can contain "consciousness" in an increasingly evolved way. Roy Thurston's work is at the outer limit of this reduction to the minimum. Thurston draws parallel lines with a steel instrument to incise a surface covered with lacquer, usually in a dark color. This is a way of expressing oneself that eliminates improvisation and facile emotionalism. It requires inner discipline, control of one's own will in order to direct one's emotions and instincts toward a higher goal, a goal worth making sacrifices for.

The quest for a higher goal: this is an essential activity for human beings. Nature predestined us to carry out the cultural evolution that has enabled us to no longer be apes, but men. This is our most substantial, most profound instinct. The almost anguished desire to look up rather than down, to never be satisfied with having attained one's goal, to keep striving for a higher goal—a goal that is not possession of things or domination of other people, or the desire for power, but rather the quest for greater values within our own consciences. This is just the opposite of the cultural situation that has dominated the art world for some time, and that has great public success. The dominant cultural world no longer cares about the evolution of art; the call to a destiny richer in new experiences has been silenced.

The fifties were heroic times, when American art rocked the foundations of Europe's centuries-long supremacy. Art needed to build a new world with new ideas after the moral and material destruction of World War II: America was an example of how civic values could be real. The new generation of American artists represented in MOCA's collection has very different ideals from those of the heroes of the fifties, such as Rothko, Rauschenberg, etc.—ideals that are part of the consciousness of each, not manifested in dramatic gestures. They surrender themselves to the theater of the world; their life experience is personal, private. They must be carefully pondered to be understood. Certainly, there is a risk of seeming too humble and modest with regard to the great artists who conquered the world many years ago. But this is precisely the task of a good collector: to call attention to artists who haven't yet become part of history, who don't yet enjoy the privileges of success. Forty years ago, paintings by artists whose works are worth millions of dollars today didn't cost much because they not only failed to capture the attention of the general public but also failed to attract the interest of art professionals who had been trained in the European tradition to admire artists who were already famous.

The artists of the 1980s and 1990s should be compared with their own contemporaries, artists who were active and successful during the same years. Such a comparison will make it evident that there are radical differences not only in terms of form, but also in something much more important: the artists' conception of life, of what values are worth believing in, what goals to pursue—knowing that each one of us is called by our own conscience to do whatever good we can, whether big or small. These artists are not disillusioned; they aren't pessimists. They believe in the future because they believe that small contributions are more important than large ones.

In the unforeseeable but not too distant future, there will be a radical reversal. The predominant trends of a period that lasts for many years are never permanent; change will come. This is an absolutely natural phenomenon, necessary for renewal to occur. When a trend lasts too long, it provokes a visual tiredness that requires a change of image. But art is not subject to this necessity. Only artists who have solid roots will be able to overcome a process of selection that does not respect fleeting fame. Change will not occur in an obtrusive way, but silently, almost without anyone realizing. We will see the prices quoted from Sotheby's and Christie's slowly change, and many artists' names will simply disappear.

Showing these works from our collection, now housed at MOCA, in Isozaki's building has also been a wonderful opportunity to create a setting in which they can be seen under the best conditions. The contribution of the architecture is a determining factor. The installation of the exhibition was carried out with several basic principles in mind: to not mix different artists; to not place too many works of art in one room; to place the most striking works at points where museum visitors will see them first. These are important requisites for a good installation. Obviously, the most important thing is good quality; otherwise, the role of the museum fails. A museum shouldn't simply be an art warehouse open to the public, but rather a place where we have a new experience, where we enter a different dimension, where the highest values of the human condition can and should be experienced. The art museum takes the place of the cathedral in this sense. In old Europe, cathedrals represented the values that the community could offer to all. Today this role falls to museums. I believe that my wife and I have made a contribution toward the realization of this goal. These are works of art with which we have had an intense bond; we have a relationship with them that has never disappointed us in all these years. I hope that it can be this way for many others as well.

Rothko, Kline, and Fautrier died years ago, and Lichtenstein died in 1997. Thus the first part of our collection has also taken on the role of making artists who are no longer living present through their works. Art gives a partial form of immortality to those who practice it with total dedication, which was certainly the case for these artists, whom I had the good fortune to know and admire before they became famous. I am glad that MOCA has given me the opportunity to see their great work again. I am certain that in the future their presence will be increasingly important for the museum.

MOCA came into existence in 1980, with Pontus Hulten as Director and Richard Koshalek as Deputy Director. That was a period of great enthusiasm and great hope. Twenty years later, expectations have become reality; trails have been blazed in a young city where everything was yet to be done, especially in the world of art. Twenty years is both a long time and a short time. The goal that then seemed so lofty now seems unexceptional in a world where new museums open almost every year. Los Angeles is the second largest city in America, and one of the most famous cities in the world. It's likely that in the near future it will be deemed necessary for MOCA to take another leap forward with a building befitting a big city in a state of expansion. Far less important cities have achieved great things. Richard Koshalek's leadership brought MOCA to a high level of prestige, efficiency, and quality, and with the help of an excellent staff, he has left his mark on the institution.

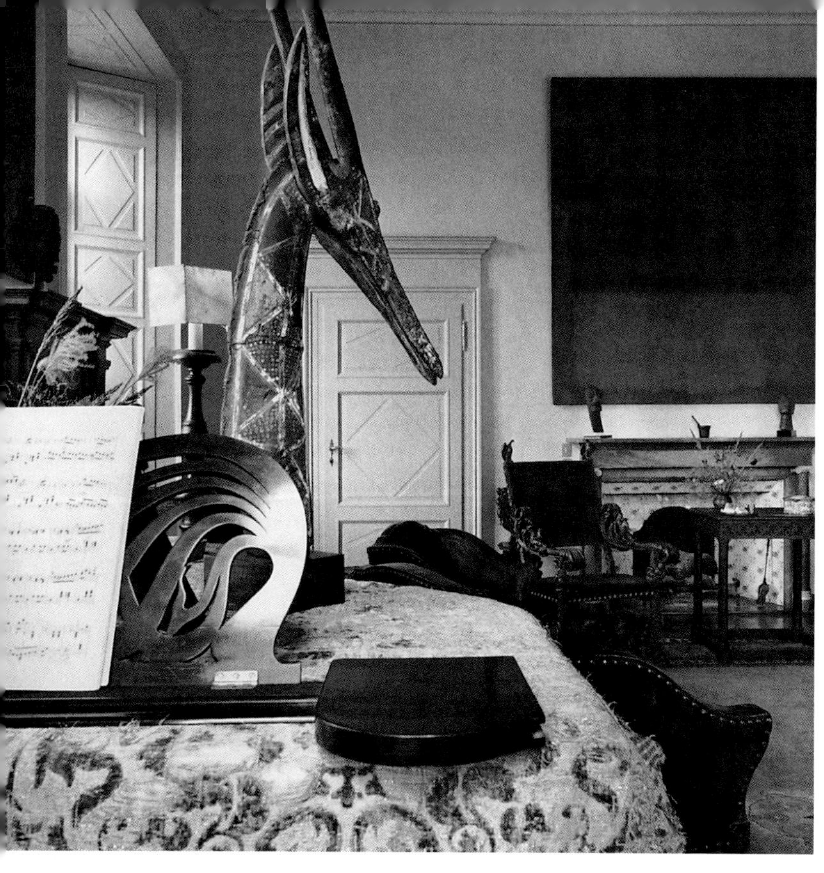

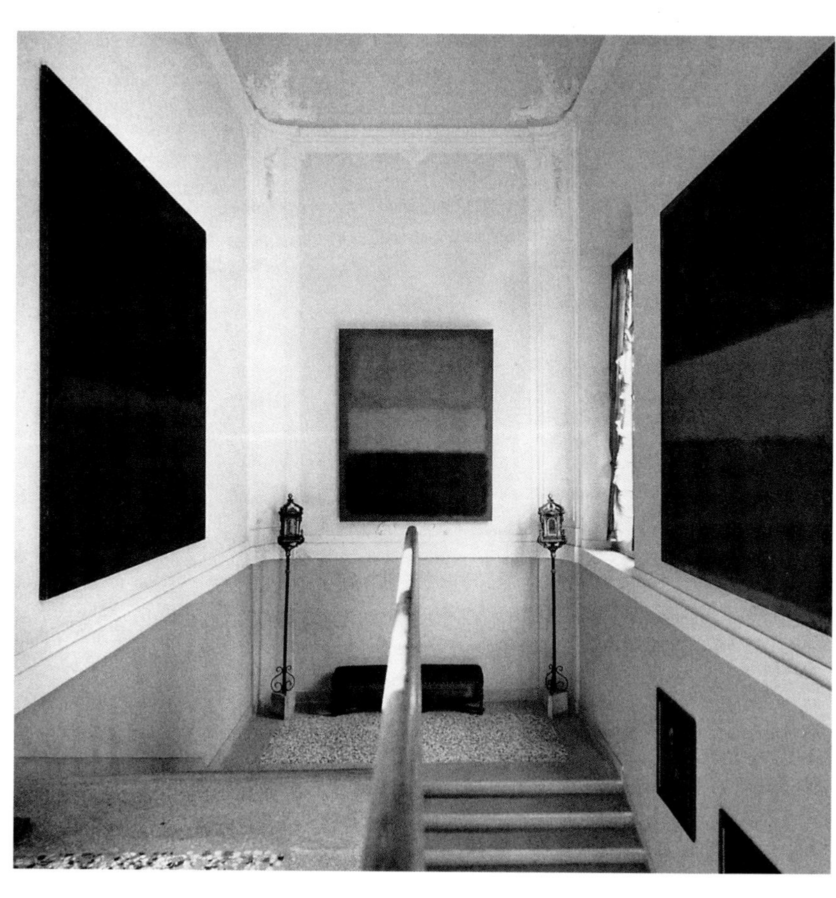

PICTURING THE COLLECTION

by Cornelia H. Butler

One cannot know everything about the world, but one can at least approach closed knowledge through the collection.[1]
Susan Stewart

Little has been written late in our century about the compulsion to collect art. While the mainstream media is fascinated by the ego and accumulation—the titillating combination of wealth, timing and chutzpah common to all good collectors—in our star-driven culture, the collector becomes a kind of enigmatic nomad. He or she seeks from (and projects upon) the art and, more rarely, the contact with artists, a spiritual or ethical reassurance: the authentic experience, truth, some reckless take on contemporary culture exclusively channeled by someone with special vision. What makes a person become interested in a work of art or career? Aside from the fascination of the chase and the seduction of discovery—both fraught with the power of economic exchange—is a strong and, I believe, innate belief in contemporary art and the spirit of experimentation. The desire to be around contemporary art is not learned but rather stumbled upon. Many of us were artists early in life and found our way to the curious activities of collecting or curating as if finding our way back to something, nurturing the conviction that participating in the presentation or collection of art is the next best thing to making it. Though a belief in the transformative power of art is problematic, there is something to the blind faith in ideas, artists, and, by extension, their residual objects. In fact, for curators, collectors, and critics, contemporary art provides a way of moving through the world, of mediating and processing the information of our time. In her recent study, Susan Stewart articulates the logic of the collection:

> To ask which principles of organization are used in articulating the collection is to begin to discern what the collection is about. . . . To arrange the objects according to time is to juxtapose personal

Interior views of the Villa Menafoglio
Litta Panza, Varese, Italy
photographed by Ugo Mulas, 1966

"

time with social time, autobiography with history, and thus to create a fiction of the individual life, a time of the individual subject both transcendent to and parallel to historical time…The collection is not constructed by its elements; rather, it comes to exist by means of its principle of organization.[2]

The liminal space comprising complex notions of the familiar and the exotic, of home and away, is brought to bear on each viewing experience. The kind of travel and probing, both geographic and philosophical, that is required to understand the complex matrix of contemporary visual production is informed by this virtual space which is occupied in the mind and life of the collector by the practice of art. Dr. and Mrs. Panza di Biumo experience art in this way. They are equally at home in the equivalent spaces of the artists' studio or a crater sculpted from the earth by the artist James Turrell, whose site-specific works they have long supported. They describe coming to New York and being struck by the peculiarly American vigor of the New York School and the transcendent intensity of paintings by Mark Rothko. They have always been most comfortable in a terrain mapped out by the artists they support and the work that interests them rather than following the idiosyncrasies of a particular market.

Based on early experiences collecting cultural material as diverse as African objects, Turkish rugs, eighteenth- and nineteenth-century Italian furniture, and living in an eighteenth-century Italian villa, the Panzas began to collect works of postwar European and American art in 1956. In a remarkable series of photographs taken in 1966 for a *Vogue* spread by the Italian fashion photographer Ugo Mulas, one of the most immediately striking things is the texture and intertextuality of the objects inhabiting the domestic realm. Dr. Panza often speaks of what he sees as the continuum of history and the evolution of art—the very un-postmodern, now unfashionably linear view of history that assimilates Western thought and art into one ascending stream of consciousness punctuated by bursts of insight. In this vision one can understand the light environments of Robert Irwin, collected by Panza in the 1970s for example, by invoking the light-filled, crystalline paintings of Vermeer. Or, more acrobatically, one can understand the resonance in a work of African tribal art by looking at the body-based works of a sculptor like Peter Shelton, whose patinated forms reconstitute an archive of the body which is as primitive as it is pop.

In the Mulas photographs, the arrangement of objects within each picture is remarkably abstract: African mask looming over *Man with White Shoes*, collapsed into *Vestigial Appendage*. Time is represented in a particularly collapsed and crystalline way. Again, according to Stewart, "The collection does not displace attention to the past; rather, the past is at the service of the collection… In the collection, time is not something to be restored to an origin; rather, all time is made simultaneous or synchronous within the collection's world."[3] Objects are truncated and the space is a flat collage of imagery. The curiously low camera angle in some of the most vertiginous pictures forces perspective in such a way that the objects of "high art" hover above eye level or are radically foregrounded.

If these serene pictures can be read as the Panza collection writ whole, as a tapestry of objects describing a coherent sensibility, one of the most striking things in formal terms is the aggressive tactility and visuality of the things in question—the hard, dark wood of the African works, the thick, luxurious carpet, the scrappy, enticing dimensionality of the Rauschenbergs, the bold verticals of the Klines, the bulky, monochromatic geometry of the Morris sculptures. There is sheer joy and indulgence in how these works have been arranged. What the Panzas have made over time is a living environment where engaging works activate the space in which they are carefully situated, and are acted upon by the surrounding cultural material. Indeed the Panzas began to understand the very architecture of their home as part of the support for the collection, inviting Sol LeWitt to make wall drawings in the stairwell and transforming the horse stables into installation spaces. One imagines what it must have been like to grow up scooting along the Robert Morris on the Turkish carpet, or playing hide-and-seek around the Combines. The brazen simplicity of Nauman's early spatial experiments must have been a wonderland for the imagination of children wandering through the former horse stables. The narrative created by these objects inhabiting the domestic realm is absolutely personal and generative.

In the early 1960s, collectors in the United States began fashioning their homes after the example of popular magazine spreads. As early as 1951, the Cecil Beaton photographs for *Vogue* of fashion models posed in front of Jackson Pollock paintings in the Betty Parsons Gallery, dressed in appropriately dramatic garb, glamorized the myth of American action painting. Hans Namuth's 1950–51 photographs of Pollock and Lee Krasner in their Long

Island studios helped construct and feed the image of the brash American artist and the liberated creative act *in situ*. In 1961, *ARTnews* magazine photographed the art collector Ben Heller's living room with Pollock's *Blue Poles* anchoring the center of the domestic realm and flanked by two unidentified African wood figures. In her illuminating study *A Taste for Pop: Pop Art, Gender, and Consumer Culture*, Cecile Whiting writes extensively about the fluid relationship between Pop art's appropriation of the domestic, feminized realm, and the way the image of the collector in popular fashion and journalistic photography was modeled after Pop art's domestic appropriations.[4] She also describes a raucous enthusiasm on the part of American collectors interested in participating in the send-up of consumer culture by allowing a certain playfulness in the public images of them in relationship to their collections. Panza would have encountered all these images as he gleaned his early information about American art from the magazines, fashion, and otherwise. While Dr. and Mrs. Panza have always maintained a high degree of modesty in relationship to the collection, and have not generally been influenced by other collectors, there is no question that they were aware of the image-making Americans and how works of art functioned in the domestic realm. What is noteworthy about the Mulas photographs is that they are virtually absent of the Panzas, with the exception of a very few touchingly arranged portraits reproduced elsewhere in this volume. The subject is the collection itself as a discreet amalgam of objects.

Claes Oldenburg's *The Store* (1961), which Panza saw in New York and from which he later purchased sixteen "painting objects,"[5] is an ingenious example of a staged confusion of consumer culture and the market for art. From the photographs of the original installation, one can glean an aesthetic of installation that influenced Panza in considering his own objects at home. Oldenburg specifically avoided museification, not only by managing the store himself—a kind of ongoing, interactive performance in which he also made objects in the back room to replace those that had sold—but also by controlling how the works were installed. As a direct critique of taste manuals and the rules of window dressing, he took great care to randomize the mix of things in the storefront to reflect the non-hierarchical arrangement of goods sold in the down-market, neighborhood shops. Over time, and with the taming of Pop art that has come with its historicization, these seminal, early works have lost some of their performative quality. But it is the spirit of Oldenburg's dense and grungy storefront installation that is traceable to the Panza's serene villa, chock-a-block with art. The Panza's clearly were struck early on by the liberated, non-hierarchical arrangement and the contingency of meanings.

Panza has on many occasions expressed his admiration for the spirit of American art at this time. The existential materiality which appealed to him in the bleak, postwar paintings of Tàpies and Fautrier, is transformed in the roughly hewn objects of Oldenburg's *Store*, George Segal's cast figures and, most physically, in Rauschenberg's "Combines." The energy of the fractured surfaces and spatial dimensions—which might be said to characterize all of the works the Panzas have collected—is reflected in the cacophony of Mulas's beautiful photographs. Interested from the start in disrupting the usual practice of collecting, the Panzas invested in an artist's oeuvre in depth. Rather than breadth, their collection initially represented the will to understand an artist's work and create greater understanding by keeping works together. The Panzas have also always viewed their collection as a growing whole. Though the majority of it has been dispersed to Los Angeles, New York, and Italy, Panza continues to talk about it as a collection in three parts comprising over 2,500 objects. The vision of art history into which he has intervened as a collector spans the early Renaissance to the present and this "family of man" view is embodied in the Mulas pictures: a domestic space lovingly transformed by art.

NOTES

1 Susan Stewart, *On Longing: Narratives of the Miniature, the Gigantic, the Souvenir, the Collection* (Durham, N.C.: Duke University Press, 1992), 161.

2 Ibid., 154–155.

3 Ibid., 151.

4 Cecile Whiting, *A Taste for Pop: Pop Art, Gender, and Consumer Culture* (Cambridge, Mass.: Cambridge University Press, 1997), 78.

5 In a letter from Panza to Green Gallery Director Richard Bellamy, February 1963, Giuseppe Panza Papers, The Getty Research Institute, Los Angeles.

1943T01969

fautrier
kline
lichtenstein
oldenburg
rauschenberg
rosenquist
rothko
segal
tàpies

COCA-COLA PLAN OR, HOW NEW YORK STOLE THE SOUL OF GIUSEPPE PANZA

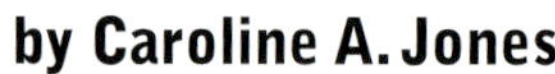
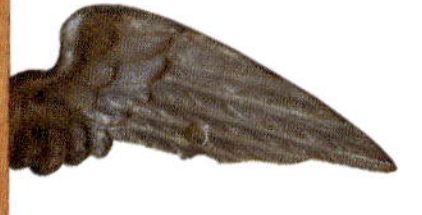

by Caroline A. Jones

We can see how power and culture were together and couldn't be split. The prince, the man of power, realized that his power didn't have any justification if there was no cultural motivation. [In the Renaissance,] the identity of good government and the cultural appreciation of the value of life was the same.
Count Giuseppe Panza di Biumo, Los Angeles, 1986

THE PLAN, THE MAN The size of a hefty trophy, *Coca-Cola Plan* announces itself with an air of fully imagined triumph (power and culture fused). The PLAN is at the top—the in-your-face king of the roost, the *kapo*, the brains, the catbird seat. Its ambitions seem modest enough: "LAY OUT STRETCHER ON FLOOR/MATCH MARKINGS AND JOIN." But as the piece begins to articulate its depth model of cultural power, its intentions go further. In the center resides the iconic heart of the plan—three trademarked Coca-Cola bottles. By 1958, their shape could be recognized, even in the dark, by a large percentage of the world's population. Flanked on either side by silvery wings, they form a triumvirate, a classical order of fluted commodity caryatids differentiated only by daubs and drips of paint. Nesting below, in what functions metaphorically as the engine room, the id, or the plinth for this programmatic prize, is a humble newell post—the carved finial from some long-abandoned banister, tilted slightly to assume the right orbital axis. Thus mounted, its concentric striations can be read as the latitudinal markings on a globe of the world.

 This is no random concatenation of urban detritus. It should not be packaged (as it was) as "merely" a dadaist gesture, whether registering Moira Roth's trenchant analysis of an "aesthetics of indifference," or indexing the world through a cool, haphazard process that Leo Steinberg brilliantly identified as a radical new "flatbed aesthetic."[1] Although it *is* cool, ironic, detached, and indexical, it is also packed with intention. Make no mistake: this *Coca-Cola*

Plan is an ambitious, calculated little package. Riding on the crest of a newly global American commodity culture, its maker (south Texas artist Robert Rauschenberg), cheerfully brandishes a proposal to take over the world.

By the time he produced *Coca-Cola Plan*, Rauschenberg had managed to launch his career with a spring exhibition planned at Leo Castelli Gallery and one in the wings (so to speak) at The Museum of Modern Art. The intensely autobiographical tenor of the artist's earlier works had waned, and by the time of this spare, lucid little "combine painting" (as he called them) Rauschenberg was addressing himself to a public he could now imagine, envisioning a realm of influence beyond Pearl Street, beyond New York, perhaps even beyond the U.S. of A. As the *Plan* notes, the indicated dimensions of its proposed "takeover" would be grander than this two-foot tall winged messenger might initially suggest. Were its instructions followed, the resulting canvas would be more than ten feet in width and eight feet in height. Structured as a triptych (as are, of course, the bottles of the combine itself), the painting plotted by the *Plan* would thus court sublimity in its dimensions (although the scale of its intended image remains unrevealed). Rauschenberg's *Plan* would result in a work competitive in size to the monumental Pollocks, Rothkos and Klines then touring Europe in the Modern's "New American Painting" show. The image on the projected canvas remains unknown (and perhaps irrelevant to the artist?)—although one might imagine Warhol's 1962 *210 Coca-Cola Bottles* as a deferred fulfillment of Rauschenberg's Plan (at slightly more modest dimensions). Coca-Cola (and its close competitor, Pepsi) had already conquered the visual culture of Rauschenberg's generation. As one British art writer commented in the London *Times*:

> The point is not whether Coca-Cola culture is wiser and nicer than wine culture: the point is that it is a culture—a set of tribal tastes and customs which implies certain values and attitudes and a conception of what life could ideally mean.... More people having a good time than have ever had a good time before. A taste for vicarious pleasure as well as vicarious cooking. Brand advertising everywhere.... A Promethean faith that nature is conquerable...expendability...standardization.[2]

Promethean faith, indeed. But a Prometheus with no Zeus to challenge his hubris. With its wings unfurled, Rauschenberg's combine presents the moral equivalent of wars' victory—postwar *bricolage* made analogous to the triumphant Hellenistic Nike from Samothrace that crowns one of the Louvre's most exalted vistas.[3] But rather than celebrate a battle won with the help of the gods, Rauschenberg's little votive is an imagined monument to a future

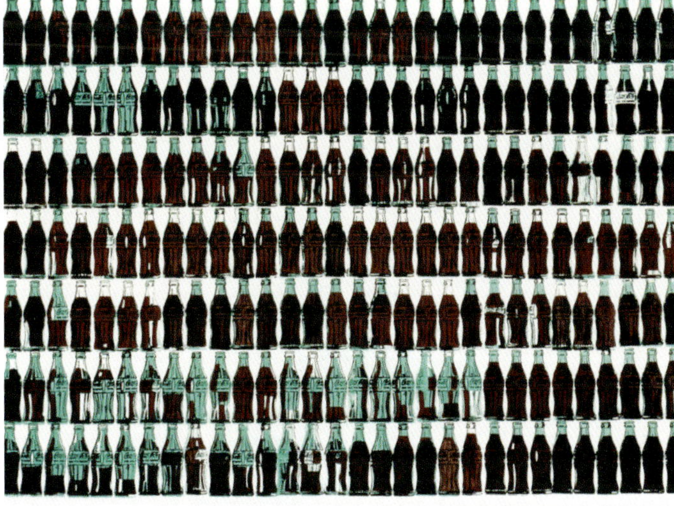

Robert Rauschenberg
Coca-Cola Plan, 1958
Combine painting
26¾ x 25¼ x 4¾ inches
The Museum of Contemporary Art, Los Angeles
The Panza Collection

Andy Warhol
210 Coca-Cola Bottles, 1962
Synthetic polymer paint and
silkscreen ink on canvas
82½ x 115 inches
The Andy Warhol Foundation, Inc./
Art Resource, New York

takeover (or a future monument to an imagined takeover—in any case, a *plan*).

With amazing good luck, the artist would find a willing accomplice to his plan in Count Giuseppe Panza, who accommodated his own grand vision to the scale of this tawdry but irrepressible *Victory of Manhattan* (purchasing the piece in 1963 from New York's Martha Jackson Gallery). For all its diminutive size, *Coca-Cola Plan* projects enormous confidence and ambition—scale trumps size. Ultimately, in weighing in with Rauschenberg's *Plan*, Panza left behind the austere struggles of European painting and put his weight behind the untried braggadocio of American art. Panza, in believing Rauschenberg's vision of a global (American) culture, helped make it so. That is the story this essay hopes to relate.

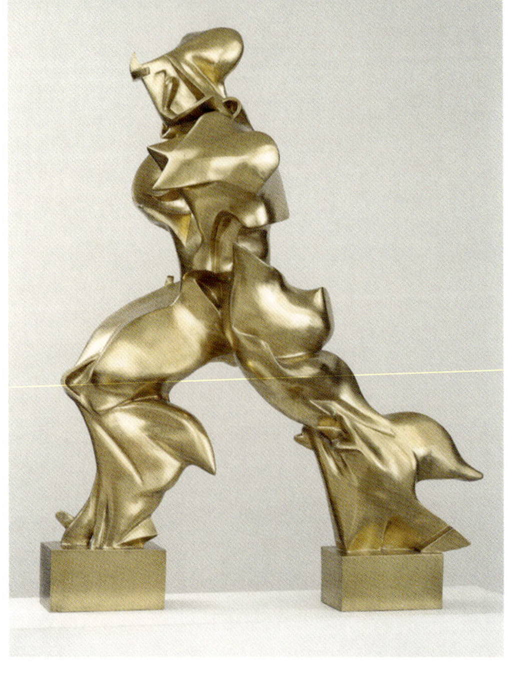

Probably unbeknownst to Rauschenberg but certainly rote to Panza, the Italian Futurists had announced similar designs on European culture during and after the first World War. Referencing precisely that rousing Hellenistic Nike of Samothrace, the *Futuristi* announced in their statements that her kind should be smashed for the lime kiln, to be replaced by their own mechanomorphic analogues of speed and steam. The symbol of success for these Italians trying to haul their country into the twentieth century was the Greeks' winged victory—significantly (as noted above), a trophy long since possessed by France, whose ownership of post-Renaissance culture both infuriated and intoxicated the Futurists. Making their own bid for control of world modernism, Futurists such as Umberto Boccioni produced dynamic figures and bottles (wine, not yet Coca-Cola) that broke the stable plinth of classical Greek form and sheathed those Hellenistic wind-whipped draperies in polished bronze. They sought "the beauty of speed…more beautiful than the *Victory of Samothrace*…."[4] Yet ironically, as with Rauschenberg a half century later, their yearning for the power and the glory of a civilization in triumphant ascension took shape as a winged, propulsive form—resembling nothing so much as the Nike herself.

The Futurists did not come to own world culture, nor did their fascist leanings endear them to subsequent historiographers of (supposedly progressive) twentieth-century modernism.[5] By the end of the *second* World War, the fate of

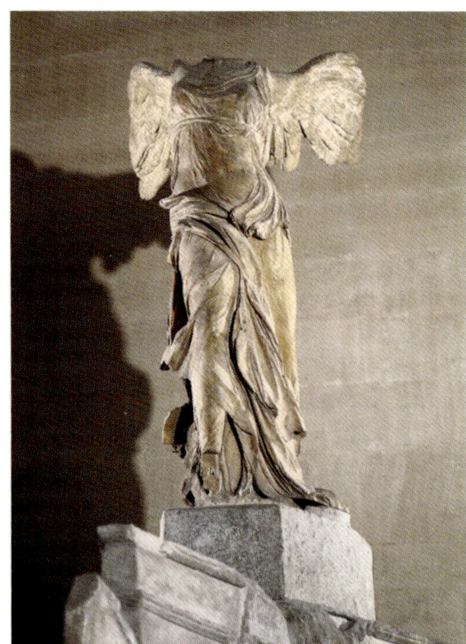

Italian modernism seemed humiliatingly certain. Seduced by a posturing imperial *Duce*, ashamed of their failure to hold onto even the most rudimentary colonial outposts, and deeply implicated in the bad business of fascism, Italian modernists had few legitimate local outlets for dreaming the future. Just how bleak cultural prospects looked can be intuited from the name Italian artists and critics gave to their first postwar movement with international aspirations: *Arte Povera*. Even this very successful curatorial congregation of avant-garde artists seemed to carry a refugee sensibility, as if to say "we, too, were victims...."[6] Their rubric and some of their works appeared with a shuffling gait and downcast eyes, as if hoping to deflect any comparison with the grand ambitions of Italy's recent bombastic past.[7]

We can speculate that after experiencing the dislocation and madness of war (and given the uncertainties of recovery), even a propertied, financially secure young man such as Giuseppe Panza (Count di Biumo) felt the dour mood in Europe. By the spring of 1956, when he moved to make his first serious acquisitions, Panza knew he wanted to leave Italy to buy contemporary art, and in Paris he took his first steps toward building one of the most extraordinary collections of contemporary art ever formed by an individual (this side of the Baroque). But in these first purchases he had not yet taken sides in the great postwar debate over the center of modernism. Drawn to the great dignity of Antoni Tàpies and the moving abjection of Jean Fautrier, Panza initially acquired what were quintessentially European paintings, still linked to the Northern tradition of the easel or cabinet picture. Panza thus entered the pervasive visual culture of postwar Europe (dominant both inside and outside the galleries)—comprised of crumbling ruins, abject and mutilated bodies, graffiti, and rags. As a vision for the future, it was bleak; the art world had not yet come to see tomorrow as envisioned by the *Coca-Cola Plan*.

At almost the same moment, however, Panza moved in a nearly opposite direction. Shortly after buying abject European tableaux by Tàpies and looking at Fautriers, he hunted down the gallery for an American artist barely known outside of New York, the abstract painter Franz Kline. Based on a single black-and-white photograph, Panza insisted on purchasing a painting barely a year old that he had never seen in person. A certain manic bravura was beginning to be an available mode of action—although initially it was entirely coextensive with its darker, more depressive self.

ABJECT BODIES

> *In some way the second World War was the end of Europe.*
> Panza, 1984

Panza was a lawyer, but when he escaped to Switzerland to avoid military duty in the German army, he was as yet "only" a student of history and philosophy. Drawn by his own account to "the problem of truth...whether knowledge is relative or absolute," Panza also stated that the "opposition of death and life" were central human and philosophical concerns of his at the time, concerns he later saw expressed in his own collecting patterns.[8] Certainly both truth and morbidity dominated Continental philosophy at the time of World War II, later crystallizing as existentialism, the mood governing Paris in the 1950s. It is safe to say that any artwork coming into view in Paris during the fifties would have been measured by an existentialist rule—certainly the art of Jean Fautrier fit that bill:

> I felt very deeply the changes taking place after the war. The rationalist vision of life and the idealist philosophy of culture had been popular in Italy. But [the war] was deeply shocking to the belief in man's rational capacities....To see how reason failed totally during the war was a great crisis for European culture.[9]

The "crisis" Panza felt in postwar Europe was represented visually in his collection by two very different artists showing in Paris in the mid-fifties: the young Spaniard Antoni Tàpies, and the mid-career Frenchman Jean Fautrier. Tàpies was the artist Panza bought first, but Fautrier was "chronologically the first artist whose works I collected...."[10] The Fautrier works Panza purchased dated primarily from 1943–44, when the artist's dark vision of human depravity met the public trauma of the occupation of France. Although Panza bought these Fautrier works

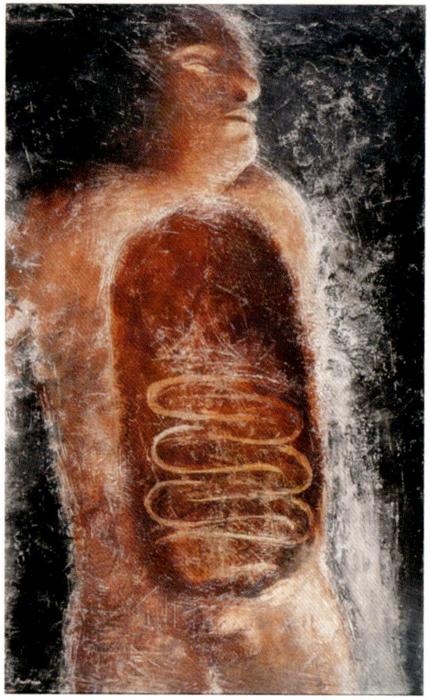

more than a decade after they had been painted, he saw them as the necessary starting point for his genealogical collection.

Flayed beef, hanging rabbit skins, and a dreaming corpse whose intestines lie open to our fascinated gaze—these were the already morbid subjects that occupied Fautrier in the late twenties. The grand Northern tradition of *vanitas* and *memento mori* (motivating artists from Rembrandt to Soutine to attempt to capture such raw food-chain realities) mingled in Fautrier's works with Surrealism and the nocturnal vision of Symbolists such as Odilon Redon. Paradoxically, Fautrier's palette *lightened* when he began the series that would be retrospectively called "Hostages"—heavily impastoed paintings begun in 1942 but named and grouped as a series only at the time of their exhibition immediately after the war in 1945. The "hostages" in question were understood by Fautrier's post-liberation audience to be those French Resistance fighters (and helpless bystanders) massacred by German soldiers (most notably in the village of Oradour-sur-Glane in Vichy, where troops killed more than 600 villagers on June 10, 1944).[11]

What must be understood about a painting such as the 1943 *Nu,* however, is the way in which its extraordinary redolence for a later, *post*-Holocaust audience must be tempered by the work's engagement with earlier themes embedded in art history in general, and Fautrier's modernism in particular. The favored Surrealist motif of erotic death (preceded in turn by fin-de-siècle fascinations with *lust morder*, *femmes fatales*, and antecedents in medieval "death and the maiden" cycles) would be a ready reference for *Nu*. Such continuities are unsettling when mapped onto the contemporaneous political, national, and ethnic violences that are invariably connected with Fautrier's work of the 1940s. Yet one can trace such links across the phases of Fautrier's production—how the erotic nudes of the twenties, their arms and legs mere stumps framing the sex and bust of the displayed woman—are brought into the present, and recontextualized as mutilated fascist victims. One must then ask how the erotics of Fautrier's sexualized corpses work when connected to the mass murder of civilians in World War II, and how such workings should be viewed in ethical terms (therapeutic or recuperative? probing or pornographic?). "Dead people who are still in some way warm bodies,"[12] as Panza described them, Fautrier's creatures of the 1940s present a flesh that softens into deliquescence, their sanguine colors betraying etymological roots that code for *blood*. Brought from the darkness of dreams into a scorching illumination that seems to have baked them into their *"haut pâté,"* Fautrier's postwar figures speak of some barely repressed carnivorous impulse, some mingling of eros and thanatos that lies at the shallow root of what passes for "civilization" in our times.

The horrifying *seductiveness* of Fautrier's abject bodies comes at us slowly, and in waves established in part by the inevitable oscillation between word (in the title) and image (floating in the mind's eye, yet also materially grounded). The sex and breasts of this nude first present themselves as shimmering veils of russet, rose, and lilac oxides layered over white (highly reflective) plaster, which has been lavished on the support in high impasto, like frosting at the local *pâtisserie*. But then the title for the work comes back into focus. The monosyllabic *Nu* connects these tinted calciferous mounds to the grand French tradition of lounging odalisques and drowsy coquettes (Boucher, Fragonard, Ingres, or Fautrier's most proximate master, Matisse). But the *abjection* of this body, its fragmentation, disorder, and stubbornly crude *bassesse*, courts what theorists such as Georges Bataille (Fautrier's contemporary and one of his collaborators) called the *informe*—a radical refusal to cohere into *"belle peinture"* (bourgeois preference and great French academic tradition). Bataille saw *bassesse* and the *informe* in social and psychological terms, "affirming that the universe resembles nothing and is only *formless*..., something like a spider or spit."[13] As Panza and other Europeans came to know Fautrier's works, in the context of the *Otages*, or displayed with the work *Dépouille*, whose title translates as "remains" (as in a corpse), their incontrovertible duality (between roseate veil of pigment and crusty, excremental base) was seen as expressing the unspeakable—as beginning to find a way to index (form) the absolute entropy of death (*informe*). And if we notice under the pearly oxides and pastes of *Dépouille* the pentimento of a cruciform shape, we can chart further doublings and dualisms (seemingly laid over a crucifixion, *Dépouille*, I suggest, also intends to render eternal life under entropy of death, absolute perfect form as the source of formlessness, and formlessness the origin of form).[14] Thus whatever the motives of Fautrier, however we might retrospectively judge his sincerity by attempting to adjudicate between "expression" and "confection,"[15] we are trapped. Forced to realize our implication in a circuit of desire, violence, and an undeniable spectacularity, we confront the fact that the hovering shapes we have been puzzling over (in *Nu*, in *Dépouille*, or in the hostages) each resolve themselves into a fetishized lozenge of death, a real *"cadavre exquis."*

Are the famed *Otages* (hostages), any different? Perhaps they are not so cruel, because the sensuality of their surfaces is immediately contradicted by the violence performed on the most expressive of all images: the human face. The mutilated faces of these heads immediately invoke layers of myth—echoing figures of Cyclops, apocalyptic lambs, and other cultural icons in whom the eyes (seat of the soul) are rearranged into monstrous singularity (*Head of a Hostage, No. 1*) or transcendental multiplicity (*Head of a Hostage, No. 14*). These hostage heads are also in the more stable convention of portraiture, a genre whose ties to libido are more effectively obscured. Viewing them as anonymous portraits (portraits of individuals made anonymous through violence), we are prepared to secure these figures in a heroic narrative of resistance, death, and immortality through art. But such heroism does not happen. If these are portraits, they are stripped to the bone of Being. No Renaissance hats, walking sticks, or views of distant vineyards—we view only disembodied heads, eyes fixed open in perpetuity or scratched into blindness, demanding us to witness a self in erasure, an individual whose social markers have been peeled away (and thereby subsumed into the rafts of "displaced persons" massing in postwar Paris at the time). As with the nudes, Fautrier's hostage heads are unsettlingly intimate paintings, but their ethical address is radically different. "Life-size" in their tight surrounds, they do not seduce so much as confront, staring back at us as they must have stared back at their sequestered maker while he tenderly layered plaster, papier mâché, washes, and oxides to create some appropriate evocation of each ravaged, nameless face. Some would argue that the endless repetition of these hostage heads is an appallingly market-driven commodification of Nazi murder; I would submit that their very massification begins to evoke the technological horror of those manufactured deaths.[16]

In this reading, Fautrier's hostage paintings find their fulfillment in the later musings of French philosophers such as Emmanuel Lévinas and Vladimir Jankélévitch who, confronted with the knowledge of absolute evil's eradication of the Other, felt compelled to theorize the implications of Nazi terror for subjectivity itself.[17] If some would suspect Fautrier's hostage paintings of being insincere or exploitative on the basis of their maker's *intention*, I would propose that these works manage nonetheless to command sincerity in the viewer (on the part of the *recipient*, the maker of their meaning in culture). The interpretive shift demanded here is tantamount to the demands Jankélévitch and Lévinas placed on existential philosophy itself, their "ultimate and exemplary challenge to the solitude of Being, a rigorous and moving testimony of one's infinite obligation to the other person" (written of Lévinas, but descriptive of Jankélévitch as well).[18] The face-to-face confrontation with the Other, for Lévinas in particular, was the absolute refutation of the isolation implied in Heideggerian theories of Being (the moral authority of which had already been shaken by Heidegger's apparent Nazism before and during the war). For Lévinas, and seemingly for Fautrier, "the face signifies in the fact of summoning, of *summoning me*, ... the idea of the Infinite is to be found in my responsibility for the Other."[19] As late as 1962, a collector such as Panza still felt the force of this summons (made material in Fautrier's heads)—a summons reiterated by Jankélévitch in 1965, refusing to "forgive and forget," to move on, to *get over it*.

To ask what kind of thinking and feeling Fautrier's paintings stimulate in the viewer is to shift our analysis from the isolated artist of genius (philosophically parallel to existential Being) to the face of the Other, a move that calls us to our ethical senses as unavoidably *summoned*. Although one cannot attribute to art (merely a representation, after all) the presence of a living human (whose face, Lévinas argues, cannot be seen as a "representation"), I would argue that something like this empathetic and projective attribution is taking place in the viewer affected by Fautrier's works. To the extent that Fautrier's paintings call to us, they do so *not* on the basis of the artist's moral authority, but on the grounds of our own ethical engagement with the Other.

We have imperfect access to Panza's motivations in acquiring these Fautrier canvases as the "earliest paintings chronologically" for his collection. Certainly, he experienced these works in terms of their "expression" of Fautrier's existential doubt and the depressive mood of postwar Paris (in other words, he took them as neither cynical nor mutely Other, but as windows onto Fautrier's motivation as an anti-fascist protesting Nazi horror): "In Europe before and during the second World War, the artist was just one person outside a situation which was contrary to his morals." The intimate size of the hostage paintings spoke to Panza not of our intimate yet universal responsibility for the Other, but of the artist's political and existential isolation: "The only way to be safe was to be alone with the small canvas, and it did not make sense to make it bigger."[20] Fautrier, then, was the ground zero of Panza's contemporary collection not because his paintings already signaled a shift from expression to reception, but because he still represented for Panza the necessary first stage of an artist's (or a collector's) absolute isolation in culture. The hostages were both a call to historical memory, an injunction "never to forget" that Panza accepted, and they were remnants of an isolated, existential artistic identity that was soon to be retooled. Their modest proportions and horrific themes were, as Panza already could have guessed when he first bought them in 1959, in dramatic contrast to painting made in other parts of the world (New York, as just one obvious example). Fautrier's paintings were made when large ambitions could not yet be imagined or perceived in anything but the most fearful and fascistic terms.

Antoni Tàpies was manifestly of a different generation than Fautrier, closer to Panza in age and in his mode of negotiating with modernism's dark side. When he first came to Paris in 1950, Tàpies was only twenty-seven. Fautrier, by contrast, was then entering his third decade as a professional painter, surrounded by the staunch veterans of the ruling *Écoles* (whether *de Paris* or *de France*) and newly credited with the birth of *l'art informel*. Fautrier's dark paintings were part of what Tàpies experienced as established influences, and clearly, the "*haut pâté*" of Fautrier's wartime paintings contributed directly to the signature mode of production Tàpies would develop when he returned to Barcelona after his year abroad. The abjection of Fautrier's works was not their paramount message, however, for from the older painter's dark vision Tàpies forged a transcendent faith in universal abstraction, linking him to Rothko and other New York painters whom Panza would soon come to admire.

When Panza purchased Tàpies's painting in 1957, the young Spaniard had only just concluded his first Parisian one-man gallery show. But perhaps in part because of his "provincial" origins, Tàpies was forced to engage in an international art world. Unlike Fautrier (but like his countrymen Picasso, Gris, and to a certain extent Miró), this Spanish artist had to leave Spain to be known at all. Thus, Tàpies worked tirelessly to organize exhibitions that showed his own increasingly monumental abstract works alongside other canvases he found congenial: paintings by Alberto Burri, Willem de Kooning, Dubuffet, Pollock, and Wols; he wrote inspiring texts about the universalism of abstraction; he traveled to the opening of each of his exhibitions. At the same time, his internationalism was always marked by constructions of an irreducible *Spanishness*; critics never failed to display a sense of amazement at the emergence of this young, modern, and seemingly abstract Catalan painter from the darkness of Franco's Spain.

Tàpies's production was thus always perceived through two optics. Anchored to primitivist tropes that had long freighted Spanish painting in a modernism centered on Paris, his work was also tied to the rising fortunes of international abstract art (linked politically to democracy). Early writings reveal this duality. The first is from the spring 1957 exhibition at Martha Jackson Gallery in New York from which Panza bought one of his first Tàpies paintings. Although the brief biography identifies Tàpies as "now established as a member of the School of Paris" (still a high mark of internationalism), the text goes on to suggest the essentially *Spanish* character of his work:

> Somber colors, sensitive line, richly textured surface enhance the essentially romantic concept of
> the painting of ANTONIO TÀPIES. Authority and exactness combine with the stark mood of Spain.[21]

An even more acute parallax occurs in an unsigned typescript found in Panza's correspondence with the artist, opening with a grand paean to Tàpies as master of the "school of Altamira:"

> For them, as they stated in their manifesto, the Magdalenian cave of art of the northwest of their country was a symbol "of living art, of art outside historical time, of art above all nationalism, representative of painting which fused forms and experience and revealed a great capacity for synthesis."

Here, then, the primitivism that always accompanies views of Spain is immediately linked to "art outside historical time, …art above all nationalism." Such modernist primitivism was, already by Tàpies's youth, a well-established trope that painters from Dubuffet to the American Abstract Expressionists were using to excellent effect. What is surprising is that the unknown author of this panegyric to Tàpies's non-nationalist painting then goes on to forge autochthonic connections between the artist and the "Spanish Earth," a linkage that explains "that austerity of palette" that is a "wide native tradition that runs from Zurbarán and earlier down through Juan Gris to present day Spanish painting."[22]

These dualities should not surprise us, for they inhere in the early paintings themselves, and in the persistent confusion over their titles. When Panza purchased *Ochre-Brown with Black Crack, No. XVIII,* as it is now known, it was called *Beast*—signaled not only by Martha Jackson's label on its verso, but also by Panza's terse telegram after her show: "BUY TÀPIES BEAST."[23] *Beast* is a fine postwar title—primitivist, raw, hinting at the untrammeled barbarity just under the veneer of civilized human behavior, resonating perfectly with recent histories of hostages and other ravaged semi-human states. *Ochre-Brown*, by contrast, signals an allegiance to the cool rule of abstraction. Similarly, another work in the Panza collection was at one time given the loaded title of *Perforated Body,* now called simply *Blackish Ochre with Perforations.* The trajectory implied here is similar to the development of Abstract Expressionist painters such as Clyfford Still, Mark Rothko, or Jackson Pollock, whose titles of the forties were dramatic declamations (Still's *Jamais!*, Rothko's *Antigone* or *Primeval Landscape*, Pollock's *Totem* paintings, or *She-Wolf*), giving way to ostensibly neutral colors and numbers by the 1950s (*Black on Dark Sienna* or *No. 1, 1950*).[24] Rarely did the American painters' titles change in designating *the same canvas*, however. For this fluidity we have both Tàpies and Panza to thank.[25]

Without the ability to conduct the elaborate scholarship needed to adjudicate among these competing interpretive "frames," we must look to the paintings themselves, to general comments by their erudite maker, and to evidence of their viewers' responses. Tàpies's apparent flexibility about titles betrays his general conviction about where meaning is made in art: "The painting is simply a 'support' that invites the viewer to participate…. So, the 'theme' can be found in the painting, or it can reside solely in the mind of the spectator."[26]

Whether we choose to designate his 1957 tableau as *Perforated Body* (as Panza did sometime before his collection came to the Museum) or *Blackish Ochre with Perforations* (as it is titled in the Tàpies catalogue raisonné), we observe a layered surface covered with cement and oil (and possibly also marble dust, latex, sand, gravel, hair, pigment). It takes its place in the magisterial corpus begun after the artist's return from Paris, when he began the well-known early "matter" paintings, here designated as one of his "walls." The "wall" motif was the artist's central revelation of the 1950s, fulfilling what he came to believe was his destiny *and* identity ("tàpies" being Catalan for "wall"), and distinguishing Tàpies's austere abstract vision from the legions of *informel* imitators then on the scene: "Each canvas [had been] a battlefield on which the wounds were to multiply over and over again, to infinity. And then came the surprise. All that frenetic movement, all that gesticulation [suddenly] came together in a uniform mass. What had been burning ebullition transformed itself on its own into static silence."[27]

The "uniform mass" typical of Tàpies's surface was built up horizontally, but displayed vertically. This unorthodoxy (in the context of European easel painting) and the description of the canvas as a "battlefield" suggest the depth of Tàpies's interest in Jackson Pollock and the agonistic, gestural branch of American Abstract Expressionism (marking, again, the incremental difference of Tàpies's works from French *Tachisme*, which remained, for all its gestural explosiveness, a kind of cabinet painting). Yet gesturalism, repeated (the sheer multiplication of "wounds" on the skin of the canvas), risked bathos, and Tàpies ensured that the body-as-canvas oscillated between insisting on its presence and retreating behind the "uniform mass" of barely differentiated matter. As I have suggested, this was not a straight trajectory, but a dualism or oscillation inherent in Tàpies's work. From *Beast* and *Perforated Body* to *Ochre-Brown* or *Blackish Ochre* was not a direction, but a dual focus. Smoothly reticent works such as *Todo Blanco (All White)* and *Grey and Black Cross* **precede** *Beast* by two years, defying the Abstract Expressionists' evolution from agonism to abstraction. The "walls" series did not represent a sealing off of the body, but a way of signaling its simultaneous rupture and endurance:

> Separation, cloistering, the wailing wall, prison, witness to the passing of time, smooth surfaces, serene and white, tortured surfaces, old and decrepit …traces of love, pain, disgust, disorder; the romantic prestige of ruins…twisting and tortures, quartered bodies, human remains; the equivalent of sounds, clawings, scrapings, explosions, shots, blows, hammerings, cries, reverberations, …battlefield; garden; playing field…[28]

The walls' multiple associations are amply demonstrated in *Blackish Ochre*. The painting's once placid horizontal surface has been upended and dragged earthward; pocked and wrinkled; even its pigmentation suggests weathered skin (as Panza clearly believed). Like the corridor in Jean Cocteau's Surrealist film *Beauty and the Beast*, Tàpies's wall comes alive, only to reveal itself as a corpse. The work's bottom half offers a sagging, ulcerated tumescence whose "abstract" markings have been laboriously worked to elicit a visceral response in the viewer (literally—our empathy is experienced in the viscera). The painting's perforations bear blackened edges, and seem to have been burned into the "skin" of the painting; some are glazed with a touch of varnish that suggests fatal leachings of plasma from this skin. Clearly it is not merely the presence of the cross in so many of Tàpies's paintings that gives them an underlying thematic of Christian martyrdom, for in oscillation with abstraction one can see the "wall" of this canvas, with its slightly curving top and sides, as an abused skin. As Octavio Paz wrote in his "Ten Lines for Antoni Tàpies," "Incarnations, disincarnations:/ your painting is the veil of Veronica/with that faceless Christ that is time."[29] Veil of Veronica that is both face and facelessness, marking both death and its transcendence into eternal life, Tàpies's paintings confront us again with the abject Other. Summoned by these evocations of abjection, we are called to a self in history—very different from the operations of sublimity Panza sought and found in New York painting from the same epoch.

BROKEN BAROQUE

> *Kline was the opposite [of the Europeans]… just an eruption of energy going up to the sky. [And] when you look at the color of Rothko, you feel the space is endless, just as when you look inside yourself…Rothko's work has no boundaries.*
> Panza, 1984

There is a persistent and delicious anecdote about Panza's acquisition of his first painting by Franz Kline (his first painting by an American). In Panza's account:

> [My] first important purchase was made in the spring of 1956 in Paris, when I bought several paintings by Antoni Tàpies. In September, or perhaps October, I read an article in the magazine *Civiltà delle Macchine*, which means *The Civilization of Machinery*. It was a good magazine, published by the state-owned steel industry. There were some illustrations of paintings which had some relationship to industry, such as Charles Sheeler's. There was also a Franz Kline because it looked like a steel structure, only broken. And I was impressed by this image. I read that the painting was from the Sidney Janis Gallery in New York. I wrote to ask for photographs of Franz Kline's work, and through them I selected the first painting, which is *Buttress*. The price was about $550. I asked Sidney Janis to reduce it to $500. He agreed.[30]

The story has all of Panza's charm—the crystalline accuracy, the wide-ranging intelligence (why was the son of a wine merchant and estate manager reading a steel magazine?), the trenchant observations ("like a steel structure, only broken"), even the evident pleasure over a good bargain. Luckily for the art historian, the magazine in question did feature Kline's work—although later than Panza recalls. It was not until May of 1957 that Panza could have seen Kline illustrated in *Civiltà delle Macchine*, on a single page, with a brief essay by Achille Perilli, "Franz Kline's Signs and Images".[31] Panza must have moved swiftly, for by the end of that year both *Buttress* and *Ilza* were on his walls.

Panza's robust recollection of Kline's work in a magazine about heavy industry is significant. But this is not just any magazine about heavy industry. There is simply no analogue in the United States for *Civiltà delle Macchine*, whose first issue in 1953 grouped articles on Italian industrial productivity with essays on Calder, Leonardo, the electric motor, and commentary on the implications of untrammeled mechanization by Siegfried Giedion and Lewis Mumford. In reading the wry, learned commentaries ("Trademarks are the tests of economic life, very seldom they are the demonstration of our ideals") and poetic offerings (a satiric poem on the subject of Maxwell's equations), one comes to a sense of *Civiltà* as a rational, capitalist continuation of the Futurists' project: erudite, aristocratic, experimental, and oriented entirely toward a technological future. Modernism is not a futile project here, but the only choice for an Italy intent on rebuilding after the war. Astonishing as it may seem for a magazine apparently funded by the Italian state, things large and innovative were cheerfully attributed to other nations—increasingly Americans. In a 1956 essay on advanced sculpture, for example, the (Italian) author describes the various national pavilions at the Biennale, concluding with a sigh, "The many sculpture halls in the Italian Pavilion give off a dusty air of restoration, indicative of the crisis of values in which Italian sculpture is now struggling, tied down to old patterns of style...." By contrast, the same author reports on Kline's work a few months later: "Perhaps it is too soon to say how far these images in black and white can go, to what extent they can be symbols and modes of our reality, but we can safely acknowledge them to be our time, our life, our poetry."[32]

Thus for Panza, Kline became the perfect bridge between the depressed, quasi-existential mood of Europe (expressed both in Fautrier's abject faces and Tàpies's scarred body/"battlefields") and what Panza was groping toward: something other than the "dusty air of restoration," something with its eyes on the future, something optimistic—a grandness of vision and ambition that might best be called Baroque (albeit a Baroque of "broken steel" set against a vast and impersonal landscape dominated by American civil engineering).

> I loved Franz Kline because it reflected my state of mind....This man was looking for something which was impossible to have but which he desperately needed. This kind of tension was my

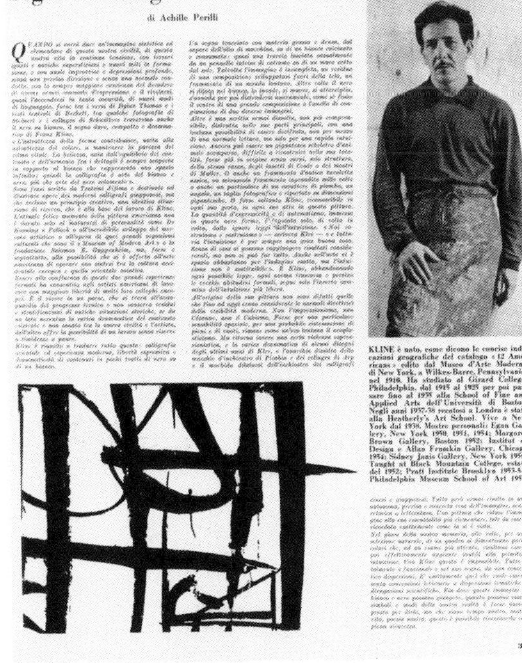

Achille Perilli's essay
"Franz Kline's Signs and Images,"
in the Italian steel industry trade magazine,
Civiltà delle Macchine 5, no. 3
(May–June 1957)
The article features Kline's *Cardinal*, 1950,
printed sideways.

condition, and I felt close to his art for this reason.... I was fascinated by life in America, by the landscape, by a way of living that was more free.... When I went back to Italy, I believed America was starting a new kind of civilization.[33]

The newness of that civilization was celebrated in the *Civiltà delle Macchine* essay, where Kline was described as breaking utterly with Impressionism, Cézanne, and Cubism (the three French modernisms that had marked Italy most permanently). "Without concessions to literature, thematic dispersions or scientific diversions," Kline's painting is so modern and "so 'functional' that nothing can be lost."[34]

As Panza noted, European paintings were still small (recall his comment on Fautrier, "the only way to be safe was to be alone with the small canvas, and it did not make sense to make it bigger"). Although his first Kline was not a large one, it was big enough:

> [*Buttress*] is small for Kline, but it was already bigger than the European standard. Before the war there was the belief that a small painting was better than a large one.... To make something small was to produce something more perfect, more beautiful. Perhaps it came from the impact of Baroque paintings in the churches in Italy. They were big paintings but with little meaning.[35]

The meaning Panza found in Kline's work was rich and sustaining, fueling his purchase of a dozen paintings in less than a decade. The bond between them is suggested by Kline's scrawl on the back of *Black and White*, painted in 1957: "DON'T FORGET: *PANZA*." The canvas made it to Italy by the following year.

Panza's Klines are particularly architectonic. *Buttress* makes this obvious, and Panza's recollection of this painting in conjunction with "a steel structure—but broken" is made manifest in its restless, cantilevered form. *Tower*, the earliest of Kline's works to enter Panza's collection, is typical of Panza's choices—strongly vertical, the form of the "tower" surges up from below, its internal energies straining against the narrow borders of white pigment. Like most of the early canvases Kline produced before he could afford artists' pigment, *Tower*'s image is built up of many thin layers of household enamel. *Pentimenti* (particularly along the left edge) betray earlier stages of the image in which broad black brushstrokes entered and exited at the canvas's edges, forming the shape of a tilted cross whose remnants are still visible within the picture's interior rectangular "frame." Blacks are highly variable, from glossy

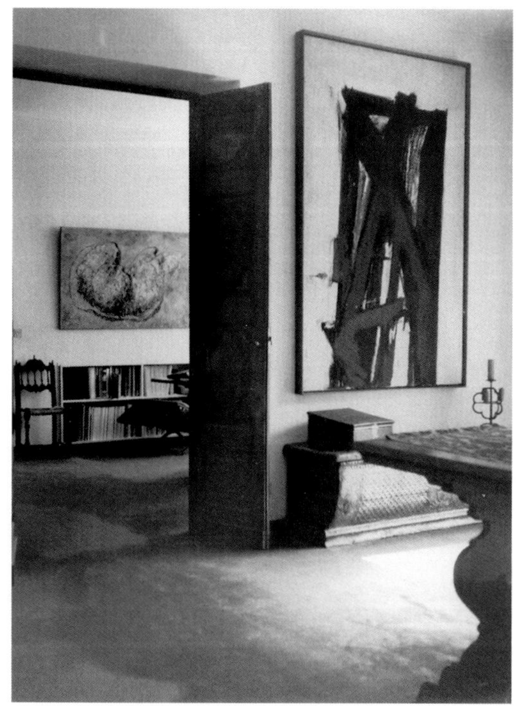

and hard (creating a kind of foreground) to rough, dry-brushed, scraped, or occluded by white overpainting (suggesting a background layer fading into mist). Much grey remains from this impassioned overpainting, and the tracts of white have now aged to ivory, giving *Tower* the tenebrous depths and shallow atmospheric perspective that characterizes Kline at his best.

Panza installed *Tower* in a semi-public room of his home in Italy, visible along with Fautrier's *Dépouille*, which stretched over a bookcase. Though the Kline is roughly as wide as the Fautrier, it is much taller. More than life-size, its scale is even more monumental in relation to Fautrier's intimate "remains," coiled in upon themselves protectively (as if it were not already too late) versus the aggressive, centrifugal tension crammed into Kline's picture. The juxtaposition of the two sharpens in our mind the contrast Panza himself felt between the "focused concentration of expression" in Europeans' small canvases, and "the energy revealed by the sign [Kline] made on the canvas, not only with the hand but by moving the arm and the body."[36] The open gestures laid down initially to begin a painting like *Tower* were later constrained by the painter's choice to impose a limit at the canvas's framing edge. Expanding edges of the cruciform were painted out, a border of white imposed. This pictorial device dams and channels "the energy revealed by the sign," and such pictures spoke to the Italian collector explicitly about the compressed urbanism of Kline's adopted island, Manhattan:

> The experience of these paintings is like looking at the city of New York when we arrive from Europe: it is a completely different situation. We see a vertical city and have a great feeling, just an eruption of energy going up to the sky. We don't know where this energy will lead... the sky is something without limit. But this energy is also an unlimited human energy. This human strength that we feel in New York is something very powerful, and Kline's constructions in black and white represent this situation.[37]

Even thirty years later, Panza spoke of his experience of New York in terms that were identical to those he used to describe the effect of Kline's paintings: "I was very impressed the first time I went to New York. For me it really was a new world... a city struggling for things impossible to possess but that it was trying to have anyway." (Recall that Kline "was looking for something which was impossible to have but which he desperately needed.") In Panza's view, for both Manhattan and for Kline "the only goal was the infinite."[38]

The "struggle for the infinite" was clear in Panza's view of Kline; as we have seen, it also motivated Tàpies's balancing act between the furious wounds of a "battleground" and the mute, pulverized dust of the cosmos. Panza's next major acquisition of paintings by Mark Rothko also employed the dialectic of struggle, but only in order to strive for its ultimate resolution in art—a synthesis between chaos and culture we call the Sublime.

It is likely that Panza became acquainted with Rothko's work through its inclusion in numerous exhibitions in Italy: first, the twenty-ninth Venice Biennale (in the spring of 1958), then in the provocative "New American Painting" show that traveled to Milan that same summer, and finally in a one-man show that appeared in Rome in January 1960; (Panza's first Rothko purchases date from 1960, and two were acquired from Galleria Blu in Milan). The younger Italian critics were swift to celebrate "*le illuminazioni di Rothko*" (Rothko's illumination) with its "*struttura materica della luce*" (material or materialized structure of light),[39] but others were dour in their assessments. Critics were particularly skeptical of the loaded baggage carted by "the New American Painting:" "It is not new. It is not painting. It is not America... Droppings of paint, sprayings, burstings, lumps, squirts, whirls, rubs and marks, erasures, scrawls, doodles and kaleidoscope backgrounds. When will they send us a real American show?"[40] These epithets, however, targeted the seeming chaos of "Action Painting." Rothko's hovering, luminescent rectangles were exempt, as representatives of a very different aspect of contemporary art in the 1950s ("Field Painting," only awkwardly grouped with its gestural cohort in Abstract Expressionism). It was admirably encyclopedic of Panza to acquire Rothko *and* Kline, one exemplar of Field painting along with one gesture painter. All of Panza's Rothkos were acquired in two short years—but by then the collector had amassed a group of at least seven large, classic paintings dating from 1953 to 1960.

Rothko's signature style had been established for more than a decade by the early 1950s. *No. 61 (Rust and Blue)* (1953) and *Violet and Yellow on Rose* (1954) suggest the range of referents, from landscape to body, that could be packed into the seemingly narrow range of Rothko's fugue-like series. The slow complexity of these brooding paintings confirms the linguistic inadequacy of the color-names they are assigned; the term "blue," for example, hardly contains the nuances of Rothko's translucent films and haze of cool hues; "red" is even more inadequate to the changes rung on this primary color. Variations in the texture of brushstrokes, the opacity or transparency of a given tone, the density of accumulated paint, its apparent wetness (fat with oil) or dryness (lean with turpentine)—all contribute to the resulting harmony or dissonance. The rich indigo of the bottom section of *Rust and Blue* (sometimes known as *Brown, Blue, Brown on Blue*) was an early decision (revealed by the small drips of other colors accidentally scattered over its thin, scrubbed-looking surface); above it is a feathered cerulean layered over another, deeper lapis blue. These masses of blue, extending to the edges of a large canvas, are experienced as absorptive, almost literally oceanic realms ("I paint large in order to be intimate," as Rothko said). Their inevitable associations with land- (or sea-) scape are not denied by the rest of the painting, but certainly become complicated by the turgid maroon (called either brown or rust) that presses down from above. Similarly, *Violet and Yellow* presents this same top-heavy composition, but here the landscape associations are less prevalent than sensations of a body, aerated and expanded over the membrane of the canvas (a "midriff" in peach dividing its torso-like proportions, suggestive of the figurative impulse at the base of much of Rothko's earlier work).[41] As these two canvases reveal, Rothko's achievement was to *fuse* landscape and the body. The existential trope of man and void collapses into the Sublime narrative of man's atomization and absorption by the oceanic Other (mother/Nature)—the body pulverized and extended out into the surrounding vastness.

Rothko and others in his generation (such as Barnett Newman, Jackson Pollock, and Ad Reinhardt) were quite self-conscious in their engagement with the discourse of the Sublime. In addition to his efforts to collapse body into landscape, Rothko routinely used the "dark, fuscous" colors alluded to by eighteenth-century writers attempting to categorize the cultural dynamic of Sublimity.[42] His canvases were meant to be hung in suites around the viewer, intended variously to surround, absorb, quiet, and perturb the complacent gaze. The matte brown at the center of *Purple Brown* (1957), for example, takes us on a disturbing journey into an atmospheric "dead zone;" our dissolution into this void is halted only by the surprisingly solid "lintel" of paint bisecting the painting's unequal halves. The softly-feathered violet framing edges usher us past the weeping plinth at the bottom of the canvas, finally delivering us into the world of the gallery once again. We are aware of ourselves as having been dissolved and put together again, enlarged by the process. This journey (through the paces of the Sublime) is not unlike that proffered by Fautrier or Tàpies, but its resolution is entirely different. If Rothko's pictures are successful, we are confronted not with the face of the Other, or the cosmic void, but with ourselves. It was, I venture to suggest, a goal entirely in keeping with the insulated faith American painters had come to find in themselves and their culture. It was a faith that undergirded the "New American Painting" show through which Rothko's work was first shown in Italy, and at least Panza seems to have been convinced. As one of his young correspondents, the budding French critic Pierre Restany, put it in describing French reactions to the Rothko and his cohort, "if even the most relentless of the 'Europeanizers' haven't admitted that there exists '*une peinture américaine*,' at least they have been forced to recognize that there is 'some painting' in America!"[43]

Restany didn't reveal whether he was one of these "*européanisants*." Declaring to Panza that "*La supériorité de Pollock est manifeste*," he felt that the other paintings in the American show revealed a double academicism—one revealed in second-generation gesture painting, the other in what he called "*abstrait sérielisant*" (serializing abstract painters). The winners, he opined, were the most vehement of the "*geste physique*" painters—although Rothko gets an honorable mention "even though [his works are] very badly installed." By May of 1960, however, Restany is no longer amused by Rothko's omnipresence in Europe (had news of Panza's Rothko purchases from Janis or Galleria Blu reached Paris?); indeed, the Frenchman sounds very cross with his Italian collector friend, berating him for focusing so exclusively on the American field painter. "Don't buy mediocre Rothkos," he urges. "I think it would be a better sell to save up for a beautiful Matthieu or a Hartung…of the best class."[44] Given Restany's efforts to promote French painting (particularly works by *Les Nouveaux Réalistes*, the movement for which he was the primary Cicero), he must have found it even more annoying that Panza's immediate move after Rothko was to Rauschenberg, a protean artist from the U.S. whose efforts in monochrome, assemblage, early conceptual art, and other genre-bending productions paralleled and often anticipated work by Restany's preferred Parisians.[45]

> *Rothko's work is the exploration of the feeling hiding in each person… But Rauschenberg explores*
> *other aspects…such as memory…Rauschenberg uses objects as images to make this relationship*
> *[between past and present.]*
> Panza, 1984

To whom a collector turns for advice is always interesting, and significant. Surely Restany hoped to play a large role in forming Panza's collection, yet for all his feverish and informative letters, the French critic seems to have accomplished little after first brokering meetings with Tàpies and Fautrier.[46] Panza's introduction to Rauschenberg came by very different means, and his persistent efforts to acquire the young American's work betrays a conversion that was swift, sudden, and complete. It was a conversion instigated by the most unlikely of holy men—an avant-garde composer dubbed "Frankenstein" by the Italian press: Rauschenberg's friend, collaborator, and mentor, John Cage.[47]

Cage had been brought to Milan in the fall of 1958 by the Italian National Radio (at the behest of Italian composer Luciano Berio), where he was meant to produce innovative compositions using electronic tape. He did this, but he also appeared on an immensely popular Italian television quiz show, where he successfully answered five weeks of questions about mushrooms (his choice), performed both music and theater works, and won the hearts of the Italian public and 8,000 lire. *Inter alia*, he made it his business to meet Panza, who invited the now-famous composer to his home, where Cage persuaded him of the importance of Rauschenberg and Jasper Johns.

Since buying his "mail-order Kline," Panza preferred to buy paintings that he had seen in person, and tried to secure the opportunity of choosing from a wide selection of available works. Johns proved too difficult (his paintings were claimed by local New Yorkers as soon as they were finished), but Rauschenberg was still possible. Panza doggedly pursued views of Rauschenberg's work (which would not become widely known in Italy until 1964, when the young Texan stunned the world by taking first prize at the Venice Biennale). Finally Panza was able to see Rauschenberg's painting *Kickback* at the 1959 *Documenta* in Kassel (many months after Cage's recommendation).[48] The painting had been loaned from the collection of William Rubin (destined to become director of the painting and sculpture department at The Museum of Modern Art), whose brother Lawrence was an art dealer happy to manage the sale.[49]

The record of Panza's ongoing hunt for Rauschenberg objects is impressive, and occasionally amusing. Fellow Italian Leo Castelli (Rauschenberg's dealer and the primary gatekeeper to his work) proved particularly obstinate. Castelli, expatriated to New York, found his self-appointed task of convincing *Americans* to support these artists daunting enough; he simply could not believe that some Milanese lawyer was serious about buying a Rauschenberg. A chronicle of their one-sided correspondence (Panza's pleas to Castelli are not here) tells the tale:

> *10 Apr 1959*—"Thank you so much for your letter of April 7, and for your interest in the work of
> Rauschenberg. His work is in great demand here, and there is hardly anything of importance that I
> would have available for the moment…."
> *30 Jan 1960*—"Forgive me for not answering your letters sooner. But the purchase of a Rauschenberg
> painting, especially by a collector who is not in New York, presents quite a problem. Rauschenberg
> is a rather slow producer…. Since you seem so anxious to have one of Rauschenberg's works, I will
> send you shortly two or three photographs…"
> *15 Apr 1960*—Castelli congratulates Panza on the purchase of Rauschenberg's *Winter Pool*
> (the work never made it into Panza's collection)—"Alfred Barr would have bought it [for The Mu-
> seum of Modern Art….]"
> *23 Apr 1960*—"Your letter of April 20th surprises me." (Panza seems to have refused *Winter
> Pool*.) "You do not seem to realize a few things: Rauschenberg does not manufacture paintings but
> each one of them is an invention. He therefore produces about fifteen of them a year. The demand
> for them is very great….with Johns he is now considered the best painter of the younger generation,

and probably the equal of some of the older ones. This is not only the opinion of Americans but also of Europeans. [It is] impossible to sell you at this time any other paintings of Rauschenberg's—there simply aren't any left. Please don't feel under any obligation as far as the purchase of *Winter Pool* is concerned. In the case of Rauschenberg I'm always very happy to get back one of his paintings."
10 May 1960—"Thank you for your letter of April 30 and for the photos of your country house."
24 Sept 1960—Castelli is glad Panza is buying *Broadcast* (another work that is not in Panza's collection). "I cannot tell you how much I look forward to your imminent visit to New York."
30 Mar 1961—Castelli has been to Panza's villa, where he praises "the amazing Rauschenberg room." The two are now friends.

One of the first paintings Castelli sold Panza was *Factum I*, but neither buyer nor dealer were sufficiently sensitive to Rauschenberg's intentions to keep this painting together with its pendant, *Factum II*. The wry point of each painting lies precisely in its mimicry of its twin. Every collage element, every "spontaneous" brushstroke, every drip seems applied with that authentic gestural emotion required of the true Abstract Expressionist painter—but its literal *duplicity* renders a devastating critique. It is not even exactly a matter of *reproduction* (although collage elements address that condition), for we cannot say, without their Roman numerals to order them, which canvas is the "original" and which the "copy." (Rauschenberg himself claimed to have made them simultaneously, adding elements to each incrementally as they stood side by side in his studio.) As with many other works of this period, *Factum* reveals its maker to have been steeped in a reappraisal of the ironic work and wit of Marcel Duchamp, an emerging hero for Johns and Cage as well as Rauschenberg himself.

Even the single *Factum* bought by Panza in 1960 reveals the density of meaning characteristic of Rauschenberg's work. The ostensibly neutral "flatbed" plane of the canvas, which initially seems primed like an offset-lithograph press to receive and transmit whatever random images drift into view,[50] reveals itself quickly to have a strong intelligence behind the wheel. The enormous red "T" at the

Robert Rauschenberg
Factum I, 1957
Combine painting
61½ x 35¾ inches
The Museum of Contemporary Art, Los Angeles
The Panza Collection

picture's lower right (the logical terminus of the literate Western viewer's sauntering gaze) might also code for twin: twin canvases, but even within those canvases twin trees, twin Eisenhowers, twin calendars, twin conflagrations— even twin dates (dated 1957 by cataloguers, the work includes a clipping from 2 December 1957 and calendar pages for 1958). In Panza's extensive collection of Rauschenberg's early work, *Factum* marks a transitional period in which personal references can be found, but no longer dominate. In seeking out earlier works, such as Rauschenberg's untitled "combine," known colloquially as *Man with White Shoes* (1955), Panza showed himself to be interested not only in Rauschenberg's more general public address, but in the personal trajectory that lay behind it.

Family photographs, letters from home, newspaper clippings, clothing, bed linens—the list of seemingly intimate personal possessions that Rauschenberg was willing to incorporate into these earlier works stimulates a troubled curiosity in the attentive viewer. Was making the piece a way of cutting these family ties, or an attempt to preserve them forever? Certainly few works, if any, had sold at the time he was making the untitled "combine." But the decision to paste a child's love letter to the surface of one's artwork would seem to end any personal association with the sender, and to announce the beginning of a more anonymous public life.

The "combine" designation for these works is also ambiguous, since what is being combined has never been made explicit by the artist (although the standard account mentions their indeterminate status between painting and sculpture). Walking around *Untitled (Man with White Shoes)*, henceforth *Man*, does present *combined* views: dim interior within brilliant exterior, juxtapositions of black and white, objects and reproductions, transparency and opacity, gestural hand painting and printed textiles. Perhaps most intriguingly for the notion of an object-triggered "memory" Panza described in these works, *Man* also combines Rauschenberg's discarded past with tokens of a deeply desired future.

Space constraints prohibit an exhaustive account of *Man*'s referents, but a few threads will reveal something of the complexity here. On the "face" of the object (as it is usually installed) there is a progression, from top left to top right, of a family photograph (it seems to be Rauschenberg's sister Janet), through images of the statue of Liberty, a parachute landing, and an Old Master reproduction, the last directly above a newspaper clipping reporting on the silver wedding anniversary of Rauschenberg's parents, who claim "a son Milton, an art student in New York City, and a daughter Janet." There is some precedent for linking these disparate images into a narrative (the artist's fascination with such gambits is revealed by his own *Rebus* paintings from 1956, one of which Panza purchased).[51] The linked narrative suggests a trajectory—from home to Liberty (and a safe escape), an arc that peaks with the parachute's dramatic landing, coming down to be anchored by Art, the tethers of one's former name (Milton), and the bonds of parental love (for spouse and children).[52] On the inner roof of the lower section of the combine (above the chicken— is it cock or hen?) is another clipping, this one advertising the charms of "Louisiana's 1953 Yambilee Queen," none other than Rauschenberg's younger sister Janet, in this image considerably more mature. The "Yam Queen," as Rauschenberg himself affectionately called her forever after, looks down pertly from her beauty-queen bathing suit onto the densely packed surface behind, under, and beyond the stuffed bird. Here paint, striped fabric, more clippings on the senior Rauschenbergs' silver wedding anniversary, fake grass, da Vinci reproductions, and various versions of the American flag (a favored theme of Jasper Johns, occurring here in a "twinned" form of back-to-back Old Glory) are all surmounted by a comic strip. The comic figures' exchange seems to summarize the artist's achievement and recapitulate his ambition. One character asks, "Ever seen this before?" and the other responds: "Never, Honest, I never saw. . . ." Stepping back from such close readings, the massed ephemera merges into that "pedestrian" mix of hues and bits of information Rauschenberg called the "no-color" of people passing in the street.[53] At this more distant view, the work's larger themes emerge. Precisely against the foil of the pedestrian and banal, how gleaming, how perfectly *elegant* is the young man whose photograph graces the open side of *Man*, how charming he appears with his white bucks and nonchalant posture, hovering above that reflective surface that serves beautifully the narcissist's loving gaze! This Southern dandy is surely Rauschenberg's ideal (for himself, and as a lover/twin)—but the artist has also seen fit to mock his own besotted vision. Yes, there is tenderness: inside the work's *sanctum sanctorum,* its inner chamber veiled by gold and black scrim, are the love object's white shoes, their sweet empty socks tumbling out, backed by a pink satin square and placed on a rough but immaculately white ground—but right below this cozy icon of domesticity and sanctioned seduction is, well, the chicken. Hen or cock, the associations are humbling (and

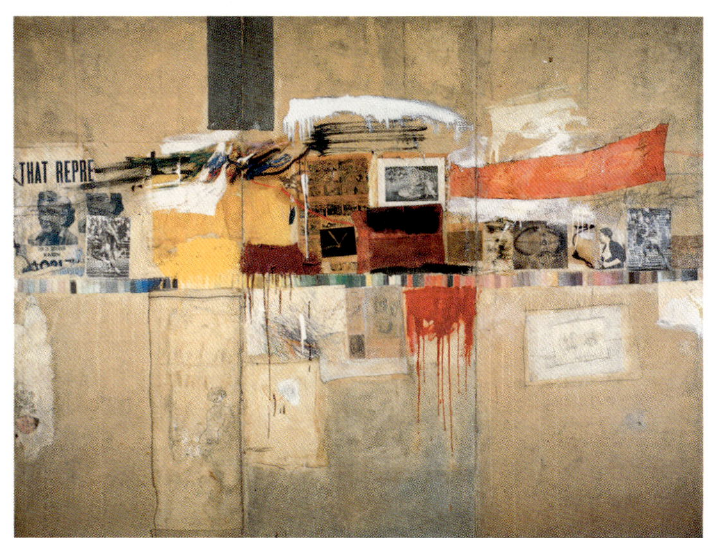

Robert Rauschenberg
Rebus, 1955
Combine painting: oil, paper, fabric,
pencil, crayon, newspaper, and
printed reproductions on three canvases
96 x 130½ inches
Private collection

multiplied at the work's top where one can find an image of a rooster, feathers flattened by surrounding floodwater and presumably "mad as a wet hen.") A red cork dangles, connecting the two registers, and only really visible from the side. From this side view, one perceives the underlying logic of the work's syntax.[54] The scrim sections render their contents somehow quotational and abstract: veiled shoes, satin, mirror, fowl, cork. An object/image poem, *Man* is deeply personal in its origins, yet it achieves a level of generalized longing that speaks more broadly. In Rauschenberg's own trajectory, it sets the terms for the "rebus" paintings' still more general address, and for *Coca-Cola Plan*'s unabashed claim on the world.

The rebus is a word picture game whose victor finds meaning in a chain of linked icons whose order is crucial. The rebus-maker desires brevity, but not at the cost of the visual (the letter "I" is never preferable to the picture of an eye). Some have tried to parse Rauschenberg's larger *Rebus* painting literally, translating its bits of ephemera into a long, implausible sentence: "That reproduces sundry cases of childish and comic coincidences to be read by eyes opened finally to a pattern of abstract problems…"[55] It seems more likely that the "Rebus" games Rauschenberg intends do not hold a single verbal payoff. Certainly *Small Rebus* has more visual rhyming, twinning, and punning than verbal cues. Note, for example: the paired bulls (above and below the central register of hardware store paint chips); the gracefully twisting gymnasts paired with the contorted dog (frozen in death under the ashes of Pompeii, as the gymnasts are frozen by flash photography); the line drawing of a handless (timeless?) clock at the far left, echoed by the line drawing of the mind's memory sites at the far right. Again, it is not a sentence that can be parsed but a trajectory—"read" from left to right, as paintings are in our literate Western society, the entire compositional arc of the painting (underscored by the direction of Rauschenberg's dragged yellow and blue lines) moves from the baroque drapery of Titian's *Europa* at lower left, over the fence of industrial color, past the nightmarish clock and agonistic bullfight to culminate in the triumphant runner (circled decisively in Rauschenberg's black calligraphy).[56] Our terminus, our anti-climax, our fisherman's deadweight, is the photograph of (Rauschenberg's) family, hovering over the map of memory that itself floats just above Death (in its material precipitate, the cast of the long-dead Pompeiian dog).

Buried at dead center of *Small Rebus*'s lower register, amidst the various symbols and icons of troubles and transcendence, are two maps, confronting one another and bifurcating the painting. At left is a portion of the U.S., linked visually to a smattering of grey "action" strokes. At right is a map of the Warsaw Pact countries, veiled by one long black drip and a fragment of black-barred gauze fabric. This small commentary on the implacable divisions between Cold War opponents is the only suggestion of the world-thinking that would later appear in *Coca-Cola Plan*. As yet, its maker has yet to catch the smell of victory that *Plan* finds "in the air," nor did its buyer know that he was soon to invest in art that would blithely take that victory for granted. Although it hadn't yet been named, Pop art was soon to establish its beachhead in Panza's heart.

POPULAR MECHANICS

> *Instead of making copies of a Greek Venus, it is perhaps more interesting to make copies of a container of Coca-Cola.... Though the Venus is something fine, we are more interested in something more relevant than this ideal realization of a human body.*
> Panza, 1984

If Rauschenberg's work represents the conjunction of object-image and memory, Claes Oldenburg's has always mined the object's sexuality—or rather, the *human* sexuality cathected onto our manufactured objects. Oldenburg admitted in 1963 (as any ad man in the postwar period might have), that "The strangest influence on my thought was Freud... I may be called... a practicing or everyday surrealist, which is what Freud was."[57] Sexuality is too broad a term, however, for the erotics of Oldenburg's vision. These are not simple entries in a dimestore dream dictionary with its literalism and pidgin Freudian equivalents ("Train: see Banana"). Oldenburg's discovery of a world between the sexual and the commodity fetish gathers its force from an affectionate alienation from American commodity culture. Like Panza, the Swedish-born Oldenburg (who moved to Chicago at the sentient but impressionable age of seven) views the blandishments of American mass culture from a slight distance. The vulgar energy of it all delights and amazes him, but the dance of commodities (what I'm calling "popular mechanics") must be met with an acute intelligence, the artist peeling away the layers of naturalized ideology to reveal the raw thrummings of libido at the heart of the machine.

The very notion of "Pop" art, a name invented by a British critic and inspired by London artists' use of images from American advertising, was meant to encompass a range of tawdry pleasures—"popular" art (an epithet hurled against bourgeois decorations by generations of avant-gardists), "pop" culture (the pleasures of those baby-boom teens described as "bobby-soxers" and "gum-chewers"), artificial beverages and confections (soda "pop," "pop"-sicles, Tootsie "Pops," lollypops), and even the explosive sound of a toy gun (a "pop" gun).[58] The name only caught on internationally by the mid-sixties, but the global manifestations of what would later be grouped by the term began in the mid- to late 1950s (Brits and Europeans appearing as members of a generation marked by the *Coca-Cola Plan*).[59] The "New Realism," as it was also known, was universally understood to be embroiled with one thing: American commodity culture, spreading globally along with U.S. government aid and military prowess—what one London critic had described as a "Coke Climate." Initially, however, this climate was saturated only by the *images* of commodity culture. For the British artists who first spawned it and probably for most Italians in the early 1960s, Pop art represented the phantasmagorical and unattainable promise of American advertisements—not lived experience but imagined plenitude.

Oldenburg's objects resonated beautifully with this somewhat simulacral European perspective on America.[60] Unlike the slick icons Andy Warhol produced (which were also simulacral, but to whose deadpan cool Panza did not respond), Oldenburg's messy, hapless, shopworn pseudo-retail objects form a corpus "that twists and extends and accumulates and spits and drips, and is heavy and coarse and blunt and sweet and stupid as life itself," as the artist announced in his famous manifesto of 1961.[61] Enlarging the "spits and drips" appearing on the bottles of Rauschenberg's *Coca-Cola Plan*, Oldenburg's *Pepsi-Cola Sign* does not announce the imminent victory of American commodity culture, but seems to evoke a time in which that culture will be as ancient (and respected? and destroyed?) as a Roman ruin, echoing what theorist Fredric Jameson has called postmodernism's "nostalgia for the present."[62] Oldenburg's *Pepsi* seems older, more experienced, and certainly more mournful than Rauschenberg's bright Cola trinity. Enormous, its letters are raised like a battered tin emblem scavenged from a billboard, layered with slapdash brushstrokes of household enamel as gestural and expressionist as a Kline. This poetic "Pop" expressionism is one that has given up its claims on sublimity, however. It is part of Oldenburg's theatrical life experiment, *The Store*, and like all *Store* objects it is "born in contorted drawings of the female figure and in female underwear and legs, dreams of the proletarian Venus, stifled yearnings which transmute into objects, brilliant colors and grossly sensuous surfaces."[63] *Pepsi-Cola Sign* and the other *Store* "goods" remain in the world, rather than transcending it, working to reveal the operations of commodity fetishism while still summoning the mesmeric power of things.

The Store did not spring full-blown from Oldenburg's libido, but mutated from a set of themes (the Street, the Store, the Home) that occupied him in the first few years of the 1960s. Since moving permanently to New York from Chicago, Oldenburg's own tropism toward theater had found strong reinforcement from a group of young artists following the theories and teaching of John Cage.[64] Allan Kaprow, Jim Dine, Red Grooms, and others were energetically blurring the boundaries between art and life, painting and theater, objects and actions, music and noise. Thus it was natural that Oldenburg's first serious exhibition should be a collaboration (with Jim Dine) and that the objects in it should be called "paintings in the shape of theater."[65] These strange hybrids, which seemed not *assemblages* of found objects and paint (as with Rauschenberg) but some kind of uneasy morphological union of a thing and its image, continued to materialize: on their own, as props in performances, and as those same events' "residual objects"—hybrids that might be described with equal accuracy as "theater in the shape of painted objects." Oldenburg's project aimed to animate the emotional nexus of commodity fetishism, not merely its triggering images.

The first version of *The Store* was a mural-like installation in "Environments, Situations, Spaces," a group show held in the spring of 1961 at Martha Jackson Gallery. The unsold objects from the exhibition were then moved to Oldenburg's new workspace, a storefront in Manhattan's lower East Side, where the artist first conceived of opening his studio as *The Store* in December of that year. Extended through January 1962, the *Store*'s proprietor and manufacturer was Claes Oldenburg, but the industrial "sponsor" was Oldenburg's *döppelganger*, his corporate projection, the "Ray-Gun Manufacturing Company."[66]

Exactly when Panza encountered this phantasmagorical "retail opportunity" is documented in Panza's papers. Scribbled on a calendar page labeled "Reminders for today, Weds Oct 3" are the words "Oldenburg 107 East 2nd st go down 2nd Ave." The first invoice for Oldenburg works, issued by the Green Gallery, is dated November 6, 1962—suggesting that Panza's October visit was in that same year. But Panza would not then have seen all the *Store* goods in Oldenburg's studio, for by October they were part of the Green Gallery's uptown re-installation. What seems evident is that Panza did his shopping both up- and downtown, acquiring, in the end, over sixteen objects produced by Oldenburg for different incarnations of the *Store*.[67]

Panza says little about the antiseptic Green Gallery installation; his memories recreate most powerfully the ambience of the first *Store* as Oldenburg had presented it in the storefront of the "Ray Gun Mfg. Co.":

> It was a beautiful experience. To reach the *Store* we had to go through the Jewish section in downtown New York, which was full of shops selling second-hand dresses. You had the strange feeling... so different from what you saw in the shops on Fifth Avenue. The Oldenburg *Store* was on a small street, after the Jewish section. It was glowing with beautiful color.... The contrast was strange, very moving.[68]

Claes Oldenburg
Poster for *The Store,* 1961
Three-color woodcut printed on cardboard
28¼ x 22⅛ inches
Collection of Claes Oldenburg and
Coosje van Bruggen

Installation view of Oldenburg's solo exhibition
at Green Gallery, New York,
24 September–20 October 1962

While the gallery director, Richard Bellamy, presented the works to Panza with tongue-in-cheek ("'Candies in a Box'—so beautiful and gooey, Signor Panza…"[69]), it is evident that Panza was struck not by the works' humorous mimicry of shiny, delectable goodies, but by their uncanny manipulation of the commodity's lived experience and emotional life. "These poor objects, which had lived so long with somebody who didn't use them anymore, so closely linked to individual lives, were changed into something brilliant by Oldenburg's strong, pure colors."[70] The items that spoke to Panza were not primarily "shop items" (such as they were—the pastry-case tarts, suit jackets on hangers, sides of beef). Rather they were objects that appeared already imprinted by human use; particularly humans such as the "tired businessman" Matisse had once envisioned as the grateful recipient of his art.

Shirt with Objects on a Chair, Blue Pants and Pocket Objects on Chair, Umbrella and Newspaper, and *Breakfast Table* are all scenarios of this type. The defeated tie, the fat, spray-painted key, the abandoned cufflinks and opened wallet—all evoke the landscape of the traveling salesman, that quintessential American anti-hero immortalized by Arthur Miller.[71] No one needs to read these newspapers to understand them. The soft, folding version with the umbrella (lovingly sewn by Oldenburg's wife, painter Pat Muchinski) is stamped with a single letter (an authorial "C"); the plaster and muslin variant on the breakfast table is scumbled with illegible paint. Their muteness both reduces and elevates such objects: reduces them to the status of props, and elevates them to the level of universals. These, Oldenburg seems to suggest, are the essential attributes of socialized man, the portals to his subjectivity as a capitalist citizen of the world. Standing in Panza's living room, we might wait forever for this Willie Loman to return—until we realize that *we* are the missing subject of these tableaux.

The poignancy of these uncradled stuffs reminds us of Oldenburg's mortuary edge, and his ambition to make "a cemetery of industrial objects."[72] For the viewing subjects constructed by the piece, it is just one more "nail in the coffin" to realize that the embalmed industrial object here is the American white-collar worker himself. Panza recalls the same mortuary sensibility, but supplies a happier ending: "…the context [of the *Store*] was important, influential.… When you were inside the *Store*, you saw the same objects in a different dimension, *like seeing a person who came back to life*."[73] I submit that resurrection is not the necessary outcome of our desires for these commodities—although that was certainly the promise of the Coca-Cola Plan.

During that fateful visit to Manhattan to see Oldenburg's *Store*, Panza also met with Castelli to see firsthand the works of James Rosenquist and Roy Lichtenstein, photos of which Castelli and his wife Ileana Sonnabend had shown Panza a few months earlier in Italy. Although grouped with Oldenburg in all standard histories of Pop art, these artists produce works that are radically different. Cool, cerebral, and ironic (terms particularly appropriate for Lichtenstein), their canvases are, above all, *paintings*—smooth surfaces on which images hover like projections from an adman's dream. These, far more than Oldenburg's lumbering *Pepsi-Cola Sign*, are the beneficiaries of the victory celebrated by Rauschenberg's *Coca-Cola Plan*. Appropriately enough, there is "Cola" in Rosenquist's *Vestigial*

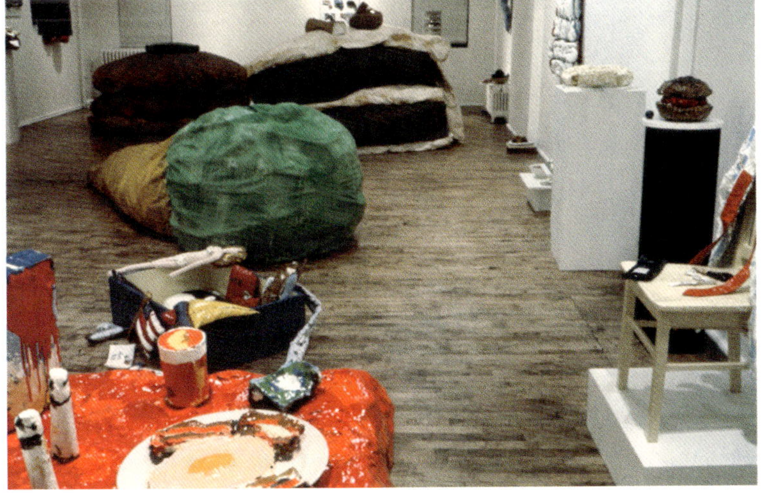

Appendage—but it is neither bottle nor nostalgic fragment of the real. It is *pure spectacle*, its momentary appearance just sufficient to ensure "product recognition" and the Pavlovian body reflexes of a hand reaching for cash and a mouth salivating for soda.

Oldenburg, too, deconstructs commodity fetishism—but his very expressionism returns his works to the realm of humanistic social realism.[74] Rosenquist, former billboard painter that he is, doesn't "comment on" advertising so much as speak its mother tongue—the airbrushed photographic tonalities, the acid hues, the "jazzy" cropping, the gloss and sheen—these visual "memes" are the primordial alef-bets of Madison Avenue's postwar visual vocabulary. Crucially, however, Rosenquist does not leave us there, in the suspended and naturalized gaze of imagined plenty. With his insistent disruption of the advertisement's visual syntax, and through other recurring devices of estrangement, the artist surfaces the (famously) subliminal messages that drive commodified desire.

Attention to the joints and disjunctions of these paintings tells us a great deal. Seemingly at the heart of *Vestigial Appendage* (though actually near its upper right corner), Rosenquist has pressed a carefully jigsawed piece of plywood into the composition, bounded by the boy's leg, the "Cola" cap, and the seductive smile of this week's *Giaconda*. The plywood (its harsh grain still visible) is painted a dull industrial gray, physically locked into the composition so tightly that paint oozes up around every side. This "appendage" may be vestigial, but its work in the image is important. It visually connects the truncated boy's phallic rocking-toy handle with the sinuous lines of the corporate logotype, as if the thinly veiled sexuality of the boy's action will result in a "signature," identity-as-logo, signed on the vault of commodity heaven. But the plywood wedge, although it connects boy and sign, also separates them. Butting up against the woman's mouth and obscuring the implied trajectory between *phallos* and *logos*, the grey block also stands as a rigid barrier to the empowered gesture fantasized here, reminding us that this boy's wish (of re-production in all its senses) is mediated by *her*—by various hers, all sundered and boxed and ready to perform the fetish's primary psychological function of guarding the ever-vulnerable phallus.[75]

Lichtenstein does not choose to probe such charged psychological terrain, and his were the last Pop objects to enter Panza's collection (and among the first to be pruned).[76] In Panza's view, Lichtenstein "gives cultural dignity to images that don't have any."[77] This was certainly high praise, but it may be that the cool, conceptual qualities of Lichtenstein's work (Panza saw them as a kind of classicism) served only to set the stage (or whet the appetite) for the collector's shift to the unmitigated conceptualism of Minimal art (and its sequelae, which would occupy the remaining years of Panza's collecting activity). A fitting coda to the first phase of Panza's career as a collector, Lichtenstein's works negotiated with the power of graphic representations of humanity (going all the way back to French modernism, as had Fautrier) but did so through the filter of reproductive technologies. "In a way I think of myself as an abstract painter," Lichtenstein said, and the seemingly mechanized, monochromatic icons in Panza's collection support that view.[78]

Standing Rib and *The Grip* have been linked to the macho tough-guy posturing of Abstract Expressionism (muscle and strength being key terms of praise for heroic Action Painting). Like Rauschenberg's *Factum* paintings, however, they are satires; their mannerism, their quotational quality, and their very *reproducibility* provides a mordant critique of the authenticity of the gesture.[79] By lavishing his considerable analytic abilities on the most banal graphic conventions (how to render flesh marbled with fat, or a thumbnail's cuticles, in

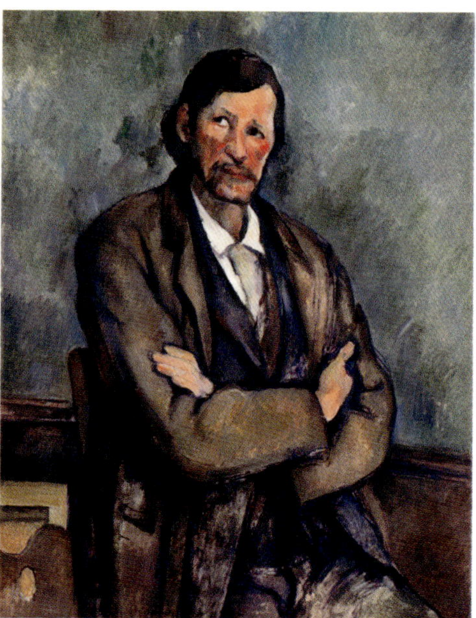

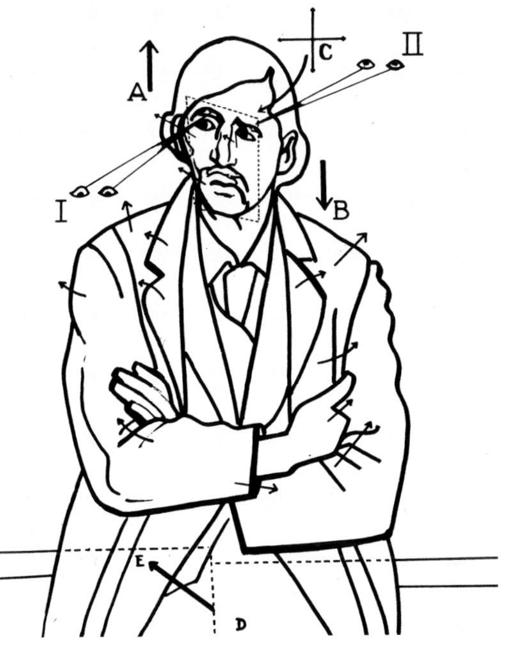

the barest and most efficient way), Lichtenstein creates a double logic of signs. Initially we see these works as interrogating the commodity system itself: the generic, standardized slab of meat, for example, floating in a sterile white void, all connection to its animal origins severed so that it can be processed by factory technologies (and presumably savored without guilt). After the barest pause, however, we begin to see past "content" and "representation" to view Lichtenstein's deadpan forms as being not just about commodity desires, but also pictorial ones. It is not just food being processed, but our visual appetites being met by the crisp, iconic culture of the corporate logotype.[80] Clean lines, classic modernist coloring (the Bauhaus's own black, white and red), good "gestalt" (the comprehensible contour), and *reproducibility* are necessary qualities, Lichtenstein suggests, not just for advertising logotypes, but for *art*. *Standing Rib* takes the time-honored convention of the still life (*nature morte*, as the French so aptly put it: those moist fish by Chardin, Rembrandt's gut-wrenching sides of beef) and presents the genre with its brand-new 1960s face.

Lichtenstein's "mechanics" were not all popular. Panza got the wit and insight of *Man with Folded Arms* (a.k.a. *Cézanne*), but the butt of Lichtenstein's joke was not amused. At first level, the painting celebrates the iconic qualities of Cézanne's painting, *Man with Crossed Arms* (c. 1899). Lichtenstein has both exaggerated the figure's length and extended the canvas's vertical axis, but more significantly, he has "punched" the figure out of its background and rendered it in thick, linear black and white to increase its brand-name iconicity (brand-name as in the common manner of speaking about an artwork as being "a Cézanne," much like "a Fiat," "a Hoover," "a Frigidaire"). What Panza would doubtless have known, however, is that Lichtenstein's joke goes much further. It was not Cézanne who came back from the grave to complain about this appropriation, but the very much alive author of *Cézanne's Composition*, Erle Loran. Lichtenstein appropriated Loran in part to critique the latter's rather pedestrian formal analyses, revealing that Loran was himself one of the minions turning Cézanne's mysterious paintings into a "brand." Loran was, perhaps predictably, furious, but Panza was intrigued. For Panza, Lichtenstein's work interrogated "an archetypal model…an intellectual transformation of something common," and it seemed to him that in the artist's uncompromising simplifications he had returned to modernism's only future: namely, determining what remained convincing in the conventions of visual art.[81] The fact that Lichtenstein was an American painter, here seizing the future from its prewar stranglehold by French modernism, surely didn't hurt. Loran, in his essay "Cézanne and Lichtenstein: Problems of 'Transformation'," violently disagreed.[82]

Although now obscure, Loran's 1943 analyses of Cézanne's painting were deft enough to persuade legions of American readers of the profound link between the French artist's nineteenth-century modernism and twentieth-century abstraction (most notably, Picasso's Cubism). And Loran was neither hostile to contemporary art nor undyingly loyal to the French. In Loran's view (obviously indebted to critics such as Clement Greenberg), the great momentum of French modernism had continued after the war—but not in France. It had been transferred irrevocably to the avant-garde of American painters working in the Abstract Expressionist vein.[83] For Loran, as for Panza, American

Paul Cézanne
Man with Crossed Arms, c. 1899
Oil on canvas
36¼ x 28⅞ inches
Solomon R. Guggenheim Museum, New York

Diagram of Cézanne's *Man with Arms Folded*
from Erle Loran's 1943 book,
Cézanne's Composition
(University of California Press)

art represented the future—but Loran's views remained mired in a Cold War politics that had long since lost its relevance to the globalizing artists of Lichtenstein's generation (and found no place in Panza's own views). In Loran's strident critique, Lichtenstein was foolishly jeopardizing the respect other countries had finally granted American culture by simply echoing "the crassness, the vulgarity, the depressing tawdriness of modern advertising art...." identified, of course, with that *other* part of American culture, that part that was increasingly global (as opposed to merely international). For Panza, Lichtenstein's insouciant confidence gave him no trouble at all. It was all part of the plan—the Coca-Cola Plan. Everything would be all right, life would go on, and people would make their free-market choices in a global frame of mind.

• • •

EPILOGUE Panza was proved both right and wrong in sharing the vision of the future predicted by that Coca-Cola Plan. As interviewers endlessly solicited, his perspicuous choices (of stimulating works by barely known artists whose prices were still in the three figures) were certainly proven "right" from the standpoint of investment. Appreciating in value more astoundingly than Panza real estate, and more solid as an asset than the Panza wine-dealing business had ever been, the Panza collection (which totaled more than 600 objects by the end of the 1970s) could have provided the capital for a substantial start-up company in the 1980s or 90s—if Panza had wanted to auction it off. But this loyal citizen had wanted primarily to see his collection, conveyed "at a greatly reduced price," installed in a fine setting provided by his own (or even some other) European country.[84] This was the hurdle that finally proved the limitations of the Coca-Cola Plan, however. Panza was wrong in expecting other Italians and fellow Europeans to see the future as he did—in a globalism developed from initially American terms.

As others have recounted, this most painful lesson came to Panza from his negotiations with politicians in Italy, specifically left-wing progressive politicians from nearby Turin whom Panza knew and trusted. As plans grew firmer for Panza's gift of a large group of Minimalist objects, the regional administrator canceled the planned transfer. Ironically, it was because of local pressure from other contenders for the "global"—the internationally minded artists of Turin's own *Arte Povera* group whom Panza had never included in his high-profile collection.

The view of American art as initiating the global—what I have named, in Rauschenberg's shorthand, the "Coca-Cola Plan"—collapses many problematic issues and minimizes the very substantial post-colonial critique of U.S. arrogance on earth. And the limitations of this view are also evident in the failure of Panza's collection to escape from the gravitational pull of its first, best, and most stubbornly local audience here in the United States. But Panza's astonishing vision (and we must never lose our wonder at this Italian's extraordinary connection with objects that began from a profoundly local, New York view of American culture) has, I have argued, other lessons to teach us. The movement from postwar abjection, to sublimity, to uneasy celebration of free marketry, is a cultural arc that has been traced in the works that Giuseppe Panza chose as constituting his own very personal view of humanity's future. But it is a trajectory that also marked what we normally think of as "more important" spheres of economic and political activity during this same period.[85] Such enlargements cannot be expanded here. But it has been the task of this essay to hint at those parallel trajectories, and to wonder at their implications for the next millennium, where globalism leaves the mechanical, the print-based, and the photographic, and enters its next, electronic phase.

NOTES

1   Moira Roth, "The Aesthetic of Indifference," *Artforum* 16, no. 3 (November 1977): 46–53; Leo Steinberg, "Reflections on the State of Criticism," *Artforum* 10, no. 7 (March 1972): 37–49. See also his *Other Criteria: Confrontations with Twentieth-Century Art* (Oxford: Oxford University Press, 1972).

2   David Sylvester, "Art in a Coke Climate," *The Sunday Times Magazine* (London)(26 January 1964): 14, 17. Spelling Americanized.

3   Since I have invoked intention, it is pertinent to note that Rauschenberg could easily have seen the Nike when he was in Paris studying at the Académie Julian in 1948.

4   Filippo Tommaso Marinetti, "The Foundation and Manifesto of Futurism" (1909), anthologized in Charles Harrison and Paul Wood, *Art in Theory: 1900–1990* (Oxford: Blackwell, 1992), 147.

5   Panza recalls the Futurists, in particular, as seeming entirely irrelevant to the future of culture during his childhood: "…in the 1930s there was very little interest left in Futurism. Most people considered Futurism a strange idea, there wasn't much interest in it anymore."Giuseppe Panza, interviewed by Christopher Knight, in *Art of the Fifties, Sixties and Seventies: The Panza Collection* (New York: Rizzoli; and Los Angeles: The Museum of Contemporary Art, 1986), 27.

6   I say "curatorial collection" because the name *Arte Povera* was coined by a critic, Germano Celant, who put the first exhibitions and publications together. Some of his first publications linked young Italian artists with contemporaneous New Yorkers such as Richard Serra (whose identification with powerful industrial processes would otherwise seem to preclude his inclusion under the rubric "poor art"). For the "victim" role in *Arte Povera* one thinks, for example, of Giuseppe Penone's comic, mysterious, yet somehow also abject and mournful pieces in which regular spuds are exhibited alongside casts of carved potatoes depicting ears, mouths, or disembodied hands.

7   The history of *Arte Povera* in Italy is only beginning to be written. Here my interest is in what Panza, as a collector living near Turin (the movement's home base), may have made of its complex relations with international art movements. Significantly, he seems to have determined that he would not participate in the development—perhaps because it was too homegrown? For an interesting view of *Arte Povera*, its history, and Germano Celant's writing of same, see Dan Cameron, "Anxieties of Influence: Regionalism, *Arte Povera*, and the Cold War," *Flash Art*, no. 164 (May/June 1992): 75–81.

8   Panza to Knight, op. cit., 27.

9   Ibid., 20–21

10   Giuseppe Panza, interviewed by Kerry Brougher in October 1984, as published in *The Museum of Contemporary Art: The Panza Collection* (Los Angeles: The Museum of Contemporary Art, 1985), n.p.

11   See William Allen, "Fautrier's Path to Abstraction," *Kunst & museumjournaal* 1, no. 5 (1990): 34–40; and Jacqueline Lafargue et al., *Fautrier 1898–1964*, exh. cat. (Paris: Musée d'art moderne de la Ville de Paris, 1989). See also Dr. Keith Comess, "The Massacres at Tulle and Oradour-sur-Glane,"website:www.ualberta.ca/~dreinbol/oradour.html.

12   Panza to Brougher, op. cit.

13   On the *informe,* Bataille continues: "informe [formless] is not only an adjective having a given meaning, but a term that serves to bring things down in the world, [which otherwise requires] that each thing have its form." Bataille, "Informe," in *Documents* 1, no. 7 (1929): 392, translated in Bataille, *Visions of Excess: Selected Writings, 1927–1939* (Minneapolis: University of Minnesota Press, 1985), 31, and cited by Yve-Alain Bois and Rosalind Krauss in their indispensable *Formless: A User's Guide* (Cambridge, Mass.: Zone Books and The MIT Press, 1997), 5 (translation slightly modified here). By coupling abjection and the *informe* in a sentence about Fautrier citing Bataille, I violate all the orders established by Bois and Krauss (perhaps I can claim a certain operation of Bataille's irreverant "quack" or belch in this impertinent disregard for their unimpeachable *author*ity). More to the point, however, the spatial and discursive constraints of the present catalogue will not permit a sustained argument on my part about how the abject and the *informe* might be connected (which I believe them to be, despite the authors' objections, with the abject a specific kind of formlessness that violates the body's boundaries) or how Fautrier might, for average viewers in the 40s and 50s, be seen to perform that connection. Certainly I concur with the authors' judgment of Fautrier as courting kitsch, and refer readers to their discussions in *Formless* on pages 21, 121–22, *et passim*. See more on "insincerity" below. For Fautrier's engagement with Bataille, see *Madame Edwarda*, by Pierre Angelique [Georges Bataille] and illustrated by Jean Perdu [Jean Fautrier] (Paris: Chez le Solitaire, 1945), "Nouvelle version revue par l'auteur et enrichie de trente gravures….," copy number 63 at Houghton Library, Harvard University.

14   The cross is observable in the presence of the painting, and exactly subtends the prostrate, fetus-like form on the surface of *Dépouille*. Seen together with its *pentimento, Dépouille* is a Deposition painting, all the more fascinating since its basic form, in Fautrier's vocabulary, is a naked, erotically amputated female like the one traced in *Nu*.

15   As mentioned above, Bois and Krauss (in *Formless*, op. cit.) see Fautrier's paintings as knowingly kitsch—and thus laudably *informe* in their mocking of bourgeois notions of "expression" with an ironic

falsehood. Although they offer trenchant analyses of Fautrier's *forms*, ultimately they pin their judgment of his irony or knowingness largely on Jean Dubuffet's competitive and spleenish complaints about Fautrier's dandyish persona at the opening of the *"Otage"* exhibition (apparently Fautrier appeared in snakeskin shoes), 258 n. 21; for Dubuffet's spleen see the fuller text of the letter in *Jean Fautrier* (Paris: Musée d'art moderne, 1989), 22. More compelling as an argument for the kitsch value of these paintings would be discussion of their situation in the market (as it is in the realm of the commodity that kitsch operates, after all). It is the cool operation of the market that commodifies outrage into kitsch. Here one would want to chronicle the appearance and progression of the paintings' theme—the first *Otage* paintings grouped, titled, and signed for the show at René Drouin in 1945 (exhibited with canvases newly titled *Oradour, Massacre, Cadavre,* many dated for the show as 1945, but subsequently backdated as painted from 1942–44), their extraordinary success propelling Fautrier into heroic position as one of the leaders of *l'art informel* (a movement the painter disavowed), the subsequent momentum of the market extending at least to 1956 with the artist's update, *Tête de partisan, Budapest.* The capacity of market negotiations to deflate any notions of "expressionist sincerity" emerges in Fautrier's correspondence with Panza, whom the painter consistently importunes to buy one "grand otage" or another, or even works by other artists he is willing to sell for the right price. See Jean Fautrier's undated, handwritten letter regarding "un grand otage (50)" and his willingness to sell Panza his Wols, Panza Papers, Getty Research Institute, Acc. #940004 Series IIA, Box 108, folder 9.

16 Here I am arguing explicitly against Bois and Krauss, who see Fautrier's interest in reproduction as fundamentally cynical, particularly in light of his later "Multiple Originals" series. I want to hold on here to the possibility that in 1945, when they were first shown, and 1959, when Panza seems to have first bought them, the hostage paintings called up different readings of reproduction.

17 See Emmanuel Lévinas, *Collected Philosophical Papers,* translated by Alphonso Lingis (Dordrecht, The Netherlands: Martinus Nijhoff, 1987), and Vladimir Jankélévitch, *"Pardonner?"* (1966), "Should We Pardon Them?," translated by Ann Hobart, reprinted as foreword, *Critical Inquiry* 22, no. 3 (Spring 1996): 552–572.

18 Séan Hand, "Preface," in *The Lévinas Reader* (Oxford: Blackwell, 1989), v.

19 Emmanuel Lévinas, "Beyond Intentionality," as cited by Séan Hand in his introduction to *The Lévinas Reader,* ibid., 5. See also Lévinas, "Meaning and Sense," in *Collected Philosophical Papers,* op. cit., particularly section 7, "Sense and Ethics:" "How is the face not simply a *true representation* in which the other renounces his alterity? …a face imposes itself upon me without my being able to be deaf to its call or to forget it, that is, without my being able to stop holding myself responsible for its distress. Consciousness loses its first place."(96–97)

20 Panza to Brougher, op. cit.

21 Exhibition brochure, Martha Jackson Gallery, 14 March 1957. Panza Papers, Getty Research Institute, Acc. #940004 Series IIA, Box 148, folder 2.

22 Typescript manuscript in Antoni Tàpies correspondence (undated and unsigned), Panza Papers, op. cit., Box 148, folder 15.

23 Undated, the telegram is in the Panza Papers, op. cit., Box 148, folder 8. What might be a response from Martha Jackson Gallery (thanking Panza for the telegram) is dated 4 February 1958, but Lynda Bunting's catalogue raisonné of the Panza collection has *Animal* entering the collection in 1957, so it is possible that the dated Jackson telegram refers to a different communiqué. See Lynda Bunting, *Giuseppe Panza Collection, The Museum of Contemporary Art Los Angeles: A Catalogue Raisonné;* M.A. Thesis, California State University at Northridge, California. The vagaries of the painting's title seem particularly intractable here. Bunting notes that the Tàpies catalogue raisonné [Anna Agustí, *Tàpies, The Complete Works; Vol. 1: 1943–1960* (New York: Rizzoli, 1989), 284 no. 572] accepts the title *Animal,* although *Beast* is both noted on the Martha Jackson gallery label and published with the work's first reproduction. All other authors refer to the work as *Ochre-Brown.*

24 I say ostensibly, because both Pollock and Barnett Newman arranged things so as to have a disproportionate number of paintings bearing the title *Number 1.*

25 The origin of these titles is unclear; however, *Beast* is certainly the title under which the painting was first shown, illustrated, and bought by Panza.

26 Tàpies, "Communication on the Wall," translation of "Comunicació sobre el mur," in Antoni Tàpies, *La pràctica de l'art* (Barcelona: Edicions Ariel, Esplugues de Llobregat, 1970), 125–130, and cited in Carmen Giménez, *Tàpies,* exh. cat. (New York: Solomon R. Guggenheim Museum, 1995), 46.

27 Tàpies, "Comunicació sobre el mur," in Giménez, ibid., 47.

28 Ibid., 48.

29 Octavio Paz, translated by Eliot Weinberger, in *The Collected Poems of Octavio Paz* (New York: New Directions, 1987), 573, as quoted by Dore Ashton, "Matter and Spirit: The Art of Antoni Tàpies," in Giménez, op. cit., 37. Although I take the quote from Ashton, I disagree completely with her reading of the poem, and of Tàpies's work in

general, as "always critical" of Christianity. In my reading, the Christian symbolism is yet one more oscillation between universalism and a (Catholic, Spanish) groundedness in Tàpies's work.

30 Panza to Knight, 22.

31 Achille Perilli, "Segni e immagini di Franz Kline," *Civiltà delle Macchine* 5, no. 3 (May–June 1957): 33. *Civiltà delle Macchine* began publication in 1953, under the auspices of the "Gruppo Industriale della Società Finanziaria Meccanica FINMECCANICA, Roma," which seems to have been a trade group or consortium of Italian industries. Just before the issue that included the short essay on Kline, the publisher switched to IRI, the Industrial Reconstruction Institute. It would be very interesting indeed to learn whether any Marshall Funds or other foreign development monies supported this publication.

32 Achille Perilli, "Scultura all'avanguardia," *Civiltà delle Macchine* 5, no. 5 (September–October 1956): 17–21 (English summary provided on page 81); Achille Perilli, "Segni e immagini di Franz Kline," op. cit. (English summary on page 82).

33 Panza to Knight, 22, 23.

34 Achille Perilli, "Segni e immagini di Franz Kline," op. cit., 33, 82. The quotes are from "Franz Kline's signs and images," the English summary of Perilli's article; paraphrases are my own translations from the Italian text.

35 Panza to Knight, 22.

36 Panza to Brougher, n.p.

37 Ibid.

38 Panza to Knight, 23–24.

39 Toni Toniato, "Le illuminazioni di Rothko," *Evento*, 3/4 (1958): 31.

40 Leonardo Borgese, for *Corriere della Sera*, quoted in the American edition of *Time* magazine, "American Abstraction Abroad," 72, no. 5 (4 August 1958): 40.

41 See the thesis of Anna Chave, who argues that Rothko's early figurative impulses are carried over into the later paintings, which can be read as depositions, crucifixions, and the like. *Mark Rothko: Subjects in Abstraction* (New Haven, Conn.: Yale University Press, 1989).

42 Edmund Burke, *A Philosophical Inquiry into the Origin of Our Ideas of the Sublime and Beautiful, With a Discourse Concerning Taste*, 2nd ed. (London: N. Hailes, John Bumpus et al., 1824); see also Immanuel Kant, *Observations on the Feeling of the Beautiful and Sublime*, translated by John T. Goldthwait (Berkeley, Calif.: University of California Press, 1960).

43 Pierre Restany to Panza, "Paris 11 fèvrier [1959]," Panza Papers, op. cit., Series I, Box 68, folder 7 (Restany Correspondence). The translations of Restany's letters are my own.

44 Pierre Restany to Panza, "31 mai 1960," Panza Papers, op. cit. The translation of the French, which I have attempted to paraphrase effectively, is mine.

45 To his credit, it must be said that Restany never openly pushes the "New Realist" works on Panza, at least in writing.

46 The evidence for even this influence is slight—however letters mention various luncheons with Tàpies and other Spanish abstractionists; a postcard from 11 December 1958 illustrates a Fautrier (*Otage #7*, not one of Panza's), and a brief note in Restany's letter of 4 February (1959, by virtue of its mention of "New American Painting") refers to a meeting with Fautrier. It was in 1959 that the first Fautrier painting seems to have entered Panza's collection, although the 1958 postcard refers to "*suo Fautrier*." Restany correspondence, Panza Papers, op. cit.

47 For the importance of Cage and the significance of the "Frankenstein" moniker, see my "Finishing School: John Cage and the Abstract Expressionist Ego," *Critical Inquiry* 19, no. 4 (Summer 1993): 628–665, especially 631. For an excellent account of the Italian sojourn, see Calvin Tomkins, *The Bride and the Bachelors: Five Masters of the Avant-Garde (Duchamp, Tinguely, Cage, Rauschenberg, Cunningham)* (New York: Viking Penguin, 1965), 130–133.

48 Panza tells the story of the painting's acquisition to Knight, op. cit., 26. He is quoted as referring to the painting as *Kick Back* rather than *Kickback*, but this is the only reference to an alternate spelling. The Documenta in question was in the summer of 1959.

49 With his pride in the hunt, Panza has enjoyed telling the story that he got the painting from Larry Rubin for $750. (See Knight, 26.) In fact, correspondence shows that Rubin's Galerie Neufville initially invoiced Panza for $2,500 for *Kickback*, "*de mon frère en New York*." Panza Papers, op. cit., Box 140, folder 16, invoice and letter 30 May 1960.

50 These metaphors are drawn from Leo Steinberg's important early criticism of Rauschenberg. See Steinberg, "Reflections on the State of Criticism," *Artforum* 10, no. 7 (March 1972): 37–49.

51 See, for example, Charles Stuckey's "Reading Rauschenberg," *Art in America* 65, no. 2 (March/April 1977): 77–84; and Roberta Bernstein, "Robert Rauschenberg's 'Rebus'," *Arts Magazine* 52, no. 5 (January 1978): 138–41.

52 The parachute would come to be a signature icon for Rauschenberg, cropping up as a kind of aerofoil sailing behind him in his 1964 performance piece named, appropriately enough, *Parachute*. The flattened umbrellas in numerous works are also visual puns of the parachute.

53 After turning from monochrome circa 1954, Rauschenberg increasingly sought this "pedestrian" color. See Calvin Tomkins, *The*

Bride and the Bachelor, op. cit., 215.

54 This is the side Panza turned toward the courtyard, so that the piece would inevitably be photographed with the shoes facing mutely toward the open window. See "At Home With Art: The Villa of Count Giuseppe Panza di Biumo," *Art in America* 58, no. 5 (September/October 1970): 102.

55 See Charles Stuckey, "Reading Rauschenberg," op. cit., 82.

56 If one were to literalize this "sentence," one might come up with "No time [for] bullfight, win horse"—hardly worth the trouble. Something like this message is already suggested visually and much more powerfully by Rauschenberg's decision to drag a line from the bullfight over and down to a violent explosion of red, to which a patch of scab-like, excremental brown has been added. Similarly, the lower register of the painting harbors things-to-be-transcended, or acts of transcendence themselves—but not a parse-able sentence. Titian's *Rape of Europa* (a classical myth on the theme of gendered violence) shows Europa straining to escape her fate (the reproduction seemingly held aloft by the straining arms of a gymnast doing a handstand), next to a photograph of a man whose face has been rubbed out, above a map of the United States butted up against one showing the Warsaw Pact countries (more violence in need of mitigation), swans (emerging from ugly ducklings), mold spores (life from decay), and a triad of gymnasts who move visually from low squats to rope-climbing heights—the message is clear enough: that only the attempt to make art and culture can stem humanity's propensity for conflict.

57 Claes Oldenburg, "LA Notes 1963," as quoted in Coosje van Bruggen, *Claes Oldenburg: Nur Ein Anderer Raum* (Frankfurt am Main: Museum für Moderne Kunst, 1991), 105. Van Bruggen also notes that Oldenburg's interest in fetishism was "stimulated" (her word) by reading *Sexual Aberrations* by William Stekel.

58 Lawrence Alloway is the British critic who circulated the name "Pop" for the new tendency, Richard Hamilton one of the London artists (see his 1956 collage for the "This Is Tomorrow" exhibition, titled *Just what is it that makes today's homes so different, so appealing?* and featuring a Tootsie-brand lollypop bearing the logo "POP!"); see also Eduardo Paolozzi's *I Was a Rich Man's Plaything,* 1947, in which a gun makes the harmless and hence humorous "POP!" sound—all discussed in David Robbins, ed., *The Independent Group: Postwar Britain and the Aesthetics of Plenty,* exh. cat. (Cambridge, Mass.: The MIT Press, 1990), 68, 97.

59 See Marco Livingstone, ed., *Pop Art: An international perspective* (New York: Rizzoli; and London: The Royal Academy of Arts, 1991).

60 For the case that Oldenburg's view of the United States was always a view from *outside:* "The erotic or the sexual is the root of 'art,' its first impulse. Today sexuality is more directed, or *here where I am in Am[erica] at this time,* towards substitutes f.ex. clothing rather than the person, fetishistic stuff, and this gives the object an intensity and this is what I try to project." Notes from 1962 (at the height of "Store Days,") as cited in van Bruggen, op. cit., 90. Emphasis added.

61 "I am for an art..." manifesto, reprinted in Germano Celant et al., *Claes Oldenburg: An Anthology* (New York: Guggenheim Museum, 1995), 97.

62 See Jameson's classic *Postmodernism, or, The Cultural Logic of Late Capitalism* (Durham, North Carolina: Duke University Press, 1991), and the more specific "Nostalgia for the Present," *South Atlantic Quarterly* 88, no. 2 (Spring 1989): 517–37. A useful gloss is offered by Arjun Appadurai, *Modernity at Large: Cultural Dimensions of Globalization* (Minneapolis: University of Minnesota Press, 1996).

63 Claes Oldenburg, *Notes* (Los Angeles: Gemini G.E.L., 1968), as quoted in Germano Celant, "Claes Oldenburg and the Feeling of Things," in *Claes Oldenburg: An Anthology,* op. cit., 23.

64 As well as the theatrical writings of Antonin Artaud, the dance innovations of Merce Cunningham, Julian Beck's Living Theater, and so forth.

65 Paul Schimmel, "Leap into the Void: Performance and the Object," in Schimmel et al., *Out of Actions: Between Performance and the Object, 1949–1979* (Los Angeles: The Museum of Contemporary Art, 1998), 68. The phrase occurred in a press release, presumably written by Oldenburg, for the "Ray Gun Show" he installed with Jim Dine at the Judson Gallery (the basement of the Judson Church in downtown Manhattan), February-March 1960.

66 "RAY GUN 1. Kid's toy. 2. Seeing through walls. 3. The universal angle. Examples: Legs, Sevens, Pistols, Arms, Phalli—simple Ray Guns. Double Ray Guns: Cross, Airplanes. Absurd Ray Guns: Ice Cream Sodas. Complex Ray Guns: Chairs, Beds. 4. Anagrams and homophonies: Nug Yar (New York). ReuBen (Gallery). 5. Accidental references: A moviehouse in Harlem. A nuclear testing site in the Sahara (Ragon). 6. What ever is needed. A word ought to be useful. 7. Cryptic sayings: 'All will see as Ray Gun sees.' 'The name of New York will be changed to Ray Gun.' 'When Ray Gun shoots no-one dies.' 8. Talismanic, fetishistic functions." "Ray Gun motto—to annihilate-illuminate.... Celebrating potency and all kids' affairs." Notes, 1961, as cited in Celant et al., op. cit., 40, with additional Notes in van Bruggen, op. cit., 13.

67 The date of the visit as fall 1962 is corroborated by Panza's recollections in interviews, and also by Richard Bellamy's letter of February 1963 referring to Panza's studio visit to Oldenburg as having already taken place. See Panza Papers, op. cit., Box 138, folders 1 and 18.

68 Panza to Knight, 28, 29.

69 Unsigned letter included with Green Gallery invoice dated 6 November 1962, Panza Papers, op. cit., Box 138, folder 1.

70 Panza to Knight, 29.

71 *Death of a Salesman* was first performed on 10 February 1949, and has been in continuous revival around the world ever since. Roy Lichtenstein takes on this same theme in his *Calendar*, dated the same year as Oldenburg's *The Store*. Measuring the days of this regulated capitalist soul, Lichtenstein's *Calendar* bears the scrawl "out of town" on one of its central pages.

72 Oldenburg, from a 1975 exhibition catalogue published by the Walker Art Center, Minneapolis, as cited in Celant, *Claes Oldenburg: An Anthology*, op. cit., 5.

73 Panza to Knight, 30. Emphasis added.

74 This question of "expressionism" in Oldenburg is supported by the fact that when the artist submitted illustrations to a fledgling *Playboy* magazine around 1955, they were rejected "as too socially conscious and too problematic" for their audience. Van Bruggen, op. cit., 7.

75 To rehearse Freud's classic theory in brief: the little (boy) child, upon first glimpsing his mother's sex, immediately connects her absence-of-a-penis to his fears of losing his own, particularly through a feared retribution by the father at the son's Oedipal desires for the mother. In order to ward off this fear, the boy must substitute some *object* for the mother's "missing member"—her shoe, perhaps, or that little fur wrap on the end of her bed. This, then, becomes the fetish: the totemic substitute for the woman's *lack*, as Jacques Lacan described it. This model of fetishism and "castration anxiety," much debated by feminists, Lacanians, and post-Freudians of one stripe or another, was a classic chestnut of 1950s analytic and popular literature.

76 Panza's wife Giovanna never liked Lichtenstein's work as much as those of other artists, and *Engagement Ring* was one painting she persuaded Panza to deaccession early on. He traded this and two other paintings by Lichtenstein for three Rosenquists. See Panza's recollections to Knight, 28.

77 Ibid.

78 Lichtenstein interviewed by Christopher Andreae, "Trying to shock—himself," *Christian Science Monitor* (18 September 1969): Section II, 11.

79 Soon after, Lichtenstein would produce the *Brushstrokes* paintings, even more direct satires of the "spontaneous" Abstract-Expressionist gesture.

80 See my *Machine in the Studio* (Chicago: The University of Chicago Press, 1996), for a fuller articulation of this argument.

81 Panza to Brougher, op. cit. In this argument about modernism, I am paraphrasing Michael Fried's deeply influential arguments of the period, since reissued in his *Art and Objecthood* (Chicago: The University of Chicago Press, 1999). For further discussion of Fried's formalism and its impact, see my "Paradigms *Perdu*, The Artworld and Kuhn," forthcoming in *Critical Inquiry*.

82 Erle Loran, "Cezanne [sic] and Lichtenstein: Problems of 'Transformation'," *Artforum* 2, no. 3 (September 1963): 34–35.

83 For the most thorough chronicle of this, see Serge Guilbaut, *How New York Stole the Idea of Modern Art*, trans. Arthur Goldhammer (Chicago: The University of Chicago Press, 1983). The present essay's title is an homage to Guilbaut.

84 Panza to Knight, 66.

85 In shorthand, and as only one example: Germany's move from Marshall Plan abjection, to "Economic Miracle," to the collapse of Eastern Europe and self-anointed leadership of the next (free-market/capitalist but also new age/Green) millennium.

I would like to acknowledge the generous assistance of many individuals: Lynda Bunting, who shared with me her catalogue raisonné of the Panza collection; curator Connie Butler and the Registration staff at The Museum of Contemporary Art; Peter Galison, collaborator and covivant, who helped me parse French handwriting; tireless Jaimey Hamilton, my research assistant; Amelia Jones, exceptional art historian, sister, and, with Tony Sherin, stalwart host; Ms. Xiaohua Li of the Harvard University Library; Charles Merewether and the staff of the Getty Research Institute.

Jean Fautrier's combinations of paint, paper, and canvas are emotionally charged works inspired by the unsettling atmosphere of France during the mid-1940s. Ambiguous and troubling, these anthropomorphic forms developed out of Fautrier's reaction to the horrors of WWII and his uncanny proximity to the atrocities. Labeled *art autre* or "other art" by French critic Michel Tapié, Fautrier's paintings are characterized by the simplification of form and rich, plastic surfaces.

Born in Paris in 1898, Fautrier was raised by his father, whose sudden death in 1908 forced the young boy to move to London and take up residence with his mother. His burgeoning artistic skills gained him admittance to London's Royal Academy School at the young age of fourteen. However, Fautrier found the Academy's instruction to be overly traditional and he subsequently enrolled in London's Slade School of Fine Art. This curriculum also proved disappointing, and he stopped attending classes in favor of painting on his own. In 1917, upon the outbreak of WWI, Fautrier was drafted into the French military and sent to fight at the front line. During the war, he was exposed to harmful gas and sustained irreparable lung and eye injuries, which granted him a medical discharge in 1921. Shortly thereafter, Fautrier settled in Paris and resumed painting.

Fautrier's work of the 1920s is highly expressive and shows evidence of two of his major influences, the nineteenth-century English painter J.M.W. Turner and the twentieth-century French painter Chaïm Soutine. These paintings, which are violent and dark investigations of sublime landscapes and decaying animals, achieved a considerable amount of commercial success throughout Paris. In 1924 Fautrier held his first one-person show of paintings at the Galerie Visconti in Paris and soon established a contract with the well-known Paris art dealer, Paul Guillaume. Fautrier's art production was not limited to painting, and in 1928 he created a series of thirty-four lithographs to illustrate Dante's *Inferno*.

Fautrier's financial security began to waver in the 1930s, which resulted in a substantial reduction of his artistic output. He began to spend the majority of his time and resources skiing and in 1934 moved to the French Alps resort town of Tignes and became a ski instructor. Upon the outbreak of WWII Fautrier abandoned the mountain town and returned to Paris in 1940. Actively involved in the war resistance, Fautrier was arrested by the Germans in 1943 and imprisoned briefly. He was able to return to Paris and was granted refuge in Dr. Lesavoureux's sanatorium where he resumed painting.

Fautrier was given the upper floor of the sanatorium's Velleda tower as a painting studio during the final years of the war. This tower was surrounded by a thicket of trees in which the Germans would torture and ultimately execute their prisoners. Although Fautrier was

JEAN
fautrier

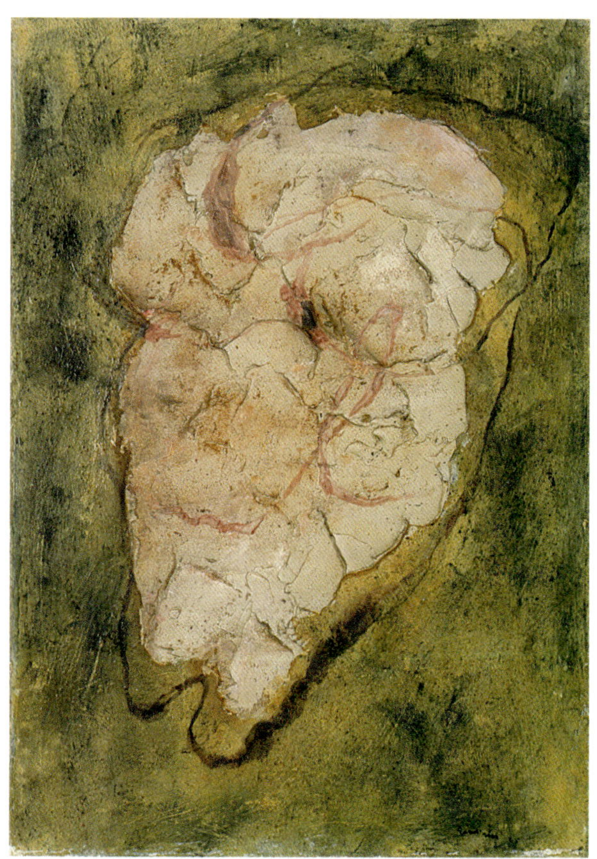

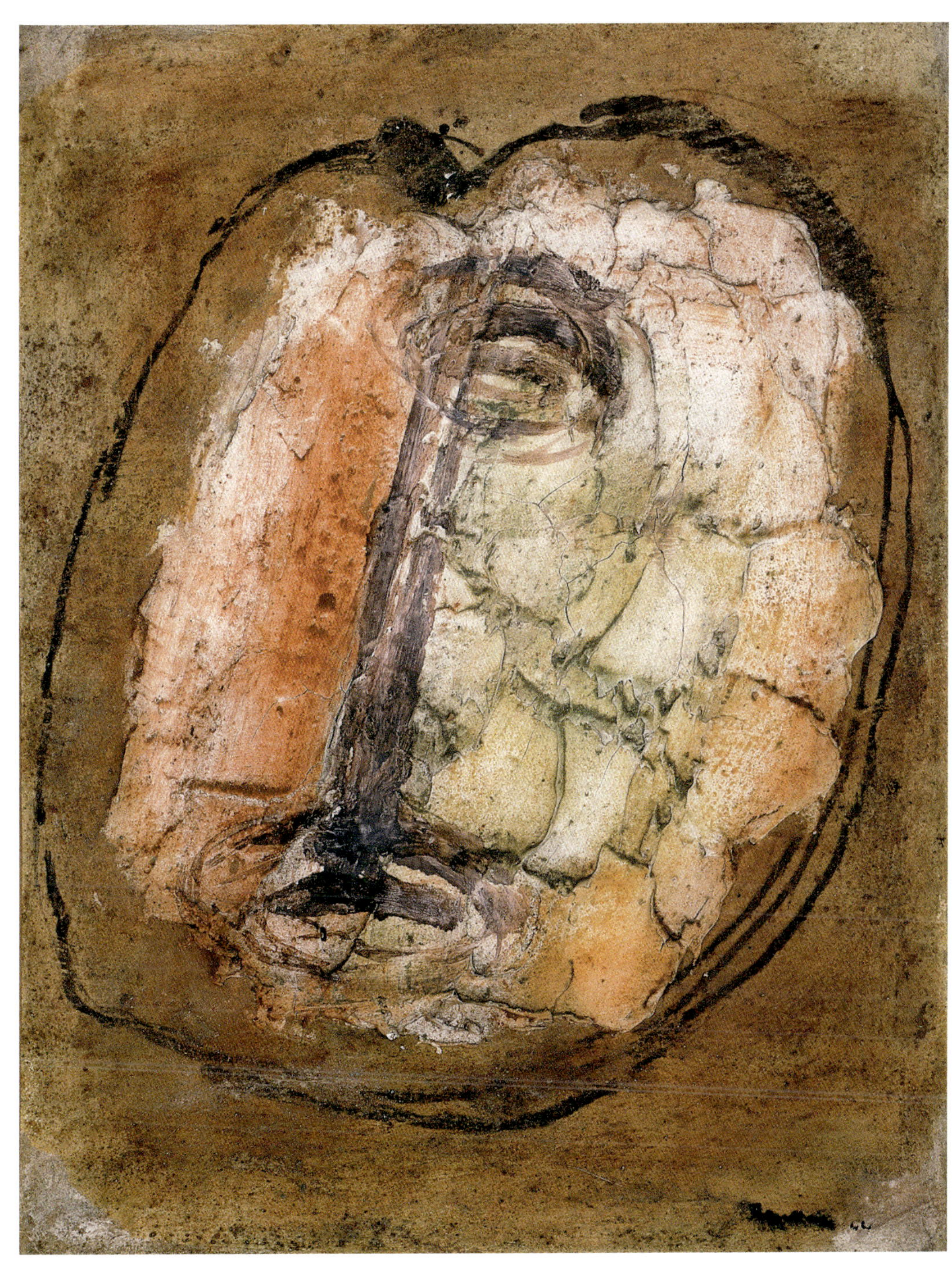

Head of a Hostage, No. 1, 1944, mixed media on paper mounted on linen, 14 x 10½ inches, (85.15)

Nu, 1943, oil on paper, 21½ x 15 inches, (84.2)

unable to actually see these horrendous acts, he was able to hear bullets ricocheting off the trees and the cries of human victims. Wracked by his exposure to human cruelty, Fautrier painted a series of small panels titled *Otages (Hostages)* that function as physical manifestations of the horrors that literally surrounded him. *Nu* (1943) is a loose representation of a human face in three-quarter view, whose ambiguity and lack of detail creates a garish and frightening figure. *Head of a Hostage, No. 14* (1944) draws upon its title for visual clues. All facial features have been obliterated by the abstraction of the form, the countenance has been replaced with a variegated line, and the result is a shape whose remains eerily reference a human head.

These pieces were created by Fautrier's own unique method, which began by gluing paper to canvas. Upon this paper he applied a thick paste, coated it with a colored powder, and permanently adhered it to the surface with varnish. The distressed surface that resulted from this technique, as seen in *Head of a Hostage, No. 1,* adds an emotional dimension to the work. The weathered and battered facade resonates within the subject and imbues it with an aura of torment. *Dépouille* (1945) was also made by this process, and the tactile nature of the materials enriches the piece with another layer of significance. It is Fautrier's interest in materiality that has historically positioned him as a precursor to the *Art Informel* school of painting.

Much of the work from this period is small and intimate in size. Probably dictated in part by the availability of materials during the war and Fautrier's own limited space within the sanatorium, works such as *Profile* (1945), for example, measure 10½ x 8¼ inches and are barely larger than a standard sheet of paper. The diminutive size is successful in yielding objects that are quiet, almost secretive glimpses into human darkness.

Fautrier's work gained international recognition in the mid-1950s and was included in *Documenta 2* in Kassel, Germany in 1959. At the Venice Biennale in 1960 he was awarded the Grand Prize. This later work, which retained the same emotional charge, became increasingly simplified in both form and content. Fautrier died in the small town of Châtenay-Malabry on the outskirts of Paris in 1964. —R.M.

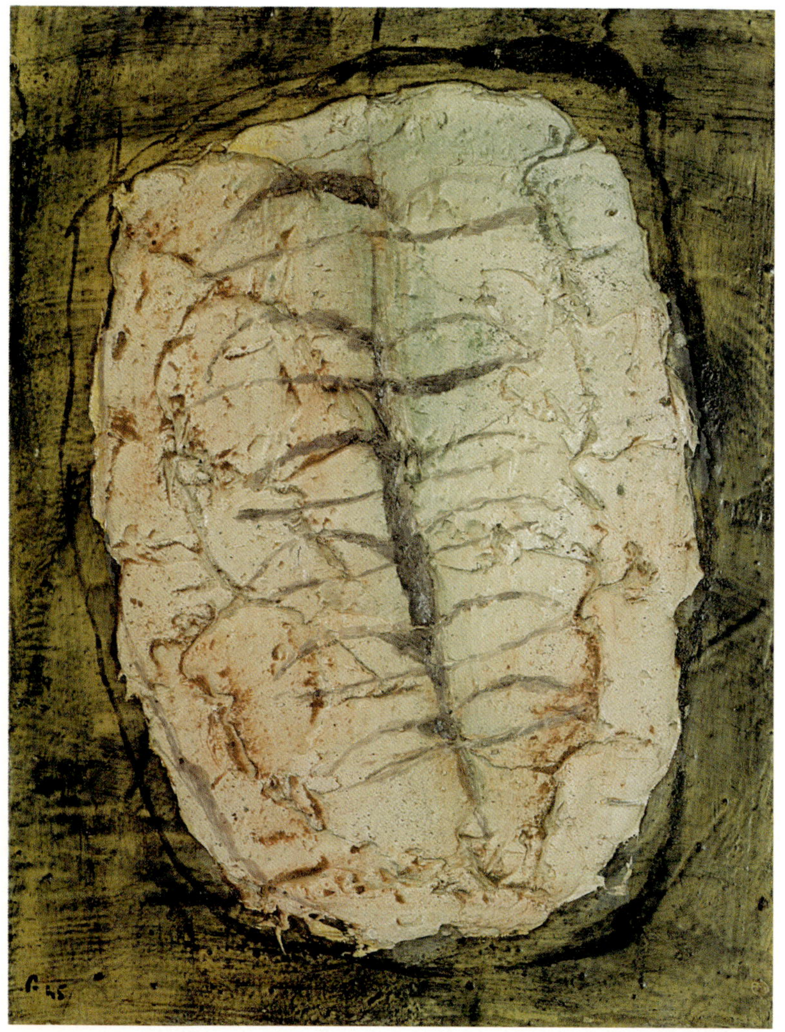

Head of a Hostage, No. 14, 1944, oil on paper, 13¾ x 10½ inches, (85.16)

Dépouille, 1945, mixed media on paper mounted to linen, 45 x 57 inches, (86.80)

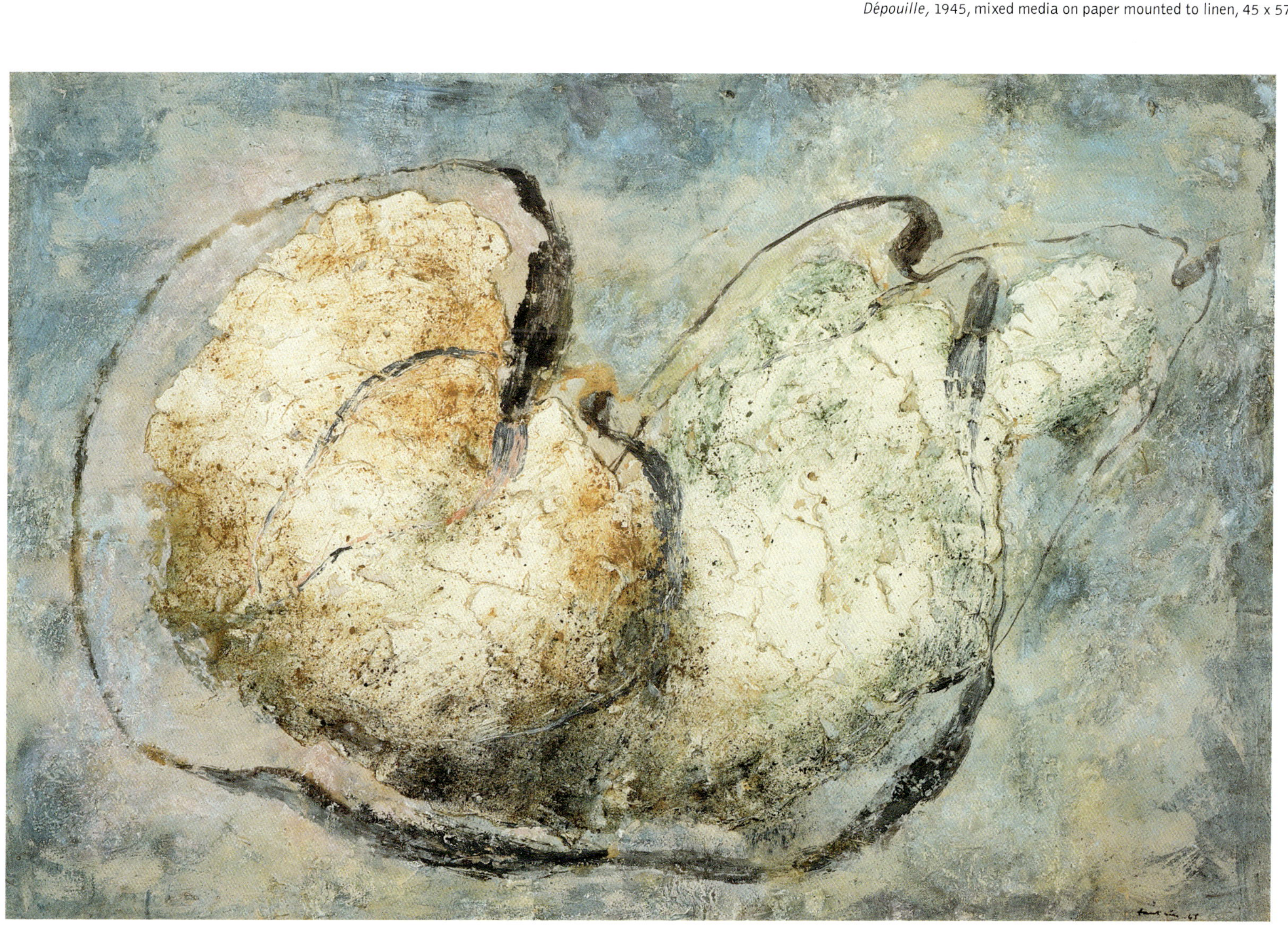

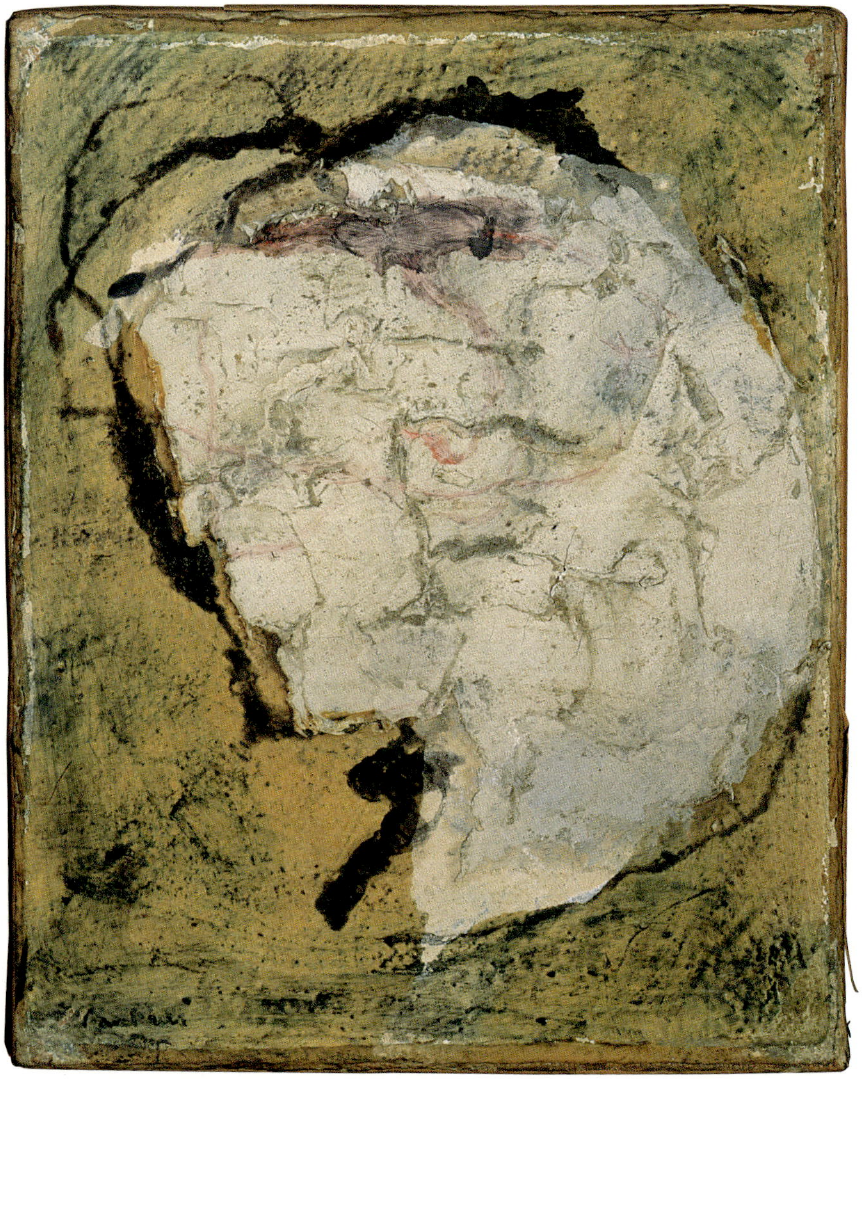

Profile, 1945, oil on canvas, 10½ x 8¼ inches, (88.3)

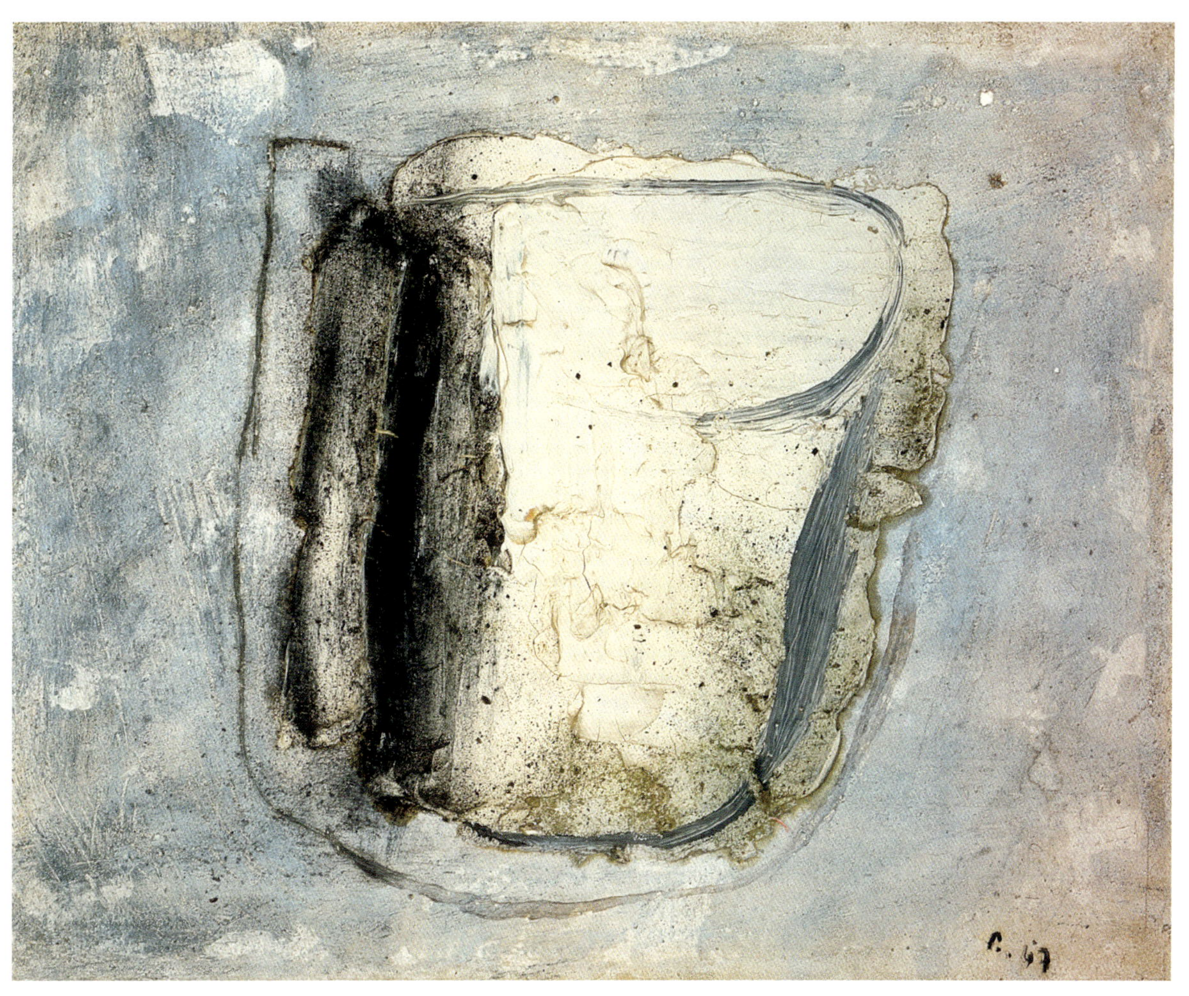

The Pot, 1947, oil on paper, 13½ x 16 inches, (87.5)

Franz Kline's dynamic and gestural abstractions positioned him as one of the key figures associated with the Abstract Expressionist movement that dominated American art production in the mid-1950s. Together with Jackson Pollock and Willem de Kooning, these artists were nicknamed "action painters" whose non-objective imagery expressed the action by which these dramatic and often emotional works were made. Although not a formally structured or self-proclaimed group, these painters worked and socialized in close proximity and established a shared artistic language. Action Painting is considered to be the first artistic movement with definitive American roots.

Born in the coal-mining region of eastern Pennsylvania, Kline displayed considerable talent as a cartoonist and illustrator as a young man.[1] The core of his formal training occurred during his two-year enrollment at Heatherley's School of Fine Art in London where he studied illustration with Steven Spurrier. Due in part to the European political climate of the 1930s, Kline returned to the United States and, in 1939, moved to New York City. At this time Kline's subject matter was focused on portraits, still lifes, cityscapes, and interior scenes. Taverns and saloons throughout New York commissioned him to paint lively murals rendered in Kline's vigorous, expressionistic style, a style that would continue to define his artistic production regardless of its content.

According to Elaine de Kooning, Kline's leap into abstract painting occurred in 1948 when he projected one of his quick, gestural sketches onto his studio wall and realized its possibilities as a large-scale painting.[2] Working from drawings he made on pages of city-issued telephone books, Kline would affix the study to a piece of cardboard, post it next to his canvas, and follow it as a guide. He was not interested in an exact reproduction; rather than projecting the drawing to be traced, or laying the composition out along a grid, he relied on his eye and gesture to recreate the basic structure and overall mood of the original sketch. Kline worked rapidly, painting black over white over black with large housepainting brushes and energetic movements. These black-and-white abstractions, for which Kline is best known, are filled with the vitality of their making.

Often jarring and disharmonious, Kline endeavored to create paintings in which the traditional methods of pictorial arrangement were dismantled and overturned. In *Black Iris* (1961) the overall geometry of the work is compromised by the solidity of pigment in the lower-left region. The verticality of *Sabro II* (1959–60) is challenged by the painted horizontal that rests quietly along the bottom-most portion of the frame. For Kline these were opportunities to explore a forced and awkward arrangement of space in which there is little distinction between figure and ground. The painting *Ilza* (1955) exemplifies

FRANZ

kline

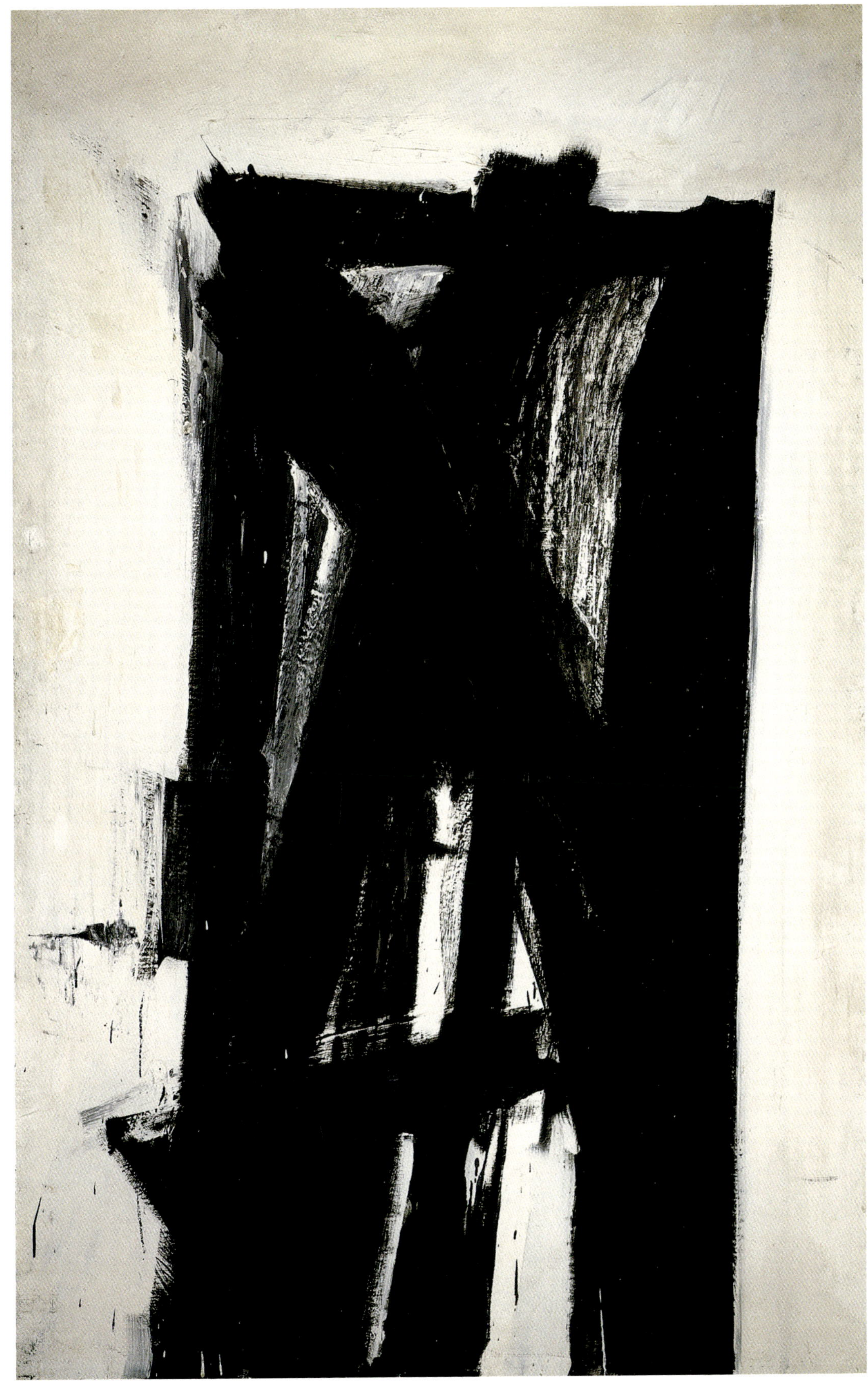

Tower, 1953, oil on canvas, 81⅜ x 51¹⁵⁄₁₆ inches, (85.17)

this complex layering of pigment in which neither black nor white can be labeled background or foreground, and the blacks, whites, and transitional grays exist in a symbiotic relationship upon the canvas.

The titles of these black-and-white abstractions suggest underlying themes, although the connections remain enigmatic. During the 1950s, New York was one of the many American cities undergoing postwar urban renewal, making scaffolding, cranes, beams, and planks all part of the everyday visual landscape. Kline's interest in this aspect of American renovation found its way into the titles of many of his works including *Buttress* (1956), *Tower* (1953), and *Monitor* (1956). More specifically, he sometimes titled the paintings after names of cities including *Hazelton* (1957) (a city in eastern Pennsylvania just south of Kline's hometown of Wilkes-Barre) and *Orleans* (1959) (a French city south of Paris).

In 1956, after the opening of Kline's first one-person show at the Sidney Janis Gallery, he commented to his friend Leo Steinberg, "I'm always trying to bring color into my paintings, but it keeps slipping away and so here I am with another black show."[3] Thus, after six years of investigating abstraction purely through black and white, Kline ceded to the exploration of color. It has been suggested that Willem de Kooning's influence led to Kline's first color abstraction *Black and Green* (1956) which later took the name *De Medici*. *Alva*, made two years later in 1958, is unusual in its inclusion of pink and yellow rather than the green and red that dominated the majority of Kline's color work. The composition of this piece is not about color, but it receives color as a harmonious additive to the black-and-white abstraction.

Kline spent the next five years creating black-and-white as well as color compositions, maintaining his energetic strokes and fluidity of expression regardless of the hues. In 1962 the artist was diagnosed with a recurring heart condition which led to his first heart attack that February. He was unable to continue painting and died three months later at New York Hospital. —R.M.

1 *Franz Kline: The Jazz Murals,* exh. cat. (Bucknell, Pennsylvania: Center Gallery, 1989).
2 Harry F. Gaugh, *Franz Kline* (New York: Abbeville Press, 1985), 84–85.
3 Letter from Leo Steinberg, Nov. 16, 1978, in Harry F. Gaugh, "Franz Kline: The Abstractions with Color," in *Franz Kline: The Color Abstractions,* exh. cat. (Washington D.C.: The Phillips Collection, 1979).

Thorpe, 1954, oil on canvas, 62 x 43⅜ inches, (88.8)

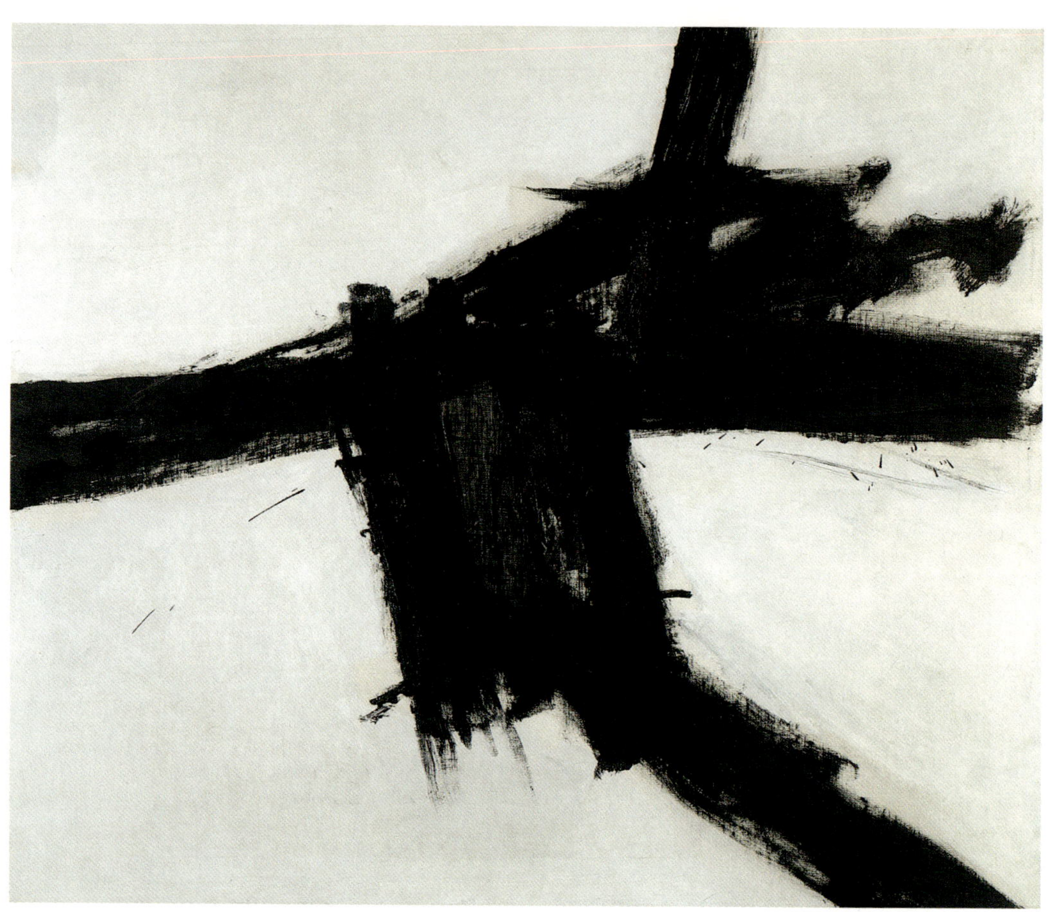

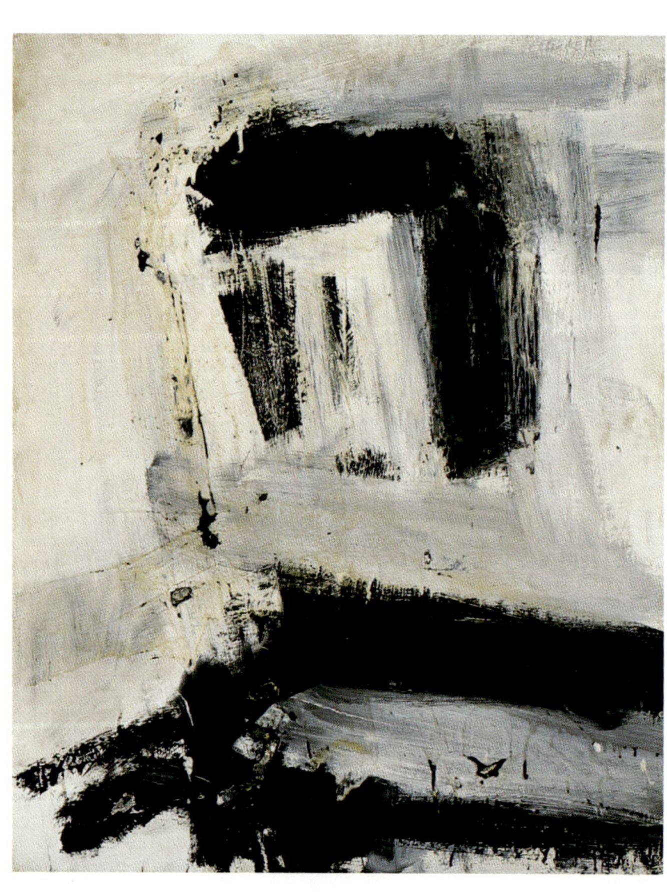

Ilza, 1955, oil on canvas, 41⅛ x 33 inches, (88.6)

Buttress, 1956, oil on canvas, 46½ x 55½ inches, (86.9)

Monitor, 1956, oil on canvas, 78¾ x 115¼ inches, (85.18)

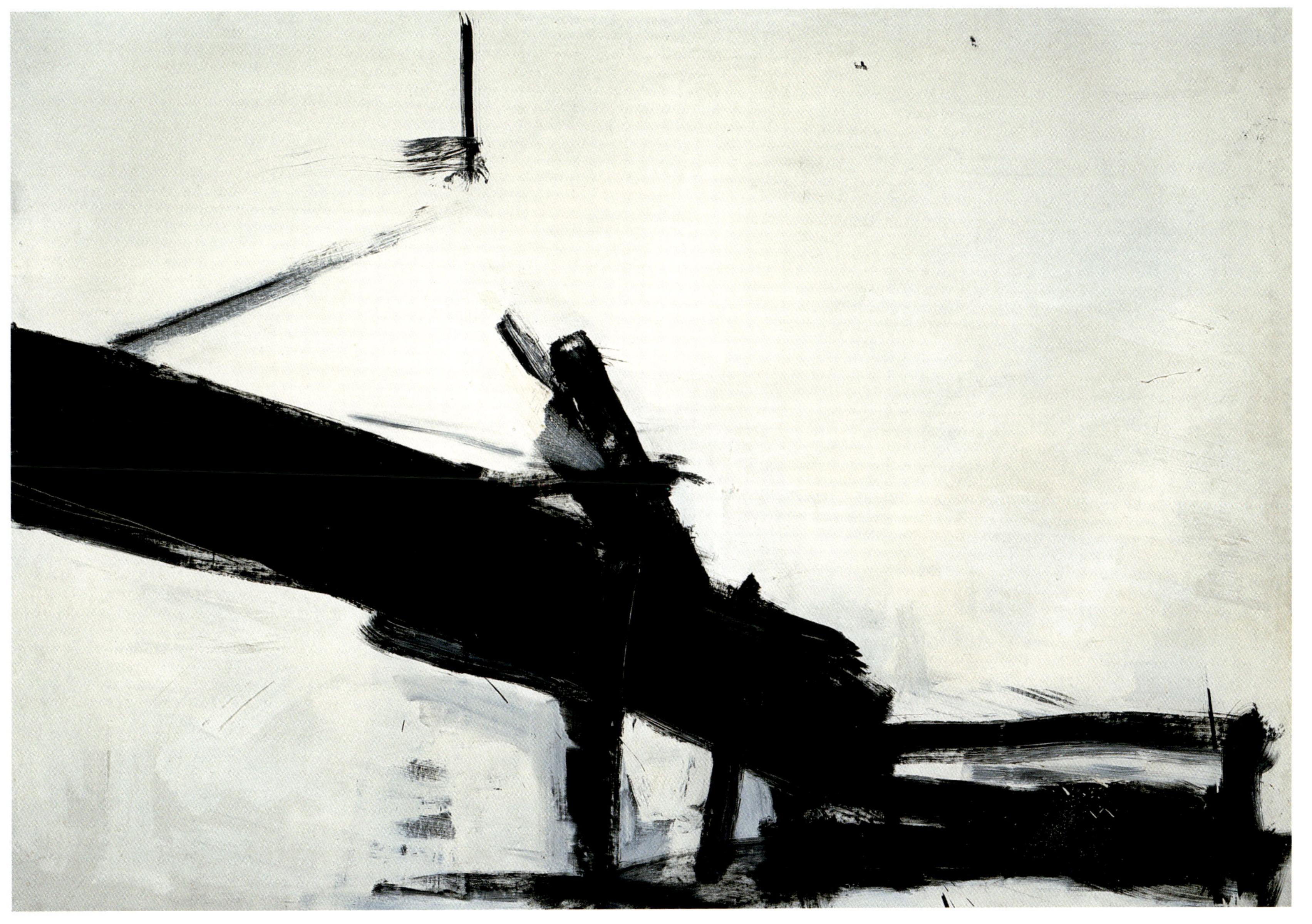

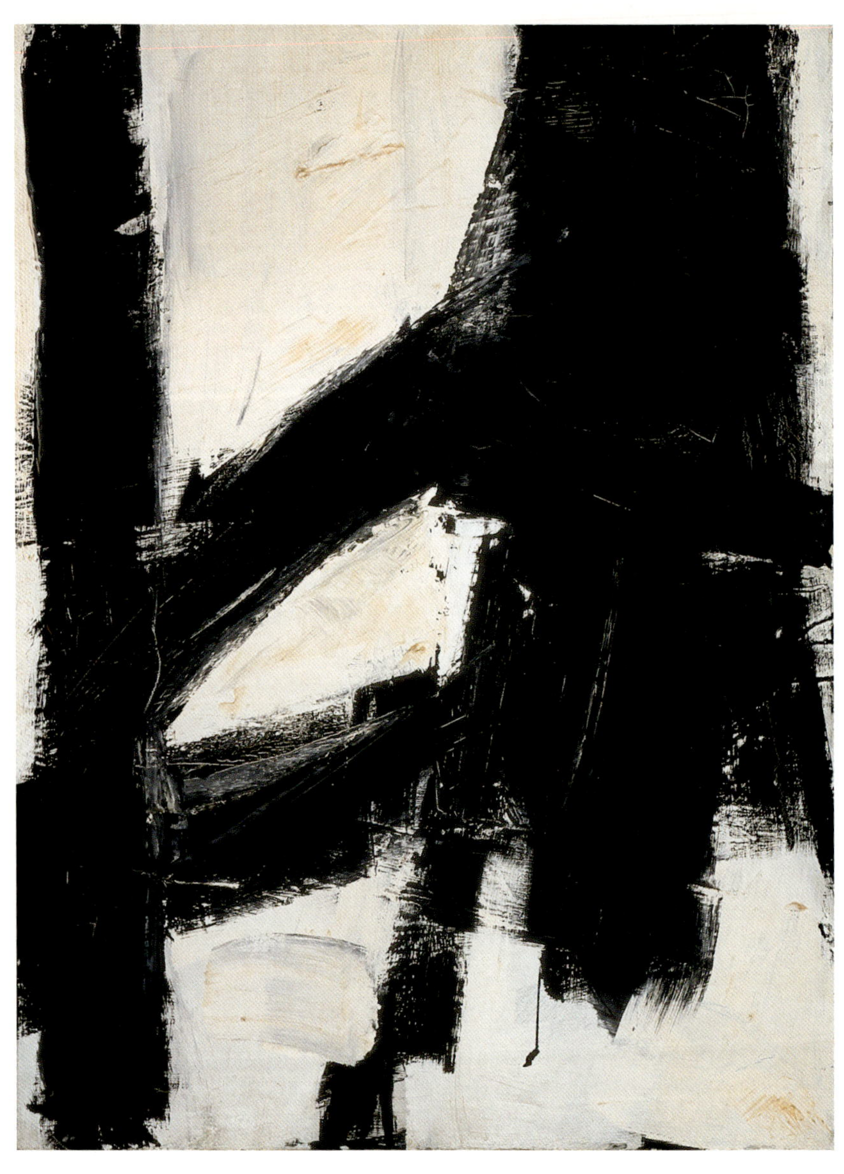

Black and White, 1957, oil on canvas, 32 x 24 inches, (88.5)

Hazelton, 1957, oil on canvas, 41¼ x 78 inches, (87.6)

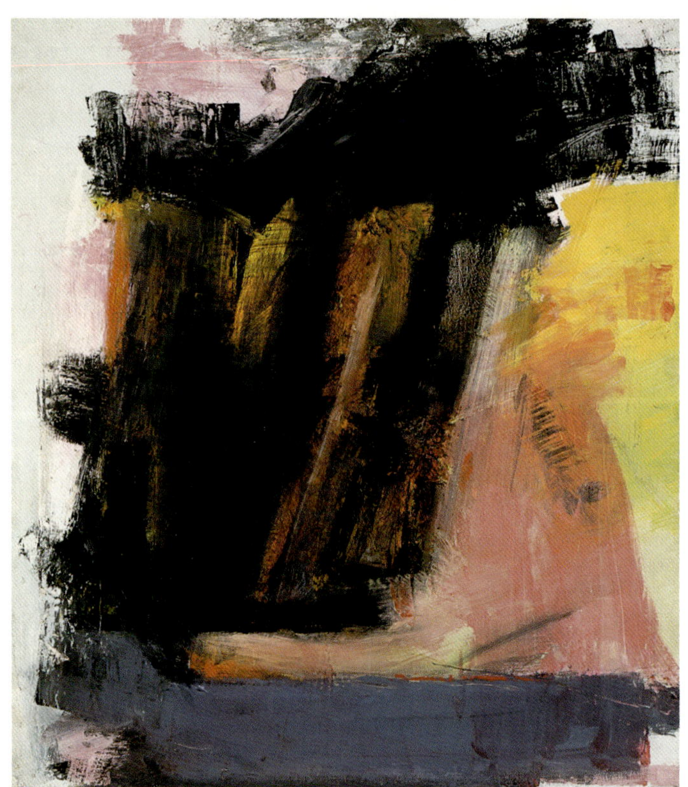

Alva, 1958, oil on canvas, 40¼ x 36⅛ inches, (88.4)

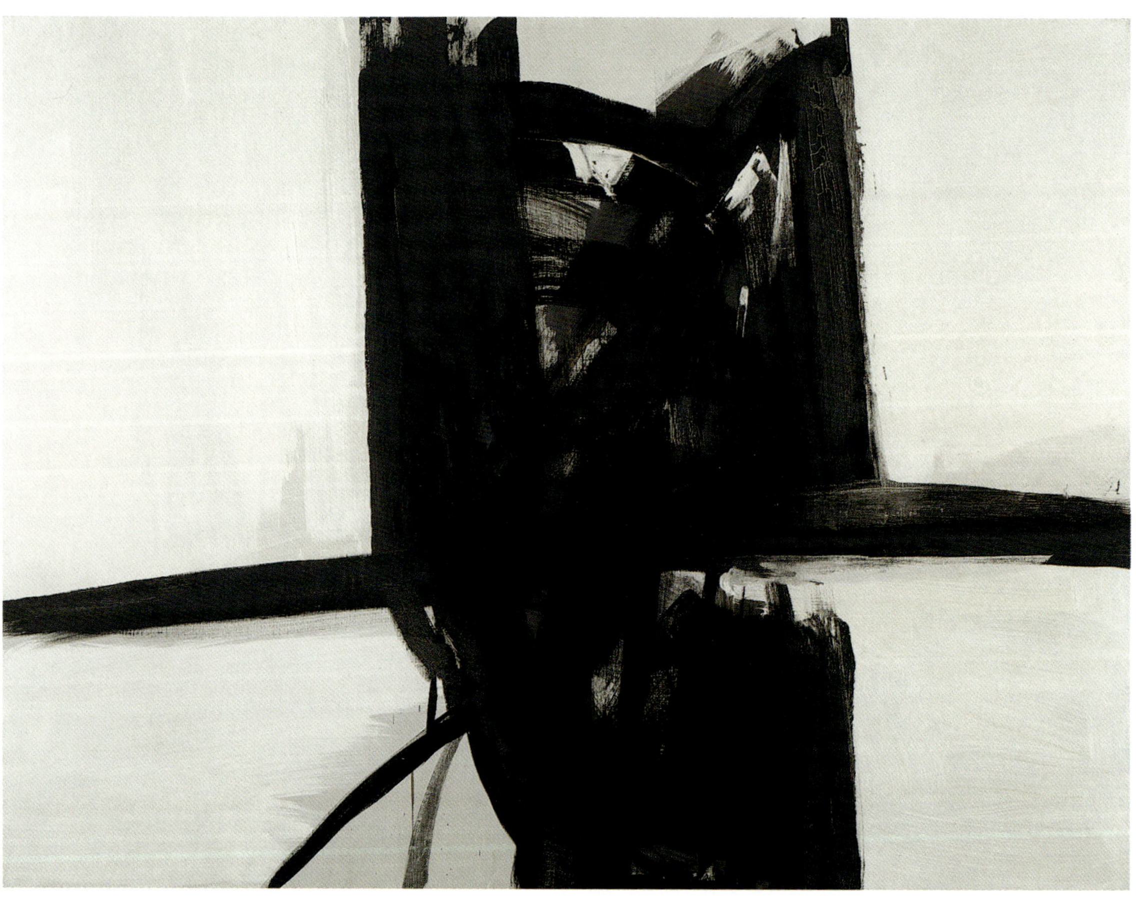

Orleans, 1959, oil on canvas, 101 x 76 inches, (86.10)

Line Through White Oblong, 1959, oil on canvas, 60¼ x 81 inches, (87.7)

Sabro II, 1959–60, oil on canvas, 62 x 78½ inches, (88.7)   *Black Iris,* 1961, oil on canvas, 108¼ x 79½ inches, (84.3)

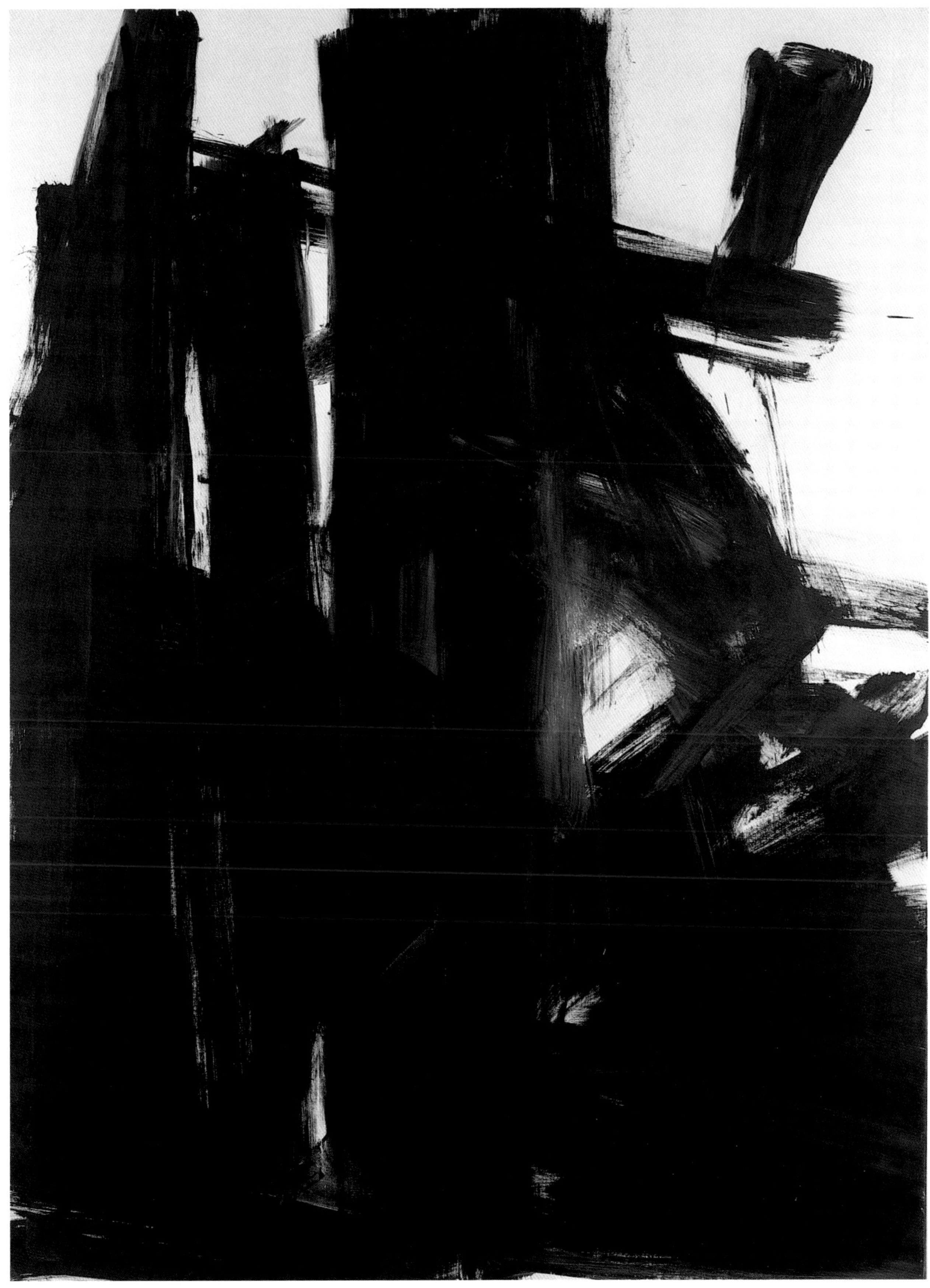

Whether freely appropriating images from the popular world of advertisements, comic strips, and press, or directly quoting the work of modern art giants like Picasso and Cézanne, Roy Lichtenstein has built an oeuvre that represents these subjects through the visual vocabulary of mass production. His art ocuppies the uneasy gap between high art and the commercial art of easy comprehension (and consumption), but withholds the accompanying moralization one expects. These paintings do not simply denegrate the high and elevate the low. As Lichtenstein himself asserts, "I want my images to be as critical, as threatening, and as insistent as possible…As visual objects, as paintings—not as critical commentaries about the world."[1]

Lichtenstein's background as an engineering draftsman may have been formative in his creation of pristine paintings emulating machine-made surfaces, which he began in 1961. Choosing images that had already been rendered two-dimensionally, Lichtenstein painted from studies, making as little change as possible from the original. The early works, which include the four featured here, were crafted with turpentine-soluble paint, allowing the artist to erase any trace of his process and precisely mimic a detached, anonymous texture free of facture.

Despite the technique's commercial look, Lichtenstein never abandoned the language of the painter. By manipulating and exploring compositional, scale, and color issues critical to the artist's craft, Lichtenstein's paintings problematize the seemingly oversimplified forms they appear to depict. In *Man with Folded Arms* (1962), Lichtenstein directly quotes a diagram, published in Erle Loran's 1943 book, *Cézanne's Composition*, which attempted to explain the complexity of Cézanne's compositional methods. Faithful to this black-and-white diagram and its unmodulated, graphic lines, Lichtenstein enlarged the original to an unwieldy scale. Inserting a rhythmic, dizzying backdrop of Benday dots, the formal, abstract qualities of the painting begin to overwhelm the eye as it becomes lost in a tangle of lines that no longer read as the folds of the man's suit.

This tension between the immediately legible and the abstract continues in Lichtenstein's early works. In addition to his adaptations of paintings by famous artists (1961–69), Lichtenstein worked on a series depicting inexpensive, mass-produced objects painted in stark black and white. Almost melodramatic in scale and composition, *Calendar* (1962) features an open desk calendar, magnified and floating on a black background. The one-to-one relationship of canvas to subject at such a monumental scale seemingly elevates the banal calendar, but also renders the subject as meaningless or beside the point. The calendar, drawn with precise, flat lines, appears to be rendered at a slightly oblique angle, displaying the "volume" of the sheets of the book. However, Lichtenstein exaggerates

lichtenstein

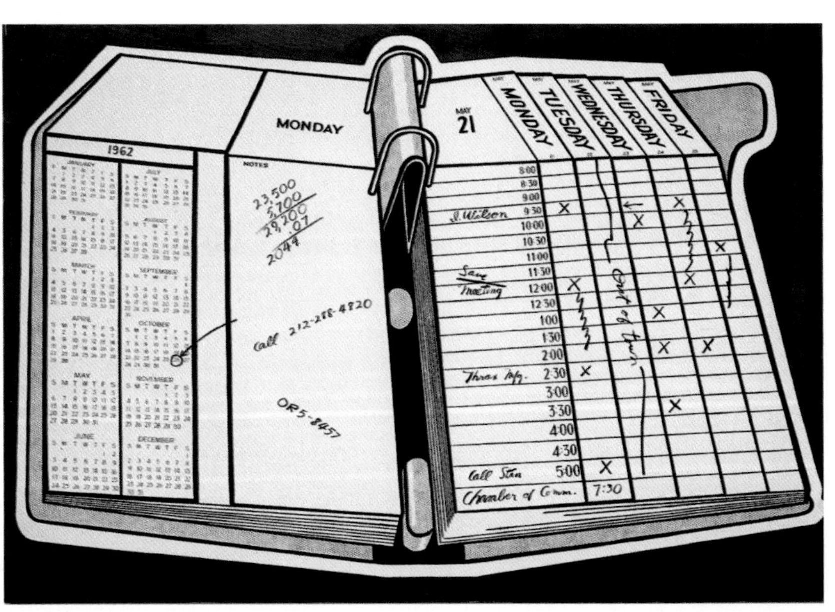

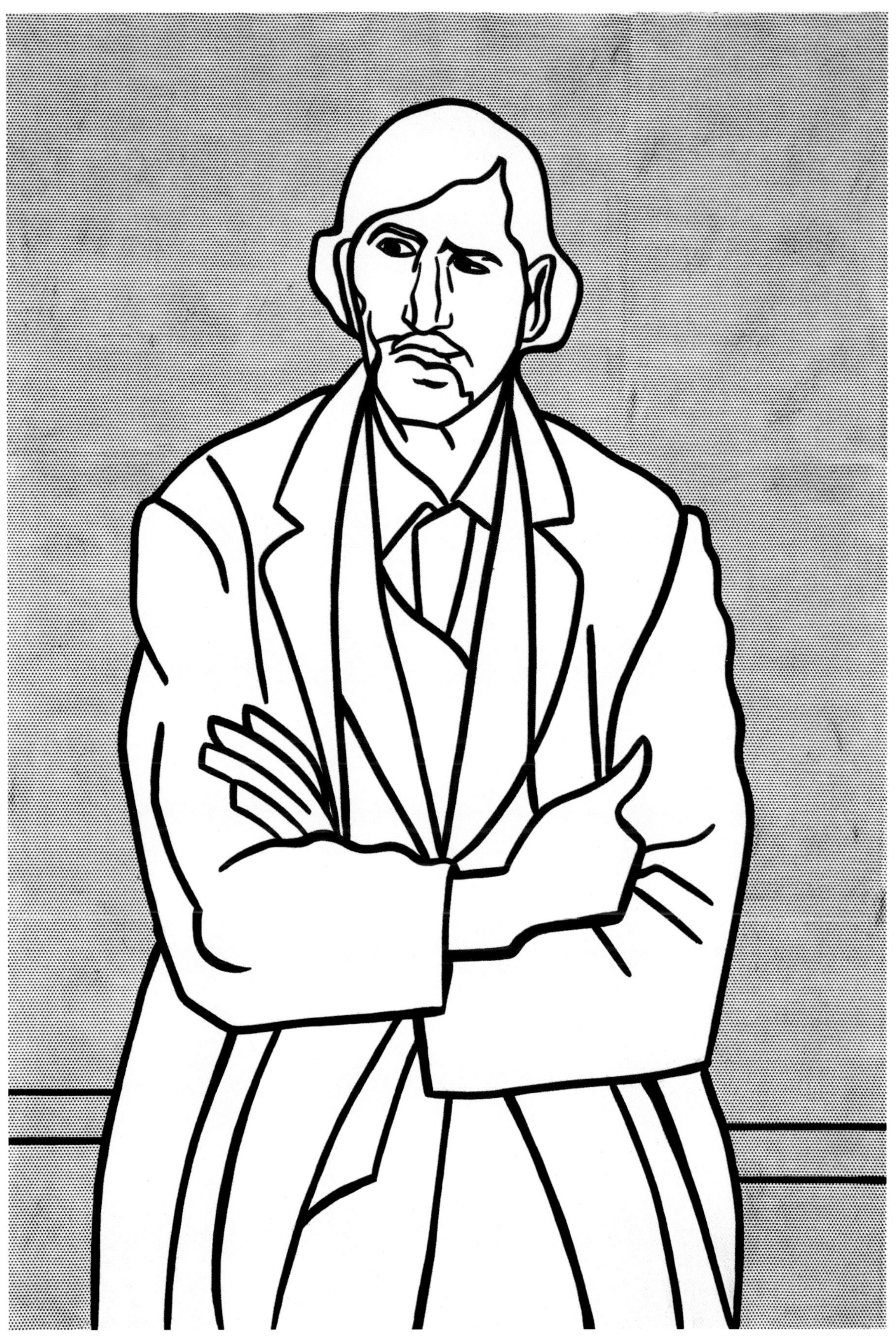

Calendar, 1962, oil on canvas, 48½ x 70 inches, (85.19)   *Man with Folded Arms,* 1962, oil on canvas, 70 x 48½ inches, (84.4)

its jutting center binder and corresponding fold, suggesting a slightly different perspective. Isolated on a black background except for the strange white border cut around the book, the image both recedes into, and emerges from, the black "space," becoming both illegible as a flat reproduction and as a representational painting.

Painted in red on an undefined, red space, *The Grip* (1962) is one of several works Lichtenstein made depicting hands or feet, cropped abruptly, performing mundane tasks. The hand here, "colored" with Benday dots, grips a tool. Once again, Lichtenstein places his extremely formalistic, flatly rendered object into pictorial question. The blocks of red, meant to indicate shading in the palm and, rather arbitrarily, along the knuckles, begin to punch visual holes in the hand, as they begin to disappear into the backdrop of red. This pictorial confusion is furthered by the circle created by the tool's shape, the interior of which is not outlined, becoming a circular form of white that stands brazenly on its own. *Standing Rib* (1962) continues in the same vein as the three above-mentioned series, itself part of a series of paintings isolating food in a central composition. As much about abstraction as it is a flat depiction of the marbled meat, *Standing Rib* perches uncertainly, anchored in its space only by its back tip curiously meeting the right edge of the canvas.

Lichtenstein's subject matter extends to everything in the visual world. A comical standardization takes place, where a Cézanne masterpiece and a piece of meat carry the same relative value and are treated with the same rigorous, and violent, hand. Referring to his choices in subject matter, Lichtenstein explained, "I use them for purely formal reasons."[2] Indeed, the artist's apparent adoption of the manner in which commercial use of images flattens and mechanistically renders them anonymous is judiciously paired with strictly painterly decisions to strip bare and brutally expose the formal elements without losing the essence of the *original* "appropriation." Working through compositional, perspectival, and representational issues, Lichtenstein returns the subjects to the realm of painting, granting them an aesthetic orientation foreign to their original condition. —J.H.

[1] Lichtenstein, quoted in John Coplans, "An Interview with Roy Lichtenstein," *Artforum* 2, no. 4 (October 1963): 31.

[2] Lichtenstein, in an interview with G[ene]. R. Swenson, "What Is Pop Art?," *ARTnews* 62 (November 1963): 63.

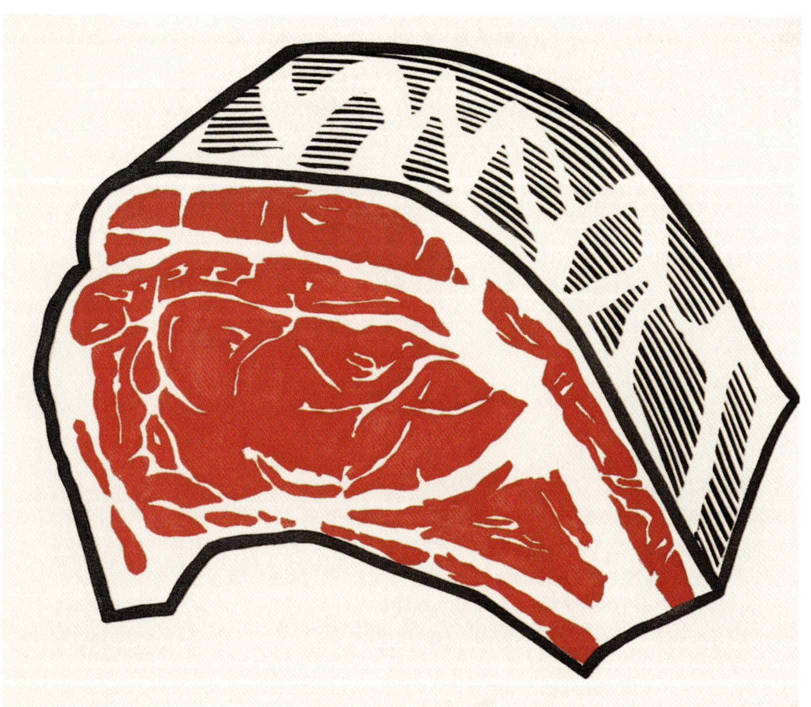

Standing Rib, 1962, oil on canvas, 21¼ x 25¼ inches, (86.11)

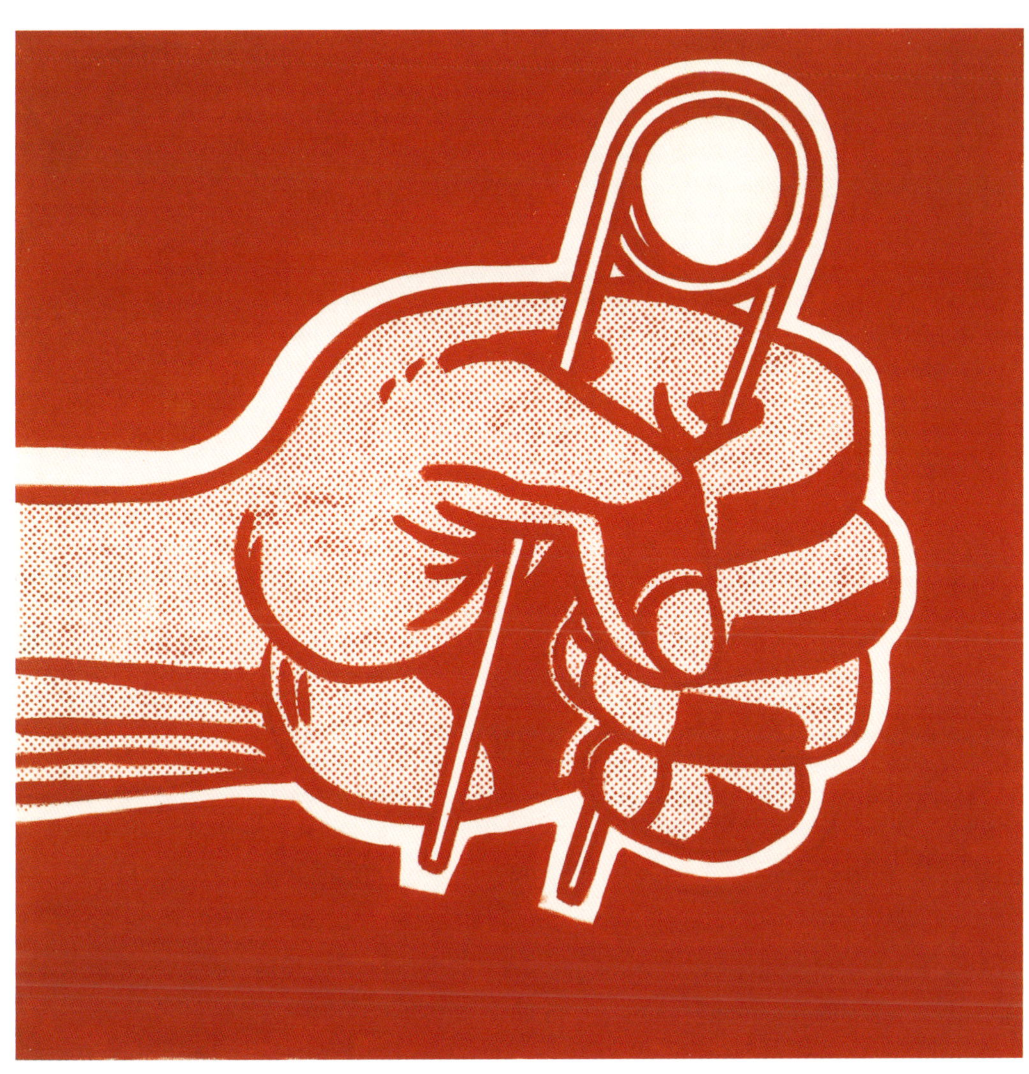

The Grip, 1962, oil on canvas, 30 x 30¼ inches, (87.8)

"I am for an art that is political-erotical-mystical, that does something other than sit on its ass in a museum… I am for an art that takes its form from the lines of life itself, that twists and extends and accumulates and spits and drips, and is heavy and coarse and blunt and sweet and stupid as life itself."[1]

In 1961, Claes Oldenburg wrote his declaration, "I Am for an Art." It was a year during which performance art, Happenings, and Pop art were all on the rise, with Oldenburg, to varying degrees, involved in all three. Searching for an art that created a correspondence between art and life by eluding the barriers in between, Oldenburg infected his work with a fervent desire to record one's times, and to recreate elements in the barrage of life experienced. Never an attack on American materialst culture (as Pop art was expected to do), Oldenburg's work in fact displayed an intense love and celebration for the city environment in all of its absurdity, grittiness, vulgarity, glut, and richness. The artist prowled the streets, looking and absorbing the world like a reporter on a beat (incidentally, the very job Oldenburg left in Chicago before moving to New York and its art world).

On December 1, 1961, in time for the Christmas season, Oldenburg opened *The Store* in a rented storefront on the Lower East Side of Manhattan. A simulacrum of the American variety store, offering the possiblity of discovering exciting, desirable things, "…the store means for [Oldenburg]: [his] consciousness.…"[2] The artist presented himself as both manufacturer and shopkeeper, cramming the storefront full of the objects he made in the back out of plaster-soaked muslin over chicken-wire armatures, then painted brightly. The items—unwearable clothes and inedible food—were displayed as if they retained the function of their models: pastries sat in glass display cases, food waited on serving dishes, dresses hung, and shoes stood on display stands. The "merchandise" was offered with un-gallery-like prices like $69.95. Oldenburg took Pop art's language of advertisements to a new level, as the artist and his objects were promoted in printed business cards and posters for *The Store*. Putting into question the object's function, Oldenburg sought to blur the line between art and consumable object, art viewer and consumer, art and life.

Blue and Pink Panties, *Bride Mannikin*, *Chocolates in Box (Fragment)*, *Cigarettes in Pack (Fragment)*, *Green Stocking*, *Man's Shoe*, *Mu Mu*, *Pepsi-Cola Sign*, and *Pentacostal Cross* were among the items on sale at *The Store*. They vary in scale, from a large but familiar Pepsi-Cola sign to the ridiculous proportions of a box of chocolates (a fragment, no less), nearly four by three feet in dimension. Painted with garish artificial colors, the objects are tasteless, both in vulgarity and physical appeal (nasty, solid plaster dripping with enamel paint). Their surfaces

CLAES
oldenburg

Blue and Pink Panties, 1961, plaster soaked muslin, 62¼ x 34¾ x 6 inches, (87.13)

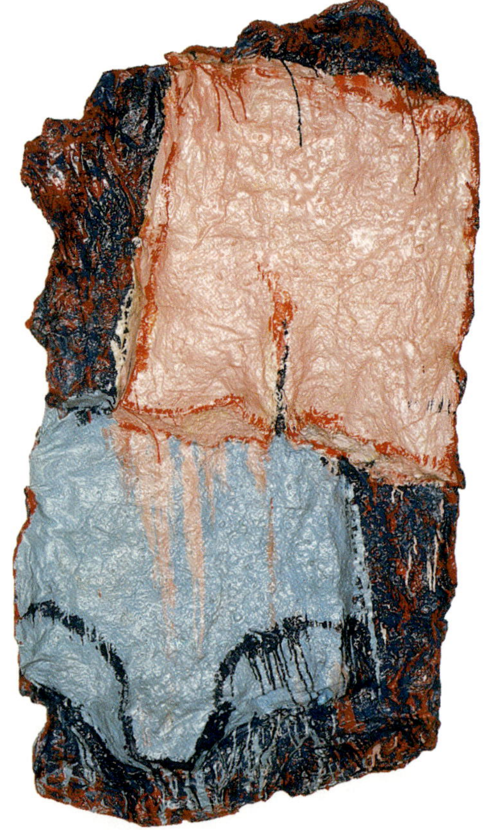

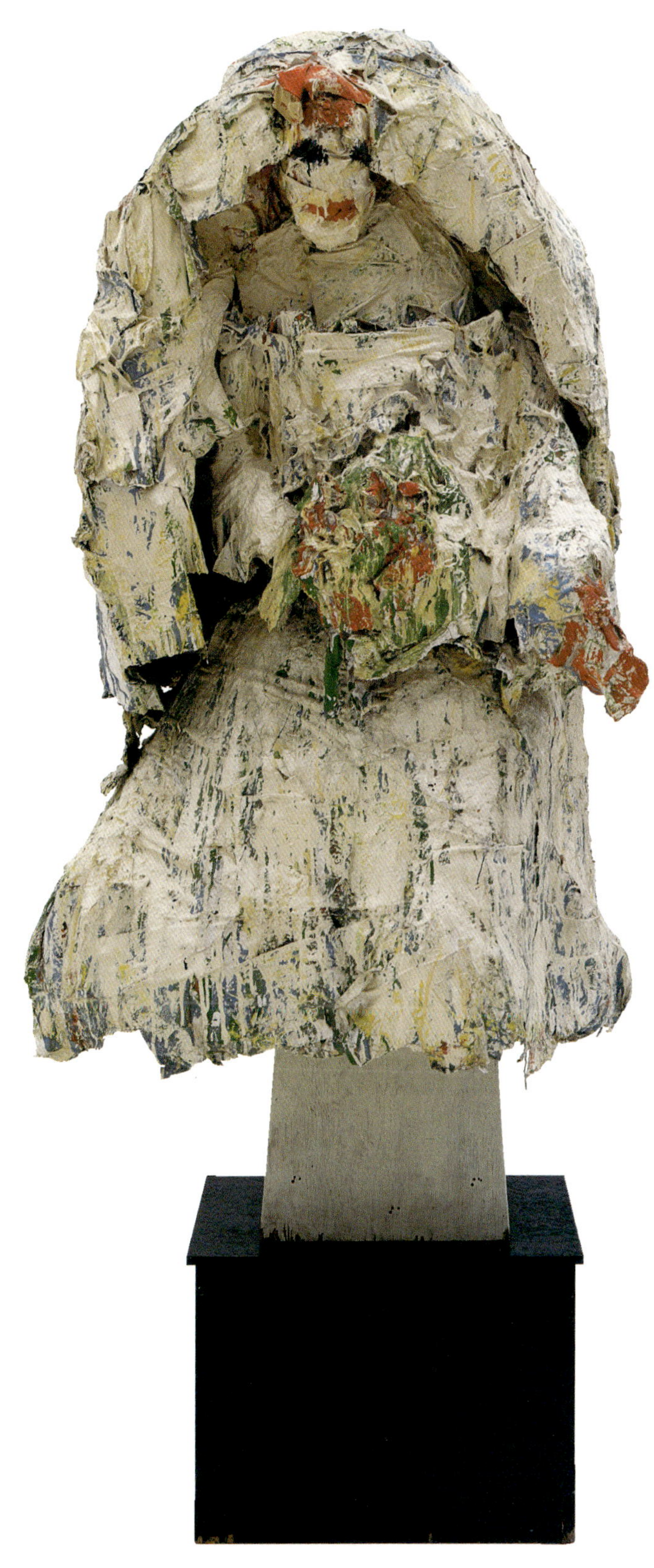

Bride Mannikin, 1961, plaster soaked muslin, 61 x 37¼ x 36¾ inches, (85.20)

glisten, almost as if shellacked to contain the energetic, expressionist handling of paint drips, splatters, and impasto. Plaster and paint are layered, one on top of the other, building a texture both sensuous and revolting. It is a painting not just to detail the floral bouquet of the *Bride Mannikin* or the fabric pattern on the *Mu Mu*, but to revel in the sheer joy of painterliness and the action of recreation.

The following year, Oldenburg continued to create objects for *The Store*, which would move from its Lower East Side location and travel in different incarnations. *Blue Pants and Pocket Objects on Chair, Breakfast Table, Pie à la Mode, Umbrella and Newspaper,* and *Shirt with Objects on a Chair* are identical in vein to those created in 1961, with the exception of the introduction of ready-made props: the chair on which the pants hang, the umbrella paired with the created newspaper; the table diplaying the breakfast. All of the objects of both 1961 and 1962, alternating between relief and free-standing sculptures, dissolved the boundaries between painting and sculpture. Oldenburg's art is far from the cold, detached posturing of which Pop art is often accused: it is instead a passionate effort to capture the abundance of the material world in full, not through distillation but through a whole-hearted embrace. —J.H.

1 Oldenburg, as quoted in *Claes Oldenburg: An Anthology* (New York: Solomon R. Guggenheim Museum; and Washington, D.C.: National Gallery of Art, 1995), 96.
2 Oldenburg, as quoted in *Claes Oldenburg: An Anthology,* 130.

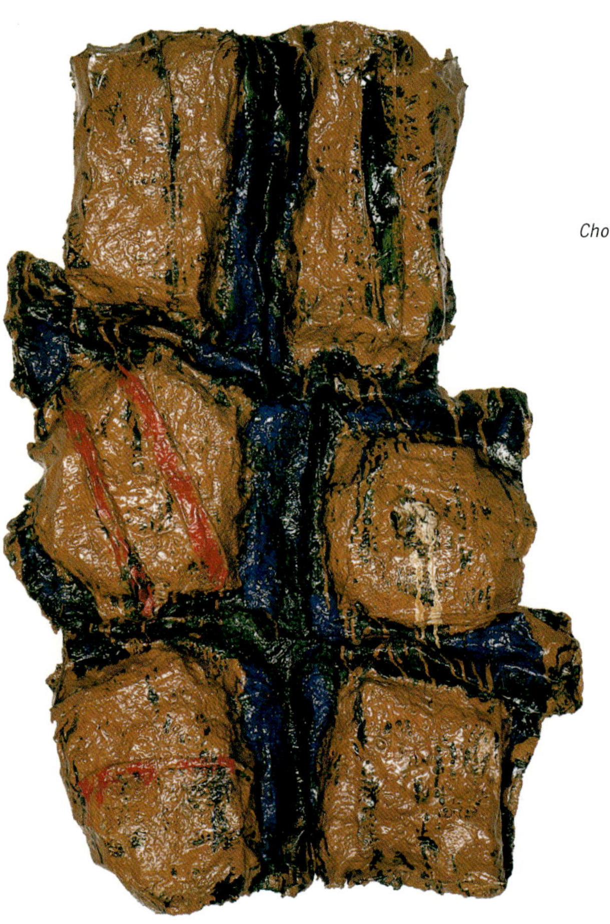

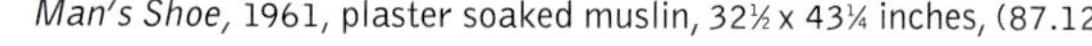

Chocolates in Box (Fragment), 1961, plaster soaked muslin, 44 x 32 x 6 inches, (87.9)

Man's Shoe, 1961, plaster soaked muslin, 32½ x 43¼ inches, (87.12)

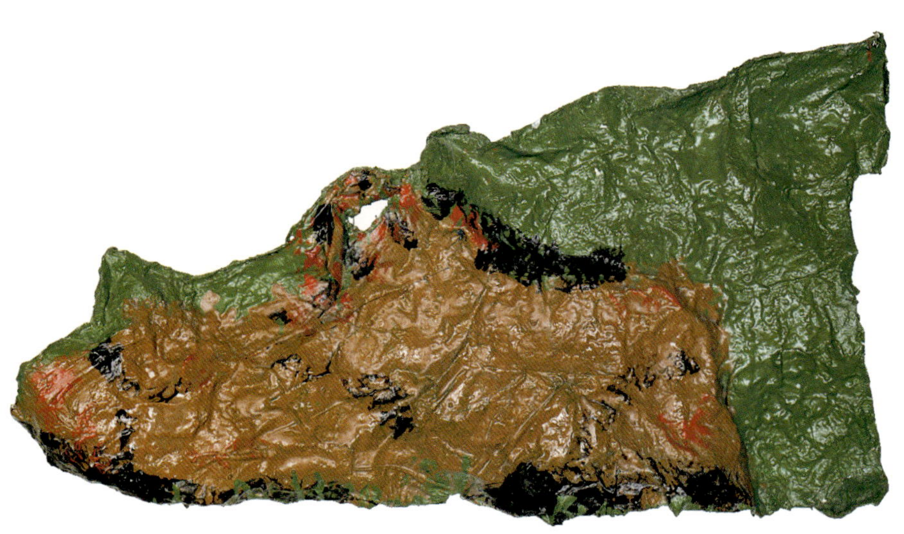

Green Stocking, 1961, plaster soaked muslin, 43¼ x 18 inches, (86.13)

Cigarettes in Pack (Fragment), 1961, plaster soaked muslin, 32¼ x 30¾ x 6¼ inches, (86.12)

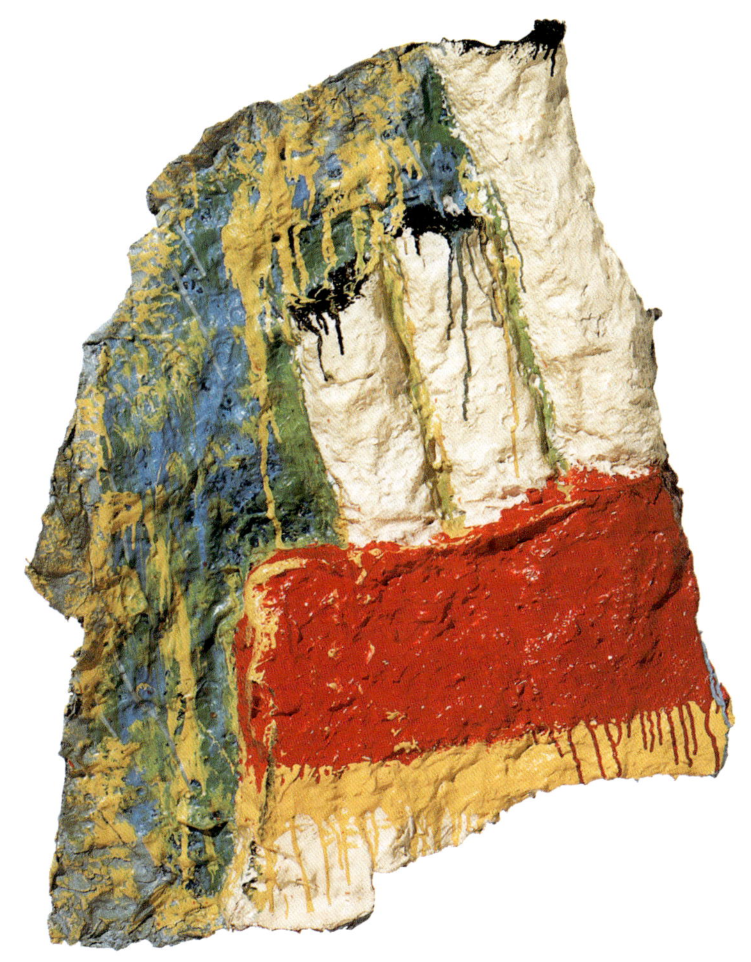

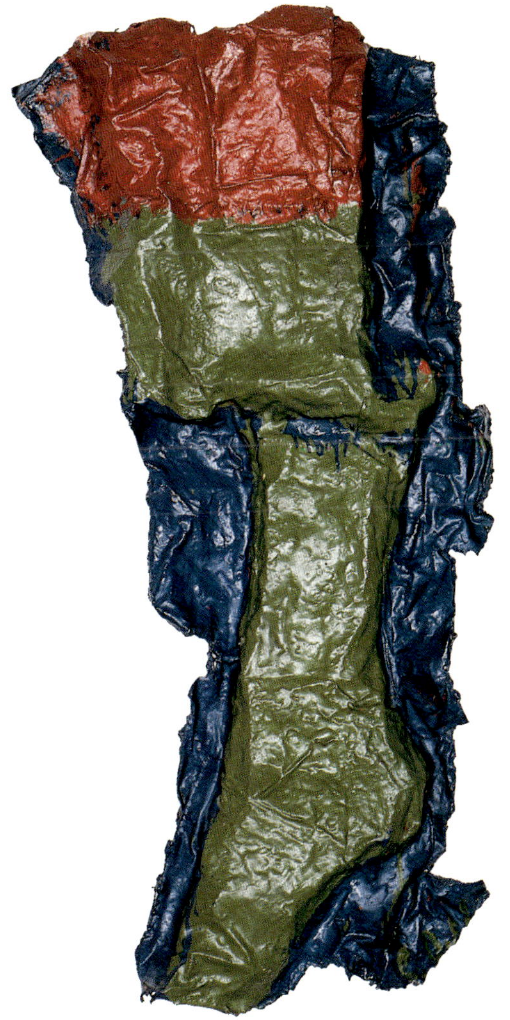

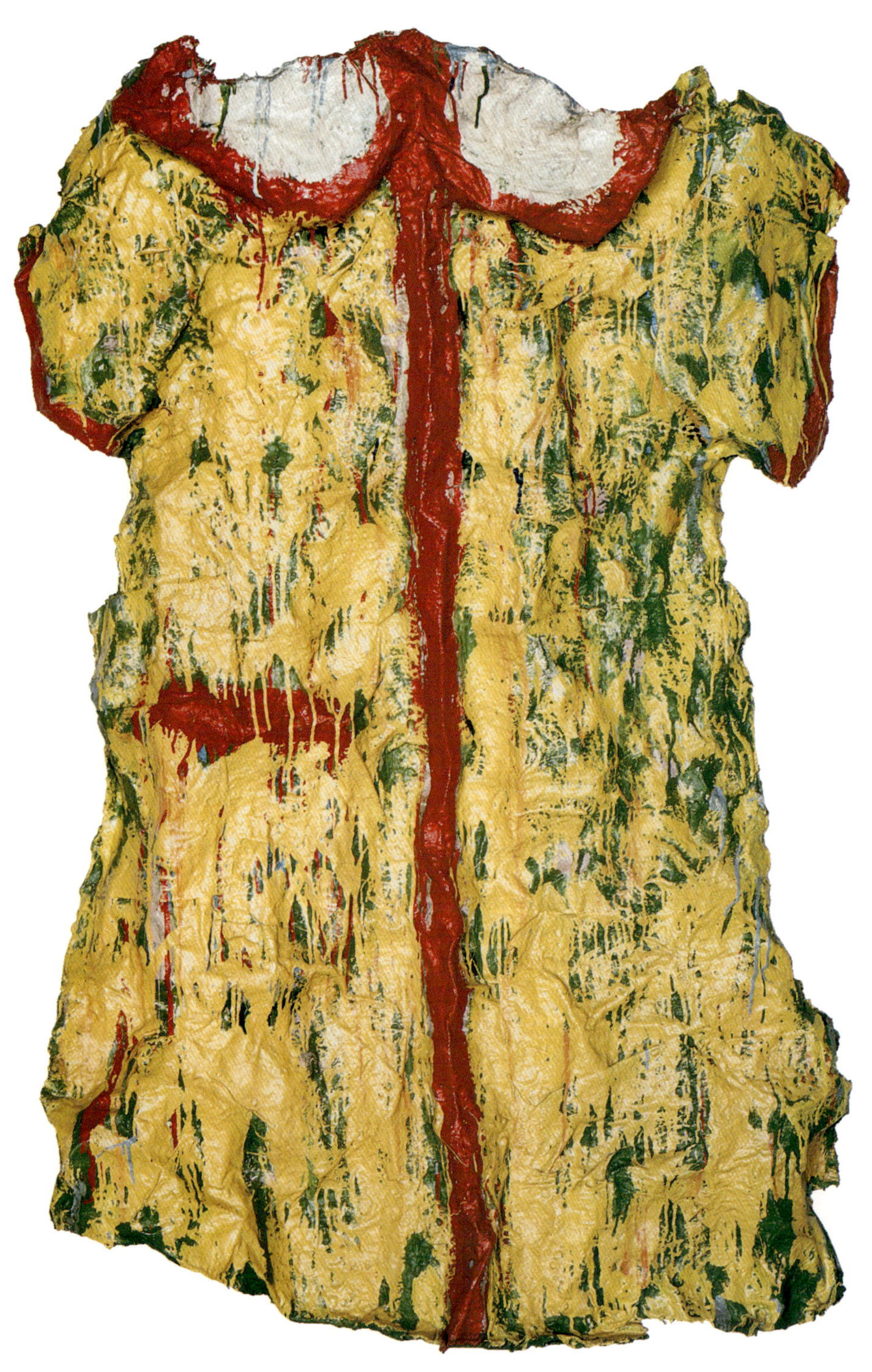

Mu Mu, 1961, plaster soaked muslin, 63¼ x 41¼ x 4 inches, (84.5)

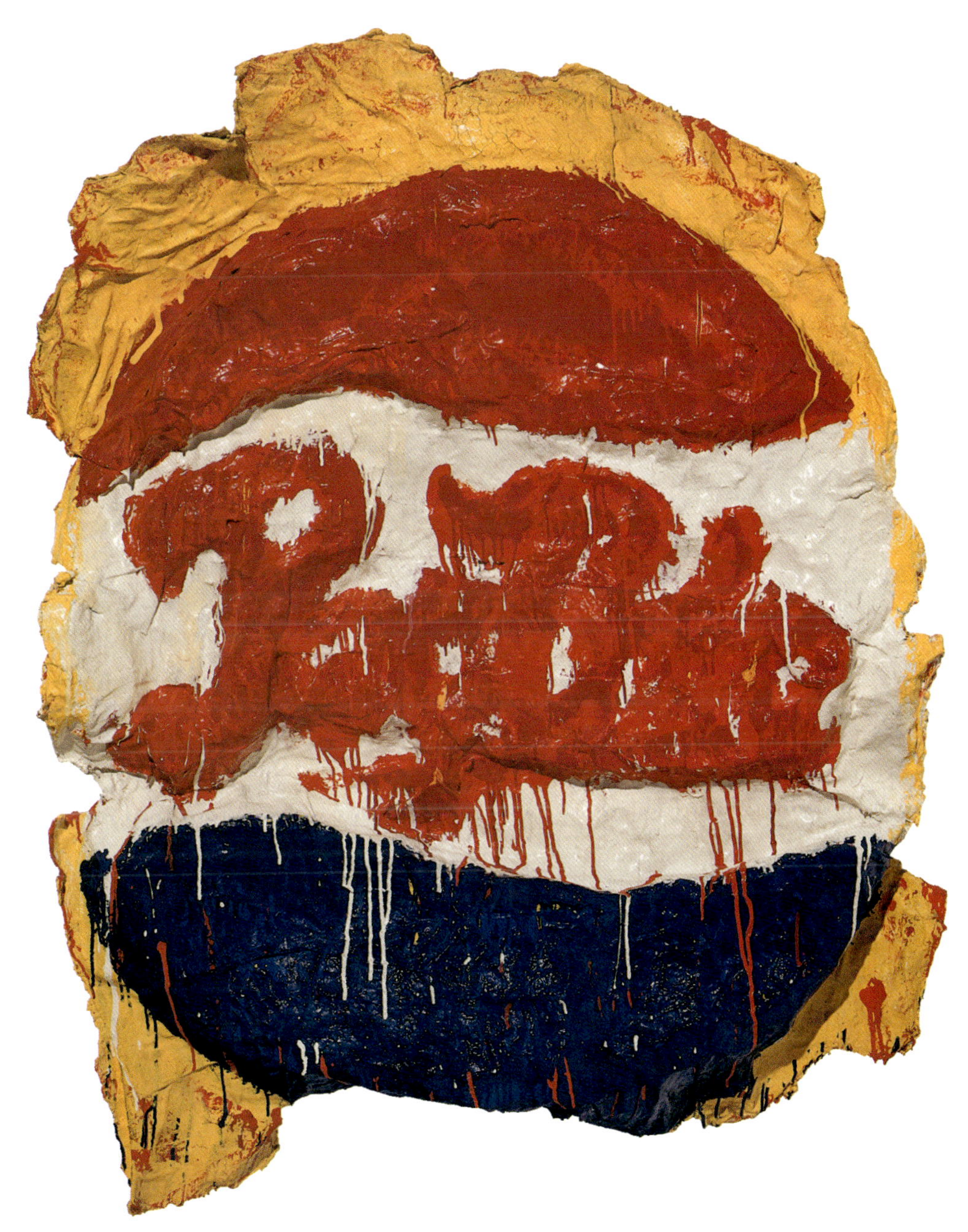

Pepsi-Cola Sign, 1961, plaster soaked muslin, 58¼ x 46½ x 7½ inches, (85.21)

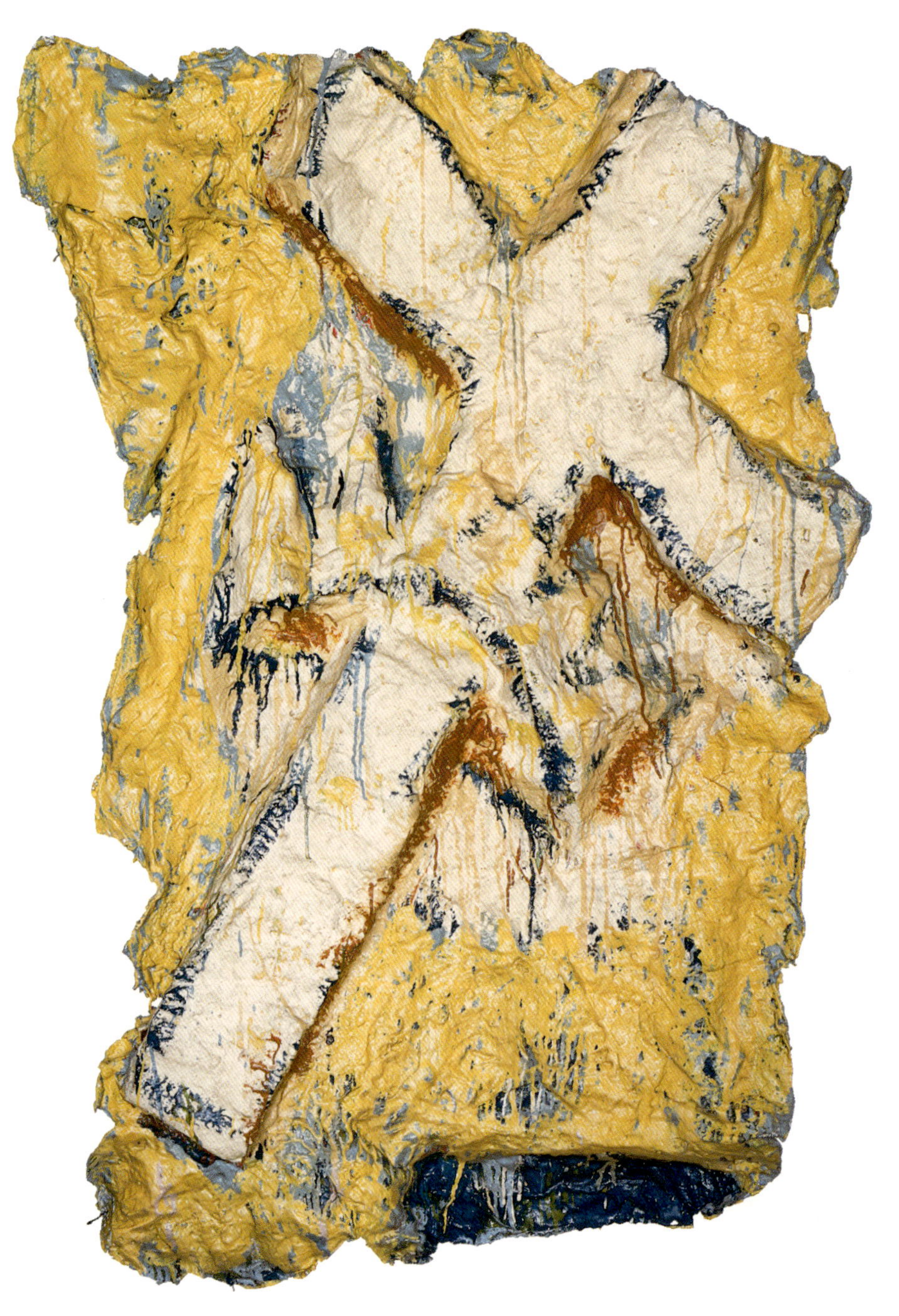

Pentacostal Cross, 1961, plaster soaked muslin, 52¾ x 40½ x 6 inches, (87.14)

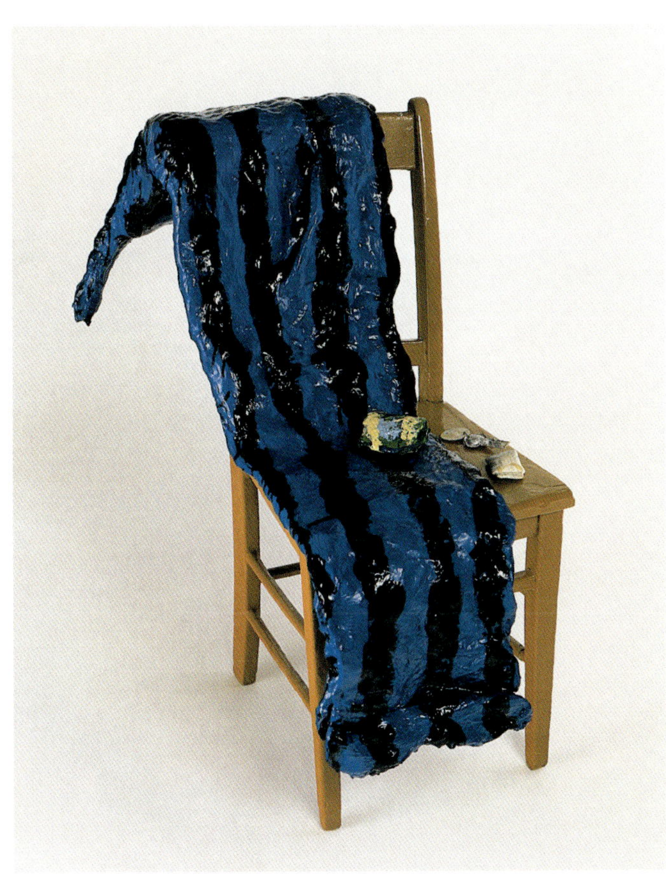

Blue Pants and Pocket Objects on Chair, 1962, plaster soaked muslin, 37 x 17 x 26¾ inches, (87.15)

Shirt with Objects on a Chair, 1962, plaster soaked muslin, 39¾ x 30 x 25 inches, (84.6)

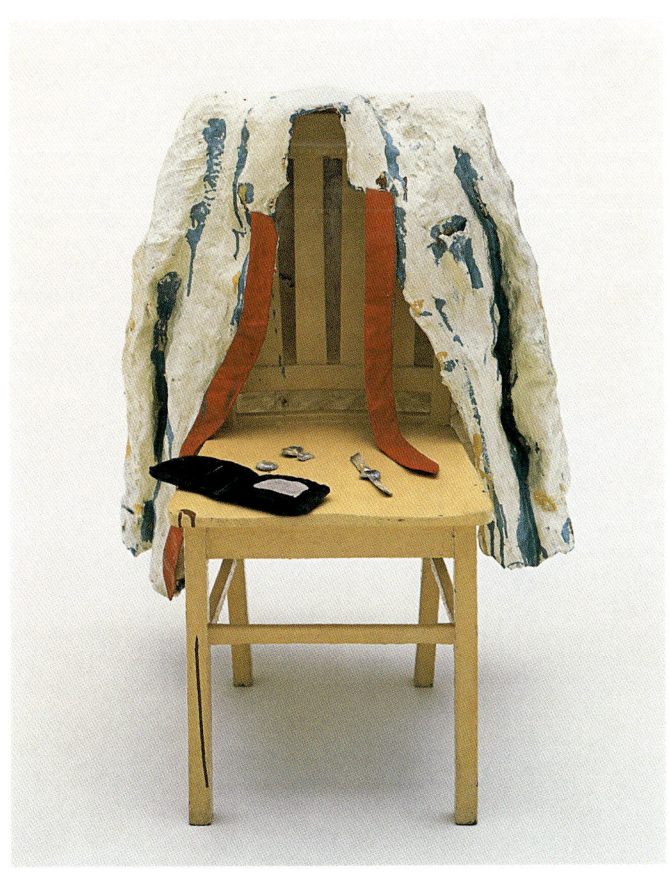

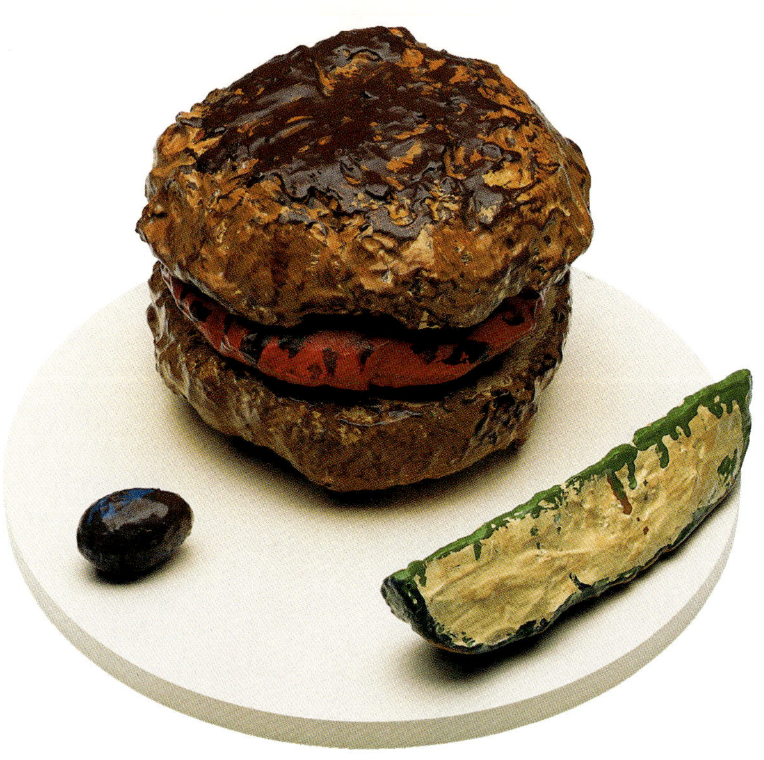

Hamburger with Pickle and Olive, 1962, plaster soaked muslin, 7 x 9 x 9 inches, (87.10)

Pie à la Mode, 1962, plaster soaked muslin, 20 x 13 x 19 inches, (88.9)

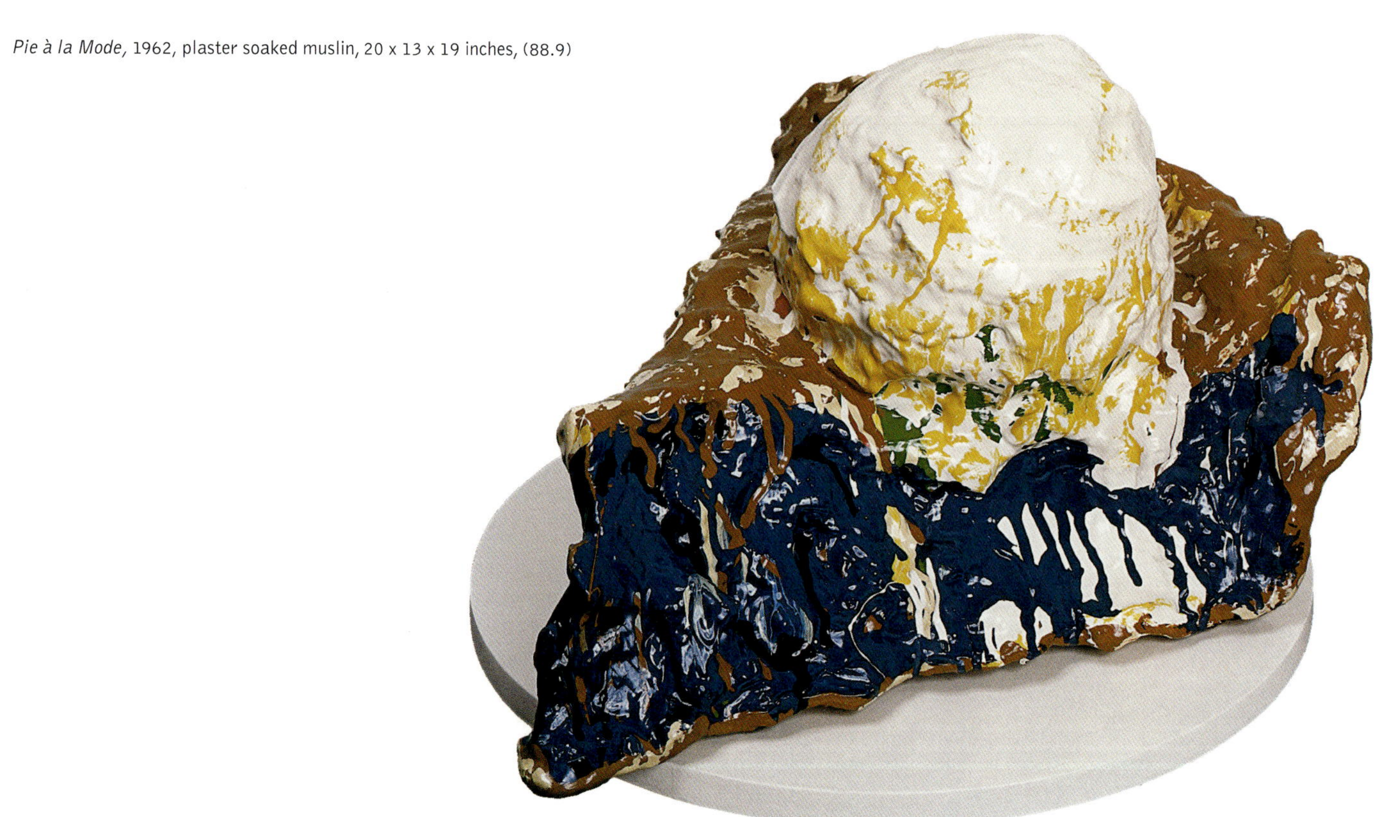

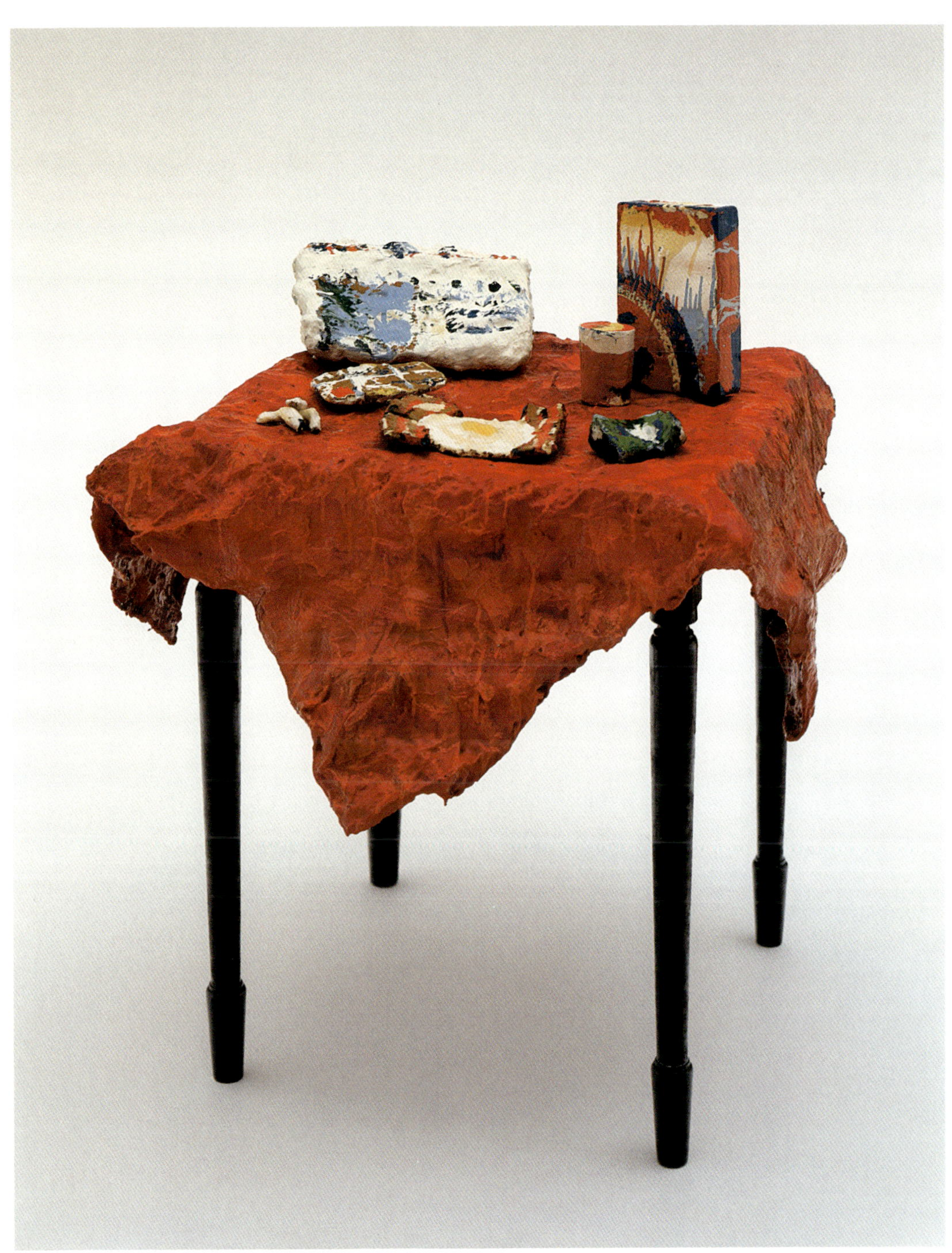

Breakfast Table, 1962, plaster soaked muslin, 34½ x 35½ x 34½ inches, (86.14)

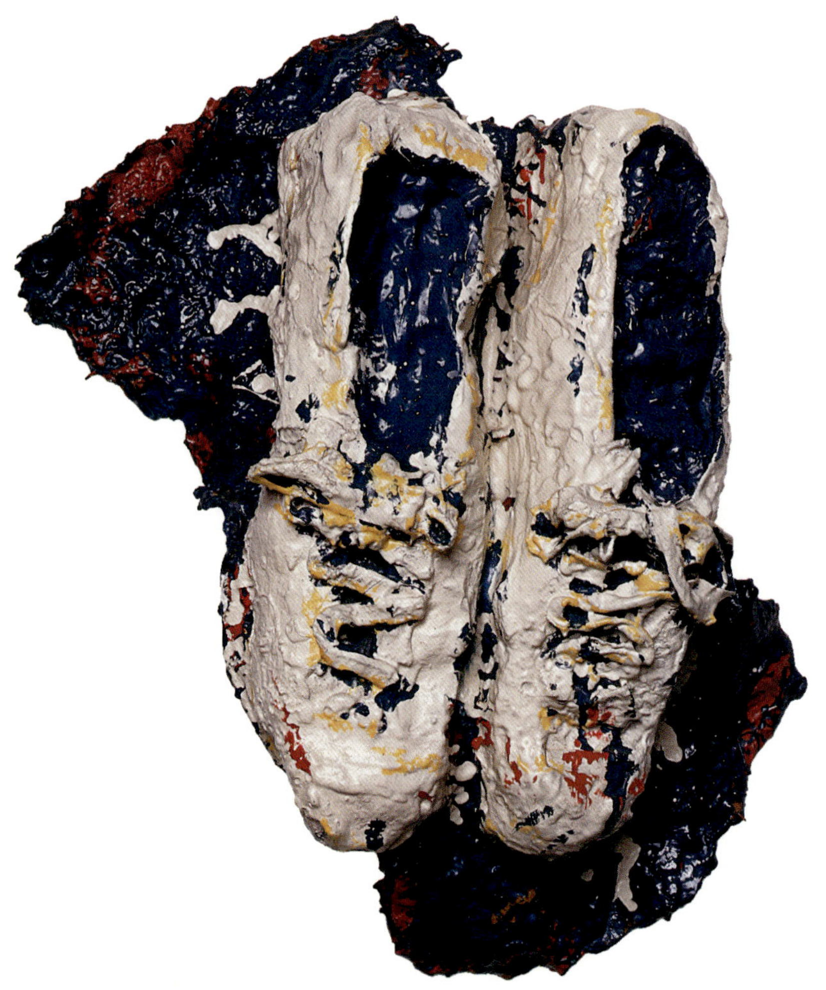

White Gym Shoes, 1962, plaster soaked muslin, 24 x 24 x 10 inches, (87.11)

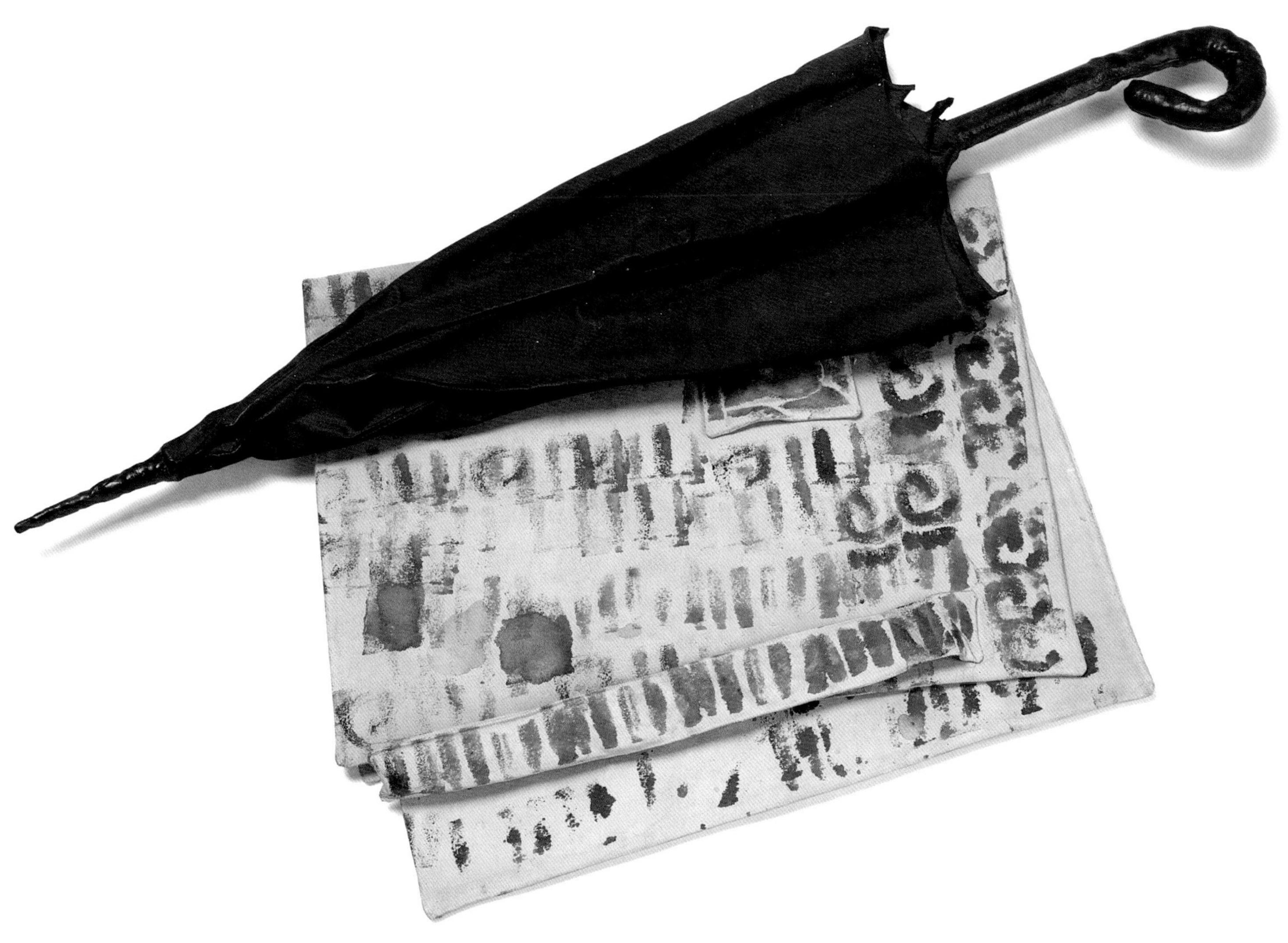

Umbrella and Newspaper, 1962, plaster soaked muslin, 38½ x 19½ x 6 inches, (87.16)

Robert Rauschenberg's unique and innovative approach to materials, methods, and artistic practice redirected postwar American art and secured his place as one of the most influential artists of this century. At a time when artistic expression was dominated by the subjective and emotional paintings of the New York Abstract Expressionists such as Willem de Kooning and Jackson Pollock, Rauschenberg created paintings that did not call upon his own emotions, tastes, or ideas as the controlling elements of production.

Born in Port Arthur, Texas, in 1925, Rauschenberg's attention to painting began when he arrived at Black Mountain College in 1948 to study with Josef Albers. Albers was to have an important effect upon the young artist who learned from him color, line, and most importantly, discipline. In the summer of 1952 Albers's teachings on color theory and optical experimentation fueled Rauschenberg's monumental all-white and all-black paintings. His contemporaries at Black Mountain College included the composer/writer John Cage and the choreographer/dancer Merce Cunningham, both of whom were influential and lifelong artistic collaborators. Also during the early 1950s Rauschenberg experimented with photographic processes and large-scale figurative photograms made by positioning figures and objects upon light-sensitive blueprint paper. These eerie and evocative life-size, camera-less images signaled what would become a lifetime dedication to experimental procedures and materials.

Five years after moving to New York, Rauschenberg met Jasper Johns, and in the summer of 1955 moved into a space above him in a loft building on Pearl Street in lower Manhattan. For the next six years the two artists were in constant contact, sharing ideas, offering criticism, and giving each other the permission to create whatever they could imagine. Indicative of this period is the painting *Factum I,* made in tandem with *Factum II* in 1957 as an exercise. One painting was created from pure spontaneous gesture (in the spirit of Abstract Expressionism) and the second was an attempt to copy the first. After discerning no visible difference between the marks in each painting, Rauschenberg began to more seriously question notions of sentiment, personality, and authorship. As a further departure from personal taste Rauschenberg started combining found objects, photographs, and typographical elements with painted segments to create works that were free, aleatory, and open to a myriad of interpretations.

These "Combine" paintings, begun in the mid-1950s, can be loosely categorized into freestanding Combines and Combine paintings. One of the major paintings in this body of work is *Small Rebus* made after his seminal work *Rebus* in 1956. Divided in half by an ersatz color scale, *Small Rebus* is a vivid assembly of collaged

ROBERT

rauschenberg

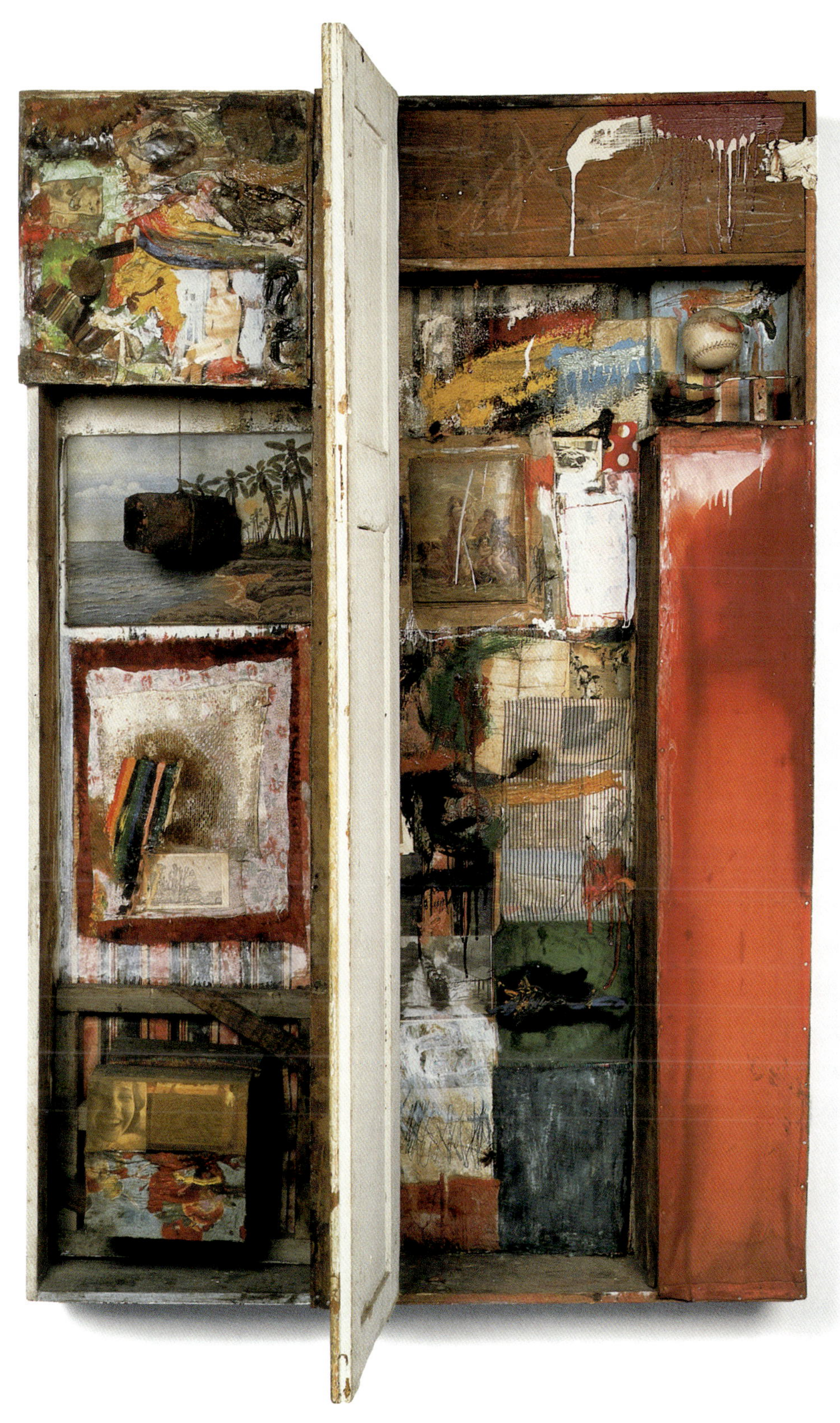

Interview, 1955, combine painting, 72¾ x 49¼ inches, (85.22)

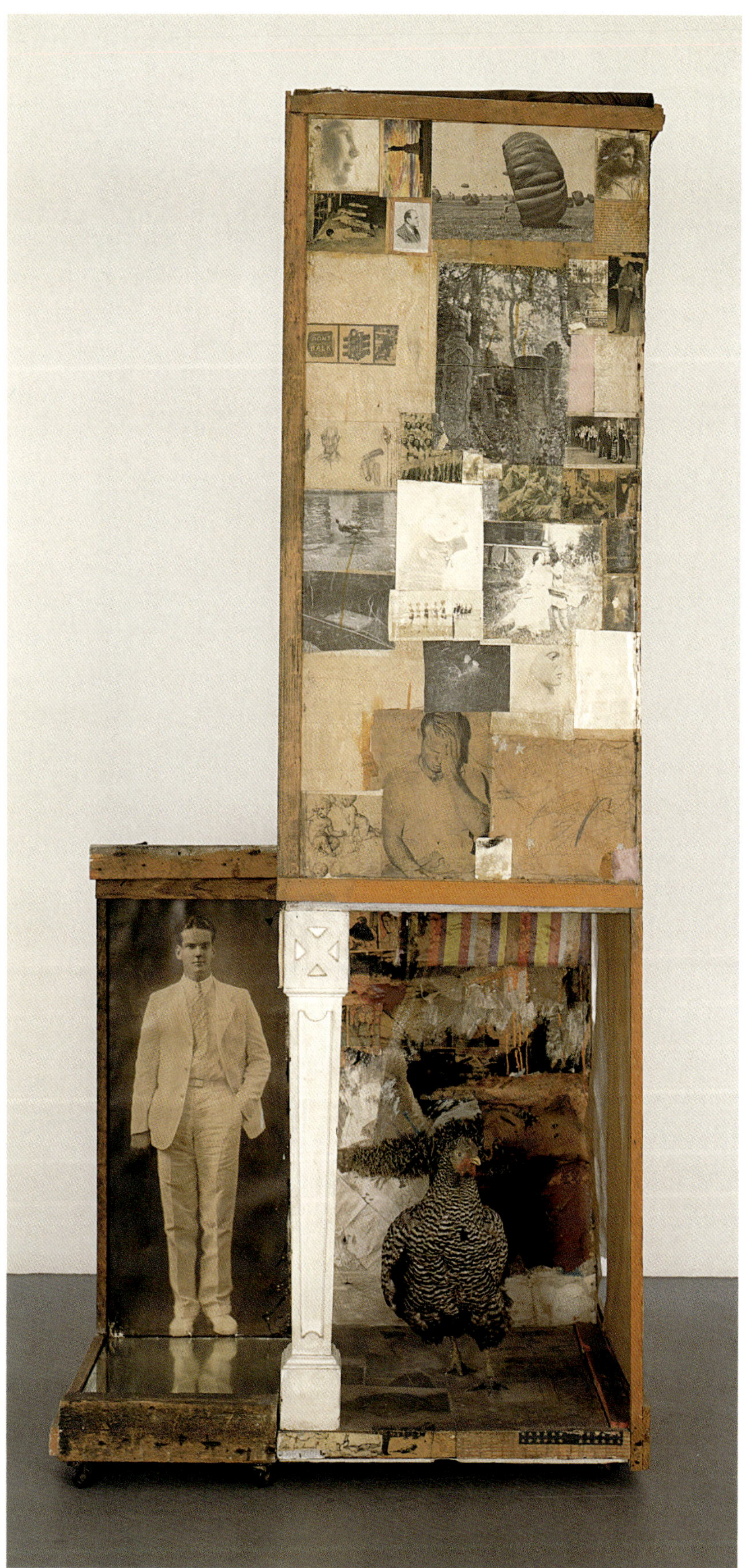

elements that are unified by their placement and over-painting, but whose meaning is not linear or fixed. Other Combine paintings in the Panza Collection include *Painting with Grey Wing* (1959), *Inlet* (1959), and *Kickback* (1959). Although there are similarities of style among these works, each has its own tenor and unique narrative potential.

Larger three-dimensional objects were incorporated into some of Rauschenberg's Combines, which expanded the works' parameters and possibilities beyond the two-dimensional picture plane. *Coca-Cola Plan* (1958) is an elegant, winged sculpture that playfully evokes comparisons to the *Nike of Samothrace,* while inspiring a generation of Pop artists with its uninhibited use of Coke bottles. Rising to over seven feet, *Untitled Combine (Man with White Shoes)* (1955) intrigues the viewer with its many crevices, mirrors, and unexpected elements such as a pair of painted men's shoes and a stuffed hen. Rauschenberg's critics regarded his unabashed utilization of

Untitled Combine (Man with White Shoes), 1955, combine painting, 86½ x 37 x 26¼ inches, (84.7)

every-day objects, including the metal bucket found in *Gift for Apollo* (1959), as shocking, outrageous, and inappropriate. However, his supporters were numerous and, beginning in 1959, the market for his work was strong.

Rauschenberg often utilized architectural elements as part of his Combine's support structure. The knotted linens, miniature ladder, and reorganized bed frame which make up *Trophy III (For Jean Tinguely)* (1961) are interwoven and assembled within the construct of a wooden windowpane. *Interview* (1955) is divided vertically by a swinging door and the moment of intrigue occurs at the fulcrum of this shifting plane—it appears as if the door has just been opened to offer us a momentary view of the contents. These found architectural details, such as columns, windows, and doors, have an innate physicality that grants the Combines a solid framework. Additionally, the reference to architecture is introduced into works that also include the disciplines of photography, printmaking, and painting.

The period in which these Combines were made represents a short, albeit very important, period in Rauschenberg's prolific career. In 1962, Rauschenberg made his first lithograph at Universal Limited Art Editions (ULAE), and printmaking, including silkscreen, became his primary method of including photographic materials seamlessly into his work. Throughout the 1960s Rauschenberg was actively involved in performance, not only as an on-stage performer, dancer, and choreographer, but also as set, costume, and lighting designer for the Merce Cunningham Dance Company, among others. Since the 1970s he has worked primarily in series, including the Hoarfrost series for which he transferred photographs onto fabric and draped it loosely upon the wall. And in 1984 Rauschenberg embarked upon a seven-year peace project called ROCI (Rauschenberg Overseas Culture Interchange) in which he traveled to politically volatile countries and made collaborative work with local artists. —R.M.

Small Rebus, 1956, combine painting, 35 x 46 inches, (87.18)

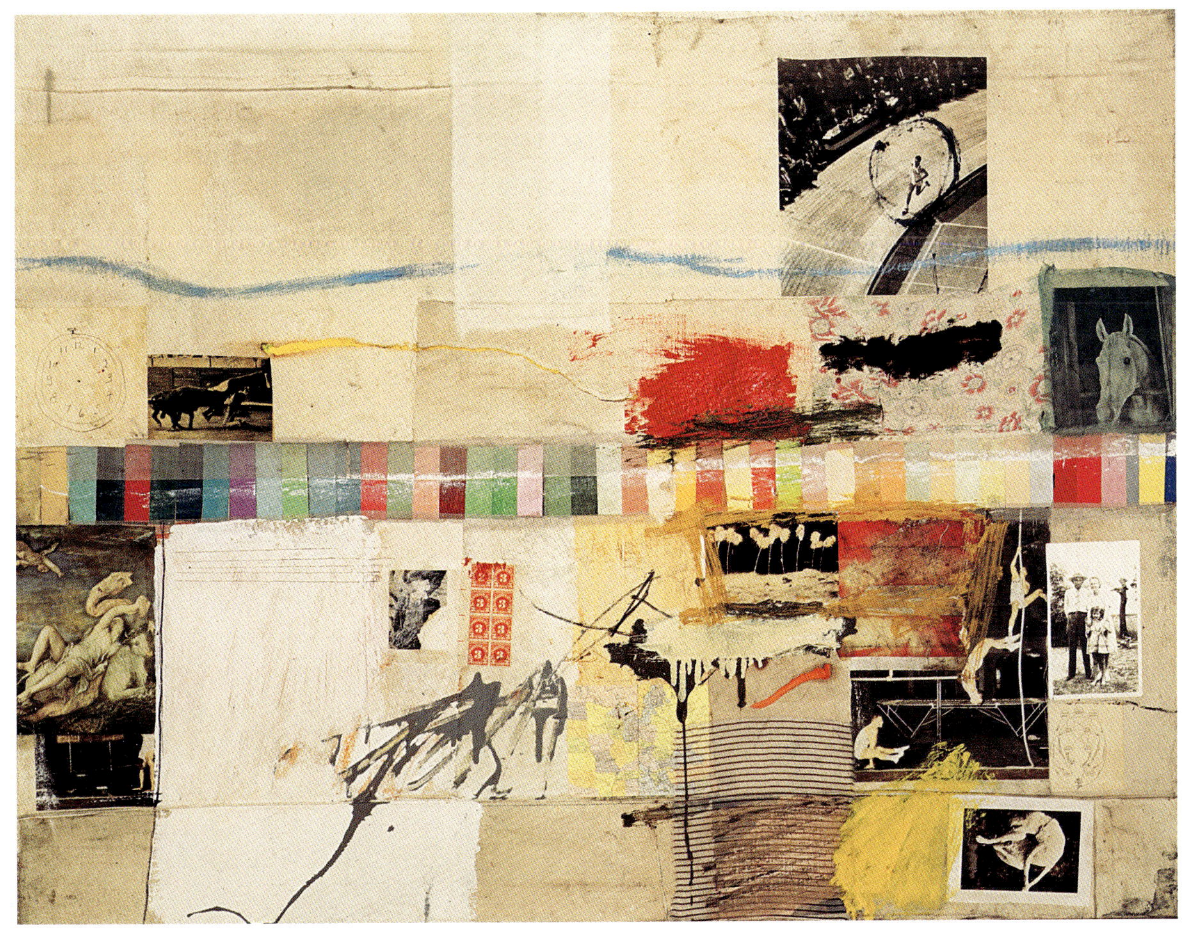

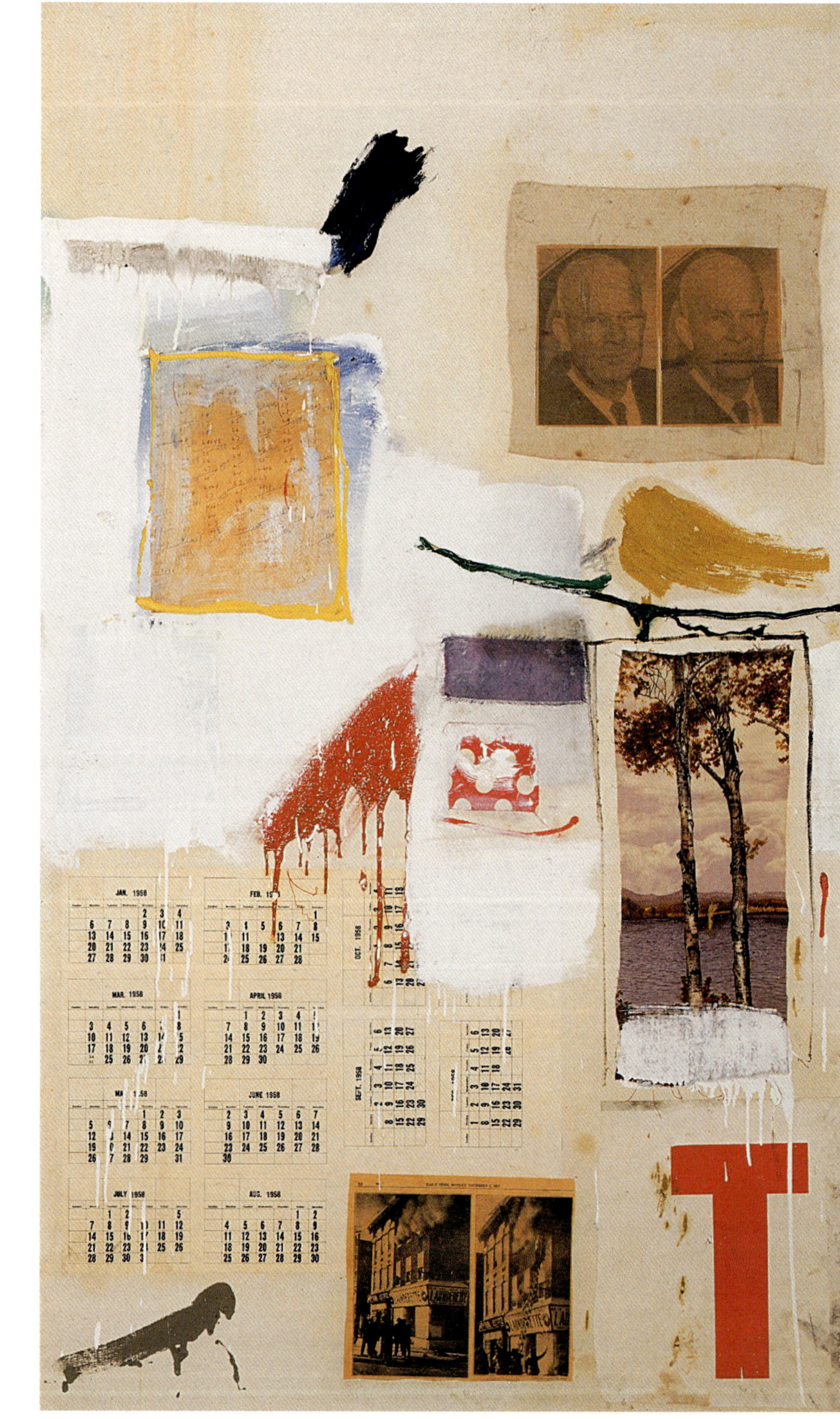

Factum I, 1957, combine painting, 61½ x 35¾ inches, (86.15)

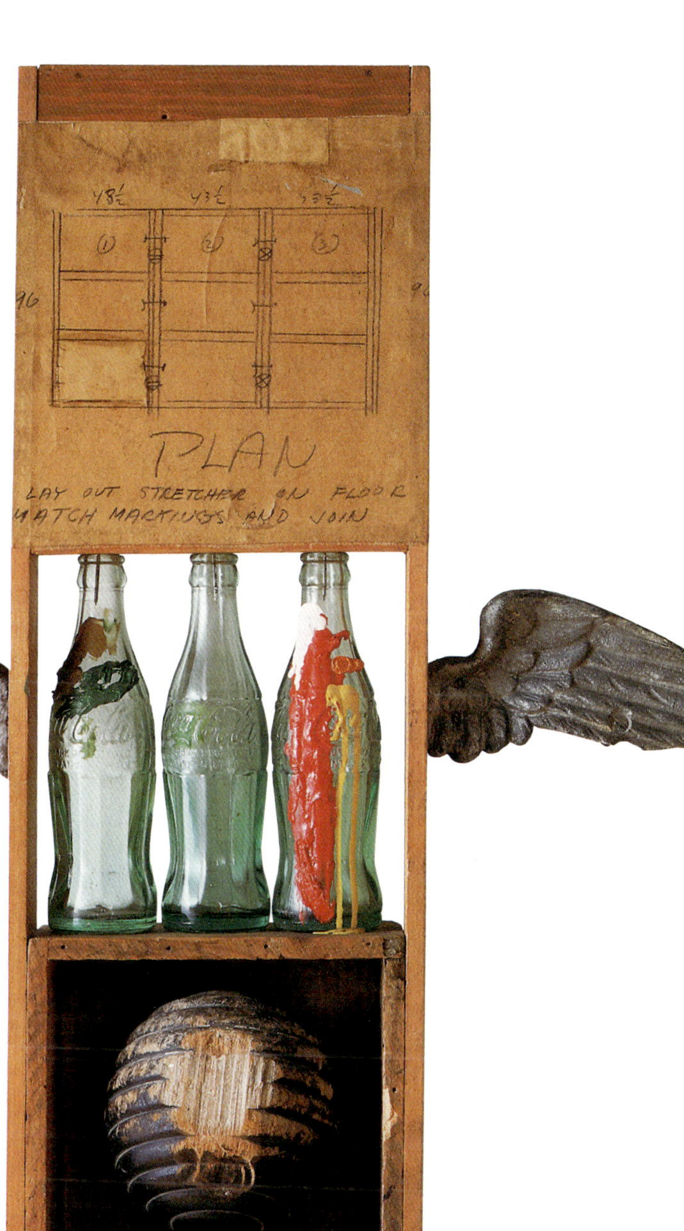

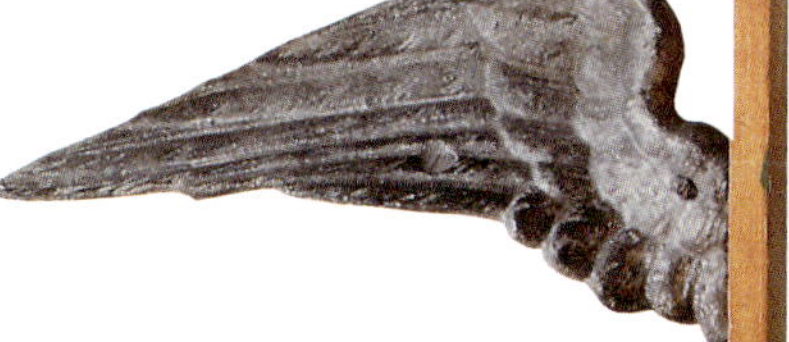

Coca-Cola Plan, 1958, combine painting, 26¾ x 25¼ x 4¾ inches, (86.16)

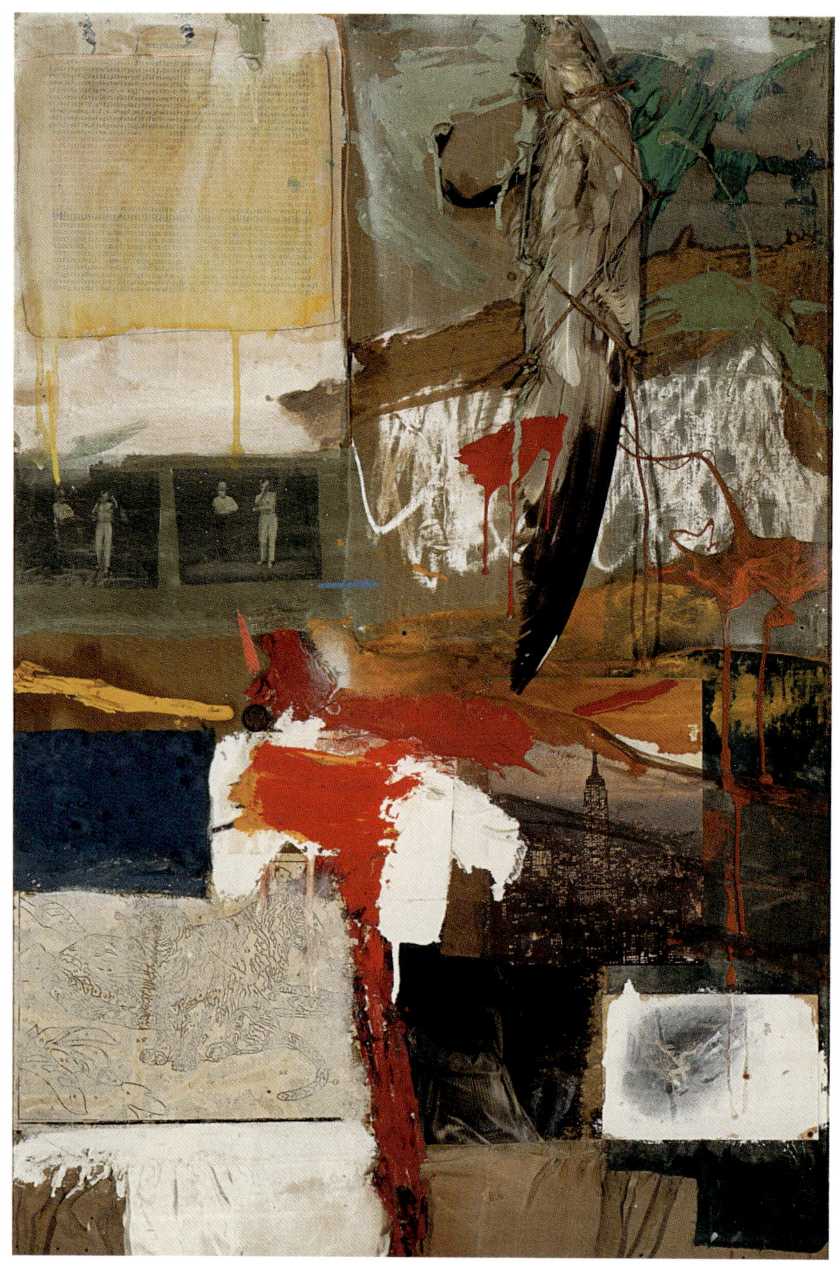

Painting with Grey Wing, 1958, combine painting, 31 x 21 inches, (86.18)

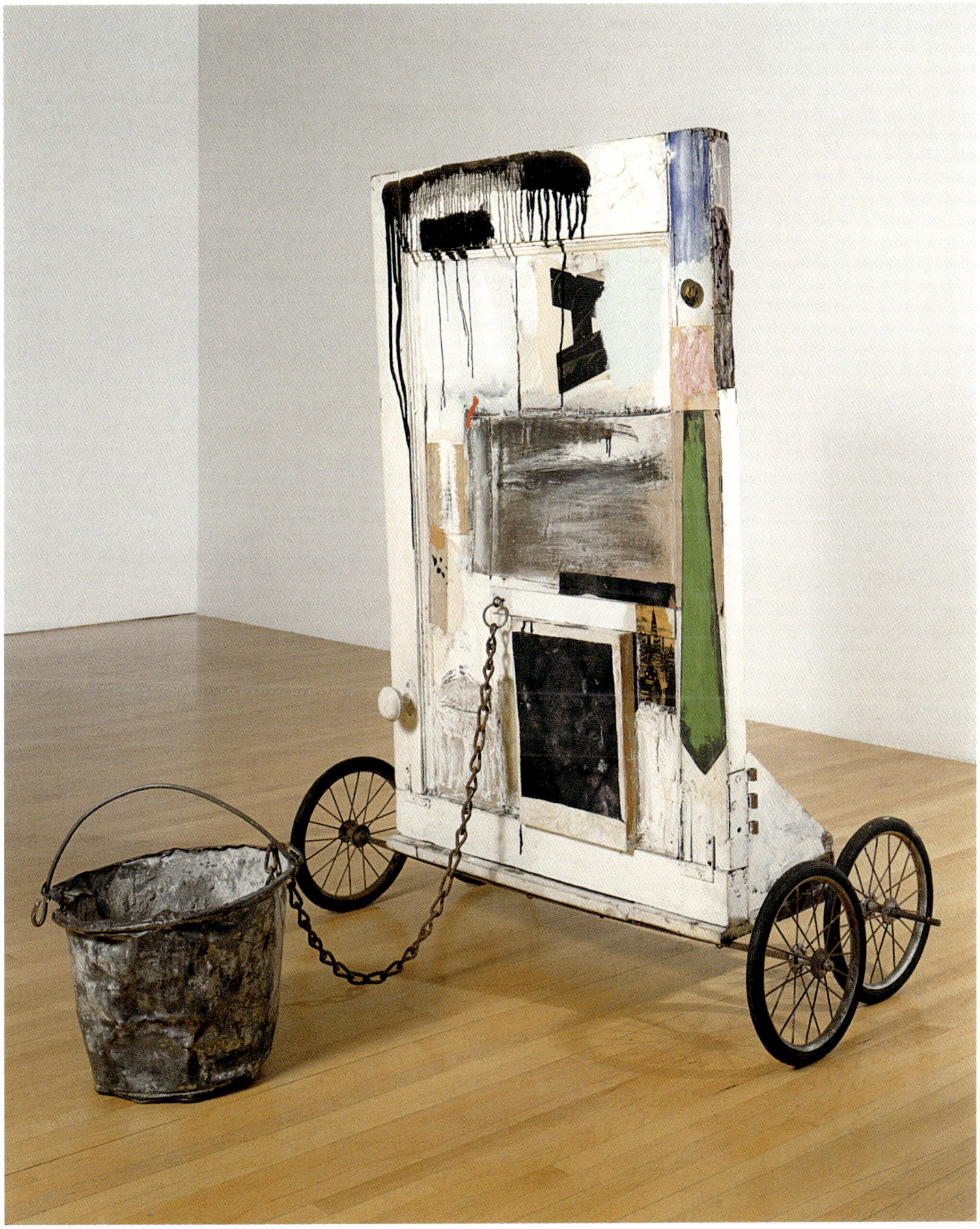

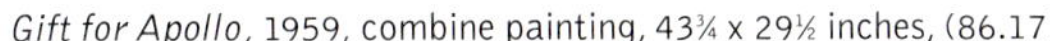

Gift for Apollo, 1959, combine painting, 43¼ x 29½ inches, (86.17)

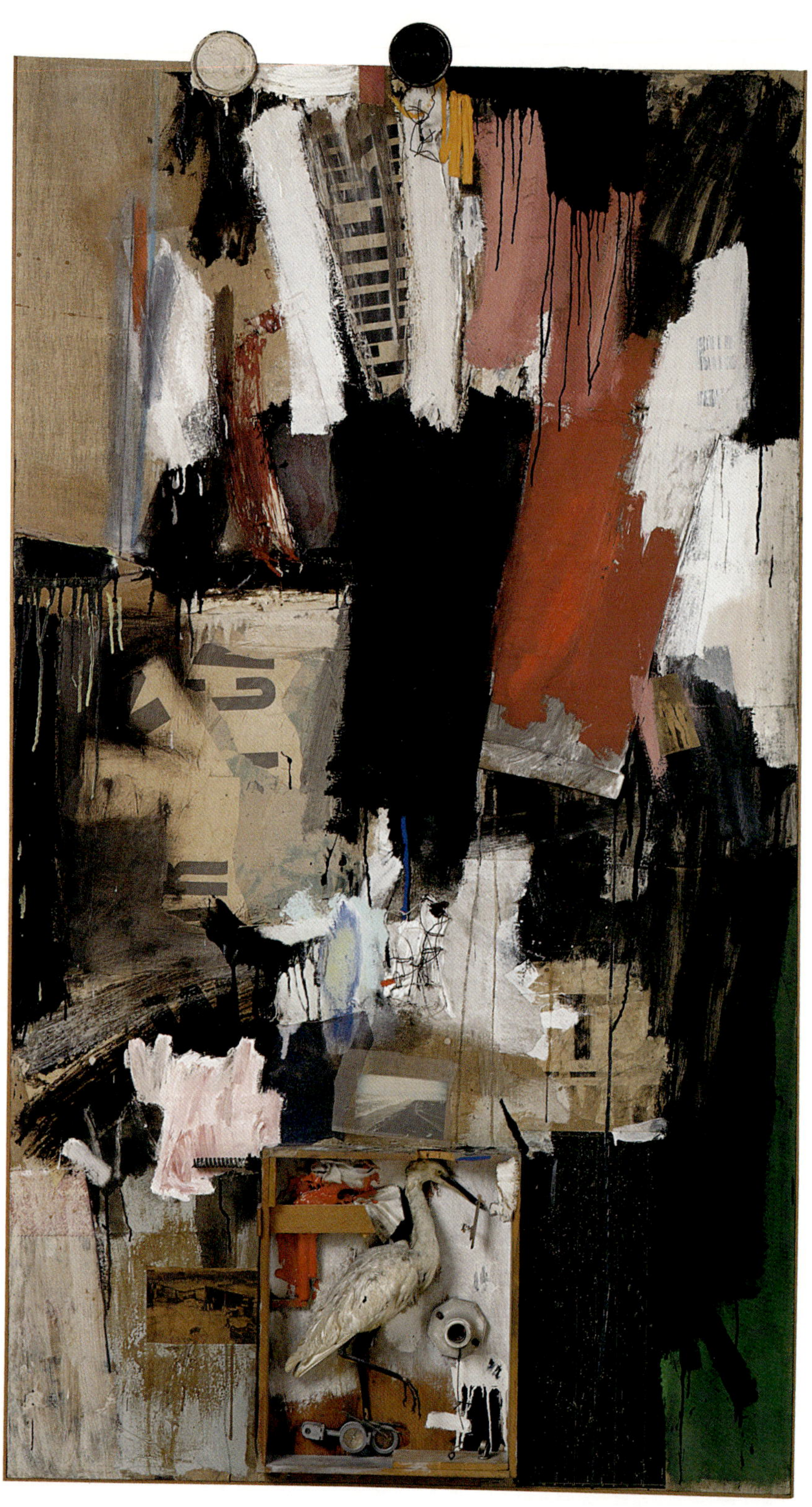

Inlet, 1959, combine painting, 84½ x 48 inches, (88.10)   *Kickback,* 1959, combine painting, 76½ x 33¼ x 2¾ inches, (87.17)

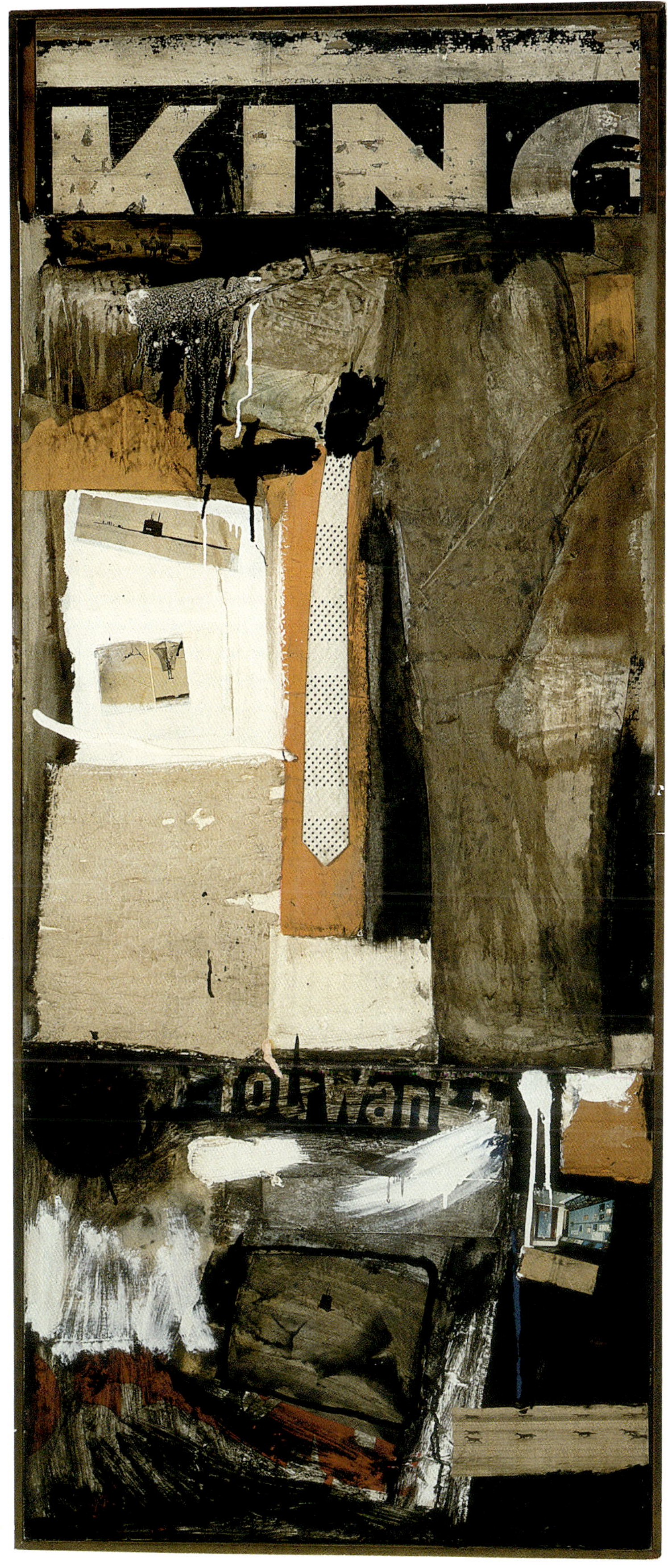

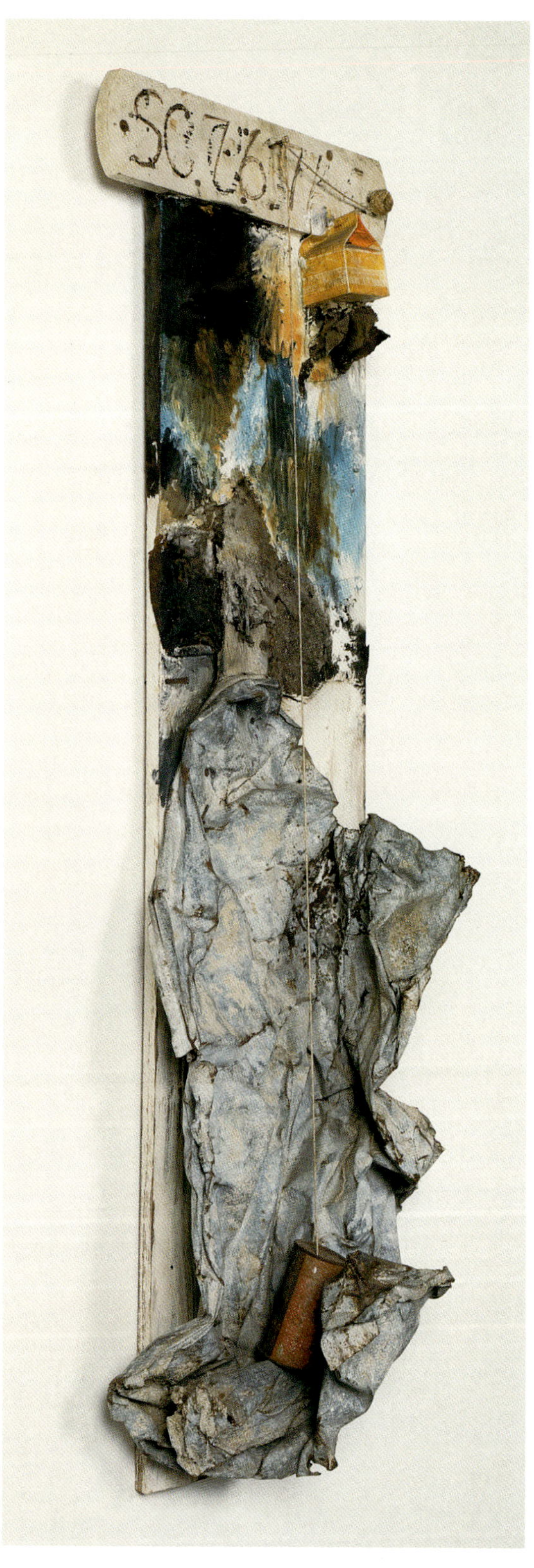

Slow Fall, 1961, combine painting, 56½ x 21 x 12 inches, (88.11)

Trophy III (For Jean Tinguely), 1961, combine painting, 96 x 65¾ inches, (87.19)

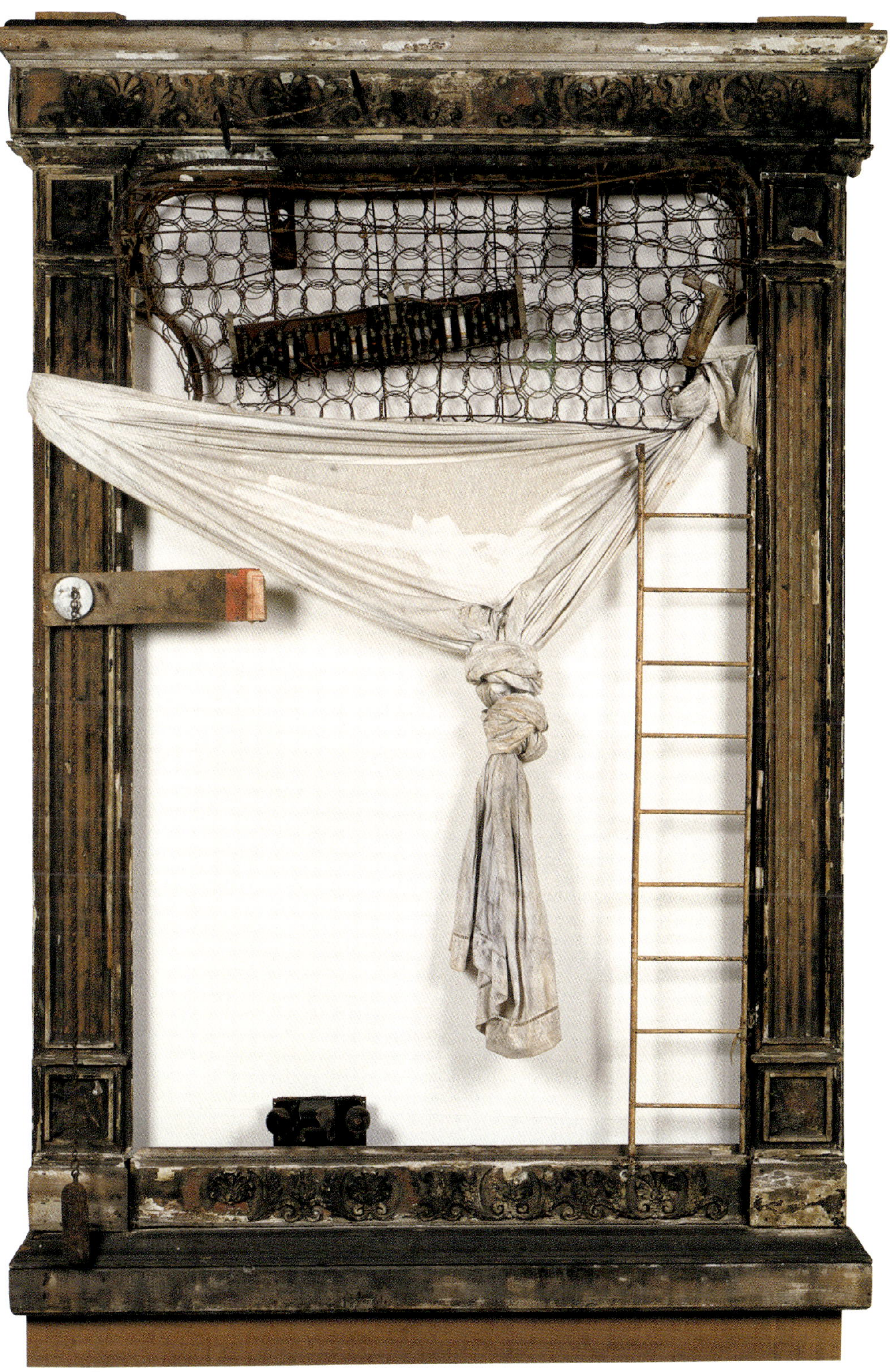

Born in North Dakota, James Rosenquist learned his craft by painting gas tanks and billboards across the Midwest while attending college. In 1955, he moved to New York City after winning a scholarship to study at the Art Students League. During the next five years, while searching for an art of his own, Rosenquist returned to painting billboards, becoming a member of Local 250 of the Sign, Pictorial & Display Union. In 1960, he permanently left this career behind to devote himself to his own painting.

In his work, Rosenquist attempts to drain images of their literal meanings rather than convey the clarity of the billboard message. Multiple images compete on the canvas, each an incomplete shard taken from magazines and advertisements. There are no discernable narratives in his paintings, for they are obscure compositions juxtaposing dissonant fragments of realistic things like abstract elements in a collage. Disruptions in color, orientation, and scale only add to the violence in his arbitrary croppings and composition. The fragmentation, at once suggestive and illusive, serves to disrupt the process of recognizing and completing each section, frustrating simple interpretations.

Rosenquist chooses to "represent" the real world by mirroring the visual effect of experiencing that world. His pictorial vocabulary is comprised of imagery from the debris of a popular, consumer culture and mass-production.

Rosenquist eschews brand names and embraces anonymous objects, finding his visual language in commonplace things. "I choose images common enough to pass without notice, old enough to have been forgotten, but not old enough to trigger nostalgia."[1]

After painting eight-foot faces and four-story letters on billboards, Rosenquist understands firsthand the power of scale and the "numbness" its brutality can elicit. His paintings, in their enormous dimensions, disorientingly remake the space of the viewer. The enlarged, individual segments within the works lose their identity and become abstract form. This development forces the viewer to feel or sense as with any other abstract work, but without the preconceptions about the form's function or strict meaning.

Rosenquist's paintings are as much about the processes of perception as anything else. "I thought I could change people's heads around by forcing them to identify these fragments at a certain rate of speed. It was a way to put mystery into my art and have the most mysterious thing be the closest, the most magnified, and the hardest to figure out."[2] In *Noon* and *Waves* (both of 1962), the fragmentation is seemingly simple in comparison to other works. Both feature a rectangle within a rectangle. *Noon*'s ground of an expansive, cloudy sky is interrupted by an inset of another sky scene: one's reading of which plane recedes, which is the detail, is muffled by the viewer's eye

JAMES

rosenquist

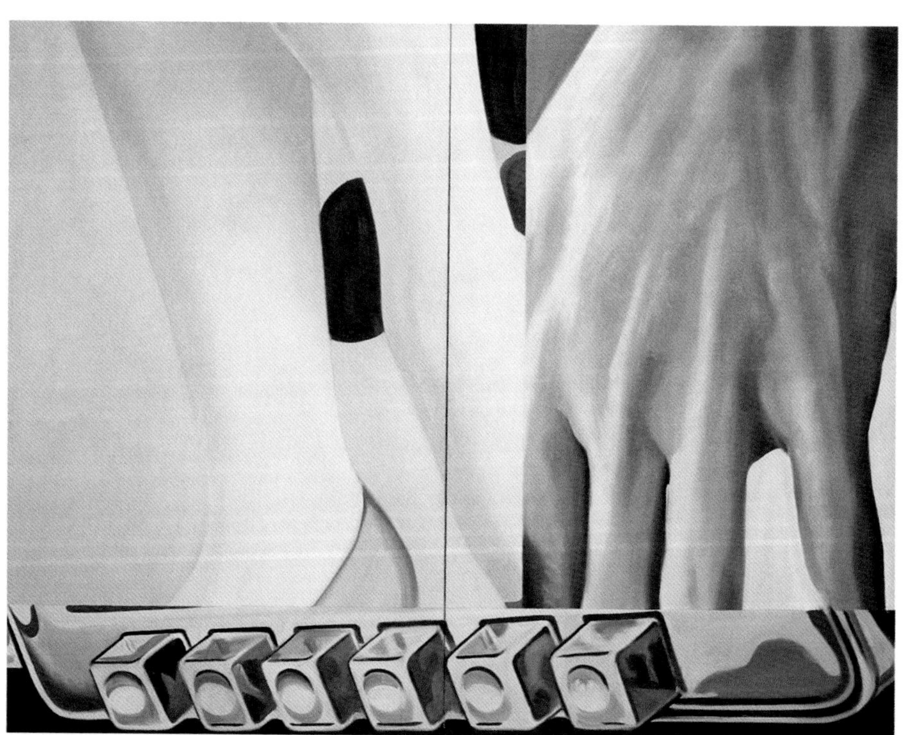

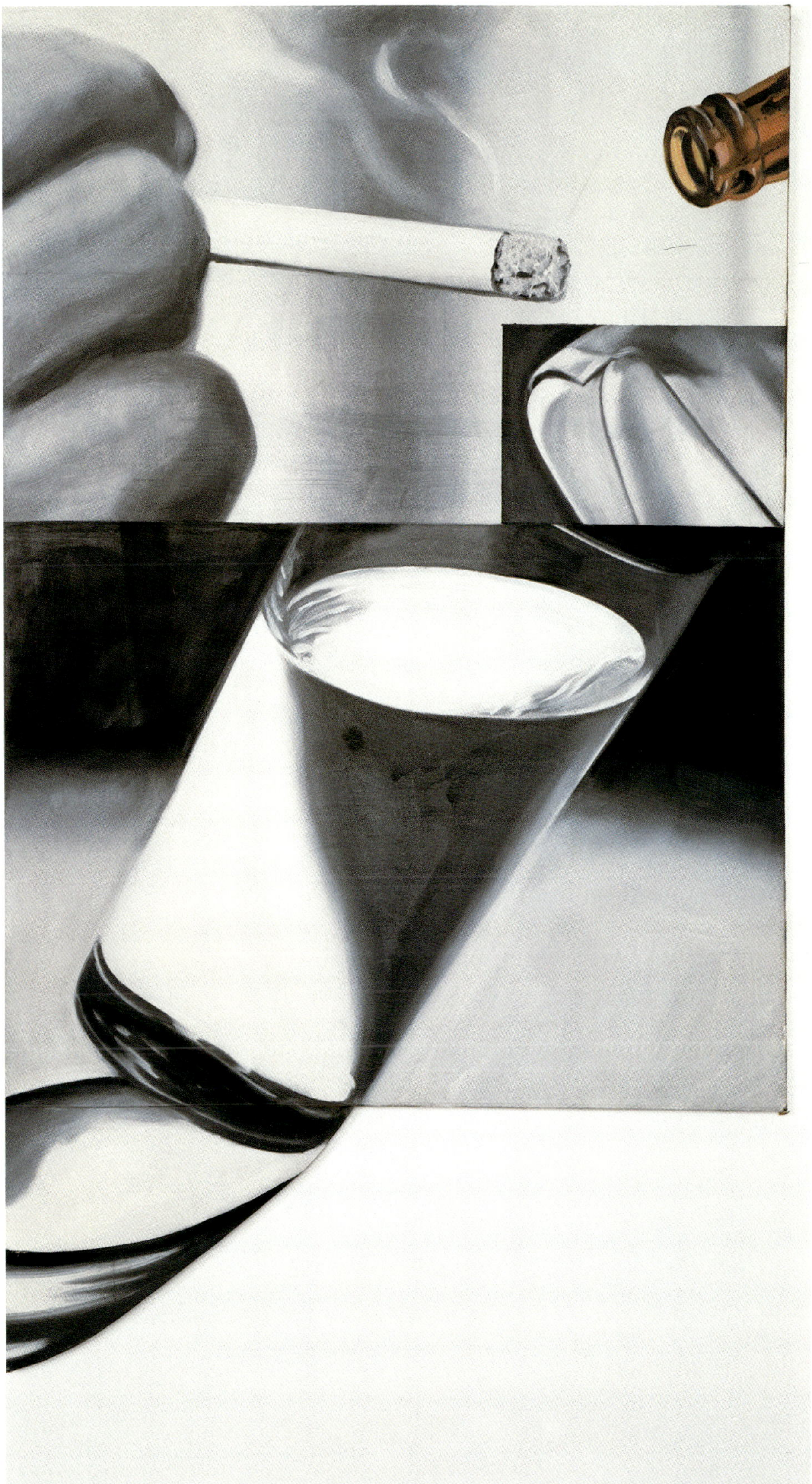

Push Button, 1961, oil on canvas, 82¾ x 105½ inches, (86.19)

White Cigarette, 1961, oil on canvas, 60½ x 35¼ inches, (87.21)

being forced to the dead-center of the painting, where the bulb of a flashlight has been placed.

In *Push Button* (1961), painted in a sensuous, grisaille palette, a magnified man's hand and the truncated legs of a woman stop abruptly at the bottom row of pushbuttons, which neither can reach or control. Does the work's anxiety stem from the threatening shadows, the menace of automation, or the dismemberment of limbs? *White Cigarette* (1961), also rendered in black-and-white with the exception of the golden-brown top of what appears to be a beer bottle, features an enlargement of a glass of water about to tip over. *Shave* (1964) features no fragmentation within the large painting, only a disturbing, oddly angled view of a man's face while shaving. Its monochromatic blue-and-yellow chiaroscuro, as well as the strange choice in composition, creates a contemplative, eerie mood.

Rosenquist abstracts nature itself in *Capillary Action* (1962), an unfragmented view of a tree in landscape. Although its grey grass looks unpromising for nourishment, the tree spouts lush green foliage amid a strangely rendered background. Spoiling the illusion, however, are the rectangles projecting several inches out from canvas, some painted one, flat color, and others painted continuously with the canvas they overlap.

There is much to connect Rosenquist to Pop art: imagery sources, palette reflecting commercial inks, and slick handling of paint, often in combination with real "found" objects. Rosenquist's work is not a critique, but a pictorial metaphor for how we see and experience things in the world. *A Lot to Like* and *Vestigial Appendage* are quintessential paintings in this sense. Depicting a world of saccharine-colored objects stripped of their selling power, they abandon traditional pictorial illusion without abandoning illusionistically painted images. Vulgar, overlapping, tense, confused, and exciting images: communication and narrative are rendered mute, frustrating vision and desire. Rosenquist's collage of life experienced makes all levels of meaning operate simultaneously into dissonance. —J.H.

1 Rosenquist, quoted in Judith Goldman, "James Rosenquist: Fragments of Fragments," *James Rosenquist* (New York: Penguin Books, 1985), 13.
2 Rosenquist, quoted in "An Interview with James Rosenquist," in Judith Goldman, *James Rosenquist: The Early Pictures, 1961–1964* (New York: Gagosian Gallery and Rizzoli, 1992), 99.

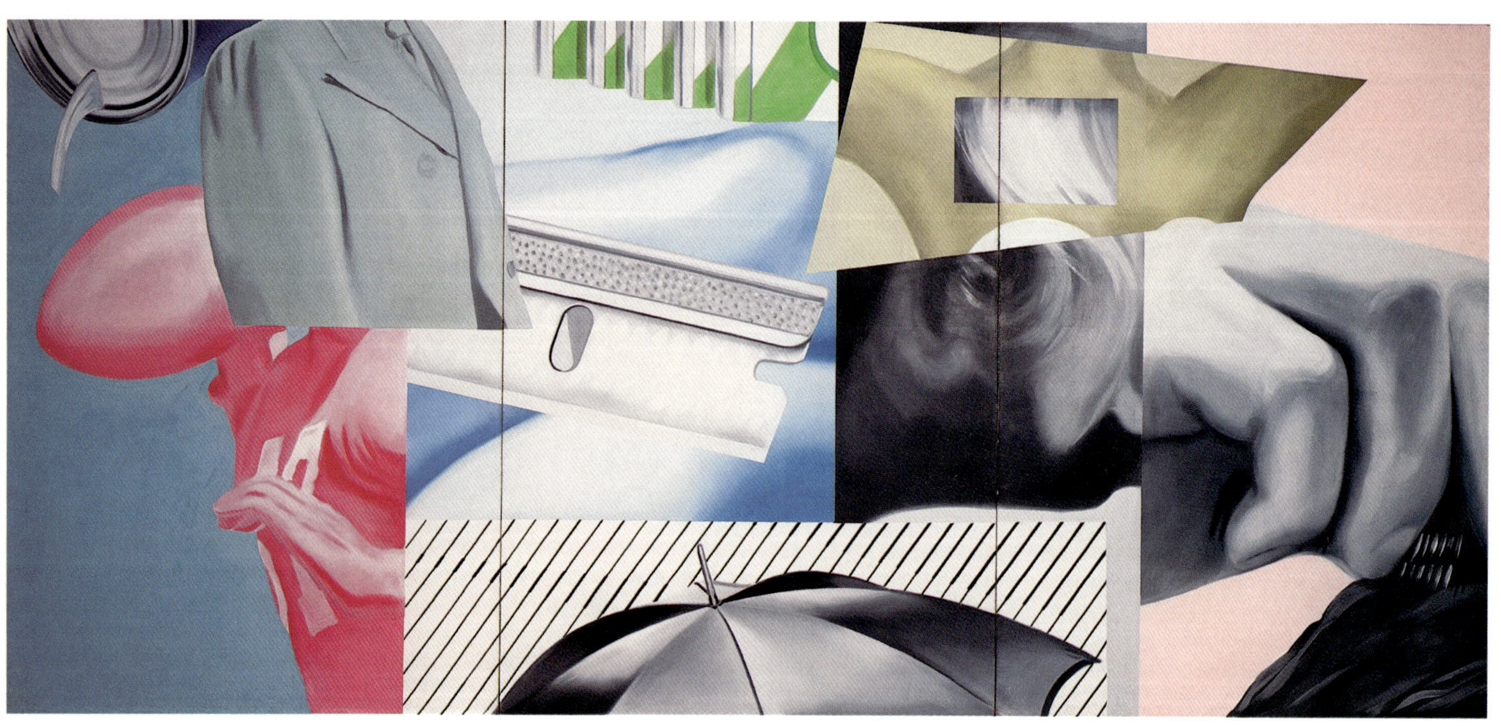

A Lot to Like, 1962, oil on canvas, 93 x 204 inches (triptych), (84.8)

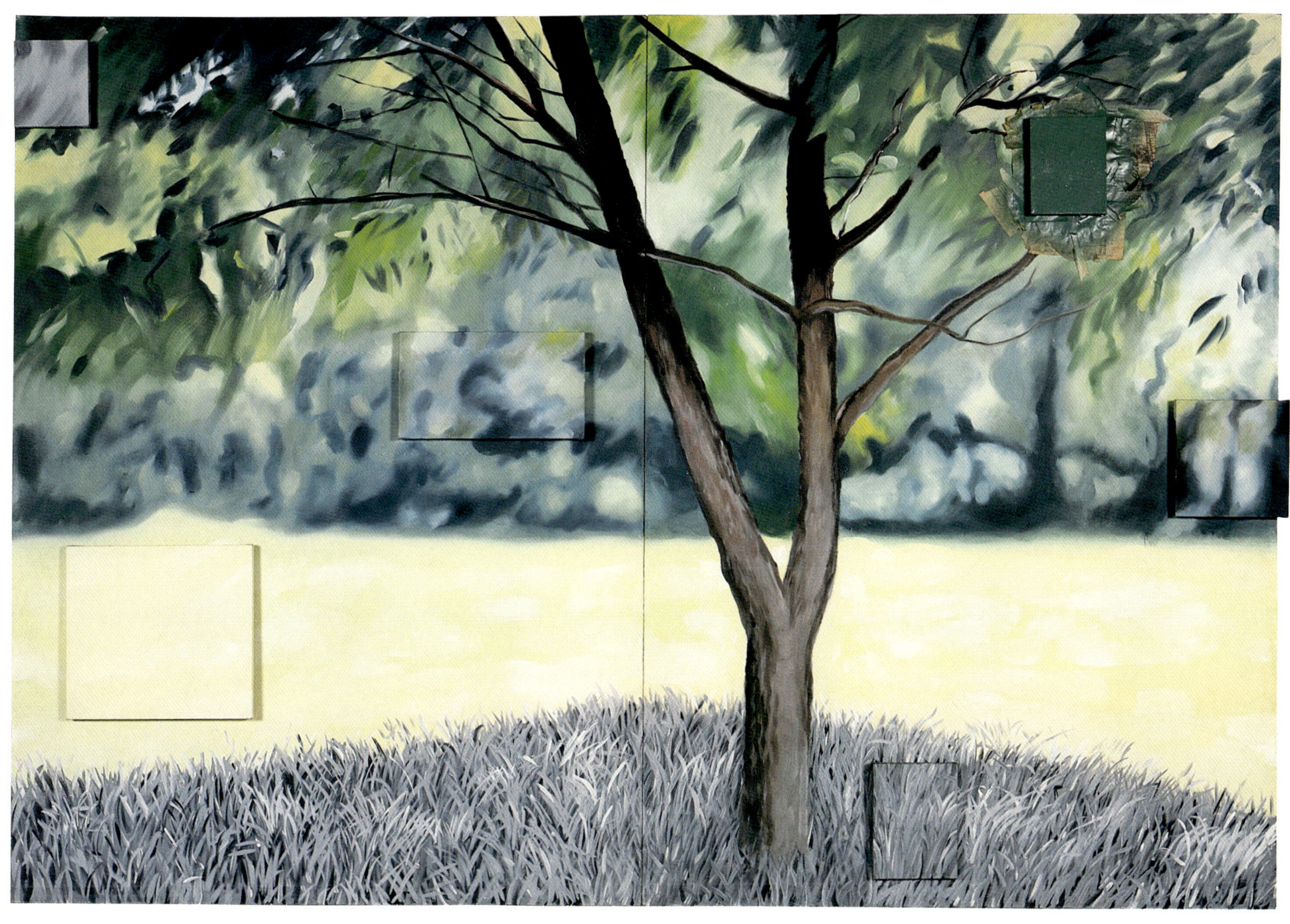

Capillary Action, 1962, oil on canvas, 92½ x 136¼ inches, (86.20)

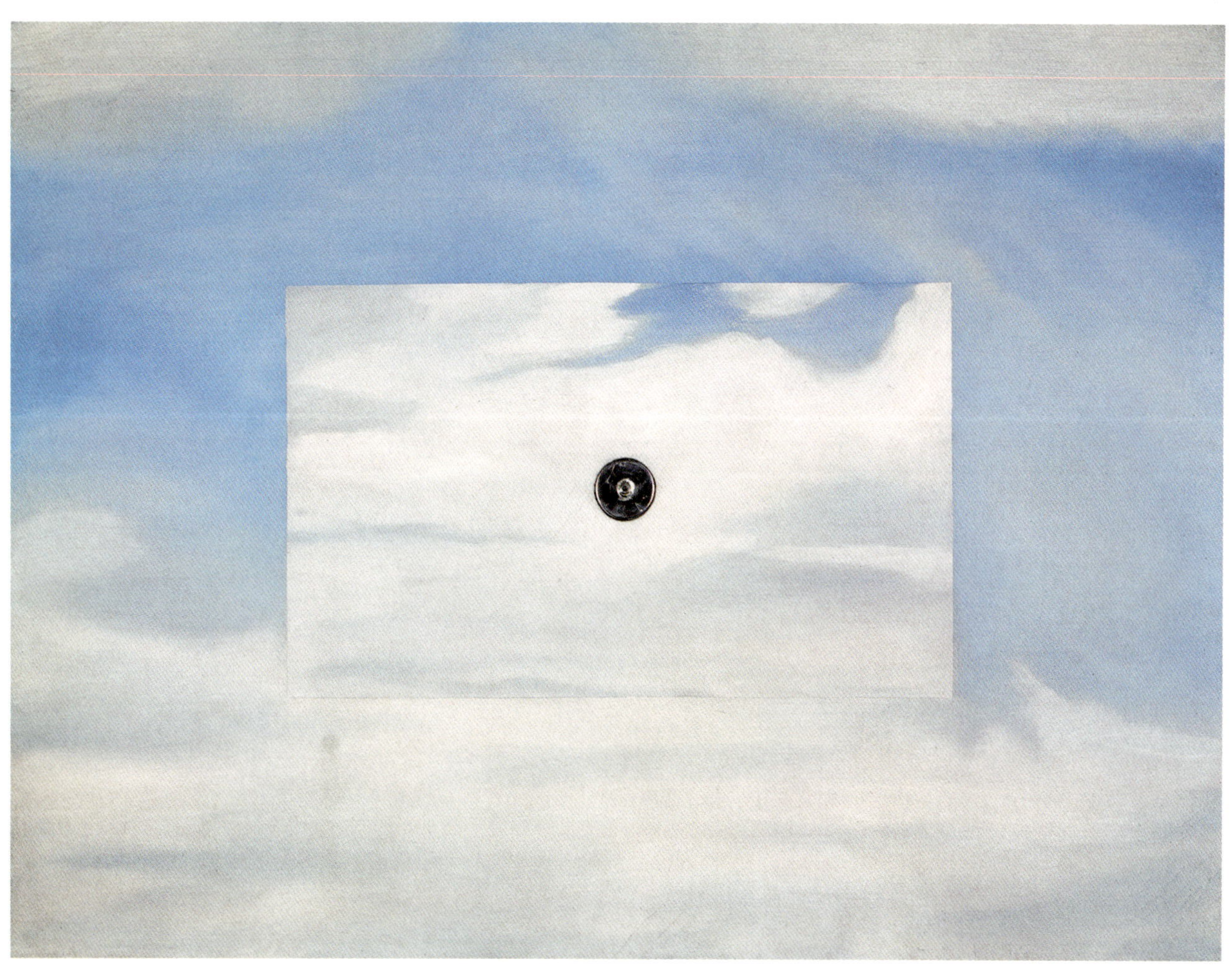

Noon, 1962, oil on canvas, 36 x 48 x 3 inches, (88.12)

Vestigial Appendage, 1962, oil on canvas, 72 x 93¾ inches, (85.23)

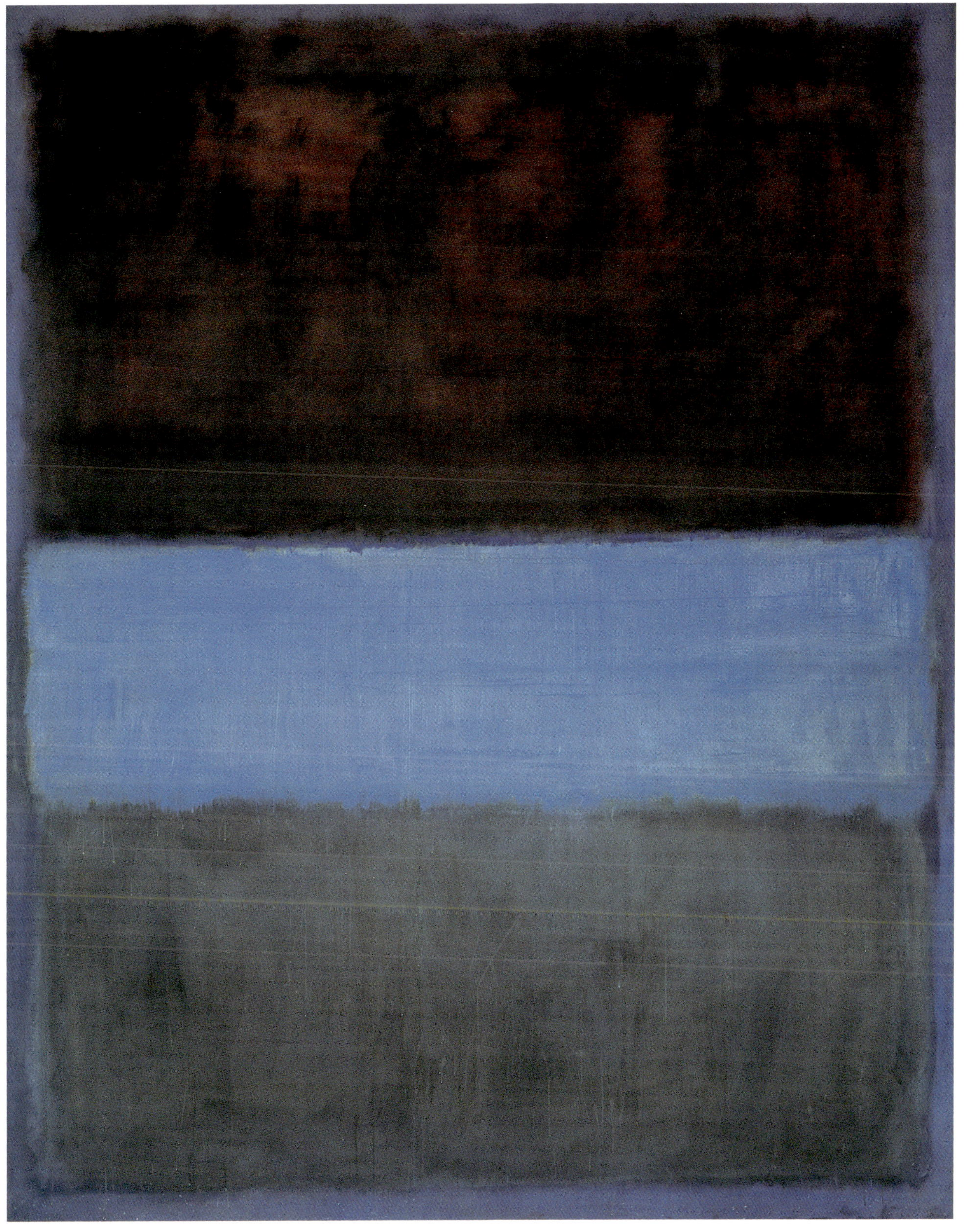

each other.

In 1957 Rothko began a marked devotion to exploring dark colors, culminating in the somber palette of his commissioned *Seagram Mural* of 1958–59. *No. 61 (Rust and Blue)* (1953) is an early exception. The blue field "framing" the work is almost squeezed out of the cool painting by large, oppressive masses of rust brown and two shades of blue. An intensity of mood and expressive energy are more palpable in *Purple Brown* (1957) and *Black on Dark Sienna on Purple* (1960). Upon looking at the works, there is a delay in perception, as the eyes adjust to the diminished but hushed light of the brackish colors. They seem to be secretive, somber, more contemplative, revealing themselves more slowly than the vibrant canvases of the early to mid-1950s. Despite the incredible variations in color, Rothko's art remained doggedly consistent and similar in composition until the end of his life in 1970. His art was less an oeuvre of individual works than one of painting a singular and inexhaustible theme, a theme "involved with the *scale* of human feeling, the human drama, as much of it as [he] can express."[5] —J.H.

Violet and Yellow on Rose, 1954, oil on canvas, 83½ x 67¾ inches, (87.22)

1 Rothko, as quoted in E.C. Goossen, "Rothko: The Omnibus Image," *ARTnews* (January 1961): 60.
2 Robert Rosenblum, "The abstract sublime," *ARTnews* 59 (May 1960): 40.
3 Rothko, as quoted in Jeffrey Weiss, "Rothko's Unknown Space," in *Mark Rothko* (Washington, D.C.: National Gallery of Art, 1998), 307.
4 Rothko, in "I Paint Very Large Pictures," (1951), reprinted in Kristine Stiles and Peter Selz, eds., *Theories and Documents of Contemporary Art: A Sourcebook of Artists' Writings* (Berkeley and Los Angeles: University of California Press, 1996), 26.
5 Rothko, quoted in *Mark Rothko*, 346.

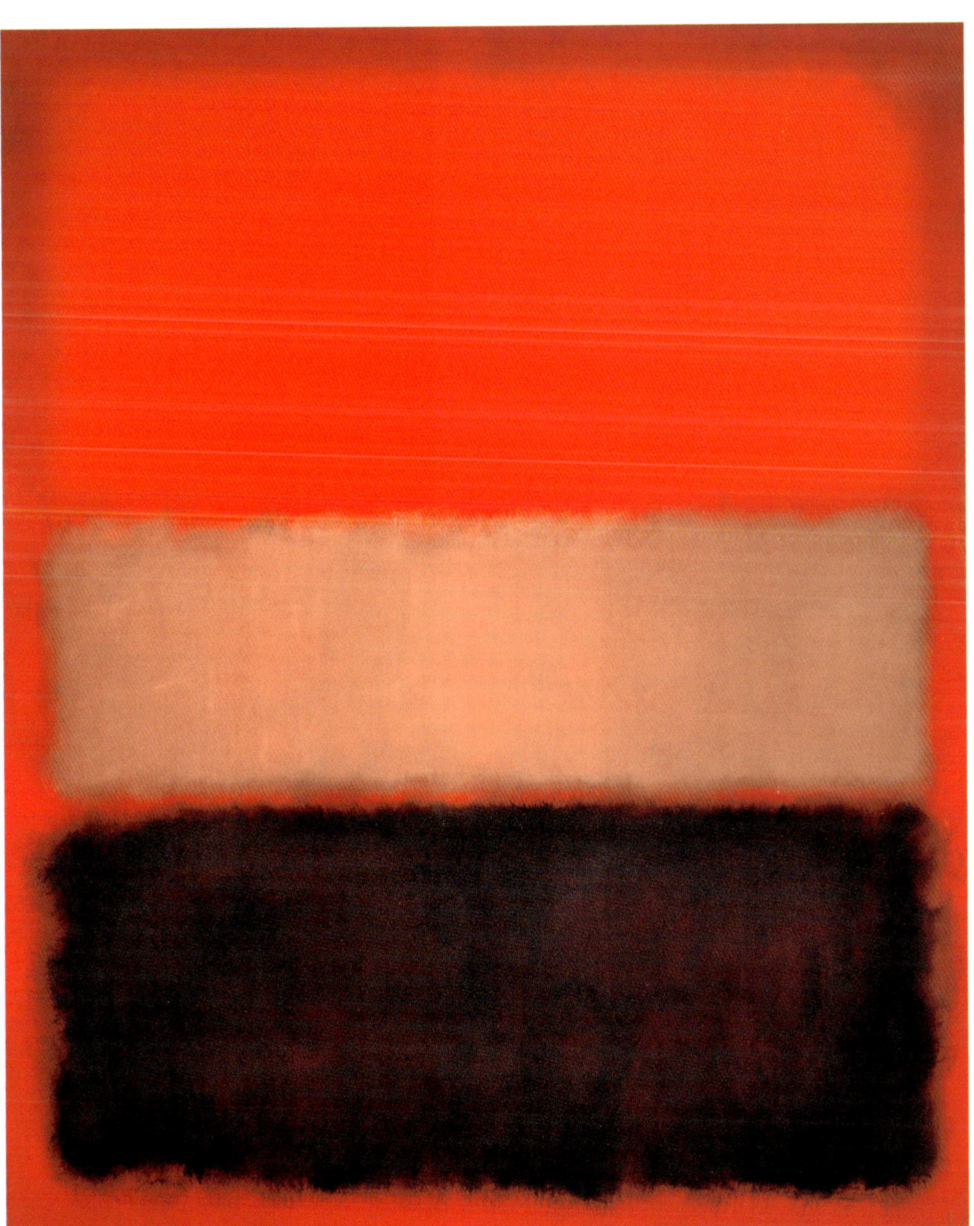

No. 46 (Black, Ochre, Red Over Red), 1957, oil on canvas, 99¼ x 81½ inches, (85.24)

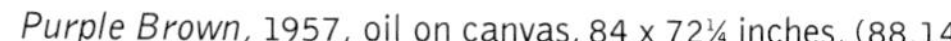

Purple Brown, 1957, oil on canvas, 84 x 72¼ inches, (88.14)

Red and Brown, 1957, oil on canvas, 69 x 43¼ inches, (88.16)

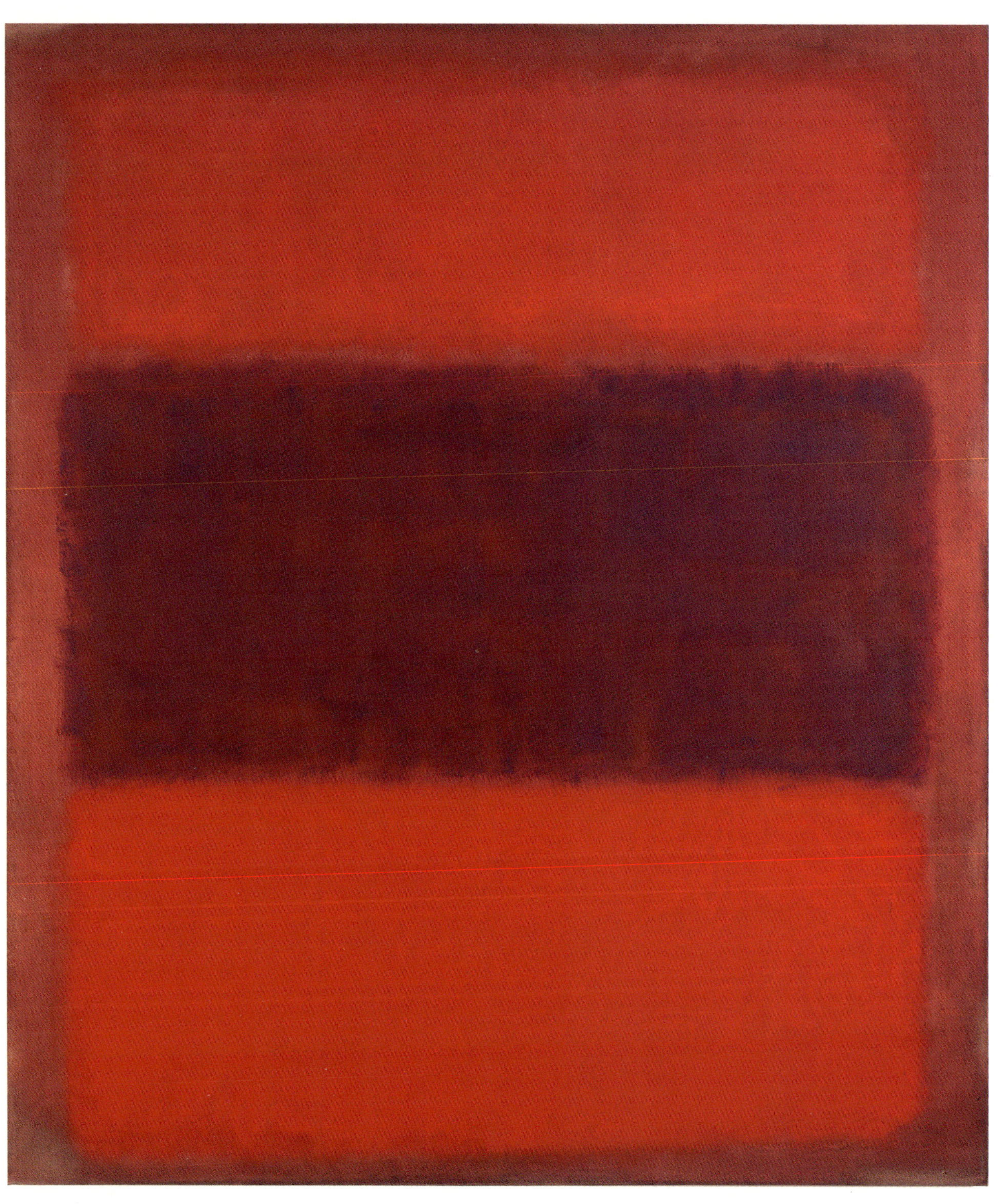

Red and Blue over Red, 1959, oil on canvas, 93 x 82¼ inches, (88.15)

Black on Dark Sienna on Purple, 1960, oil on canvas, 119¾ x 105 inches, (86.21)

Trained as a painter during the ascendency of Abstract Expressionism, George Segal eventually turned to sculpture in his frustration with the medium of painting. Although attracted to expressionism, Segal was unable to reconcile the movement's exclusion of the physical world in art with his own desire to express the qualities of experience. Stymied by this struggle, Segal left Manhattan to start a farm in New Jersey.

While in New Jersey, Segal took classes at Rutgers University, where he met Allan Kaprow. Their discussions focused on the creation of a new art, one that incorporated objects and experiences of everyday life for a total experience. In response to Jackson Pollock's paintings—and what he saw as their implied extension beyond literal dimensions into the space of the viewer—Kaprow staged his first Happening at Segal's farm in 1957. Uncomfortable with the ephemerality of Happenings, Segal began to experiment with sculpture, and its composition out of space itself, as an extension of the canvas.

After a chance discovery in 1961 of plaster-impregnated medical bandages, Segal found his method of direct casting, as well as his direction as a sculptor. His sculptures are taken from the exterior of the cast, capturing a textured, expressionistic, modeled surface, instead of the interior, which would provide a more precise physical replica. The lowly art material dries quickly into a thin and flexible shell which, after being cut off the body of the sitter, must be re-pieced together, allowing Segal manipulation of its form and gesture. The ash-preserved bodies at Pompeii are a common allusion to the casts and, although Segal objects to this association with death, his casts are indeed eerie, plaster shells of live bodies, immobilized and mute.

Plaster white, the sculptures are bloodless but somehow transcendent of the everday, often derelict furnishings or environments with which they are austerely paired. For Segal, "The trick is not to juggle them like a school exercise, but to juggle them in a way that they shiver in a sense to a real experience."[1] The life-sized work imposes an insistent presence upon the viewer: tableau vivants eerily animating space with frozen bodies and everyday objects that invade the viewer's world and scale.

By capturing situations and gestures so universal, Segal invites the viewer to project upon the work, creating a profound humanism and sympathy. In *Sunbathers on Rooftop* (1963–67), a man and a woman lie on a black platform furnished with a dilapidated skylight. A familiar scene of Manhattan in the summer, they sunbathe, fully clothed, in postures both languorous and exhausted. More intensely private in mood is *Man in the Armchair* (1969). Shoulders slumped with resignation, a man sits in weighty, quiet contemplation. This unremarkable moment in time is given permanence with a pervading, pregnant silence that surprisingly induces a state of mind, of alienation. —J.H.

1 Segal, in *Studio International* 174, no. 893 (October 1967): 147.

segal

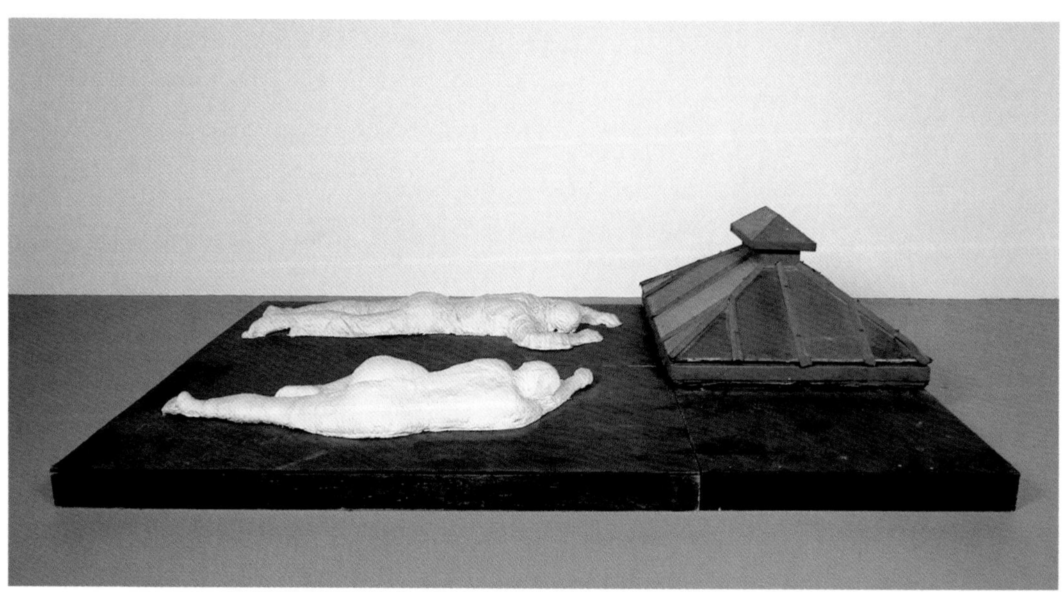

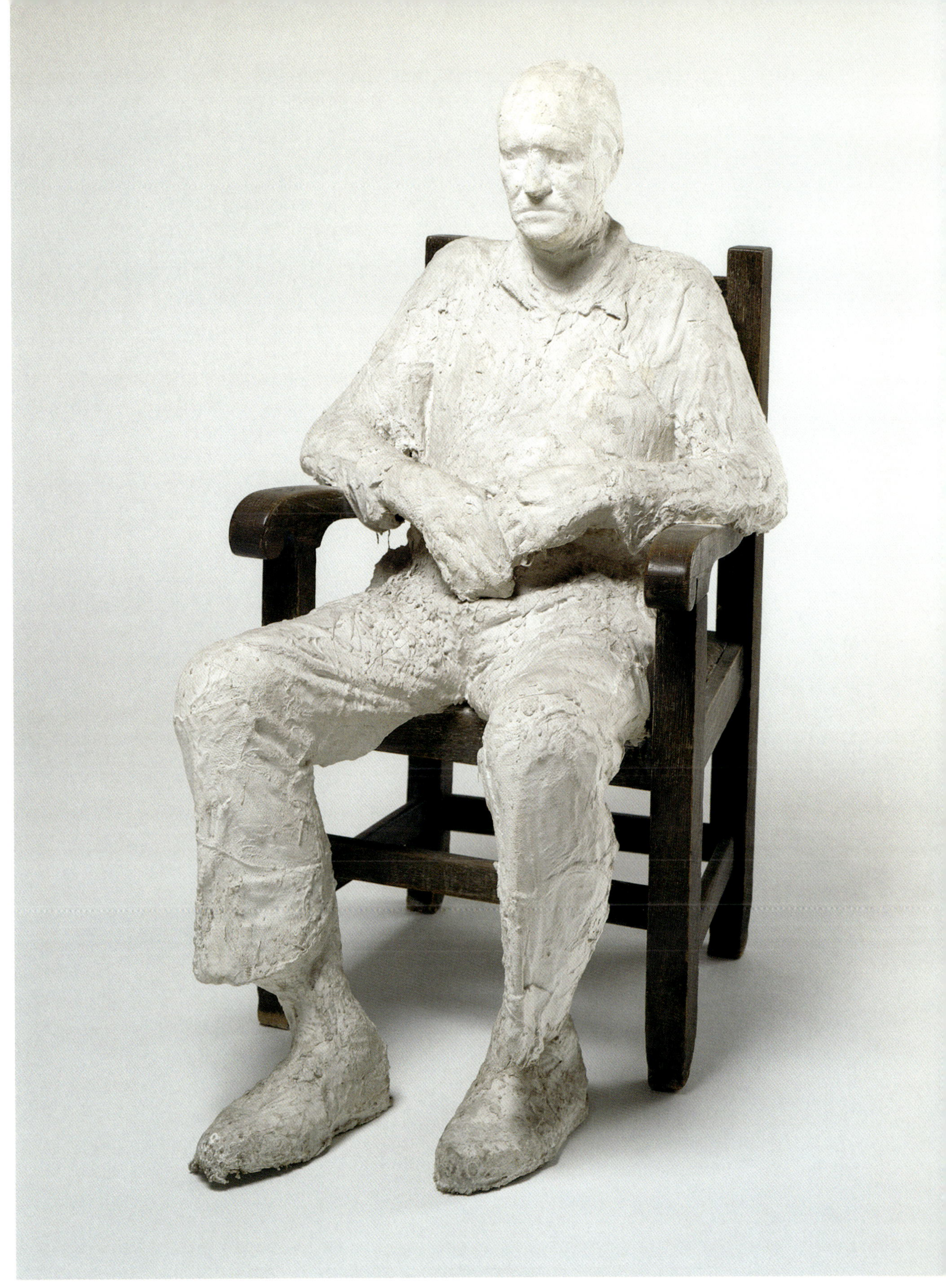

Man in the Armchair, 1969, plaster and wood, 49½ x 30 x 31½ inches, (87.23)

Antoni Tàpies, considered one of the most important, postwar Spanish artists, employs abstraction and a concentrated use of texture to produce paintings that are beautiful yet ambiguous. Tàpies is most closely associated with *Art Informel*, which emerged as an avant-garde style in Europe during the early 1950s. Characterized by the thick, almost sculptural surfaces of their canvases, artists such as Hans Hartung and Pierre Soulages created paintings in which the identifying content was not the imagery or pictorial structure, but the materials used. This concentrated focus upon matter was rooted in the idea that the work's physical content would cause the viewer to transcend the object and experience an emotional reaction.

Born to a middle-class family in Barcelona, Spain, in 1923, Tàpies's tranquil childhood was abruptly interrupted by the outbreak of the Spanish Civil War in 1936. This gruesome and destructive war finally ended in the spring of 1939, leaving the country torn both physically and mentally. One year later, at the age of seventeen, Tàpies suffered a near-fatal heart attack brought on by tuberculosis and was sent into Spain's rural countryside to convalesce. During his influential two-year recovery, Tàpies honed his drawing skills, became versed in non-Western philosophies including Veda and Zen Buddhism, and read Nietzsche, Ibsen, and Dostoevsky.

Returning to Barcelona in 1943 with no specific direction, Tàpies enrolled in law school at the University of Barcelona. However, he also participated in drawing classes at the Acadèmia Valls in the Carrer de Jonqueres and soon his dedication to the arts far exceeded that of law. In 1947 he began to regularly associate with a small group of artists known as the *Blaus,* some of whom had been in close contact with the Parisian Surrealists in the 1930s. Through one of the members, Tàpies made the acquaintance of Joan Miró, and the two formed a lasting and important friendship. The influence of both Miró and Paul Klee are evident in the early work of Tàpies, which incorporates dreams, automatism, and other elements of Surrealism.

These "magical paintings" brought Tàpies international recognition. In 1952 they were shown in Pittsburgh at the Carnegie International, the Venice Biennale, and Laietanes Gallery in Barcelona. In 1953 Martha Jackson began showing this work in her New York gallery and three years later Tàpies had series of exhibitions at the Stadler Gallery in Paris. However, as early as 1952, Tàpies's outlook began to shift. Sparked in part by his 1951 meeting with Picasso in France, Tàpies began to experiment with color studies and the simplification of forms. Abstractions ensued that were characterized by unusual textures produced by the combination of materials including paint, sand, varnish, and powdered marble. Rich and tactile surfaces with bits of collage and incised portions characterized this work, which came to be the

ANTONI

tàpies

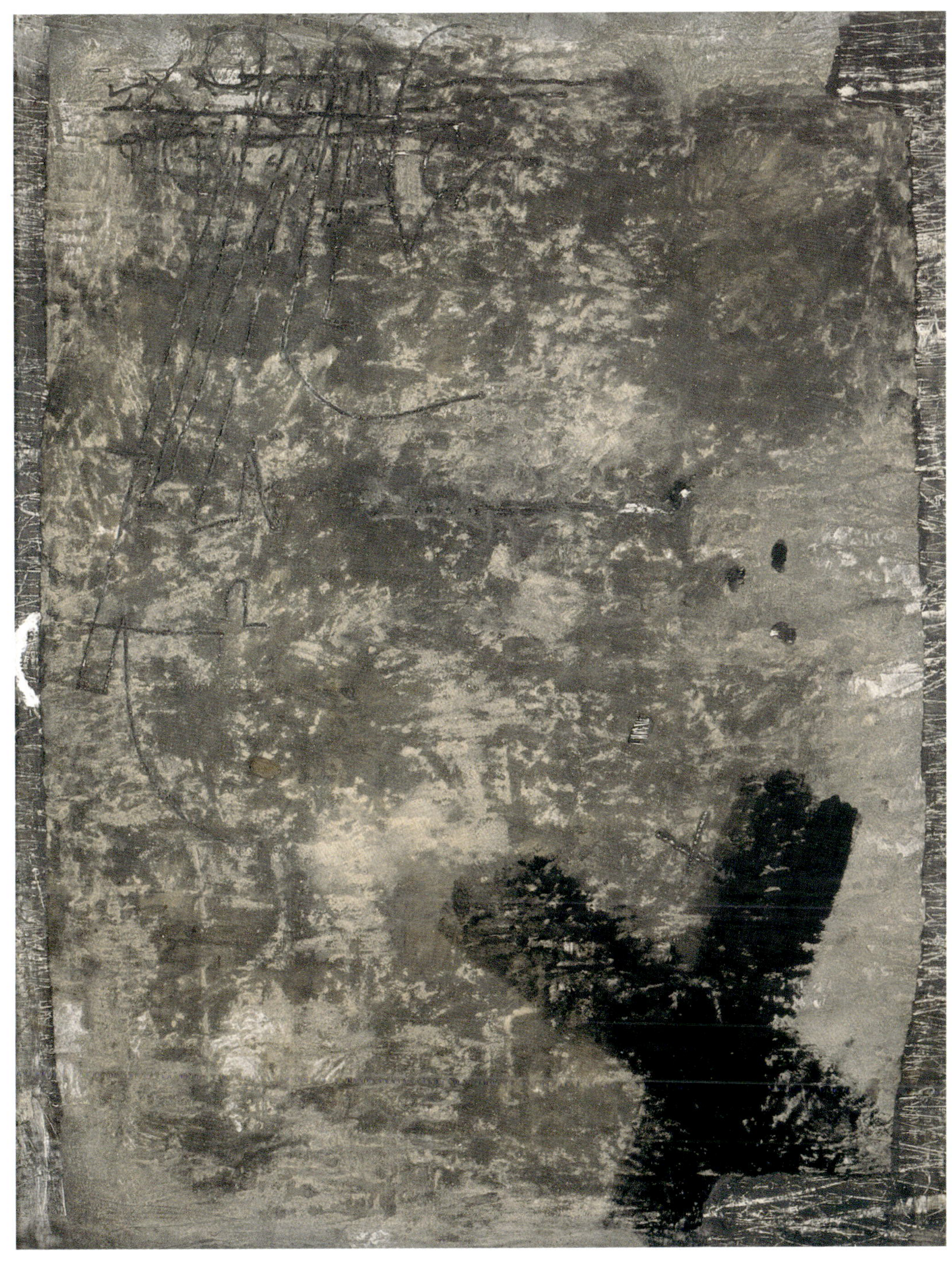

Grey with Black Cross. No. XXVI, 1955, mixed media on canvas, 57⅛ x 44⅝ inches, (88.20)

style for which Tàpies is best known.

Hammered Grey (1959), *Ochre-Sand. No. LXVIII* (1957), and *Ochre-Brown with Black Crack. No. XVIII* (1956) are among the artist's densely textured works referred to as "matter paintings." Limited in palette, these works are frequently compared to walls, upon which Tàpies has left his mark. The wall functions as a metaphor for enclosure, confinement, escape, and freedom—ideas that are at the heart of Tàpies's personal experience. He states, "If I were to recount how I became gradually aware of this evocative power of walls, I would have to go back a long time. They are memories that date from my adolescence and my childhood spent confined between the walls where I spent the war years."[1] With deepened marks or inlaid objects, as in *Grey Painting with Reddish Sign* (1958), or *The Broken Plate. Homage to Gaudí. No. IX* (1956), the idea of "writing on the walls" is realized.

In addition to textural effects, Tàpies also includes symbolic marks into his paintings. In the lower portion of both *Grey with Black Cross. No. XXVI* (1955) and *Grey Relief Perforated with Black Sign. No. X* (1955) there is a large, black cross. While this mark could be regarded as simple graffiti, the cross is a loaded symbol whose reference to Christianity is undeniable. In *Reddish Painting* (1958), Tàpies's marks are more anthropomorphic, and the image loosely resembles a headless torso with visible interior organs. The vertical form of *Blackish Ochre with Perforations* (1956–58) alludes to a human body whose lower organs have been physically pierced. While there are indeed allusions to these ideas, the lack of specificity grants them a power that is palpable. Tàpies's desire for ambiguity is a critical component to his work. This notion is felt strongly in *All White. No. II* (1955), *Marble-Worker's Sand with Six Footprints* (1959), and *Grey on White. No. LXV* (1956), all of whose beautiful, non-referential surfaces allow the mind to wander and float through the constructed void. —R. M.

1 Manuel J. Borja-Villel, "Writing On the Wall," in *Tàpies: Comunicació Sobre el Mur.* Exh. cat. (Barcelona: Fundació Antoni Tàpies, 1992), 291.

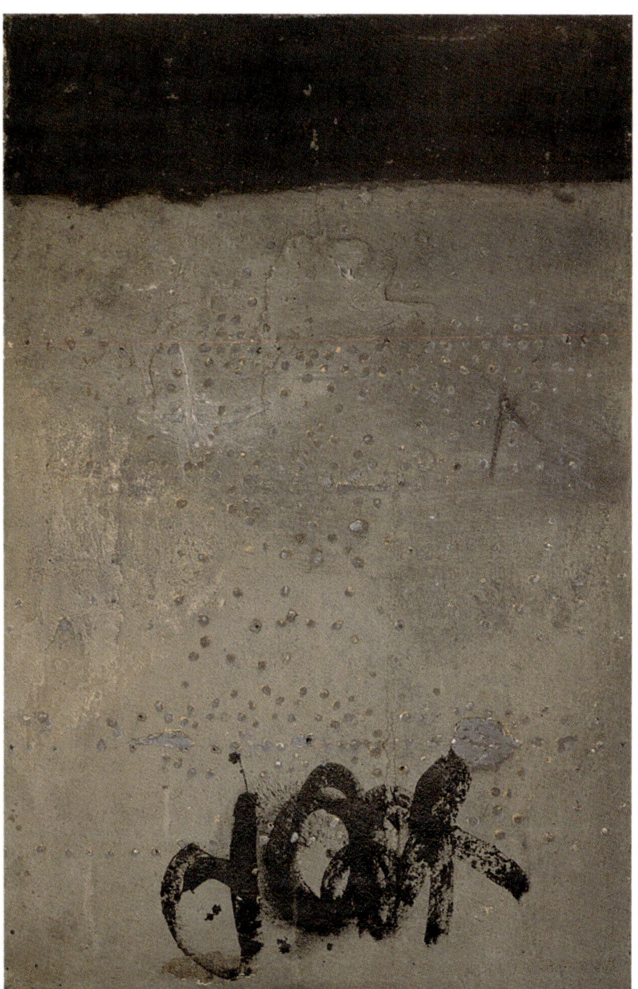

Grey Relief Perforated with Black Sign. No. X, 1955, mixed media on canvas, 57⅝ x 38 inches, (88.22)

All White. No. II, 1955, mixed media on canvas, 57½ x 38 inches, (84.10)

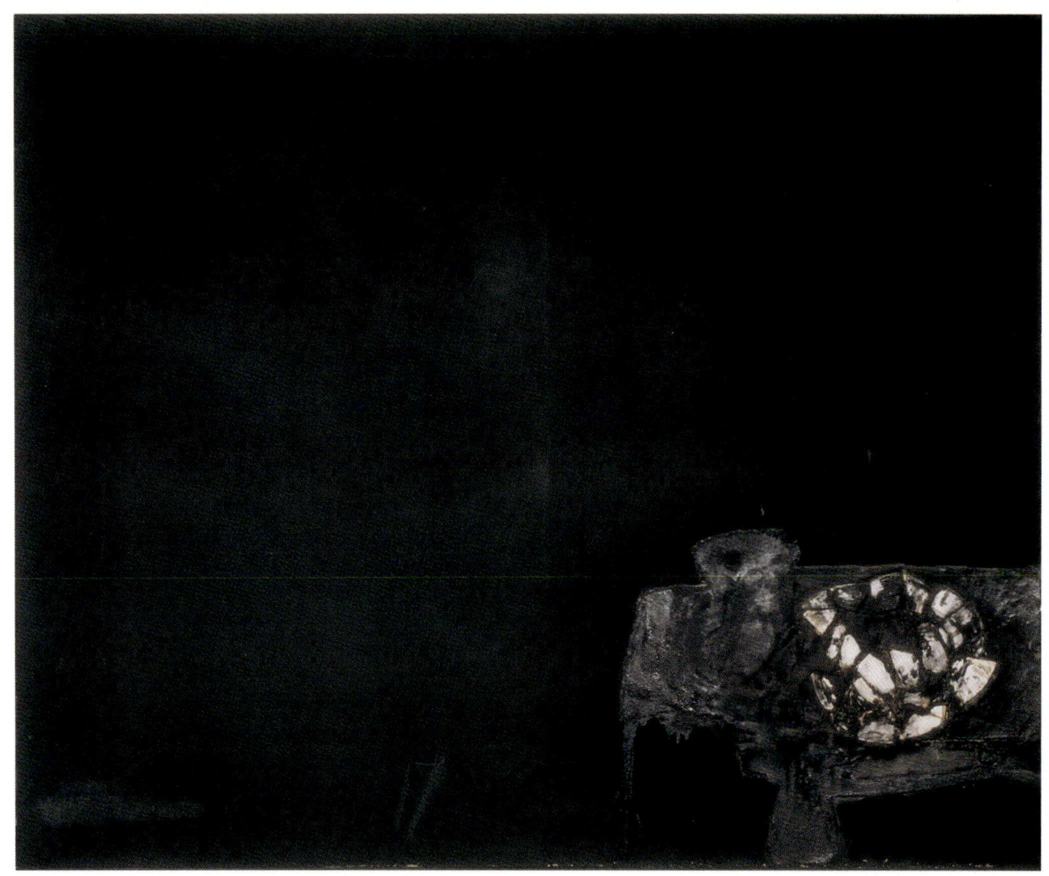

The Broken Plate. Homage to Gaudí. No. IX, 1956, mixed media on canvas, 51⅛ x 63⅝ inches, (88.19)

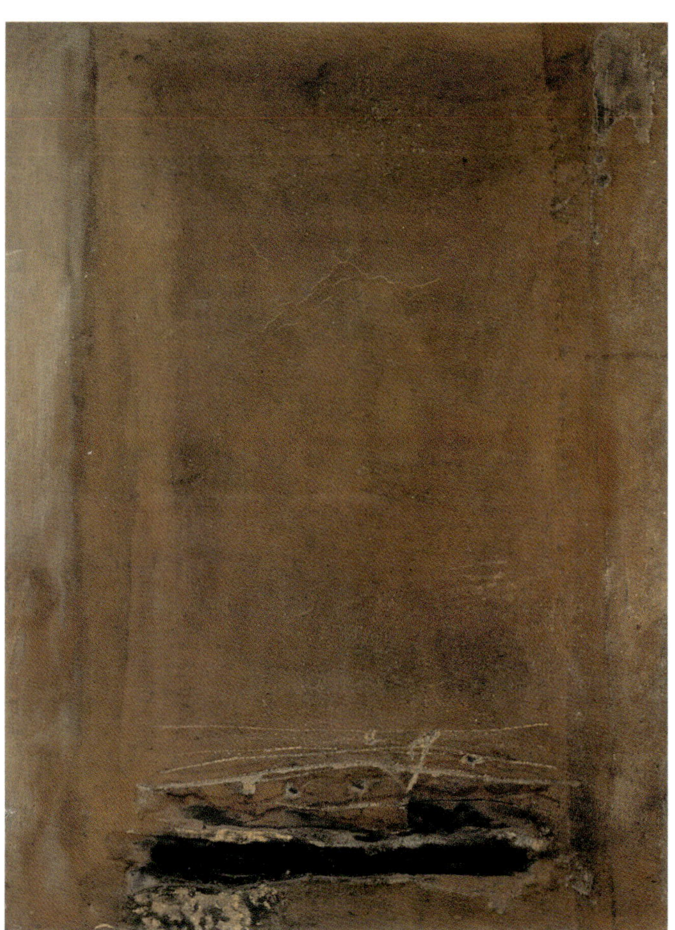

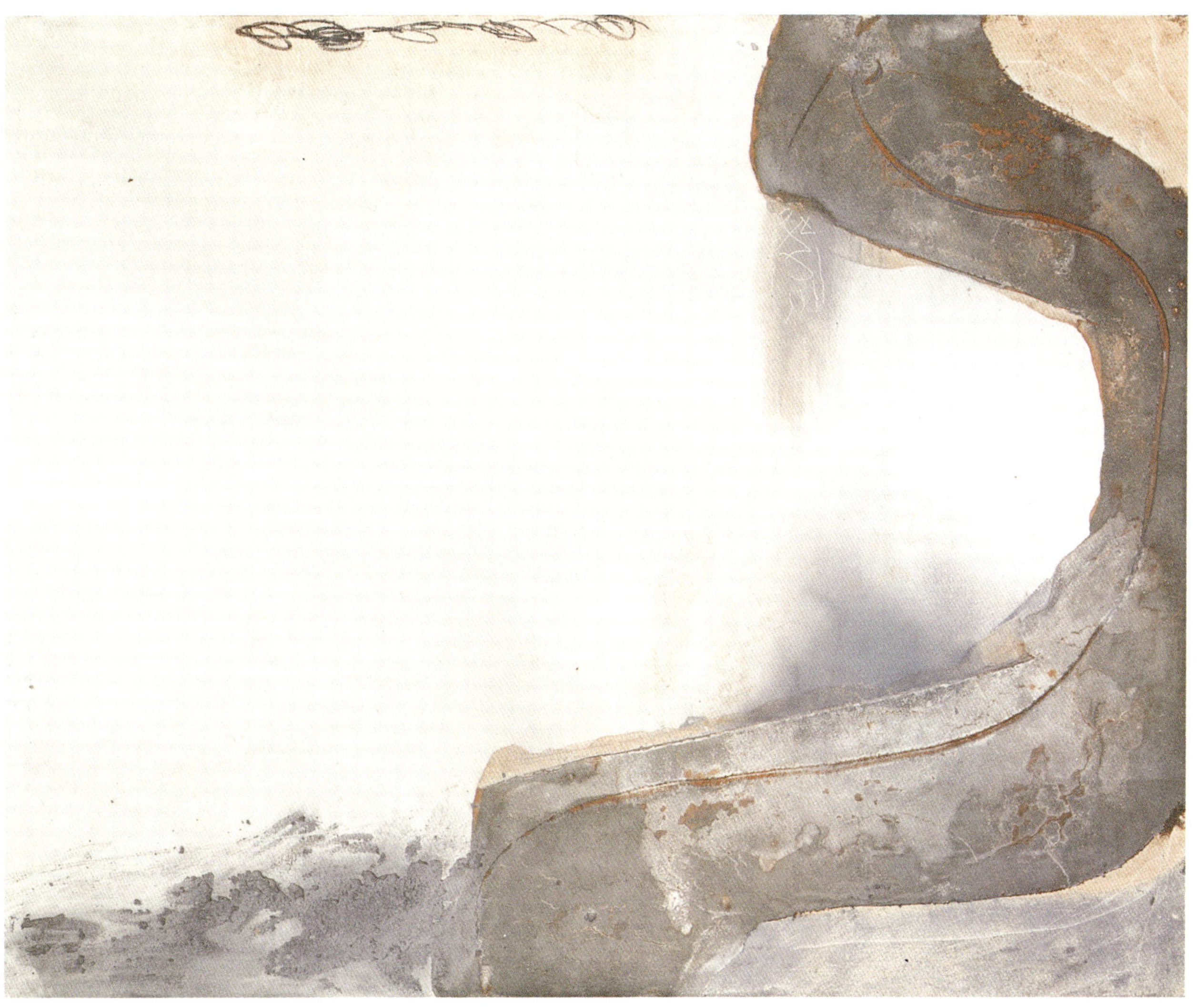

Ochre-Brown with Black Crack. No. XVIII, 1956, mixed media on canvas, 51¼ x 38⅛ inches, (88.18)

Grey on White. No. LXV, 1956, mixed media on canvas, 51¼ x 63¾ inches, (85.25)

Brown-Grey Composition. No. XIII, 1955, mixed media on canvas, 35⅛ x 51¼ inches, (88.21)

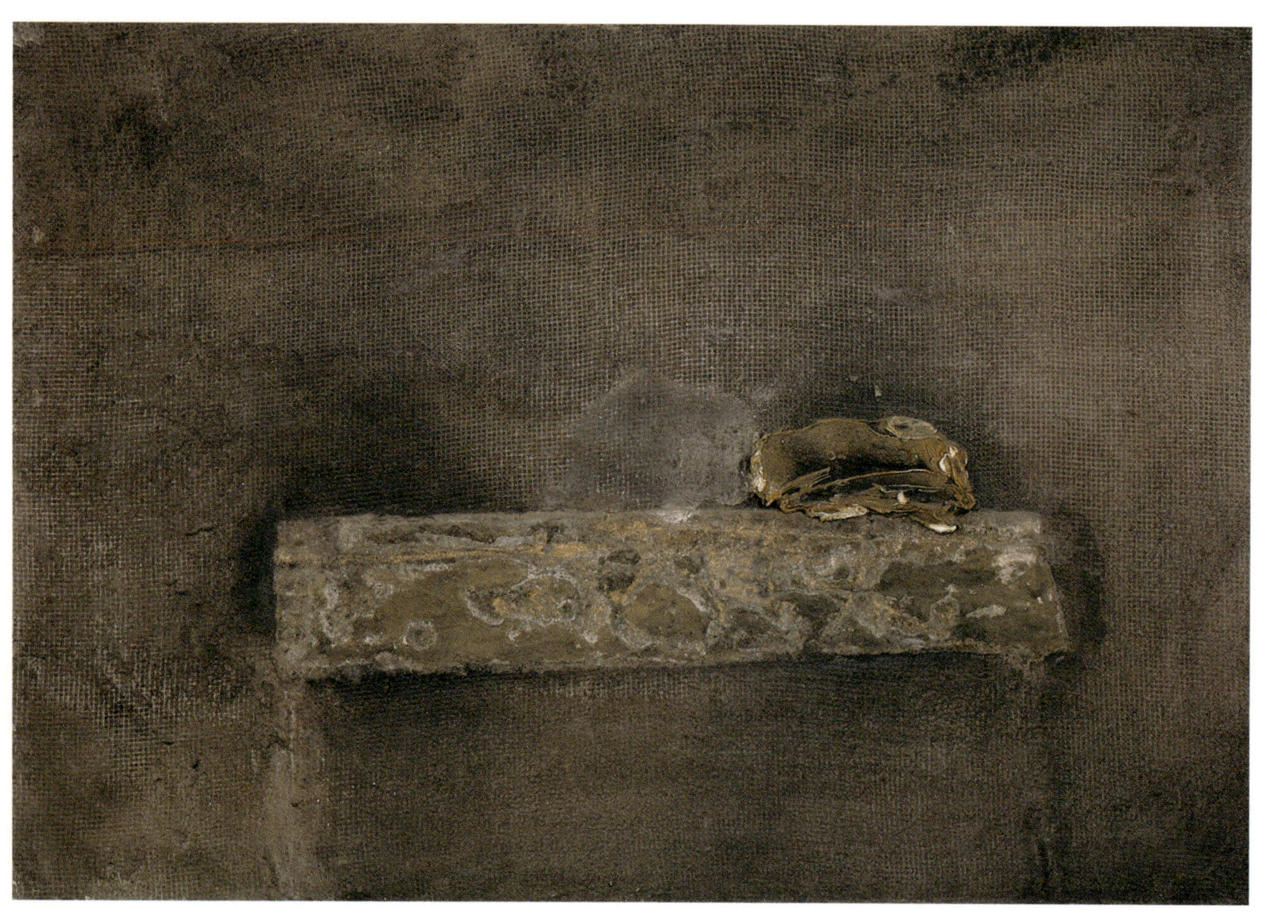

Animal, 1956, mixed media on canvas, 21¼ x 32 inches, (88.23)

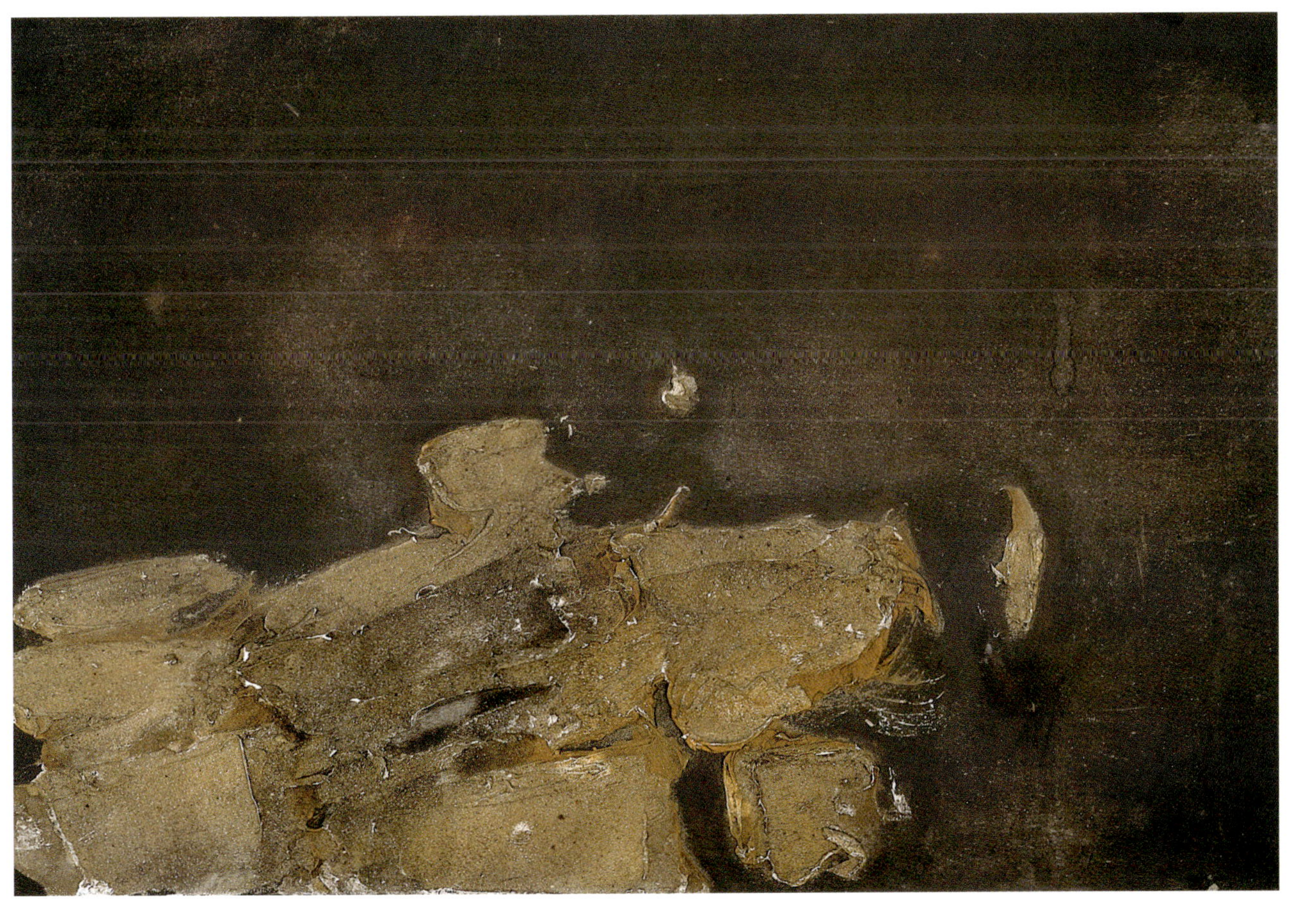

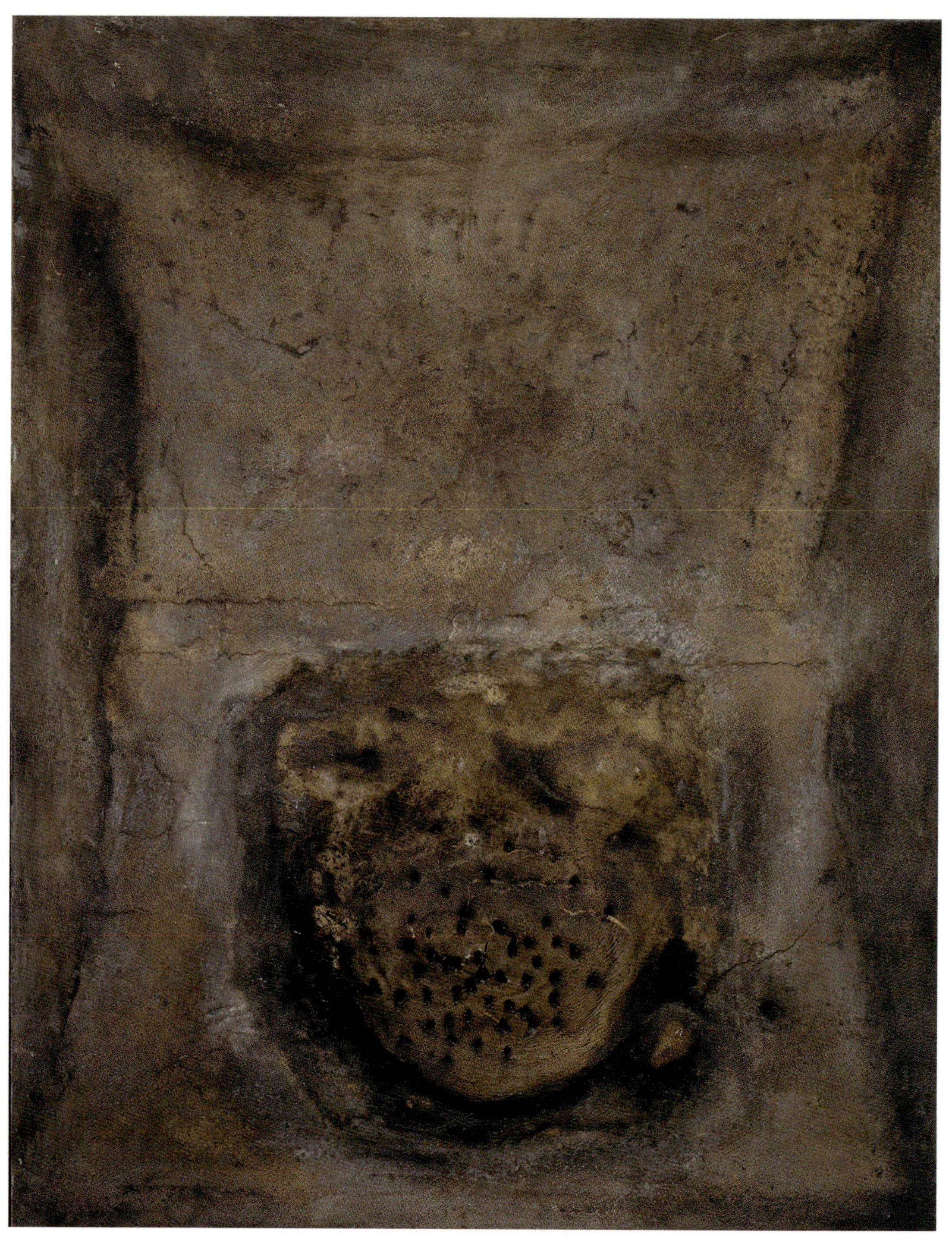

Blackish Ochre with Perforations, 1956–58, mixed media on canvas, 57⅜ x 44⅞ inches, (88.24)

Ochre-Sand. No. LXVIII, 1957, mixed media on canvas, 76¾ x 51 inches, (86.23)

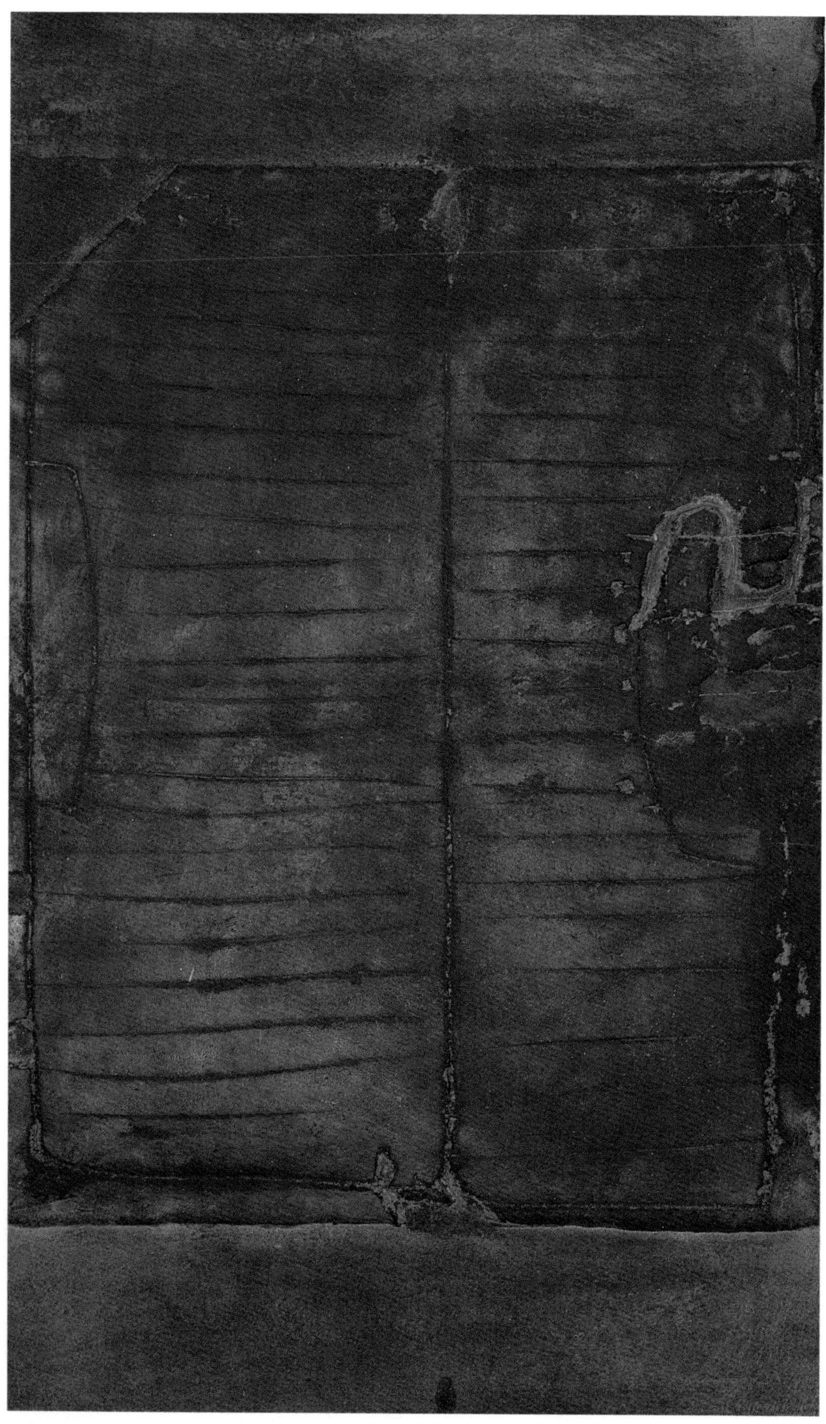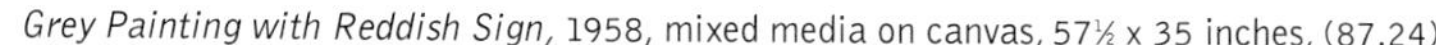

Grey Painting with Reddish Sign, 1958, mixed media on canvas, 57½ x 35 inches, (87.24)

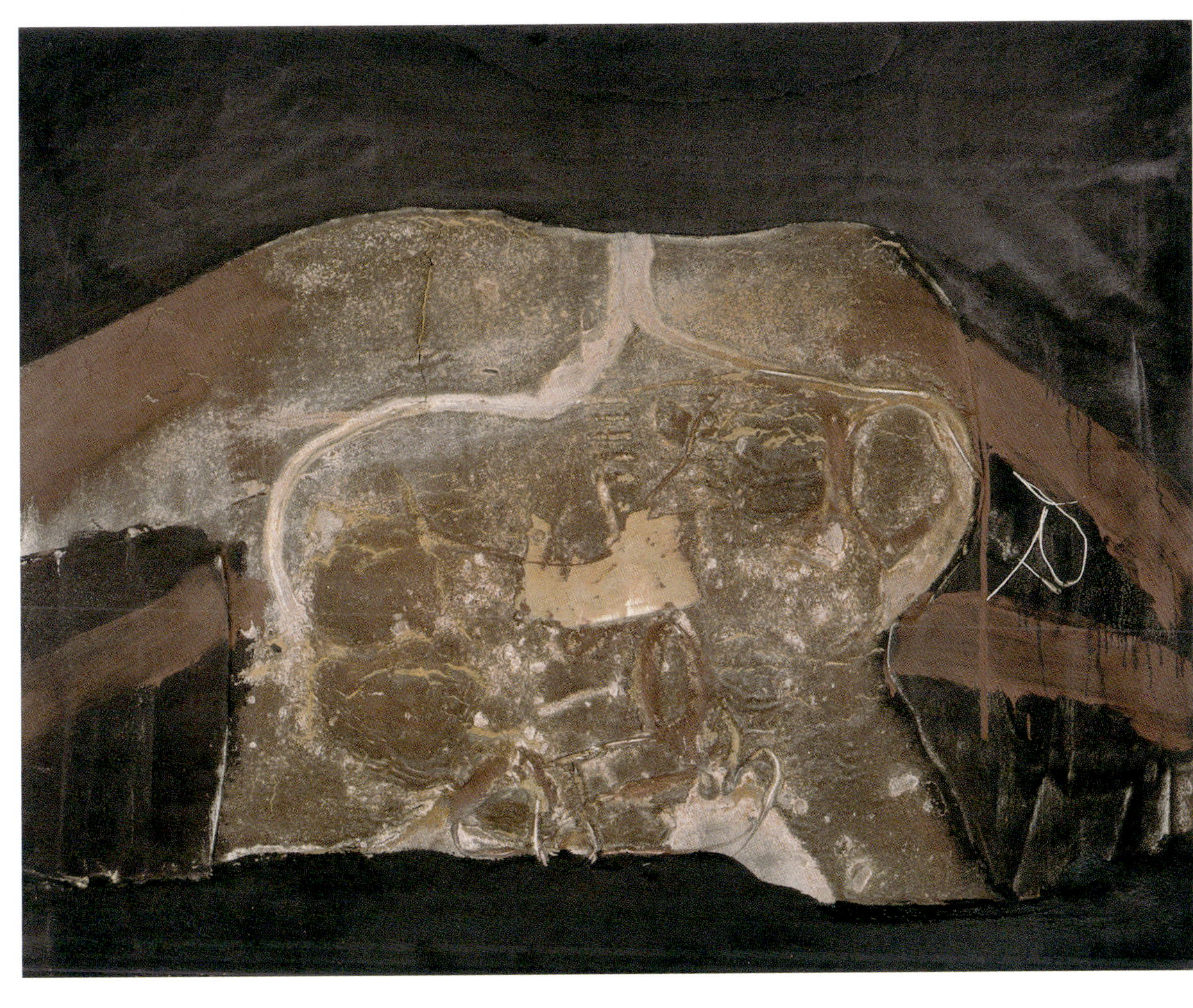

Reddish Painting, 1958, mixed media on canvas, 45 x 57⅞ inches, (88.25)

Marble-Worker's Sand with Six Footprints, 1959, mixed media on canvas, 102½ x 76½ inches, (88.17)

Hammered Grey, 1959, mixed media on canvas, 45½ x 35 inches, (85.26)

1982T01993

carroll
g.colson
j.colson
griffin
lere
mahoney
rudel
shelton
therrien
thurston

1982T01993

END OF THE CENTURY ART: PRODUCTION IN LOS ANGELES

by Kenneth Baker

Among the reasons to collect contemporary art is the prospect of forming an interpretive context for individual objects, even for an entire body of work. For decades Giuseppe Panza di Biumo has collected on a scale that would make such a framing of reception feasible. Yet Panza insists that it is objects in their singularity that interest him, not the intellectual patterns or artistic genealogy they may form. Yet when we examine *en bloc* his recent gifts to MOCA of works by Los Angeles artists, we cannot help but scan the whole ensemble for clues to understanding particular pieces. We resist the idea that a collection is merely a portrait of one man's taste. Contemporary art itself has taught us to regard taste as obsolete and to seek linkages among artworks, even if we cannot fully explain them.

Our sense of what an art object is—not just of its meaning but of its very being—can vary dramatically depending on the context in which we encounter or interpret it. In collecting American art made since the mid-fifties, Panza has favored work that appears to insist on its autonomy, work whose claims on our attention seem to owe little or nothing to reference beyond itself. The eighties and nineties works by Los Angeles artists in Panza's latest gift to MOCA may therefore strike us as a departure. In aesthetic terms, some of these works have a reductive bent: the paintings of Roy Thurston and Ron Griffin, the sculpture of Robert Therrien and Mark Lere. Yet even some of the sparest pieces in the recent Panza gift raise questions of content and reference that more minimalistic art tries to nullify.

How far afield in contemporary culture must we look for parameters of interpretation: how far back into art history, how searchingly within popular culture? How deeply should we look into the modern history of ideas or into the personal history of ideas behind our own response? To what extent, if any, does a work seem to solicit completion by interpretive engagement?

Consider the work of Gregory Mahoney. It makes some sense if we merely recall how popular consciousness of ecology has intensified in the past thirty years. Mahoney's *Untitled (Time Study)* (1992), for example, is a pair of long, narrow, rusted steel elements that hang edge to edge on a wall. One half is pictorial, the other sculptural. Twelve tiny images of the earth comprise the left panel. They are like clock faces for time zones: successive two-hour snapshots of a day's planetary rotation. Mahoney has made his little planet views by stenciling oceans of white salt on the rusted steel ground to silhouette land masses. The second element, of similar dimensions, hangs just to the right: a rusted steel channel that brims with granular salt. The optical pulse of the earth-profiles might lead us to think of the primal saline affinity between the oceans and our own bloodstreams. The salt deposits also evoke evaporation, which may bring to mind the doomsday prospect of a world freshwater shortage or, even more apocalyptically, of the oceans vaporizing through some solar, nuclear, or meteoric catastrophe. Meanwhile, the process aspect of Mahoney's piece eats away at our complacent sense of the earth's image as a human creation. In one sense, the earth as a concept and as the object of mapping is a human cultural construction; in a more profound sense, the whole human world is the earth's creation.

Of course nothing says that Mahoney's planetary stop-frames represent moments in human history. They might just as readily refer to times before or after humankind's tenure here. (Mahoney likes to use found steel because its corrosion evokes processes that occur independent of human will.) In the long view of geophysical time, representation itself is a very recent phenomenon which may prove to be very short-lived.

Mahoney's *Untitled (Time Study)* will have added depth for anyone who knows the work of Robert Smithson (1938–1973), which Mahoney acknowledges as a source. Mahoney's trough of salt echoes the open metal boxes that Smithson filled with geological matter, with maps appended to indicate where the material had been collected. Smithson called such pieces "non-sites" and placed them in gallery settings as tokens of modern culture's inevitable loss of terrestrial awareness.

For Smithson, map and territory were not just confused, they set up a dialectic that we misread in such a way as to treat them both as unreal. The only answer to this modern abstractedness, he believed, was an "entropic" art that pointed continually to the predestined collapse of all forms of order. Mahoney, however, is more interested in maps as places where information design meets the chance-determined forms of land mass or of geopolitical boundary, as we see in *Deconstructing Pacific* (1992), his salt-on-steel projection of a Pacific Ocean map.

Any geographic map is a figure for humankind's capacity to take a detached view of its situation. This detachment is close to the root of all of science's discoveries and technology's tributary double-edged marvels. As expressions of the capacity to construct a "view from nowhere," as Thomas Nagel calls objectivity, maps are emblems of humanity's unique position as the self-conscious witness to nature that nature itself has evolved. The aerial point of view that maps—and metaphorically, all intellectual abstractions—postulate is also at issue in Mahoney's *Bad Water Periphery* (1992). A grid of four wall-mounted, steel plates, open at the center, *Bad Water Periphery* has a fixed order given by the cardinal points of the compass. The words "north," "east," "south," and "west," written in salt, appear clockwise at the four plates' respective outermost edges. All the direction names are horizontal and parallel, indicating the work's intended disposition on the wall. Yet the words "east" and "west" do not seem to dictate that the work be placed on a wall that runs east to west, for "north" and "south" would correspond literally to our, or the object's, orientation only if it were placed on the floor and we stood at its center. The work thus reminds us that our compass when looking at most art is the conventions of spectatorship: upright posture, frontal address, refraining from touch, feeling for focal distance.

At first *Bad Water Periphery* looks as if it might refer to the modernist lineage of pictorial abstraction. But it concerns not pictorial form so much as the cardinal directions of an abstract order that may or may not dovetail with impersonal circumstances, like the beliefs by which we orient ourselves cognitively. The work gestures to a

Robert Smithson
Mirage No. 1, 1967
Nine units of mirrored glass
36⅛ x 255⅛ inches overall
The Museum of Contemporary Art, Los Angeles
Purchased with funds provided by the
Collectors Committee

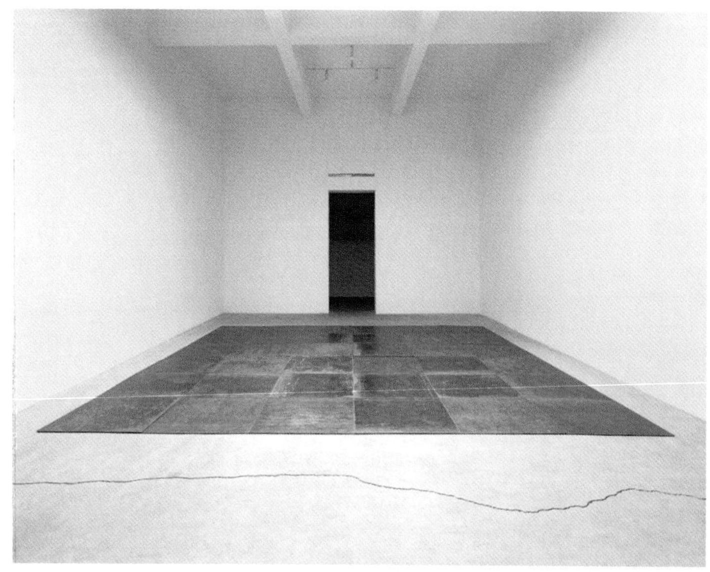

different sort of abstractedness, closer to what Smithson decried: the fact that most art treats our geographical orientation as irrelevant. In Asian art traditions, the four directions (plus the center) have ancient symbolic associations as well as their own iconography. But, as Mahoney reminds us, to the modern Western mind the compass points are barren. At most they evoke political or economic polarities and vague flavors of cultural difference.

Another possible art reference point for Mahoney's *Bad Water Periphery* is the gridded-metal floor sculpture of Carl Andre (which is also something more than abstract). Andre famously declared that, for him, sculpture is a matter of place, not of things, though most of his work takes the form of material units arrayed indoors. Mahoney's *Bad Water Periphery* may imply a critique of Andre's idea of sculpture as place.

In view of the preponderance it once had in the Panza Collection, American Minimal art seems like the obvious basis for considering the younger Los Angeles artists that have interested Panza more recently. Yet if there are assumptions common to the work of the younger artists, they are far from the faith in clear vision expressed by Minimalism's systematic emptying out of form. Peter Shelton, Mark Lere, Robert Therrien, Ross Rudel, and Lawrence Carroll all seem to share the view that no form or medium, invented or found, can be free of discursive or metaphoric associations.

The Minimalists tried to eliminate metaphor because it was a filter on perception. They believed that metaphor postponed or derailed a clarity that was both artistically and socially necessary. Perception of things in metaphorical terms, the thinking went, was tacitly allied with corrupt systems of marketing and opinion management, whose agenda was to keep anything and everything from being seen for what it is. To reject metaphor, then, was an act not only of artistic lucidity, but of social responsibility. For beneath the networks of response and meaning that society imposed, some of the Minimalists believed, lay an unstructured immediacy—or one structured neurobiologically, rather than by history—that promised the recuperation of our politically stultified humanity. That viewpoint itself now seems like a utopian period artifact, the product of a time when anti-war sentiment was ascendant, along with hopes that institutionalized injustice and hypocrisy might be undone.

In the 1960s, underlining the distinction between people and things, between thought and its objects, seemed crucial. The treatment of people as things was shorthand for the readiness to make war, punish dissent, ignore injustice, and govern by propaganda. Hence the emphasis, particularly in New York painting and sculpture, on making it difficult to project human content onto art objects or extract it from them. Only a phenomenology of perception, and an art that furthered it, might hope to undercut the reigning order of signs.

The social background of the eighties and nineties has been dramatically different from that out of which Minimalism arose. (The general difference in cultural ethos between the East Coast and West is probably telling as well.) After the wave of cynicism that followed the Vietnam War and Watergate, a new resignation set in: the assumption that nothing could undercut the ruling sign systems because—as the deconstructionists would have it—they are what we and the world are made of. Soon the Hollywood conservatism of Ronald Reagan brought the Cold War background into the foreground. Boundaries between propaganda and fact dissolved into a new delirium of nationalist, capitalist righteousness.

Meanwhile, in the academic realm, the very concept of reality was purportedly "exposed" as proprietary and aggressive: to use it at all was to make a move in a never-ending contest to justify some structure of power, whether intimate or institutional. After 1989, the polarities and pieties of the Cold War were abruptly replaced with clashing fundamentalisms: the religious, which believes in the stabilizing power of hierarchy and codified belief; and market fundamentalism, with its faith in covetous self-interest as the propellant of a planetary consumer society better ruled by corporations than by states.

In the 1960s, the great threats to humanity seemed to be the arms race, with the military adventurism of the superpowers in the international arena, and racism and consumer mindlessness in the American domestic sphere. By 1990, it looked as if the threat of the bomb and the allure of consumerism had won the Cold War. For, as the arms race and its fealty bankrupted the communist economies, nothing created more popular discontent in the Eastern Bloc than endless deferral of shopping for the sake of the garrison state.

The thing that seemed most nearly to unite humankind in a post-Cold War world was the desire to emulate the wasteful, acquisitive American way of life. (The fundamentalist backlash against this headlong materialism is little better than its twisted inversion.) Against this background, the Minimalist insistence on distinguishing between people and things, the human and the inhuman, seems idealized, dogmatic, almost pointless. When people identify most passionately with what they own or hope to own, when advertising depicts a world of gratified desires so seamlessly and unremittingly that it eclipses unrepresented reality altogether, we should not be surprised to find artists teasing out a new human content that seems to have reinfused every object, even abstract systems such as maps, geometry, and software.

From a psychoanalytic angle, consumer society is more than a convergence of mass production, non-stop promotion, and international trade. It makes concrete the mind's compulsive processing of fantasy as trade-offs of attachment and aversion. The adhesion of thoughts and emotions to things figures in the work of Therrien, Lere, Rudel, Shelton, and Greg Colson. In various ways these artists express amusement or fascination with the capacity of things to appear inherently—yet not objectively—meaningful.

Therrien and Lere make objects that seem deliberately to call Minimal sculpture to mind: forms whose simplicity stops just short of purging them of evocativeness. The stopping short expresses not restraint, but resignation to the fact that reference is inescapable. No "pure," non-referential form is possible now (if it ever were), so intricately cross-referenced have the culture and our common consciousness of it become. Reductive form in art now does not culminate in blank-slate experience, it sets off echoes of a history of reductive forms in art and of their influence on interior decoration, clothing design, and architecture.

Therrien's big inverted bronze plinth, *No Title* (1988), for instance, quavers between looking like an oversize piece of furniture (perhaps a bench), a colossal architectural capstone, and a mid-scale homage to the sculpture of Tony Smith. (Mid-scale, that is, relative to the respective proportions of Smith's maquettes and his full-blown pieces.) Therrien's sculpture proposes that figural and historical references are equally unavoidable—overlapping interpretive schemes that no artist working nowadays can outrun. Make something that resembles a work of sixties Minimalism as closely as this sculpture does and it will either be taken for a period piece or be read as quotational.

More importantly, Therrien's sculpture does not imply that the disparate readings we may give it have a critical structure to them. Nothing indicates that it is better, say, for a sculpture to resemble a Tony Smith or a Scott Burton than to resemble a piece of loft furniture. Such associations in Therrien's work reflect or propose no hierarchy of values. Minimalism could aspire to produce sculpture without metaphysics because in its day the faith prevailed that people's ways of living expressed some coherent and binding, even if unarticulated, logic of values. The personal was the political, as the saying goes. Today, all the old ideological back stories that undergirded such a logic ring hollow. Advertising and entertainment are America's spiritual life now, as Andy Warhol foresaw. They may be without moral or metaphysical substance, but they are replete with cross-references. More and more often we see television commercials that refer to other commercials and entertainment echoing entertainment, even print ads that reference other print ads, rather than realities outside their orbit, bolstering the superstition that there is nothing worth noticing outside their orbit.

An absence of intellectual anxiety distinguishes Therrien's and Lere's rejoinders to the Minimalism of Joel Shapiro, a New Yorker. Shapiro reinjected Minimalist geometry with figurative content, but always with a subtext of morbid physical comedy that boils down to a fear of falling or of falling apart. The threat of physical incoherence in Shapiro's art is his formal shorthand for the fear that one's intellectual scheme, too, will come unglued, that nothing makes the linkages among values and ideas anything better than arbitrary.

The notes of anxiety in Therrien's and Lere's work invoke a fear that is almost the opposite of what we sense in Shapiro's art: a fear of depth, of experience suddenly unfolding repressed dimensions of memory or of unexpected, unwanted realization. When Therrien makes a wall sculpture that resembles a giant Dutch door (*No Title* (1988)), it may make us think momentarily of a wall prop piece by Richard Serra, but it lacks the rigorous physical logic of Serra's art and flavor of structural menace.

The Therrien might even cause us to think of Ludwig Wittgenstein's notion of "hinge" concepts: that we have to leave certain beliefs unquestioned so that other beliefs can turn on them. In Wittgenstein's thinking, what matters is not the content of beliefs, but that some necessarily provide leverage to others. (This is the sort of thing that causes some readers to judge Wittgenstein an anarchic relativist.) If we have Minimalism in mind, Therrien's "doors" may even read as a figure for mind and body swinging in and out of unison.

But Therrien's piece reads more straightforwardly as a monument to a peculiarly American neighborly ambivalence. It evokes the sort of withdrawal that Robert Frost had in mind when he proposed that "good fences make good neighbors": the door half-ajar, whether below or above we cannot be sure, uncertainly inviting, promising some

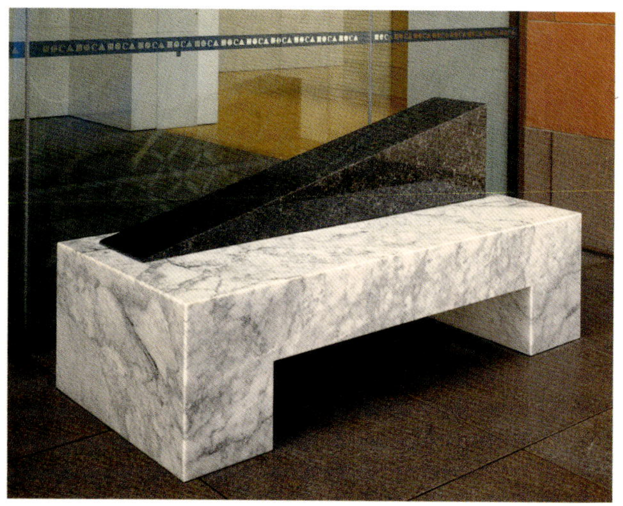

sort of equability by its half-and-half division, yet only vaguely. The piece's bigger-than-life scale can make us feel small, which leads us to infer that the work and our response may have sources in childhood memory. Of course, Therrien's piece is not really a door at all: it neither blocks nor gives access to anyplace. Rather, it is a sculptural cipher for the way artworks can make us feel excluded or clued-in, depending on how intelligible they seem to us.

In a similar vein are the taller of Therrien's "columns," in silvered bronze and the darkly patinated bronze respectively, both known by *No Title* (1988). Both pieces hover between seeming to contain something that their stature keeps (most of) us from seeing and being pedestals for something more significant than themselves, which is missing. Both can cause us to feel insufficiently large, and translate that sensation into an echo of childlike inadequacy. And both recall the way some of Constantin Brancusi's work makes us wonder how to distinguish sculpture from pedestal, or in what sense we must. But the activation of childlike anxiety through scale is key. It reminds us that the present moment in time subsumes our past experience in ways we cannot articulate and that this may be a cultural process, not just a matter of individual psychology. Not just any inflation of scale or shape will cause this to happen. It does not happen in Claes Oldenburg's largest work, for example, or in Tony Smith's. To

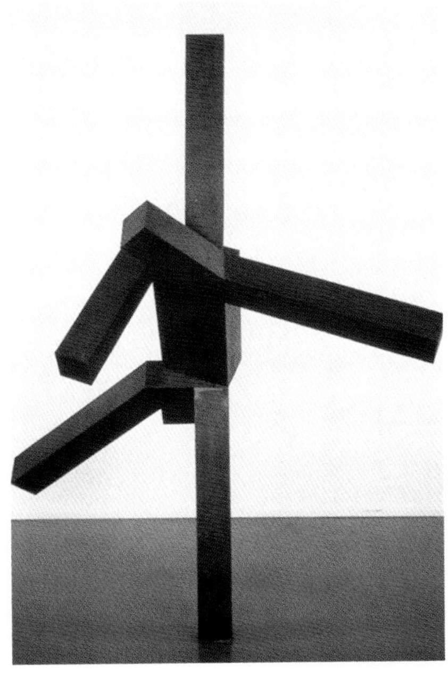

acknowledge the waves of childlike feeling that Therrien's work sets up is to intuit or recall that for a lifetime we have linked fears and wishes with physical sensations, sometimes as a way of bearing them, sometimes in the hope of ridding ourselves of the emotions when we leave the associated objects behind. The process begins, if we believe Freud, long before we acquire the language to disavow it. Therrien's useless Dutch door is a signature work in its suggestion that there is no exit from emotional give-and-take with the world of physical forms, not only because objects are so heavily coded by culture, but because that process is a bodily one.

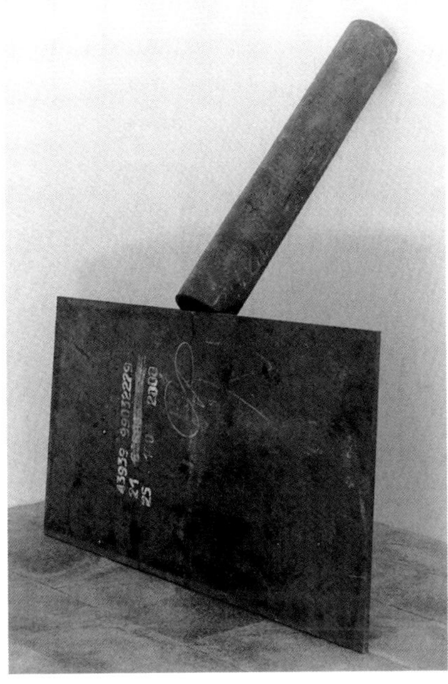

Where Therrien relies on our physical response to his objects, Lere touches more upon our feelings about anatomy and its representation. Take Lere's untitled 1994 steel piece that looks a little like a bent knee. It seems to flicker between symbolizing a whole human figure, folding at the waist, and a single dismembered leg, like an oddly angular hosiery manikin. Its third obvious reading is more bizarre: it suggests the memory of a tornado. But none of these aspects is assertive enough in itself to blot out the others or to keep us from reverting to seeing the sculpture as a mute fabrication in steel.

The two related pieces *Throat* (1987) and *Voice* (1987)—funnels with long, curved spouts that lean against the wall—make only metaphorical reference to internal anatomy, but they activate our uneasiness about what goes on inside us, unknowably. The pieces are like abstractions of human beings. Is this ruthless reduction of the human to orifice and conduit a mere artistic gambit? Is it a joke about the power of a title to get our imagination going? Or is it an icon of twentieth-century barbarism? Nothing says these possibilities are mutually exclusive.

If we approach Lere's work with this kind of uncertainty in mind, it will make our response to pieces such as *Bone Heads* (1990) and *Bladder* (1988) that much more visceral. *Bladder* (1988) seems not to be a depiction of an organ so much as a reduction of the body as a whole to a sort of vessel with an opening at either end. This is a vision equidistant from that of a torturer and that of a cultivated nihilist like Samuel Beckett. Then again, we have to wonder whether Lere intends to drive us to interpretive extremes or whether he is simply drawing psychological lightning from the culture's overheated atmosphere. And again, if we break the emotional spell of such interpretive quandaries, we are left with dumb objects that can embarrass us by their muteness.

Ron Griffin's paintings also seem to isolate the intersection of a few facets of meaning, giving us pause to wonder what links one iota of meaning with another. His *Untitled (Marlboro Series, No. 17)* (1993), for example, has a geometry of folded red on white forms that make us think of the Constructivist abstractions of a painter such as El Lissitzky. But Griffin's title tips us off that his painting has a sort of subject: a folded, flattened Marlboro cigarette carton, minus its lettering. There is a post-Pop joke here: that abstraction is not just any process of excerpting forms or colors from something given. It is what results when enough information is subtracted that we no longer recognize a familiar product design or logo at a glance. Griffin turns pictorial rhetoric once associated with utopian social projects (the Russian Revolution) to a jaded—though still very elegant—mode of abstraction. How it is made adds another layer of meaning to Griffin's work. What look like collage elements are in fact built-up layers of paint, the paint representing not only the contours but the thickness of the depicted objects.

The Griffins that echo Constructivist abstraction are tame compared with those that, if we believe their titles, describe mail pouches conforming to postal regulations for sending fecal samples. Our relief at finding these "pouches" empty is our clue that the paintings are about how easily human content can be given to ostensibly abstract form. Griffin may also be referring to a classic of conceptual art, Piero Manzoni's infamous tins of *Merda d'artista* (1961), which take literally the Freudian thought that defecation is the self-expressive root of all artistic production.

Griffin's fecal-sample-pouch paintings imply that formalist abstraction teaches us a defensive way of seeing, of blotting out the content with which everything in the cultural realm is overloaded. They also sound again a minor theme of works in the Panza gift: fear of what is inside—the subjective, the sediment of memories, the anatomical reality unswayed by vagaries of culture, except those of drugs and diet.

Another way to think about the generational difference between 1960s and 1990s artists is to recall the implicit assumption of much Minimalist art that some ground of uncoded immediacy underlay culture's imprints on subjective experience. Several of the Los Angeles artists collected here work as if no such ground plane of immediacy is available now, nor ever was. Perhaps most reminiscent of that impossible ideal, which has resurfaced in modernism periodically, is the work of Lawrence Carroll. The reminiscence in his case is critical, not nostalgic, for Carroll's paintings look timeworn. They seem steeped in a fetid climate of human presence, despite having no apparent autographic or

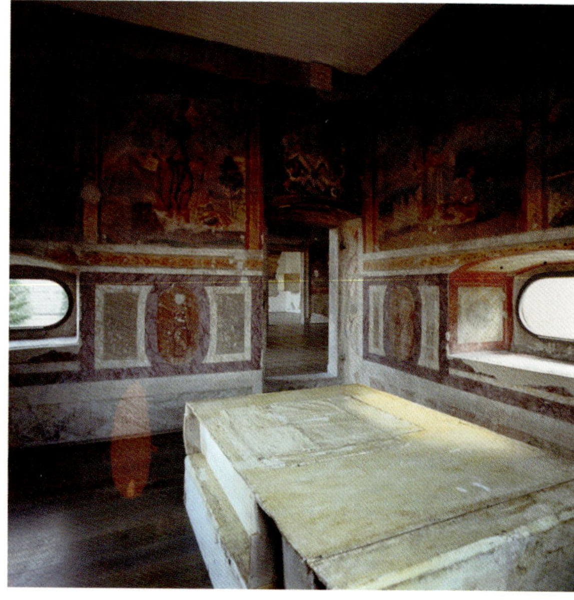

other reference. Some of his pieces suggest segments cut from rundown apartment walls and bandaged with canvas to form slablike paintings. Unlike most art, Carroll's work seems to occupy space apologetically. His paintings may hang at knee level or hug the corner of a room or stack up, like the three panels of *Along the Ground* (1992), as if to spare themselves unnecessary exposure. *Along the Ground* brings to mind the traditional triptych structure of Christian altarpieces. But it gives the impression of being an anti-altarpiece: an object that not only negates the possibility of transcendent significance, especially of Christian redemptive martyrdom, by intimating that it suffers its own

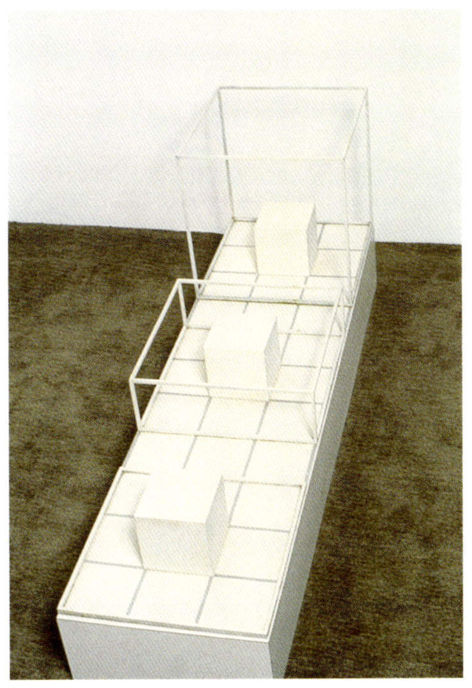

visibility. A hostile critic might accuse Carroll of displacing into abstract painting the preoccupation with abjection that was fashionable in art at the turn of the 1990s. But Carroll's work is more disturbing, more disillusioning, than that. It suggests that we cannot look at anything without projecting sentience onto it. This animism may be part of what has always made pictorial representation compelling. It may even be the basis of empathy. But it also keeps us in a cognitive muddle about our own limits, about where ourselves end and what is not ourselves begins.

Carroll's work seems to solicit not attention but company. It seems to ask that we suffer along with it the passage of time. It conveys this impression partly by appearing to be in poor repair with no strong focus to structure our attention to it. By its subtle plea we stand with it in no better position with respect to time. Suppose our belief that time is ours to use or waste, to save or lose, is a delusion. Then so are our dreams of being actors in history, however peripheral. Read this way, Carroll's work seems closer to Joseph Beuys taking the connotative temperatures of substances and things than to, say, Robert Ryman dwelling on facture and tints of white.

Carroll is not the only artist here who questions the value of sharp focus and its incitement or enhancement of action. The bizarre constructions of Greg Colson put the very possibility of concentration in doubt. Theorists of modernism from Walter Benjamin and Siegfried Kracauer to Clement Greenberg and John Berger viewed concentration as the last bastion of the individual mind's integrity where mass society and popular culture impose the rule of corrupting distraction. Robert Morris picked up this theme when he said that his early Minimalist work was an effort to make an object with only one quality.

From a distance, Colson's *Beaumont* (1990) is a flat, irregular lattice of wood and metal strips that looks like a piece of post-Minimalist sculpture. It might be a structure of found materials cobbled together in rejoinder to the idealizing implications of the Minimalist grid as we find it in the work of Sol LeWitt or Agnes Martin. But up close, the crossbars of *Beaumont* turn out to be labeled with names. We recognize that what looked at first like a purely arbitrary structure is really a road map, a structure whose arbitrariness plots a complex social history. We might also see *Beaumont* as a makeshift bridge across the cultural distance between cubist and post-cubist construction in the manner of Pablo Picasso or Kurt Schwitters and American folk art. The aesthetic dissonance in it is as much that of class friction as of formal contradiction. If artworks mirror their anticipated audience, then this one, like much of Colson's work, is cracked in a very particular way.

Colson's *Memorial Coliseum* (1991) appears to be an old wood cabinet door with a broad band of white enamel across its lower half. It might be an example of kitchen abstraction, except that its blankness is punctuated by an elliptical pattern of tiny labels that map the seating in a stadium. Like his *Schaefer Stadium* (1991), this piece evokes a mind to which spectatorship brings thoughts of sports before, or along with, thoughts of art. The mass audience for sports is counterposed to the intimate public that artworks attract, or could be expected to attract until museums began to become mass entertainment centers.

In the context of the Panza gift Colson's constructions suggest that we have no illuminating way to map onto one another the disparities of experience and knowledge that class divisions, or even our own scattered interests, create. Colson seems not to find this a reason for pessimism. It is a plain American fact which we might as well

Lawrence Carroll
Installation view at Villa Menafoglio Litta,
Panza di Biumo,
Biumo Superiore, Varese, Italy, 1996

Sol LeWitt
B 2-5-8 (s), 1967
Painted aluminum
13½ x 48¾ x 13½ inches
The Museum of Contemporary Art, Los Angeles
Gift of Lannan Foundation

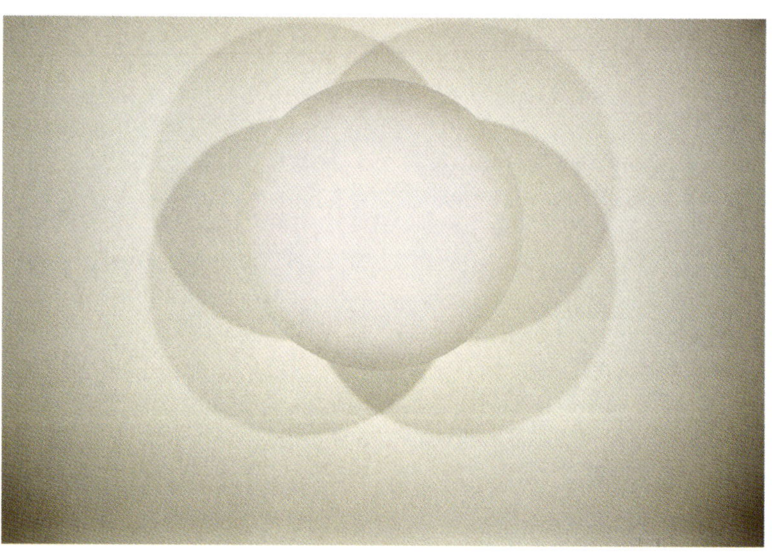

make light of as not. Colson's *Estimate* (1988) may be his most economical expression on that point. In it, a white retracting spool tape measure—a pocket symbol of American know-how—leaves function behind as it twists upward around an armature into a whimsical dome, a sort of architectural doodle halfway between an igloo and something dreamed up by Buckminster Fuller.

Jeff Colson works a vein very different from that of his brother Greg, though he too flouts the Minimalist faith that vivifying an art object's materiality will cause viewers to focus and intensify their attention to it. Jeff Colson's pieces appear to be abstract paintings, and paint is indeed among their ingredients. But the more closely we study them, the less they conform to our conventional sense of what counts as painting.

Colson's *Untitled* (1991), for example, is blanketed by a fine, square grid. From a distance, the grid looks drawn, but a closer look reveals that it has been routed or incised into the picture's wood surface, and that the surface is composed of wood squares about the size of floor tiles. Parts of the fine grid are smeared and clotted with black. One square section looks like an insert because it and it alone is dotted with white circles. Several of Colson's pieces contain similar components that look as if they are makeshift substitutes for uniform structures that were unavailable when needed. A glance at the list of the work's materials makes this "painting" seem even less pictorial: besides enamel, it contains plaster, bondo (an adhesive), charcoal, gesso, and motor oil. Its strangest element is a circular form that resembles a small, shallow, bottomless flower pot, or perhaps a large telescope eyepiece, sans lens. Countersunk in the object's surface, it exposes the wall behind. Seeming to offer direct insight into the art object, this element has us look right through it. This aperture, which has counterparts in other Colsons, is a device to disarm interpretation worthy of Jasper Johns.

Colson assembles and treats parts of his work so as to make us wonder often whether we are seeing something

138

salvaged, recycled, or custom made. Yet little seems to be at stake in these distinctions. The confusion seems to matter as much to Colson as any possible resolution of it, as if the point were merely to keep our imagination circulating, like an old horse that needs a smattering of exercise to stay alive, no matter how plodding.

Found objects figure in quite a few works in Panza's recent gift to MOCA, but in Ross Rudel's sculpture we cannot tell whether what we see is found, industrially fabricated or handcrafted. Some of Rudel's wall pieces are intended to be hung at a height that puts them out of reach. The sensory information that might tell us what kind of thing we are seeing is deliberately withheld, as if the sculpture were abstract icons of the fact that human knowledge has limited reach. Paradoxically, Rudel's sculptures evoke organic forms: heads, polyps, the jointed thoraxes of ants, or chains of complex molecules. The scale of objects such as *Untitled No. 107* (1992) and *Untitled No. 115 (White)* (1992) makes it hard to decide whether they are meant to be read. Are they models of things normally unavailable to the senses or idealizations of familiar forms? In any case we cannot rest easy with the notion that they are merely abstract. They are disquieting presences that hover between surrealism and a nostalgic ideal of formal asperity. (Some seem indebted to the early plastic pieces of Robert Irwin.) Like the work of Therrien, Carroll, and Lere, Rudel's suggests that there is no longer any distance to which forms can withdraw to be "pure," that is, free of all reference.

The paintings of Roy Thurston come nearest to standing outside the storm of cultural cross-references. The grooved surfaces of his imageless, monochrome paintings do not bring anyone else's work to mind, except perhaps that of Yaacov Agam. To call Agam an Op artist is to pay him a compliment. Agam's abstract work enjoyed a certain popularity because it was painted on evenly beveled wood surfaces that showed the viewer different compositional aspects depending on his position. The how and why of looking at this work were readily apparent and people enjoyed exercising the obvious choices it offered.

Thurston's paintings also have a low relief of parallel striations that affects their appearance as our vantage point changes. But unlike Agam's paintings, or Ad Reinhardt's or Mark Rothko's, Thurston's pictures are gleaners of light. They have none of the translucency or glow that we customarily associate with the Light and Space art of people such as Irwin, James Turrell, or Larry Bell. Instead, they concern the perceived speed of light as we catch it gliding over the surfaces of things. In making a theme of these elusive perceptions—which we find articulated nowhere else in contemporary culture—Thurston's paintings suggest that we should rethink how objects occupy time. Modernist critical language acknowledges the way objects occupy space, but assumes that only we occupy time. Thurston's paintings, like Carroll's, suggest that we may overestimate our capacity to affect what happens.

Of the Los Angeles artists in the recent Panza gift to MOCA only Peter Shelton seems free of ambivalence about the human content of his work, although he never comes close to making what could be called a portrait. Shelton's work can even be grotesque in its abbreviation of anatomy. He never describes a face, as if to reinforce the sense that our inability to see our own faces is the price each of us pays for living from the inside out. We might see his art as a struggle to find adequate expression for that paradoxical condition.

Pieces such as *bigfeet* (1985–90), *ironmitts* (1986), and *copperneck* (1986–89) seem to objectify uncomfortable bodily sensations as lived from within: feelings of inertia, ham-handedness or difficulty swallowing that words do not put across. An enlarged shape in Shelton's sculpture, such as the long neck of *copperneck* or the extended arm of *onelongsleeve* (1988–89), suggests heightened awareness due to pain or morbid self-consciousness. Such pieces bring us full circle to the question with which we began: how far afield must we look for the frame of reference in which artworks exfoliate meaning. Even when academic answers are available, gut feeling has to be our guide, the level of feeling toward which Shelton typically drives. His are the representative works in the Panza gift if any are, for trust in gut feeling is an attribute of every great collector that no schooling or financial position can provide.

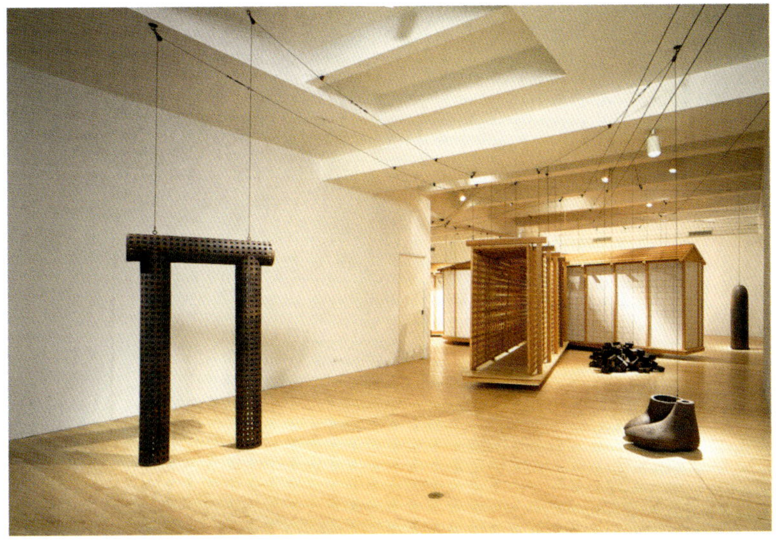

Robert Irwin
Untitled, 1965–67
Sprayed acrylic lacquer on shaped aluminum
60 inches diameter
The Museum of Contemporary Art, Los Angeles
Gift of Lannan Foundation

Peter Shelton
Installation view of
floatinghouseDEADMAN, 1985–86
Exhibition at Louver Gallery, New York,
6 January–3 February 1990
Courtesy of L.A. Louver, Venice, California

Lawrence Carroll's monumental, boxlike structures are quiet meditations on transition, allusion, and the passage of time. The geographic duality of having been born in Australia and schooled in California has allowed Carroll to work outside of the conventional art historical norms that dominate Europe and the East Coast of the United States. While his art production rejects strict classification as painting or sculpture, critics have suggested that Carroll's work be aligned with the tradition of Robert Ryman, whose reductive paintings emphasize materiality. Interested in everything from the supporting structure to the paint on the surface, Ryman adheres to a primarily monochromatic palette which allows for the rigorous pursuit of these formal concerns.

Carroll's works, *Untitled* (1992) (16½ x 23¼ x ¾"), and *Untitled* (1992) (3½ x 14½ x 38½"), exemplify similar concerns by calling attention to both surface and structure. All of his sculptures are built around a wooden core that is systematically covered with canvas, wax, and oil paint in a pale cream-colored palette. Carroll gathers and combines fragments of leftover materials which he turns inside out, cobbles together, and refashions to render solid structures that both hang and lean against the wall. This desire to utilize bits, pieces, and parts is a sensibility that appears to come from his upbringing, about which he states, "My parents were immigrants. They were always holding on…They were not interested in making things new, only in making things whole—functional, modest."[1]

The massive, hollow structures are emblematic of the work that has come to define Carroll's oeuvre. Hung upon the wall just inches above the floor, these works have a looming and magnificent presence in the sheer nature of their size and girth. Standing ten feet tall and two feet deep, *As She Dressed* (1990–91) causes the viewer to ponder the work's role as a possible container for something extraordinary—real or imagined. The layered nature of the boxes within *Along the Ground* (1992) endows the piece with a mystifying aura and causes the viewer to automatically question its hidden surfaces and concealed spaces. Inherently mysterious and obliquely narrative in their titles, these works reveal an interest in ideas beyond the physical exploration of surface, texture, paint, and form.

Untitled (1992) (24¾ x 37 x 11") and *Untitled* (1992) (24¾ x 38¼ x 54½") introduce tin as a significant element within the work. In these works Carroll's minimal palette is not sacrificed, but taken to the other end of the spectrum in order to offer a suggestive contrast to cream-colored canvas that dominates his work. His palette is meant to resemble raw canvas so that his pieces always appear to be at the nascence of their existence, a strategy that grants them an optimism inherent in origination. Lawrence's tin shares the unworked

LAWRENCE

carroll

As She Dressed, 1990–91, oil, wax, canvas, and wood, 120 x 54½ x 23½ inches, (94.29)

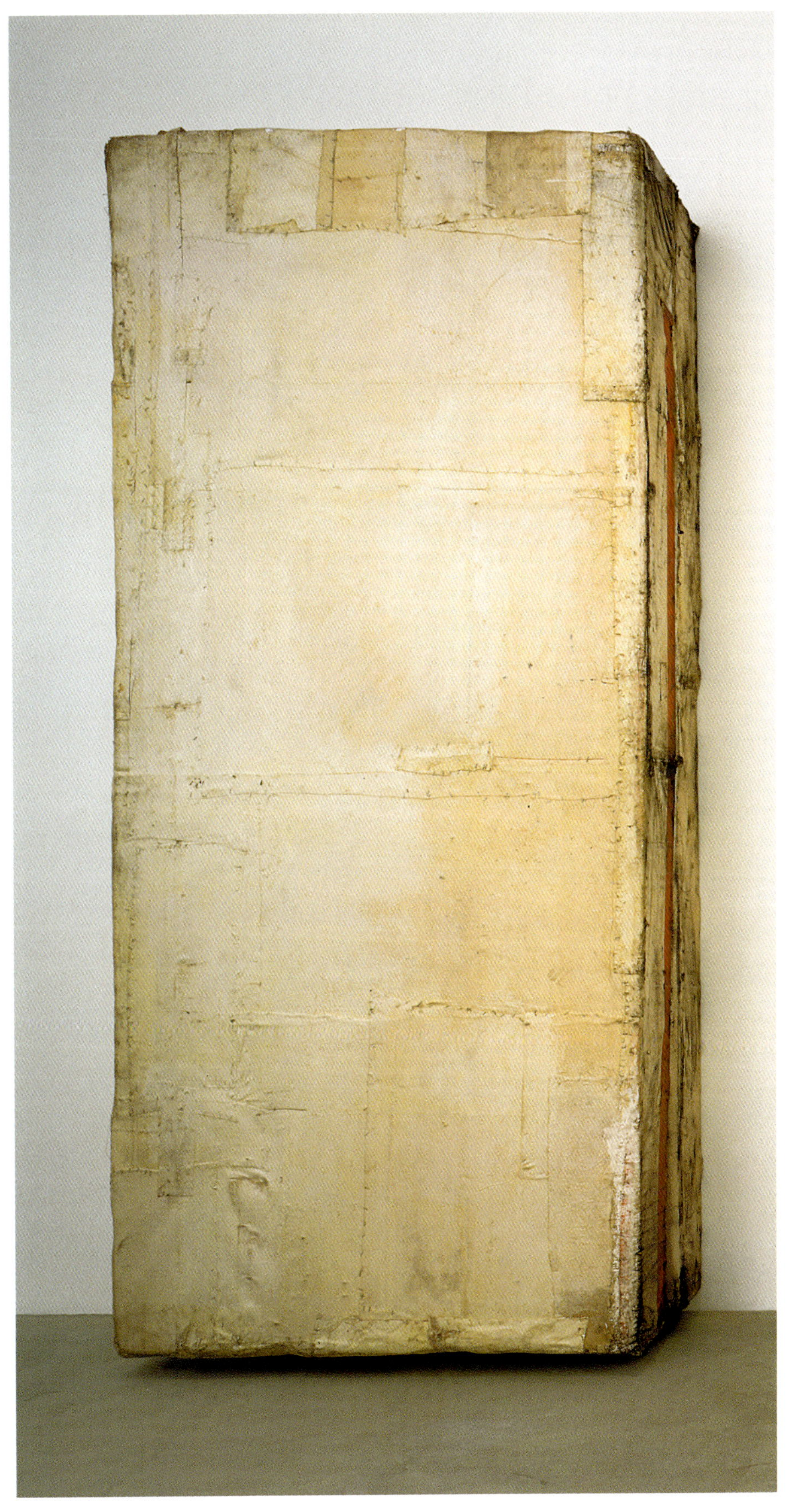

quality of the canvas and reaffirms the status of these objects as open and mutable.

Coyly occupying the corner of the room is a diminutive work *Untitled* (1991–92) (11½ x 36 x 72"). This work occupies the wall, floor, and surrounding space, its boundary demarcated with a layer of off-white paint. By intervening in the architecture of the gallery this work activates the space, engages the viewer, and blurs the line between painting and sculpture. Referred to as his "folded" paintings these sculptural works, bent over and under, exist within a space whose transformation grants the work a tangible sense of magnitude equal to that commanded by the immense and imposing boxes. These quiet and thoughtful sculptures, both large and small, are filled with meaning, illusion, and ultimately a mysterious presence. —R.M.

[1] Lawrence Carroll, quoted in Richard Milazzo, "In Memory of Our Feelings," in *Lawrence Carroll*, exh. cat. (Stuttgart: Galerie Der Stadt Stuttgart, 1998), 61.

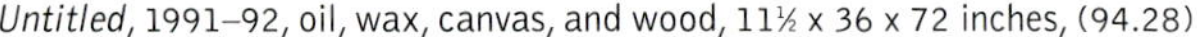

Untitled, 1991–92, oil, wax, canvas, and wood, 11½ x 36 x 72 inches, (94.28)

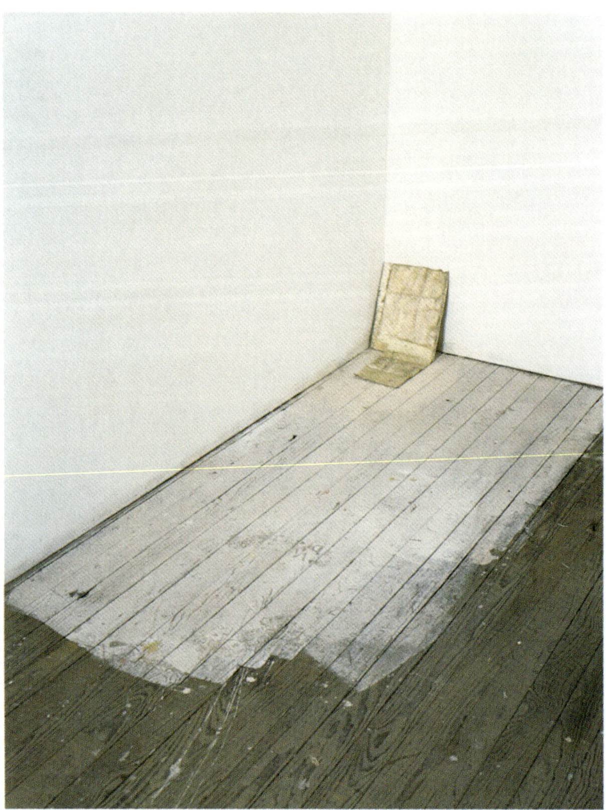

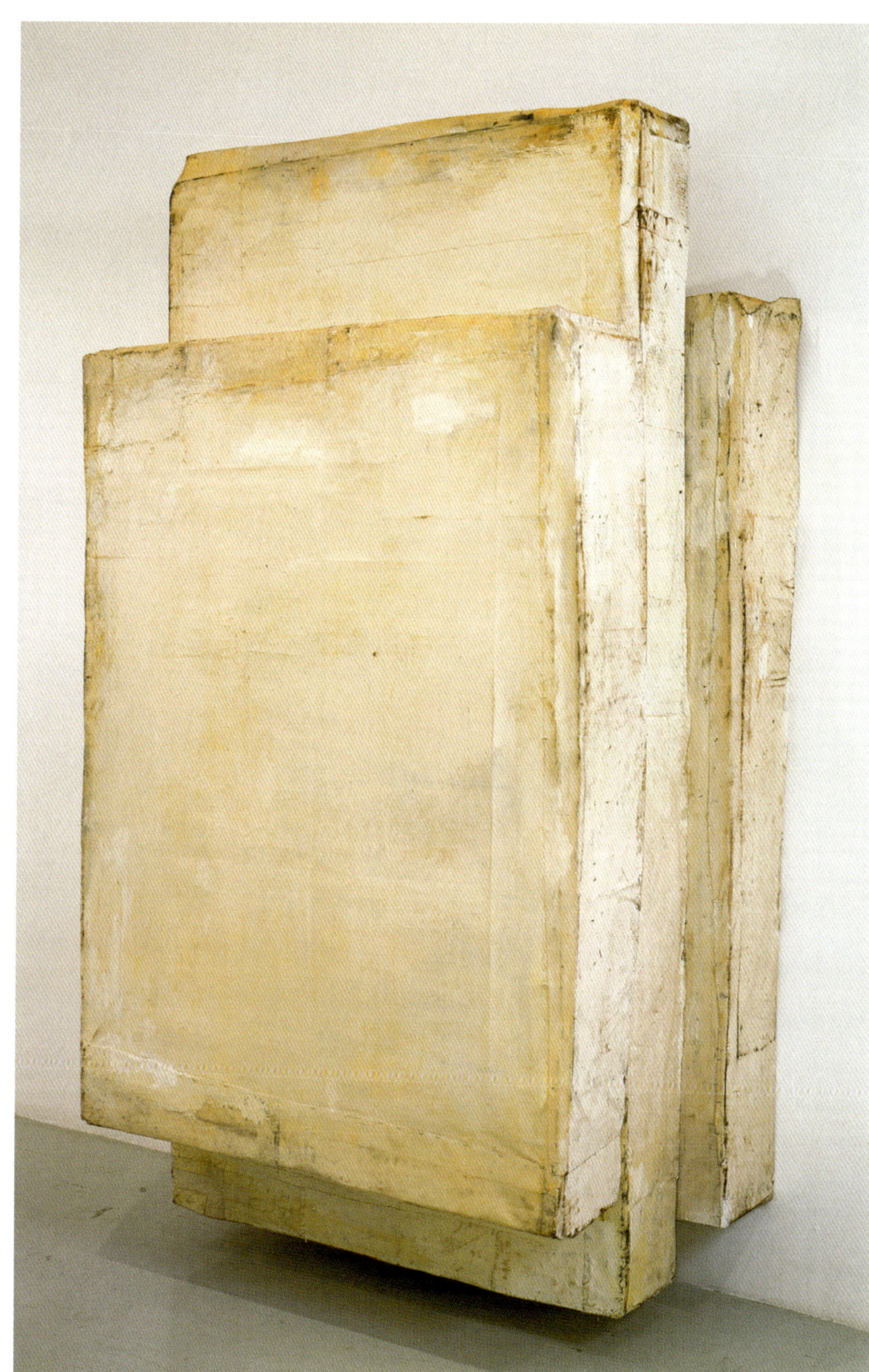

Along the Ground, 1992, oil, wax, canvas, and wood, 120 x 60 x 36 inches, (94.32)

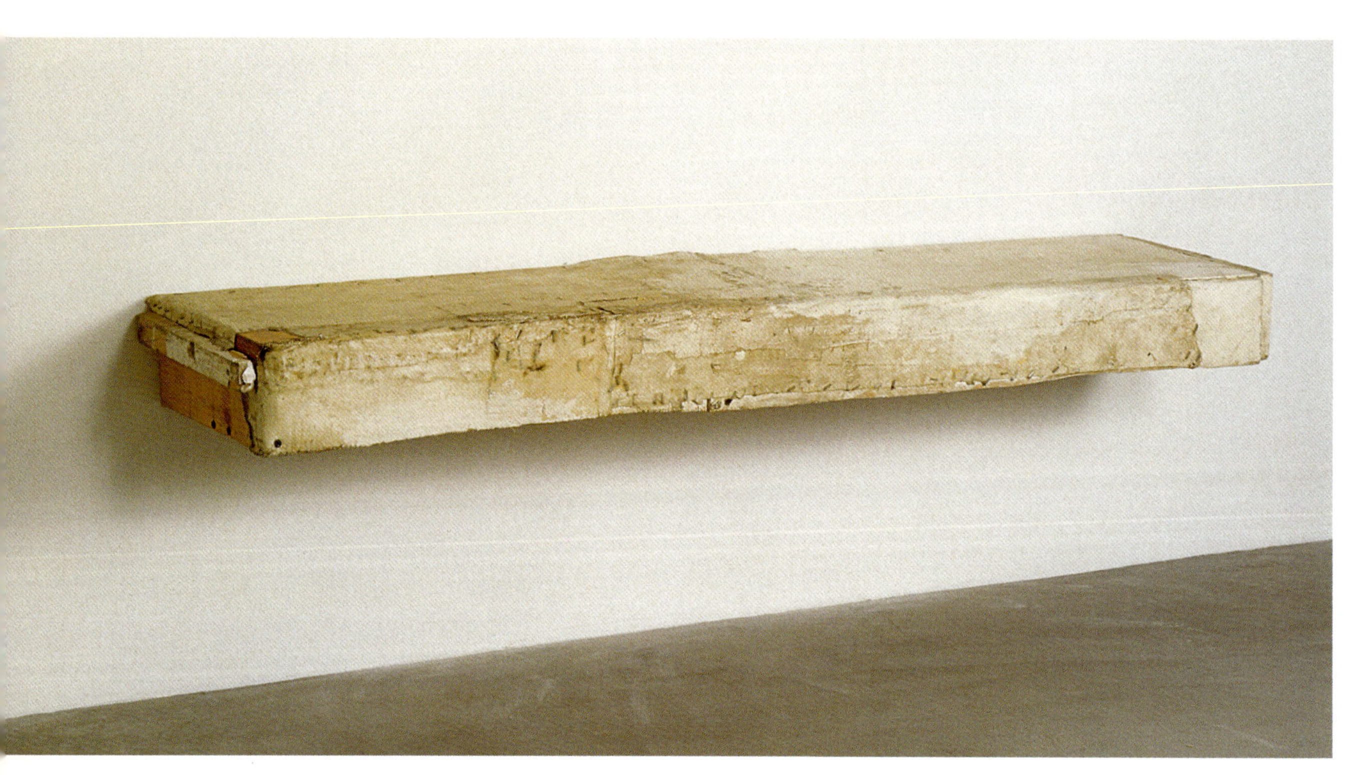

Untitled, 1992, oil, wax, canvas, wood, and paint, 3½ x 14½ x 38½ inches, (94.26)

Untitled, 1992, oil, wax, canvas, wood, and steel, 24¼ x 38¼ x 54½ inches, (94.27)

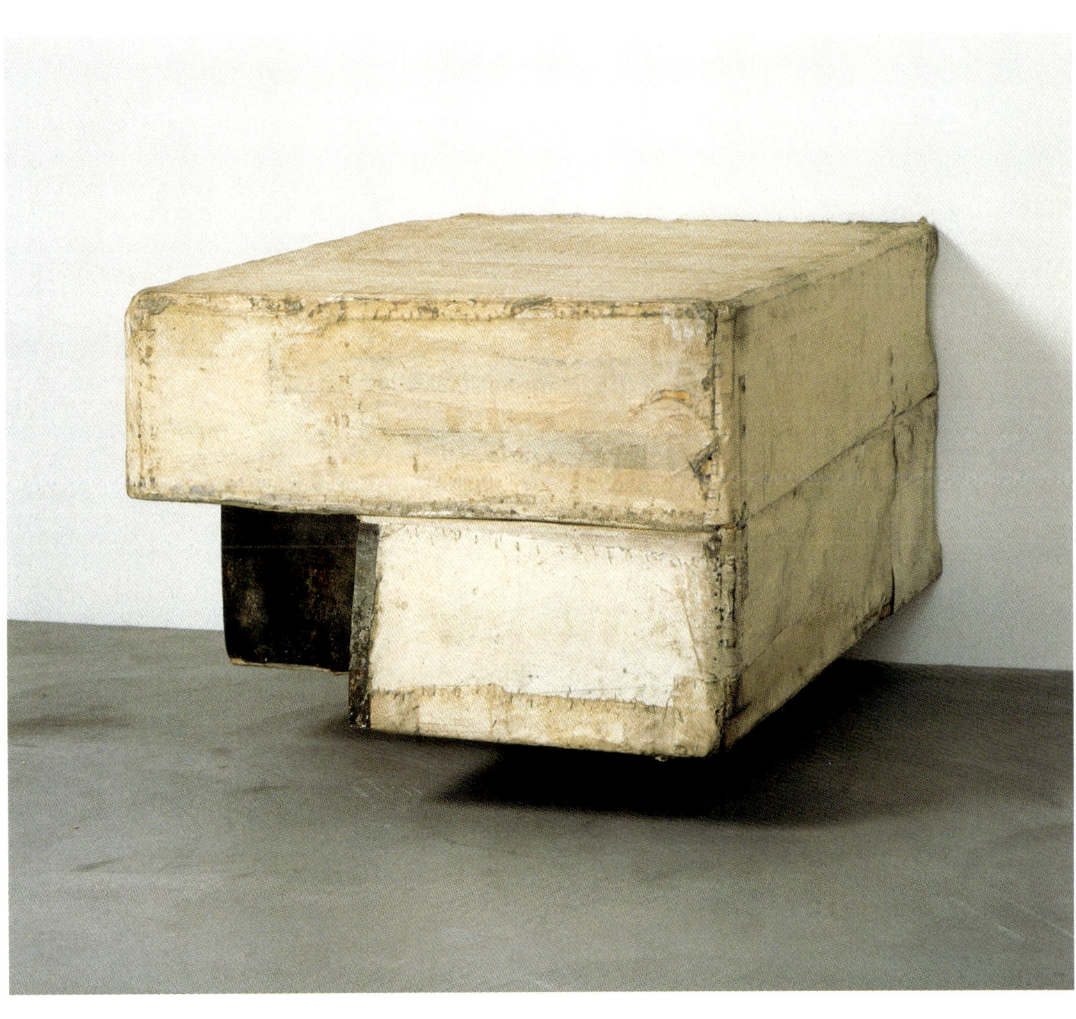

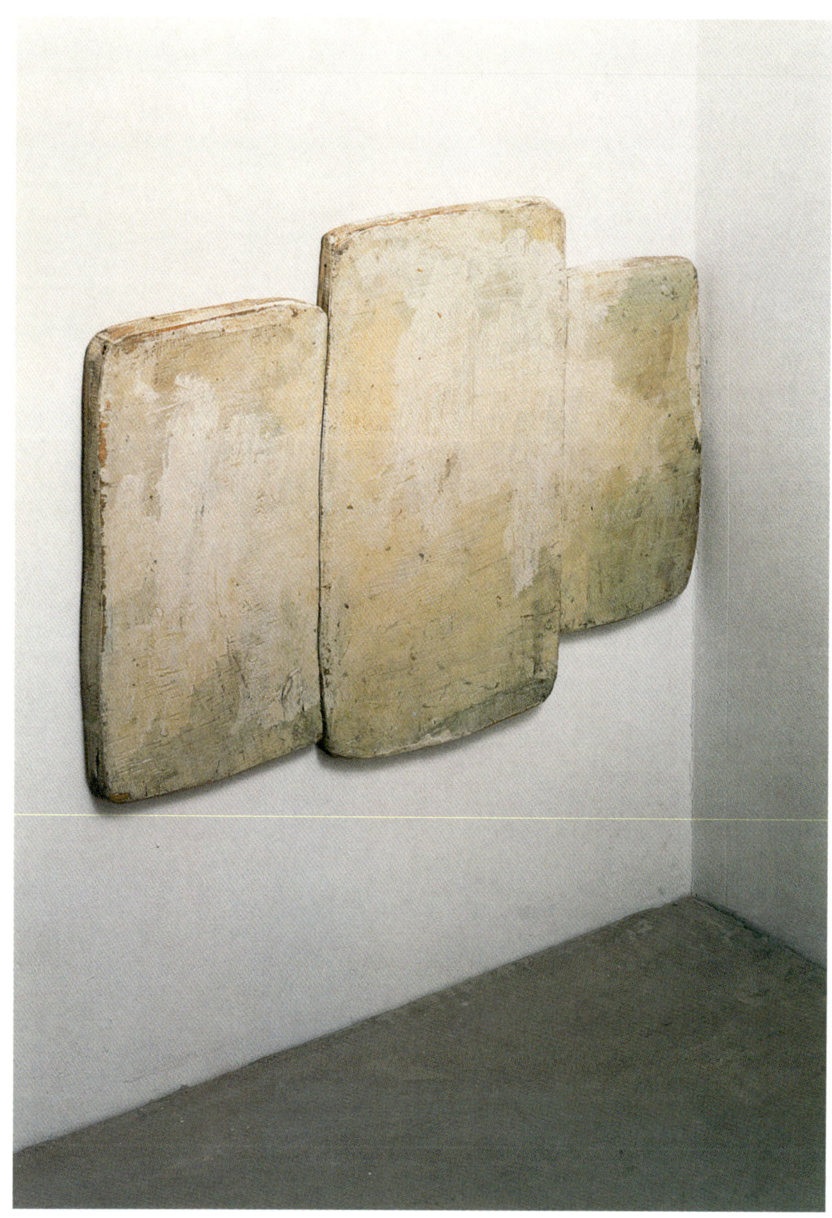

Untitled, 1992, oil, wax, and wood, 16½ x 23¼ x ¾ inches (triptych), (94.30)

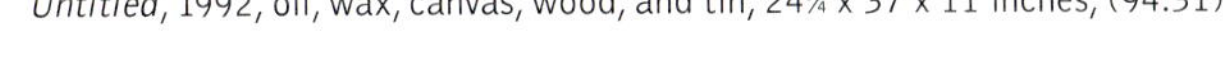

Untitled, 1992, oil, wax, canvas, wood, and tin, 24¾ x 37 x 11 inches, (94.31)

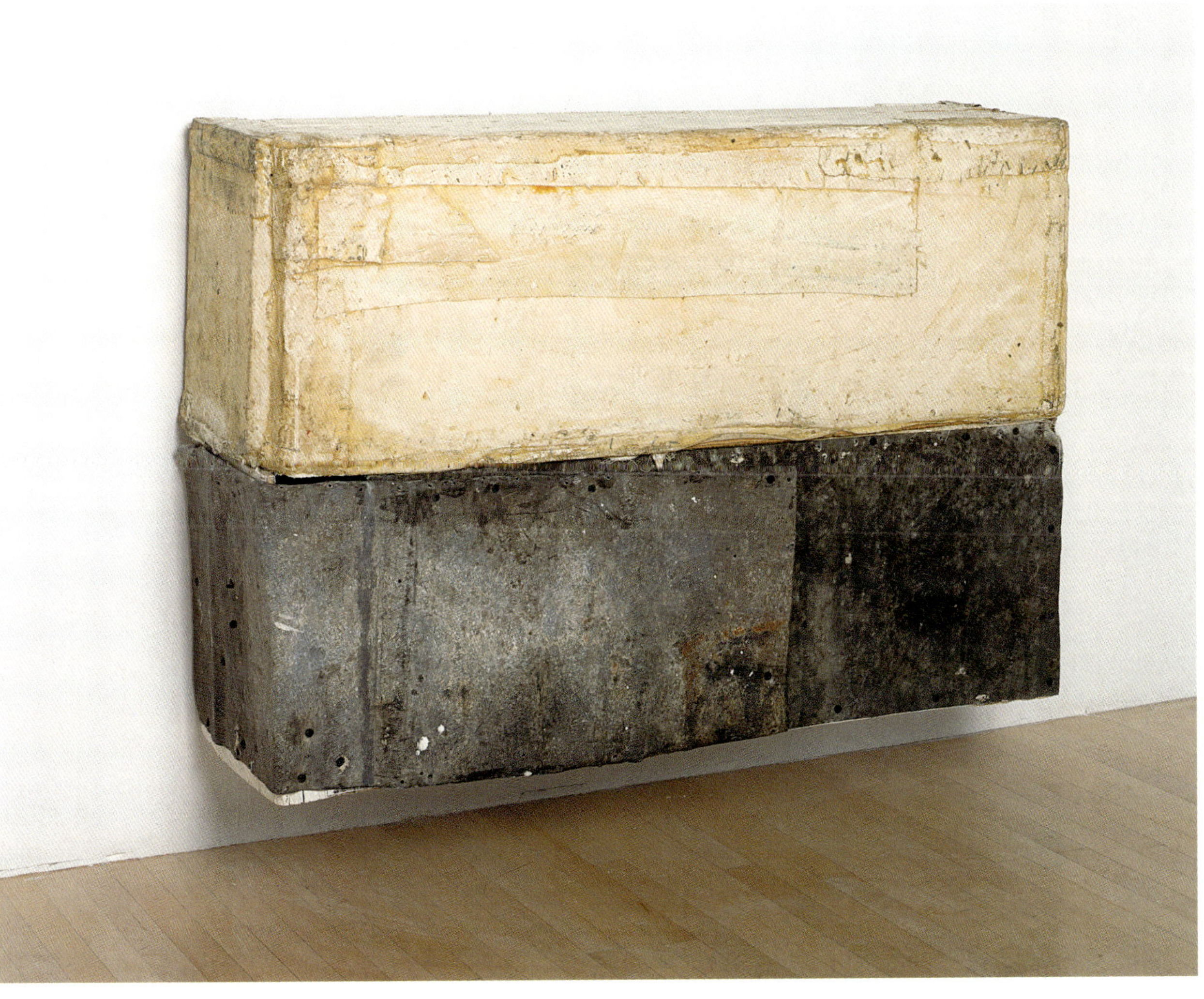

By combining urban detritus—including scraps of wood, shards of metal, and bits of plastic—Greg Colson makes order out of chaos. His assemblages, which hang from the wall and sit upon pedestals, recycle and reuse found objects that have been casually discarded. As evidenced by the tripartite piece *Stacked Hub* (1987), Colson seeks out items whose original purpose is no longer served and combines them in a formally clever way. This method of art production follows in the spirit of Kurt Schwitters and Robert Rauschenberg who composed cast-off materials into aesthetically complex collages and combines. Contemporaneously, British artists Tony Cragg and Bill Woodrow also gather and assemble secondhand materials to yield their own elaborate and emotive constructions.

Colson's investigation of order is echoed in his utilization of organizational tools such as maps, diagrams, plans, and measuring instruments. In *Mobile* (1992), street names and the marks that represent them have been printed in a muddled cluster on top of the convex side of a metal platter. On the front of a boxlike structure that protrudes from *Evansville* (1992), a small map has been printed that shows streets and highways, but is strangely void of text. *Beaumont* (1990) is an arrangement of wood and metal strips that resembles the avenues and boulevards of an anonymous town. In each of these pieces the maps do not serve the customary purpose of clearly charting a city. Instead, Colson has appropriated the language of maps and manipulated their signs and symbols to create a compelling visual interplay.

Colson investigates another type of mapping in two pieces that thematically make use of the sports arena. Both *Memorial Coliseum* (1991) and *Schaefer Stadium* (1991) are enlarged diagrams of sports facilities in which the text that designates the bathroom, the field, the seat numbers, etc., has been cut out and adhered to pieces of wood. These bulky, awkward, three-dimensional diagrams have little efficacy; their practical application is clearly irrelevant—it is instead the visual usefulness of the guides' syntax that is manipulated and explored. Colson exploits the random relationship between sign and signifier by juxtaposing maps and guides with metal dishes and wooden planks.

A different sort of organizing element, the ruler or tape measure, is featured in Colson's piece *Estimate* (1988). The metal conical structure which stands at the core of this piece has been carefully wrapped with white measuring tape. The futility of measuring an object's circumference with a tape measure is comical and this piece reflects the humor that runs subtly throughout Colson's work. By ingeniously employing rulers, maps, and diagrams toward a visual end, Colson causes us to question familiar linguistic arrangements and encourages us to explore their potential as a visual language. —R.M.

GREG
colson

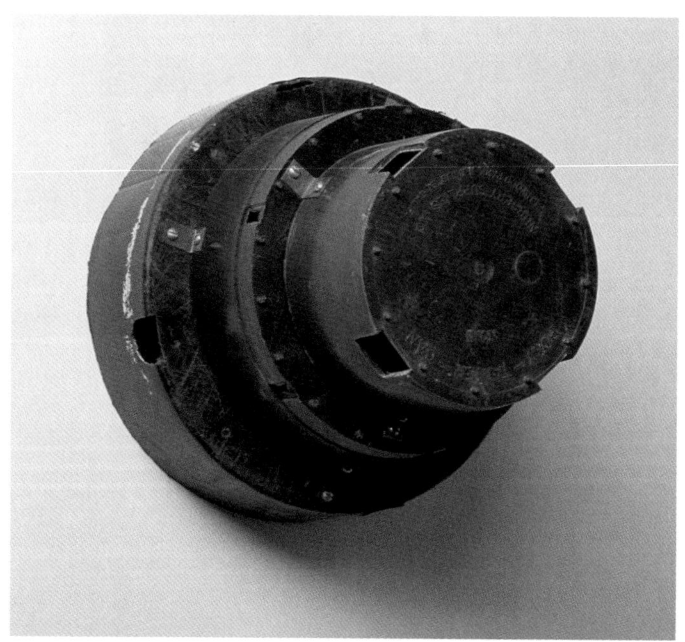

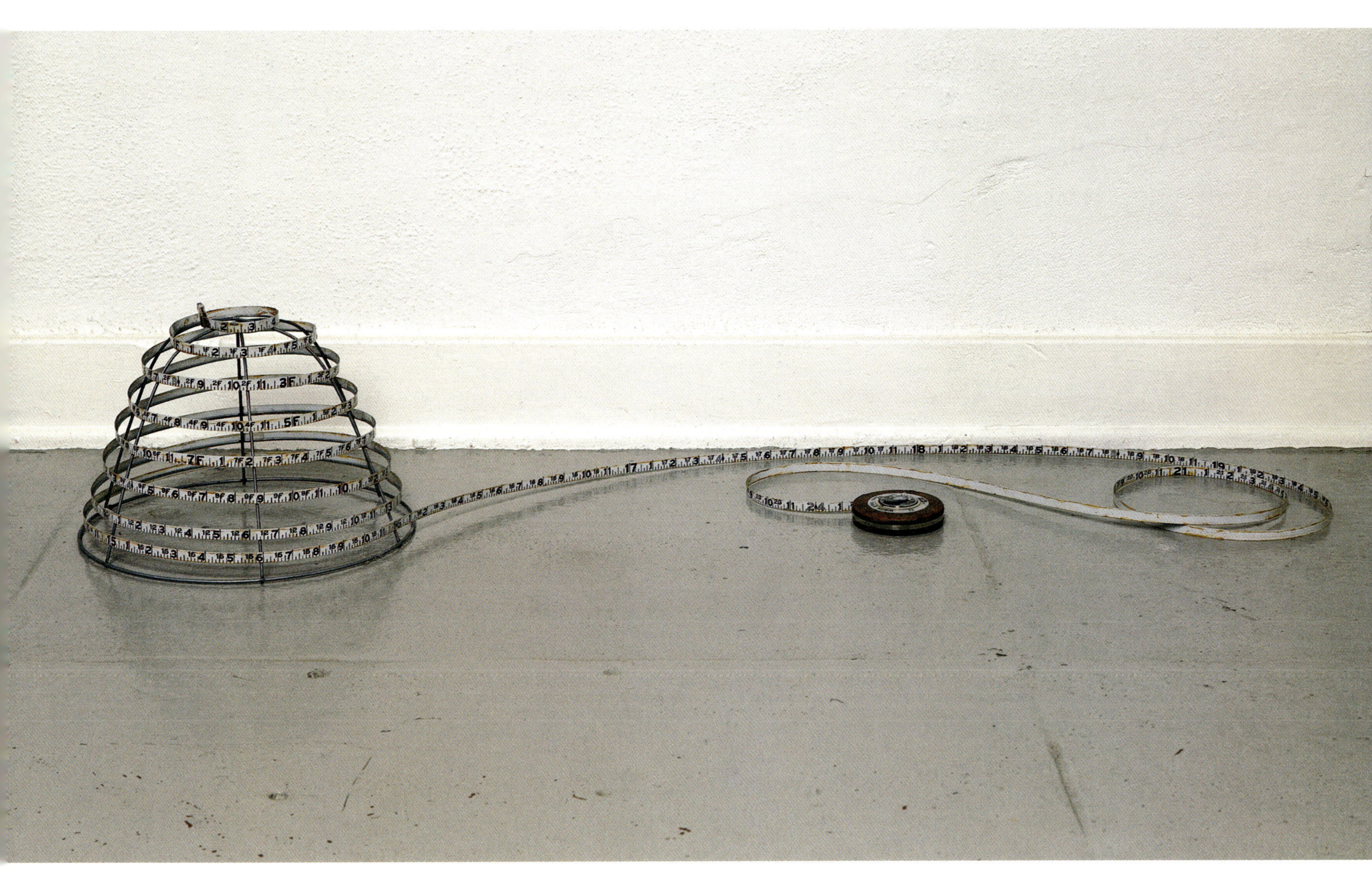

Estimate, 1988, plastic and tape, 9¼ x 52½ x 18 inches, (94.33)

Stacked Hub, 1987, plastic and metal, 9¾ inches diameter x 9¾ inches, (94.34)

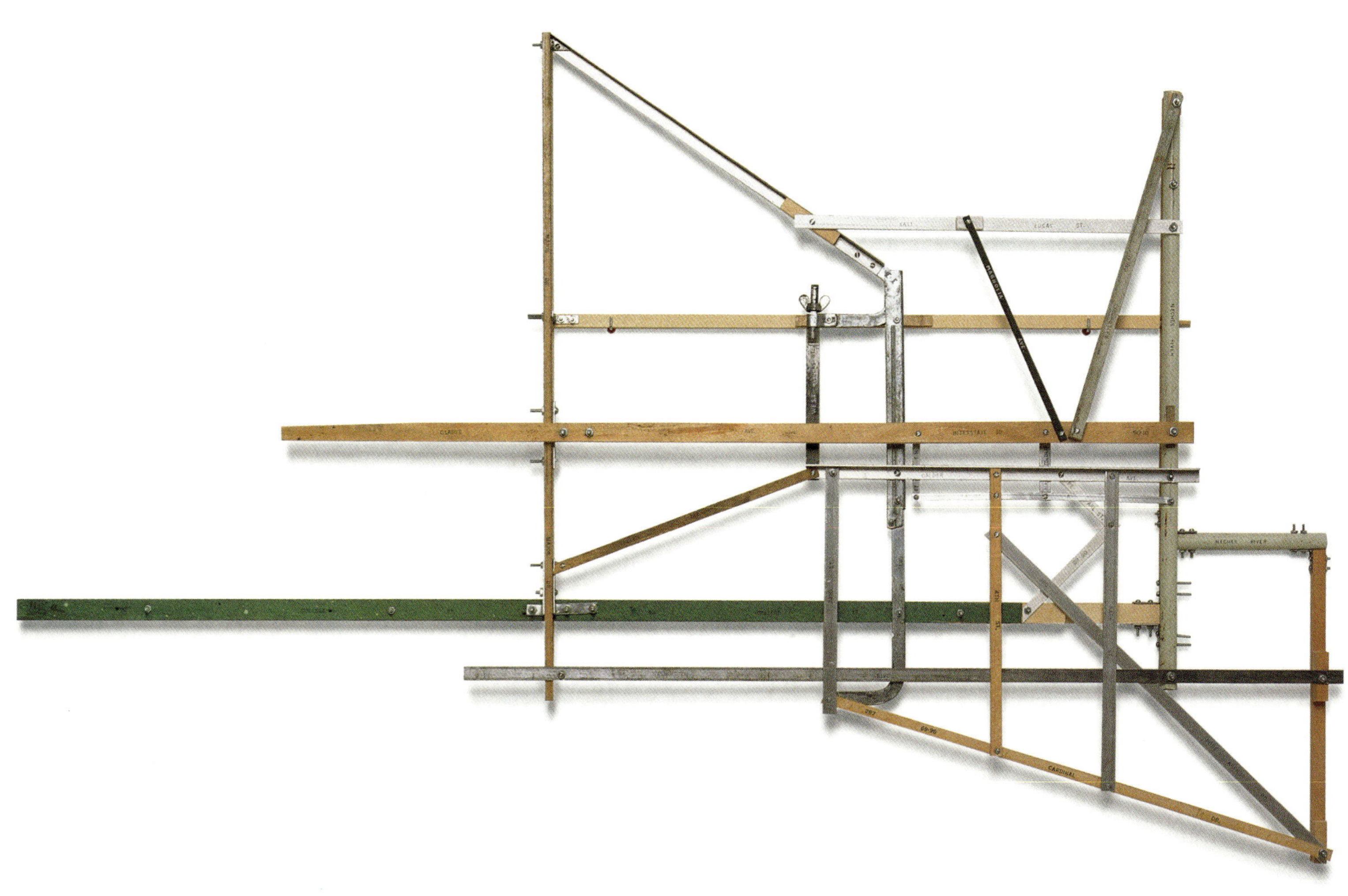

Beaumont, 1990, ink and enamel on metal and wood, 31 x 50 x 1½ inches, (94.39)

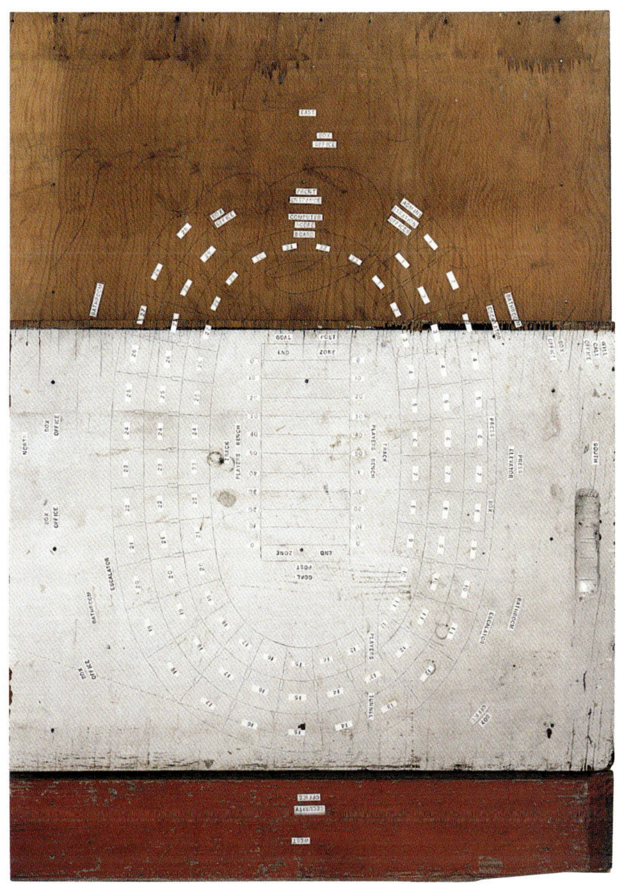

Memorial Coliseum, 1991, ink, paper, and wood, 27 x 19 x 1½ inches, (94.35)

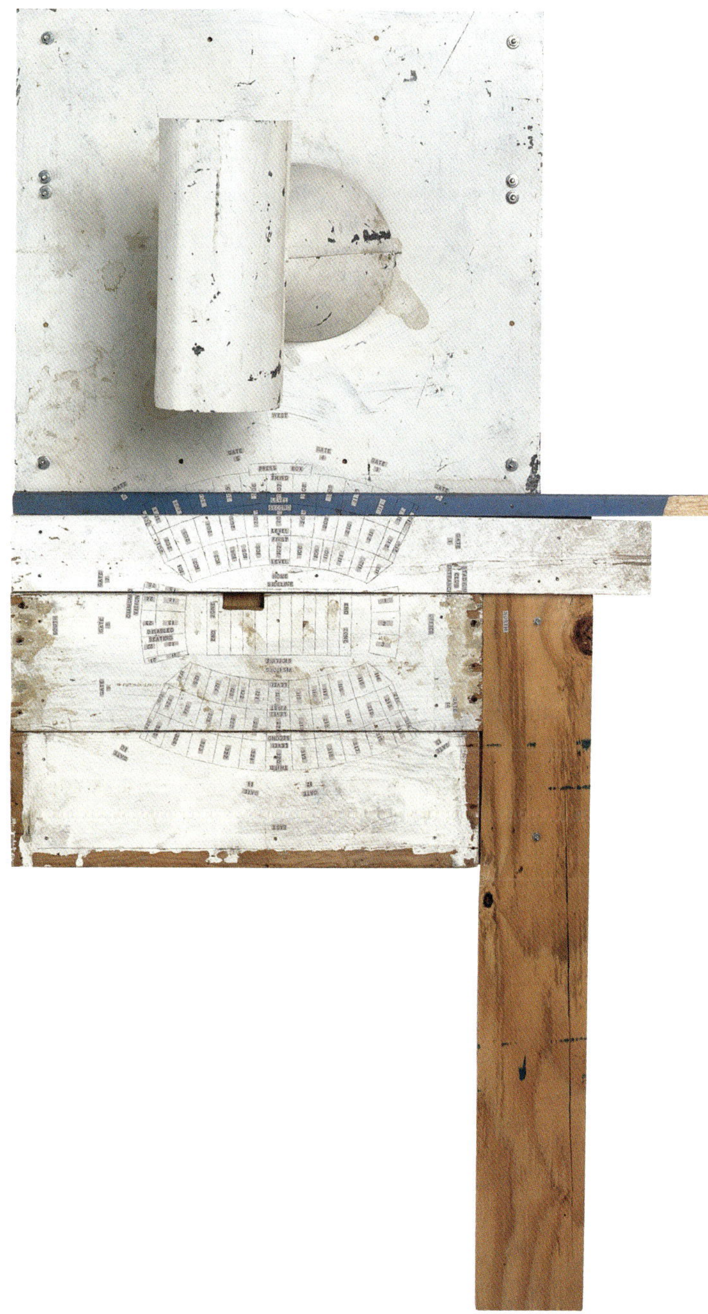

Schaefer Stadium, 1991, ink, paper on wood and metal, 43¼ x 24½ x 8¼ inches, (94.36)

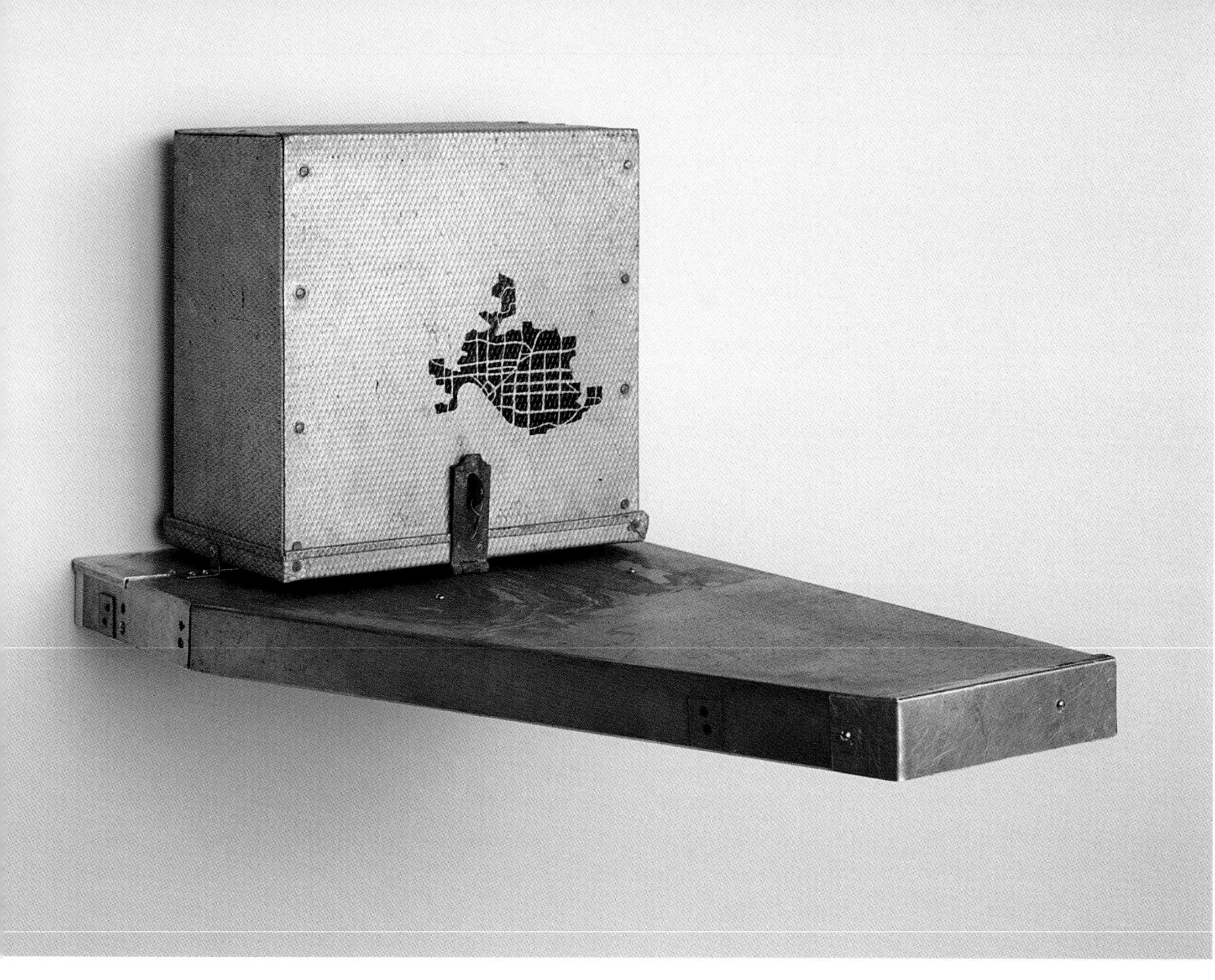

Evansville, 1992, enamel on metal and wood, 12 x 13¼ x 23¼ inches, (94.38)

Mobile, 1992, ink on metal, 10 x 3 inches, approximately, (94.37)

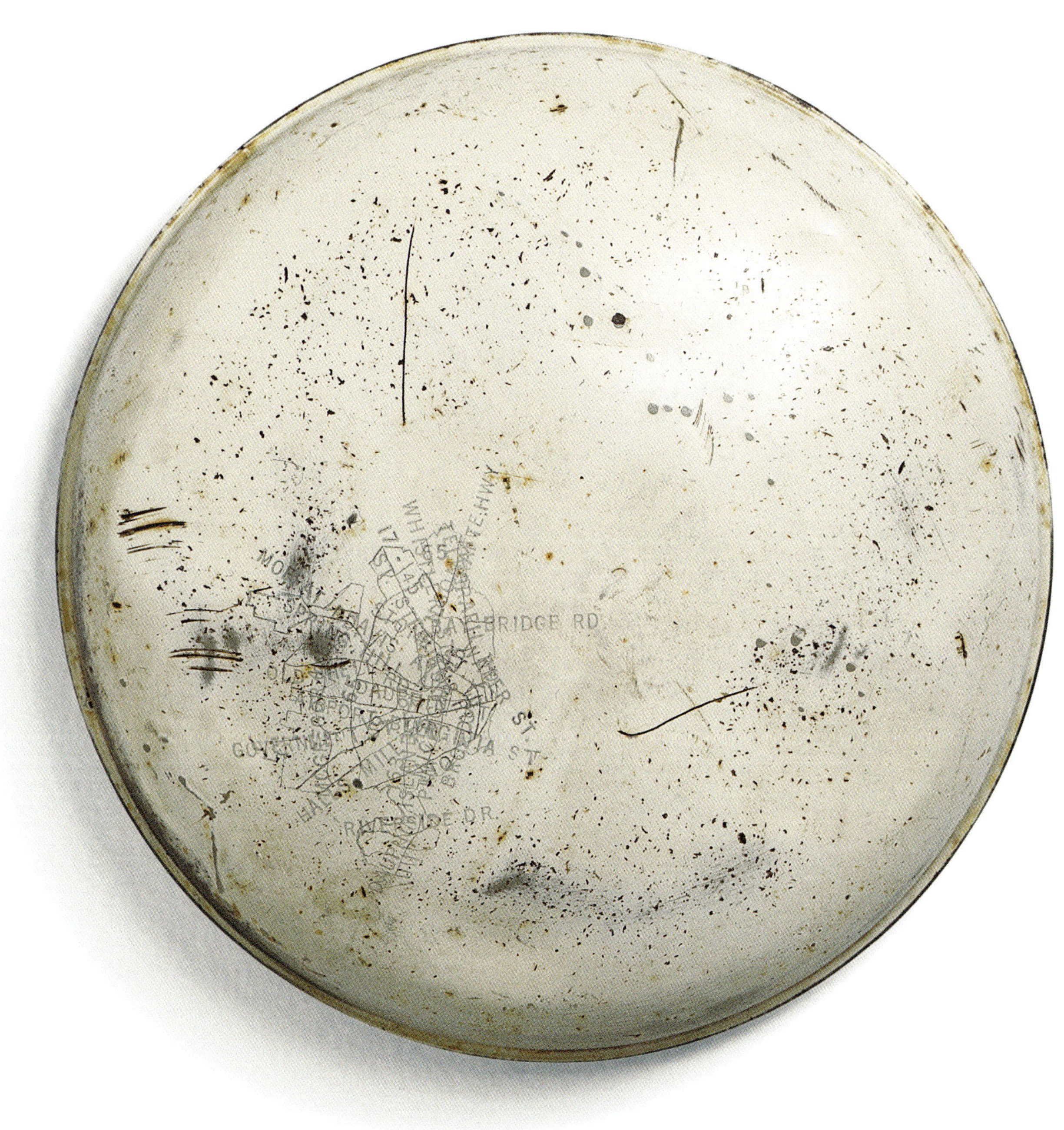

BAYSBRIDGE RD

Jeff Colson's plywood and plaster constructions are a layered complexity of pattern, texture, and color. Interested in dimensionality, Colson creates sculptures for various modes of presentation including works that are freestanding, those that are strategically balanced between the floor and the wall, and pieces that hang upon the wall in the manner of painting. Generated from Colson's homemade routers, potters' wheels, and lathes, his floor pieces consist of beautifully rendered, wooden ellipses formed into singular orbs with colored striations and varied patinas. His craft is impeccable, and these pieces, though a composite of multiple parts, exude a striking sense of mass and solidity.

Using the grid as a point of departure, Colson combines squares and rectangles to create the grounds from which his wall pieces emerge and take shape. Referencing the formal properties of Minimalism, *Untitled* (1992) (48 x 48") is composed of sixteen plywood squares that have been arranged into a grid and carved into smaller intersections of vertical and horizontal lines. The top white layer has been incised to expose a black reticulum below and circles of yellow, orange, and gray have been over-painted in a roving cluster within the lower, left-hand portion of the piece. Colson's juxtaposition of the quad and the sphere is further explored in *Untitled* (1992) (37 x 35½"), *Untitled* (1992) (35½ x 31½"), and *Untitled* (1991) (28½ x 57"). By confining the circular shapes to one square, or by painting them an alternating red and blue, Colson accentuates the shapes' structural differences and creates a lively interplay between the forms.

His polychromatic palette and variegated surface makes the artist's hand evident. Utilizing crude materials such as plywood, plaster, bondo, and motor oil aligns Colson with the pragmatism of the California assemblage tradition, exemplified by the work of George Herms and Edward Kienholz.[1] The commonality of these materials grants the pieces a natural accessibility, and their surfaces, with deep grooves and joined parts, provides the viewer with multiple points of entry. After entering the piece, the eye is strategically led along the incised lines, around the circles, and to the areas with concentrated visual activity, where it rests momentarily, and then continues its exploration.

Untitled (1991) (28½ x 57"), *Untitled* (1992) (28¾ x 28¾"), and *Untitled* (1992) (54½ x 54½") also employ the grid as a starting point. These works are complex assemblies of rectangles and squares upon which Colson has painted thick lines and heavy circles with dense, inky motor oil. These black marks gravitate towards a small circular opening in each piece that has been fortified with graduated plywood rings similar to those found in Colson's floor pieces. This sculptural element imbedded within the paintings echoes the complexity of the surfaces and Colson's passion for industrial craft. —R.M.

---

[1] Anne Ayres, *Material Consequence,* exh. cat. (Los Angeles: Otis Art Institute of Parsons School of Design, 1990), 4.

JEFF
colson

Untitled, 1991, plaster, plywood, bondo, charcoal, gesso, motor oil, and enamel, 40¾ x 40¾ inches, (94.40)

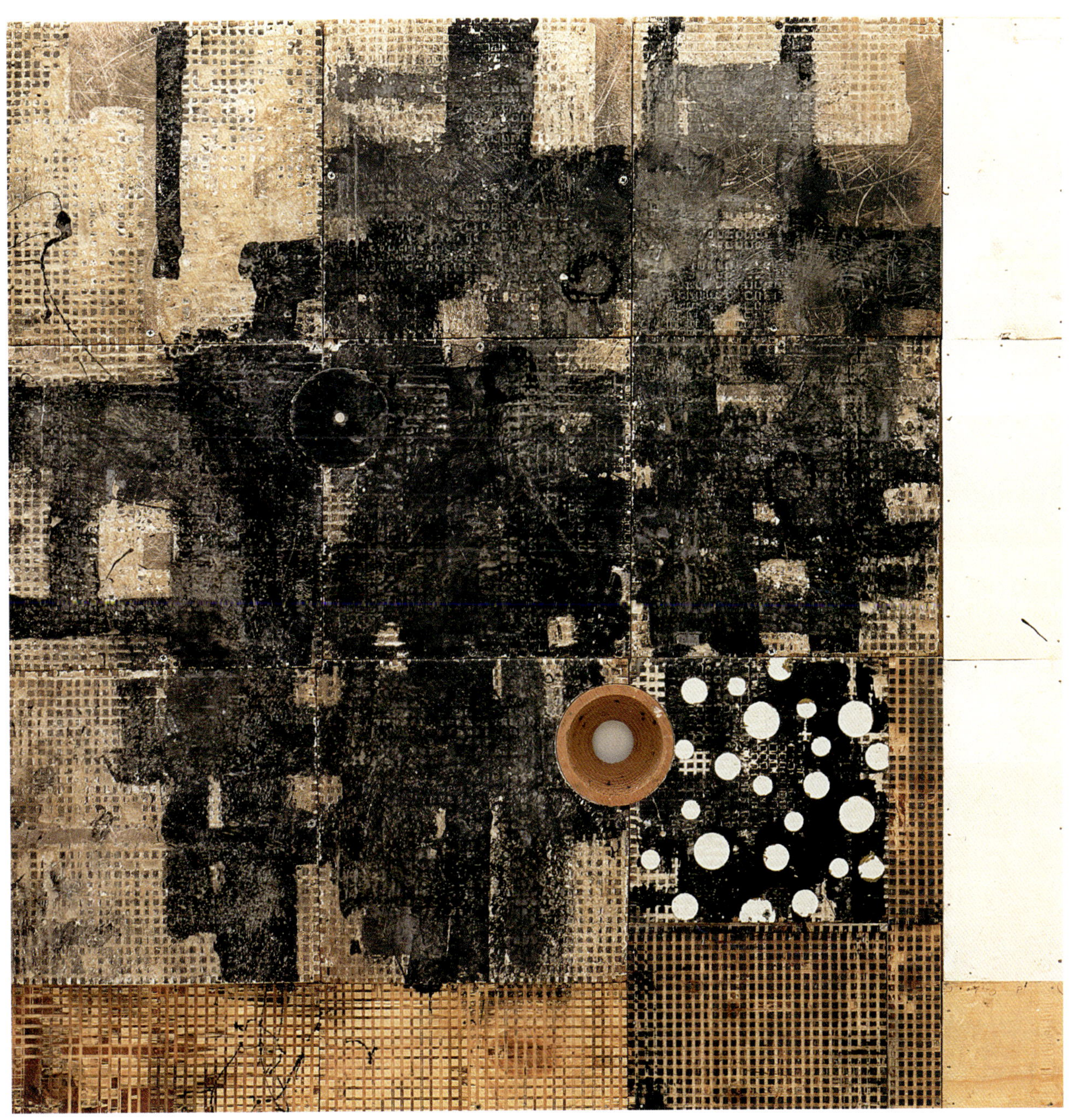

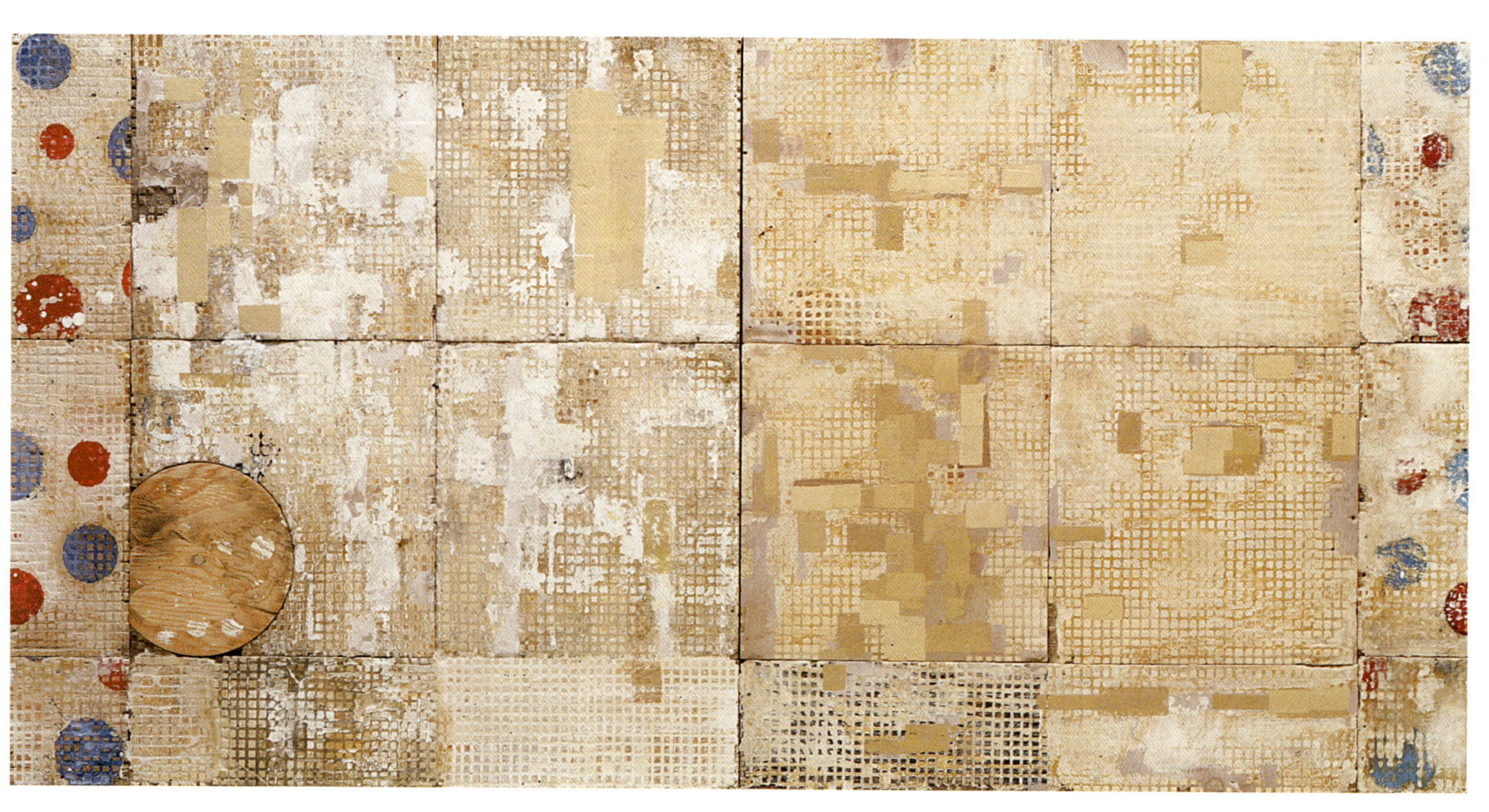

Untitled, 1991, plaster, plywood, bondo, enamel, and motor oil, 28½ x 57 inches, (94.41A,B)

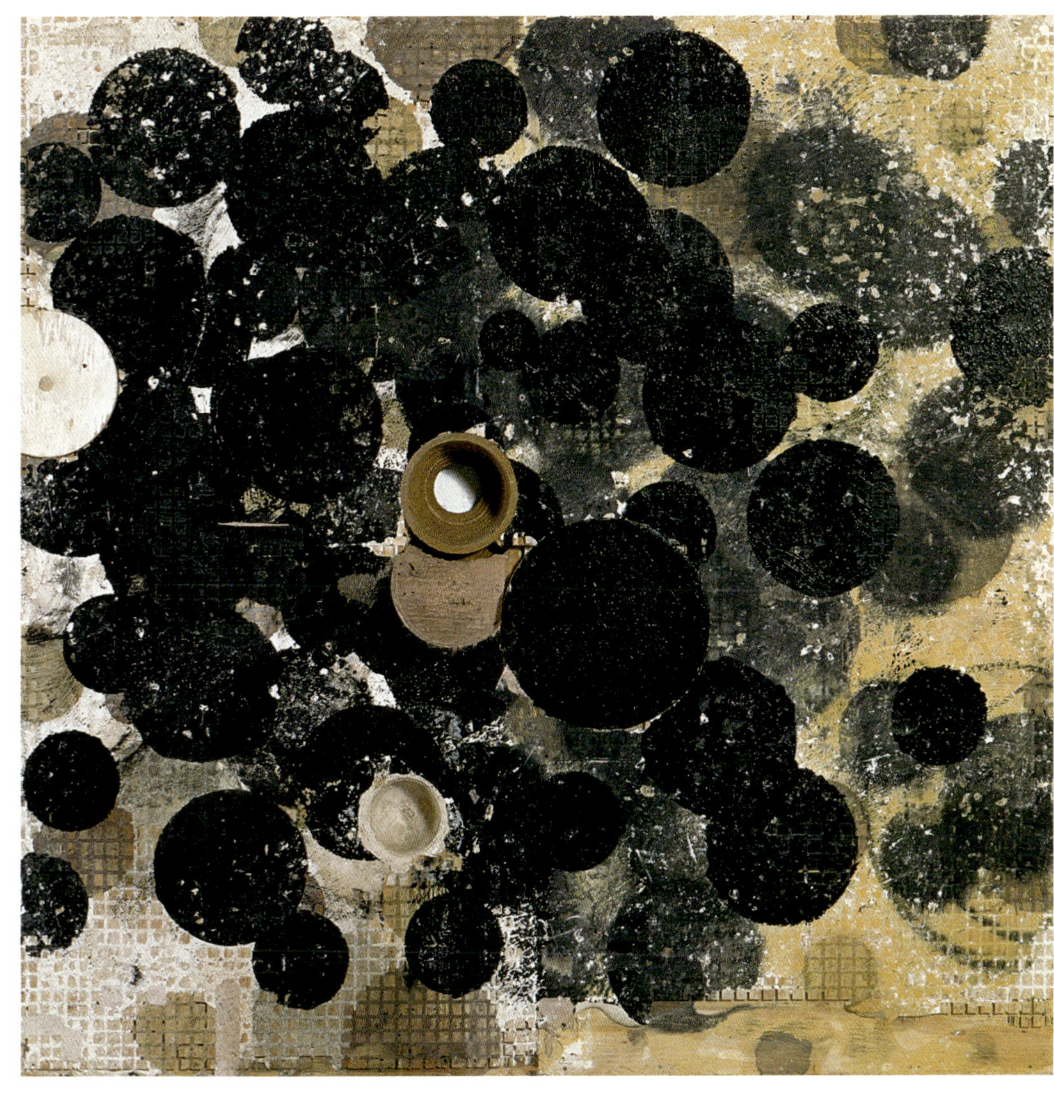

Untitled, 1992, plaster, plywood, bondo, motor oil, enamel, and charcoal, 28¾ x 28¾ inches, (94.42)

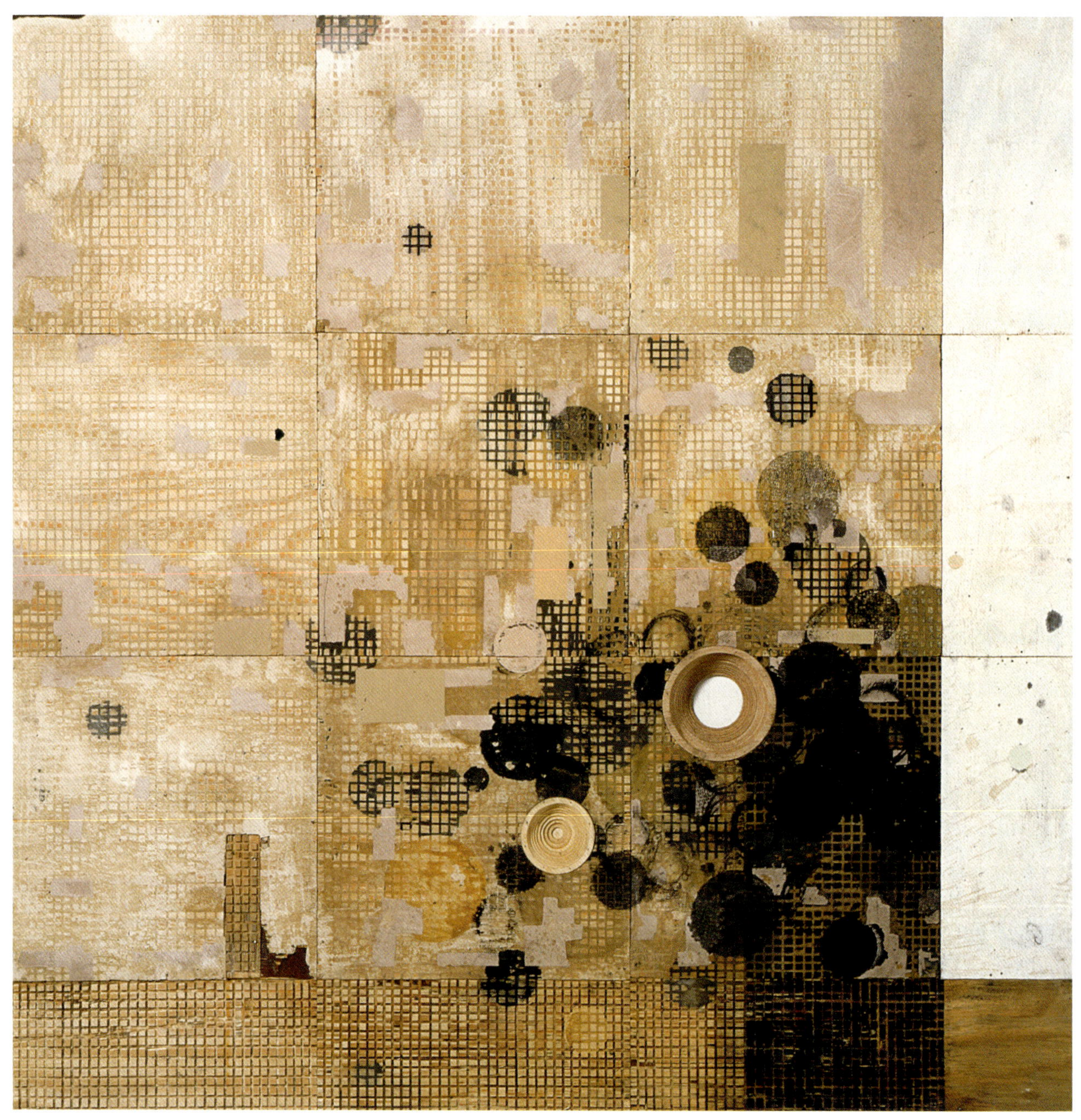

Untitled, 1992, plaster, plywood, bondo, charcoal, gesso, motor oil, and enamel, 54½ x 54½ inches, (94.43)

Untitled, 1992, plaster, plywood, bondo, motor oil, and enamel, 35½ x 31½ inches, (94.44)

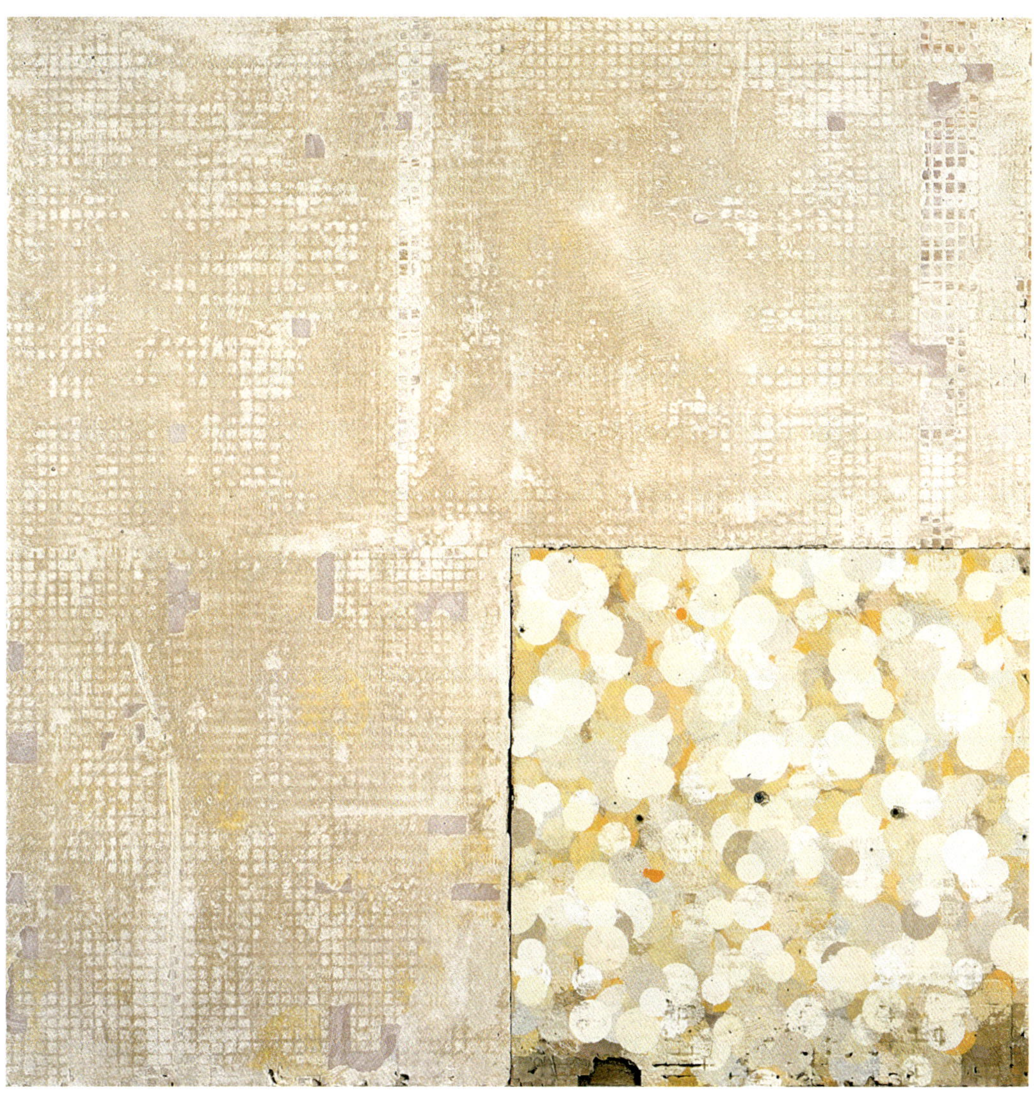

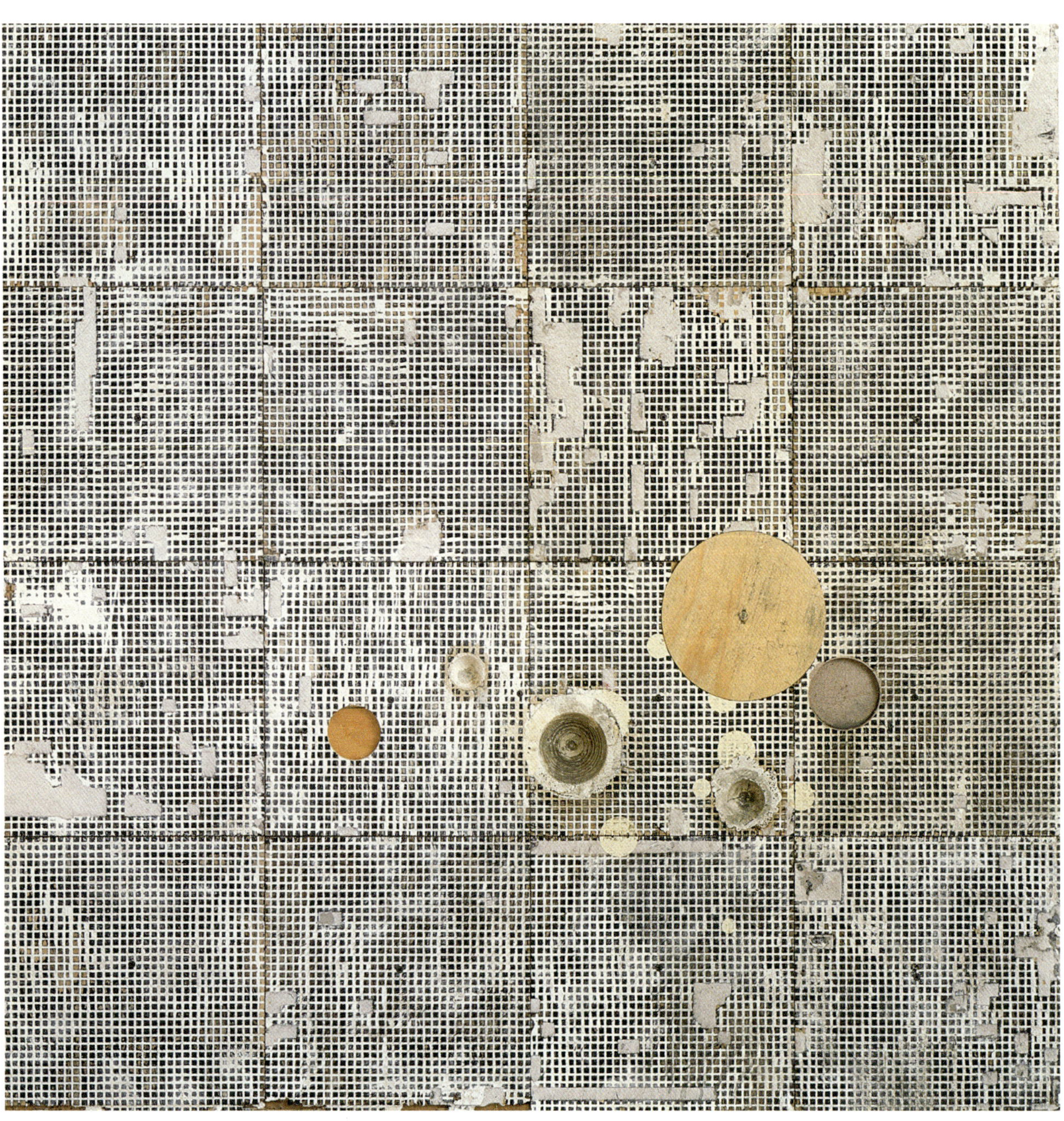

Untitled, 1992, plaster, plywood, bondo, motor oil, and enamel, 48 x 48 inches, (94.45)

Untitled, 1992, plaster, plywood, bondo, motor oil, and enamel, 37 x 35½ inches, (94.46)

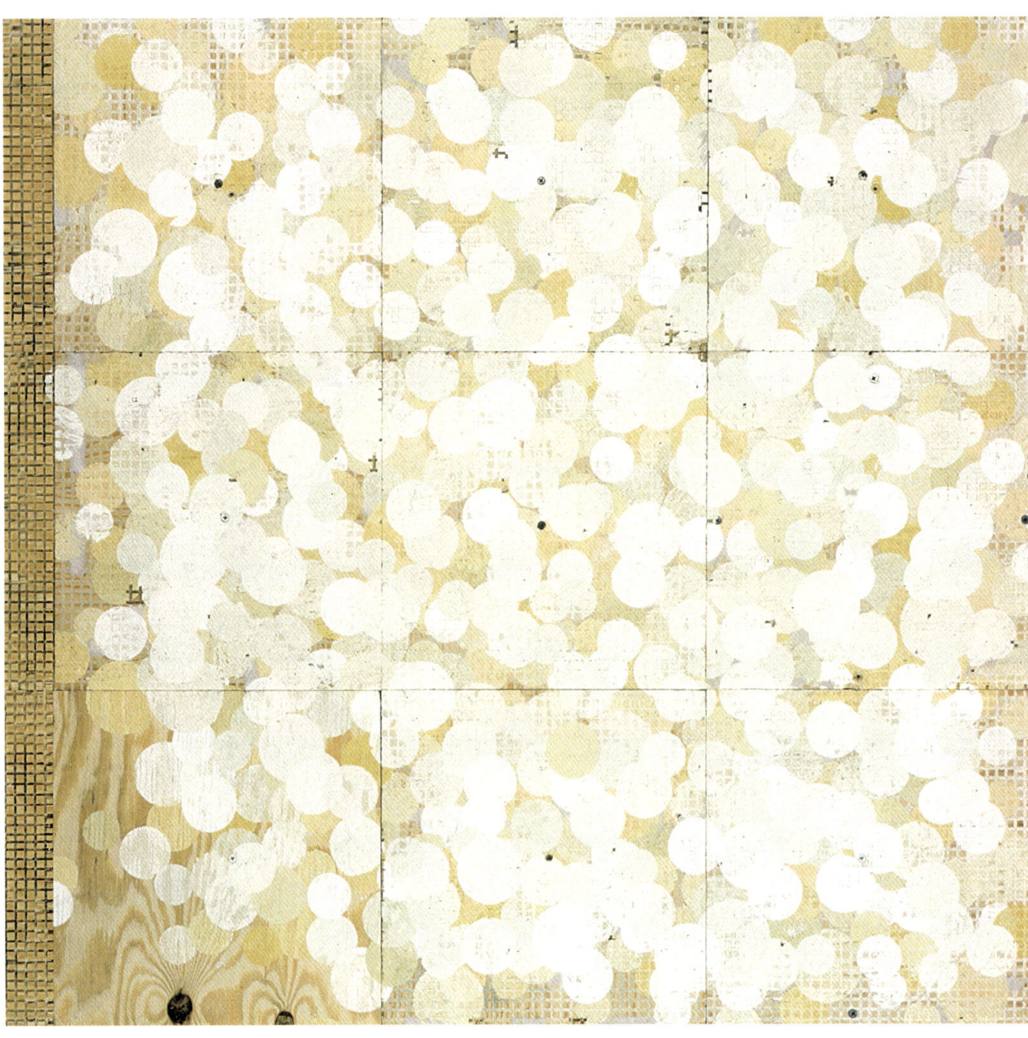

Ron Griffin's paintings of tickets, envelopes, cake boxes, and gum wrappers are illusory combinations of polymers and paint. By using consumer goods as his visual vocabulary Griffin references the tradition of New York Pop artists Andy Warhol and Roy Lichtenstein, who looked upon advertisements and mass media as viable sources for art production. However, Griffin's method is rooted in his own experience of the landscape, primarily the Mojave Desert in California where he travels, hikes, and camps, inevitably coming across the detritus of marginal culture. This desert, which sits on the edge of a major metropolis, is a rich source for abandoned objects including mobile homes, cars, bikes, and on a smaller scale wrappers, packets, and even personal letters which Griffin culls with an eye for the inherent formal richness of the texture, color, and compositional possibilities.

Griffin's *trompe l'oeil* paintings of these small popular culture containers such as *Untitled (Marlboro Series No. 9)* (1993) and *Untitled (Marlboro Series No. 17)* (1993) require close examination. At first glance they appear to be cigarette boxes that have been dismantled, flattened, and simply adhered to a panel with a shiny varnish. However, the tangible object is nowhere present in the painting, only its painted representation. Griffin recreates the dimensionality of these compressed boxes with multiple layers of enamel that he then paints in detail to yield a striking resemblance to the original object.

Interested in the raw beauty of design and construction found in today's packaging he states, "The industrial producer of millions of containers has no idea of their aesthetic qualities that the artist unveils and praises." [1] His investigations, which erase any deterioration or weathering, bring this beauty to the fore and assert its status within the realm of art.

The act of recreating a mass-produced object encourages the viewer to not only consider its visual components, but also its metaphorical allusions. The work *Air France* (1993) is a representation of a flight ticket whose position within a frame invites careful scrutiny. The small rectangular piece of paper is not only a ticket, but also a poetic symbol of the complete experience of travel. *Mailing Pouch Designed to Meet the U.S. Postal Service Regulations for Fecal Samples* (1993) is specific in its reference and conjures up a curious narrative while revealing Griffin's strong sense of humor and subtle social critique that runs concurrent with the work.

Different from Griffin's appropriations that are virtually void of text, *Work Song* (1993) and *SIC* (1993) explore the possibilities of word as image and the hidden significance in found texts which are part of our cultural vernacular. The piece *Work Song* consists of a bicolored wooden structure that has been inscribed with a poem that parodies a familiar biblical passage. The stanzas, rendered in ink, are arranged in a left justified

RON
griffin

Air France, 1993, spray primer, ink and golden msa on panel, 54 x 36 x 3½ inches, (94.52)

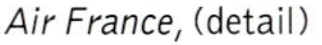

Air France, (detail)

square that is poised centrally along a fifteen and a half-foot piece of wood whose color is divided into two hues along a wavering horizon line. The poem ends with "sic" which reveals that the quoted words are written exactly according to the original poem regardless of mis-pellings, improper grammar, or unusual subject matter. This singular word is showcased in Griffin's piece of the same title, *SIC* where the word stands alone on a piece of wood hung horizontally upon the wall. Almost lost amid the ten-foot expanse of wood grain "sic" does not follow any writing and in fact refers to the divided col-oration of the wood itself. These wooden structures used by Griffin have not been changed or manipulated in any way, but were found in the lumber yard bearing these beautiful, colored segments.

Griffin's work, which emerges from his love of leftover landscapes and its contents, also explores issues of originality and appropriation. By recreating mass-produced packaging and quoting passages of anonymous prose Griffin grants meaning and value to these over-looked artforms. While the act of appropriation is often used as a means to question and negate notions of mas-terpiece, Griffin's work does just the opposite — it makes resonant, poetic icons from the everyday. —R. M.

1 *The Panza di Biumo Collection: Some Artists from the 80s and 90s,* exh. cat. (Trento, Italy: Museo di Arte Moderna e Contemporanea di Trento e Rovereto, 1996), 72.

SIC, 1993, ink on wood, 6½ x 130¼ x 1⅜ inches, (94.49)

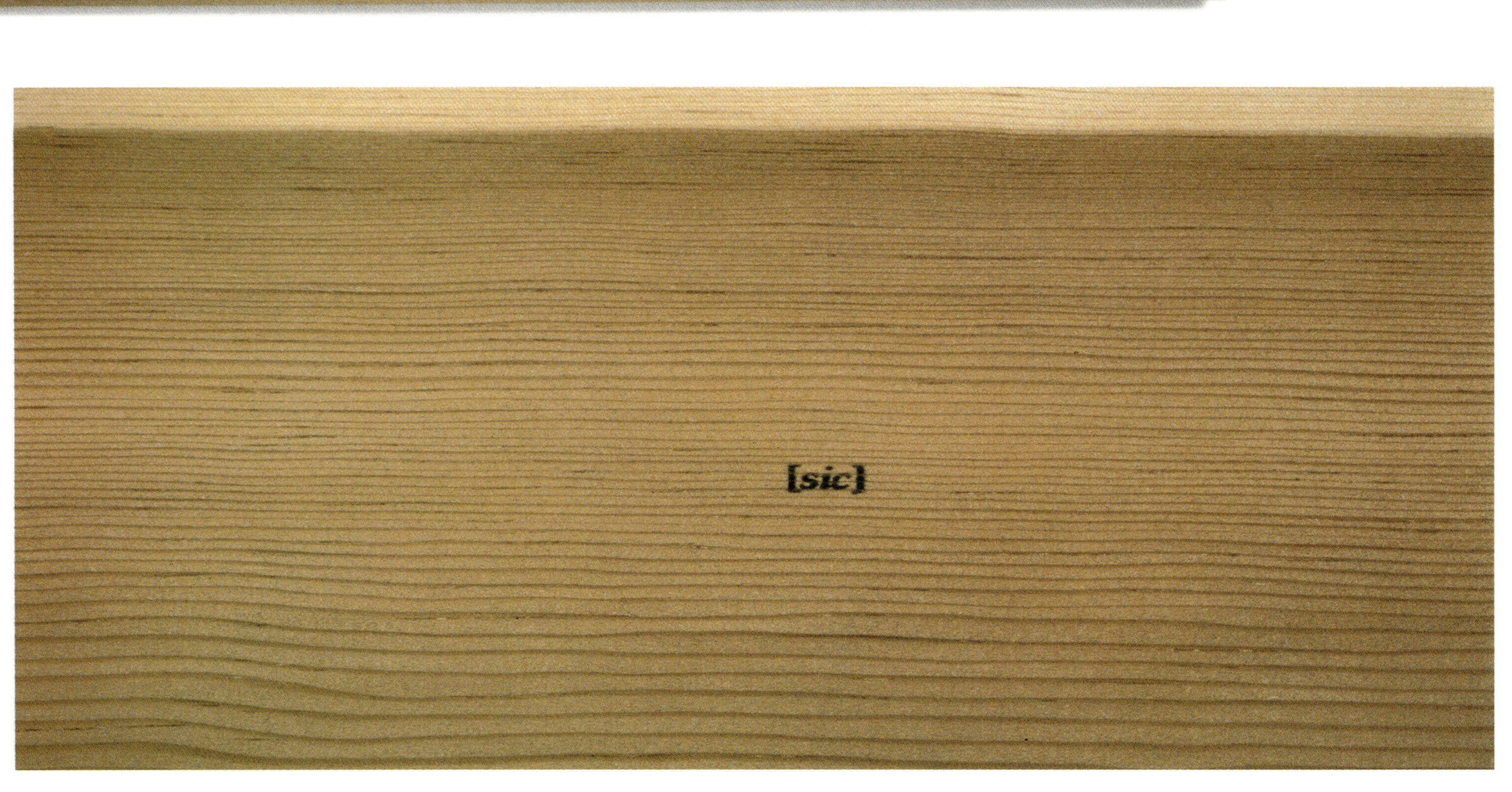

SIC, (detail)

Mailing Pouch Designed to Meet the U.S. Postal Service Regulations for Fecal Samples, (detail)

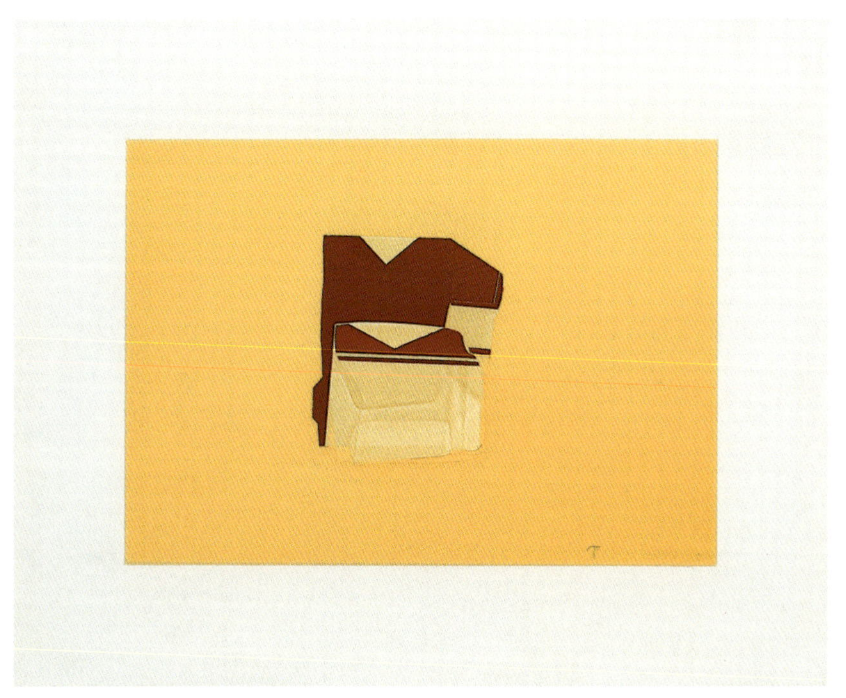 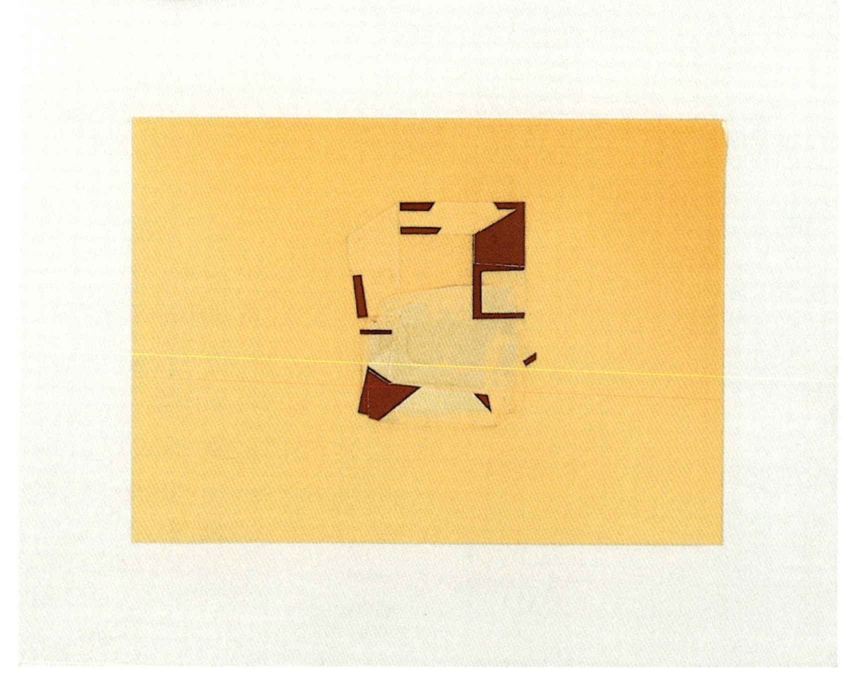

Untitled (Marlboro Series No. 9), 1993, spray primer, polyurethane and varnish on two panels, 11¼ x 14¼ x 1¾ inches each, (94.48)

Untitled (Marlboro Series No. 17), 1993, spray primer and polyurethane on panel, 42 x 36 x 3½ inches, (94.50)

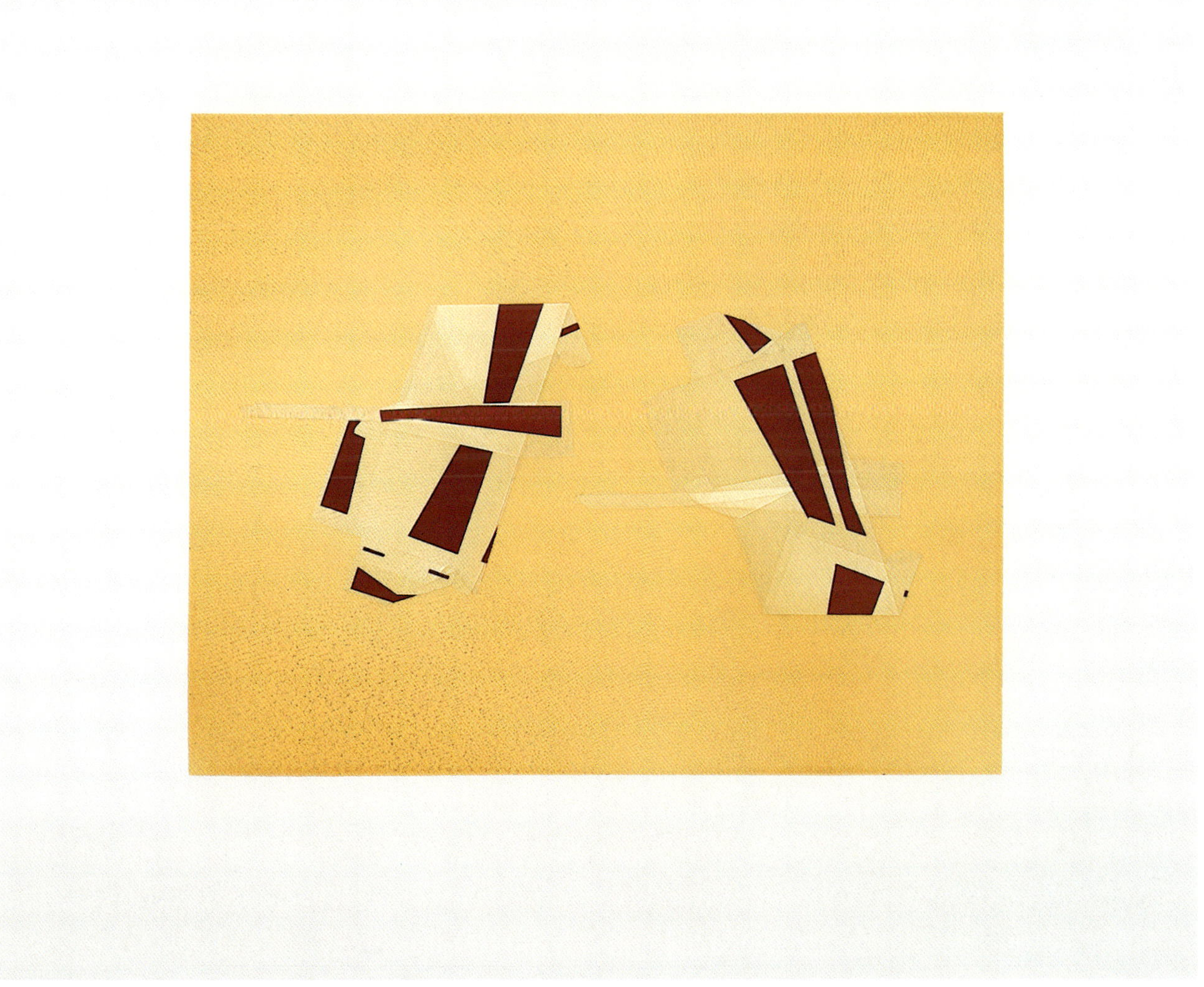

MOHAVE PSALM

CHAPMAN is my shepherd; I shall not think.
HE maketh me to assume the position with my socks off;
HE leadeth me beside my locker;
HE restoreth my faith in bolt-cutters.
HE leadeth me in the paths of paranoia for HIS ego's sake.
Yeah, though I walk through the gates of Corporate Security,
I still fear THY evil; for THOU still work here:
THY rod and THY staff they intimidate me.
THOU preparest a false case against me
in the absence of my accusers:
THOU anointeth my reputation with unfounded accusations
and my cup runneth over with indignation.
Surely deception and illegalities
will follow me all the days of my life
and I will dwell in the house of self-righteous fascism
forever. [sic]

Work Song, (detail)

168

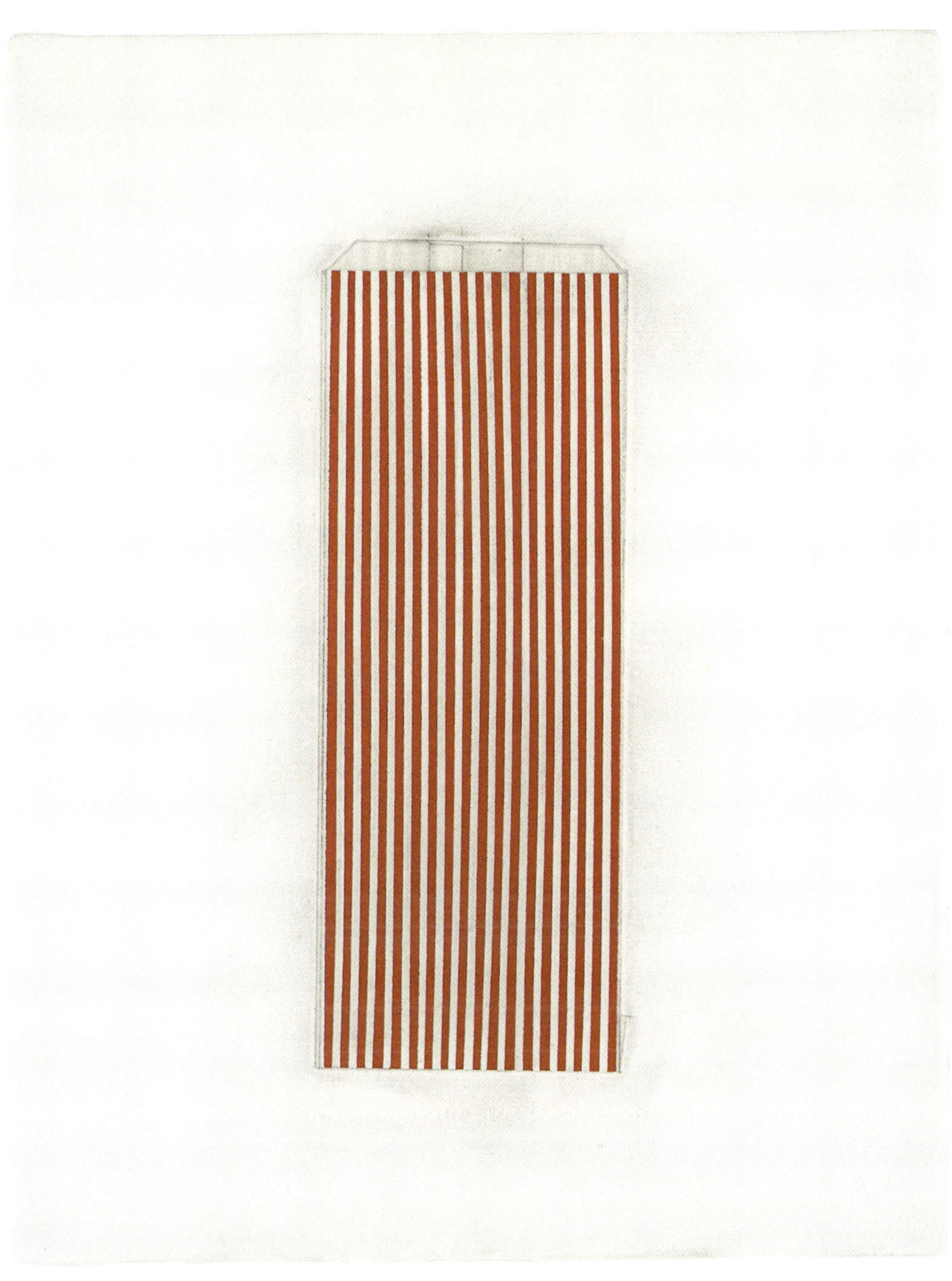

Untitled (Popcorn Bag), 1993, enamel and varnish on panel, 14 x 11 x 1¾ inches, (94.53)

In 1978 Mark Lere, building upon his interest in the vocabulary of theater and notions of the stage, began to construct "metaphorical spaces" by recreating the individual rooms that composed his apartment in Los Angeles. These "Room Stages" strategically synthesized the two seemingly disparate artforms of architecture and sculpture. The confluence resulted in pieces of non-functional architecture that prompted sculptural considerations within the gallery. The inevitable discussion surrounding these constructions was how the space appeared to influence the emotions, productivity, and behavior of its potential occupant.

In the early 1980s, Lere turned his attention to the creation of individual objects, though he continued to explore ideas of theatricality established by the earlier work. He rejected the use of pedestals and conceived of the floor as one large stage upon which all the objects were to be placed. By carefully choreographing the works' positioning he endeavored to encourage a dialogue among the various pieces situated in an installation-like setting. Lere's spatial theories were influenced, in part, by Barry Le Va's *Distribution Pieces* from the late 1960s. The apparent randomness of Le Va's pieces was in fact a strategic and calculated placement meant to promote the most fluid discourse among the objects present. The shift in Lere's production ushered in the transition from the making of a public theatrical space into a private metaphorical space. [1]

As part of the second generation to react against Minimalism, Lere was interested in the possibilities of suggestive imagery within the medium of sculpture. Objects made in the early 1980s such as *Black Spout* (1983) or *Bladder* (1988), while not referential to one specific narrative, are metaphorical in nature. These structures allude to the water contained within them and reveal Lere's investigation of naturally occurring substances, patterns, and phenomena.

In *Coil* (1987), Lere manipulated aluminum into self-enveloping curves whose implied momentum refers to the whirling force created by a tornado. Lere, a native of the Great Plains of North Dakota and raised in eastern Colorado, lived with the reality of this weather phenomenon as a condition of his geography. Interested in motion, natural phenomena, and the visual components of landscape, Lere's tornado-like objects resonate with the irony inherent in making permanent a fleeting spectacle. The pieces *Voice* and *Throat*, both from 1987, also experiment with this swirling tunnel shape. However, in these works the bodies have been streamlined and elongated with an exaggerated opening at the apex much like a trumpet, horn, or old-fashioned gramophone.

Lere's involvement with less-traditional materials such as Masonite, plastic, and fiberglass connects him loosely to the likes of Giovanni Anselmo and the Italian

MARK

lere

Black Spout, 1983, painted wood, 13 x 13¼ x 17¼ inches, (94.54)

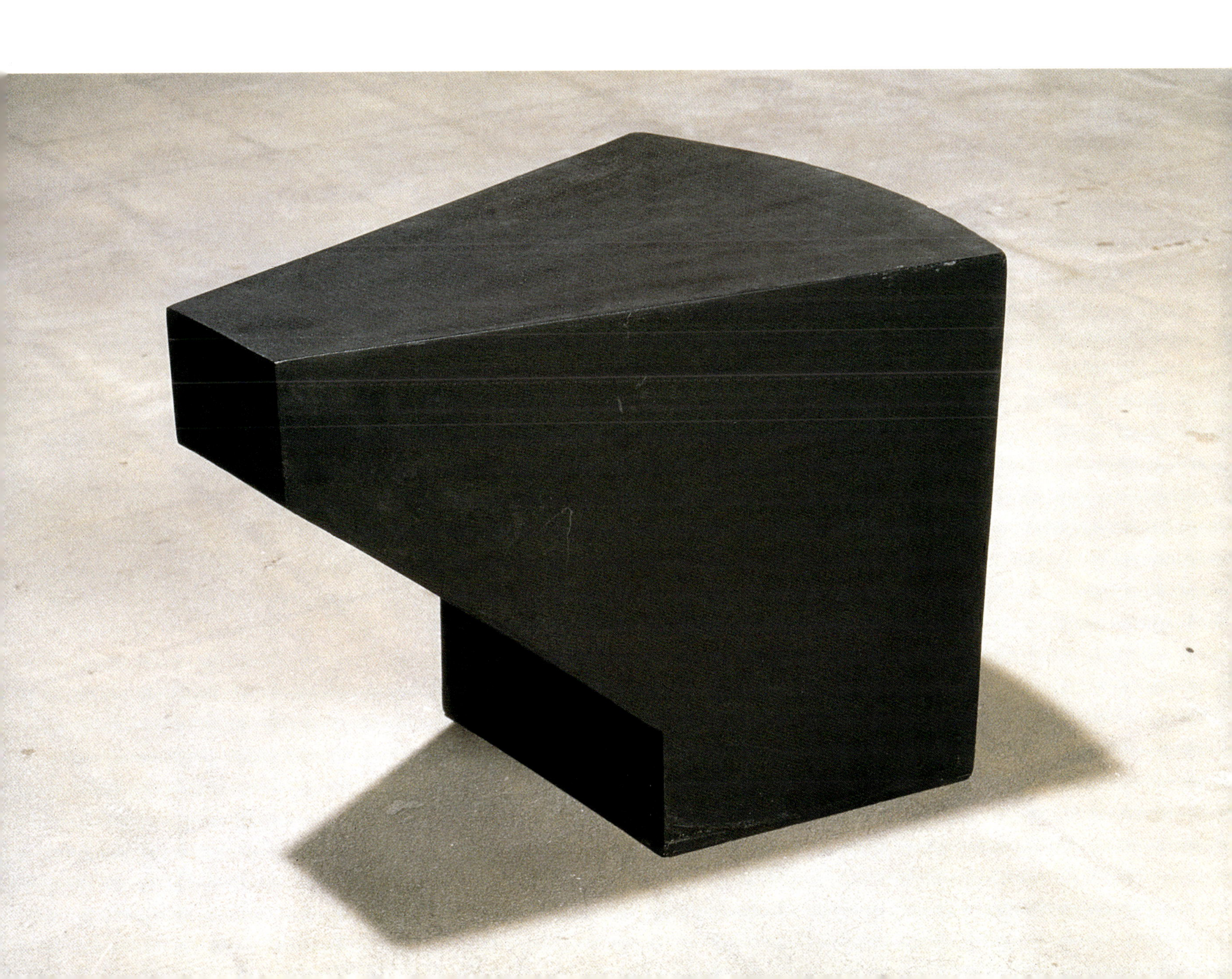

movement *Arte Povera*. Trained as a carpenter, Lere's
intimate knowledge of structure led to a simple approach
to construction in which he does not defy the nature
of his materials, but allows them to dictate the ultimate
form of the piece. The apparent roughness of his objects,
as seen in his piece *Bone Heads* (1990), is in direct
contrast, if not a conscious reaction, to the slick "finish
fetish" which once defined Los Angeles sculpture. Indeed,
it is Lere's utilization of metaphor and narrative that
distinguishes his work from the glossy and impersonal
abstractions of his Los Angeles predecessors. —R.M.

1 Frances Colpitt, "Mark Lere," in *Mark Lere:
New and Selected Work,* exh. cat. (Los Angeles:
The Museum of Contemporary Art, 1985), 20.

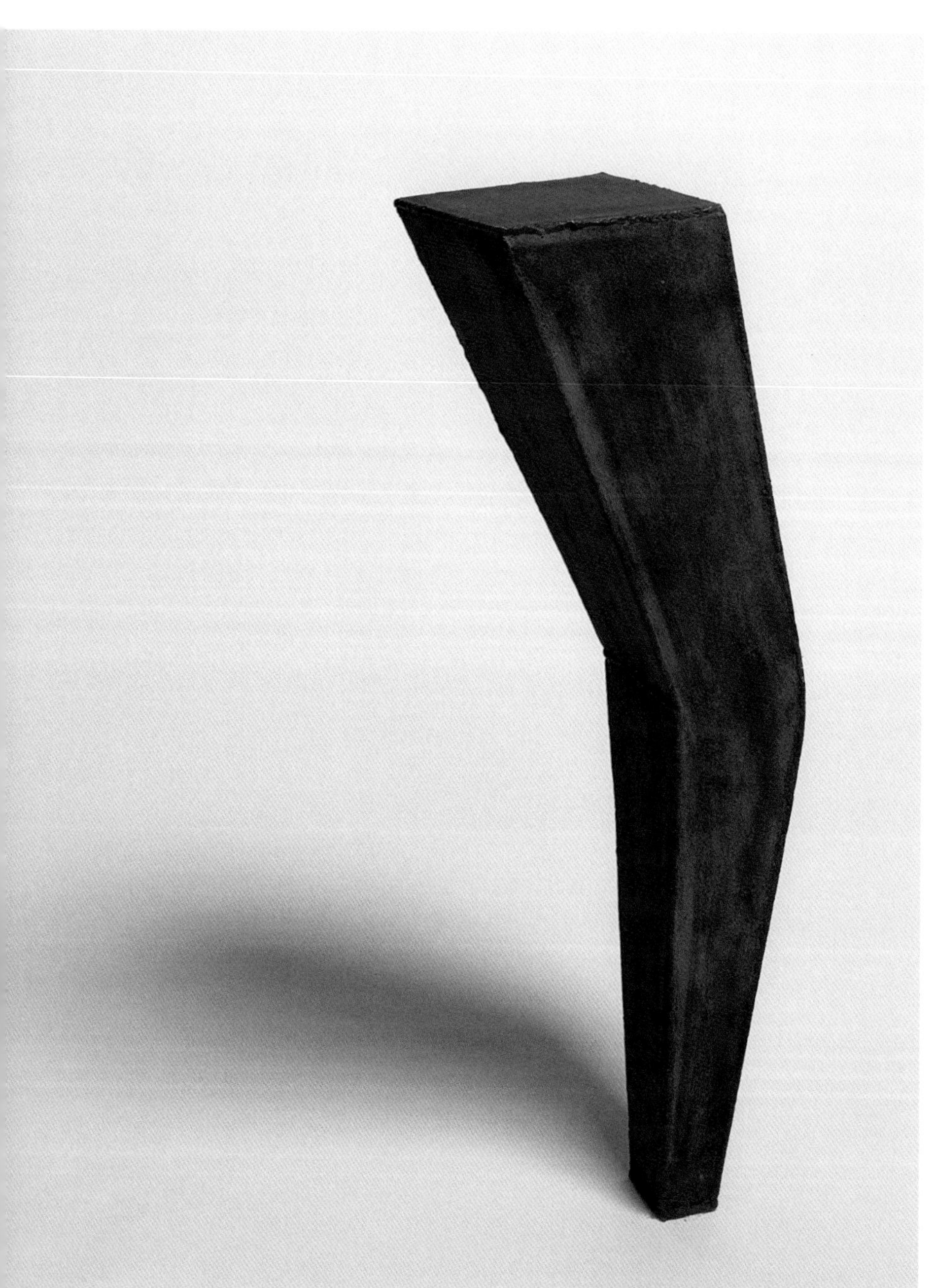

Untitled, 1984, mild steel, 36 x 9 x 11 inches, (94.55)

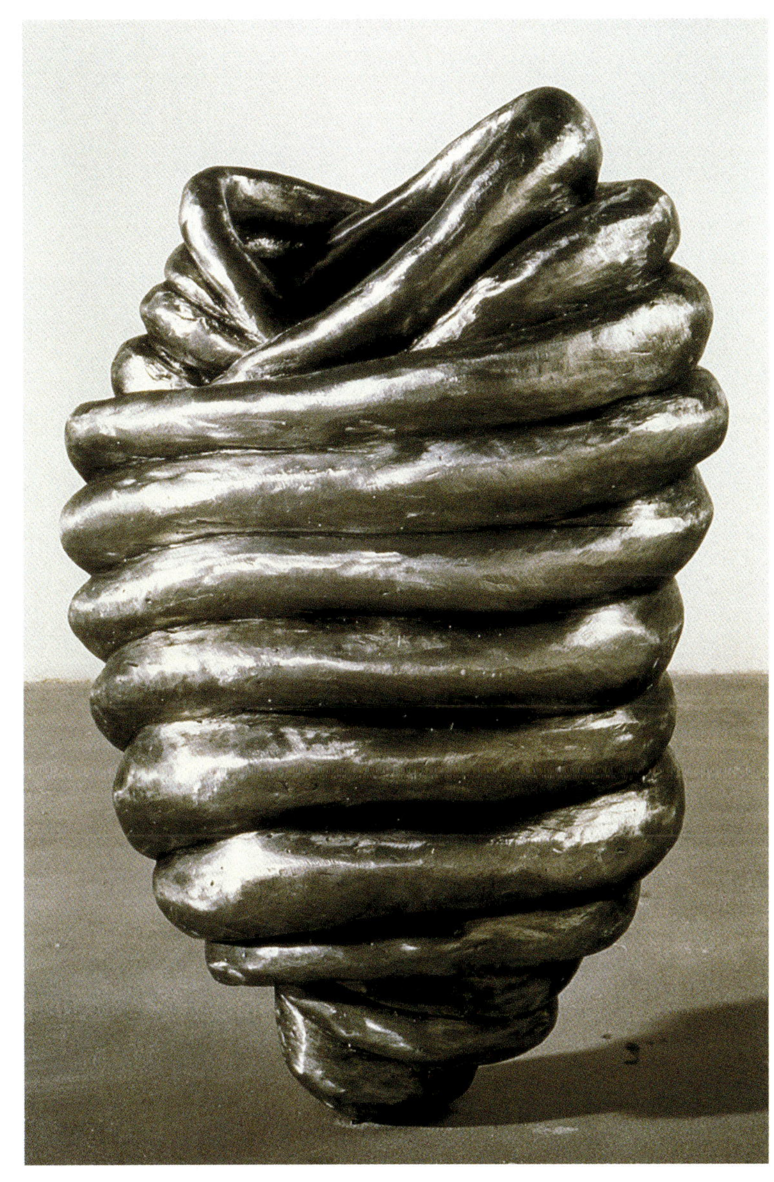

Coil, 1987, aluminum, 32½ x 21¼ x 14½ inches, (94.58)

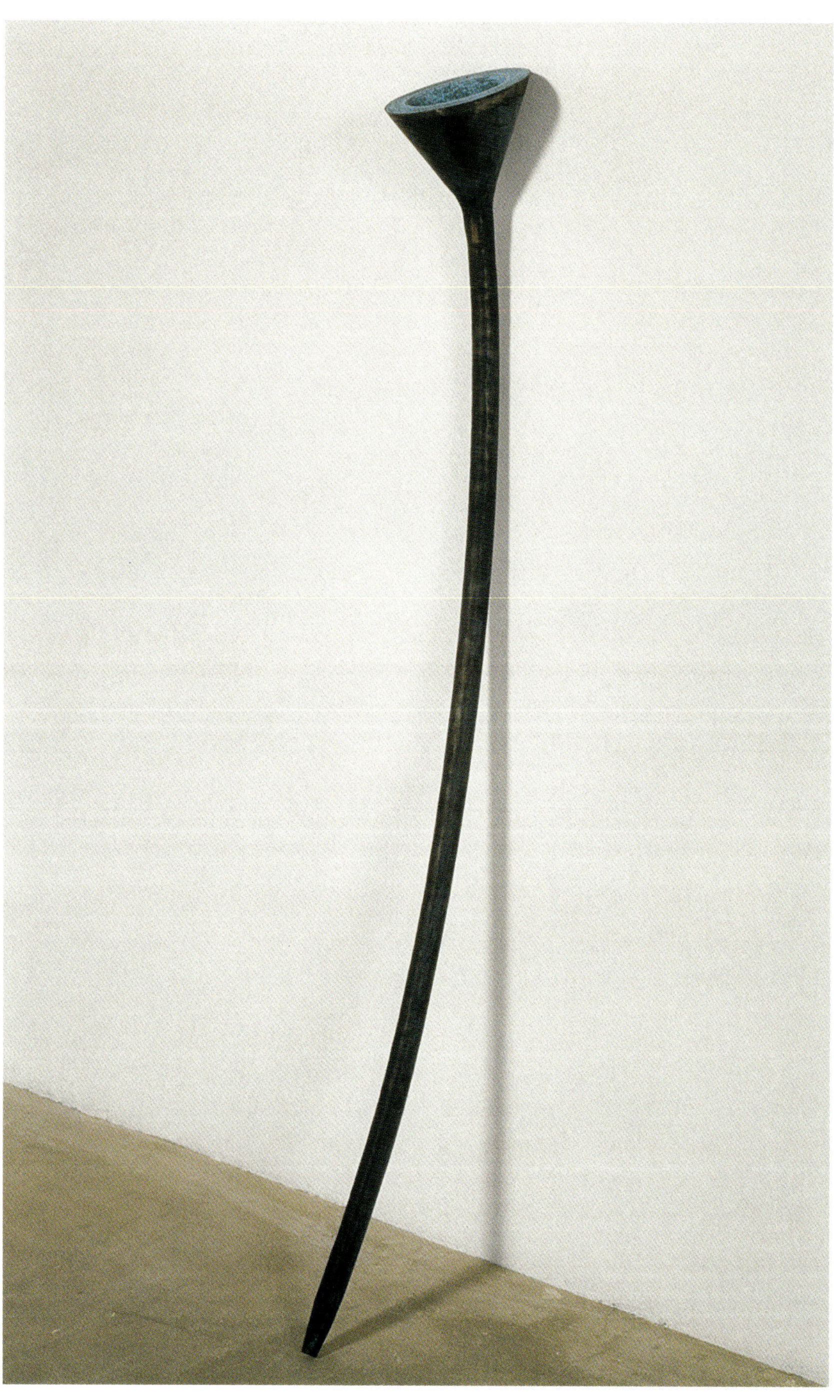

Throat, 1987, bronze, 66 x 8 inches, (94.57)

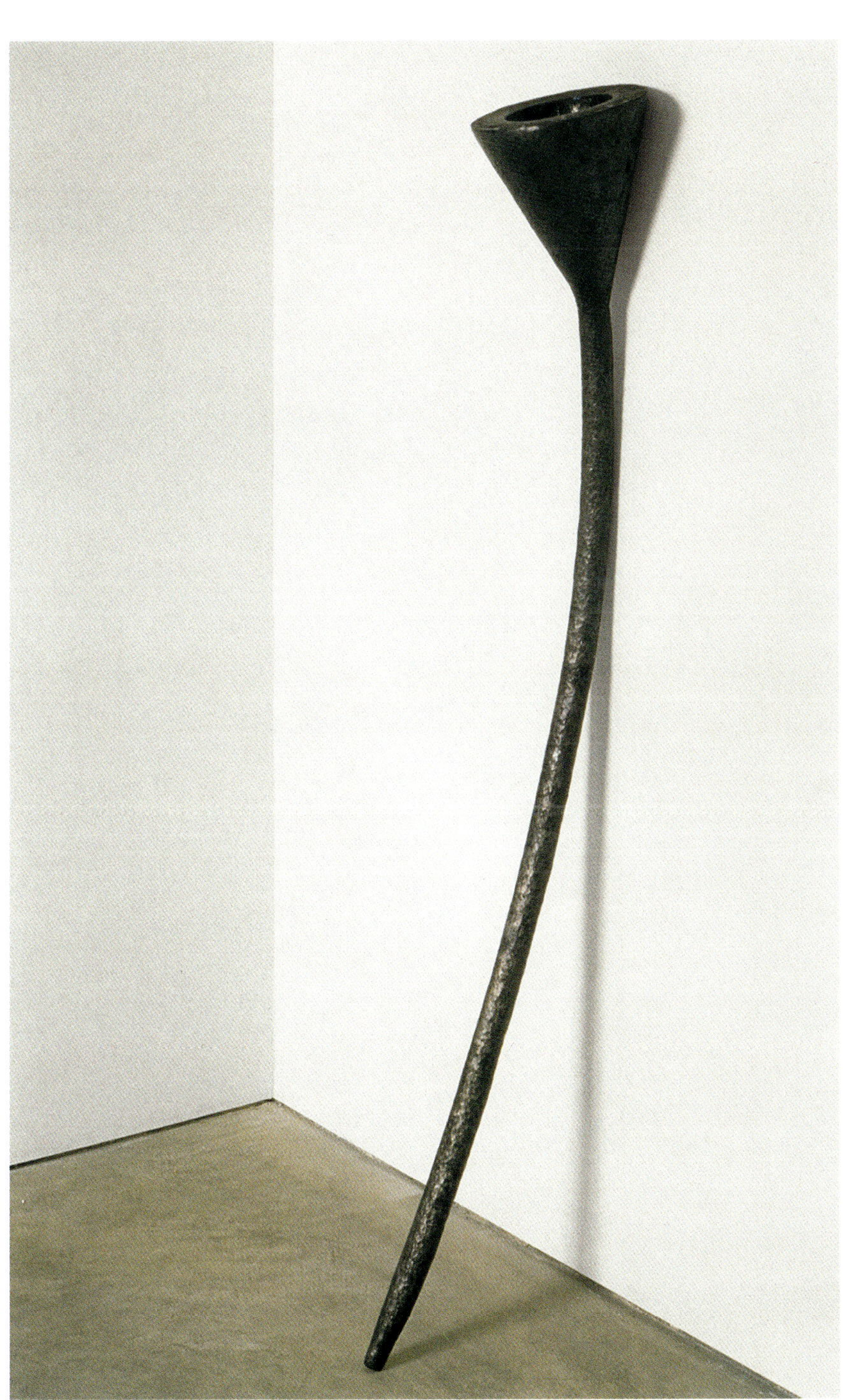

Voice, 1987, lead over aluminum, 72 x 12 x 12 inches, (94.56)

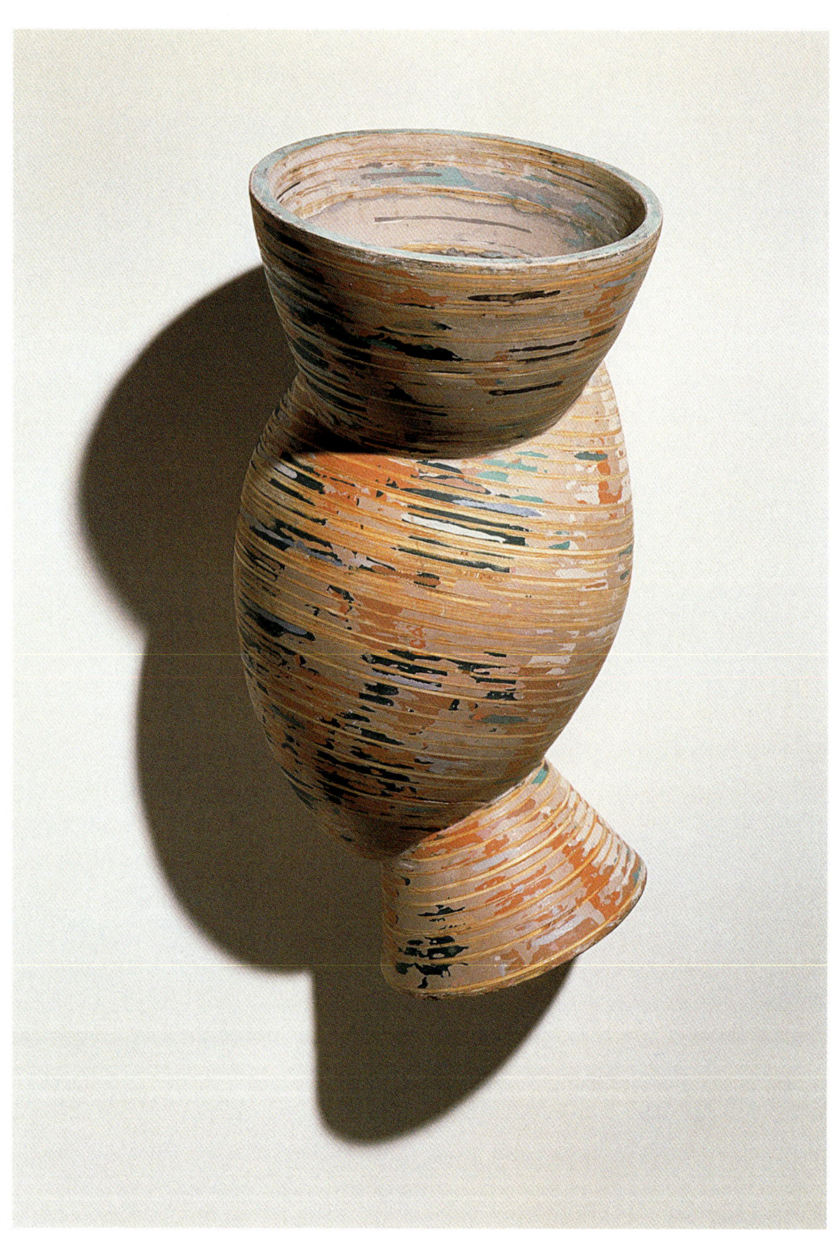

Bladder, 1988, fiberglass over wood, 31½ x 16 x 17 inches, (94.59)

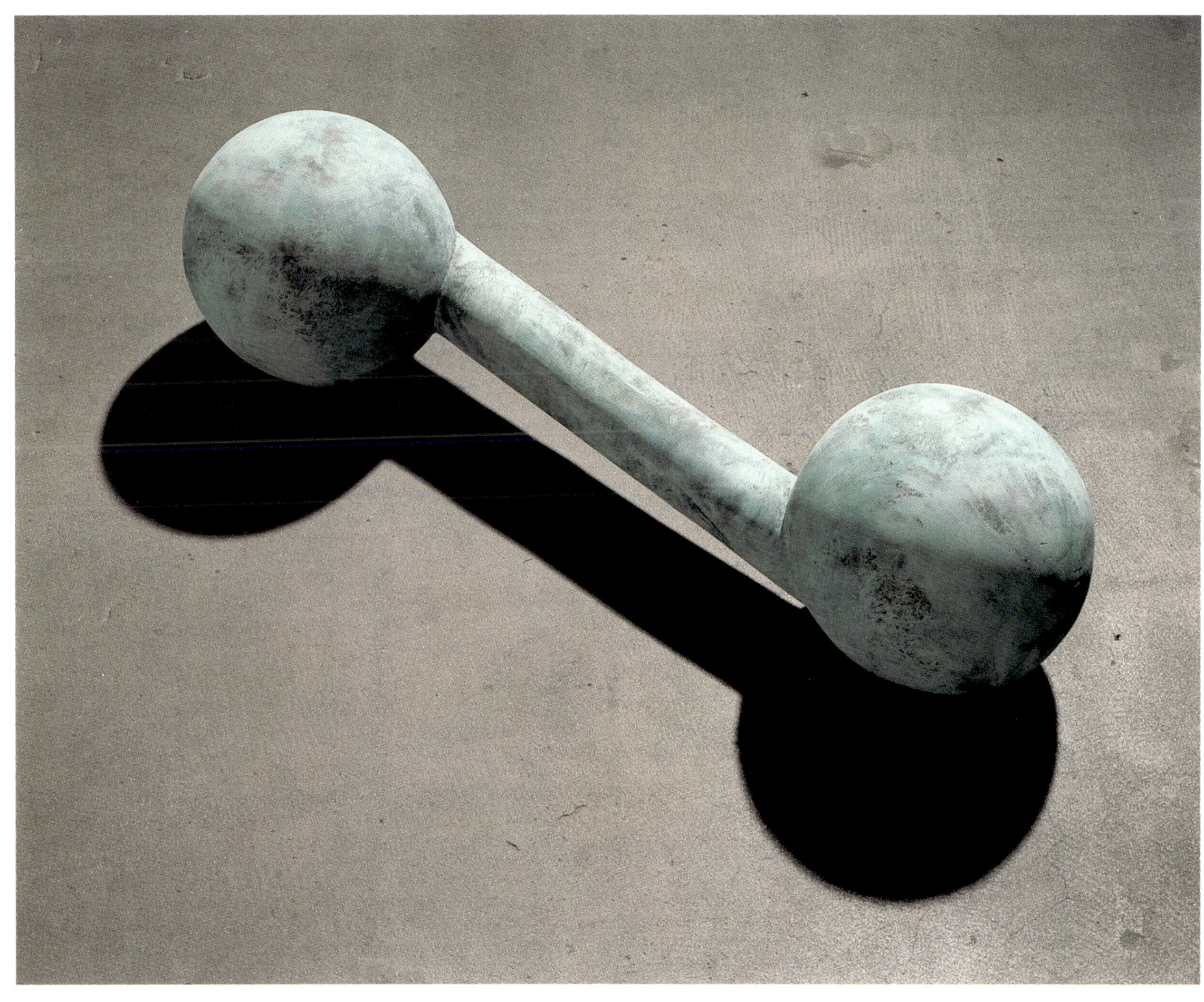

Bone Heads, 1990, cast bronze, 10 x 16 x 40½ inches, (94.60)

Gregory Mahoney's carved shapes of rusted steel, washes of alkaline salt, and sharp bursts of cobalt blue originate from his intimate relationship with the diverse California landscape, which includes forest, mountains, ocean, and desert. Mahoney's primary interest lies in Southern California's Death Valley, which provides both inspiration and a rich source of building materials. Influenced by the Earth Artists of the 1970s including Robert Smithson and Michael Heizer, who took their artistic practice out of the studio and into the land, Mahoney turned his attention to the landscape early in his career and has been drawing upon it ever since.

His chief material is steel, a manufactured product of the most common metal on earth, iron. By choosing such an abundant natural resource, Mahoney's work is inextricably linked to the earth's composition. To further emphasize this relationship he works with gritty, reddish, oxidized steel that has been subjected to the harsh environs of the desert, rather than newly manufactured, shiny steel. Often he employs materials already found in this condition, but Mahoney also places pieces of steel within the environment knowing that they will oxidize, rust, and develop a rich patina. *Deconstructing Pacific* (1992) begins with a rusted steel base that Mahoney has cut into consecutive crescents intended to mimic a divided and flattened globe. On this base continents are rendered with a mixture of sediment and cement, and the

Pacific Ocean is composed with a wash of alkaline salts from Death Valley. It is these natural elements that comprise Mahoney's palette; only when he needs to render sky or water, as in *In The Pacific (Blue)* (1992), does he use paint—always cobalt blue.

Death Valley, located on the eastern border of south-central California, is the lowest, hottest, and driest region in the Western Hemisphere. About 5,000 years ago, the valley floor was occupied by a shallow lake that has since evaporated leaving only traces of its existence in the form of a white glimmering salt pan. Nearly 550 square miles of Death Valley lie below sea level, and the lowest point on land in the Western hemisphere, at 282 feet below sea level, falls within the area near Badwater, California. Mahoney's two-dimensional sculpture, *Sea Level/Bad Water* (1991) charts the section of the valley that is below sea level. This mapping creates a beautiful shape, eerily reminiscent of the banks of an unknown sea. A more literal interpretation of this area is manifest in *Sea Level* (1991), which is Mahoney's rusted steel re-creation of the official national park sign.

Bad Water Periphery (1992) consists of four hard-edged squares which have formal parallels to the hard-edge abstraction of artists Ellsworth Kelly and Leon Polk Smith. However, this piece is referential and coolly understates the importance of the four coordinates (north, south, east, and west) as a means of surviving

GREGORY

mahoney

Sea Level, 1991, weathered steel, cement, alkali, and salt, 13¾ x 59⅝ inches, (94.61)

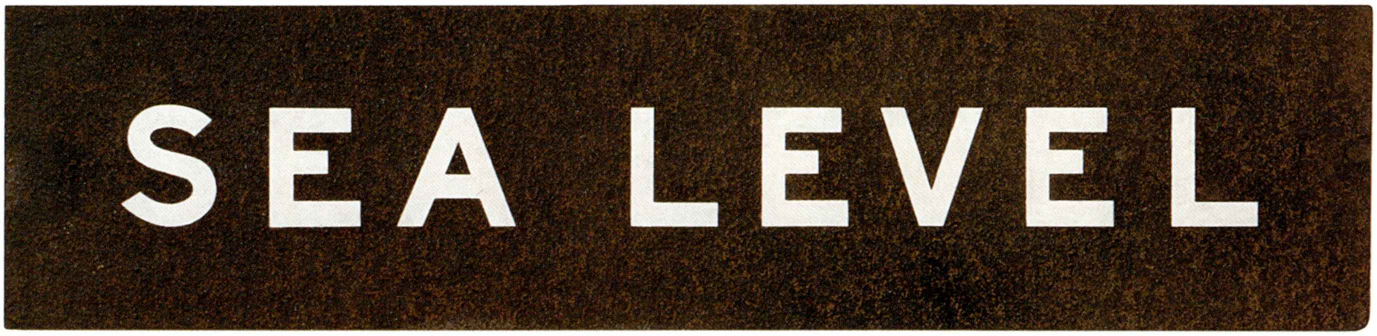

SEA LEVEL

one of the hottest and most unforgiving places on earth. To create *North (Constellation)* (1992), ball bearings that have been rendered useless with the addition of salt are installed into the wall in the shape of the Big Dipper and the Little Dipper. While generally appreciated for their beauty and mystery in the night sky, these constellations have also served as crucial mapping devices for millions of years.

In *Untitled (Time Study)* (1992), the earth is presented at twelve different points throughout its axial rotation. Mahoney's relationship with time falls outside of our day-to-day frame of reference; in his work, time both provides structure and operates metaphorically. Interested in sustained duration, conditional effects upon materials over time, and sites that have shifted monumentally over the earth's history, Mahoney takes into consideration the multifarious relationship human beings have to the natural landscape and the passage of days, seasons, years, or millennia. —R.M.

Sea Level/Bad Water, 1991, weathered steel, cement, alkali, and salt, 57½ x 13½ inches, (94.62)

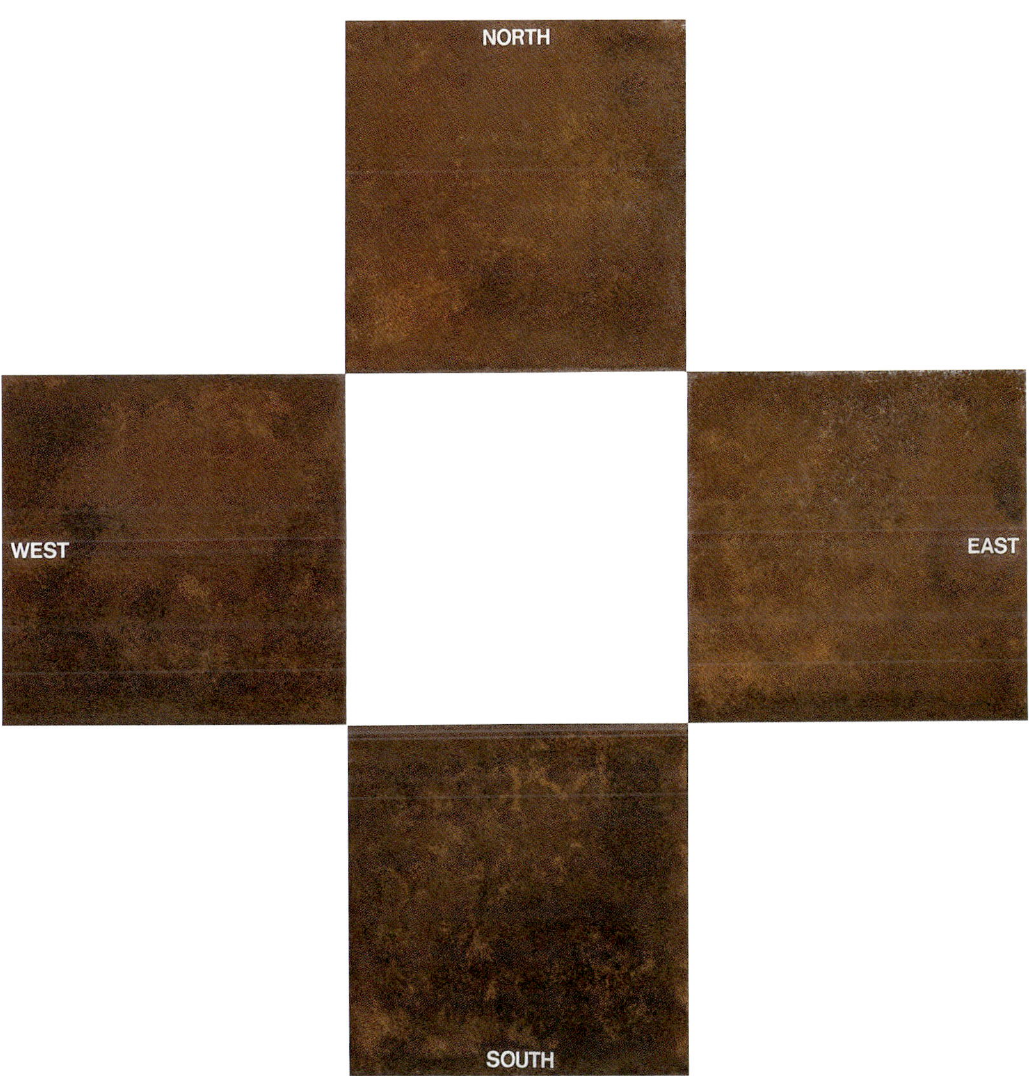

Bad Water Periphery, 1992, rusting steel, sediment, alkali, and salt, 69 x 69 inches, (94.66)

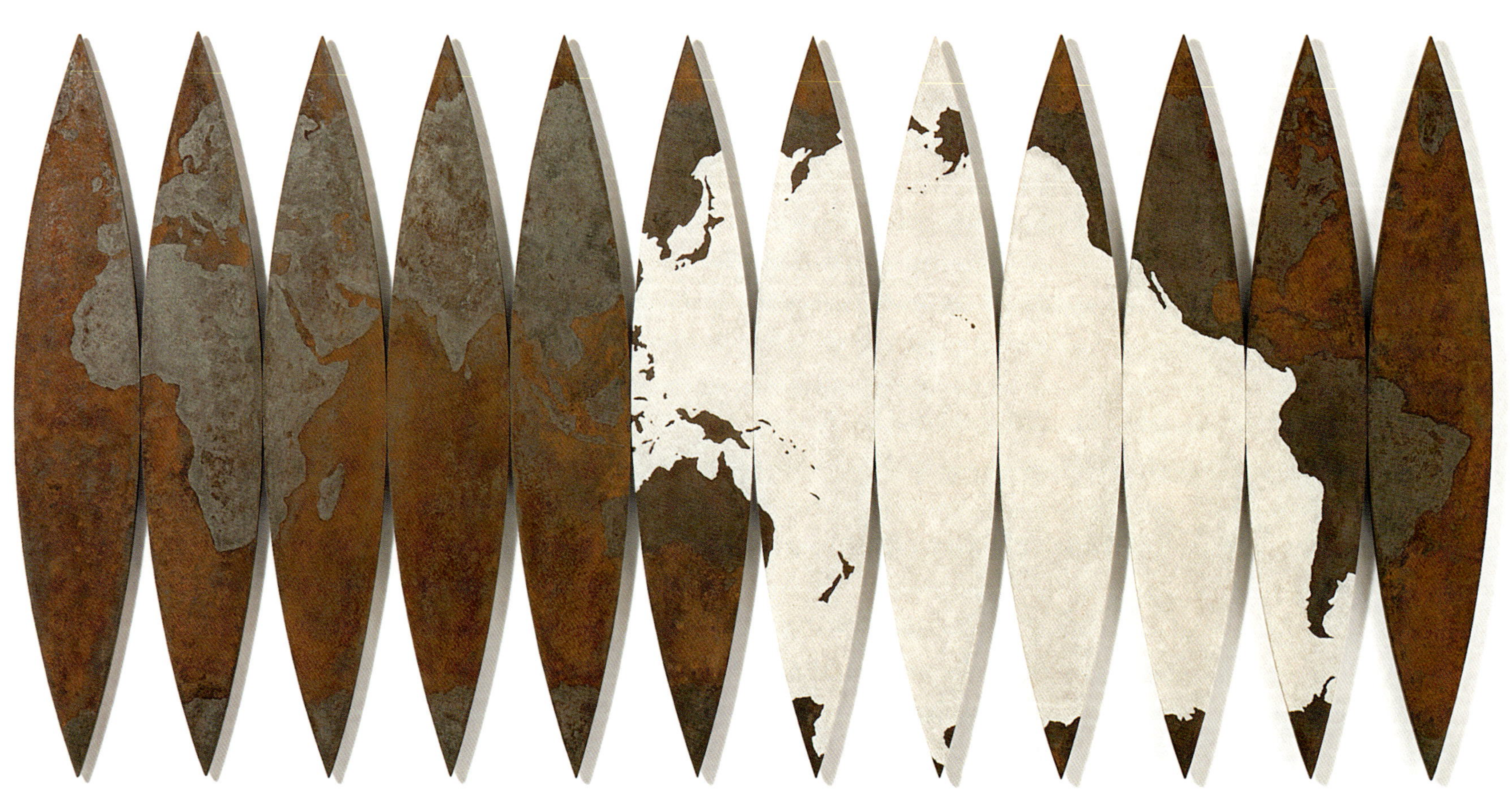

Deconstructing Pacific, 1992, rusting steel, cement, sediment, alkali, and salt, 46½ x 95½ inches, (94.65)

In The Pacific (Blue), 1992, formed steel, oil paint, pumice, and pigment, 31 inches diameter x 4 inches, (94.67)

North (Constellation), 1992, fourteen bearings filled with salt, dimensions variable, (94.63)

Untitled (Time Study), 1992, found steel, oil paint, alkali, and salt, 18 x 98 x 3½ inches, (94.64)

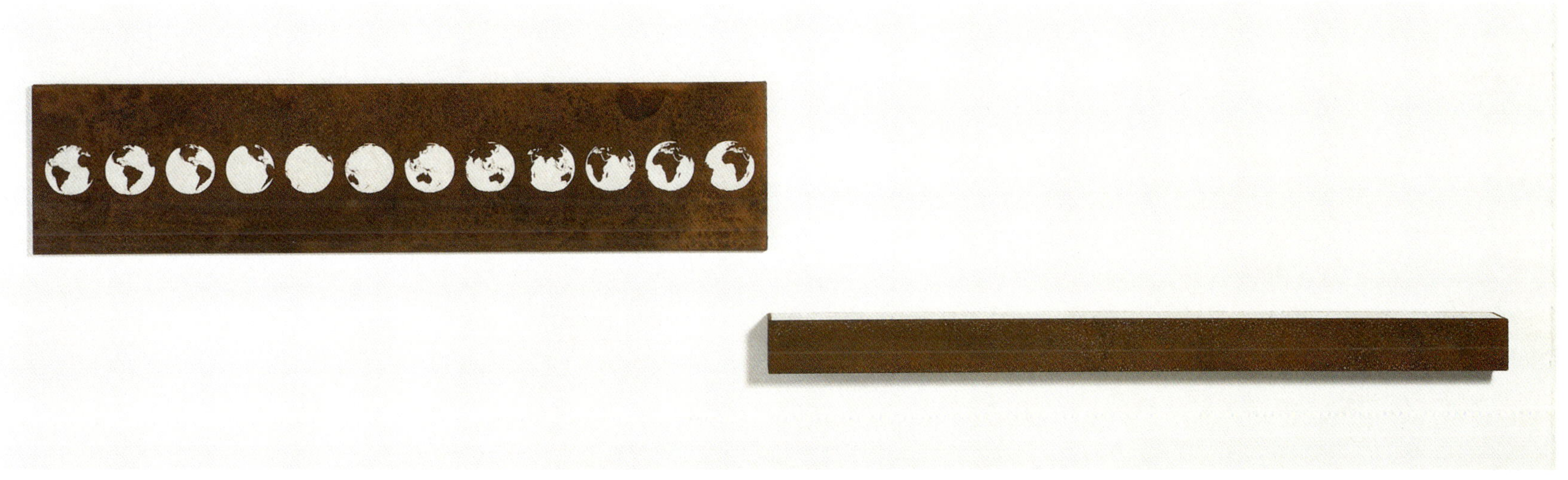

The organic sculptures of Ross Rudel emerge from the wall and slink across the floor, subtly and deliberately occupying the space that surrounds them. These soft, smooth, and rounded forms are contrary to the vocabulary of the hard-edged cube that so dominated sculptural production of the 1960s. Together with Charles Simonds and Carole Seborovski, Rudel's work has been aligned with the body-art genre of sculpture making and has been described as "erotic abstraction."[1] His anthropomorphic forms, although anatomically ambiguous, are corporeal and sensual. His interest in primordial forms with sleek and glossy surfaces also reflects an extension of modernist sculptural ideas explored earlier in this century by Constantin Brancusi.

Many pieces in Rudel's oeuvre embody his interest in variations on the form of the sphere. Mounted on the wall, these shapes appear to emerge from the vertical planes that support them, blurring the figure/ground relationship and activating the surrounding wall space as part of the sculptural whole. *Untitled No. 108 (Black)* (1992) is a solid black sphere that shines with polished luster from its perch upon the wall. Covered with a textured fabric and painted over in a flat white, *Untitled No. 115 (White)* (1992) is a slightly smaller sphere with a visibly patterned and tactilely exotic surface. The same expanding, bulbous shape is echoed in Rudel's *Untitled No. 107* (1992); here, however, a deep and narrowly sloping orifice erupts from just below the middle section of the creamy white orb. This ominous opening appears unsteady, supple, and strangely capable of expansion.

Rudel's sculptures are alive with harnessed potential energy. *Untitled No. 129* (1993) is a curvilinear dowel upon which dark wooden spheres and lightly colored separators have been stacked. It extends aggressively from the wall and challenges the surrounding space. A variation on this form is manifest in *Untitled No. 126* (1993), a black columnar sculpture made of large spheres and separating partitions; it too projects challengingly into the viewer's space. Spreading out along the floor, *Untitled No. 132* (1993) is a series of wooden pods, encased in nylon stockings, that appears to be dividing, blossoming, and growing in numbers. Each of these works moves the eye around and beyond its structural form, as we are led to consider the work's interaction with, and activation of, its encompassing space.

The sensuality and inherent motion of Rudel's sculptures are facilitated in part by the artist's choice of materials. He uses carved wood as the core of all of his sculptures, enabling him to mine the organic and animate quality inherent to this natural resource. Energy exudes from these luscious bodily forms, masquerading as living and breathing organisms with a sensuality that has been momentarily contained. —R.M.

ROSS
rudel

1 Suzanne Ramljak, "The Art of Seduction: Suzanne Ramljak Makes a Case for Erotic Abstraction," *Sculpture* 14, no. 5 (September–October 1995), 32–33.

Untitled (Pole), 1986, stained wood, 68 x 3¼ x 3¼ inches, (94.68)

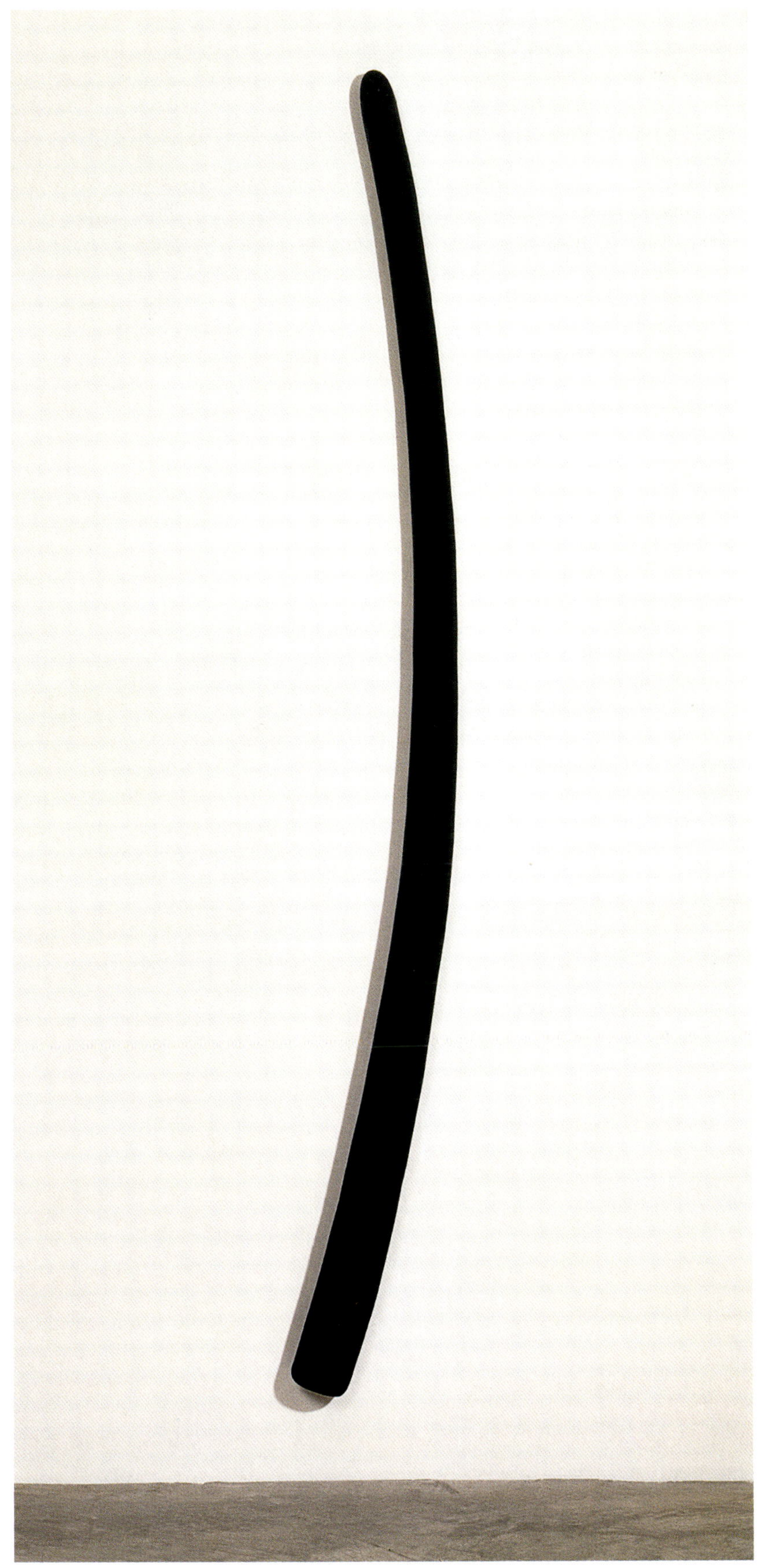

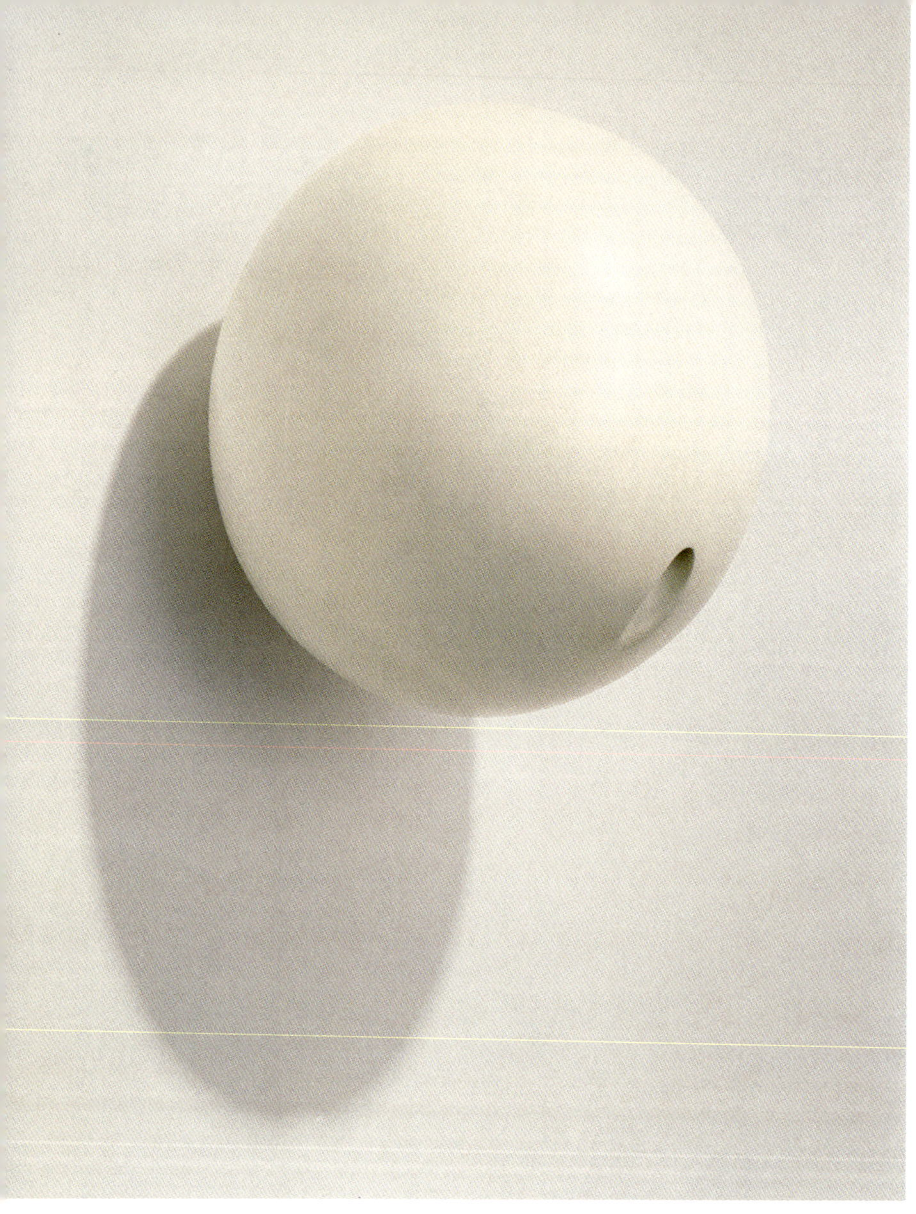

Untitled No. 107, 1992, enamel on wood, 13 x 10½ x 13 inches, (94.69)

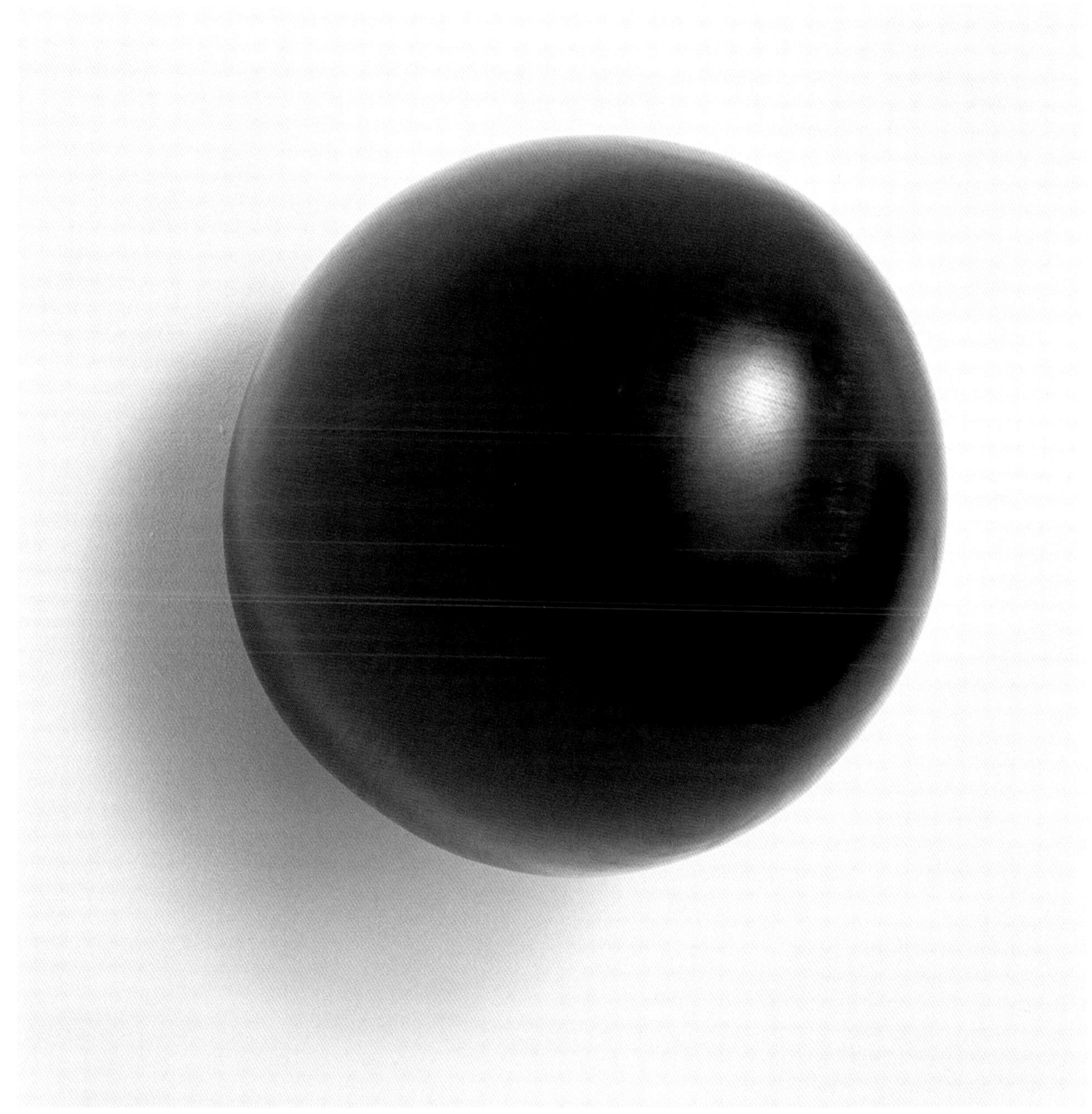

Untitled No. 108 (Black), 1992, stained wood, 14 x 14 x 15 inches, (94.70)

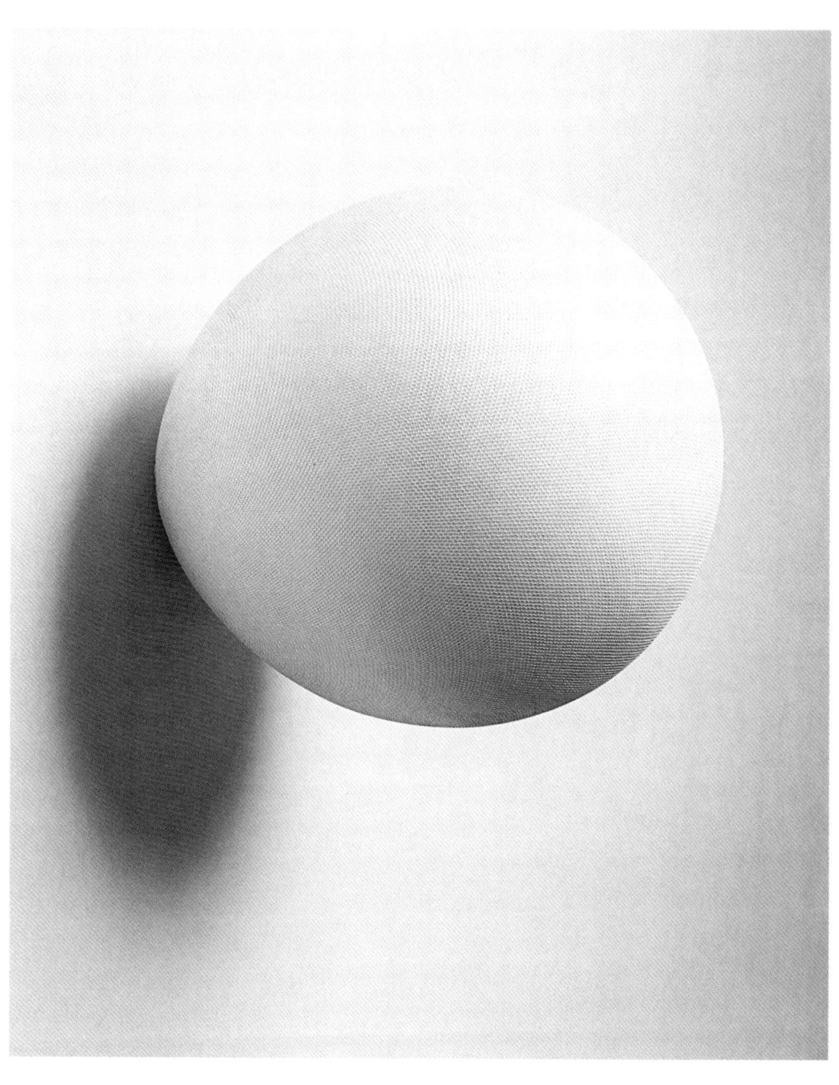

Untitled No. 115 (White), 1992, wood, fabric, and enamel, 11 x 11 x 12½ inches, (94.71)

Untitled No. 126, 1993, stained wood, 7 x 7 x 20 inches, (94.74)

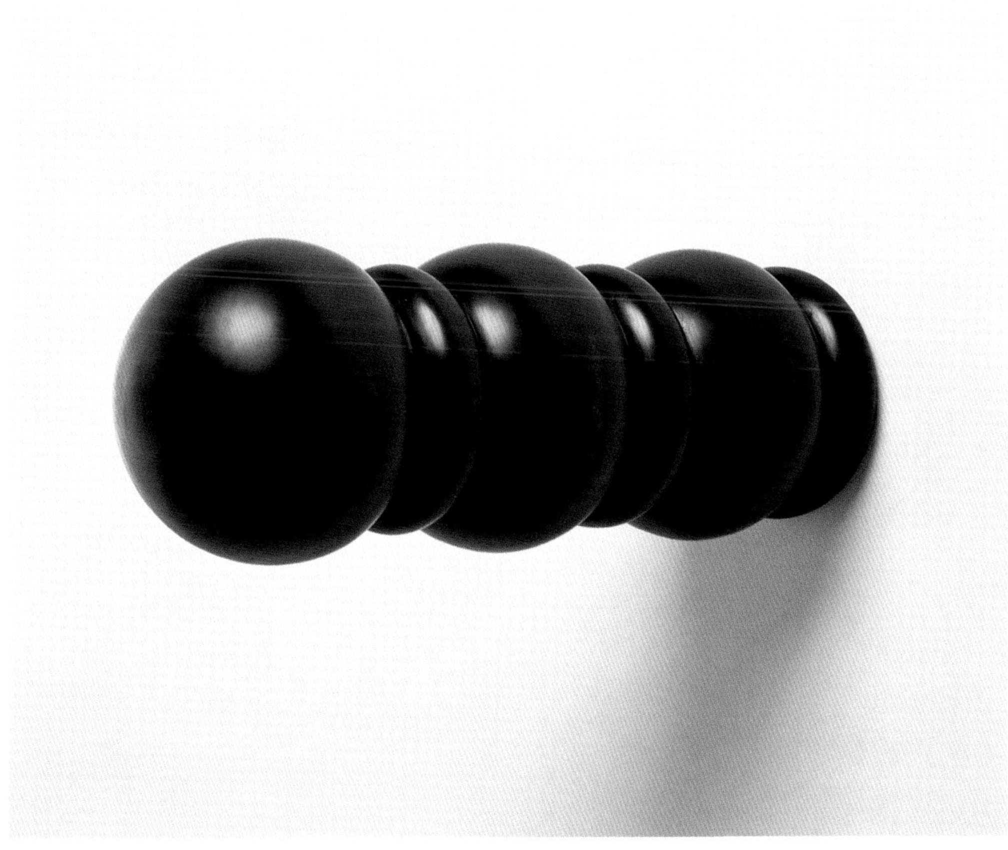

Untitled No. 129, 1993, wood, nylon stocking, resin, and adjustable steel rod, 8 x 80 x 90 inches, (94.73)

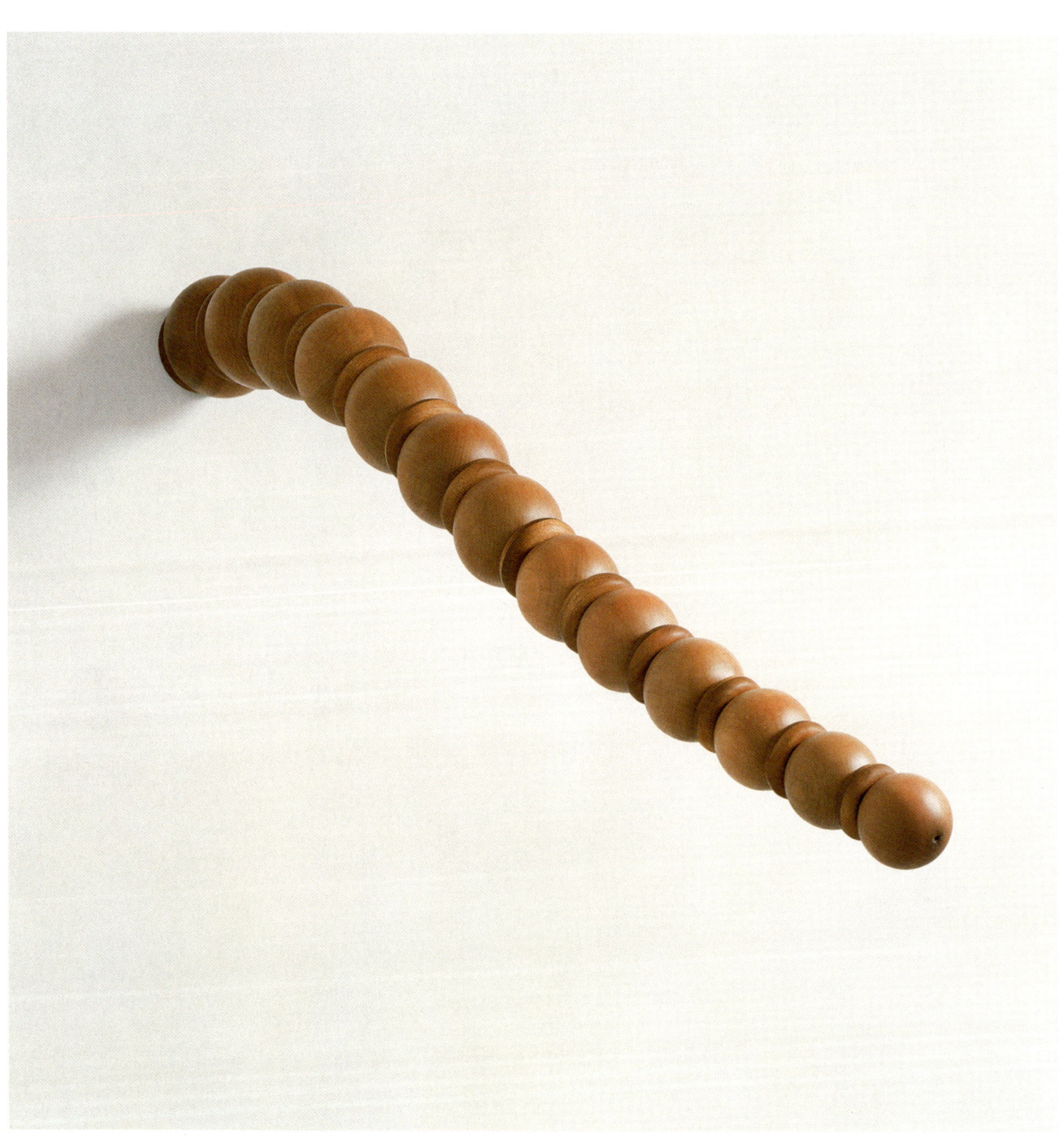

Untitled No. 132, 1993, wood, nylon stocking, resin, steel rings, and wire, 105 x 13 x 5 inches, (94.72)

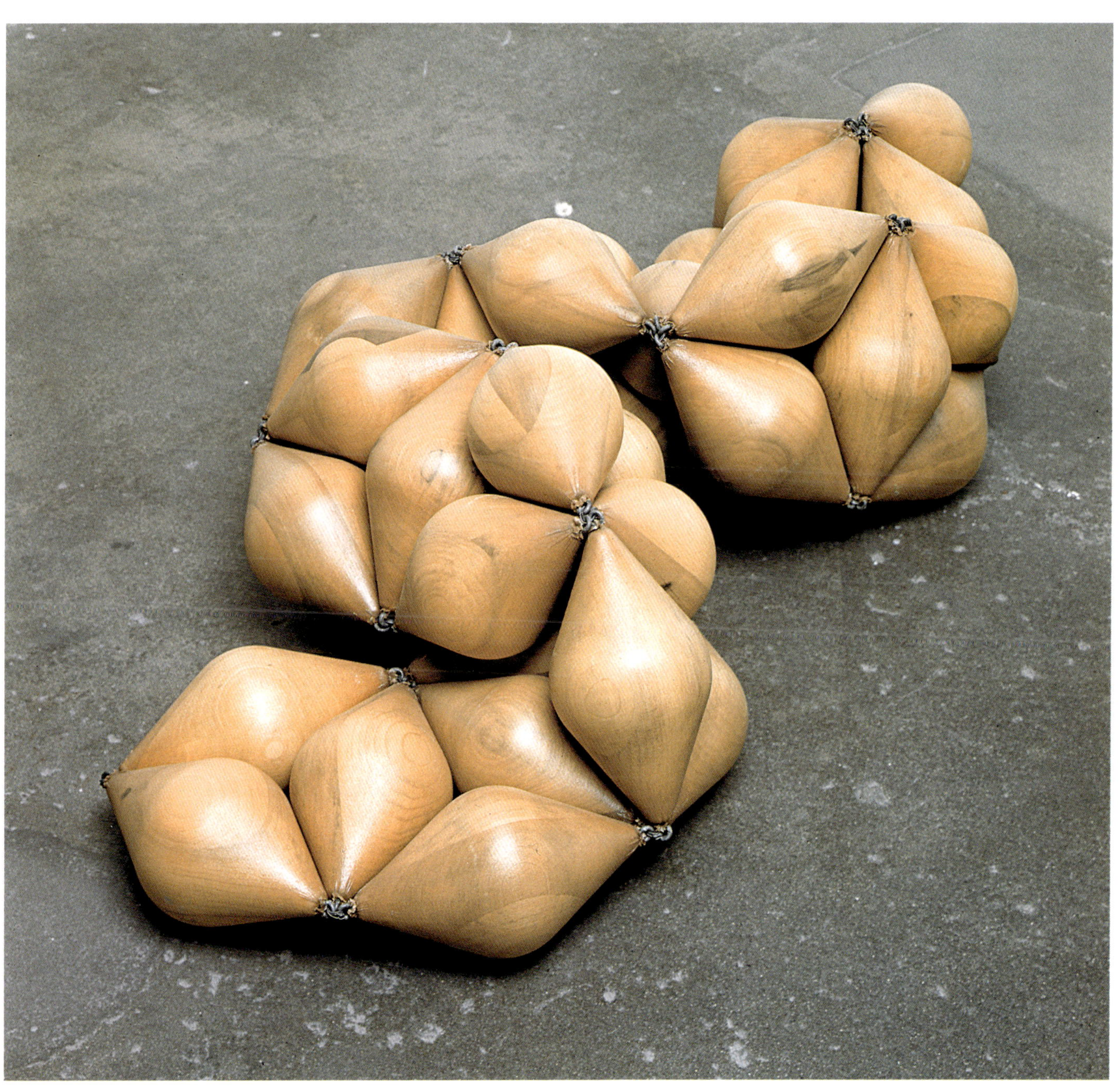

As singular sculptural works or parts of a larger whole, Peter Shelton's oversized objects and suspended forms reach out from the wall, hang from the ceiling, and glide above the floor. Using the traditional materials of sculpture, including iron, bronze, and wax, Shelton's objects, and their combination, set up spatial anomalies that call into question both the surrounding space and its occupants.

The sculpture *bigfeet* (1985–90), which currently stands alone, originally existed as a component of the monumental installation *floatinghouseDEADMAN,* made for exhibition at the gallery of the University of Massachusetts at Amherst in 1985. In this work the abstracted feet behaved as counterweights or "deadmen" to a full-scale Japanese-style house made from paper and wood. Attached to this structure, along with other objects, these sculptural weights counterbalanced the house and allowed it to hover several inches above the gallery floor. This multi-faceted, three-dimensional arrangement actively blurred the boundaries between sculpture and architecture by weighing one against the other and erasing the divide.

In a different manner from the traditional sculptural portrayal of the human figure, Shelton's investigation focuses on those objects that cover, envelop, and hide the body or otherwise exemplify ideas of weight and mass, and presence and absence of form. Rather than rendering the curve of a bare arm or the slope of a neck three-dimensionally, Shelton creates exoskeletal outlines or armatures that take the form of exaggerated capes, gloves, and blouses, as in *ironmitts* (1986), *bmantle* (1987–89), and *onelongsleeve* (1988–89). These objects belie the seeming inflexibility of their materials by appearing soft, supple, and eerily alive. They allude to the negative space that takes shape in midair, and ultimately it is the viewer's imagination that creates the neck, hands, and torso to which these structures so eloquently refer.

The relationship between vessels and conduits is an underlying theme that runs throughout Shelton's sculptural work. This focus speaks to an interest in the way in which energy, water, or ideas are channeled among various holding cells, gaining momentum and leading to disintegration. This issue reverberates through *copperneck* (1986–89), *TUBEpipe* (1986–88), and *CURVEDTUBEbentpipe* (1989), where the pipes and vessels actually suggest plumbing and metaphorically allude to passage. A more literal translation of these ideas is realized in Shelton's large installation *thingsgetwet* where many of the objects, ranging from stacks of books to a scattering of teeth, are bathed in water that flows from small, carefully placed pipes. The incorporation of this natural element is meant to "challenge the materiality and certainty of the object"[1] and allude to the eventual disintegration of organic materials.

PETER

shelton

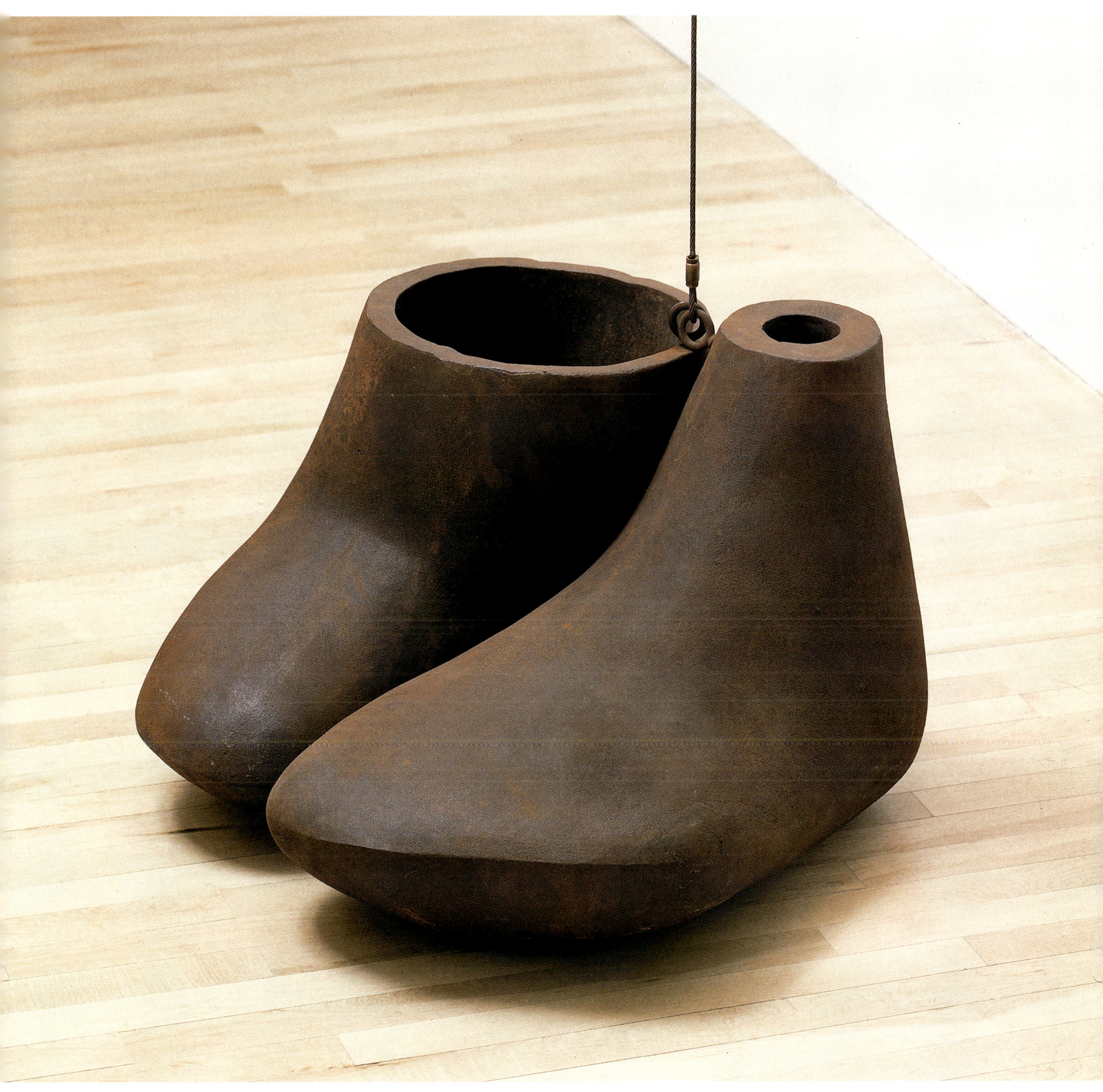

bigfeet, 1985–90, cast iron, ed. ⅔, 16 x 18 x 22 inches, (94.79)

There is an open-ended, narrative element intrinsic
to Shelton's work that clearly reveals his own reaction to
the canon of Minimalism and also his relationship to
a particularly idiosyncratic history of West Coast sculpture, which includes figures as diverse as Bruce Conner
and Mowry Baden. Having studied briefly with environmental artists Robert Irwin and James Turrell at Pomona
College in the early 1970s, Shelton is also aligned with
those artists who were interested in spatial presence
and the physicality of light. The way in which an object
might effect the viewer was a key concern to these
artists and an impetus for the progressively more anthropomorphic objects created by Shelton. In an effort to
imbue objects with human content, he departs drastically
from the pure abstract forms of his Minimalist predecessors. Intellectually paired with Bruce Nauman and
Joel Shapiro, and formally akin to Alberto Giacometti and
Louise Bourgeois, Shelton's consideration of weight,
presence, and space makes an ideal arena for the emergence of a compelling and flexible narrative. —R.M.

1 Carol S. Eliel, "An Armature for Our Desires,"
in *Peter Shelton: bottlesbonesandthingsgetwet*,
exh. cat. (Los Angeles: Los Angeles County Museum of Art, 1994), 31.

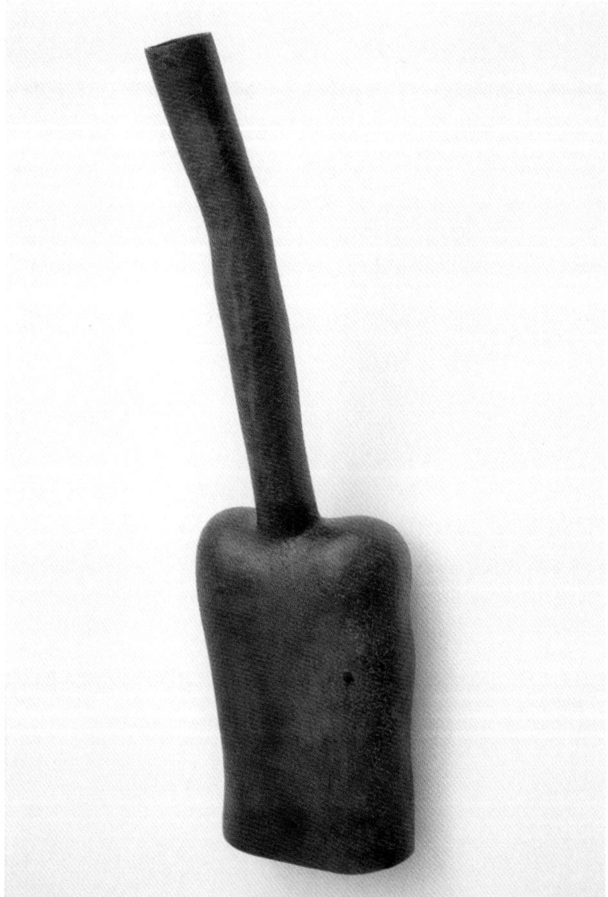

copperneck, 1986–89, bronze, 54 x 16 x 21 inches, (94.81)

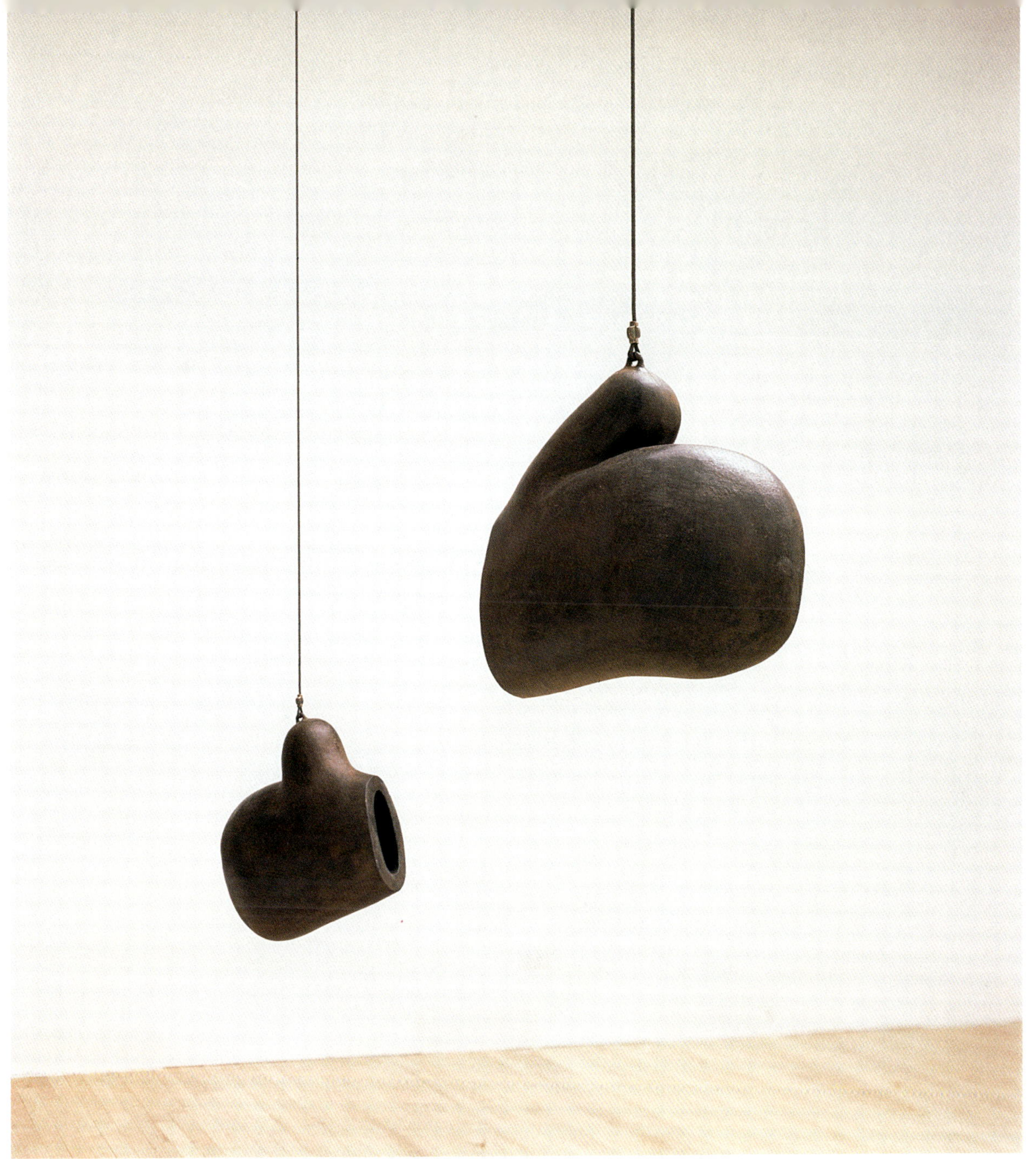

ironmitts, 1986, cast iron, two pieces: 13 x 13 x 5 inches and 12 x 11½ x 7 inches, (94.80)

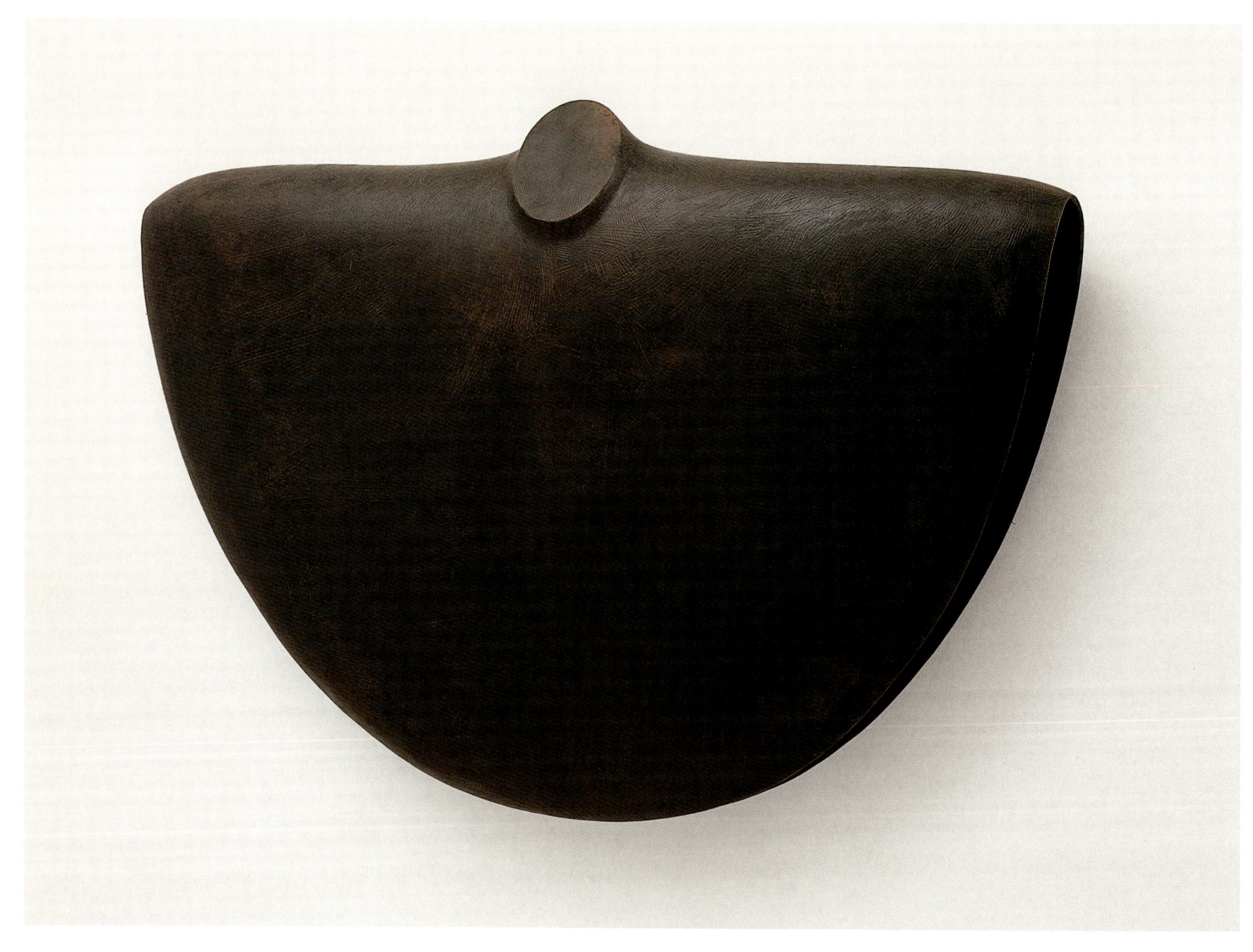

bmantle, 1987–89, bronze, 37½ x 47½ x 5½ inches, (94.78)

CURVEDTUBEbentpipe, 1989, cast bronze, 46½ x 90 x 20½ inches overall, (94.76)

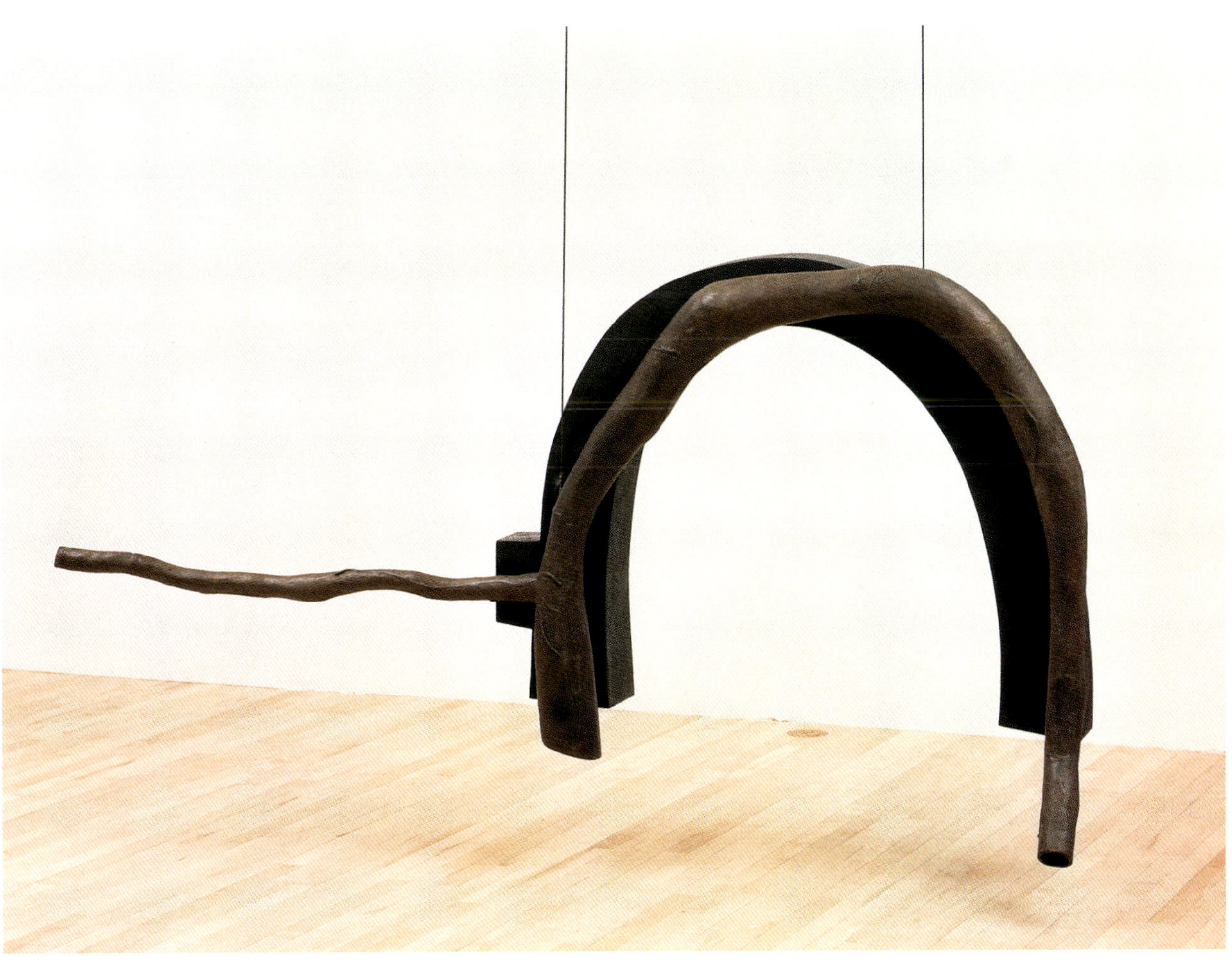

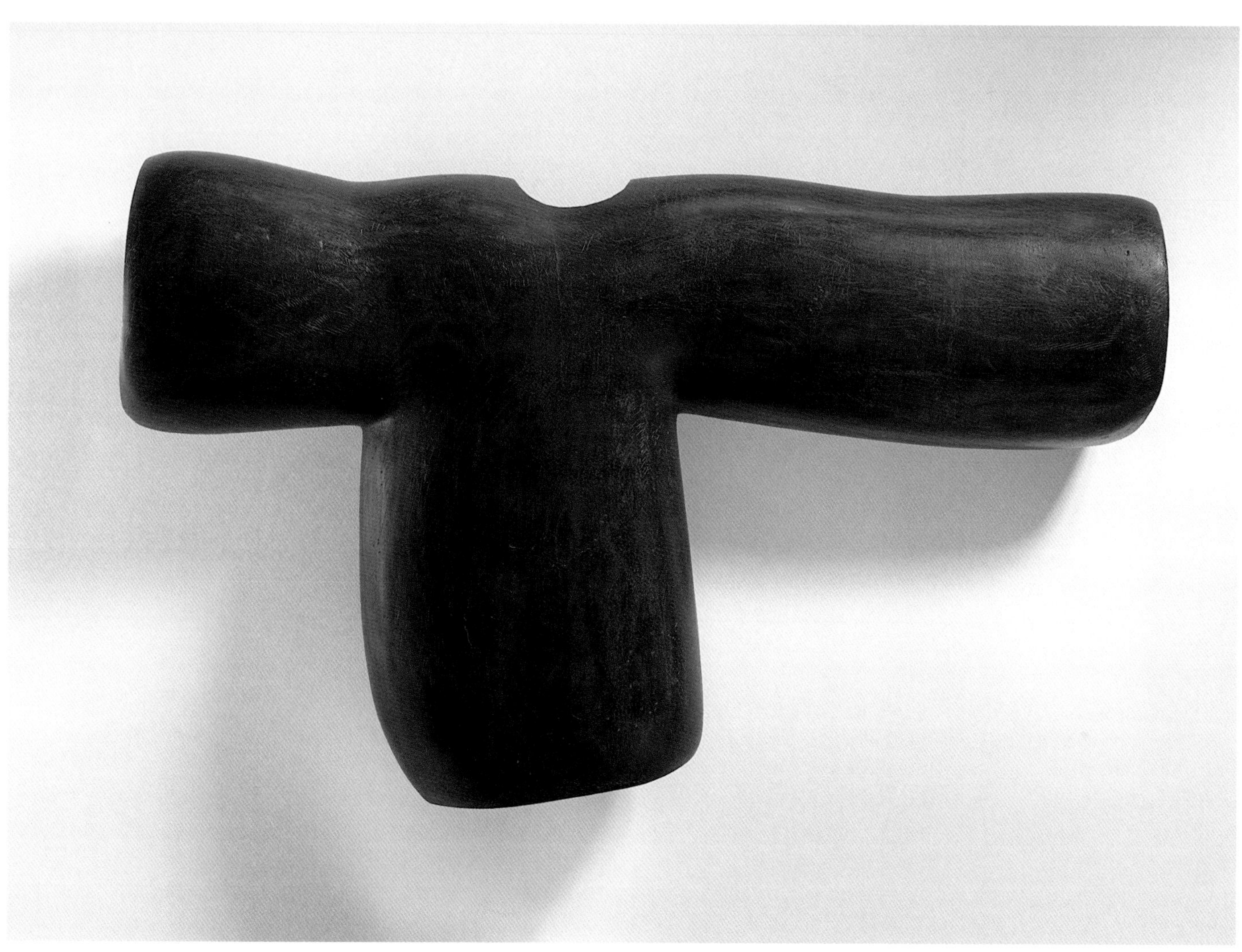

onelongsleeve, 1988–89, cast copper, 28 x 47½ x 8 inches, (94.75)

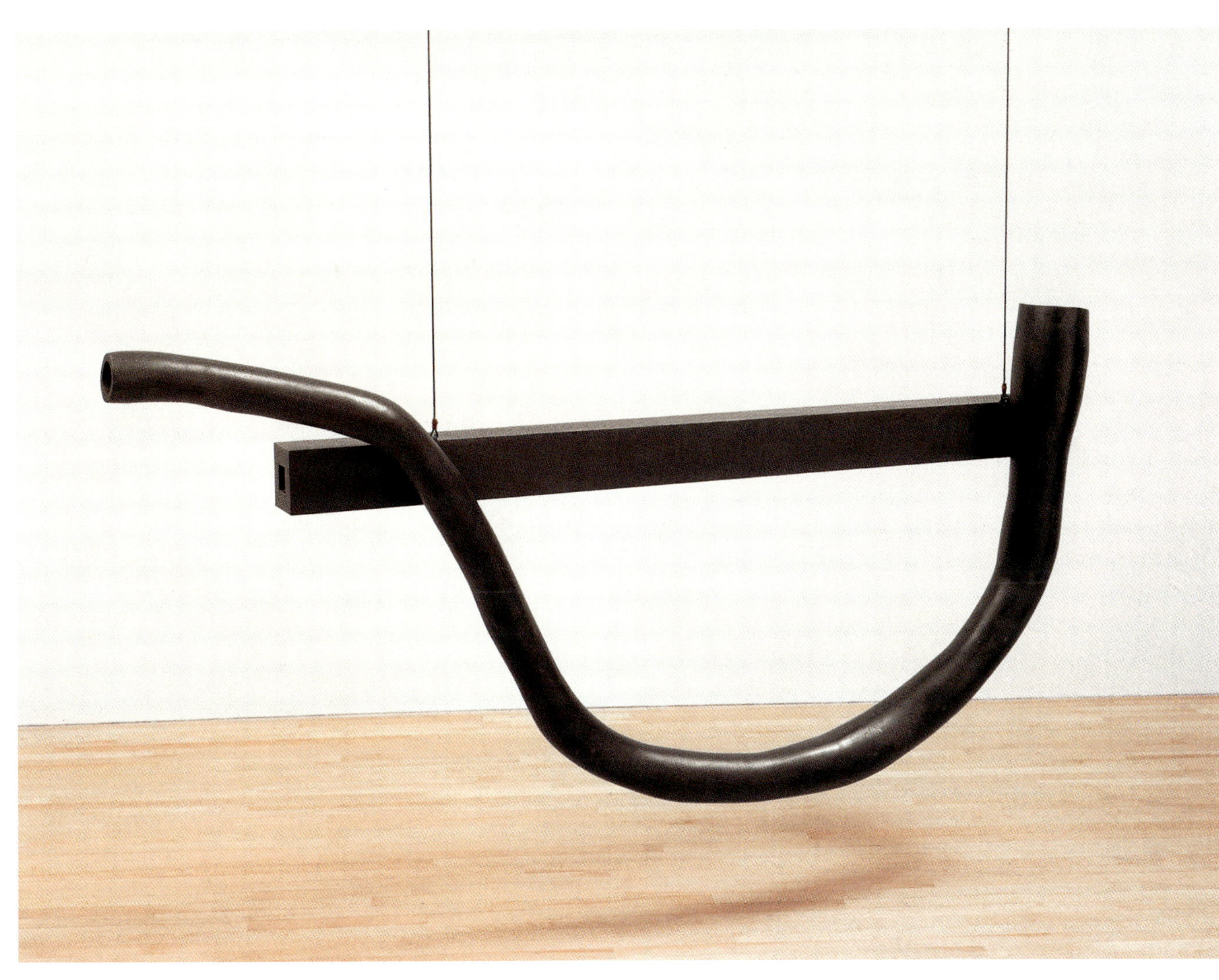

TUBEpipe, 1986–88, cast iron and steel, 38 x 85 x 11 inches, (94.77)

In the early 1970s Robert Therrien emerged as a sculptor whose work repudiated the stylistic principles of Minimalism that had dominated art production of the previous decade. Exemplified by the works of Carl Andre and Donald Judd, Minimalist artists sought to explore abstraction by creating extremely simplified shapes and surfaces that were deliberately neutral and void of any external associations. Therrien and his post-Minimalist contemporaries such as Joel Shapiro and Richard Tuttle executed three-dimensional objects that departed from the reductive vocabulary of Minimalist sculpture. Influenced in part by the sensuality of Claes Oldenburg's early soft sculptures, the post-Minimalists created simplified formal objects that were referential, emotional, and affective.

Therrien creates, and sometimes repeats, shapes that develop out of his own experience and sensibility. *No Title* (1988) (109½ x 34½ x 44½") formally resembles a set of Dutch doors similar to a pair at his grandfather's house that had intrigued him as a child.[1] Recalling the balanced interplay between the perpendicular forms, Therrien set out to recreate the shapes based on his childhood memory. The psychological and often surrealistic possibilities inherent in domestic objects is a theme that has been explored by other sculptors, such as American artist Robert Gober and British artist Rachel Whiteread. While Therrien's primary interest lies in the object's contour, his work is far from pure abstraction— each piece hangs in the balance between the representational and the conceptual.

Throughout his career, Therrien has utilized a variety of compelling shapes that are consistently part of his sculptural vocabulary. This fact complicates the chronology of his oeuvre because any imagery, contour, or form might be recycled or reinvented at any time. Take *No Title* (1982) (61 x 23¾ x 24"), *No Title* (1988) (89 x 40 x 40"), *No Title* (1988) (73 x 31¼ x 31¼") and *No Title* (1988) (20 x 47¼ x 37"), for example. Made over the course of six years, each of these four works has a similar keystone shape, but differs dramatically in size. Architecturally this shape is the central wedge of an arch that structurally locks its parts together, and is metaphorically the central supporting element of a whole. This variation on a theme is reminiscent of Minimalism's interest in serial production, a strategy that is further enhanced by Therrien's coy evasion of the naming process. By avoiding titles, each piece subverts its own status as an individual masterpiece and instead augments a body of work that is in constant flux.

Therrien's interest in tone and surface is an integral part of his production. He rigorously seeks out a complimentary color for each shape and often applies it repeatedly, among layers of material and pigment, to yield the desired muted exterior. The luminosity of his

No Title, 1982, oil and wax on wood, 61 x 23¾ x 24 inches, (94.85)

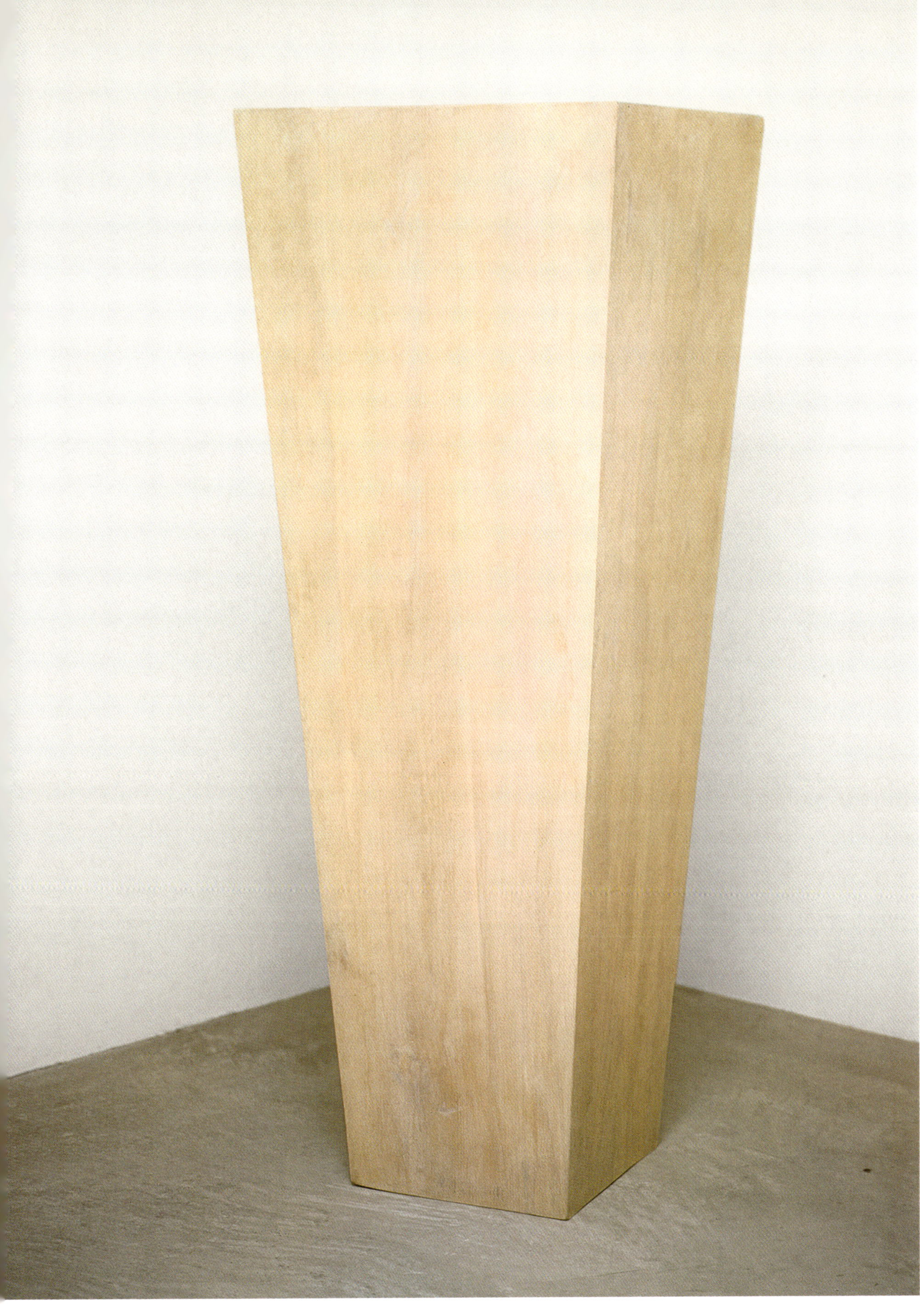

surfaces creates a tranquility that is compelling and provocative. *No Title* (1986) (41 x 46 x 13½") and *No Title* (1986–87) (41 x 46 x 13½") are both rectangular objects adorned with metallic bells along the bottom edge. However, although the two pieces have the same dimensions and are rendered with the same medium, subtle differences reveal that they are not exact replicas of each other, but unique objects.

While Therrien's attention to surface is particular to painting, and his works are often hung on the wall as such, the spatial complexity of his work is akin to the challenges of sculpture. Ideally installed with particular attention to the complex interaction between works hung alone on the wall and those placed upon the floor, the works are not routinely placed at eye level, but at varying heights determined by the individual work's size and intended association. The intrinsic duality between Therrien's interests in surface and space makes it impossible to categorize his work as either painting or sculpture— rather, it is a sophisticated hybrid of the two. —R.M.

1 Margit Rowell, "Ordinary–Extraordinary: The Work of Robert Therrien," in *Robert Therrien*, exh. cat. (Madrid: Museo Nacional, Centro de Arte Reina Sofia, 1991), 16.

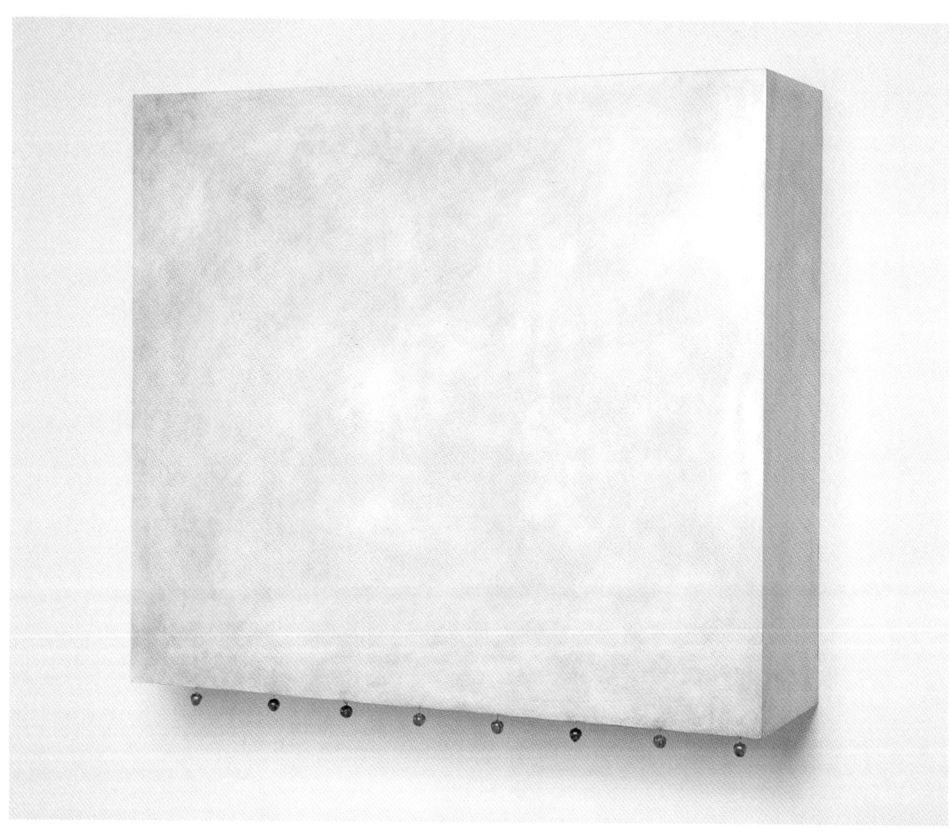

No Title, 1984–86, enamel on metal and silver on brass, 41 x 46 x 13½ inches, (94.84)

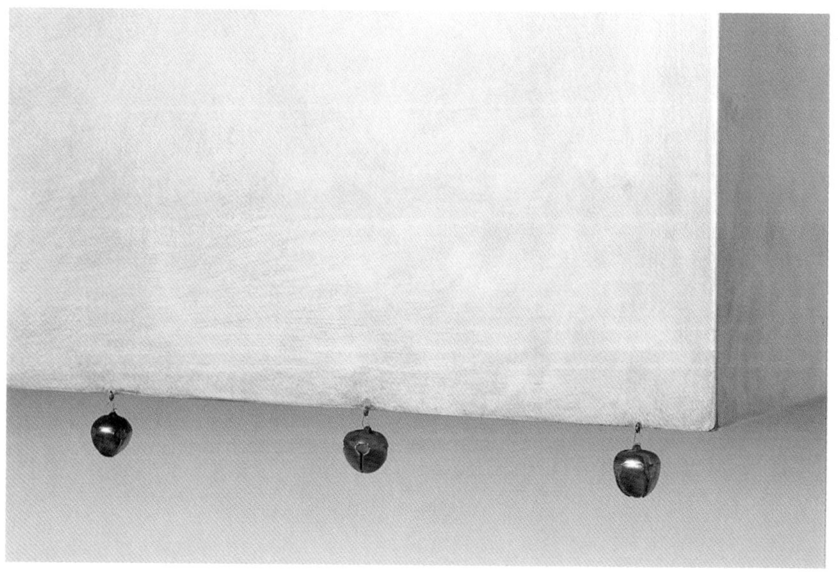

No Title, (detail)

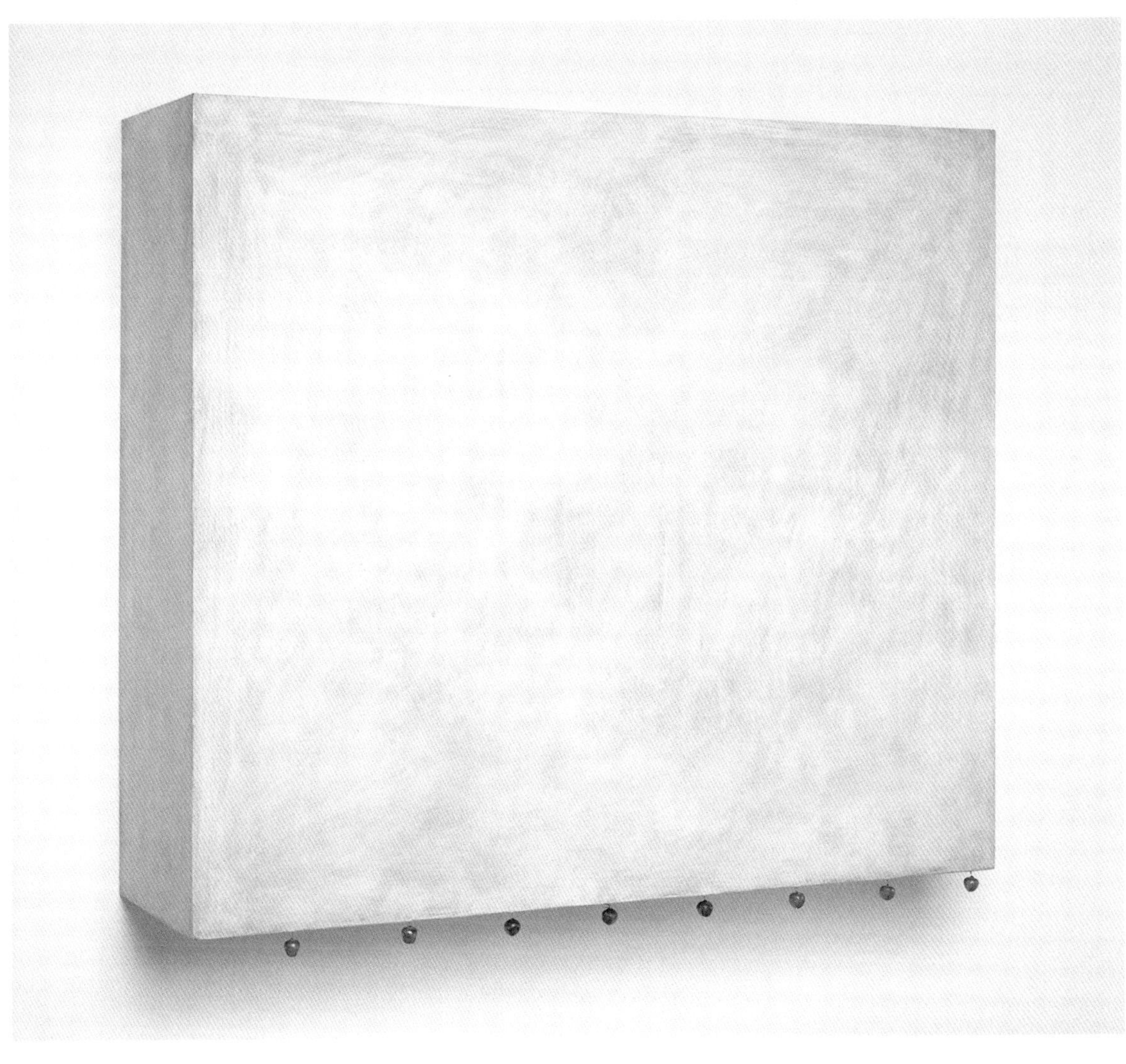

No Title, 1986–87, enamel on metal and silver on brass, 41 x 46 x 13½ inches, (94.86)

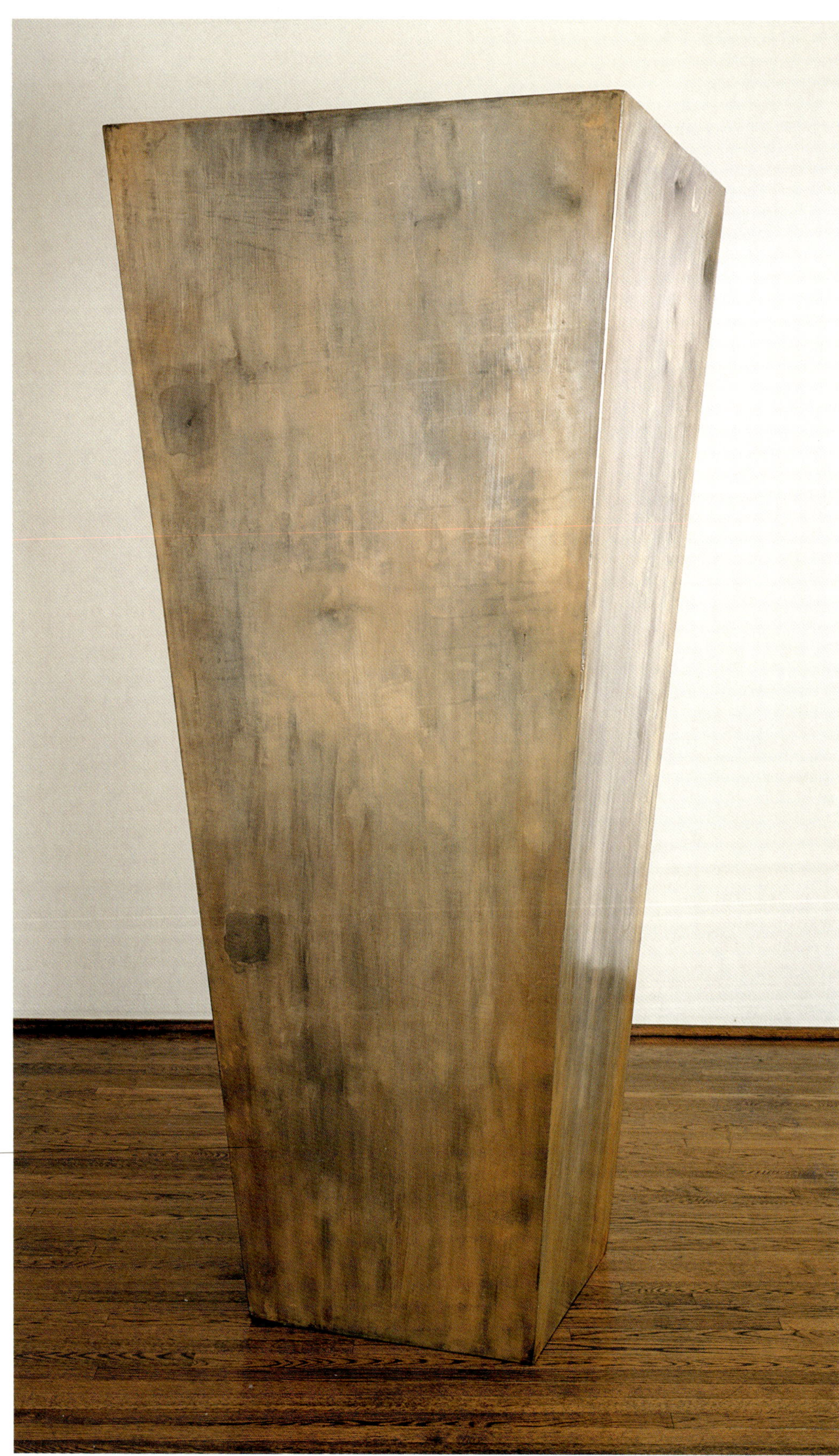

No Title, 1988, silver on bronze, 89 x 40 x 40 inches, (94.82)

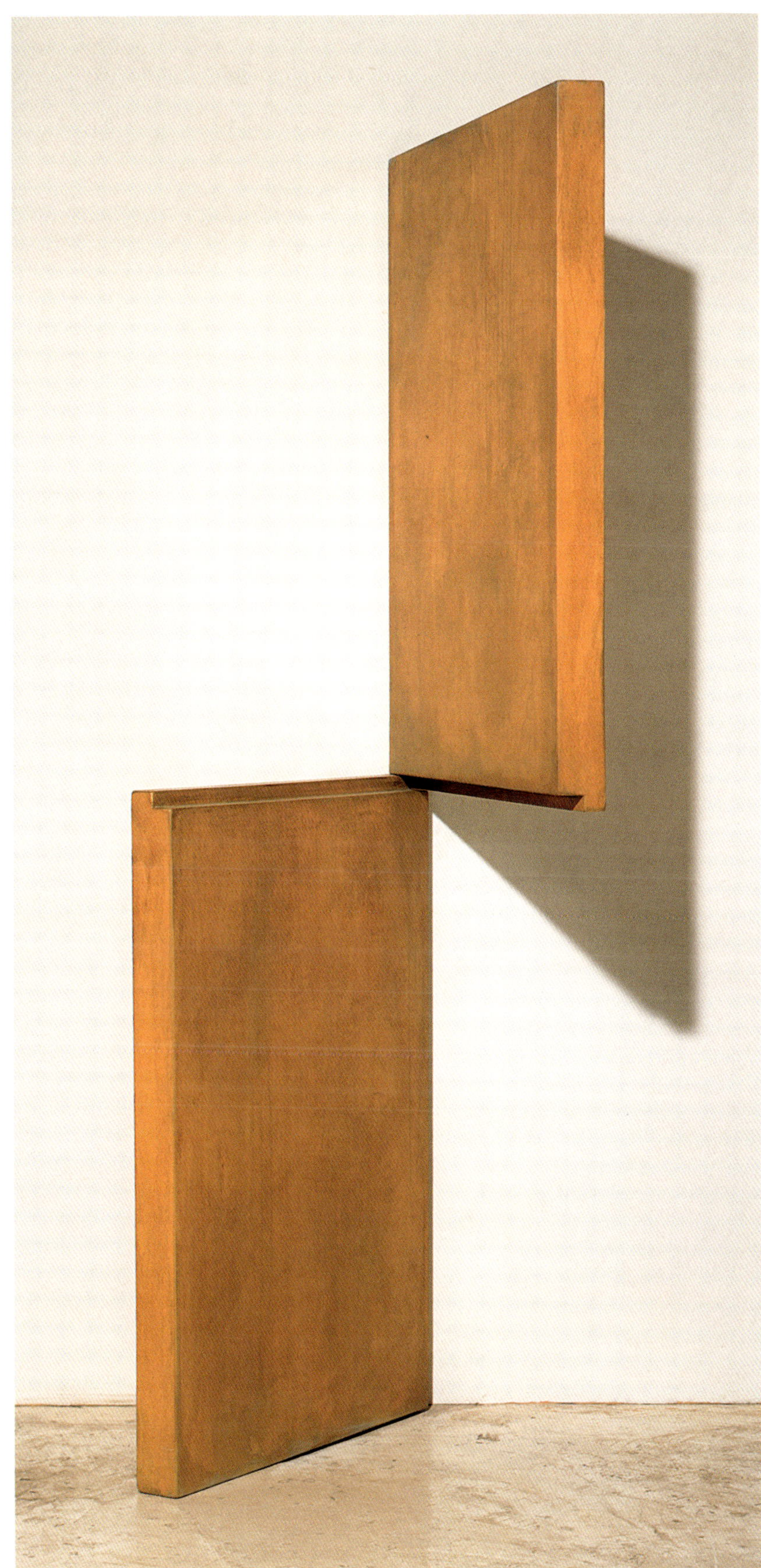

No Title, 1988, lacquer on wood, 109½ x 34½ x 44 inches, (94.83)

No Title, 1988, bronze and mixed media, 20 x 47¼ x 37 inches, (94.87)

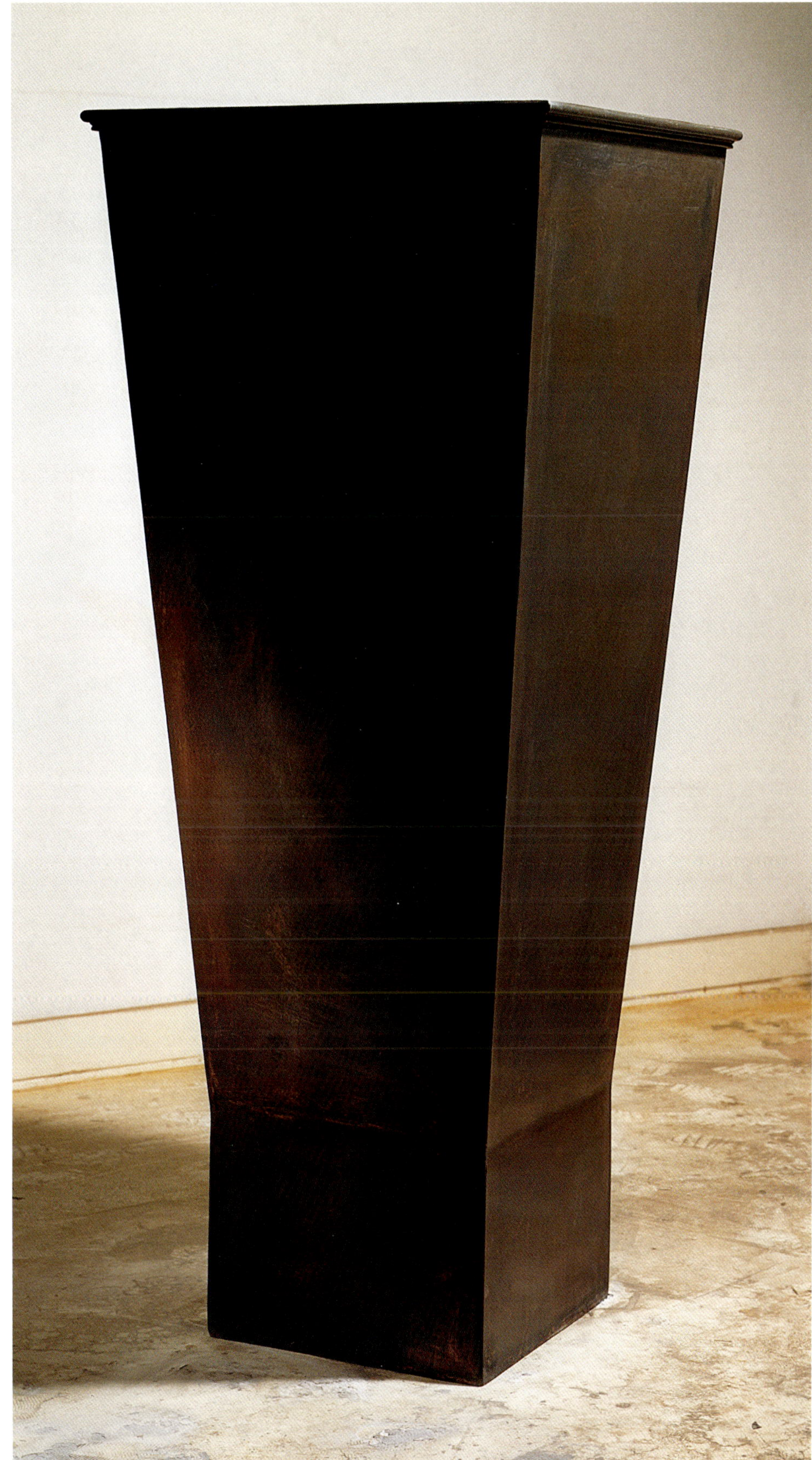

No Title, 1988, bronze and mixed media, 73 x 31¼ x 31¼ inches, (94.88)

Roy Thurston's rectangular wall pieces, though commanding in size, are quiet explorations in subtlety, reflection, and transformation. Their rich and even surfaces appear almost machine made, and consequently invoke notions of the two- and three-dimensional abstractions that dominated Los Angeles art in the mid-to-late 1960s. Known as the "Los Angeles look," this sculptural style was explored by such artists as Robert Irwin, Craig Kauffman, and John McCracken and is seen as Southern California's own hybrid of Minimalism's abstraction and the manufactured appearance of Pop art. While Thurston's work hovers between painting and sculpture, he actually emerged from the discipline of painting and remains interested in pushing and exploring the possibilities within the boundaries of that medium. He cites the influence of West Coast painters such as John McLaughlin whose "hard-edge" painting style is typically angular, balanced and, while restrained in palette, develops a great warmth.

Believing strongly in the apolitical nature of art and the idea that painting is not an effective political vehicle, Thurston's work relates to the interaction between his created objects and their surroundings. He states "the painting is not representational, it is actual. It becomes an area for the actual interaction of light and matter, the elucidation of simple phenomena."[1] Intended for domestic spaces in which the viewer can experience the work under varying light conditions and atmospheric moods, these pieces necessitate sustained exposure for ultimate comprehension. His approach to the painted surface is straightforward and begins with the application of multiple layers of lacquer upon smooth plywood or panel surfaces. On this plane he carefully incises grooves that vary in width, direction, and depth and span the entire length, width or portion of each painting. Created in numerous ways, these handmade marks differ slightly in appearance, from silky smooth lines to mottled excisions reflecting the speed in which they are carved and the tools used by the artist. However, the overall uniformity of marks conveys a highly linear and thus manufactured appearance.

In the piece *89–3* (1989) the grooves are subtle, but serve to catch and bend the light in just the right way to cause a slight shift in the color of the surface. Here the work's monochromatic nature, of which we are convinced from a distance, is challenged when the striations shimmer in a spectrum of blues from cerulean to cobalt. Equally vivid is *#R* (1988), its surface rich with layers of lacquer that fluctuate in sheen and hue depending upon the viewer's position. In this work graphite has been added to the lacquer giving the piece a metallic luster. Much like textiles, the tint, finish, and texture of which shift among various viewpoints, these pieces are not flat color planes, but multifarious amalgams of

ROY
thurston

#P, 1986, butyrate lacquer on birch plywood, 60 x 24 x ¾ inches, (94.90)

color, light, and reflection. Made with a certain type
of lacquer (chosen by Thurston due to its viscosity and
composition), his palette became secondary to those
concerns and consists of whatever was available and the
combinations thereof.

The works *#P* (1986), *#V* (1988), and *89–10* (1989)
are each composed of dark earthy tones that yield a
subdued and contemplative reaction. Standing five feet
tall and two and a half feet wide, this group of paintings
is proportioned to the average human torso. Hung
just inches above the floor, they are easily accessible to the
viewer. If the light permits, it is possible to see a very
faint reflection of oneself within the lustrous finish of the
piece—a possibility that suggests a correlation between
the work and a full-length mirror hung on the wall. This
shape, used by Thurston for its familiarity, also estab-
lishes the notion that whatever is seen within the painting
is an interaction between the viewer, the painting's
surface, and the environment. Shifting and changing, the
work fluctuates throughout the days, seasons, and years
as it continues to offer a range of subtly varied experiences
with space and light. —R.M.

1 Roy Thurston, "A Text by Roy Thurston,"
Spazio Umano (Milan) (February 1987): 37.

#V, 1988, butyrate lacquer on birch plywood, 60 x 26⅛ x ¾ inches, (94.91)

#R, 1988, butyrate lacquer with graphite on panel, 80 x 35¼ x 1¾ inches, (94.89)

89–4, 1989, butyrate lacquer with dry pigment on birch plywood, 60 x 30 inches, (94.93)

89–10, 1989, butyrate lacquer on birch plywood, 60 x 28 inches, (94.95)

89–3, 1989, butyrate lacquer on birch plywood, 60 x 28 inches, (94.92)

90–1 (detail)

90–1, 1990, butyrate lacquer on birch plywood, 60 x 28 inches, (94.94)

Selected Exhibition Chronologies and Bibliographies

LAWRENCE **carroll**

born in Melbourne, Australia, 1954
lives and works in New York and Los Angeles
education Otis Art Institute, Los Angeles, 1980
Art Center College of Design, Pasadena, California, 1976–80
Moorpark College, Moorpark, California, 1972–75

selected one-person exhibitions

1999 Galerie Karsten Greve, Paris
Project Room, Ace Gallery, New York
1998 Galerie Alexander Sies, Düsseldorf, Germany
Galerie Buchmann, Cologne, Germany
Galerie der Stadt Stuttgart, Stuttgart, Germany
Lawing Gallery, Houston, Texas
1997 Galleria Gian Ferrari, Milan, and Gian Enzo Sperone, Rome
Galerie Peter Bäumler, Regensburg, Germany
Städtische Ausstellungshalle Münster, Munster, Germany
1996 *Blanket for Rothko*, Ace Contemporary Exhibitions, Los Angeles
Deweer Art Gallery, Otegem, Belgium
E una Natura Morta di Giorgio Morandi, Studio La Città, Verona, Italy
Gian Enzo Sperone, Rome
Milleventi, Turin, Italy
1995 *Drawings*, Ace Contemporary Exhibitions, Los Angeles
Lawing Gallery, Houston, Texas
Museo de Bellas Artes, Caracas, Venezuela
Paintings and Drawings, Galerie Buchmann, Cologne, Germany
Paintings and Drawings, Lawing Gallery, Houston, Texas
Studio Trisorio, Naples, Italy
1994 Galerie Buchmann, Basel, Switzerland
Grand Salon, New York
Städtische Galerie im Museum Folkwang Essen, Essen, Germany
When Things Sleep, Domaine de Kerguéhennec, Centre d'Art Contemporain, Bignan, France
1993 Städtisches Museum Abteiberg, Mönchengladbach, Germany
Jim Schmidt Contemporary Fine Art, St. Louis, Missouri
Ace Contemporary Exhibitions, Los Angeles
1992 Stux Gallery, New York
Galerie Beaumont, Lasne, Belgium
1991 Röntgen Kunst Institut, Tokyo
Galerie Baudoin Lebon, Paris
1990 Stux Gallery, New York
1989 Stux Gallery, New York
Galerie Ryszard Varisella, Frankfurt
1988 Stux Gallery, New York
Stux Gallery, Boston

selected group exhibitions

1999 *Lawrence Carroll, Sean Scully*, Lawing Gallery, Houston
1998 *Master Drawings,* Galerie Peter Bäumler, Regensburg, Germany
Panza Collection, Palazzo Ducale, Venice
Pollution, Galleria Gian Ferrari, Milan
1997 *After the Fall*, Snug Harbor Cultural Center, Staten Island, New York
La Donazione Panza di Biumo al Museo Cantonale d'Arte, Museo Cantonale d'Arte, Lugano, Switzerland
The Obsession of the Mark, Studio La Città, Verona, Italy
1996 *The Panza di Biumo Collection: some artists from the 80s and 90s*, Museo d'Arte Moderna e Contemporanea di Trento e Rovereto, Trento, Italy
Positionen, Museum Folkwang Essen, Essen, Germany
Silence, Lawing Gallery, Houston
1995 *Abstraction from Two Coasts,* Lawing Gallery, Houston
Cover to Cover, The Work Space, New York

Drawings, Ace Contemporary Exhibitions, Los Angeles
Interventions in Space, Museo de Bellas Artes, Caracas, Venezuela
Jim Schmidt Contemporary Fine Art, St. Louis, Missouri
Sperone Westwater, New York
The Spirit of the Matter, Grand Salon, New York
1994 Domaine de Kerguéhennec, Centre d'Art Contemporain, Bignan, France
Lawrence Carroll, Tony Cragg, Wilhelm Mundt, Galleria Manuela Allegrini, Brescia, Italy
A Painting Show, Deweer Art Gallery, Otegem, Belgium
The State of Things, Kölnischer Kunstverein, Cologne, Germany
1993 *Beyond Paint,* Tibor de Nagy Gallery, New York
Jours Tranquilles à Clichy, Paris, John Good Gallery, New York
Extravagant (The Economy of Eloquence), Tony Shafrazi Gallery, New York
Object Bodies, William West Clarke Emison Art Center, DePauw University, Greencastle, Indiana, and Turman Art Gallery, Indiana State University, Terre Haute, Indiana
Plötzlich ist eine Zeit hereingebrochen, in der möglich sein sollte, Kunstverein Ludwigsburg, Ludwigsburg, Germany
Private: Lawrence Carroll, Tony Oursler, Gallery F 15, Moss, Norway
Residual Hope, S.L. Simpson Gallery, Toronto
Reveillon, Stux Gallery, New York
1992 *Dealing with Art*, Künstlerwerkstatt, Munich
Documenta IX, Kassel, Germany
The New Physical Abstraction in Los Angeles, Ace Contemporary Exhibition, Los Angeles
Whiter Shade of Pale, Galerie Sophia Ungers, Cologne, Germany
Who's Afraid of Minimalism and Passport Photography?, Annina Nosei Gallery, New York
1991 Galerie Krinzinger, Vienna
1990 *All Quiet on the Western Front?*, Galerie Antoine Candau, Paris
Galerie Ghislaine Hussenot, Paris
Galerie Schmela, Düsseldorf, Germany
Mayor Rowan Gallery, London
Musée des Beaux-Arts, Brussels
1989 *Einleuchten*, Deichtorhallen, Hamburg, Germany
Galerie Ryzaard Varisella, Frankfurt
Holtegaard Museum, Vedaek, Denmark
Pre-Pop/Post-Appropriation, Stux Gallery, New York
De Rozeboomkamer, Beeld-en-Route Foundation, Diepenheim, Holland
1988 *Art at the End of the Social*, Rooseum, Malmö, Sweden
The New Poverty II, Meyers/Bloom Gallery, Los Angeles
Off White, Diane Brown Gallery, New York
1987 Bronx Museum of the Arts, Bronx, New York
Gallery 3, Hoboken, New Jersey
Gallery 503 Broadway, New York
Miniatures, Stux Gallery, Boston
Juried Exhibition, City Without Walls, Newark, New Jersey
P.S. 122, New York
Philip Stanbury Gallery, New York
Queens Museum of Art, Flushing Meadows, New York
Sweet Briar College, Sweet Briar, Virginia
1986 City Without Walls, Newark, New Jersey
Silvermine Guild Arts Center, New Caanan, Connecticut
1985 Now Gallery, New York
1983 Hanson Gallery, Santa Barbara, California
1982 University Gallery, California State University at Fullerton, Fullerton, California
1976 Art Center College of Design, Pasadena, California
1972 Moorpark College, Moorpark, California

selected bibliography

After the Fall—Aspects of Abstract Painting Since 1970. Exh. cat. Staten Island, New York: Snug Harbor Cultural Center, 1997.
Archer, Michael. "I Don't Like Eggs: Janet Green, British Collector, on Art and the Art World." *Artscribe* (Summer 1990).
Art at the End of the Social. Exh. cat. Malmö, Sweden: Rooseum, 1988. Essay by Tricia Collins

and Richard Milazzo.

Bild-Skulpturen. Exh. cat. Aachen, Germany: Ludwig—Forum für Internationale Kunst, 1996. Essays by Ulrich Schneider and Hugo Jung.

Bonetti, David. "Lawrence Carroll." *The Boston Phoenix* (22 January 1988).

Collins, Tricia, and Richard Milazzo. "Post-Appropriation and the Romantic Fallacy." *Tema Celeste* (September 1989): 36–43.

——. "Translation." *Juliet Magazine,* no. 45 (December 1989).

——. "From Kant to Kitsch and Back Again." *Tema Celeste* (January–February 1991): 76–80.

Dealing with Art. Exh. cat. Munich: Künstlerwerkstatt, 1992.

Decter, Joshua. "Pre-Pop Post-Appropriation: Stux Gallery." *Flash Art,* no. 146 (May/June 1989): 113.

Dell'Ara, Renzo. "Solo a Furia di Bussare l'Arte Vince." *Il Giorno* (14 September 1996).

Documenta IX. Exh. cat. Kassel, Germany: Museum Fridericianum Kassel, 1992.

Frank, Peter. "Dialectic Material." *Los Angeles Magazine* (November 1989).

Gandini, Emanuela. "Messe da Parte le Figure Ecco le Silenti Geometrie." *Il Giorno* (14 September 1996).

"A Gift of Los Angeles Artists for a Los Angeles Museum—A Gift from the Panza's." *The New York Times* (11 April 1994).

Imdahl, Georg. "Im Studiolo Jetzt Die Mochromie." *Frankfurter Allegmeine Zeitung* (20 April 1999).

Intervenciones en el Espacio. Exh. cat. Caracas, Venezuela: Museo de Bellas Artes, 1998.

Kampmann, Matthias. "Die vergifteten Bilder." *Westfalischer Anzeiger* (5 September 1996).

Kandel, Susan. "Gracefully Disrupting Space." *Los Angeles Times* (23 December 1993).

——. "Altogether There." *Los Angeles Times* (4 July 1996).

Karmel, Pepe. *The New York Times* (5 January 1996).

Kreter, Sabine. "Schwimmende Gedichte in Bronze." *Westfalische Nachtrichten* (30 November 1996).

Kuspit, Donald. "Lawrence Carroll: Stux Gallery." *Artforum* 28, no. 5 (January 1990): 137.

——. "The Dialectic of Decadence." In *Revillon*. New York: Stux Press, 1993.

The Last Decade: American Artists of the Eighties. Exh. cat. New York: Tony Shafrazi Gallery, 1990. Essay by Tricia Collins and Richard Milazzo.

Lawrence Carroll. Exh. cat. New York: Stux Gallery, 1988. Essay by Robert Pincus-Witten.

Lawrence Carroll. Exh. cat. Mönchengladbach, Germany: Städtisches Museum Abteiberg, 1993. Essay by Jerry Saltz.

Lawrence Carroll. Exh. cat. Bignan, France: Domaine de Kerguéhennec, Centre d'Art Contemporain, 1994.

Lawrence Carroll. Exh. cat. Otegem, Belgium: Deweer Gallery, 1996.

Lawrence Carroll. Exh. cat. Milan: Gian Ferrari Arte, in collaboration with Gian Enzo Sperone, Rome, 1997.

Lawrence Carroll. Exh. cat. Cologne: Galerie Buchmann, 1998.

"Lawrence Carroll: Die positive Kraft des Unvollkommen." *Münstersche Zeitung* (30 November 1996).

Lawrence Carroll—E una natura morta di Giorgio Morandi. Exh. cat. Verona, Italy: Studio La Città, 1996.

"Lawrence Carroll in Stuttgart." *Stuttgart Zeitung-Kultur* (12 September 1998).

Lawrence Carroll, Sean Scully. Exh. cat. Houston: Lawing Gallery, 1998.

Lawrence Carroll, Tony Cragg, Wilhelm Mundt. Exh. cat. Brescia, Italy: Galleria Manuela Allegrini, 1994.

Lawrence Carroll's Panel Paintings and the Optimism of Failure. Exh. cat. New York: Stux Gallery, 1990. Essay by Terry Myers.

Mahoney, Robert. "Lawrence Carroll." *Arts Magazine* 64, no. 5 (January 1990): 102.

Meneghelli, Luigi. "Tanto per Farsi un'Idea dell'Arte Attuale." *L'Arena* (6 November 1996).

Muchnic, Suzanne. "MOCA gets Major Gift—Works by 10 Local Artists." *Los Angeles Times* (26 October 1994): F1.

Myers, Terry R. "Lawrence Carroll's Boxes." *Arts Magazine* 63, no. 4 (December 1988): 66–69.

The New Poverty II. Exh. cat. Los Angeles: Meyers/Bloom Gallery, 1998. Essay by Tricia Collins and Richard Milazzo.

Object Bodies. Exh. cat. Greencastle, Indiana: William West Clarke Emison Art Center, DePauw University; and Terre Haute, Indiana: Turman Art Gallery, Indiana State University, 1993. Essay by Terry R. Myers.

Off White. Exh. cat. New York: Diane Brown Gallery, 1988. Essay by Tricia Collins and Richard Milazzo.

Pagel, David. "The New Physical Abstraction in Los Angeles." *Tema Celeste* (Winter 1993): 79.

The Painting Show. Exh. cat. Otegem, Belgium: Deweer Art Gallery, 1994. Essay by Jo Coucke.

Panza Collection. Exh. cat. Lugano, Switzerland: Museo Cantonale d'Arte, 1995.

The Panza di Biumo Collection: some artists from the 80s and 90s. Exh. cat. Trento, Italy: Museo di Arte Moderna e Contemporanea di Trento e Rovereto, 1996. Essays by Gabriella Belli and Giuseppe Panza di Biumo; entries and biographies.

Peterson, William. "Physical Abstraction: On Some Abstract Painting in Los Angeles." *Artspace* (December 1992): 53–60.

Pincus-Witten, Robert. "Entries: Concentrated Juice and Kitschy Kitschy Koons." *Arts Magazine* (February 1989).

Posca, Claudia. "Lawrence Carroll. Städtische im Museum Folkwang, Essen." *Kunstforum International* (January-April 1995).

Pre-Pop Post-Appropriation. Exh. cat. New York: Stux Gallery, 1989. Essay by Tricia Collins and Richard Milazzo.

Puvogel, Renate. "Lawrence Carroll—Städtishes Museum, Mönchengladbach." *Kunstforum International* (May–August 1993).

——. "The State of Things, Kölnischer Kunstverein." *Kunstforum International* (January-April 1995).

Residual Hope. Exh. cat. Toronto: S.L. Simpson Gallery, 1993. Essay by Sharon Brooks.

Rimanelli, David. "Pre-Pop Post-Appropriation at Stux Gallery." *Artforum* (May 1989).

Sandqvist, Gertrud. "Privat." *Parkett,* no. 37 (1993): 148–154.

Sanzenobi, SZ. "Collezione Panza di Biumo: Artisti degli Anni '80–'90." *N4* (September–October 1996).

Schmidt-Wulffen, Stephan. "Lawrence Carroll." *Kunstforum* (January–February 1990).

Schwalb, Claudia. "Integrating Anxiety." *Cover Magazine* (November 1989).

Schwendenwien, Jude. "Pre-Pop Post-Appropriation." *Tema Celeste* (April–June 1989).

Smith, Roberta. "Lawrence Carroll." *The New York Times* (20 October 1989).

The State of Things. Exh. cat. Cologne, Germany: Kölnischer Kunstverein, 1994. Essay by Udo Kittlemann.

Temin, Christine. "Romance Is in the Galleries." *The Boston Globe* (23 March 1989).

Ventavoli, Bruno. "Panza di Biumo, Randomante del Bello." *La Stampa* (26 September 1996).

Vettesse, Angela. "24 Ore." *Il Sole* (17 January 1999).

GREG **colson**

born in Seattle, Washington, 1956
lives and works in Los Angeles
education M.F.A., Claremont Graduate School, Claremont, California, 1980
B.F.A., California State University, Bakersfield, California, 1978

selected one-person exhibitions

1999	Griffin Contemporary, Venice, California
	Gian Enzo Sperone, Rome
	John Berggruen Gallery, San Francisco
1998	Griffin Contemporary, Venice, California
	1000 Eventi, Milan
1997	Angles Gallery, Santa Monica, California
1996	Krannert Art Museum, University of Illinois, Champaign, Illinois
1995	Angles Gallery, Santa Monica, California
1994	Kunsthalle Lophem, Brugges, Belgium
	Sperone Westwater, New York
1993	Angles Gallery, Santa Monica, California
1992	Gian Enzo Sperone, Rome
1991	Sperone Westwater, New York
	Konrad Fischer Gallery, Düsseldorf, Germany
1990	Sperone Westwater, New York
	Angles Gallery, Santa Monica, California
1988	Lannan Museum, Lake Worth, Florida
	Angles Gallery, Santa Monica, California
1987	Angles Gallery, Santa Monica, California

selected group exhibitions

1999   *Recent Sculpture*, Griffin Contemporary, Venice, California
1998   *Collaboration/Transformation*, Fred Jones Jr. Museum of Art, University of Oklahoma,
            Norman, Oklahoma
        Wood, Fisher Landau Center, Long Island City, New York
1997   *100 Years of California Art*, Orange County Museum of Art, Newport Beach, California
        Book Obsession, Tel Aviv Museum of Art, Tel Aviv, Israel
        CA 90001-185, W 139, Amsterdam
        Paper Works, Sperone Westwater, New York
        Structures: Buildings in American Art, 1900–1997, John Berggruen Gallery,
            San Francisco
1996   *The Empowered Object*, Hunsaker/Schlesinger Fine Art, Santa Monica, California
        Limited Edition Artists' Books, Brooke Alexander, New York
        Tangles, Otis Gallery, Otis College of Art and Design, Los Angeles
        Six Projects: Robert Therrien, Ed Moses, Peter Shelton, Greg Colson, Bobbie
            Greenfield Gallery, Santa Monica, California
1995   *een actuele privé-verzameling*, Sint-Lukasgalerij, Brussels
        Presence: Recent Portraits, Angles Gallery, Santa Monica, California
        Too Cool: Assemblage and Finish Fetish in Los Angeles, Laguna Art Museum, Laguna
            Beach, California
        Uncommon Objects, Kathleen Shields Contemporary Art Projects, Albuquerque,
            New Mexico
1994   Art on the Map, Chicago Cultural Center, Chicago
        Artist's Books from The Lapis Press, Kohn Turner Gallery, Los Angeles
        Mapping, The Museum of Modern Art, New York
1993   *The Return of the "Cadavre Exquis,"* The Drawing Center, New York
        The Spirit of Drawing, Sperone Westwater, New York
        Vancouver Collects, Vancouver Art Gallery, Vancouver, British Columbia, Canada
1992   *Colson, Kuitca, Wegman*, Sperone Westwater, New York
        Colson, Pardo, Murakami, Tower, Mars Gallery, Tokyo
        Drawn in the 90s, Katonah Art Museum, Katonah, New York
        How It Is, Tony Shafrazi Gallery, New York
        Oddly: 4 Los Angeles Artists, Oakland Museum, Oakland, California
1991   *Dots*, Angles Gallery, Santa Monica, California
        New American Art: Beyt, Colson, Wool, Ho Gallery, World Art, Hong Kong
        Third Newport Biennial: Mapping Histories, Newport Harbor Art Museum, Newport
            Beach, California
1990   *12th International Biennial of Drawings: Working Drawings from Sculptors*, Museum
            of Modern Art, Rijeka, Yugoslavia
        Laboratory, Russian Museum, St. Petersburg, Russia
        Je viens de chez la charcutier, Galerie Ghislaine Hussenot, Paris
1989   *Containers*, Shoshana Wayne, Santa Monica, California
        Greg Colson, Peter Greenaway, Nicolas Rule, Nicole Klagsbrun, New York
        Outer Limits, Holly Solomon Gallery, New York
1988   *Black and White Abstraction*, Angles Gallery, Santa Monica, California
        Bocanegra, Colson, Scarpitta, Craig Cornelius Gallery, New York
        Excavations, Otis Institute of Parsons School of Design Art Gallery, Los Angeles
1987   *New Painting and Sculpture*, Angles Gallery, Santa Monica, California
        White Work, Angles Gallery, Santa Monica, California

bibliography

Anderson, Michael. "Greg Colson at Angles." *Art in America* 77, no. 7 (July 1989): 144–145.
Baker, Kenneth. "Just Odd Enough: Four L.A. Artists' Work Raises Questions in Oakland Show."
    San Francisco Chronicle (14 June 1992): 47.
Becker, Shizuyo. "From Los Angeles." *Bijutsu Techo* (Japan) (July 1993): 126.
Butler, Brian. "Greg Colson: Angles Gallery." *New Art Examiner* 16, no. 7 (March 1989): 53.
Clearwater, Bonnie. "Lettre de Los Angeles." *Art Press*, no. 146 (April 1990): 86.
Colson, Greg. "Colson's Corner." *LAICA Journal*, no. 30 (September–October 1981): 56.
——. "Colson's Corner." *LAICA Journal*, no. 31 (Winter 1981): 72.
——. "Colson's Corner." *LAICA Journal*, no. 32 (Spring 1982): 72.
——. "Colson's Corner." *LAICA Journal*, no. 33 (Summer 1982): 72.
——. "Colson's Corner." *LAICA Journal*, no. 34 (Fall 1982): 72.
——. "Colson's Corner." *LAICA Journal*, no. 35 (Winter 1983): 64.
——. "Projects by Greg & Jeff Colson." *LAICA Journal,* no. 35 (Winter 1983): 58–63.
Contemporary Art Series: Greg Colson. Exh. cat. Urbana-Champaign, Illinois: Krannert Art
    Museum and Kinkead Pavillion, University of Illinois, 1996. Essay by David Pagel.
Curtis, Cathy. "Oddball Organizations." *Los Angeles Times* (17 October 1990): F5.
Dubrow, Norman. "The Neo Tendencies of the Late 1980s." *Drawing* 12, no. 6 (March-April
    1991): 121–125.
Frank, Peter. "Greg Colson, Jeff Colson, Reinhard Voigt, Lienhard von Monkiewitsch: 'New
    Paintings and Sculpture.'" *L.A. Weekly* (29 January–4 February 1988): 43.
——. "Pick of the Week: Excavations." *L.A. Weekly* (16–22 December 1988): 125.
——. "Pick of the Week." *L.A. Weekly* (2–8 May 1997): 138.
Gardner, Colin. "The Art Galleries: Santa Monica." *Los Angeles Times* (22 May 1987): VI,14.
——. "Colson's semantic playground: Artist evokes dance of chaos and form." *Los Angeles
    Herald Examiner* (16 December 1988): 48.
Geer, Suvan. "They Connect." *Los Angeles Times* (23 July 1991): F7.
"Goings on About Town." *The New Yorker* 67, no. 6 (1 April 1991): 12.
Greg Colson. Exh. cat. Lake Worth, Florida: Lannan Museum, 1988. Essay by Bonnie Clearwater.
"Greg Colson, Dockings" *The Print Collector's Newsletter* 26, no. 2 (May–June 1995): 64.
Heartney, Eleanor. "Greg Colson: Sperone Westwater." *ARTnews* 89, no. 5 (May 1990): 210.
Hunt, David. "Greg Colson at 1000eventi." *Flash Art* (Italy) (October-November 1998): 130–132.
——. "Spotlight: Greg Colson." *Flash Art* 31, no. 203 (November-December 1998): 105.
Kosenko, Peter. "Greg Colson: Angles Gallery." *Art Papers* 19, no. 3 (May–June 1995): 37–38.
"L.A. Scoop: The Cool Art Crop." *W* (5 September 1988).
Maclay, Cathrine. "Ambiguity and Amusement from Four Los Angelenos." *San Jose Mercury
    News* (22 May 1992): 48.
Mahoney, Robert. "Greg Colson." *Arts Magazine* 64, no. 8 (April 1990): 109–110.
Mapping. Exh. cat. New York: The Museum of Modern Art, 1994. Essay by Robert Storr.
Mapping Histories: Third Newport Biennial. Exh. cat. Newport Beach, California: Newport
    Harbor Art Museum, 1991. Essay by Buzz Spector.
Marzahl, Kevin. "Greg Colson: Krannert Art Museum." *New Art Examiner* 24, no. 6 (March
    1997): 47–48.
Melrod, George. "Greg Colson at Sperone Westwater." *Art in America* 82, no. 9 (September
    1994): 112.
Miles, Christopher. "Greg Colson at Griffin Contemporary Exhibitions." *Artweek* 29, no. 5 (May
    1998): 23.
Muchnic, Suzanne. "Making Book." *Connoisseur* (July 1991): 28–29.
——. "California Currents: Artists Choose Artists—Ed Ruscha and Greg Colson." *ARTnews* 90,
    no. 9 (November 1991): 98.
——. "MOCA Gets Major Gift—Works by 10 Local Artists." *Los Angeles Times* (26 October
    1994): F1, F6.
Nesbitt, Lois E. "Greg Colson: Sperone Westwater." *Artforum* 28, no. 8 (April 1990): 173.
Oddly. Exh. cat. Oakland: Oakland Museum, 1992. Essay by Paul Tomidy.
Pagel, David. "Object Lessons: The Assemblages of Greg Colson." *Arts Magazine* 64, no. 2
    (October 1989): 40–43.
——. "Vibrant Multiculturalism at Newport Biennial." *Los Angeles Times* (10 October 1991): F6-F7.
——. "Greg Colson: Homage to the Repairman." *Los Angeles Times* (15 April 1993): F6.
Rubin, Jane. "Greg Colson at Angles and Otis-Parsons." *Art Issues*, no. 3 (April 1989): 28.
Russell, John. "Greg Colson." *The New York Times* (12 January 1990): C27.
Saltz, Jerry. "Greg Colson: Liberating Materials from Materiality." *Flash Art,* no. 152
    (May/June 1990): 150.
Smith, Roberta. "Greg Colson, Peter Greenaway, Nicolas Rule." *The New York Times*
    (8 December 1989): C26.
——. "These Are the Faces to Watch." *The New York Times* (5 January 1990): C21.
——. "Greg Colson." *The New York Times* (29 March 1991): C20.
Snow, Shauna. "Conceptualist Greg Colson Puts His Faith in Intuition." *Los Angeles Times*
    (16 September 1990): 90.
Spada, Sabina. "Greg Colson—1000eventi, Milan." *Tema Celeste* (October–December 1998).
Stephens, Richard. "Greg Colson, Tim Hawkinson and Robert Millar." *Visions* 3, no. 3 (Spring
    1989): 30.
Watten, Barrett. "In the In-Between: Oddly at the Oakland Museum." *Artweek* 23, no. 18 (18
    June 1992): 16–17.

JEFF **colson**

born in Santa Ana, California, 1957
lives and works in Yucca, California
education Claremont Graduate School, Claremont, California, 1980
B.F.A., California State University, Bakersfield, California, 1979

selected one-person exhibitions

1999 Griffin Contemporary, Venice, California
John Berggruen Gallery, San Francisco
1998 Angles Gallery, Santa Monica, California
Griffin Contemporary, Venice, California
1994 Angles Gallery, Santa Monica, California
1993 John Good Gallery, New York
1992 Angles Gallery, Santa Monica, California
1991 Galerie Karsten Greve, Paris
1990 Angles Gallery, Santa Monica, California
1989 Angles Gallery, Santa Monica, California

selected group exhibitions

1999 *Drawn From Artists' Collections*, The Drawing Center, New York, and University of
California, Los Angeles, Hammer Museum of Art and Cultural Center, Los Angeles
Edward Ruscha, Robert Therrien and Jeff Colson, Leo Castelli Gallery, New York
John Berggruen Gallery, San Francisco
Recent Sculpture, Griffin Contemporary, Venice, California
1998 *California Current*, Rare, New York
Griffin Contemporary, Venice, California
1996 *The Empowered Object*, Hunsaker/Schlesinger, Santa Monica, California
1995 *A California Collection*, Hunsaker/Schlesinger, Santa Monica, California
1994 *In Plain Sight: Abstract Painting in Los Angeles*, Blue Star Art Space,
San Antonio, Texas
John Good Gallery, New York
1993 *Paintings*, Mars Gallery, Tokyo
Vancouver Collects, Vancouver Art Gallery, Vancouver
1991 *Dots*, Angles Gallery, Santa Monica, California
LA 1990: Selected Views, California State University, Bakersfield, California
Squaresville, Angles Gallery, Santa Monica, California
Works on Paper, John Good Gallery, New York
1990 *Laboratory,* Russian Museum, St. Petersburg, Russia
Material Consequence, Otis Gallery, Otis College of Art and Design, Los Angeles
Sculpture, Angles Gallery, Santa Monica, California
1989 *Works on Paper: A Changing Exhibition*, Angles Gallery, Santa Monica, California
1988 *Black & White Abstraction,* Angles Gallery, Santa Monica, California
1987 *New Painting and Sculpture*, Angles Gallery, Santa Monica, California
1983 *The Lewis Building Artists*, California State University, Bakersfield, California
1980 Libra Gallery, Claremont Graduate School, Claremont, California
1979 California State University, Bakersfield, California

bibliography

Anderson, Michael. "Material Consequence: Otis/Parsons Gallery, Los Angeles."
Contemporanea 3, no. 5 (May 1990): 101.
Channin, Richard. "Jeff Colson at Angles." *Art in America* 77, no. 6 (June 1989): 184.
Colson, Greg. "Projects by Greg & Jeff Colson." *LAICA Journal,* no. 35 (Winter 1983): 58–63.
DiMichele, David. "Fat Chance: Jeff Colson at Angles Gallery." *Artweek* 25, no. 22 (17
November 1994): 16.
Donohue, Marlena. "Galleries." *Los Angeles Times* (31 March 1989): VI, 20.
Frank, Peter. "Art Pick of the Week: Andres Serrano; Vito Acconci; Dennis Oppenheim;
David Amico; Tim Hawkinson; Jeff Colson; Patrice Claire." *L.A. Weekly* (13–19 July
1990): 128.
In Plain Sight: Abstract Painting in Los Angeles. Exh. cat. San Antonio: Blue Star Art Space,
1994. Essay by Frances Colpitt.
Material Consequence. Exh. cat. Los Angeles: Otis Art Institute of Parsons School of Design,
1990. Essay by Anne Ayres.
McKenna, Kristine. "Minimalism Focus of 'Material Consequences.'" *Los Angeles Times* (12
February 1990): F5.
Miles, Christopher. "New Work." *Art Papers* 22, no. 6 (November 1998).
Muchnic, Suzanne. "MOCA Gets Major Gift–Works by 10 Local Artists." *Los Angeles Times*
(26 October 1994): F1, F6.
——. "Art Notes: Brotherly Debut." *Los Angeles Times* (8 December 1996): 55.
Selwyn, Marc. "Jeff Colson: Angles Gallery." *Flash Art* 23, no. 154 (October 1990): 157–158.
Vancouver Collects. Exh. cat. Vancouver: Vancouver Art Gallery, 1993.
Vogel, Carol. "Los Angeles Art is Given to a Los Angeles Museum." *The New York Times*
(4 November 1994): B9.

JEAN **fautrier**

born in Paris, 1898
died Châtenay-Malabry, France, 1964
education Royal Academy School, London, 1912
Slade School of Fine Art, London

selected exhibition history

1996 *Jean Fautrier,* Musée National Fernand Léger, Biot, France
Mücsarnok, Budapest, Hungary
1993 *Art and Liberation: Paintings & Sculpture in Post-war Paris 1945–1955,* Tate
Gallery, London
1992 *The European Presence in the Permanent Collection,* The Museum of Contemporary
Art, Los Angeles
Jean Fautrier, Gemälde und Zeichnungen, Kunsthandel Wolfgang Werner, Bremen,
Germany
1990 *The Decisive Years: 1945–1960,* The Museum of Contemporary Art, Los Angeles
1989 *Selections from the Permanent Collection,* The Museum of Contemporary Art,
Los Angeles
Constructing a History: A Focus on MOCA's Permanent Collection, The Museum of
Contemporary Art, Los Angeles
Fautrier, 1898–1964, Musée d'Art Moderne de la Ville de Paris, Paris
1988 *Postwar Abstraction: 1945–1960,* The Museum of Contemporary Art, Los Angeles
1987 *Jean Fautrier. Gemälde, Skulptur, Radierungen,* Museum Insel Hombroich, Neuss,
Germany
1985 *Jean Fautrier, Bilder 1926–1930,* Galerie Thomas Borgmann, Cologne. Traveled to
Galerie Neuendorf, Hamburg
The Panza Collection, The Museum of Contemporary Art, Los Angeles
1980 *Jean Fautrier. Gemälde, Skulpturen und Handzeichnungen,* Josef-Haubrich-Kunsthalle
Köln, Cologne
1976 *Jean Fautrier, Ölbilder 1925–1959,* Galerie Thomas Borgmann, Cologne. Traveled to
Galerie Neuendorf, Hamburg
1973 *Jean Fautrier,* Kunstverein, Hamburg
1971 *Aspetti dell'informale,* Ente Provinciale per il Turismo, Bari, and Pinacoteca
Provinciale, Bari, Italy
1969 *Jean Fautrier: oeuvre grave, oeuvre sculpte,* Galerie Engelberts, Geneva
1968 *Venice Biennale,* Venice
1964 *Jean Fautrier. Rétrospective,* Musée d'Art Moderne de la Ville de Paris, Paris
1963 *Jean Fautrier. Malningar 1921–1963,* Moderna Museet, Stockholm
1961 *Tokyo Biennale,* Tokyo
La Pittura moderna straniera nelle collezioni private Italiane, Galleria Civica d'Arte
Moderna, Turin, Italy
1960 *Venice Biennale,* Venice
Galerie L'Immagine, Turin, Italy

La Sala Nebli, Madrid
Jean Fautrier: pittura e materia, Il Saggiatore, Milan
1959 *documenta 2,* Kassel, Germany
Galerie Hanover, London
La Loggia, Bologna
Galerie Minami, Tokyo
1958 Galerie Apollinaire, Milan
1957 *30 années de figuration informelle,* Galerie Rive Droite, Paris
Lithographies 1928–1958, Galerie André Schœller, Paris
Sidney Janis Gallery, New York
1956 *Nus,* Galerie Rive Droite, Paris
Gallery Lolas, New York
1955 *Objets,* Galerie Rive Droite, Paris
1945 *Les Otages, peintures et sculptures de Jean Fautrier,* Galerie René Drouin, Paris
1942 Galerie Poyet, Paris
1933 *L'Enfer,* Galerie de la Nouvelle Revue, Paris
1930 Galerie Le Centaure, Brussels
1929 Galerie des Quatre-Chemins, Paris
1928 Galerie Georges Bernheim, Paris
1924 Galerie Visconti, Paris
1923 Galerie Fabre, Paris
1922 *Salon d'Automne,* Paris

selected bibliography

Aeply, Jeanine. "Les originaux multiples." *Cahiers bleus* 2 (1982).
Alvard, Julien. "Fautrier." *Cimaise* 2, no. 4 (March 1955).
Arland, Marcel. "Les Otages de Fautrier." *Le Vingtième Siècle* (8 November 1945).
Berne-Joffroy, André. "Les objets de Jean Fautrier." *La Nouvelle Revue Française* (May 1955).
Brandi, Cesare. "La pittura di Fautrier." *Il Punto* (1959).
Bucarelli, Palma. "Jean Fautrier (la forma dell'informe)." *La Sera* (16 April 1958).
De Solier, René. "Fautrier." *Monde Nouveau* (July 1956).
Fautrier, 1898–1964. Exh. cat. Paris: Musée d'Art Moderne de la Ville de Paris, 1989.
Jean Fautrier. Exh. cat. Biot, France: Musée National Fernand Léger, 1996.
Jean Fautrier. Exh. cat. Cologne: Josef-Haubrich-Kunsthalle, 1980. Essay by Siegried Gohr.
Jean Fautrier. Exh. cat. Hamburg: Kunstverein, 1973. Essay by Hans Gerd Tuchel.
Jean Fautrier, Bilder 1926-1930. Exh. cat. Cologne: Galerie Thomas Borgmann, 1985.
Jean Fautrier. Gemälde, Skulptur, Radierungen. Exh. cat. Neuss, Germany: Museum Insel Hombroich, 1987.
Jean Fautrier. Gemälde, Skulpturen und Handzeichnungen. Exh. cat. Cologne: Josef-Haubrich-Kunsthalle, 1980.
Jean Fautrier, Gemälde und Zeichnungen. Exh. cat. Bremen: Kunsthandel Wolfgang Werner, 1992.
Jean Fautrier. Malningar 1921–1963. Exh. cat. Stockholm: Moderna Museet, 1963
Jean Fautrier: oeuvre grave, oeuvre sculpte. Exh. cat. Geneva: Galerie Engelberts, 1969.
Jean Fautrier, Ölbilder 1925–1959. Exh. cat. Cologne: Galerie Thomas Borgmann, 1976.
Jean Fautrier: pittura e materia. Exh. cat. Milan: Il Saggiatore, 1960. Essay by Palma Bucarelli.
Jean Fautrier: Rétrospective. Exh. cat. Paris: Musée d'Art Moderne de la Ville de Paris, 1964. Essays by Jean Paulhan and André Berne Joffroy.
Jouffroy, Alain. "Jean Fautrier." *Arts* 16 (February 1955).
Knight, Christopher. *Art of the Sixties and Seventies: The Panza Collection.* New York: Rizzoli International Publications, 1988.
Les objets de Fautrier. Exh. cat. Paris: Galerie Rive Droite. Essay by Jean Paulhan.
Les Otages, peintures et sculptures de Jean Fautrier. Exh. cat. Paris: Galerie René Drouin, 1945. Essay by André Malraux.
Limbour, Georges. "Mignardises et cadavres." *France-Observateur* 24 (February 1955).
Malraux, André. "Exposition Fautrier." *La Nouvelle Revue Française* (February 1933).
Mason, Rainer Michael. *Jean Fautrier: les éstampes: nouvel essai de catalogue raisonné.* Geneva: Cabinet des éstampes, 1986.
Mazars, Pierre. "Fautrier fait une petite révolution dans la peinture, Meinungen von Fernand Léger, Jacques Villon, Roger Chastel, André Lhote, Jean Paulhan, René Drouin, Nacenta." *Figaro Littéraire* (25 November 1950).
Paroles à propos des nus de Fautrier. Exh. cat. Paris: Galerie Rive Droite, 1956. Essay by Francis Ponge.
Paulhan, Jean. "Grâce et atrocité de Fautrier." *XXème Siècle* 11 (December 1958).
Peyré, Yves. *Fautrier: ou les outrages de l'impossible.* Paris: Editions du Regard, 1990.
Ponge, Francis. *Note sur Les Otages, peintures de Fautrier.* Paris: Pierre Seghers, 1946.
Ragon, Michel. "Les objects de Fautrier." *Cimaise* (April 1955).
Réponse à un ami américain. Exh. cat. New York: Gallery Lolas, 1956. Essay by André Malraux.
Restany, Pierre. "Un appartement milanais consacré à trois peintres: Fautrier, Kline et Tàpies." *Plaisir de France* 374 (January 1970).
——. "L'Autre face de l'art. L'Aventure de l'objet." *Domus,* no. 583 (June 1978).
Tapié, Michel. "Fautrier: The 'Multiple originals.'" *Paris News Post* (January 1951).
——. "Fautrier paints a picture." *ARTnews* (December 1955).
Verdet, André. "Le tragique de l'humour chez Fautrier." *XXème Siècle* (January 1957).
Wallard, Daniel. "Les Otages de Fautrier." *Poésie* (January 1946).
Wheeler, Daniel. *Art Since Mid-Century: 1945 to the Present.* New York: Vendome Press, 1991.
Zahar, Marcel. "Fautrier, ou de la puissance des ténèbres." *Formes* 7 (July 1930).

RON griffin

born in Pomona, California, 1954
lives and works in Los Angeles
education M.F.A., California Institute of the Arts, Valencia, California, 1988
B.A., University of California, Irvine, California, 1986

selected one-person exhibitions

1999 Hosfelt Gallery, San Francisco
1998 Hosfelt Gallery, San Francisco
1990 Los Angeles Contemporary Exhibitions (LACE), Los Angeles
1988 California Institute of the Arts, Valencia, California
1987 California Institute of the Arts, Valencia, California

selected group exhibitions

1999 Hosfelt Gallery, San Francisco
1998 *Handmade,* Jelmoni Studio, Piacenza, Italy
1997 *Collaboration/Transformation: Lithographs from the Hamilton Press,* Montgomery Gallery, Pomona College, Claremont, California
La Donazione Panza di Biumo al Museo Cantonale d'Arte, Museo Cantonale d'Arte, Lugano, Switzerland
Panza Collection, Sa Llonja, Palma de Mallorca, Spain
Steve Keister, Jonathan Seliger, Ron Griffin, Patricia Faure Gallery, Santa Monica, California
Wood Work, Fisher Landau Center, Long Island City, New York
1996 *Painting as Object,* Studio La Città, Verona, Italy
The Panza di Biumo Collection: some artists from the 80s and 90s, Museo d'Arte Moderna e Contemporanea di Trento e Rovereto, Trento, Italy
1993 *First Sightings,* Denver Art Museum, Denver, Colorado
Gala Centennial Celebration, Denver Art Museum, Denver, Colorado
Salad Days, Margo Leavin Gallery, Los Angeles
Selections from the Permanent Collection, Centro Cultural Arte Contemporáneo, Mexico City
With Light, Galerie Lelong, New York
1987 *Panic in the Streets,* Video production for the bi-weekly *Low Cal Cable Show,* California Institute of the Arts, Valencia, California
1985 *Expressions of the Human Figure,* Muckenthauler Cultural Center, Fullerton, California

bibliography

"Art Pick of the Week: Sharon Ellis, Ron Griffin & Pamela Goldblum; Goldblum/Kaisershot." *L.A. Weekly* (26 January–1 February 1990).

Baker, Kenneth. "Griffin Polished but Wry." *San Francisco Chronicle* (22 January 1998): E1.
——. "Sculptures Made of Paint: Down-Home Abstraction." *San Francisco Chronicle* (12 June 1999).
Barbierei, Natasha. "Fatto a mano: confronto tra culture; Due artisti californiani e due piacen-
tini alla 'Jelmoni.'" *Liberta* (Piacenza, Italy) (7 April 1998).
Bonetti, David. "Gallery Watch." *San Francisco Examiner* (29 January 1998).
Colleccio' Panza di Biumo Anys 80 I 90, Llonja. Exh. cat. Mallorca, Spain: Govern Baleara,
Conselleria d'Educacio, Culgura !Esports, 1997.
The Panza di Biumo Collection: some artists from the 80s and 90s. Exh. cat. Trento, Italy:
Museo d'Arte Moderna e Contemporanea di Trento e Rovereto, 1996. Essays by
Gabriella Belli and Giuseppe Panza di Biumo; entries and biographies.
The Panza di Biumo Donation. Exh. cat. Lugano, Switzerland: Museo Cantonale d'Arte, 1997.
Essays by Marco Franciolli and Maddalena Disch; bibliographies, exhibition histories.

FRANZ **kline**

born in Wilkes-Barre, Pennsylvania, 1910
died in New York, 1962
education Heatherley's Art School, London, 1936–38
Boston University, Boston, 1931–32
Boston Art Students League, Boston

selected exhibition history

1994 *Franz Kline: Black & White 1950–1961*, The Menil Collection, Houston
1989 *Franz Kline: The Jazz Murals*, Center Gallery, Bucknell University, Lewisburg,
Pennsylvania
1985 *The Vital Gesture: Franz Kline in Retrospect*, Cincinnati Art Museum, Cincinnati, Ohio
1984 *Kline: Paintings and Drawings*, Marisa del Re Gallery, New York
1980 *Das Bild einer Geschichte 1956/1976; Die Sammlung Panza di Biumo*, Kunstsammlung
Nordrhein-Westfalen, Kunstmuseum Düsseldorf, and Kunsthalle Düsseldorf,
Düsseldorf, Germany
1979 *Franz Kline: The Color Abstractions*, Phillips Collection, Washington, D.C.
1977 *Franz Kline: The Early Works as Signals*, State University of New York, Binghamton,
New York
Kline Works on Paper, The Mayor Gallery, London
1976 *Homage to Franz Kline*, Bell Art Gallery, Brown University, Providence, Rhode Island
1975 *Franz Kline*, David McKee Gallery, New York
1974 *Franz Kline: Selected Works*, Allan Stone Gallery, New York
1968 *Franz Kline 1910–1962*, Whitney Museum of American Art, New York
1967 *Franz Kline Estate: Paintings and Drawings*, Marlborough-Gerson Gallery, New York
1963 *Franz Kline*, Dwan Gallery, Los Angeles
Franz Kline, Stedelijk Museum, Amsterdam
Franz Kline Memorial Exhibition, The Museum of Modern Art, New York
Kline, La Tartaruga Galleria d'Arte, Rome
Kline Memorial Exhibition, Sidney Janis Gallery, New York
1962 *Continuity and Change, 45 American Abstract Painters and Sculptors*, Wadsworth
Atheneum, Hartford, Connecticut
Eleven Abstract-Expressionist Painters, Sidney Janis Gallery, New York
Franz Kline, Galerie Lawrence, Paris
Franz Kline Memorial Exhibition, Washington Gallery of Modern Art, Washington, D.C.
Ten American Painters, Sidney Janis Gallery, New York
1961 *64th American Exhibition*, Art Institute of Chicago, Chicago
American Abstract Expressionists and Imagists, Solomon R. Guggenheim Museum,
New York
Franz Kline, Arts Club of Chicago, Chicago
Franz Kline, The Collector's Gallery, New York
Franz Kline and Phillip Guston, Dwan Gallery, Los Angeles
Kline, New Arts Gallery, Atlanta

Kline, Sidney Janis Gallery, New York
Ten American Painters, Sidney Janis Gallery, New York
1960 *60 American Painters, 1960: Abstract Expressionist Painting of the Fifties*, Walker Art
Center, Minneapolis
Guggenheim International Award Exhibition, Solomon R. Guggenheim Museum,
New York
Kline, Sidney Janis Gallery, New York
Nine American Painters, Sidney Janis Gallery, New York
XXX Venice Biennale, Venice
1959 *Eight American Painters*, Sidney Janis Gallery, New York
1958 *Franz Kline*, Galleria del Naviglio, Milan
Franz Kline, Sidney Janis Gallery, New York
Kline, La Tartaruga Galleria d'Arte, Rome
Nature in Abstraction, Whitney Museum of American Art, New York
The New American Painting, organized by International Program of The Museum of
Modern Art, New York
1957 *American Paintings 1945–57*, Minneapolis Institute of Arts, Minneapolis, Minnesota
Eight Americans, Sidney Janis Gallery, New York
1956 *12 Americans*, The Museum of Modern Art, New York
American Artists Paint the City, XXVIII Venice Biennale, Venice
Franz Kline, Sidney Janis Gallery, New York
Modern Art in the United States, Tate Gallery, London
Recent Paintings by Seven Americans, Sidney Janis Gallery, New York
1955 *The New Decade: 35 American Painters and Sculptors*, Whitney Museum of American
Art, New York
1954 *Franz Kline*, Egan Gallery, New York
Franz Kline, Institute of Design, Chicago
Third Annual Exhibition of Painting and Sculpture, Stable Gallery, New York
Younger American Painters: A Selection, Solomon R. Guggenheim Museum, New York
1953 *Fine Arts Festival*, Women's College, University of North Carolina, Greensboro,
North Carolina
Second Annual Exhibition of Painting and Sculpture, Stable Gallery, New York
1952 *Franz Kline*, Margaret Brown Gallery, Boston
1951 *American Vanguard Art for Paris Exhibition*, Sidney Janis Gallery, New York
Franz Kline, Egan Gallery, New York
1950 *Franz Kline*, Egan Gallery, New York
Talent 1950, Kootz Gallery, New York
Young Painters in U.S. and France, Sidney Janis Gallery, New York
1946 *Annual Exhibition*, National Academy of Design, New York
1945 *Annual Exhibition*, National Academy of Design, New York
1944 *Annual Exhibition*, National Academy of Design, New York
1943 *Annual Exhibition*, National Academy of Design, New York
1942 *Annual Exhibition*, National Academy of Design, New York

selected bibliography

Action/Precision: The New Direction in New York. Exh. cat. Newport Beach, California:
Newport Harbor Art Museum, 1984. Essay by Paul Schimmel.
Alloway, Lawrence. "Signs and Surface: Notes on Black and White Painting in New York."
Quadrum 9 (1960): 49–62.
——. "Franz Kline's Estate." *Arts Magazine* 41 (April 1967): 40–43.
Alvard, Julien. "Franz Kline." *Aujourd'hui* 47 (October 1964): 4–9.
Ashton, Dore. "Art." *Arts and Architecture* 73 (April 1956): 3, 10–12.
——. "Art." *Arts and Architecture* 75 (July 1958): 10, 31–33.
——. *The New York School: A Cultural Reckoning*. New York: Viking Press, 1973.
Brach, Paul. "Fifty-Seventh Street in Review." *Art Digest* 26 (1 December 1951): 19.
Butler, Barbara. "Franz Kline." *Arts Magazine* 34 (April 1960): 55.
——. "Franz Kline in Retrospect." *Arts Magazine* 37, no. 4 (January 1963): 30–33.
Campbell, Lawrence. "Reviews and Previews." *ARTnews* 53 (Summer 1954): 54.
Conley, Tom. "Accent Grave, Kline and Blanchot." *Sub-Stance* 14 (1976): 77–91.
Crehan, Hubert. "Inclining to Exultation." *Art Digest* 28 (1 May 1954): 15, 33.
Creeley, Robert. "A Note on Franz Kline." *Black Mountain Review* 1 (Winter 1954): 23–32.
——. "The Art of Poetry X." *Paris Review* 44 (Fall 1968): 173–74.
Das Bild einer Geschichte 1956/1976; Die Sammlung Panza di Biumo. Exh. cat. Düsseldorf:
Kunstsammlung Nordrhein-Westfalen, Kunstmuseum Düsseldorf, and Kunsthalle

Düsseldorf, 1980. Essay by Germano Celant.

Dawson, Fielding. *An Emotional Memoir of Franz Kline*. New York: Pantheon, 1967.

de Kooning, Elaine. "Subject: What, How or Who?" *ARTnews* 54 (April 1955): 26–29.

——. "Two Americans in Action: Franz Kline, Mark Rothko." *ARTnews Annual* 56 (November 1957): 88–97.

——. "Franz Kline: painter of his own life." *ARTnews* 61, no. 7 (November 1962): 28–31, 64–69.

Farber, Manny. "Art." *Nation* 171 (11 November 1950): 445.

"Fifty-Seventh Street in Review." *Art Digest* 25 (1 November 1950): 20–21.

Fish, John. "Franz Kline." *The Village Voice* (14 March 1956): 10.

Franz Kline. Exh. cat. Chicago: Arts Club of Chicago, 1961.

Franz Kline. Exh. cat. Paris: Galerie Lawrence, 1962.

Franz Kline. Exh. cat. Los Angeles: Dwan Gallery, 1963. Essay by Jules Langsner.

Franz Kline. Exh. cat. New York: David McKee Gallery, 1975.

Franz Kline. Exh. cat. New York: Marisa del Re Gallery, 1984.

Franz Kline, 1910–1962. Exh. cat. New York: Whitney Museum of American Art, 1968. Essay by Robert Goldwater.

Franz Kline: Art and the Structure of Identity. Barcelona: Antoni Tàpies Foundation, 1994.

Franz Kline: Black & White 1950-1961. Exh. cat. Houston: The Menil Collection, 1994. Essay by David Anfam.

Franz Kline: The Color Abstractions. Exh. cat. Washington, D.C.: The Phillips Collection, 1979. Essay by Harry F. Gaugh.

Franz Kline: The Early Works as Signals. Exh. cat. Binghamton: University Art Gallery, State University of New York, 1977. Essays by Albert Boime and Fred Mitchell.

Franz Kline: The Jazz Murals. Exh. cat. Lewisburg, Pennsylvania: Center Gallery, Bucknell University, 1989. Essay by Robert Metzger.

Franz Kline, Memorial Exhibition. Exh. cat. Washington, D.C.: Washington Gallery of Modern Art, 1962. Essay by Elaine de Kooning.

Franz Kline, A Retrospective Exhibition. Exh. cat. London: Whitechapel Gallery, 1964. Introduction and interview by Frank O'Hara.

Franz Kline: Selected Works. Exh. cat. New York: Allan Stone Gallery, 1974.

Franz Kline: Works on Paper. Exh. cat. London: The Mayor Gallery, 1977. Essay by Thomas B. Hess.

Friedman, B.H. "Current and Forthcoming Exhibitions." *Burlington Magazine* 98 (March 1956): 177.

Gaugh, Harry F. "Kline's Transitional Abstractions, 1946–50." *Art in America* 62, no. 4 (July-August 1974): 43–47.

——. "Franz Kline's Romantic Abstraction." *Artforum* 13, no. 10 (Summer 1975): 28–37.

——. "Franz Kline at University Art Gallery, SUNY." *Art in America* 65 (September–October 1977): 123.

——. *Franz Kline*. New York: Abbeville Press, 1985.

——. "Franz Kline: The Man and the Myths." *ARTnews* 84, no. 10 (December 1985): 61–67.

Genauer, Emily. "Critic Deplores New Art of Nothing-ness." *New York Herald Tribune* (11 March 1956): 10.

——. "Franz Kline: Mirror on Violence." *New York Herald Tribune* (8 December 1963): 43.

Goldwater, Robert. "Reflections on the New York School." *Quadrum* 8 (1960): 17–36, 77.

——. "Art Chronicle: Masters of the New." *Partisan Review* 29 (Summer 1962): 29, 416–20.

——. "Franz Kline: Darkness Visible." *ARTnews* 66, no. 1 (March 1967): 38–43, 77.

Goodnough, Robert. "Kline Paints a Picture." *ARTnews* 51 (December 1952): 36–39.

Greenberg, Clement. "Art Chronicle: Feeling Is All." *Partisan Review* 19 (January–February 1952): 92–102.

Hamill, Pete. "Beyond the Vital Gesture." *Art and Antiques* 7 (May 1990): 117.

Hasegawa, Sabro. "The Beauty of Black and White." *Bokubi* (Tokyo) 12, no. 4 (1951).

Hess, Thomas B. "Seeing the Young New Yorkers." *ARTnews* 49 (May 1950): 23.

——. *Abstract Painting, Background and American Phase*. New York: Viking, 1951.

——. "Franz Kline." *ARTnews* 55 (March 1956): 51.

——. "Reviews and Previews:" *ARTnews* 57 (Summer 1958): 14.

——. "Is Today's Artist With or Against the Past?" *ARTnews* 57 (September 1958): 40, 58.

——. "Franz Kline." *ARTnews* 60 (January 1962): 46–47, 60–61.

——. "The Convertible Oyster." *New York Magazine* 8 (7 April 1975): 68-70.

Hopkins, Budd. "Franz Kline's Color Abstractions: Remembering and Looking Afresh." *Artforum* 17 (Summer 1979): 37–41.

Judd, Donald. "Franz Kline." *Arts Magazine* 36, no. 5 (February 1962): 44.

Karp, Ivan C. "The Unweary Mr. Franz Kline: Artist without Metaphysics." *The Village Voice* (7 March 1956): 10.

Kees, Welden. "Art." *Nation* 170 (6 May 1950): 430–31.

Kinglsey, April. "Conflict in Color." *Newsweek* 94 (6 August 1979): 78–79.

Kline. Exh. cat. Rome: La Tartaruga Galleria d'arte, 1958.

Kline. Exh. cat. Atlanta: New Arts Gallery, 1961.

Kline. Exh. cat. Rome: La Tartaruga Galleria d'arte, 1963.

Kline Memorial Exhibition. Exh. cat. New York: Sidney Janis Gallery, 1963.

Kline: New Paintings by Franz Kline. Exh. cat. New York: Sidney Janis Gallery, 1960.

Kline, Elizabeth V. "Editor's Letters." *ARTnews* 61, no. 9 (January 1963): 6.

Kramer, Hilton. "Franz Kline: Turning Art Into Academic History." *The New York Times* (6 October 1968): B35.

Kuh, Katharine. *The Artist's Voice: Talks with Seventeen Artists*. New York: Harper and Row, 1962.

Langsner, Jules. "Franz Kline, Calligraphy and Information Theory." *Art International* 7, no. 3 (March 1963): 25–29.

McBride, Henry. "No Exit at the Whitney." *ARTnews* 51 (April 1952): 36–37, 64.

McDarrah, Fred W. *The Artist's World in Pictures*. New York: E.P. Dutton, 1961.

Munson, Gretchen T. "Reviews and Previews." *ARTnews* 49 (November 1950): 48.

The New American Painting. Exh. cat. New York: The Museum of Modern Art, 1958. Essay by Alfred H. Barr, Jr.

The New Decade: 35 American Painters and Sculptors. Exh. cat. New York: Whitney Museum of American Art, 1955. Edited by John I.H. Baur.

Nordland, Gerald. "Requiem in Black and White." *Frontier* 12 (July 1962): 13, 21–23.

O'Doherty, Brian. "Art: The Opposite Sides of the Coin Are Displayed." *The New York Times* (7 December 1961): 49.

Oeri, Georgine. "Notes on Franz Kline." *Quadrum* 12 (1961): 93–102.

O'Hara, Frank. "Franz Kline Talking." *Evergreen Review* (Autumn 1958): 58–64.

Porter, Fairfield. "Franz Kline." *ARTnews* 50 (December 1951): 46.

Preston, Stuart. "Chiefly Modern." *The New York Times* (11 March 1956): 14.

Quattro Artisti Americani: Guston, Hofmann, Kline, Roszak. Exh. cat. Venice: XXX Biennale, 1960. Essays by Adelyn D. Breeskin and Kenneth B. Sawyer.

Read, Sir Herbert, and Harvard H. Arnason. "Dialogue on Modern U.S. Painting." *ARTnews* 59 (May 1960): 32–36.

Richard Brown Baker Collects! Exh. cat. New Haven, Connecticut: Yale University Art Gallery, 1975. Essay by Theodore E. Stebbins, Jr.

Robbins, Daniel and Eugenia. "Franz Kline: Rough Impulsive Gesture." *The Studio* 167 (May 1964): 186–89.

Rodman, Selden. *Conversations with Artists*. New York: Devin-Adair, 1957.

——. "Important Abstractionist." *Cosmopolitan* 146 (February 1959): 66-69.

Russell, John. "Kline's Effulgent Abstractions." *The New York Times* (18 March 1979): 31.

——. "Art: Franz Kline Show." *The New York Times* (11 May 1984): C20.

Sandler, Irving. *The Triumph of American Painting*. New York: Praeger, 1970.

——. *The New York School: The Painters and Sculptors of the Fifties*. New York: Harper and Row, 1978.

Sawin, Martica. "An American Artist in Japan." *Arts Digest* 29 (1 August 1955): 12–13.

——. "In the Galleries: Franz Kline." *Arts Magazine* 32, no. 10 (September 1958): 57–58.

Schuyler, James. "Reviews and Previews." *ARTnews* 59 (April 1960): 12.

——. "As American as Franz Kline." *ARTnews* 67, no. 6 (October 1968): 30–33, 58–59.

Sieberling, Dorothy. "The Varied Art of Four Pioneers." *Life* (16 November 1959): 74–83, 85–86.

S[iegel], J[eanne]. "In the Galleries." *Arts Magazine* 41 (March 1967): 56.

Steinberg, Leo. "Month in Review." *Arts Magazine* 30 (April 1956): 42-45.

Sylvester, David. "Franz Kline 1910–1962: An Interview with David Sylvester." *Living Arts* 1 (Spring 1963): 3–13.

Tannous, David. "Report from Washington." *Art in America* 67 (July 1979): 24–25.

Twelve Americans. Exh. cat. New York: The Museum of Modern Art, 1956. Essay by Dorothy C. Miller.

Wright, Martha McWilliams. "Washington Letter." *Art International* 23 (September 1979): 81.

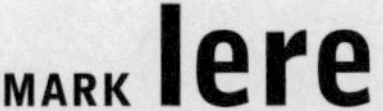

MARK **lere**

born in LaMoure, North Dakota, 1950
lives and works in Los Angeles
education M.F.A., University of California at Irvine, Irvine, California, 1976
B.F.A., Metropolitan State College, Denver, Colorado, 1973

selected one-person exhibitions

1996   Weatherspoon Art Gallery, University of North Carolina at Greensboro, Greensboro, North Carolina

1992   *Mark Lere: Works in Two Dimensions*, Margo Leavin Gallery, Los Angeles

1991   *Mark Lere Sculpture*, Greg Kucera Gallery, Seattle, Washington

1990   *Mark Lere: New Sculpture*, Margo Leavin Gallery, Los Angeles

1989   North Dakota Museum of Art, Grand Forks, North Dakota

1988   *Mark Lere: Recent Sculpture*, John Berggruen Gallery, San Francisco
       Liz Larner Sculpture/Mark Lere Drawings, Margo Leavin Gallery, Los Angeles

1987   *Mark Lere*, Margo Leavin Gallery, Los Angeles

1986   *Mark Lere: Recent Sculpture*, Margo Leavin Gallery, Los Angeles
       Mark Lere Sculpture, Hewlett Gallery, Carnegie Mellon University, Pittsburgh
       Mark Lere: Sculpture/Installation, Temple Gallery, Temple University, Philadelphia

1985   *Mark Lere*, University of California, Irvine, California
       New and Selected Work, The Museum of Contemporary Art, Los Angeles

1984   *Halo/Wheel*, Public exhibition commissioned by The Museum of Contemporary Art, Los Angeles

1983   Sonoma State University, Sonoma, California
       Installation, San Diego, California
       Los Angeles Municipal Art Gallery, Los Angeles
       Riko Mizuno Gallery, Los Angeles

1982   California State University, Los Angeles

1980   Riko Mizuno Gallery, Los Angeles

1976   Arts Gallery, University of California, Irvine, California

selected group exhibitions

1995   *25 Years: An Exhibition of Selected Works*, Margo Leavin Gallery, Los Angeles
       Between Reality and Abstraction: California Art at the End of the Century, Art Museum of South Texas, Corpus Christi, Texas
       California: In Three Dimensions, California Center for the Arts Museum, Escondido, California
       From Behind the Orange Curtain, Muckenthaler Cultural Center, Fullerton, California

1993   *A Complete Hand of One Suit*, Donna Beam Fine Art Gallery, University of Nevada at Las Vegas, Las Vegas
       In Search of Form, Weatherspoon Art Gallery, University of North Carolina at Greensboro, Greensboro, North Carolina

1992   *California: North and South*, Aspen Art Museum, Aspen, Colorado
       Gli anni Ottanta e Novanta dalla Collezione Panza di Biumo, Museo Cantonale d'Arte, Lugano, Switzerland
       Objects of Affection: Small-Scale Paintings, Sculpture, Works on Paper, John Berggruen Gallery, San Francisco

1991   *20th Century Collage*, Margo Leavin Gallery, Los Angeles. Traveled to Centro Cultural Arte Contemporáneo, Mexico City, and Musée d'Art Moderne et d'Art Contemporain, Nice, France
       The Artist's Hand, A. P. Giannini Gallery, Bank of America, San Francisco. Traveled to San Diego Museum of Art, San Diego, California
       Big Objects, Tacoma Art Museum, Tacoma, Washington
       Contemporary Bronze, Process and Object, Atlanta College of Art, Atlanta
       Different Stories, Newport Harbor Art Museum, Newport Beach, California
       Evocative Objects, California State University, Fine Arts Gallery, Los Angeles
       Individual Realities, Sezon Museum of Art, Tokyo. Traveled to Tsukashin Hall, Osaka, Japan
       Large Scale Works on Paper, John Berggruen Gallery, San Francisco
       Sculpture Exhibition, Margo Leavin Gallery, Los Angeles

1990   *Lead & Wax*, Stephen Wirtz Gallery, San Francisco

New Sculpture, Eve Mannes Gallery, Atlanta
Recent Acquisitions, John Berggruen Gallery, San Francisco

1989   *American Sculptors: New York & Los Angeles*, Kamakura Gallery, Tokyo
       Endangered Industries, Mary Ryan Gallery, New York

1988   Ace Contemporary Exhibtions, Los Angeles
       Discreet Formalities, Greg Kucera Gallery, Seattle, Washington
       Figurative Impulses, Santa Barbara Museum of Art, Santa Barbara, California
       Southern California Summer 1988, Cirrus Gallery, Los Angeles
       Summer Sculpture Exhibtion at Monadnock, John Berggruen Gallery, San Francisco

1987   *Avant-Garde in the 80s*, Los Angeles County Museum of Art, Los Angeles
       Individuals: A Selected History of Contemporary Art, 1945–1986, The Museum of Contemporary Art, Los Angeles
       Lead, Hirschl & Adler Modern, New York
       Prints, Hirschl & Adler Modern, New York
       Sculpture Arenas, Mandeville Gallery, University of California, La Jolla, California
       Two Exhibtions of Contemporary Southern California Art, Taipei Fine Arts Museum, Taipei, Taiwan; and Los Angeles Municipal Art Gallery, Los Angeles

1986   *Fabricated, not found*, Loughelton Gallery, New York
       Installation: 1982–1986, Installation, San Diego, California
       Paintings and Sculpture by Candidates for Art Awards, American Academy and Institute of Arts and Letters, New York
       Pasadena Collects: The Art of Our Time, Art Center College of Design, Pasadena, California
       Prospect 86, Frankfurter Kunstverein, Frankfurt
       Sculpture and Works in Relief, John Berggruen Gallery, San Francisco
       A Southern California Collection, Cirrus Gallery, Los Angeles

1985   *Anniottanta (the 80's)*, Galeria Communale d'Arte Moderna, Bologna, Italy
       MARK LERE/menisucs. . . ex machina/MARC PALLY, Fine Art Gallery, University of California, Irvine, California
       Mile 4, Chicago Sculpture International, Chicago
       Outdoor Sculpture, Margo Leavin Gallery, Los Angeles
       Small Monuments, Tyler Gallery, Tyler School of Art, Temple University, Philadelphia

1984   *American Sculpture*, Margo Leavin Gallery, Los Angeles
       Aperto '84, 1984 Venice Biennale, Venice
       Constructed Metal, University of California, Santa Barbara, California
       Contemporary Landscapes, Hunsaker/Schlesinger, Los Angeles
       Landscape, Marianne Deson Gallery, Chicago

1983   *Artists and the Theater*, Herbert Palmer Gallery, Los Angeles
       The Nancy Yewell Collection, Baxter Art Gallery, California Institute of Technology, Pasadena, California
       Sixteen Months at Art Center, Art Center College of Design, Pasadena, California

1982   Cirrus Gallery, Los Angeles
       Hang 8: Southern California Artists, Foundations Gallery, New York
       Sculpture '82, Sonoma State University, Sonoma, California
       Security Pacific Bank Collection, Los Angeles Municipal Art Gallery, Los Angeles
       Visiting Artists: 10 Years, Claremont Graduate School, Claremont, California

1981   *Anti-Static*, Baxter Art Gallery, California Institute of Technology, Pasadena, California
       The Big Drawing Show, Newspace Gallery, Los Angeles
       Gallery Artists, Riko Mizuno Gallery, Los Angeles
       Southern California Artists, Los Angeles Institute of Contemporary Art, Los Angeles

1980   *Tableaux*, Los Angeles Institute of Contemporary Art, Los Angeles
       Architectural Sculpture, Fine Arts Gallery, Mount St. Mary's College, Los Angeles

1979   *Visual and Musical Permutations*, Fine Arts Gallery, University of California, Irvine, California

1978   *1001 Current Directions in Southern California Art*, Los Angeles Institute of Contemporary Art, Los Angeles

1976   *A December Drawing Show*, Floating Wall Gallery, Santa Ana, California

bibliography

Anderson, Michael. "Mark Lere: sculpture and drawing at Margo Leavin Annex." *L.A. Weekly* (28 March–3 April 1986): 43.

Anniottanta. Exh. cat. Milan: Galleria Salamon Augstoni Algranti, 1985.

Apgar, Katie. "Drawing by 20 artists." *Artweek* 6, no. 44 (20 December 1975): 6.

Baker, Kenneth. "Sculpture that Looks like Sculpture." *San Francisco Chronicle* (22 June 1988): E2.

——. "Physical Precision." *Artspace* (September/October 1990): 40–45.

Bianchi, Tom. "Controlled Violence." *Artweek* 14, no. 16 (23 April 1983): 7.

Blaine, Michael. "Architectural Spoof and Satire." *Artweek* 11, no. 34 (18 October 1980): 20.

Bonetti, David. *San Francisco Examiner* (21 September 1990): C-2.

Brunson, Jamie. "Quirky Materials, Diverse References." *Artweek* 19, no. 25 (9 July 1988): 3.

Burchett, Debra. *Journal: A Contemporary Art Magazine* (October/November 1978).

Burstein, Joanne. "Sculpture '82: The Parallel Current." *Artweek* (10 April 1982): 1.

Clark, Vicky A. "Two from LA." *Dialogue* 10, no. 1 (January/February 1987): 32–33.

Contemporary Southern California Art. Exh. cat. Taipei, Taiwan: Taipei Fine Arts Museum, 1987.

Cotter, Holland. "Eight Artists Interviewed." *Art in America* 75, no. 5 (May 1987): 162–179.

Delgado, Michael. "Pick of the Week: Mark Lere." *L.A. Weekly* (9–15 September 1983): 98.

Drohojowska, Hunter. "Pick of the Week: Tableau at LAICA." *L.A. Weekly* (15–21 February 1980): 44.

Failing, Patricia. "MOCA: Los Angeles Gets its Long-Awaited Museum of Contemporary Art—Or At Least A Temporary Contemporary." *ARTnews* 82, no. 8 (October 1983): 105–109.

Faust, Wolfgang Max. "Prospekt 86 Die Lehre als Mittel." *Wolkenkratzer* (November/December 1986): 53–54.

Frank, Peter. "Art Pick of the Week: Mark Lere, Doug Edge, 'Cont-text.'" *L.A. Weekly* (26 October–1 November 1990): 130.

From Los Angeles . . . DAVID AMICO Paintings . . . MARK LERE Sculpture. Exh. cat. Pittsburgh: Hewlett Gallery, Carnegie Mellon University, 1986. Interview by Elaine E. King.

Geer, Suvan. "Close Encounters with Sculptures by Mark Lere." *Los Angeles Times* (31 October 1990): F4.

Giovannini, Joseph. " Architecture as Sculpture: LAICA presents art you can walk through, see into, climb." *Los Angeles Herald Examiner* (10 November 1980): B1, B6.

Glueck, Grace. "Artful L.A.: New Museums-Collectors-Artists." *The New York Times Magazine* (23 November 1986): F34–39.

Hughes, Robert. "Getting On the Map." *Time* 129, no. 2 (12 January 1987): 78–81.

Ianco-Starrels, Josine. "L.A. Sculptors in Venice Biennale." *Los Angeles Times* (13 May 1984): 95.

Installation: 1981–1986. Exh. cat. San Diego, California: Installation, 1986.

Jacki, Apple. "The Language of Objects in an Unknown Land." *Artweek* 16, no. 14 (6 April 1985): cover, 1.

Kelley, Jeff. "San Diego Art Review: Installation of Conical Fantasy." *Los Angeles Times* (25 November 1983): VI1, VI2.

Knight, Christopher. "Bridging the Gap: Sculpture and architecture." *Los Angeles Herald Examiner* (28 September 1980): E9.

——. "Breaking the tyranny of the automobile." *Los Angeles Herald Examiner* (26 August 1984): E1, E7.

——. "Unveiling the State of L.A.'s Art: What we'll see when LACMA and MOCA open new buildings." *Los Angeles Herald Examiner* (21 September 1986): E1, E6.

Komac, Dennis. "Spiralling Forces." *Artweek* 14, no. 40 (26 November 1983): 4.

Lewis, Louise. "Experiences in Tableaux." *Artweek* 11, no. 7 (23 February 1980): 5.

Madoff, Steven Henry. "Sculpture Unbound." *ARTnews* 85, no. 9 (November 1986): 103–109.

Mark Lere: New and Selected Work. Exh. cat. Los Angeles: The Museum of Contemporary Art, Los Angeles, 1985. Essays by Frances Colpitt and Kerry Brougher; biography and bibliography.

Mark Lere: Sculpture/Installation. Exh. cat. Philadelphia: Tyler Gallery, Temple University, 1986. Introduction by Julie Courtney, essay by Suzanne Muchnic, interview by Elaine E. King.

Morera, Daniela. "Art of Los Angeles." *Vogue Italia* (October 1986): 270–277.

Muchnic, Suzanne. "Sculpture Becomes a Structure." *Los Angeles Times* (27 October 1980): F1, F6.

——. "Mark Lere: Mizuno Gallery." *Los Angeles Times* (21 November 1980): F7.

——. "Mark Lere at Margo Leavin Gallery." *Los Angeles Times* (14 March 1986): D12.

Pincus, Robert. "Portrait, Nature and Symbols on Exhibition at Barnsdall Park Gallery." *Los Angeles Times* (15 September 1983): F6.

Prospect 86. Exh. cat. Frankfurt: Frankfurter Kunstverein, 1986. Essay by Suzanne Muchnic.

Reveaux, Tony. "Mark Lere." *Artweek* 22, no. 44 (26 December 1991): 12.

Sculpture Arenas: Chris Burden, Kenneth Capps, Jill Giegerich, Mathieu Gregoire, Margaret Honda, Mark Lere. Exh. cat. La Jolla, California: Mandeville Gallery, University of California, San Diego, 1987. Essay by Michael McManus; biographies.

Selwyn, Marc. "La dynamique de l'art." *Beaux Arts Magazine,* no. 42 (January 1987): 89.

——. "New Art L.A." *Flash Art,* no. 141 (Summer 1988): 112–113.

Smallwood, Lyn. "Visual Arts/They might be functional." *Seattle Weekly* (12 June 1991): 61.

Stein, Donna. *Between Reality and Abstraction: California Art at the End of the Century.* Los Angeles: The Hillcrest Foundation, 1995.

"WCSD Sculpture Exhibit an Educational Event," *Los Angeles Times* (April 18 1987).

Wilson, William. "'Tableaux' L.A. Institute of Contemporary Art." *Los Angeles Times* (1 February 1979): 85.

——. "'Tableau': Rooms for Improvement." *Los Angeles Times* (24 February 1980): 85.

——. "Lere's Halo/Wheel." *Los Angeles Times* (4 September 1984): F1, F3.

Wolf, Leslie. "Pick of the Week: American Sculpture." *L.A. Weekly* (27 July–2 August 1984): 128.

Woodard, Josef. "Abstracting the Figure." *Artweek* 19, no. 42 (10 December 1988): 9

Wortz, Melinda. "Crawling, like Alice, down the rabbit hole." *ARTnews* 78, no.1 (January 1979): 71–74.

——. "Artists the Critics Are Watching." *ARTnews* 80, no.5 (May 1981): 87–88.

ROY **lichtenstein**

born in New York, 1923
died in New York, 1997
education Art Students League, New York, 1940
B.F.A., Ohio State University, Columbus, 1940–1943, 1946
M.F.A., Ohio State University, Columbus, 1946–1949

selected one-person exhibitions

1999   *Roy Lichtenstein: Interiors*, Museum of Contemporary Art, Chicago
     Roy Lichtenstein: Sculpture and Drawings, Corcoran Gallery of Art, Washington, D.C.

1998   *Roy Lichtenstein*, Foundation Beyeler, Basel, Switzerland

1997   *Roy Lichtenstein: New Paintings*, Galerie Lawrence Rubin, Zurich, and Anthony d'Offay Gallery, London
     Roy Lichtenstein: Recent Drawings and Sculpture, Richard Gray Gallery, Chicago

1994   *Roy Lichtenstein: Nudes*, Leo Castelli Gallery, New York
     The Prints of Roy Lichtenstein, National Gallery of Art, Washington, D.C. Traveled to Los Angeles County Museum of Art, Los Angeles; and Dallas Museum of Art, Dallas, Texas

1993   *Roy Lichtenstein,* Solomon R. Guggenheim Museum, New York. Traveled to The Museum of Contemporary Art, Los Angeles; The Montreal Museum of Fine Art, Montreal; Haus der Kunst, Munich; Deichtorhallen, Hamburg; Les Expositions du Palais des Beaux-Arts, Brussels; and Wexner Center for the Arts, Columbus, Ohio

1992   FAE Musée d'Art Contemporain, Lausanne, France. Traveled to Tate Gallery, Liverpool, England
     Roy Lichtenstein: Interiors, Collages, Galerie Ulysses, Vienna
     Roy Lichtenstein: Three Decades of Sculpture, Guild Hall Museum, East Hampton, New York
     Interiors, Leo Castelli Gallery, New York, and 65 Thompson Street, New York

1991   Galerie Beyeler, Basel, Switzerland

1989   *Roy Lichtenstein: Bronze Sculpture 1976–1989*, 65 Thompson Street, New York
     Roy Lichtenstein: "The Mirror Paintings," Mary Boone Gallery, New York

1988   *Lichtenstein's Picassos: 1962–1964*, Gagosian Gallery, New York
     Roy Lichtenstein: Imperfect, Heland Wetterling Gallery, Stockholm

1987   *The Drawings of Roy Lichtenstein*, The Museum of Modern Art, New York. Traveled to Museum Overland, Amsterdam; Tel Aviv Museum, Tel Aviv; The Douglas Hyde Gallery, Trinity College, Dublin; Schirn Kunsthalle, Frankfurt; Museum of Modern Art, Oxford, England; and Corcoran Gallery of Art, Washington, D.C.

1986   *Roy Lichtenstein: Sculptures and Graphics 1980–1986*, Heland Thordén Wetterling Galleries, Stockholm

1985   *Roy Lichtenstein as Sculptor: Recent Works 1977–1984*, Columbus Museum of Art, Columbus, Ohio

1984   *Roy Lichtenstein: Eight New Paintings*, Richard Gray Gallery, Chicago

Roy Lichtenstein: Paintings, Leo Castelli Gallery, New York

1982   *Roy Lichtenstein—Paintings*, The Parrish Art Museum, Southampton, New York

1981   *Roy Lichtenstein 1970–1980*, The Saint Louis Art Museum, St. Louis, Missouri. Traveled to Seattle Art Museum, Seattle; Whitney Museum of American Art, New York; Fort Worth Art Museum, Fort Worth, Texas; Museum Ludwig, Cologne; City of Florence, Italy; Musée des arts décoratifs, Paris; Fundacion Juan March, Madrid; and Sezon Museum of Modern Art, Karuizawa, Japan

Roy Lichtenstein: New Works, Leo Castelli Gallery, New York

1980   *Roy Lichtenstein Graphic Work: 1970-1980*. Whitney Museum of American Art, Downtown Branch, New York

Roy Lichtenstein: Recent Paintings, The Mayor Gallery, London

1979   Leo Castelli Gallery, New York

1978   Ace Gallery, Los Angeles

Roy Lichtenstein: The Modern Work, 1965–1970, The Institute of Contemporary Art, Boston

1977   Leo Castelli Gallery, New York, and Blum Helman, New York

Roy Lichtenstein: Gemälde und Graphik 1962–1977, Mannheimer Kunstverein, Mannheim, Germany

Roy Lichtenstein Sculpture, The Mayor Gallery, London, and Leo Castelli Gallery, New York

1976   *Roy Lichtenstein: New Paintings*, The Mayor Gallery, London

1975   Leo Castelli Gallery, New York

Roy Lichtenstein: Sculpture 1967–68; Entablature Paintings, 1974–75, Ace Gallery, Los Angeles

Roy Lichtenstein: Zeichnungen, Nationalgalerie, Berlin. Traveled to Neue Galerie—Sammlung Ludwig, Aachen, Germany

1974   Galerie Mikro, Berlin

Margo Leavin Gallery, Los Angeles

The Mayor Gallery, London

Roy Lichtenstein: Artist's Studio Paintings, Leo Castelli Gallery, New York

1973   Galerie Beyeler, Basel, Switzerland

Roy Lichtenstein: Still Lifes, Leo Castelli Gallery, New York

1972   Contemporary Arts Museum, Houston

Leo Castelli Gallery, New York

1971   Irving Blum Gallery, Los Angeles

Roy Lichtenstein: Mirror Paintings, Leo Castelli Gallery, New York

1970   Galerie Ileana Sonnabend, Paris

Roy Lichtenstein: Graphics, Reliefs and Sculpture, 1969–1970, Art Gallery, University of California, Irvine

1969   Castelli Graphics, New York

Guggenheim Museum, New York. Traveled to Nelson-Atkins Museum of Fine Arts, Kansas City; Museum of Contemporary Art, Chicago; Seattle Art Museum, Seattle; and Columbus Gallery of Art, Columbus, Ohio

1968   *Roy Lichtenstein: Exhibitions of Paintings and Sculpture*, The Contemporary Arts Center, Cincinnati

1967   Irving Blum Gallery, Los Angeles

Leo Castelli Gallery, New York

Pasadena Art Museum, Pasadena, California, in collaboration with Walker Art Center, Minneapolis

Stedelijk Museum, Amsterdam. Traveled to Tate Gallery, London; Kunsthalle Bern, Bern, Switzerland; and Kestner-Gesellschaft, Hannover, Germany

1966   *Works by Roy Lichtenstein*, Cleveland Museum of Art, Cleveland, Ohio

1965   Galerie Ileana Sonnabend, Paris

Roy Lichtenstein: Brushstrokes and Ceramics, Leo Castelli Gallery, New York

1964   Ferus Gallery, Los Angeles

Galleria Il Punto, Turin, Italy

Landscapes, Leo Castelli Gallery, New York

1963   Ferus Gallery, Los Angeles

Galerie Ileana Sonnabend, Paris

Leo Castelli Gallery, New York

1962   Leo Castelli Gallery, New York

1959   *Paintings: Lichtenstein*, Condon Riley Gallery, New York

1957   John Heller Gallery, New York

1954   John Heller Gallery, New York

1953   *Recent Paintings: Roy F. Lichtenstein*, John Heller Gallery, New York

1952   Art Colony Galleries, Cleveland, Ohio

1951   *Roy Lichtenstein*, Carlebach Gallery, New York

selected group exhibitions

1993   *Hand-Painted Pop: American Art in Transition 1955–1962*, The Museum of Contemporary Art, Los Angeles. Traveled to Museum of Contemporary Art, Chicago; and Whitney Museum of American Art, New York

1991   *High and Low: Modern Art and Popular Culture*, The Museum of Modern Art, New York. Traveled to Art Institute of Chicago, Chicago; and The Museum of Contemporary Art, Los Angeles

Pop Art, Royal Academy of Arts, London. Traveled to Museum Ludwig, Cologne; Museo Nacional Centro de Arte Reina Sofia, Madrid; and Museum of Fine Arts, Montreal

Roy Lichtenstein/Frank Stella, Galerie Beyeler, Basel, Switzerland

La sculpture contemporaine après 1970, Fondation Daniel Templon, Musée Temporaire, Fréjus, France

1990   *Image World: Art and Media Culture*, Whitney Museum of American Art, New York

1989   *La Collezione Sonnabend. Dalla Pop Art in poi*, Galleria Nazionale d'Arte Moderna, Rome. Traveled to Museo Nacional Centro de Arte Reina Sofia, Madrid; CAPC Musée d'Art Contemporain de Bordeaux, France; and "Zeitgeist" Gesellschaft Hamburger Bahnhof, Berlin

1988   *The Turning Point: Art and Politics in Nineteen Sixty-eight*, Cleveland Center for Contemporary Art, Cleveland, Ohio

1987   *Comic Iconoclasm*, Institute of Contemporary Arts, London. Traveled to Douglas Hyde Gallery, Dublin; Cornerhouse Gallery, Manchester; and Louisiana Museum of Modern Art, Humlebaek, Denmark

Made in U.S.A.: An Americanization in Modern Art, The '50s and '60s, University Art Museum, University of California at Berkeley, Berkeley, California. Traveled to Nelson-Atkins Museum of Art, Kansas City; and Virginia Museum of Fine Arts, Richmond, Virginia

1984   *Blam! The Explosion of Pop, Minimalism, and Performance 1958–1964*, Whitney Museum of American Art, New York

1974   *American Pop Art*, Whitney Museum of American Art, New York

1971   *Art and Technology*. Los Angeles County Museum of Art, Los Angeles

1969   *Pop Art*, Hayward Gallery, London

The Spirit of the Comics, Institute of Contemporary Art, University of Pennsylvania, Philadelphia

1964   *Neue Realisten und Pop Art*, Akademie der Künste, Berlin

1963   *Mixed Media and Pop Art*, Albright-Knox Art Gallery, Buffalo, New York

The Popular Image, Institute of Contemporary Arts, London, in collaboration with Galerie Ileana Sonnabend, Paris

Six Painters and the Object, Guggenheim Museum, New York. Traveled Los Angeles County Museum of Art, Los Angeles; Minneapolis Institute of Art, Minneapolis; University of Michigan Museum of Art, Ann Arbor; Rose Art Museum, Brandeis University, Waltham, Massachusetts; Museum of Art, Carnegie Institute, Pittsburgh; Columbus Gallery of Fine Arts; and Art Center in La Jolla, California

1955   *Lichtenstein-Penfield-Miller*, Art Colony Galleries, Cleveland, Ohio

selected bibliography

Alloway, Lawrence. "Roy Lichtenstein's Period Style: From the 'Thirties to the 'Sixties and Back." *Arts Magazine* 42, no. 1 (September–October 1967): 24–29.

——. "Roy Lichtenstein." *Studio International* 175, no. 896 (January 1968): 25–31.

——. "On Style: An Examination of Roy Lichtenstein's Development, Despite a New Monograph on the Artist." *Artforum* 10, no. 7 (March 1972): 53–59.

——. *Roy Lichtenstein*. New York: Abbeville Press, 1983. Interview with Lichtenstein.

Amaya, Mario. "Scaling the Heights: De Kooning into Lichtenstein." *Studio International* 196, no. 1004 (1984): 41–42.

Art of Two Ages: The Hudson River School and Roy Lichtenstein. New York: Mi Chou Gallery, 1962.

Baro, Gene. "Roy Lichtenstein: Technique as Style." *Art International* 12, no. 9 (November 1968): 35–38.

Bernard, April, and Mimi Thompson. "Roy Lichtenstein." *Bomb*, no. 14 (Winter 1986): 22–27.

Boime, Albert. "Roy Lichtenstein and the Comic Strip." *Art Journal* 28, no. 2 (Winter 1968–69): 155–59.

Brenson, Michael. "The Changing World of Roy Lichtenstein." *The New York Times* (10 August 1982): 9.

Brewster, Todd. "Pop Primer: Roy Lichtenstein's Monumental Mural Explains the Modern Movement." *Life* 9, no. 6 (June 1986): 75–79.

Busche, Ernst A. *Roy Lichtenstein: Das Frühwerk 1942–1960.* Berlin: Gebr. Mann, 1988.

Calas, Nicolas. "Roy Lichtenstein: Insight through Irony, the Guggenheim Retrospective." *Arts Magazine* 44, no. 1 (September–October 1969): 29–33.

Campbell, Lawrence. "Roy Lichtenstein." *ARTnews* 50, no. 3 (May 1951): 56–57.

——. "Roy Lichtenstein." *ARTnews* 62, no. 7 (November 1963): 12–13.

Canaday, John. "The Lichtenstein Retrospective." *The New York Times* (20 September 1969): 25.

Coplans, John. "An Interview with Roy Lichtenstein." *Artforum* 2, no. 4 (October 1963): 31.

——., ed. *Roy Lichtenstein.* New York and Washington, D.C.: Praeger, 1972.

Cortlett, Mary Lee. *The Prints of Roy Lichtenstein: A Catalogue Raisonné, 1948–1993.* New York and Washington, D.C.: Hudson Hills Press in association with the National Gallery of Art, 1994.

Dalí, Salvador. "How an Elvis Presley Becomes a Roy Lichtenstein." *Arts Magazine* 41, no. 6 (April 1967): 26–31.

Deitcher, David. "Lichtenstein's Expressionist Takes." *Art in America* 71, no. 1 (January 1983): 84–89.

Denson, G. Roger. "Roy Lichtenstein." *Flash Art* , no. 150 (January–February 1990): 130–31.

De Salvo, Donna, and Paul Schimmel. *Hand-Painted Pop: American Art in Transition 1955–1962.* Los Angeles: The Museum of Contemporary Art, 1992. Essays by David Deitcher, De Salvo, Stephen C. Foster, Dick Hebdige, Linda Norden, Schimmel, Kenneth E. Silver, and John Yau.

Diamonstein, Barbaralee. "Pop Art, Money, and the Present Scene: An Interview with Roy Lichtenstein and Leo Castelli." *Partisan Review* 45, no. 1 (1978): 80–93.

The Drawings of Roy Lichtenstein. New York: The Museum of Modern Art, 1987. Essay by Barbara Rose.

Edgar, Natalie. "Roy Lichtenstein." *ARTnews* 61, no. 1 (March 1962): 14.

Esterow, Milton. "Roy Lichtenstein: 'How Could You Be Much Luckier Than I Am?'" *ARTnews* 90, no. 5 (May 1991): 85–88, 90–91.

Fried, Michael. "New York Letter." *Art International* 7, no. 9 (5 December 1963): 66–68.

Glaser, Bruce. "Oldenburg Lichtenstein Warhol: A Discussion." *Artforum* 4, no. 6 (February 1966): 20–24.

Glueck, Grace. "Blam! To the Top of Pop." *The New York Times* (21 September 1969): 31.

——. "New York: Visual Riches and Recessionary Blues." *Art in America* 5, no. 2 (March–April 1971): 42–47.

Gopnik, Adam. "The Wise Innocent." *The New York Times* 69, no. 37 (8 November 1993): 119–23.

Gruen, John. "Roy Lichtenstein: From Outrageous Parody to Iconographic Elegance." *ARTnews* 75, no. 3 (March 1976): 39–42.

Hahn, Otto. "Roy Lichtenstein." *Art International* 10, no. 6 (Summer 1966): 64, 66–69.

Hamilton, Richard. "Roy Lichtenstein." *Studio International* 175, no. 896 (January 1968): 20–24.

Haskell, Barbara. *Blam! The Explosion of Pop, Minimalism, and Performance 1958–1964.* New York: Whitney Museum of American Art, 1984. Text by Haskell, essay by John G. Hanhardt.

Heartney, Eleanor. "Roy Lichtenstein: Master of the Benday Dot." *ARTnews* 86, no. 6 (Summer 1987): 210.

Hess, Thomas B. "New Realists." *ARTnews* 61, no. 8 (December 1962): 12–13.

High and Low: Modern Art and Popular Culture. New York: The Museum of Modern Art, 1990. Texts by Kirk Varnedoe and Adam Gopnik.

Indiana, Gary. "The Disappearing Mural." *Art in America* 72, no. 3 (March 1984): 102–07.

Jodidio, Philip. "A Question of Appearances: Talk with Roy Lichtenstein." *Connaissance des arts*, no. 349 (March 1981): 61.

Johnson, Ellen H. "Lichtenstein: The Printed Image, at Venice." *Art and Artists* 1, no. 3 (June 1966): 12–15.

——. "The Lichtenstein Paradox." *Art and Artists* 2, no. 10 (January 1968): 12–15.

Johnston, Jill. "Roy Lichtenstein." *ARTnews* 63, no. 8 (December 1964): 15.

Judd, Donald. "Roy Lichtenstein." *Arts Magazine* 36, no. 7 (April 1962): 52–53.

——. "Roy Lichtenstein." *Arts Magazine* 38, no. 2 (November 1963): 32–33.

——. "Roy Lichtenstein." *Arts Magazine* 39, no. 3 (December 1964): 66.

Kozloff, Max. "Art." *The Nation* 197, no. 14 (2 November 1963): 284–87.

——. "Dissimulated Pop." *The Nation* 199, no. 17 (30 November 1964): 417–19.

——. "Lichtenstein at the Guggenheim." *Artforum* 8 , no. 3 (November 1969): 41–45.

Kuspit, Donald B. "Lichtenstein and the Collective Unconscious of Style." *Art in America* 67, no. 3 (May–June 1979): 100–05.

Lichtenstein's Picassos: 1962–1964. New York: Gagosian Gallery, 1988. Essay by Henry Geldzahler.

Linker, Kate. "Roy Lichtenstein." *Artforum* 25, no. 10 (Summer 1987): 113–14.

Lippard, Lucy. "New York Letter." *Art International* 10, no. 1 (January 1966): 93.

Livingstone, Marco, ed. *Pop Art.* London: Royal Academy of Arts, 1991. Essays by Dan Cameron, Constance W. Glenn, Thomas Kellein, Livingstone, Alfred Pacquement, and Evelyn Weiss.

Loran, Erle. "Cézanne and Lichtenstein: Problems of 'Transformation.'" *Artforum* 2, no. 3 (September 1963): 34–35.

Pincus-Witten, Robert. "Roy Lichtenstein, Castelli Gallery." *Artforum* 9, no. 9 (May 1971): 75.

Ratcliff, Carter. "Lichtenstein: Creating Art from Art." *Harper's Bazaar*, no. 3240 (November 1981): 32, 34, 38, 72.

——. "The Work of Roy Lichtenstein in the Age of Walter Benjamin's and Jean Baudrillard's Popularity." *Art in America* 77, no. 2 (February 1989): 110–23, 177.

——. "Roy Lichtenstein: Donald Duck et Picasso." *Art Press*, no. 140 (October 1989): 12–19.

Roberts, Keith. "Roy Lichtenstein and the Popular Image." *Burlington Magazine* 117, no. 880 (July 1976): 515.

Rose, Barbara. "Pop Art at the Guggenheim." *Art International* 7, no. 5 (25 May 1963): 20–22.

——. "Pop Art Revisited." *Art International* 8, no. 10 (December 1964): 48–49.

Rose, Barbara, and Irving Sandler. "Sensibility of the Sixties." *Art in America* 55, no. 1 (January–February 1967): 44–57.

Roy Lichtenstein. Los Angeles: Ferus Gallery, 1963.

Roy Lichtenstein. Pasadena, California: Pasadena Art Museum, in collaboration with Walker Art Center, Minneapolis, 1967. Essay and interview by John Coplans.

Roy Lichtenstein. Amsterdam: Stedelijk Museum, 1967. Essay by Wim Beeren, interview by John Coplans.

Roy Lichtenstein. London: Tate Gallery, 1968. Text by Wieland Schmied, interviews by John Coplans, David Pascal, Alan Solomon, Raphaël Sorin, and Gene R. Swenson.

Roy Lichtenstein. Houston: Contemporary Arts Museum, 1972. Essay by Lawrence Alloway.

Roy Lichtenstein. Lausanne, France: FAE Musée d'Art Contemporain, with Tate Gallery Liverpool, England, 1992. Essay and interview by Charles A. Riley II.

Roy Lichtenstein: Exhibitions of Paintings and Sculpture. Cincinnati: The Contemporary Arts Center, Cincinnati, 1968.

Roy Lichtenstein/Frank Stella. Basel, Switzerland: Galerie Beyeler, 1991.

Roy Lichtenstein: Gemälde und Graphik 1962–1977. Mannheim, Germany: Mannheimer Kunstverein, 1977. Interview by John Coplans.

Roy Lichtenstein: Interiors. Chicago: Museum of Contemporary Art, 1999. Texts by Robert Fitzpatrick, Dorothy Lichtenstein, Leo Castelli, Cassandra Lozano, and Sidney B. Felsen.

Roy Lichtenstein—Paintings. Southampton, New York: The Parrish Art Museum, 1982.

Roy Lichtenstein: The Modern Work, 1965–1970. Boston: The Institute of Contemporary Art, Boston. Essay by Elisabeth Sussman.

Russell, John. "Lichtenstein Has Not Lost His Power to Provoke." *The New York Times* (18 December 1983): 33.

Schaff, David. "A Conversation with Roy Lichtenstein." *Art International* 23, no. 9 (January–February 1980): 28–29.

Schwabsky, Barry. "Roy Lichtenstein." *Flash Art*, no. 135 (Summer 1987): 97.

Seiberling, Dorothy. "Is He the Worst Artist in the U.S.?" *Life* 56, no. 5 (31 January 1964): 79–83.

Siegel, Jeanne. "Thoughts on the 'Modern Period.'" In Siegel, *Artwords: Discourse of the 60s and 70s.* Ann Arbor, Michigan: University of Michigan Research Press, 1985, 191–96.

Six Painters and the Object. New York: Guggenheim Museum, 1963. Text by Lawrence Alloway.

Smith, Philip. "Roy Lichtenstein: Interview." *Arts Magazine* 52, no. 3 (November 1977): 26.

Smith, Roberta. "Roy Lichtenstein." *Artforum* 13, no. 6 (February 1975): 63–64.

Solomon, Deborah. "The Art behind the Dots." *The New York Times Magazine* (8 March 1987): 42–46, 107, 112.

Sorman, Guy. "Roy Lichtenstein roi du Pop." *Le Figaro Magazine* (Paris), no. 14775 (22 February 1992): 67–70.

Stich, Sidra. *Made in U.S.A.: An Americanization in Modern Art, The '50s and '60s.* Berkeley, California: University Art Museum, 1987. Text by Stich; essays by Ben H. Bagdikian, James E.B. Breslin, and Thomas Schaub.

Swenson, Gene R. "What Is Pop Art?: Answers from Eight Painters, Part I." *ARTnews* 62, no. 7 (November 1963): 24–27, 60–64.

Sylvester, David. "Roy Lichtenstein: 'The Iconic Lichtenstein Who Takes Soulful Subjects and

Paints Them with Cool.'" *Vogue* 154, no. 5 (15 September 1969): 142, 144–45, 168–69.

Taylor, Paul. "Roy Lichtenstein: Naïveté Allowed You to Do a Lot of Work, Now I Don't Know How Anyone Does Anything." *Flash Art* 22, no. 148 (October 1989): 87–91.

Tillim, Sidney. "Lichtenstein's Sculpture: '…Primary Structures in Its Rococo.'" *Artforum* 6, no. 5 (January 1968): 22–24.

Tomkins, Calvin. "The Antic Muse." *The New Yorker* (17 August 1981): 80–83.

Tomkins, Calvin, and Bob Adelman. *Roy Lichtenstein: Mural with Blue Brushstroke.* New York: Harry N. Abrams, 1988. Ed. Margaret Donovan and Anne Yarowsky. Essays by Pari Stave and Tomkins, interwith by Adelman.

Tuchmans, Phyllis. "Pop! Interviews with George Segal, Andy Warhol, Roy Lichtenstein, James Rosenquist, and Robert Indiana." *ARTnews* 73, no. 5 (May 1974): 24–29.

Waldman, Diane. "Remarkable Commonplace."*ARTnews* 66, no. 6 (October 1967): 28–31, 65–67.

——. *Roy Lichtenstein: Drawings and Prints.* London and New York: Chelsea House, 1969.

——. *Roy Lichtenstein.* New York: Harry N. Abrams, 1972. Essay and interview by Waldman.

——. *Roy Lichtenstein.* New York: Rizzoli, 1993.

——. *Roy Lichtenstein.* New York: Solomon R. Guggenheim Museum, 1993.

GREGORY **mahoney**

born in Los Angeles, 1955
lives and works in Los Angeles
education B.F.A., University of Southern California, Los Angeles, 1980

selected one-person exhibitions

1995	Angles Gallery, Santa Monica, California
1993	Angles Gallery, Santa Monica, California
1992	Angles Gallery, Santa Monica, California
1991	Galerie Karsten Greve, Paris
	Angles Gallery, Santa Monica, California
1990	Angles Gallery, Santa Monica, California
1988	Fuller/Gross Gallery, San Francisco
	Lang & O'Hara, New York
1987	Burnett Miller Gallery, Los Angeles
1986	Fuller Goldeen Gallery, San Francisco
1985	Burnett Miller Gallery, Los Angeles
1984	Leila Ivy Gallery, New York

selected group exhibitions

1998   *The Edward R. Broida Collection, A Selection of Works,* Orlando Museum of Art, Orlando, Florida
Outside/Inside, Trans America Pyramid Gallery, San Francisco
Vault of Heaven, El Camino College Art Gallery, Los Angeles

1996   *The Panza di Biumo Collection: some artists of the 80s and 90s*, Museo d'Arte Moderna e Contemporanea di Trento e Rovereto, Palazzo delle Albere, Trento, Italy

1995   *Between Reality and Abstraction: California Art at the End of the Century*, Art Museum of South Texas, Corpus Christi, Texas
The Panza di Biumo Donation: European and American Art '83–'93, Museo Cantonale d'Arte, Lugano, Switzerland

1994   *Mapping*, University of North Texas Art Gallery, Denton, Texas. Traveled to Contemporary Arts Forum, Santa Barbara, California; and Nevada Institute for Contemporary Art, Las Vegas, Nevada

1992   *California: North/South*, Aspen Art Museum, Aspen, Colorado
Group Show, Lemberg Gallery, Birmingham, Michigan

1991   *12th International Biennial of Drawings: Working Drawings from Sculptors*, Museum of Modern Art, Rijeka, Yugoslavia
Squaresville, Angles Gallery, Santa Monica, California

1990   Cirrus Gallery, Los Angeles
Earth, Krygier/Landau, Santa Monica, California
Laboratory, Russian Museum, St. Petersburg, Russia
Referential Drawings, Angles Gallery, Santa Monica, California

1989   *Works on Paper: A Changing Exhibition*, Angles Gallery, Santa Monica, California

1988   *Black and White Abstraction*, Angles Gallery, Santa Monica, California

1987   *Summer Invitational*, Burnett Miller Gallery, Los Angeles
Synthesis: An Aspect of Contemporary Exhibitions, Fuller/Goldeen Gallery, San Francisco

1986   *Abstracted Landscapes*, Robbin Lockett, Chicago
American Painting 1950s–1980s, Marilyn Pearl Gallery, New York
New California Painting: Dealers Choice, Rancho Santiago College, Los Angeles
Pasadena Collects: the Art of Our Time, Art Center College of Design, Pasadena, California
Recent Abstraction, Burnett Miller Gallery, Los Angeles

1985   *Painting and Sculpture*, Angles Gallery, Santa Monica, California
Selections, Fuller/Gross Gallery, San Francisco
Three from Paris, Three from L.A., Angles Gallery, Santa Monica, California

1983   *14 Artists Out of Line*, Gallery 8336, Los Angeles

1982   Independent Contemporary Exhibitions, Los Angeles

bibliography

12th International Biennial of Drawings: Working Drawings from Sculptors. Exh. cat. Rijeka, Yugoslavia: Museum of Modern Art, 1991.

Between Reality and Abstraction: California Art at the End of the Century. Exh. cat. Corpus Christi, Texas: Art Museum of South Texas, 1995.

Boisset, Maiten. *Beaux Arts*, no. 99 (March 1992): 99.

Clothier, Peter. "At the Hard Edge: California Abstraction Then and Now." *ArtCoast* (March-April 1989): 40–49.

Colpitt, Frances. "Santa Monica: Gregory Mahoney at Angles." *Art in America* 78, no. 10 (October 1990): 221, 223.

Gardner, Colin. "Los Angeles: Gregory Mahoney." *Artforum* 26, no. 3 (November 1987): 145.

"Gregory Mahoney." *Spazio Umano* (February 1988): 126–133.

Grimes, Nancy. "Gregory Mahoney: Lang & O'Hara." *ARTnews* 87, no. 5 (May 1988): 181.

Hugo, Joan. "The Elements of Landscape." *Artweek* (16 November 1985): 5.

Hammond, Pamela. "Los Angeles: Gregory Mahoney." *ARTnews* 89, no. 7 (September 1990): 171.

Jouannais, Jean-Yves. *Art Press* (February 1992): 96.

Muchnic, Suzanne. "MOCA Gets Major Gift—Works by 10 Local Artists." *Los Angeles Times* (26 October 1994): F1.

Muchnic, Suzanne, and Gary Kamiya. "California Currents: Artist Choose Artists: Sam Francis and Gregory Mahoney." *ARTnews* 90, no. 9 (November 1991): 99.

The Panza di Biumo Collection: some artists from the 80s and 90s. Exh. cat. Trento, Italy: Museo d'Arte Moderna e Contemporanea di Trento e Rovereto, 1996. Essays by Gabriella Belli and Giuseppe Panza di Biumo; entries and biographies.

The Panza di Biumo Donation: European and American Art '83–'93. Exh. cat. Lugano, Switzerland: Museo Cantonale d'Arte, 1995.

Tamblyn, Christine. "Reviews." *ARTnews* (December 1988): 171.

Vogel, Carol. "Inside Art." *The New York Times* (4 November 1994): C24.

——. "Los Angeles Art Is Given to a Los Angeles Museum." *The New York Times* (4 November 1994): B9.

born in Stockholm, 1929
lives and works in New York
education Yale University, New Haven, Connecticut, 1946–50
Art Institute of Chicago, Chicago, 1950

selected exhibition history

1999   *The American Century: Art & Culture 1950–2000*, Whitney Museum of American Art, New York
Claes Oldenburg/Coosje van Bruggen, Museo Correr, Venice
The Museum as Muse, The Museum of Modern Art, New York

1998   *Claes Oldenburg: Printed Stuff*, Madison Art Center, Madison, Wisconsin. Traveled to Columbus Museum of Art, Columbus, Ohio; and Detroit Institute of Arts, Detroit
Out of Actions: Between Performance and the Object, 1949–1979, The Museum of Contemporary Art, Los Angeles. Traveled to MAK-Austrian Museum of Applied Arts, Vienna; Museu d'Art Contemporani, Barcelona; and Museum of Contemporary Art, Tokyo

1997   *The Age of Modernism: Art in the Twentieth Century*, Martin-Gropius-Bau, Berlin
Allegory, Joseph Helman Gallery, New York
Claes Oldenburg Drawings and Notebook Studies 1961–1996, Susan Inglett Gallery, New York
Future, Present, Past, Venice Biennale, Venice
Homage to R. Mutt, Garth Clark Gallery, New York
Objects of Desire: The Modern Still Life, The Museum of Modern Art, New York. Traveled to Hayward Gallery, London
Proof Positive: Forty Years of Contemporary American Printmaking at ULAE, 1957–1987, Corcoran Gallery of Art, Washington, D.C. Traveled to Armand Hammer Museum of Art and Cultural Center at the University of California at Los Angeles; Sezon Museum of Art, Tokyo; and Kitakysyu Municipal Museum of Art, Kitakysyu City, Japan
Skulptur: Projekte in Münster, Westfälisches Landesmuseum für Kunst und Kulturgeschichte, Münster, Germany

1995   *Beat Culture and the New America 1950–1965*, Whitney Museum of American Art, New York. Traveled to Walker Art Center, Minneapolis; and DeYoung Memorial Museum, San Francisco
Claes Oldenburg: An Anthology, National Gallery of Art, Washington, D.C. Traveled to The Museum of Contemporary Art, Los Angeles; Solomon R. Guggenheim Museum, New York; Kunst- und Austellungshalle der Bundesrepublik Deutschland, Bonn; and Hayward Gallery, London
Drawing the Line, Whitechapel Art Gallery, London

1994   *Claes Oldenburg: Books and Ephemera, 1960–1994*, Printed Matter, New York
Claes Oldenburg/Coosje van Bruggen Large-Scale Projects: Drawings and Sculpture, Pace Wildenstein, New York
Drawing on Scultpure, Cohen Gallery, New York
Sculptors' Maquettes, The Pace Gallery, New York

1993   *American Art in the Twentieth Century: Painting and Sculpture 1913–1993*, Martin-Gropius-Bau, Berlin. Traveled to Royal Academy of Arts, London
Artists at Gemini G.E.L, Gemini G.E.L. at Joni Moisant Weyl, New York
Claes Oldenburg: "The Store" Drawings 1960–1963, Galerie Busche, Berlin
Materia, Imagen y Concepto: Un Recorrido por el Arte Contemporáneo Internacional, Galería Namia Mondolfi, Caracas

1992   *Claes Oldenburg: Multiples 1964–1990*, Portikus, Frankfurt. Traveled to Lenbachhaus, Munich; Hochschule für Angewandte Kunst, Vienna; Musée Municipal, La Roche-sur-Yon, France; and Musée d'Art Moderne Saint-Etienne, Saint-Etienne, France
Claes Oldenburg: New York, The Pace Gallery, New York
Die frühen Zeichnungen, Museum für Gegenwartskunst, Basel
Hand-Painted Pop: American Art in Transition 1955–62, The Museum of Contemporary Art, Los Angeles. Traveled to Museum of Contemporary Art, Chicago; and Whitney Museum of American Art, New York
In the Studio, Walker Art Center, Minneapolis
Transform: Bild Object Skulptur in 20. Jahrhundert, Kunstmuseum and Kunsthalle, Basel

1991   *The Pop Art Show*, Royal Academy of Arts, London. Traveled to Museum Ludwig, Cologne; Centro de Arte Reina Sofía, Madrid; and Montreal Museum of Fine Arts, Montreal

1990   *A Complete Survey of Sculptures in Edition 1963–1990*, Carl Solway Gallery, Cincinnati
High & Low: Modern Art and Popular Culture, The Museum of Modern Art, New York. Traveled to Art Institute of Chicago, Chicago; and The Museum of Contemporary Art, Los Angeles
Lithographs from Gemini G.E.L., 1988–1990, Castelli Graphics, New York

1989   *From the Entropic Library*, Musée d'Art Moderne, Saint-Etienne, France
Magiciens de la Terre, Musée National d'Art Moderne, Centre Georges Pompidou, and La Grande Halle, La Villette, Paris

1988   *Drawings 1959–1988*, Palais des Beaux-Arts, Brussels. Traveled to Musée d'Art Contemporain, Nîmes, France; and IVAM Centre Julio González, Valencia, Spain
The Knife Ship, The Museum of Contemporary Art, Los Angeles
Props, Costumes and Designs from the Performance Il Corso del Coltello *by Claes Oldenburg, Coosje van Bruggen, Frank O. Gehry*, Margo Leavin Gallery, Los Angeles

1987   *Comic Iconoclasm*, Institute of Contemporary Art, London
Le couteau navire décors, costumes, dessins: Il Corso del Coltello *de Claes Oldenburg, Coosje van Bruggen et Frank O. Gehry*, Musée national d'art moderne, Centre Georges Pompidou, Paris
Made in U.S.A.: An Americanization in Modern Art, The '50s and '60s, University Art Museum, University of California at Berkeley, Berkeley. Traveled to Nelson-Atkins Museum of Art, Kansas City; and Virginia Museum of Fine Arts, Richmond, Virginia
Piano/Hammock, Galerie Konrad Fischer, Düsseldorf

1986   *El Cuchillo Barco*, Palacio de Cristal, Parque del Retiro, Madrid
The Knife Ship, Solomon R. Guggenheim Museum, New York

1984   *Blam! The Explosion of Pop, Minimalism and Performance 1958–1964*, Whitney Museum of American Art, New York

1982   *Documenta 7*, Kassel, Germany

1980   *Large-Scale Projects 1977–1980*, Leo Castelli Gallery, New York
Pop Art: evoluzione di una generazione, Instituto di Cultura di Palazzo Grassi, Venice
Urban Encounters: Art, Architecture, Audience, Institute of Contemporary Art, University of Pennsylvania, Philadelphia

1978   *Sculptures, 1971–1977*, Margo Leavin Gallery, Los Angeles

1977   *Claes Oldenburg: Drawings, Watercolors and Graphics*, Stedelijk Museum, Amsterdam. Traveled to Musée National d'Art Moderne, Centre Georges Pompidou, Paris; and Moderna Museet, Stockholm
The Mouse Museum/The Ray Gun Wing: Two Collections/Two Buildings by Claes Oldenburg, Museum of Contemporary Art, Chicago. Traveled to Phoenix Art Museum, Phoenix; St. Louis Art Museum, St. Louis; Museum of Fine Arts, Dallas; Whitney Museum of American Art, New York; Rijksmuseum Kröller-Müller, Otterlo, The Netherlands; and Museum Ludwig, Cologne
Richard Gray Gallery, Chicago
Documenta 6, Kassel, Germany
Skulptur: Ausstellung in Münster, Westfälisches Landesmuseum für Kunst und Kulturgeschichte, Münster, Germany

1976   Leo Castelli Gallery, New York

1975   *Oldenburg: Six Themes*, Walker Art Center, Minneapolis. Traveled to Denver Art Museum, Denver; The Seattle Art Museum, Seattle; Institute of Contemporary Art and Hayden Gallery, Boston; and The Art Gallery of Ontario, Toronto
Zeichnungen von Claes Oldenburg, Kunsthalle Tübingen, Tübingen, Germany. Traveled to Kunstmuseum Basel, Basel; Städtische Galerie im Lenbachhaus, Munich; Nationalgalerie, Berlin; Staatliche Museen Preussicher Kulturbesitz, Berlin; Kaiser Wilhelm Museum, Krefeld, Germany; Museum des 20. Jahrhunderts, Vienna; Kunstverein Hamburg, Germany; Städelsches Kunstinstitut und Städtische Galerie, Frankfurt; Kestner-Gesellschaft, Hannover, Germany; and Louisiana Museum of Modern Art, Humlebaek, Denmark

1974   Leo Castelli Gallery, New York
The Lipstick Comes Back, Yale University Art Gallery, Yale University, New Haven, Connecticut
Poets of the Cities, New York and San Francisco, 1950–1965, Museum of Fine Arts, Dallas. Traveled to San Francisco Museum of Art, San Francisco; and Wadsworth Atheneum, Hartford, Connecticut

1973   Minami Gallery, Tokyo
Recent Prints, M. Knoedler & Co., New York

1972   *Documenta 5*, Kassel, Germany

1971 *Object into Monument*, Pasadena Art Museum, Pasadena, California. Traveled to
University Art Museum, University of California at Berkeley, Berkeley; Nelson-
Atkins Museum, Kansas City; Des Moines Art Center, Des Moines, Iowa; Philadelphia
Museum of Art, Philadelphia; and Art Institute of Chicago, Chicago

1970 Sidney Janis Gallery, New York

1969 *Chicago Show*, Richard Feigen Gallery, Chicago
The Museum of Modern Art, New York. Traveled to Stedelijk Museum, Amsterdam;
Städtische Kunsthalle, Düsseldorf; and Tate Gallery, London
Pop Art, Hayward Gallery, London

1968 *Documenta 4*, Kassel, Germany
Irving Blum Gallery, Los Angeles
São Paulo IX: Environment U.S.A. 1957–1967, Museu de Arte Moderna, São Paulo,
Brazil. Traveled to Brandeis University, Waltham, Massachusetts

1967 *Dine, Oldenburg, Segal*, Art Gallery of Ontario, Toronto. Traveled to Albright-Knox Art
Gallery, Buffalo, New York
Projects for Monuments, Museum of Contemporary Art, Chicago
Sidney Janis Gallery, New York

1966 Robert Fraser Gallery, London
Moderna Museet, Stockholm

1964 *4 Environments by 4 New Realists*, Sidney Janis Gallery, New York
*XXXII International Biennial Exhibition of Art: Four Germinal Painters—Four Younger
Artists*, Venice Biennale, Venice,
Amerikansk pop-konst, Moderna Museet, Stockholm. Traveled to Louisiana Museum of
Modern Art, Humlebaek, Denmark; and Stedelijk Museum, Amsterdam
Galerie Ileana Sonnabend, Paris
Nieuwe Realisten, Haags Gemeentemuseum, The Hague. Traveled to Museum des 20.
Jahrhunderts, Vienna; Akademie der Kunst, Berlin; and Palais des Beaux-Arts, Brussels
The Pace Gallery, Boston
Sidney Janis Gallery, New York

1963 *Americans 1963*, The Museum of Modern Art, New York
Dwan Gallery, Los Angeles
Three Young Americans, Allen Memorial Art Museum, Oberlin College, Oberlin, Ohio

1962 Green Gallery, New York
My Country 'Tis of Thee, Dwan Gallery, Los Angeles
New Realists, Sidney Janis Gallery, New York

1961 *Environments, Situations, Spaces*, Martha Jackson Gallery, New York
The Store, 107 East 2nd Street, New York

1960 *The Street*, Reuben Gallery, New York

1959 *Below Zero*, Reuben Gallery, New York
Drawings, Sculptures, Poems by Claes Oldenburg, Judson Gallery, Judson Memorial
Church, New York

selected bibliography

Adrien, Dennis. "New York: Claes Oldenburg." *Artforum* (May 1966): 50.

Alloway, Lawrence. "Hi-way Culture: Man at the Wheel." *Arts Magazine* (February 1967):
28–33.

Ashton, Dore. "Exhibition at the Green Gallery." *Studio International* (January 1963): 25–26.

——. "Four Environments, Exhibition at Janis Gallery." *Arts & Architecture* (February 1964): 9.

Baro, Gene. "Claes Oldenburg, or the Things of This World." *Art International* (20 November
1966): 41–43, 45–48.

Battcock, Gregory. "In the Galleries: Claes Oldenburg." *Arts Magazine* (May 1967): 56.

Bourdon, David. "Claes Oldenburg's Store Days." *The Village Voice* (28 December 1967).

Canady, John. "Oldenburg as the Picasso of Pop." *The New York Times* (28 September 1969).

Celant, Germano, et al. *Claes Oldenburg: An Anthology*. New York: Guggenheim Museum, 1995.
Texts by Germano Celant, Mark Rosenthal, and Dieter Koepplin.

Celant, Germano, Coosje van Bruggen, and Claes Oldenburg. *The Course of the Knife/Il Corso
del Coltello*. Milan: Electa, 1986.

——. *A Bottle of Notes and Some Voyages*. New York: Rizzoli, 1988.

Coplans, John. "Pop Art USA." *Artforum* (October 1963): 27–30.

——. "The Artist Speaks: Claes Oldenburg." *Art in America*, no. 2 (March 1969): 68–75.

Fahlström, Öyvind, and Ulf Linde. "Claes Oldenburg at the Moderna Museet, Stockholm: Two
Contrasting Viewpoints." *Studio International* (December 1966): 326–29.

Finch, Christopher. "Notes for a Monument to Claes Oldenburg." *ARTnews* (October 1969): 52–56.

Foote, Nancy. "Oldenburg's Monuments to the Sixties." *Artforum*, no. 5 (January 1977): 54–56.

Forge, Andrew. "Store Days." *Studio International* 175 (March 1968): 162–63.

Fried, Michael. "New York Letter." *Art International* (25 October 1962): 59–65, 74–76.

Friedman, Martin. *Oldenburg: Six Themes*. Minneapolis: Walker Art Center, 1975. Interview
with the artist.

Gablik, Suzi. "Protagonists of Pop: Five Interviews Conducted by Suzi Gablik." *Studio
International* 178 (July 1969): 9–16.

Glueck, Grace. "Soft Sculpture or Hard—They're Oldenburgers." *The New York Times Magazine*
(21 September 1969): 28–29.

Graham, Dan. "Oldenburg's Monuments." *Artforum* (January 1968): 30–37.

"A Happening." *Scene* (August 1962): 13–14.

Haskell, Barbara. *Claes Oldenburg: Object into Monument*. Pasadena, California: Pasadena Art
Museum, 1971.

Haywood, Robert. "Demon in the Kitchen: Oldenburg's Alterations." *Art in America* (October
1995): 86–92, 139.

Hopkins, Henry T. "Abstract Expressionism." *Artforum* (Summer 1964): 59–68.

Johnson, Ellen H. "The Living Object." *Art International* (25 January 1963): 42–45.

——. "Oldenburg's Poetics: Analogues, Metamorphoses and Sources." *Art International* (20
April 1970): 42–45.

——. *Claes Oldenburg*. New York: Penguin Books, 1971.

Johnson, Ken. "Report from New York, Big Top Whitney." *Art in America* (June 1995): 39–55.

Johnston, Jill. "Art Without Walls: Three New York Exhibitions." *ARTnews* (April 1961): 36,
57.

——. "Off-Off Broadway: 'Happenings' at Ray Gun Mfg. Co." *The Village Voice* (26 April
1962): 10.

——. "Exhibition at Oldenburg and Green Gallery." *ARTnews* (May 1962): 55.

Judd, Donald. "In the Galleries: Claes Oldenburg." *Arts Magazine* (September 1964): 63.

Knight, Christopher. "The Percolating Mind of Oldenburg." *Los Angeles Times* (6 August
1995): 56, 59.

Kozloff, Max. "'Pop' Culture Metaphysical Disgust, and the New Vulgarians." *Art International*
(March 1962): 34–36.

——. "New York Letter." *Art International* (September 1962): 33–35.

——. "New Works by Oldenburg." *The Nation* (27 April 1964): 445–46.

——. "Art: Dissimulated Pop." *The Nation* (30 November 1964): 417–49.

——. "Art: Store Days and Assemblage, Environments, Happenings." *The Nation*, no. 205 (3 July
1967): 27–29.

Kuspit, Donald. "Documenta: Claes Oldenburg." *Artforum* (October 1982): 84–85.

Linker, Kate. "Public Sculpture: Pursuit of the Pleasurable and Profitable Paradise." *Artforum*
(March 1981): 64–73.

Lipman, Jean. "The Period Rooms—The Sixties and Seventies." *Art in America* (November
1970): 126–29.

Lippard, Lucy. "New York Letter." *Art International* (April 1965): 51.

——. "Art Outdoors, In and Out of the Public Domain." *Studio International* (March-April
1977): 83–90.

McGee, Celia. "A Pop Art Provocateur Having Monumental Fun." *The New York Times*
(1 October 1995): 41–42.

Nordland, Gerald. "Marcel Duchamp and Common Object Art." *Art International* (15 February
1964): 30–32.

Novick, Elizabeth. "Happenings in New York." *Studio International* (September 1966):
154–59.

Oldenburg, Claes. "Object: Still Life. Interview." *Craft Horizons* (September 1965): 31.

——. *Claes Oldenburg: Notes*. Los Angeles: Gemini G.E.L., 1968. Text by Barbara Rose.

——. "American: War & Sex, Etc." *Arts Magazine*, no. 8 (Summer 1967): 32–38.

Rastorfer, Darl. "Engineering Oldenburg." *Architectural Record* (March 1986): 146–51.

Reaves, A.W. "Claes Oldenburg, and Interview." *Artforum* (October 1972): 11, 27, 36–39.

Restany, Pierre. "Le nouveau réalisme à la conquête de New York." *Art International*
(25 January 1963): 29–36.

——. "Une tentative américaine de synthèse de l'information artistique: les Happenings."
Domus (August 1963): 35–42.

——. "L'autre face de l'art: Le jeu existentiel." *Domus*, no. 582 (May 1978): 41–47.

Rose, Barbara. "Dada Then and Now." *Art International* (25 September 1963): 77–79.

——. "Claes Oldenburg's Soft Machines." *Artforum* (Summer 1967): 30–35.

——. "The Origin, Life and Times of Ray Gun." *Artforum* (November 1969): 50–57.

——. *Claes Oldenburg*. New York: The Museum of Modern Art, 1970.

Rosenstein, Harris. "Climbing Mt. Oldenburg." *ARTnews* (February 1966): 21-25, 56–59.

Rugoff, Ralph. "Pumping Vinyl: Claes Oldenburg's soft-machine age." *L.A. Weekly* (21–27 July

1995): 41.
Russell, John. "Oldenburg Sees Nothing Insignificant." *The New York Times* (11 May 1974): 27.
——. "Oldenburg Again: Whimsy and Latent Humanity." *The New York Times* (6 March 1995): C9, C16.
Sandler, Irving. "Reuben Gallery." *ARTnews* (Summer 1960): 16, 59.
Seitz, William C. "Pop Goes the Artist." *Partisan Review* 30 (Summer 1963): 313–16.
——. "The Real and the Artificial: Painting of the New Environment." *Art in America* (November–December 1972): 59–72.
Siegel, Jeanne. "How to Keep Sculpture Alive In and Out of a Museum: An Interview with Claes Oldenburg on his Retrospective Exhibition at The Museum of Modern Art." *Arts Magazine* (September–October 1969): 24–28.
——. "Oldenburg's Places and Borrowings." *Arts Magazine* (November 1969): 48–49.
Smith, Roberta. "Art: Oldenburg's Works as Props for 'Il Corso.'" *The New York Times* (9 January 1987).
——. "Art in Review: Claes Oldenburg 'Books and Ephemera 1960–1994.'" *The New York Times* (16 September 1994): 29.
——. "A Pop Absurdist Who's a Happening All by Himself." *The New York Times* (6 October 1995): C1, C27.
Solomon, Alan R. "The New American Art." *Art International* (20 March 1964): 50–55.
Solway, Arthur, Thomas Lawson, Claes Oldenburg, and David Platzker. *Claes Oldenburg: Multiples in Retrospect, 1964–1990.* New York: Rizzoli, 1991.
Spencer, Charles S. "An Artist Who Paints Object with Souls." *The New York Times* (12 December 1966).
Swenson, G.R. "Reviews and Previews: Four Environments at Janis." *ARTnews* (February 1964): 8.
Sylvester, David. "The Soft Machines of Claes Oldenburg." *Vogue* (1 February 1968): 116, 209, 211–12.
Tillim, Sidney. "In the Galleries: Claes Oldenburg." *Arts Magazine* (June 1960): 53.
——. "Month in Review: New York Exhibitions." *Arts Magazine* (February 1962): 34–37.
Tomkins, Calvin. "Standup Artist." *The New Yorker* (2 October 1995): 76–79.
Trini, Tommaso. "Libri: Claes Oldenburg's 'Store Days.'" *Domus*, no. 453 (8 August 1967): [45], 51.
Van Bruggen, Coosje, Claes Oldenburg, and Rudi H. Fuchs. *Claes Oldenburg: Large-Scale Projects, 1977–1980.* New York: Rizzoli, 1980.
——. *Claes Oldenburg: Nur ein anderer Raum.* Frankfurt: Museum für Moderne Kunst, 1991.

ROBERT **rauschenberg**

born in Port Arthur, Texas, 1925
lives and works on Captiva Island, Florida
education Art Students League, New York, 1949–52
Black Mountain College, North Carolina, 1948–49 & 1951–52
Académie Julian, Paris, 1948
Kansas City Art Institute, Kansas City, Missouri, 1947

selected exhibition history

1999   *Robert Rauschenberg: Anagrams (A Pun),* PaceWildenstein, 142 Greene Street, New York
1997   *Rauschenberg: A Retrospective,* Solomon R. Guggenheim Museum & Guggenheim SoHo, New York
Robert Rauschenberg: Through the Lens, Gallery of Art, University of Missouri, Kansas City, Missouri
Robert Rauschenberg: Haywire—Major Technological Works from the 1960s, Aktionsforum, Munich
Proof Positive: Forty Years of Contemporary American Printmaking at ULAE: 1957–1997, Corcoran Gallery of Art, Washington, D.C.
From Dürer to Rauschenberg: A Quintessence of Drawing, Masterworks from the Albertina and the Guggenheim, Solomon R. Guggenheim Museum, New York
1996   *The Print and Beyond: Robert Rauschenberg Editions 1970–1995,* Robert Hull Fleming Museum, University of Vermont, Burlington, Vermont
Robert Rauschenberg: Prints 60s, 70s, 80s, Jim Kempner Fine Art, New York
Icons of the Century: Centurions, Robert Rauschenberg, Exhibit A Gallery, The Savannah College of Art and Design, Savannah, Georgia
Metamorphoses: Photography in the Electronic Age, Philadelphia Museum of Art, Philadelphia
Omaggio a Leo Castelli: Da Rauschenberg a Warhol, da Flavin a Judd. 20 artisti a New York negli anni sessanta, Padiglione d'Arte Contemporanea, Milan
Face à l'histoire: 1933–1996, Musée National d'Art Moderne, Centre Georges Pompidou, Paris
1995   *Robert Rauschenberg,* Texas Gallery, Houston
Robert Rauschenberg: Night Shades & Urban Bourbons, Galerie Beyeler, Basel, Switzerland
Robert Rauschenberg: Major Printed Works, 1962–1995, Morris Museum of Art, Augusta, Georgia
Robert Rauschenberg: New Paintings: Vydocks and Doubleluck, Reefs, Gagosian Gallery and 65 Thompson Street, New York
Robert Rauschenberg: Two Decades at Graphicstudio, Graphicstudio, University of South Florida, Tampa, Florida
Robert Rauschenberg: Sculpture, Modern Art Museum of Fort Worth, Fort Worth, Texas
Beat Culture and the New America: 1950–1965, Whitney Museum of American Art, New York
1994   *Rauschenberg: Scores (Off Kilter Keys),* Leo Castelli Gallery and 65 Thompson Street, New York
Head On: Image and Text in the Prints of Robert Rauschenberg, Archer M. Huntington Art Gallery, The University of Texas at Austin, Austin, Texas
Robert Rauschenberg, Kunstsammlung Nordrhein-Westfalen, Düsseldorf, Germany
Experimental Vision: The Evolution of the Photogram since 1919, Denver Art Museum, Denver
Duchamp's Leg, Walker Art Center, Minneapolis
1993   *Robert Rauschenberg: Photems/Fotografías,* Galería Cobo y Alexander, Madrid
The Second Hiroshima Art Prize: Robert Rauschenberg, Hiroshima City Museum of Contemporary Art, Hiroshima, Japan
1992   *Robert Rauschenberg: A Print Survey in Themes, 1952–1992,* Simmons Visual Arts Center, Brenau College, Gainesville, Georgia
Rauschenberg: Prints and Editions, 1962–1992, Leo Castelli Gallery, 578 Broadway, New York
Robert Rauschenberg: Skulpturen aus den achtziger Jahren, Alfred Kren Gallery, Cologne, Germany
Both Art and Life: Gemini G.E.L. at Twenty-five, Newport Harbor Art Museum, Newport Beach, California
Hand-Painted Pop: American Art in Transition, 1955–1962, The Museum of Contemporary Art, Los Angeles
1991   *Rauschenberg Overseas Culture Interchange: ROCI,* National Gallery of Art, Washington, D.C.
Robert Rauschenberg: The Early 1950s, Corcoran Gallery of Art, Washington, D.C., organized by The Menil Collection, Houston
Robert Rauschenberg 1974–1991: Animals and Other Themes, City Gallery of Contemporary Art, Raleigh, North Carolina
Seven Master Printmakers, Innovations in the 1980s, The Museum of Modern Art, New York
Pop Art, Royal Academy of Arts, London
1990   *Robert Rauschenberg: Paintings 1962–1980,* Lang & O'Hara Gallery, New York
Rauschenberg Overseas Culture Interchange: ROCI Berlin, Neue Berliner Galerie, Alten Museum, Berlin
Rauschenberg Overseas Culture Interchange: ROCI Malaysia, Balai Seni Lukis Negara National Art Gallery, Kuala Lumpur, Malaysia
Robert Rauschenberg, Galerie Fabien Boulakia, Paris
Robert Rauschenberg: The Silkscreen Paintings, 1962–64, Whitney Museum of American Art, New York (organized by Independent Curators, New York)
High and Low: Modern Art and Popular Culture, The Museum of Modern Art, New York
1989   *Rauschenberg Overseas Culture Interchange: ROCI Moscow,* Tretyakov Gallery, Central House of Culture, Moscow

Robert Rauschenberg, the Gemini Works: 1967–1988, Fred Hoffman Gallery, Santa Monica, California, and Manny Silverman Gallery, Los Angeles

Jasper Johns and Robert Rauschenberg: Selections from the Anderson Collection, San Jose Museum of Art, San Jose, Calfornia

Five Great American Artists: Warhol, Lichtenstein, Rauschenberg, Rosenquist, Stella, Duson Gallery, Seoul, South Korea

1988 *Robert Rauschenberg: New Pictures,* Pace/MacGill Gallery, New York

Rauschenberg Overseas Culture Interchange: ROCI Cuba, Museo Nacional de Bellas Artes, Castillo de la Fuerza and Casa de las Américas, Galleria Haydee Santa María, Havana, Cuba

1987 *Selections from Rauschenberg's ¼ Mile or 2 Furlong Piece,* The Metropolitan Museum of Art, New York

Rauschenberg: Neapolitan Glut, Galleria Lucio Amelio, Naples, Italy

Robert Rauschenberg: Works on Paper: 1970–1983, BlumHelman Gallery, New York

1986 *Robert Rauschenberg: Photographs 1949–1984,* Contemporary Arts Museum, Houston

Rauschenberg: The White and the Black Paintings 1949–1952, Gagosian Gallery, New York

Robert Rauschenberg: Drawings 1958–1968, Acquavella Contemporary Art, New York

Rauschenberg Overseas Culture Exchange: ROCI Japan, Setagaya Art Museum, Tokyo

Individuals: A Selected History of Contemporary Art, 1945–1986, The Museum of Contemporary Art, Los Angeles

1985 *Rauschenberg,* Fundación Juan March, Madrid

Rauschenberg Overseas Culture Exchange: ROCI Mexico, Museo Rufino Tamayo, Mexico City

Rauschenberg Overseas Culture Exchange: ROCI Chile, Museo Nacional de Bellas Artes, Santiago, Chile

Rauschenberg Overseas Culture Exchange: ROCI Venezuela, Museo de Arte Contemporáneo de Caracas, Caracas, Venezuela

Rauschenberg Overseas Culture Exchange: ROCI China, National Art Gallery, Beijing

Rauschenberg Overseas Culture Exchange: ROCI Tibet, Tibet Exhibition Hall, Lhasa, Tibet

Robert Rauschenberg, Work from Four Series: A Sesquicentennial Exhibition, Contemporary Arts Museum, Houston

The Museum of Contemporary Art: The Panza Collection, The Museum of Contemporary Art, Los Angeles

Transformations in Sculpture: Four Decades of American and European Art, Solomon R. Guggenheim Museum, New York

1984 *The Robert Rauschenberg Exhibition,* Gallery of the Port Arthur Public Library, Port Arthur, Texas

Rauschenberg, Galerie Beyeler, Basel, Switzerland

The First 400 Feet or More Than ⅓ a Furlong of the ¼ Mile or 2 Furlong Piece, Center for the Fine Arts, Miami

BLAM! The Explosion of Pop, Minimalism and Performance, Whitney Museum of American Art, New York

1983 *Rauschenberg/Performance: 1954–1979,* Galleria di Franca Mancini, Pesaro, Italy

The First Show: Painting and Sculpture from Eight Collections 1940-1980, The Museum of Contemporary Art, Los Angeles

1982 *Selections from 'In + Out City Limits: New York C.,'* Louisiana Museum of Modern Art, Humlebaek, Denmark

Rauschenberg in China, The Museum of Modern Art, New York

Art and Dance: Images from the Modern Dialogue 1890–1980, The Institute of Contemporary Art, Boston

1981 *Rauschenberg Photographe,* Musée National d'Art Moderne, Centre Georges Pompidou, Paris

In + Out City Limits: Charleston, Gibbes Art Gallery, Charleston, South Carolina

In + Out City Limits: Boston, Magnuson Lee Gallery, Boston

In + Out City Limits: Baltimore, Grimaldis Gallery, Baltimore

In + Out City Limits: Los Angeles, Rosamund Felsen Gallery, Los Angeles

1980 *Rauschenberg: Werke 1950–1980* [retrospective], Staatliche Kunsthalle, Berlin

Robert Rauschenberg: 1970–1980, Baltimore Museum of Art, Baltimore

Rauschenberg, University Gallery of Fine Art, The Ohio State University, Columbus, Ohio

1979 *Robert Rauschenberg: Zeichnungen, Gouachen, Collagen: 1949 bis 1979,* Kunsthalle, Tübingen, Germany

Rauschenberg: Prints/Multiples, Institute of Contemporary Art of Virginia Museum, Richmond, Virginia

The Thirty-sixth Biennial Exhibition of Contemporary American Painting: Willem de Kooning, Jasper Johns, Ellsworth Kelly, Roy Lichtenstein, Robert Rauschenberg, Corcoran Gallery of Art, Washington, D.C.

1978 *Rauschenberg,* Muzeum Narodowe w Warszawie, Warsaw

Mirrors and Windows: American Photography since 1960, The Museum of Modern Art, New York

1977 *Rauschenberg, viaggio nel dispendio,* Museo "Principe Diego Aragona Pignatelli Cortes," Naples, Italy

Robert Rauschenberg: Collagen, Grafiken, Multiples aus der Sammlung Rischner, Neue Galerie am Landesmuseum Joanneum, Graz, Austria

1976 *Robert Rauschenberg,* National Collection of Fine Arts, Smithsonian Institution, Washington, D.C.

1975 *Robert Rauschenberg: Drawings,* Visual Arts Museum, School of Visual Arts, New York

Robert Rauschenberg, Museo d'Arte Moderna Ca'Pesaro, Venice

1974 *Rauschenberg at Graphicstudio,* Library Gallery, University of South Florida, Tampa, Florida

Hoarfrosts, Leo Castelli Gallery and Sonnabend Gallery, New York

1973 *Robert Rauschenberg: Combing Drawings,* The Mayor Gallery, London

Biennial Exhibition, Whitney Museum of American Art, New York

1972 *Made in Tampa: Prints + Clay Pieces,* Castelli Graphics and Leo Castelli Gallery, New York

Seventieth American Exhibition, The Art Institute of Chicago, Chicago

1971 *Cardboards,* Leo Castelli Gallery, New York

Cardbirds, Castelli Graphics, New York

Duchamp, Johns, Rauschenberg, Cage, The Contemporary Arts Center, Cincinnati, Ohio

Art and Technology, Los Angeles County Museum of Art, Los Angeles

1970 *Rauschenberg: Graphic Art,* Institute of Contemporary Art, University of Pennsylvania, Philadelphia

Robert Rauschenberg: Prints 1948/1970, Minneapolis Institute of Arts, Minneapolis, Minnesota

Robert Rauschenberg, Kunstverein Hannover, Hannover, Germany

Robert Rauschenberg: New Work, Visual Arts Museum, School of Visual Arts, New York

1969 *Solstice,* Fort Worth Art Center, Fort Worth, Texas

Robert Rauschenberg in Black and White: Paintings 1962–63, Lithographs 1962–67, Newport Harbor Art Museum, Newport Beach, California

1968 *Robert Rauschenberg,* Stedelijk Museum, Amsterdam

Dada, Surrealism, and Their Heritage, The Museum of Modern Art, New York

Documenta 4: Internationale Ausstellung, Museum Fridericianum, Kassel, Germany

1967 *Robert Rauschenberg: Revolvers,* Leo Castelli Gallery, New York

1966 *Two Decades of American Painting,* organized by the National Museum of Modern Art and the International Council of The Museum of Modern Art, New York

The Visual Arts as Taught and Practiced at Black Mountain College, Carroll Reece Museum, East Tennessee State University, Johnson City, Tennessee

1965 *Rauschenberg at Dwan,* Dwan Gallery, Los Angeles

Robert Rauschenberg: Oracle, Leo Castelli Gallery, New York

Rauschenberg, Paintings 1953–1964, Walker Art Center, Minneapolis

1964 *Rauschenberg: Illustrations for Dante's 'Inferno,'* Whitechapel Art Gallery, London

Robert Rauschenberg, Paintings, Drawings and Combines, 1949–1964, Whitechapel Art Gallery, London

Thirty-second International Biennial Exhibition of Art, Venice

1963 *Robert Rauschenberg,* Jewish Museum, New York

Rauschenberg, Leo Castelli Gallery, New York

Rauschenberg: Première Exposition (Oeuvres 1954–1961) and Rauschenberg: Seconde Exposition (Oeuvres 1962–1963), Galerie Ileana Sonnabend, Paris

Three Young Americans, Allen Memorial Art Museum, Oberlin, Ohio

1962 *Robert Rauschenberg,* Dwan Gallery, Los Angeles

4 Amerikanare: Jasper Johns, Alfred Leslie, Robert Rauschenberg, Richard Stankiewicz, Moderna Museet, Stockholm

1962 Annual Exhibition of Contemporary Sculpture and Drawings, Whitney Museum of American Art, New York

1961 *Rauschenberg,* Leo Castelli Gallery, New York

Robert Rauschenberg, Galerie Daniel Cordier, Paris

Rauschenberg, Galleria dell'Ariete, Milan

The Art of Assemblage, The Museum of Modern Art, New York

Annual Exhibition of Contemporary American Painting, Whitney Museum of American Art, New York

1960 *Drawings for Dante's 'Inferno,'* Leo Castelli Gallery, New York
      Rauschenberg, Twombly: Zwei amerikanische Maler, Galerie 22, Düsseldorf, Germany
      New Forms—New Media One: Junk Culture as Tradition, Martha Jackson Gallery,
         New York
1959 *Rauschenberg,* Galleria La Tartaruga, Rome
      Documenta II: Kunst nach, Museum Fridericianum, Kassel, Germany
      *Première Biennale de Paris: Manifestation biennale et internationale des jeunes
         artistes,* Musée d'Art Moderne de la Ville de Paris, Paris
      Sixteen Americans, The Museum of Modern Art, New York
1958 *Robert Rauschenberg,* Leo Castelli Gallery, New York
      Beyond Painting: An Exhibition of Collages and Constructions, Alan Gallery, New York
1957 *Artists of the New York School: Second Generation,* Jewish Museum, New York
1955 *U.S. Paintings: Some Recent Directions,* The Stable Gallery, New York
1954 Egan Gallery, New York
1953 *Bob Rauschenberg: Scatole e Feticci Personali,* Galleria dell'Obelisco, Rome
      Rauschenberg: Paintings and Sculpture, Stable Gallery, New York
1951 *Paintings by Bob Rauschenberg,* Betty Parsons Gallery, New York
      Abstraction in Photography, The Museum of Modern Art, New York
      Today's Self-Styled School of New York [Ninth Street Show], Sixty East Ninth Street,
         New York

selected bibliography

*Art and Technology: A Report on the Art and Technology Program of the Los Angeles County
   Museum of Art 1967–1971.* Exh. cat. Los Angeles: Los Angeles County Museum of Art,
   1971. Introduction by Maurice Tuchman; texts by Jane Livingston and Gail R. Scott.

The Art of Assemblage. Exh. cat. New York: The Museum of Modern Art, 1961. Essay by
   William C. Seitz.

Ashbery, John. "Five Shows Out of the Ordinary: Robert Rauschenberg." *ARTnews* 57, no. 1
   (March 1958): 40, 56.

Ashton, Dore. "Fifty-seventh Street: Robert Rauschenberg." *Art Digest* 27, no. 20 (September
   1953): 21, 25.

Ashton, Dore. *Rauschenberg: XXXIV Drawings for Dante's Inferno.* New York: Harry N. Abrams,
   1969.

Biennale de Paris: Une anthologie 1959–1967. Exh. cat. Paris: Musée d'Art Moderne de la
   Ville de Paris, 1959. Introduction by Catherine Millet; interviews by Jacques Lassaigne
   and Pierre Faucheux.

Blam! The Explosion of Pop, Minimalism and Performance, 1958–1964. Exh. cat. New York:
   Whitney Museum of American Art, 1984. Essay by John G. Hanhardt.

Bourdon, David. "Pop: Bing-Bang Landscapes." *Time* 85, no. 22 (28 May 1965): 80.

Burr, James. "The Exhilarating Art of Robert Rauschenberg." *The Times* (London) (8 February
   1964): 5.

Coates, Robert M. "The Art Galleries: Robert Rauschenberg." *The New Yorker* 36, no. 8
   (1 April 1960): 158–159.

——. "The Emperor's Combine." *Time* 75, no. 16 (18 April 1960): 92.

Dada, Surrealism, and Their Heritage. Exh. cat. New York: The Museum of Modern Art, 1968.
   Essay by William S. Rubin.

Davis, Douglas. "Artist of Everything." *Newsweek* 88, no. 17 (25 October 1976): 94–99.

Duchamp, Johns, Rauschenberg, Cage. Exh. cat. Cincinnati: Contemporary Arts Center, 1971.
   Introduction by William A. Leonard; essay by Barbara Rose.

Experimental Vision: The Evolution of the Photogram since 1919. Exh. cat. Denver: Denver Art
   Museum, 1994. Essays by Thomas Barrow, Charles Hagen, and Floris M. Neusüss.

Feinstein, Roni. "The Unknown Early Robert Rauschenberg: The Betty Parsons Exhibition of
   1951." *Arts Magazine* 59, no. 5 (January 1985): 126–131.

Forge, Andrew. *Rauschenberg.* New York: Harry N. Abrams, 1972.

Hand-Painted Pop: American Art in Transition, 1955–1962. Exh. cat. Los Angeles: The
   Museum of Contemporary Art, 1992. Introductions by Paul Schimmel and Donna De
   Salvo; essays by David Deitcher, De Salvo, Stephen C. Foster, Dick Hebdige, Linda
   Norden, Schimmel, Kenneth E. Silver, and John Yau.

Hopps, Walter, and Susan Davidson. *Robert Rauschenberg: Retrospective.* Exh. cat. New York:
   Solomon R. Guggenheim Museum, 1998.

Hughes. Robert. "The Most Living Artist." *Time* 108, no. 22 (29 November 1976): 54–62.

Hughes, Robert. "The Arcadian as Utopian: Rauschenberg's Rhapsodic Energies Fill Four
   Manhattan Shows." *Time* 121, no. 4 (24 January 1983): 74, 77.

Icons of the Century: Centurions, Robert Rauschenberg. Exh. cat. Savannah, Georgia: The
   Savannah College of Art and Design, 1996. Introduction by Judith Van Baron and
   essay by Anne Swartz.

Individuals: A Selected History of Contemporary Art, 1945–1986. Exh. cat. Los Angeles: The
   Museum of Contemporary Art, 1986. Essays by Germano Celant, Hal Foster, Donald
   Kuspit, Thomas Lawson, Kate Linker, Achille Bonito Oliva, Ronald J. Onorato, and John
   C. Welchman.

Jasper Johns and Robert Rauschenberg: Selections from the Anderson Collection. Exh. cat. San
   Jose, California: San Jose Museum of Art, 1989. Introduction by I. Michael Danoff;
   essay by James Cuno.

Johnston, Jill. "The World outside His Window." *Art in America* 80, no. 4 (April 1992):
   114–25, 183.

Kotz, Mary Lynn. "Captiva: The ROCI Road Show." *ARTnews* 88, no. 6 (Summer 1989): 48, 50.

Lampert, Catherine. "Review: Robert Rauschenberg at the Mayor Gallery." *Studio International*
   185, no. 956 (June 1973): 293-294.

Larson, Kay. "Rauschenberg's Renaissance: Three Exhibitions Show Artist at a New Peak."
   New York 16, no. 1 (27 December 1982–3 January 1983): 50–56.

Lippard Lucy R. "New York Letter, April-June 1965." *Art International* 9, no. 6 (20 September
   1965): 57.

Lucie-Smith, Edward. "Three Illustrators of Dante." *The Times* (London) (11 February 1964): 13.

Mahoney, Robert. "Sculpture on the Road: Rauschenberg's ROCI." *Sculpture* 10, no. 6
   (November-December 1991): 44–49.

Metamorphoses: Photography in the Electronic Age. Exh. cat. Philadelphia: Philadelphia Museum
   of Art, 1996. Introduction by Mark Haworth-Booth; essays by Geoffrey Batchen,
   Rebecca Busselle, Ben Davis, Timothy Druckrey, Jonathan Green, and Vincent Katz.

The Museum of Contemporary Art: The Panza Collection. Exh. cat. Los Angeles: The Museum
   of Contemporary Art, 1985.

Neo-Dada: Redefining Art, 1958–62. Exh. cat. New York: The American Federation of Arts,
   1995. Essays by Maurice Berger, Susan Hapgood, and Jill Johnston.

New York Painting and Sculpture: 1940–1970. Exh. cat. New York: The Metropolitan Museum
   of Art, 1969. Organized by Henry Geldzahler; essays by Geldzahler, Michael Fried,
   Clement Greenberg, Harold Rosenberg, Robert Rosenblum, and William Rubin.

O'Hara, Frank. "Reviews and Previews: Bob Rauschenberg." *ARTnews* 53, no. 9 (January
   1955): 47.

Pincus-Witten, Robert. "New York: Robert Rauschenberg, Castelli Gallery." *Artforum* 7, no. 4
   (December 1968): 54–56.

Pop Art. Exh. cat. London: Royal Academy of Arts, 1991. Introduction by Marco Livingstone
   and Sarat Magaraj; essays by Dan Cameron, Constance W. Glenn, Thomas Kellein,
   Livingstone, Alfred Pacquement, and Evelyn Weiss, Dore Ashton, Henry Geldzahler, and
   Hilton Kramer.

Proof Positive: Forty Years of Contemporary American Printmaking at ULAE: 1957–1997.
   Exh. cat. Washington D.C.: Corcoran Gallery of Art, 1997. Introduction by Jack Cowart;
   essays by Sue Scott and Tony Towle.

Rauschenberg. Exh. cat. Basel: Galerie Beyeler, 1984. Texts by Joseph Beuys, William
   Burroughs, David Byrne, John Cage, Teeny Duchamp, and Andrei Voznesensky; statements by Rauschenberg.

Rauschenberg at Dwan. Exh. cat. Los Angeles: Dwan Gallery, 1965. Essay by Walter Hopps.

Rauschenberg at Graphicstudio. Exh. cat. Tampa, Florida: Library Gallery, University of South
   Florida, 1974. Introduction by Willard McCracken.

Rauschenberg: Graphic Art. Exh. cat. Philadelphia: Institute of Contemporary Art, University
   of Pennsylvania, 1970. Introduction by Lawrence Alloway.

Rauschenberg: Neapolitan Glut. Exh. cat. Naples: Galerie Lucio Amelio, 1987. Interview by
   Michele Bonuomo.

Rauschenberg Overseas Culture Interchange: ROCI. Exh. cat. Washington, D.C.: National
   Gallery of Art, 1991. Introduction by Jack Cowart; essays by Rosetta Brooks, José
   Donoso, Heiner Müller, Octavio Paz, Laba Pingcuo, Roberto Fernández Retamar,
   Revgeny Yevtushenko, and Wu Zuguang; by Donald Saff; statement by Rauschenberg.

Rauschenberg: Performance, 1954–1979. Exh. cat. Pesaro, Italy: Galleria di Franca Mancini,
   1983. Introduction by Franca Mancini; essays by Alberto Boatto and Nina Sundell.

Rauschenberg Photographs. New York: Pantheon Books, 1981. Foreword by Pontus Hulten and
   Robert Rauschenberg. Interview by Alain Sayag.

*Rauschenberg: Première Exposition (Oeuvres 1954–1961); Rauschenberg: Second Exposition
   (Oeuvres 1962–1963).* Exh. cat. Paris: Galerie Ileana Sonnabend, 1963. Texts by
   Lawrence Alloway, Françoise Choay, Gillo Dorfles, Alain Jouffrey, and Michel Ragon.

Rauschenberg: The White and the Black Paintings 1949–1952. Exh. cat. New York: Larry
   Gagosian Gallery, 1986. Introduction by Roberta Bernstein.

Rauschenberg: Werke 1950–1980. Exh. cat. Berlin: Staatliche Kunsthalle, 1980. Essays by Lawrence Alloway, William S. Lieberman, Götz Adriani, and Douglas M. Davis.

Robert Rauschenberg. Exh. cat. Amsterdam: Stedelijk Museum,1968. Introduction by Andrew Forge.

Robert Rauschenberg. Exh. cat. Paris: Galerie Daniel Cordier, 1961. Essay by David Myers.

Robert Rauschenberg. Exh. cat. Hannover, Germany: Kunstverein Hannover, 1970. Essay by William S. Lieberman, Lawrence Alloway, John Ciardi, Douglas M. Davis, Lucy Lippard, Manfred de la Motte, Willoughby Sharp, and Paul Wember; interview with Ken Tyler by R. Sherrill.

Robert Rauschenberg. Exh. cat. Venice: Museo d'Arte Moderna Ca'Pesaro, 1975. Essays by Daniel Abadie, David Bourdon, and Guido Perrocco.

Robert Rauschenberg. Exh. cat. Washington, D.C.: National Collection of Fine Arts, Smithsonian Institution, 1976. Essay by Lawrence Alloway.

Robert Rauschenberg. Exh. cat. Paris: Galerie Fabien Boulakia, 1990. Essays by John Cage, Michel Nuridsany, Daniel Abadie, Pierre Daix, Régis Durand, Catherine Millet, Severo Sarduy, and Nina Sundell; interview by France Huser.

Robert Rauschenberg: A Print Survey in Themes, 1952–1992. Gainesville, Georgia: Simmons Visual Arts Center, Brenau College, 1992. Text by Kathleen Slavin.

Robert Rauschenberg: Drawings 1958–1968. Exh. cat. New York: Acquavella Contemporary Art, 1986. Essay by Lawrence Alloway.

Robert Rauschenberg in Black and White: Paintings 1962–63, Lithographs 1962–67. Exh. cat. Newport Beach, California: Newport Harbor Art Museum, 1969. Introduction by Thomas H. Garver.

Robert Rauschenberg: Major Printed Works, 1962–1995. Exh. cat. Augusta, Georgia: Morris Museum of Art, 1995. Introduction by William S. Morris III; essays by J. Richard Gruber and Ann Rowson.

Robert Rauschenberg: Paintings, Drawings and Combines, 1949–1964. Exh. cat. London: Whitechapel Art Gallery, 1964. Essays by John Cage, Henry Geldzahler, and Max Kozloff.

Robert Rauschenberg: Photos In + Out City Limits: New York C. New York: Untitled Press (Universal Limited Art Edition), 1981.

Robert Rauschenberg: Photems/Fotografías. Exh. cat. Madrid: Galería Cobo y Alexander, 1993. Text by Horacio Fernández.

Robert Rauschenberg: Sculpture. Exh. cat. Fort Worth, Texas: Modern Art Museum of Forth Worth, 1995. Discussion among Pontus Hulten, Julia Brown Turrell, and Rauschenberg; interview by Brown Turrell; essay by Marjorie Welish.

Robert Rauschenberg: Selections. Exh. cat. Forth Worth, Texas: Fort Worth Art Center, 1969. Introduction by Henry T. Hopkins.

Robert Rauschenberg: The Early 1950's. Exh. cat. Houston: The Menil Collection and Houston Fine Art Press, 1991.

Robert Rauschenberg: The Silkscreen Paintings, 1962–64. Exh. cat. New York: Whitney Museum of American Art, 1990. Text by Calvin Tomkins.

Robert Rauschenberg: Through the Lens. Exh. cat. Kansas City, Missouri: Gallery of Art, University of Missouri, 1997. Essay by Richard Gruber.

Rose, Barbara. *Off the Wall: Robert Rauschenberg and the Art World of Our Time*. Garden City, New York: Doubleday & Co., 1980.

Rose, Barbara. *Rauschenberg*. New York: Vintage Books, 1987.

Rosenberg, Harold. "The Art World: Souvenirs of an Avant-Garde." *The New Yorker* 53, no. 13 (16 May 1977): 123–28.

Rosenblum, Robert. "Trend to the 'Anti-Art.'" *Newsweek* 51, no. 13 (31 March 1958): 94, 96.

Rosenthal, Mark. *Artists at Gemini G.E.L.: Celebrating the Twenty-fifth Year*. New York: Harry N. Abrams, 1992.

Schjeldahl, Peter. "Rauschenberg Just Won't Be Boxed in." *The New York Times* (31 October 1971): D21.

Story, Richard David. "Robert Rauschenberg: The Unstoppable Artist Pours Hard Work and Wild Humor into His Pop-Cultural Canvases." *USA Today* (26 January 1987): D4.

Stuckey, Charles F. "Reading Rauschenberg." *Art in America* 65, no. 2 (March-April 1977): 74–84.

The Thirty-sixth Biennial Exhibition of Contemporary American Painting: Willem de Kooning, Jasper Johns, Ellsworth Kelly, Roy Lichtenstein, Robert Rauschenberg. Exh. cat. Washington, D.C.: Corcoran Gallery of Art, 1979. Essays by Jane Livingston and Linda Crocker Simmons.

Thomsen, Barbara. "Robert Rauschenberg at Castelli." *Art in America* 61, no. 5 (September–October 1973): 112–114.

Tomkins, Calvin. *The Bride and the Bachelors: Five Masters of the Avant-Garde: Duchamp, Tinguely, Cage, Rauschenberg, Cunningham*. New York: Penguin Books, 1968.

Transformations in Sculpture: Four Decades of American and European Art. Exh. cat. New York: Solomon R. Guggenheim Museum, 1985.

Two Decades of American Painting. Exh. cat. Tokyo: The National Museum of Modern Art, 1966. Introduction by Waldo Rasmussen; essays by Lucy R. Lippard, Irving Sandler, and G.R. Swenson.

Views from Abroad/European Perspectives on American Art, I. Exh. cat. New York: Whitney Museum of American Art, 1996. Essays by Rudi Fuchs, Seamus Heaney, Hayden Herrera, and Adam D. Weinberg.

Wallach, Amei. "Art, Life and Robert Rauschenberg." *Newsday* (10 December 1990): 51–60, 66.

Whittet, G.S. "Interesting, but It Isn't Art." *Studio International* 167, no. 852 (April 1964): 158–61.

MARK **rothko**

born in Dvinsk, Russia, 1903
died in New York, 1970
education Yale University, New Haven, Connecticut, 1921–23
Art Students League, New York, 1924–26

selected exhibition history

1999 *The American Century: Art and Culture 1900–1950*, Whitney Museum of American Art, New York

1998 *Mark Rothko*, National Gallery of Art, Washington, D.C. Traveled to Whitney Museum of American Art, New York; and Musée d'Art Moderne de la Ville de Paris, Paris
Mark Rothko: The Spirit of Myth, Early Paintings from the 1930s and 1940s, Arkansas Art Center, Little Rock

1997 *The Age of Modernism: Art in the Twentieth Century*, Martin-Gropius-Bau, Berlin
Bonnard—Rothko: Color and Light, PaceWildenstein, New York

1996 *In Quest of the Absolute*, Peter Blum, New York
Mark Rothko: The Chapel Commission, The Menil Collection, Houston
Pintura Estadounidense Expresionismo Abstracto, Centro Cultural Arte Contemporaneo, Mexico City
Surrealism: Dream of the Century, Galerie Beyeler, Basel

1995 *Exploring the Unknown: Surrealism in American Art*, Rosenfeld Gallery, New York
Mark Rothko Retrospective, Kawamura Memorial Art Museum, Sakura, Japan. Traveled to Marugame Genichiro-Inokuma Museum of Art, Marugame, Japan; Nagoya City Art Museum of Contemporary Art, Nagoya, Japan; and New Tokyo Metropolitan Art Museum, Tokyo
Our Century, Museum Ludwig, Cologne

1994 *Mark Rothko: The Last Paintings*, PaceWildenstein, New York

1993 *American Art in the 20th Century: Painting and Sculpture 1913–1993*, Martin-Gropius-Bau, Berlin, and Royal Academy of Arts, London
A Century of Silence, University Art Museum, State University of New York at Binghamton, Binghamton, New York
Ils ont cité Matisse, Galerie de France, Paris
Mark Rothko: "Multiforms," Galerie Daniel Blau, Munich

1990 Galerie Beyeler, Basel
Mark Rothko: Multiforms, The Pace Gallery, New York
Mark Rothko: The Early Works, National Gallery of Art, Washington, D.C.

1989 *Mark Rothko: Kaaba in New York*, Kunsthalle Basel, Basel
Mark Rothko: The Seagram Mural Project, Tate Gallery, Liverpool, England
Paintings by Mark Rothko, Yale University Art Gallery, New Haven, Connecticut

1987 *Beuys, Klein, Rothko*, Galerie Anthony d'Offay, London. Traveled to Fundacion Caja de Pensiones, Madrid
Mark Rothko 1903–1970, Tate Gallery, London. Traveled to Museum Ludwig, Cologne

1986 *The Spiritual in Art: Abstract Painting 1890–1985*, Los Angeles County Museum of Art, Los Angeles. Traveled to Museum of Contemporary Art, Chicago; and Haags

Gemeentemuseum, The Hague

1985 *Mark Rothko: The Dark Paintings, 1969–70*, The Pace Gallery, New York

1983 *Mark Rothko: Paintings 1948–1969*, The Pace Gallery, New York

1981 *Amerikanische Malerei 1930–80*, Haus der Kunst, Munich

Mark Rothko: The Surrealist Years, The Pace Gallery, New York

1980 Orangerie des Schloss, Charlottenberg, Berlin

1978 *Abstract Expressionists: The Formative Years*, Herbert F. Johnson Museum of Art, Ithaca, New York. Traveled to Seibu Museum of Art, Tokyo; and Whitney Museum of American Art, New York

Mark Rothko 1903–1970, Solomon R. Guggenheim Museum, New York

Rothko: The 1958–1959 Murals, The Pace Gallery, New York

1977 Galleria Civica d'Arte Moderna, Mantua, Italy

Less Is More, Sidney Janis Gallery, New York

Paris—New York, Centre Georges Pompidou, Paris

1976 The Brooklyn Museum of Art, Brooklyn, New York

The Natural Paradise, The Museum of Modern Art, New York

1974 *The Great Decade of American Abstraction*, The Museum of Fine Arts, Houston

Newport Harbor Art Museum, Newport Beach, California

1971 Kunsthaus Zürich, Zurich. Traveled to Berlin, Düsseldorf, Rotterdam, London, and Paris

Galleria Martano, Turin

The Structure of Color, Whitney Museum of American Art, New York

Yale University Art Gallery, New Haven, Connecticut

1970 *Mark Rothko 1903–1970*, The Museum of Modern Art, New York

Museo d'Arte Moderno Ca'Pesaro, Venice. Traveled to Marlborough Gallery, New York

Painting in New York, Pasadena Art Museum, Pasadena, California

1966 Marlborough New London Gallery, London

1965 *The Decisive Years*, Institute of Contemporary Art, University of Pennsylvania, Philadelphia

Galleria Nazionale d'Arte Moderna, Rome

The New York School, Los Angeles County Museum of Art, Los Angeles

1963 *11 Abstract Expressionist Painters*, Sidney Janis Gallery, New York

Five Mural Panels Executed at Harvard, Solomon R. Guggenheim Museum, New York

1961 *American Abstract Expressionists and the Imagists*, Solomon R. Guggenheim Museum, New York

The Museum of Modern Art, New York. Traveled to London, Amsterdam, Basel, Rome, and Paris

Paintings for the WPA, Smolin Gallery, New York

Plariteit, Stedelijk Museum, Amsterdam

1960 *Art from Ingres to Pollock*, University Art Galleries, University of California at Berkeley, Berkeley

Paths of Abstract Art, Cleveland Museum of Art, Cleveland

The Phillips Collection, Washington, D.C.

1958 Sidney Janis Gallery, New York

1957 Contemporary Arts Museum, Houston

Eight Americans, Sidney Janis Gallery, New York

1955 Sidney Janis Gallery, New York

1954 Art Institute of Chicago, Chicago

1952 *Fifteen Americans*, The Museum of Modern Art, New York

1951 *Revolution and Tradition*, The Brooklyn Museum, Brooklyn, New York

Surrealisme en het Abstrakt: Keuzen uit de verzameling, Stedelijk Museum, Amsterdam

1950 *Annual Exhibitions of Contemporary American Painting*, Whitney Museum of American Art, New York

Betty Parsons Gallery, New York

1949 Betty Parsons Gallery, New York

The Intrasubjectives, The Samuel M. Kootz Gallery, New York

1948 Betty Parsons Gallery, New York

La Collezione Peggy Guggenheim, XXIV Biennale di Venezia, Venice

1947 *Abstract and Surrealist Art of America*, Art Institute of Chicago, Chicago

Betty Parsons Gallery, New York

1946 Mortimer Brandt Gallery, New York

San Francisco Museum of Art, San Francisco

1945 Art of This Century, New York

1944 *Abstract and Surrealist Art in the United States*, Cincinnati Art Museum, Cincinnati. Traveled to Denver Art Museum, Denver; The Santa Barbara Museum of Art, Santa Barbara; San Francisco Museum of Art, San Francisco; and Mortimer Brandt

Gallery, New York

1942 Valentin-Dudensing Gallery, New York

1933 Contemporary Arts Gallery, New York

Museum of Art, Portland, Oregon

selected bibliography

Alloway, Lawrence. "Notes on Rothko." *Art International* (1962): 90–4.

——. "The American Sublime." *Living Arts* (June 1963): 11–22.

——. "The Biomorphic Forties." *Artforum* (September 1965): 18–22.

——. "The Spectrum of Monochrome." *Arts Magazine* (January 1971): 30–33.

Anfam, David. *Mark Rothko: The Works on Canvas: Catalogue Raisonné*. New Haven, Connecticut, and London: Yale University Press, 1998.

Ashton, Dore. "Art: Lecture by Rothko." *The New York Times* (31 October 1958).

Baker, Kenneth. "Shedding Light on Rothko's Light." *The Art Newspaper* (June 1998): 24.

Breslin, James E.B. *Mark Rothko: A Biography*. Chicago: The University of Chicago Press, 1993.

——. "Terminating Mark Rothko: Biography Is Mourning in Reverse." *The New York Times Book Review* (24 July 1994): 3, 19–20.

Causey, Andrew. "Rothko Through His Paintings." *Studio International* (April 1972): 149–55.

Cavaliere, Barbara. "Notes on Rothko." *Flash Art* (January–February 1979).

Cernuschi, Claude E. "Mark Rothko's Mature Paintings: A Question of Content." *The New York Times* (20 August 1986).

Chave, Anna C. *Mark Rothko: Subjects in Abstraction*. New Haven, Connecticut, and London: Yale University Press, 1989.

De Kooning, Elaine. "Two Americans in Action: Franz Kline and Mark Rothko." *ARTnews Annual* (1958): 86–97, 174–79.

Decker, Andrew. "Rothko's Legacy." *ARTnews* (September 1989).

Fischer, Joel. "Mark Rothko: Portrait of the Artist as an Angry Man." *Harper's* (July 1970): 16–23.

Glimcher, Marc, ed. *The Art of Mark Rothko: Into an Unknown World*. New York: Clarkson N. Potter, 1991.

Glueck, Grace. "Art: Rothko as Surrealist in His Pre-Abstract Years." *The New York Times* (1 May 1981).

Goldwater, Robert. "Rothko's Black Paintings." *Art in America* (March–April 1971): 58–63.

Goossen, E.C. "The Big Canvas." *Art International* (November 1958): 45–47.

——. "Rothko: The Omnibus Image." *ARTnews* (January 1961): 38–40, 60–61.

Hayt-Atkins, Elizabeth. "Mark Rothko." *ARTnews* (May 1990).

Heron, Patrick. "Can Mark Rothko's Work Survive." *Modern Painters* 2, no. 2 (Summer 1989): 36–39.

Hess, Thomas B. "Editorial: Mark Rothko." *ARTnews* (April 1970): 29, 66, 67.

Kertess, Klaus. "Mark Rothko: Menil Collection." *Artforum* (October 1997): 96.

Kimmelman, Michael. "Rothko's Gloomy Elegance in Retrospect." *The New York Times* (18 September 1998): 31, 34.

Kingsley, April. "Mark Rothko: The Painful Evolution of a Radical." *The Village Voice* (20 November 1978).

Kozloff, Max. "The Problem of Color-Light in Rothko." *Artforum* (September 1965): 38–44.

——. "Mark Rothko." *Artforum* (April 1970): 88–89.

Kramer, Hilton. "A Pure Abstractionist: Rothko's Work in Color Conveyed Luminosity Yet an Extreme Serenity." *The New York Times* (26 February 1970): 39.

——. "Rothko—Art as Religious Faith." *The New York Times* (November 1978).

——. "Rothko's Surreal Killer May Have Been Greenberg." *The New York Observer* (15 June 1998): 1, 27.

Kuspit, Donald B. "The Illusion of the Absolute in Abstract Art." *Art Journal* (Fall 1971): 26–30.

——. "Symbolic Pregnance in Mark Rothko and Clyfford Still." *Arts Magazine* (March 1978): 120–125.

——. "The Only Immortal." *Artforum* (February 1990).

——. "The Passion of Mark Rothko." *The New York Times Book Review* (26 December 1993): 1, 21.

Levine, Edward M. "Abstract Expressionism: The Mystical Experience." *Art Journal* (Fall 1971): 22–25.

Mark Rothko. Washington, D.C.: National Gallery of Art, 1998. Texts by Jeffrey Weiss, John Gage, Barbara Novak and Brian O'Doherty, and Carol Mancusi-Ungaro.

Mark Rothko 1903–1970. London: Tate Gallery, 1987. Texts by Bonnie Clearwater, Michael

Compton, Dana Cranmer, Robert Goldwater, Robert Rosenblum, Rothko, Irving Sandler, and David Sylvester.

Mark Rothko 1949: A Year of Transition/Selections from the Mark Rothko Foundation. San Francisco: San Francisco Museum of Modern Art, 1983. Text by Karen Tsujimoto.

Mark Rothko: "Multiforms." Munich: Galerie Daniel Blau, 1993. Texts by David Anfam, Andreas Franzke, Siegfried Gohr, Rothko, and Mark Stevens.

Mark Rothko: Paintings 1948–1969. New York: The Pace Gallery, 1983. Text by Irving Sandler.

Mark Rothko: Subjects. Atlanta: High Museum of Art, 1983. Text by Anna C. Chave.

Mark Rothko: Works on Paper. Washington, D.C.: National Gallery of Art, 1984. Text by Bonnie Clearwater.

Newman, Barnett, and Neil A. Levine. "The New York School Question." *ARTnews* (September 1965): 38–41, 55–56.

Nodelman, Sheldon. "Rediscovering Rothko." *Art in America* (July 1999): 58–65.

O'Doherty, Brian. "Rothko." *Art International* (20 October 1970): 30–44.

Plagens, Peter. "Darkness into Light." *Newsweek* (1 June 1998): 68.

Putnam, Wallace. "Rothko Told Me." *Arts Magazine* (April 1974): 44–45.

Ratcliff, Carter. "Rothko: The Dark Paintings 1969-70." *The New York Times* (12 April 1985).

Read, Herbert. "An Art of Internal Necessity." *Quadrum* (May 1956): 7–22.

Rosenberg, Harold. "The Art World: Rothko." *The New Yorker* (28 March 1970): 90–95.

——. "The Art World: Death and the Artist." *The New Yorker* (24 March 1975): 69–75.

Rosenblum, Robert. "The Abstract Sublime." *ARTnews* (February 1961): 38–41, 56, 58.

——. "Isn't it Romantic?" *Artforum* (May 1998): 116–119.

Rothko, Mark. "The Ideas of Art: The Attitudes of Ten Artists on Their Art and Contemporaneousness." *The Tiger's Eye* (December 1947): 44.

——. "The Romantics Were Prompted." *Possibilities* (Winter 1947): 84.

——. "Statement." *The Tiger's Eye* (October 1949): 114.

Rubin, William. "The New York School—Then and Now, Part II." *Art International* (May/June 1958): 19–22.

——. "Mark Rothko 1903–1970." *The New York Times* (8 March 1970): 21, 22.

Sandler, Irving. "Dada, Surrealism, and Their Heritage, Part 2: The Surrealist Emigres in New York." *Artforum* (May 1968): 24–31.

——. *The Triumph of American Paintings: A History of Abstract Expressionism*. New York: Praeger, 1970.

——. "Les Irascibles." *Art Press* (January 1989).

Schaffner, Ingrid. "From Rodin to Rothko, the Artist as Tragic Hero." *Art & Antiques* (April 1994): 90.

Schjeldahl, Peter. "Shining Through." *The Village Voice* (6 October 1998): 139.

Scully, Sean. "Bodies of Light." *Art in America* (July 1999): 67–71, 111.

Seldes, Lee. *The Legacy of Mark Rothko*. New York: Holt, Rinehart and Winston, 1979.

Smith, Roberta. "Mark Rothko's Surrealistic Billows." *The Village Voice* (6 May 1981).

——. "For Rothko, It Wasn't All Black Despair." *The New York Times* (6 March 1994): 41.

Tomkins, Calvin. "The Escape Artist: A New Rothko Retrospective at the Whitney." *The New Yorker* (28 September 1998): 102–03.

Vallier, Dora. "Rothko ou l'absence de thème devenue thème." *XXème Siècle* (May 1963): 53–6.

Waldman, Diane. *Mark Rothko, 1903–1970: A Retrospective*. New York: Abrams and Solomon R. Guggenheim Museum, 1978.

Wilson, William. "Rothko: Retrospective of a Dark Journey." *Los Angeles Times* (15 July 1979).

JAMES **rosenquist**

born in Grand Forks, North Dakota, 1933
lives and works in New York and Aripeka, Florida
education University of Minnesota, 1952–54
Art Students League, New York, 1955

selected exhibition history

1998   *James Rosenquist: The Swimmer in the Econo-mist*, Deutsche Guggenheim, Berlin

1996   *James Rosenquist: A Retrospective of Prints Made at Graphicstudio 1971–1996*, Graphicstudio, University of South Florida, Tampa, Florida

James Rosenquist: Target Practice, Galerie Traddaeus Ropac, Paris

New Paper Constructions, Gemini G.E.L., Los Angeles

1995   *James Rosenquist: Gli anni novanta*, Civico Museo Revoltella, Galleria d'Arte Moderna, Trieste, Italy

James Rosenquist Paintings, Seattle Art Museum, Seattle

James Rosenquist: The Big Paintings, Pyo Gallery, Seoul

1993   Akira Ikeda Gallery, Tokyo

James Rosenquist: Recent Paintings, Alyce de Roulet Williamson Gallery, Art Center College of Design, Pasadena, California

James Rosenquist: Time Dust, The Complete Graphics, 1962–1992, Walker Art Center, Minneapolis

1992   Galeria Weber, Alexander y Cobo, Madrid

James Rosenquist: The Early Pictures 1961–1964. Gagosian Gallery, New York

1991   *James Rosenquist*, IVAM Centre Julio González, Valencia

Pop Art, Royal Academy of Arts, London. Traveled to Museum Ludwig, Cologne; Museo Nacional Reina Sofía, Madrid; and Montreal Museum of Fine Arts, Montreal

Rosenquist: Moscow—USA, Tretyakov Museum, Moscow

Twentieth-Century Collage, Margo Leavin Gallery, Los Angeles

1990   *High and Low: Modern Art and Popular Culture*, The Museum of Modern Art, New York. Traveled to Art Institute of Chicago, Chicago; and The Museum of Contemporary Art, Los Angeles

James Rosenquist, Leo Castelli Gallery, New York

James Rosenquist—Never Mind—From Thoughts to Drawing, Universal Limited Art Editions, New York

James Rosenquist: Welcome to the Water Planet, The Museum of Modern Art, New York

James Rosenquist: Welcome to the Water Planet and House of Fire 1988–89, Erika Meyerovich Gallery, San Francisco, and Richard Feigen & Company, Chicago

1989   *A Decade of American Painting, 1980–89*, Daniel Weinberg Gallery, Los Angeles

Galerie Busche, Cologne

Image World: Art and Media Culture, Whitney Museum of American Art, New York

1988   *Committed to Print*, The Museum of Modern Art, New York

James Rosenquist: New Work, Richard Feigen & Company, Chicago

James Rosenquist: Selected Lithographs, The Penson Gallery, New York

Leo Castelli Gallery, New York

Rosenquist/Memphis: Works by James Rosenquist, University Gallery at Memphis State, Memphis, Tennessee

1987   *James Rosenquist*, Galerie Daniel Templon, Paris

James Rosenquist, The Mayor Gallery, London

Made in U.S.A.: An Americanization in Modern Art, the '50s and '60s, University Art Museum, University of California at Berkeley, Berkeley. Traveled to Nelson-Atkins Museum of Art, Kansas City, Missouri; and Virginia Museum of Fine Arts, Richmond, Virginia

1986   *Definitive Statements: American Art 1964–66*, Bell Gallery, Brown University, Providence, Rhode Island. Traveled to The Parrish Art Museum, Southampton, New York

Surrealismo!, Barbara Braathen Gallery, New York

1985   *James Rosenquist Paintings 1961–1985*, Denver Art Museum, Denver. Traveled to Contemporary Arts Museum, Houston; Des Moines Art Center, Des Moines, Iowa; Albright-Knox Art Gallery, Buffalo, New York; Whitney Museum of American Art, New York; and National Museum of American Art, Washington, D.C.

1984   *El Arte Narrativo*, Museo Rufino Tamayo, Mexico City

Blam! The Explosion of Pop, Minimal, and Performance Art, Whitney Museum of
  American Art, New York
James Rosenquist: New Paintings, Heland Thorden Wetterling Gallery, Stockholm

1983 *James Rosenquist: Paintings & Works on Paper*, Van Straaten Gallery, Chicago
James Rosenquist, Leo Castelli Gallery, New York

1982 *James Rosenquist*, Colorado State University, Fort Collins, Colorado
James Rosenquist: House of Fire, Castelli-Feigen-Corcoran Gallery, New York
James Rosenquist: Paintings from the Sixties, The Mayor Gallery, London

1981 *1981 Biennial Exhibition.* Whitney Museum of American Art, New York
Internationale Ausstellung Köln 1981, Cologne, Germany
James Rosenquist, Leo Castelli Gallery, New York

1980 *Hidden Desires*, Neuberger Museum, State University of New York at Purchase,
  Purchase, New York
New Paintings and Sculpture, Castelli-Feigen-Corcoran Gallery, New York
Pop Art: Evolution of a Generation, Instituto di Cultura di Palazzo Grassi, Venice
Texas Gallery, Houston

1979 Albright-Knox Gallery, Buffalo, New York
American Pop Art, Galerie d'Art Contemporain des Musées de Nice, Nice, France
Galerie Ileana Sonnabend, Paris

1978 *American Painting of the 1970s*, Albright-Knox Art Gallery, Buffalo, New York.
  Traveled to Newport Harbor Art Museum, Newport Beach, California; Oakland
  Museum, Oakland, California; and Cincinnati Art Museum, Cincinnati, Ohio
Recent Paintings, The Mayor Gallery, London

1977 *The Dada/Surrealist Heritage*, Sterling and Francine Clark Institute, Williamstown,
  Massachussetts
Institute of Modern Art, Brisbane, Australia
New Paintings, Leo Castelli Gallery, New York
Sable-Castelli Gallery, Toronto

1976 The Greenberg Gallery, St. Louis
The Mayor Gallery, London
Paule Anglim Associates, San Francisco

1975 Leo Castelli Gallery, New York
Margo Leavin Gallery, Los Angeles

1974 *American Pop Art*, Whitney Museum of American Art, New York
Margo Leavin Gallery, Los Angeles
Max Protetch Gallery, Washington, D.C.
Paintings: 1961–1973, The Mayor Gallery, London
Pop Art, Il Segnapassi Galleria d'Arte, Pesaro, Italy

1973 High Museum of Art, Atlanta
Leo Castelli Gallery, New York
Portland Center for the Visual Arts, Portland, Oregon
Stedelijk Museum, Amsterdam

1972 Margo Leavin Gallery, Los Angeles
James Rosenquist: Gemälde—Räume—Graphik, Kunsthalle Köln, Cologne
James Rosenquist, Whitney Museum of American Art, New York. Traveled to Museum
  of Contemporary Art, Chicago

1971 *The Cologne Art Fair*, Kunsthalle Köln, Cologne
Leo Castelli Gallery, New York
Metamorphose de l'objet: Art et Anti-art 1910–1970, Palais des Beaux-Arts, Brussels

1970 Galerie Rolf Ricke, Cologne
Leo Castelli Gallery, New York
Monumental Art, Contemporary Arts Center, Cincinnati

1969 *Annual Exhibition of Contemporary American Painting*, Whitney Museum of American
  Art, New York
Leo Castelli Gallery, New York
New York Painting and Sculpture: 1940–1970, The Metropolitan Museum of Art,
  New York
Pop Art, Hayward Gallery, London

1968 *Documenta*, Kassel, Germany
Galerie Ileana Sonnabend, Paris
Leo Castelli Gallery, New York
The Machine as Seen at the End of the Mechanical Age, The Museum of Modern Art,
  New York
National Gallery of Canada, Ottawa
San Francisco Museum of Art, San Francisco

1967 *IX São Paulo Bienal*, São Paulo, Brazil
Annual Exhibition of Contemporary American Painting, Whitney Museum of American
  Art, New York
Musée des Arts Décoratifs, Paris

1966 Kunsthalle, Bern, Switzerland
Leo Castelli Gallery, New York
Louisiana Museum of Modern Art, Humlebaek, Denmark

1965 Galerie Ileana Sonnabend, Paris
International Exhibition, Instituto Torcuato di Tella, Buenos Aires
James Rosenquist, F-111, The Jewish Museum, New York. Traveled to Moderna Museet,
  Stockholm; Stedelijk Museum, Amsterdam; Staatliche Kunsthalle, Baden-Baden,
  Germany; Galleria Nazionale d'Arte Moderna, Rome
Leo Castelli Gallery, New York
Museo d'Arte Moderna, Turin

1964 *XXème Salon de Mai*, Musée d'Art Moderne de la Ville de Paris, Paris
Amerikanst Pop-konst, Moderna Museet, Stockholm
Dwan Gallery, Los Angeles
Environments by 4 New Realists, Sidney Janis Gallery, New York
Green Gallery, New York
Galerie Ileana Sonnabend, Paris
Galleria Gian Enzo Sperone, Turin

1963 *Americans 1963*, The Museum of Modern Art, New York
Annual Exhibition of Contemporary American Painting, Whitney Museum of American
  Art, New York
Green Gallery, New York
The Popular Image, Institute of Contemporary Arts, London
Six Painters and the Object, Guggenheim Museum, New York

1962 Green Gallery, New York
New Realists, Sidney Janis Gallery, New York

selected bibliography

1981 Biennial Exhibition. New York: Whitney Museum of American Art, 1981.

Adcock, Craig. "James Rosenquist: Museum of Modern Art." *Tema Celeste* (January–
  February 1991).

——., et al. *Rosenquist*. Valencia, Spain: Institut Valencia d'Art Modern, 1991.

Alloway, Lawrence. "Popular Culture and Pop Art." *Studio International* 178, no. 913 (July–
  August 1969): 17–21.

——. "Derealized Epic." *Artforum* 10, no. 10 (June 1972): 35–41.

Artner, Alan G. "Random Thoughts from 'Pop' Phenomenon James Rosenquist." *Chicago Tribune*
  (22 May 1983).

Ashbery, John. "Spaced-Out Rosenquist." *Newsweek* 97, no. 6 (9 February 1981): 84.

Ashton, Dore. "Response to Crisis in American Art." *Art in America* 57, no. 1 (January–February
  1969): 24–35.

Baker, Kenneth. "New York." *Artforum* 9, no. 5 (January 1971): 75.

Battcock, Gregory. "James Rosenquist." *Arts Magazine* 46, no. 7 (May 1972): 49–52.

Bernstein, Richard. "Rosenquist in Retrospect." *Interview* 2, no. 6 (June 1972): 36–38.

Bonami, Francesco. "James Rosenquist: Militant Pop." *Flash Art* 25, no. 165 (Summer 1992):
  102–04.

Brundage, Susan, ed. *James Rosenquist, The Big Paintings: Thirty Years, Leo Castelli*.
  New York: Leo Castelli Gallery with Rizzoli, 1994.

Burr, James. "Pop of the Billboard." *Apollo* 100, no. 154 (December 1974): 518–19.

Calas, Nicholas, and Elena Calas. "James Rosenquist: Vision in the Vernacular." *Arts Magazine*
  44, no. 2 (November 1969): 38–39.

Canaday, John. "James Rosenquist." *The New York Times* (5 April 1969): 23.

Cotter, Holland. "Advertisements for a Mean Utopia." *Art in America* 75, no. 1 (January
  1987): 82–89.

Coupland, Douglas. *"James Rosenquist: F-111."* *Artforum* 32, no. 8 (April 1994): 84–85.

Cummings, Paul. "Interview: James Rosenquist Talks with Paul Cummings." *Drawing* 5 (July–
  August 1983): 30–34.

Danto, Arthur C. "Works on Paper." *The Nation* 241, no. 4 (17 August 1985): 122–25.

Durand, Régis. "James Rosenquist: la réincarnation des images." *Art Press* 158 (May 1991):
  14–21.

Fillin-Yeh, Susan. *The Technological Muse*. Katonah, New York: Katonah Museum of Art, 1991.

Frank, Peter. "James Rosenquist." *ARTnews* 72, no. 7 (September 1973): 84–85.

Geldzahler, Henry. *James Rosenquist at Gemini*. Los Angeles: Gemini G.E.L., 1983.

——. *New York Painting and Sculpture: 1940–1970*. New York: E.P. Dutton, in association with Metropolitan Museum of Art, 1969.

——. *James Rosenquist: The Early Pictures 1961–1964*. New York: Gagosian Gallery/Rizzoli International Publications, 1992.

Glenn, Constance W. *Time Dust, James Rosenquist: Complete Graphics, 1962–1992*. Long Beach, California: University Art Museum, California State University; and New York: Rizzoli International Publications, 1993.

Goldman, Judith. *James Rosenquist*. New York: Viking Penguin, 1985.

Haskell, Barbara. *Blam! The Explosion of Pop, Minimalism, and Performance 1958–1964*. New York: Whitney Museum of American Art, 1984.

Hess, Thomas B. "The phony crisis in American art." *ARTnews* 62 (Summer 1963): 24–28, 59–60.

Heartney, Eleanor. "Mixing Cars, Girls, and Ripe Tomatoes." *ARTnews* 85, no. 3 (March–April 1986): 44–46.

——. "Rosenquist Revisited." *ARTnews* 85, no. 6 (Summer 1986): 98–103.

Hughes, Robert. "Memories Scaled and Scrambled: In New York City, a Survey of James Rosenquist." *Time* 128, no. 6 (11 August 1986): 69.

Hulten, Pontus. *The Machine as Seen at the End of the Mechanical Age*. New York: The Museum of Modern Art, 1968.

James Rosenquist: The Serenade for the Doll after Claude Debussy or Gift Wrapped Dolls and Masquerade of the Military Industrial Complex Looking Down on the Insect World. New York: Leo Castelli Gallery, New York, 1993. Statements by Rosenquist and interview by David Whitney.

Johnson, Ray. "Abandoned Chickens." *Art in America* 62, no. 6 (November–December 1974): 107–12.

Jones, Roland. "James Rosenquist: Paintings 1961–1985 at Whitney Museum." *Flash Art*, no. 131 (December 1986-January 1987): 88.

Kelly, Edward T. "Neo-Dada: A Critique of Pop Art." *Art Journal* 23, no. 3 (Spring 1964): 192–201.

Kimmelman, Michael. "From Rosenquist, A Pleasing Look at Early Pop." *The New York Times* (7 June 1992): 33.

Kozloff, Max. "Art." *The Nation* 206, no. 18 (29 April 1968): 578–80.

Kuspit, Donald. "James Rosenquist at the Whitney Museum of American Art." *Artforum* 25, no. 2 (October 1986): 128–29.

Lewallen, Constance. "Rosenquist's New Work." *Artweek* 7, no. 2 (10 January 1976): 1, 16.

Lippard, Lucy R. "James Rosenquist: Aspects of a Multiple Art." *Artforum* 4 (December 1965): 41–45.

Livingstone, Marco, ed. *Pop Art*. London: Royal Academy of Arts, 1991. Essays by Livingstone, Sarat Maharaj, Constance Glenn, Alfred Pacquement, Evelyn Weiss, Thomas Kellein, and Dan Cameron.

Michaelson, Annette. "Paris Letter." *Art International* 8, no. 9 (November 1964): 61.

The Museum of Contemporary Art: The Panza Collection. Los Angeles: The Museum of Contemporary Art, 1985.

Narrett, Eugene. "Rosenquist in Retrospect: Wrestling with the American Goddess." *New Art Examiner* 14, no. 4 (December 1986): 23–25.

Perreault, John. "Art: Too Much of the Same." *The Village Voice* 13, no. 19 (22 February 1968): 18.

——. "Art: Here & There." *The Village Voice* (4 June 1970): 17–19.

——. "'Classic' Pop Revisited." *Art in America* 62, no. 2 (March–April 1974): 64–68.

Pincus-Witten, Robert. "Rosenquist and Samaras: The Obsessive Image and Post-Minimalism." *Artforum* 11, no. 2 (September 1972): 63–69.

Ratcliff, Carter. "Reviews and Previews." *ARTnews* 69, no. 5 (September 1970): 18.

——. "Rosenquist's Rouge." *Artforum* 23, no. 10 (Summer 1985): 92–4.

Raynor, Vivien. "Art: American Imagery by James Rosenquist." *The New York Times* (14 October 1983).

Restany, Pierre. "Le nouveau réalisme à la conquête de New York." *Art International* 7, no. 1 (25 January 1963): 29–36.

Russell, John. "Pop Reappraised." *Art in America* 57, no. 4 (July–August 1969): 78–89.

——. "Persistent Pop." *The New York Times Magazine* (21 July 1974): 6–7, 25–34.

——. "Art: James Rosenquist in Retrospective." *The New York Times* (27 June 1986).

Schjeldahl, Peter. "A 'Trip' with Rosenquist." *The New York Times* (31 May 1970): 17.

——. "Entretien avec James Rosenquist." *Opus International*, nos. 29–30 (December 1971): 46–49, 114–15.

——. "The Rosenquist Synthesis." *Art in America* 60 (March–April 1972): 56–61.

Schwabsky, Barry. "James Rosenquist." *Artscribe International*, no. 60 (November–December 1986): 77–78.

Siegel, Jeanne. "An Interview with James Rosenquist." *Artforum* 10, no. 10 (June 1972): 30–34.

Smith, Roberta. "Photos and Realism." *The Village Voice* (1 November 1983): 95.

Solomon, Alan R. *The Popular Image*. London: Institute of Contemporary Arts, 1963.

Stevenson, Wade. "Rosenquist, le peintre de l'imaginaire-réel." *XXème Siècle* (Paris), no. 44 (June 1975): 155–61.

Stich, Sidra. *Made in U.S.A.: An Americanization in Modern Art, The '50s and '60s*. Berkeley, California: University Art Museum, 1987.

Swenson, G.R. "The New American Sign Painters." *ARTnews* 61 (September 1962): 44–47, 60–62.

——. "What Is Pop Art?, Part II." *ARTnews* 62 (February 1964): 41, 62–64.

——. "The F-111." *Partisan Review* 32 (Fall 1965): 589–601. Interview with the artist.

——. "Social realism in blue: an interview with James Rosenquist." *Studio International* 175 (February 1968): 76–83.

Sylvester, David. *James Rosenquist: An Exhibition of Paintings 1961–1973*. London: The Mayor Gallery, 1975.

Taylor, Paul. "Interview with James Rosenquist." *Parkett*, no. 28 (1991): 116–21.

Tillim, Sidney. "Further Observations on the Pop Phenomenon: 'All Revolutions Have Their Ugly Aspects…'" *Artforum* 4, no. 3 (November 1965): 17–19.

——. "Rosenquist at the Met: Avant-garde or Red Guard?" *Artforum* 6, no. 8 (April 1968): 46–49.

Trini, Tommaso. "E la via Rosenquist." *Domus*, no. 455 (October 1967): 46–49.

——. "At Home with Art: The Villa of Count G. Panza di Biumo." *Art in America* 58, no. 5 (September–October 1970): 102–109.

Tuchman, Phyllis. "Pop! Interviews with George Segal, Andy Warhol, Roy Lichtenstein, James Rosenquist, and Robert Indiana." *ARTnews* 73, no. 5 (May 1974): 24–29.

Tucker, Marcia. *James Rosenquist*. New York: Whitney Museum of American Art, 1972.

Varian, Elayne H. *James Rosenquist Graphics Retrospective*. Sarasota, Florida: John and Mable Ringling Museum of Art, 1979.

Varnedoe, Kirk, and Adam Gopnik. *High and Low: Modern Art and Popular Culture*. New York: The Museum of Modern Art, 1991.

Weiss, Evelyn. *James Rosenquist: Gemälde—Räume—Graphik*. Cologne: Wallraf-Richartz-Museums, 1972.

Wortz, Melinda. "James Rosenquist." *ARTnews* 77, no. 3 (March 1978): 144–45.

Yau, John. *James Rosenquist: Never Mind, From Thoughts to Drawing*. New York: Universal Limited Art Editions, 1990.

ROSS **rudel**

born in Billings, Montana, 1960
lives and works in Los Angeles
education M.F.A., University of California at Irvine, Irvine, California, 1985
B.A., Montana State University, Bozeman, Montana, 1983

selected one-person exhibitions

1999	Angles Gallery, Santa Monica, California
1998	Jack Shainman Gallery, New York
1997	Angles Gallery, Santa Monica, California
1996	Angles Gallery, Santa Monica, California
1995	Jack Shainman Gallery, New York
1993	Angles Gallery, Santa Monica, California
	Angles Gallery, Santa Monica, California
1992	Ace Contemporary Exhibitions, Los Angeles
1991	Ace Contemporary Exhibitions, Los Angeles
1990	Ace Contemporary Exhibitions, Los Angeles
1987	Dahl Fine Arts Center, Rapid City, South Dakota
1986	Irvine Fine Arts Center, Irvine, California

selected group exhibitions

1998   *Ecstasy*, Jack Shainman Gallery, New York
1997   *Curiosity Room,* Jack Shainman Gallery, New York
      La Donazione Panza di Biumo al Museo Cantonale d'Arte, Museo Cantonale d'Arte, Lugano, Switzerland
      A Hotbed of Advanced Art: Four Decades of Visual Arts at UCI, Fine Arts Gallery, University of California at Irvine, Irvine, California
      In Touch With . . ., Galerie + Edition Renate Schröder, Cologne, Germany
      Plastered, Shoshana Wayne Gallery, Santa Monica, California
      Sensuality in the Abstract, Los Angeles Municipal Art Gallery, Barnsdall Art Park, Los Angeles
1996   *Additions to the Permanent Collection,* Museum of Contemporary Art, San Diego, California
      . . .And They Call it Painting. . ., Studio La Città, Verona, Italy
      The Panza di Biumo Collection: some artists from the 80s and 90s, Museo d'Arte Moderna e Contemporanea di Trento e Rovereto, Palazzo delle Albere, Trento, Italy
1995   *California: In Three Dimensions*, California Center for the Arts Museum, Escondido, California
      Gender, Myth and Exploration, University Art Gallery, University of North Texas, Denton, Texas
      Human/Nature, The New Museum of Contemporary Art, New York
      The Language of Form, Atkinson Gallery, Santa Barbara City College, Santa Barbara, California
      The Panza di Biumo Donation: European and American Art '83–'93, Museo Cantonale d'Arte, Lugano, Switzerland
      Presence: Recent Portraits, Angles Gallery, Santa Monica, California
      Seductive Matter, Rice University Art Gallery, Houston. Traveled to Corcoran Hemicycle Gallery, Washington, D.C.
      Sexy: Sensual Abstraction in California Art, 1960s–1990s, Contemporary Arts Collective, Las Vegas, Nevada
      Skew: The Unruly Grid, Gallery 400, University of Illinois at Chicago, Chicago
1994   *Damned: Life, Death & Surface,* John Thomas Gallery, Santa Monica, California
      A Perhaps Hand, Thomas Solomon's Garage, Los Angeles
      Serious Beauty II, Stuart Katz Art Loft, Laguna Beach, California
      Some Like it Hot, Jack Shainman Gallery, New York
1992   *Oddly,* Oakland Museum, Oakland, California
1991   *Evocative Objects,* California State University, Los Angeles
      Rudels, South Dakota School of Mines and Technology, Rapid City, South Dakota

bibliography

Baker, Kenneth. "Just Odd Enough: Four L.A. Artists' Work Raises Questions in Oakland Show." *San Francisco Chronicle* (14 June 1992): 47.
Bonetti, David. "Sculptors Who Attract, Oddly Enough." *San Francisco Examiner* (11 June 1992): C1, C7.
Brock, Hovey. "Ross Rudel: Jack Shainman." *ARTnews* 94, no. 6 (Summer 1995): 128.
Curtis, Cathy. "The Galleries: Wilshire Center." *Los Angeles Times* (23 June 1989): 14.
——. "Delayed Gratification: Beyond the 'Physical' Exhibition Is a Cumulative Effect." *Los Angeles Times* (28 April 1998): F2, F3.
Cutajar, Mario. "Ross Rudel at Ace." *Visions* 5, no. 2 (Spring 1991): 43.
Darling, Michael. "Skin Deep; Damned: Life, Death and Surface at John Thomas Gallery." *Artweek* 25, no. 3 (3 February 1994): back cover.
Dubin, Zan. "Reality Based: Show Spans Decades of Hands-On Approach of UCI Art Stars." *Los Angeles Times* (11 November 1997): F1-2, F5.
Fiz, Alberto. "I consigli del conte." *Milano Finanza* (7 September 1996): 18–19.
Frank, Peter. "Pick of the Week: Ross Rudel, John Millei, Bruce Rod, Craig Deines, Some Recent Sculpture, Norman Schwab, Heidi Zin." *L.A. Weekly* (16–22 November 1990): 131.
——. "Ross Rudel, Carole Seborovski: Angles." *ARTnews* 95, no. 4 (April 1996): 141.
Galeone, Lorenza. "Ross Rudel at Jack Shainman." *Juliet Art Magazine* (April–May 1998): 71.
A Hotbed of Advanced Art: Four Decades of Visual Arts at UCI. Exh. cat. Irvine, California: The Art Gallery, University of California at Irvine, 1997. Essays by Dickran Tashijan and Catherine Lord; chronology and biographies.
Iannaccone, Carmine. "Ross Rudel." *Art Issues,* no. 32 (March/April 1994): 36.
Johnson, Ken. "Ross Rudel at Jack Shainman." *The New York Times* (20 February 1998): E38.
Koplos, Janet. "Ross Rudel at Angles." *Art in America* 84, no. 6 (June 1996): 109.

Kugelman, Kerry. "Ross Rudel at Angles and Carlos Mollura at Acme." *Artweek* 27, no. 4 (April 1996): 23.
Kutner, Janet. "Artists Explore the Issues of Human Gender." *Dallas Morning News* (30 April 1995): C.
Maclay, Catherine. "Ambiguity and Amusement from Four Los Angelenos." *San Jose Mercury News* (22 May 1992).
Oddly. Exh. cat. Oakland, California: Oakland Museum, 1992. Essay by Paul Tomidy.
The Panza di Biumo Collection: some artists from the 80s and 90s. Exh. cat. Trento, Italy: Museo d'Arte Moderna e Contemporanea di Trento e Rovereto, 1996. Essays by Gabriella Belli and Giuseppe Panza di Biumo; entries and biographies.
Pincus, Robert L. "Accessible 'California' Sculpture Proves Novel without Being Novelty." *San Diego Union-Tribune* (2 July 1995): E6.
——. "Complex's Fine Museum Makes a Case for Artful Accessibility." *San Diego Union-Tribune* (2 July 1995): E6.
Ramljak, Suzanne. "The Art of Seduction: Suzanne Ramljak makes a case for erotic abstraction." *Sculpture* 14, no. 5 (September–October 1995): 28–33.
Rebbeck, Dick. "Family of Artists Combines Forces." *The Rapid City Journal* (13 January 1991): D1.
Rockwell, Steve. "Ross Rudel at Jack Shainman." *ART International,* no. 2 (April–June 1998): 37.
Snow, Shauna. "A Santa Monica Gallery Is the Site for Chinatown Project." *Los Angeles Times* (19 July 1992): 78.
Trevisan, Giorgio. "Tante Pitture, nessuna memoria." *L'Aren* (11 July 1996).
Walsh, Daniela B. "Exhibit Marks 30 Years of UCI Art." *Orange County Register* (16 November 1997): 33.
Watten, Barrett. "In the In-Between: Oddly at the Oakland Museum." *Artweek* 23, no. 18 (18 June 1992): 16–17.

GEORGE segal

born in New York, 1924
lives and works in New Jersey
education M.F.A., Rutgers University, New Brunswick, New Jersey, 1962–63
B.A., New York University School of Education, New York, 1948–49
Pratt Institute, Brooklyn, New York, 1947–48
Rutgers University, New Brunswick, New Jersey, 1942–46
Cooper Union, New York, 1941–42

selected one-person exhibitions

1998   *George Segal: Large Scale Pastels, 1998*, Sidney Janis Gallery, New York
1997   *George Segal, A Retrospective: Sculpture, Paintings, Drawings*, Musée des Beaux-Arts, Montreal. Traveled to Hirshhorn Museum and Sculpture Garden, Washington, D.C.; The Jewish Museum, New York; and The Miami Art Museum of Dade County
      George Segal: New Sculpture and Drawings, Sidney Janis Gallery, New York
      George Segal: Works from the Bible, Skirball Cultural Center, Los Angeles
1996   *George Segal: New Photo Sculpture*, Fred Hoffman Gallery, Santa Monica, California
      George Segal: Recent 15 Years, Sezon Museum of Art, Tokyo. Traveled to Shizuoka Prefectural Museum of Art, Shizuoka, Japan; and Kawamura Memorial Museum, Sakura, Japan
1995   Ho-Am Art Museum, Seoul
      Sidney Janis Gallery, New York
1994   Lorenzelli Arte, Milan
      Sidney Janis Gallery, New York
1993   *Sequences New York/New Jersey, 1990–1993: Recent Photographs by Sculptor and Artist George Segal*, Howard Greenberg Gallery, New York
      Sidney Janis Gallery, New York
1992   *George Segal: The Graffiti Wall and Selected Works*, Neuberger Museum of Art,

Purchase College, State University of New York, Purchase, New York
Sidney Janis Gallery, New York
1991 *George Segal: Obras de 1959 a 1989/Works of 1959 to 1989*, Museo de Arte Contemporáneo de Caracas, Caracas, Venezuela
George Segal: The Holocaust, New Jersey State Museum, Trenton, New Jersey. Traveled to Memorial Art Gallery, University of Rochester, Rochester, New York
Sidney Janis Gallery, New York
1990 *George Segal: Recent Painted Sculpture*, Galerie Tokoro, Tokyo
George Segal: The Street, Gallery Ueda, Tokyo
Invasion blanche, Galerie Beaubourg, Paris
Margulies/Taplin Gallery, Bay Harbor, Florida
1989 *George Segal: Sculptures, 1958–1988*, New Jersey Center for Visual Arts, Summit, New Jersey
George Segal: Still Lifes and Related Works, Modern Art Museum of Fort Worth, Texas. Traveled to Orlando Art Museum, Orlando, Florida; Portland Art Museum, Portland, Oregon; and Whitney Museum of American Art, Fairfield County, Stamford, Connecticut
Sidney Janis Gallery, New York
1988 Riva Yares Gallery, Scottsdale, Arizona
Sidney Janis Gallery, New York
1987 Galerie Esperanza, Montreal
Richard Gray Gallery, Chicago
1986 Galerie Brusberg, Berlin
George Segal: A Sculptor's Photographs, University Art Museum, California State University, Long Beach
George Segal: Escultures i obra sobre paper, Galeria Joan Prats, Barcelona
Sidney Janis Gallery, New York
1985 Galerie Esperanza, Montreal
Galerie Maeght-Lelong, Paris
George Segal: The Drawings, Butler Institute of American Art, Youngstown, Ohio
George Segal: The Holocaust, Jewish Museum, New York
1984 Evelyn Aimis Fine Art, Toronto
Galeria Il Ponte, Rome
Sidney Janis Gallery, New York
1983 *George Segal Sculpture*, Lowe Art Museum, University of Miami, Coral Gables, Florida
Israel Museum, Jerusalem
Jewish Museum, New York
1982 Contemporary Sculpture Center, Tokyo. Traveled to Seibu Museum of Art, Tokyo; Tanakawa Museum, Karuizawa, Japan; Museum of Modern Art, Toyama, Japan; Ohara Museum of Art, Kurashiki, Japan; and National Museum of Art, Osaka, Japan
Sidney Janis Gallery, New York
1980 Akron Art Institute, Akron, Ohio
Gatoda Gallery, Tokyo
Sidney Janis Gallery, New York
1979 Hope Makler Gallery, Philadelphia
Serge DeBloe, Brussels
1978 *George Segal: Sculptures*, Walker Art Center, Minneapolis. Traveled to San Francisco Museum of Modern Art, San Francisco; and Whitney Museum of American Art, New York
Sidney Janis Gallery, New York
1977 *George Segal: Pastels, 1957–1965*, Art Galleries, California State University, Long Beach. Traveled to Fine Arts Gallery of San Diego; Modern Art Pavilion, Seattle Art Museum, Seattle; Boise Gallery of Art, Boise, Idaho; Nelson-Atkins Museum, Kansas City; and Walker Art Center, Minneapolis
Sidney Janis Gallery, New York
1976 *George Segal: Environments*, Institute of Contemporary Art, Philadelphia. Traveled to Baltimore Museum of Art, Baltimore; Nina Freudenheim Gallery, Buffalo, New York; Art Association of Newport, Newport, Rhode Island; and Santa Barbara Museum of Art, Santa Barbara, California
1975 André Emmerich, Zürich
Hopkins Center Art Galleries, Dartmouth College, Hanover, New Hampshire
1974 Galerie Onnasch, Basel Art Fair, Basel
Sidney Janis Gallery, New York
1973 *The Private World of George Segal*, Art History Galleries, University of Wisconsin, Milwaukee. Traveled to Indianapolis Museum of Art, Indianapolis, Indiana

Sidney Janis Gallery, New York
1971 Galerie Darthea Speyer, Paris
Galerie Onnasch, Cologne
Kunsthaus Zürich. Traveled to Hessisches Landesmuseum, Darmstadt, Germany; Museum Boijmans van Beuningen, Rotterdam; Städtisches Museum Leverkusen, Leverkusen, Germany; Centre national d'art contemporain, Paris; Kunsthalle Tübingen, Tübingen, Germany; and Städtische Galerie im Lenbachhaus, Munich
Sidney Janis Gallery, New York
1970 Sidney Janis Gallery, New York
Western Gallery, Western Washington State College, Bellingham, Washington
1969 Galerie Darthea Speyer, Paris
Princeton University, Princeton, New Jersey
1968 *George Segal: 12 Human Situations*, Museum of Contemporary Art, Chicago
Sidney Janis Gallery, New York
1967 Sidney Janis Gallery, New York
1965 Sidney Janis Gallery, New York
1964 Green Gallery, New York
1963 Galerie Ileana Sonnabend, Paris
Galerie Schmela, Düsseldorf, Germany
Paintings, Pastels and Sculpture, Art Gallery, Douglass College, New Brunswick, New Jersey
Rutgers University, New Brunswick, New Jersey
1962 Green Gallery, New York
1960 Green Gallery, New York
1959 Hansa Gallery, New York
1958 Hansa Gallery, New York
Rutgers University, New Brunswick, New Jersey
1957 Hansa Gallery, New York
1956 Hansa Gallery, New York

selected group exhibitions

1994 *Art américain: les années 1960–1970*, Musée d'art moderne, Saint-Etienne, France
1992 *Figures of Contemporary Sculpture (1970–1990): Images of Man*, Isetan Museum, Tokyo. Traveled to Daimaru Museum, Osaka, Japan; Hiroshima City Museum of Contemporary Art, Hiroshima, Japan
1991 *Pop Art*, Royal Academy of Arts, London. Traveled to Museum Ludwig, Cologne, Germany; Centro de Arte Reina Sofia, Madrid; and Montreal Museum of Fine Arts, Montreal
1988 *Classical Myth and Imagery in Contemporary Art*, Queens Museum, New York
Venice Biennale, Italian Pavilion, Venice
1985 *Body and Soul: Recent Figurative Sculpture*, Contemporary Arts Center, Cincinnati. Traveled to Knight Gallery, Spirit Square Art Center, Charlotte, North Carolina; Fresno Arts Center, Fresno, California; Loch Haven Art Center, Orlando, Florida; Visual Arts Gallery, Florida International University, Miami; Joslyn Art Museum, Omaha; and Jacksonville Art Museum, Jacksonville, Florida
Contemporary Bronze: Six in the Figurative Tradition, Sheldon Memorial Art Gallery, University of Nebraska, Lincoln. Traveled to Kansas City Art Institute, Kansas City, Kansas; and Des Moines Art Center, Des Moines, Iowa
Transformations in Sculpture: Four Decades of American and European Art, Guggenheim Museum, New York
1984 *Figurative Sculpture: Ten Artists/Two Decades*, University Art Museum, California State University, Long Beach
1983 *Six in Bronze*, Williams College Museum of Art, Williamstown, Massachusetts. Traveled to Carnegie Institute, Pittsburgh; High Museum of Art, Atlanta; Laguna Gloria Art Museum, Austin, Texas; and Columbus Museum of Art, Columbus, Ohio
1982 *Five Artists and the Figure: Duane Hanson, Alex Katz, Philip Pearlstein, Alice Neel, George Segal*, Whitney Museum of American Art, New York
Real, Really Real and Super Real, San Antonio Museum of Art, San Antonio, Texas
Sculpture in the 70s: The Figure, Pratt Institute, Manhattan Center, New York. Traveled to Arkansas Art Center, Little Rock; University of Oklahoma, Norman, Oklahoma; Arizona State University, Tempe, Arizona; and Dartmouth College Art Museum, Hanover, New Hampshire
1981 *Figuratively Sculpting*, P.S. 1, Long Island City, New York
Inside Out: Self beyond Likeness, Newport Harbor Art Museum,

Newport Beach, California

1980 *The Figurative Tradition and the Whitney Museum of American Art: Paintings and Sculpture from the Permanent Collection*, Whitney Museum of American Art, New York

Pop Art: evoluzione di una generazione, Palazzo Grassi, Venice

Sculptures on the Wall: Relief Sculpture of the Seventies, University Galleries, University of Massachusetts, Amherst

1978 *Art about Art*, Whitney Museum of American Art, New York

1977 *Documenta VI*, Museum Fridericianum, Kassel, Germany

1976 *200 Years of American Sculpture*, Whitney Museum of American Art, New York

Private Images: Photographs by Sculptors, Los Angeles County Museum of Art, Los Angeles

1975 *Realism and Reality*, Kunsthalle Darmstadt, Darmstadt, Germany

Sculpture: American Directions, 1945–1975, National Collection of Fine Arts, Smithsonian Institution, Washington

Traditions and Revisions: Themes from the History of Sculpture, Cleveland Museum of Art, Cleveland, Ohio

1974 *Contemporary American Artists*, Cleveland Museum of Art, Cleveland, Ohio

1973 *Contemporary American Artists*, Cleveland Museum of Art, Cleveland, Ohio

New York Collection for Stockholm, Moderna Museet, Stockholm

1971 *IVème Exposition internationale de sculpture contemporaine*, Musée Rodin, Paris

Métamorphose de l'objet: art et anti-art 1910–1970, Palais des Beaux-Arts, Brussels. Traveled to Museum Boijmans Van Beuningen, Rotterdam; Nationalgalerie, Berlin; Palazzo Reale, Milan; Kunsthalle Basel; and Musée des arts décoratifs, Paris

White on White: The White Monochrome in the 20th Century, Museum of Contemporary Art, Chicago

1970 *1970 Annual Exhibition of Contemporary American Sculpture*, Whitney Museum of American Art, New York

1970 Pittsburgh International Exhibition of Contemporary Art, Museum of Art, Carnegie Institute, Pittsburgh

Expo '70, Expo Museum of Fine Arts, Osaka, Japan

Figures/Environments, Walker Art Center, Minneapolis

1969 *La nouvelle figuration américaine: peinture, sculpture, film, 1963–1968*, Palais des Beaux-Arts, Brussels

New York Painting and Sculpture: 1940–1970, Metropolitan Museum of Art, New York

Pop Art, Hayward Gallery, London

1968 *1968 Annual Exhibition of Contemporary American Sculpture*, Whitney Museum of American Art, New York

The Sidney and Harriet Janis Collection, The Museum of Modern Art, New York

Documenta IV, Museum Fridericianum, Kassel, Germany

The Obsessive Image: 1960–1968, Institute of Contemporary Arts, London

Three Environmental Happenings, Newark Museum, Newark, New Jersey

1967 *1967 Pittsburgh International Exhibition of Contemporary Painting and Sculpture*, Museum of Art, Carnegie Institute, Pittsburgh

American Sculpture of the Sixties, Los Angeles County Museum of Art, Los Angeles. Traveled to Philadelphia Museum of Art, Philadelphia

Art of the '60s, The Museum of Modern Art, New York

Dine, Oldenburg, Segal: Painting/Sculpture, Art Gallery of Ontario, Toronto. Traveled to Albright-Knox Gallery, Buffalo, New York

Environment U.S.A.: 1957–1967, organized by the International Art Program, National Collection of Fine Arts, Smithsonian Institution, Washington, D.C., for the IX Bienal de São Paulo, Museu de Arte Moderna, São Paulo

Guggenheim International Exhibition 1967: Sculpture from Twenty Nations, Solomon R. Guggenheim Museum, New York

Original Pop Art, Städtische Kunstausstellung Gelsenkirchen, Gelsenkirchen, Germany

Protest and Hope: An Exhibition on Civil Rights and Vietnam, New School for Social Research, New York

1966 *Eight Sculptors—The Ambiguous Image*, Walker Art Center, Minneapolis

Environmental Painting and Constructions, Jewish Museum, New York

The Found Object: Can it Be Art?, Institute of Contemporary Art, Boston

1965 *Corcoran Biennial*, Corcoran Gallery of Art, Washington, D.C.

A Decade of American Drawings, 1955–1965, Whitney Museum of American Art, New York

Eleven from the Reuben Gallery, Solomon R. Guggenheim Museum, New York

Etats-Unis: sculptures du XXème siècle, Musée Rodin, Paris

The New American Realism, Worcester Art Museum, Worcester, Massachusetts

Pop and Op, Sidney Janis Gallery, New York

Pop Art and the American Tradition, Milwaukee Art Museum, Milwaukee

Pop art, nouveau réalisme, etc., Palais des Beaux-Arts, Brussels

1964 *4 Environments by 4 New Artists*, Sidney Janis Gallery, New York

10 American Sculptors of the 1963 São Paulo Biennial, Walker Art Center, Minneapolis. Traveled to Saint Louis Art Museum; and Daytona Art Institute, Daytona, Florida

1964 Annual Exhibition of Contemporary American Sculpture, Whitney Museum of American Art, New York

1964 Pittsburgh International Exhibition of Contemporary Painting and Sculpture, Museum of Art, Carnegie Institute, Pittsburgh

American Pop Art, Stedelijk Museum, Amsterdam

Amerikansk pop-konst, Moderna Museet, Stockholm

Neue Realisten & Pop Art, Akademie der Künste, Berlin

Nieuwe Realisten, Haags Gemeentemuseum, The Hague. Traveled to Museum van Hedendaagse Kunst, Ghent

Recent American Sculpture, Jewish Museum, New York

1963 *New Works II*, Sidney Janis Gallery, New York

Ten American Sculptors, organized by the Walker Art Center, Minneapolis, for the VII Bienal de São Paulo, Museu de Arte Moderna, São Paulo, Brazil

1962 *New Realists*, Sidney Janis Gallery, New York

1959 *1959 Annual Exhibition of Contemporary American Painting*, Whitney Museum of American Art, New York

Below Zero, Reuben Gallery, New York

1957 *Artists of the New York School: Second Generation*, Jewish Museum, New York

selected bibliography

Barrio-Garay, José. *George Segal: Environments*. Baltimore: The Baltimore Museum of Art, 1976.

——. *The Private World of George Segal*. Milwaukee: Art History Galleries, The University of Wisconsin at Milwaukee, 1973.

Berger, Danny. "George Segal: An Interview." *The Print Collector's Newsletter* 18, no. 3 (July–August 1987): 91–94.

Brenson, Michael. "Why Segal Is Doing Holocaust Memorial." *The New York Times* (8 April 1983): C16.

Diamonstein, Barbaralee. "George Segal." In *Inside New York's Art World*. New York: Rizzoli International Publications, 1979, 354–366.

Dine, Oldenburg, Segal: Painting/Sculpture. Toronto: Art Gallery of Ontario, 1967. Preface by Brydon Smith, essay by Robert Pincus-Witten.

Environment U.S.A.: 1957–1967. Washington, D.C.: Smithsonian Institution, 1967. Essay by William S. Seitz.

Foster, Hal. "George Segal." *Artforum* 17, no. 6 (February 1979): 66–67.

Friedman, Martin. "George Segal: A Proletarian Mythmaker." *Art International* 23, no. 9 (January–February 1980): 14–27.

Geldzahler, Henry. "George Segal." In *Recent American Sculpture*. New York: The Jewish Museum, 1964.

——. "An Interview with George Segal." *Artforum* 3, no. 2 (November 1964): 26–29.

Gelhaar, C. "Marriage Between Matter and Spirit, interview with George Segal." *Pantheon* 34 (July 1976): 231–237.

George Segal. Zurich: Kunsthaus Zürich, 1971. Introduction by Jan van der Marck, text by George Segal.

George Segal. Paris: Centre national d'art contemporain, 1972. Introduction by Jan van der Marck, texts by George Segal, Donald Judd, Allan Kaprow, Robert Pincus-Witten, and Ellen H. Johnson.

George Segal. Jerusalem: The Israel Museum, 1983. Foreword by Dr. Martin Weyl, introduction by Sam Hunter and Donald Hawthorne.

George Segal. Tokyo: Kodansha, 1993.

George Segal: 12 Human Situations. Chicago: Museum of Contemporary Art, 1968. Introduction by Jan van der Marck.

George Segal: Environments. Philadelphia: Institute of Contemporary Art, 1976. Foreword by Suzanne Delahanty, introduction by José L. Barrio-Garay.

George Segal: Escultures I obra sobre paper. Barcelona: Galeria Joan Prats, 1986. Introduction by Daniel Berger, interview with Giovanni dalla Chiesa.

George Segal: Obras de 1959 a 1989/Works of 1959 to 1989. Caracas: Museo de Arte Contèmporáneo de Caracas, 1991. Introduction by Sofía Imber, essay by

Phillis Tuchman.

George Segal: Pastels, 1957–1965. Long Beach, California: California State University, 1977. Interview with Constance W. Glenn, essay by Maudette Bell.

George Segal: Recent 15 Years. Tokyo: Sezon Museum of Art, 1996. Essays by Martin Friedman and Noboyuki Hiromoto.

George Segal: Sculptures. Minneapolis: Walker Art Center, 1978. Essays by Martin Friedman and Graham W.J. Beal.

George Segal: Street Crossing and New Painted Sculpture. Tokyo: Galerie Tokoro, 1994. Introduction by Pierre Restany.

George Segal: Works from the Bible. Los Angeles: Skirball Cultural Center, 1997.

Henry, Gerrit. "Ten Portraitists: Interviews/Statements." *Art in America* 63, no. 1 (January–February 1975): 36.

Hughes, Robert. "Invasion of the Plaster People." *Time* (27 August 1979): 68.

Hunter, Sam. *George Segal*. Barcelona: Ediciones Poligrafa; and New York: Rizzoli International Publications, 1989.

Hunter, Sam, and Don Hawthorne. *George Segal*. New York: Rizzoli, 1984.

Johnson, Ellen H. "The Sculpture of George Segal." *Art International* 8, no. 2 (20 March 1964): 46–49.

Kaprow, Allan. "Segal's Vital Mummies." *ARTnews* 62, no. 10 (February 1964): 30–33, 65.

Kramer, Hilton. "Plebeian Figures, Banal Anecdotes: The Tableaux of George Segal." *The New York Times* (15 December 1968).

Kuspit, Donald B. "George Segal: On the Verge of Tragic Vision." *Art in America* 65, no. 3 (May–June 1977): 84–85.

New Realists. New York: Sidney Janis Gallery, 1962. Texts by John Ashbery, Pierre Restany, and Sidney Janis.

Perreault, John. "George Segal: Plastered People." *The Village Voice* (24 October 1974).

Pincus-Witten, Robert. "George Segal as Realist." *Artforum* 5, no. 10 (Summer 1967): 84–87.

Recent Work by George Segal. New York: Sidney Janis Gallery, 1986. Introduction by Robert Rosenblum.

Seitz, William C. *Segal*. Stuttgart, Germany: Gerd Hatje; New York: Harry N. Abrams; and London: Thames and Hudson, 1972.

Segal. Paris: Galerie Ileana Sonnabend, 1963. Text by Michel Courtois, Allan Kaprow, and George Segal.

Segal, George, with William C. Lipke. "The Sense of 'Why Not?': George Segal on His Art." *Studio International* 174, no. 893 (October 1967): 146–149.

Tuchman, Phyllis. "George Segal." *Art International* 12, no. 7 (20 September 1968): 50–53.

———. "Interview with George Segal." *Art in America* 60, no. 3 (May–June 1972): 74–81.

———. "POP! Interviews with George Segal, Andy Warhol, Roy Lichtenstein, James Rosenquist, and Robert Indiana." *ARTnews* 73, no. 5 (May 1974): 24–29.

———. *George Segal*. New York: Abbeville Press, 1983.

Van der Marck, Jan. *George Segal*. New York: Harry N. Abrams, 1975.

"White in Art Is White?" *The Print Collector's Newsletter* 3, no. 1 (March–April 1977): 3.

PETER **shelton**

born in Troy, Ohio, 1951
lives and works in Los Angeles
education M.F.A., University of California at Los Angeles, Los Angeles, 1979
Trade Certification: Hobart School of Welding Technology, Troy, Ohio, 1974
B.A., Pomona College, Claremont, California, 1973

selected one-person exhibitions and site works

1999 L.A. Louver, Venice, California
1998 *blackelephanthouse, Peter Shelton, Dean Clough*, Henry Moore Sculpture Trust, Halifax, England
godspipes: Peter Shelton, Irish Museum of Modern Art, Dublin
sixtyslippers, University of California at Berkeley, Berkeley, California. Traveled to Madison Arts Center, Madison, Wisconsin; and Contemporary Arts Museum, Houston
1997 *oldwetbrickhouse*, Museum of Contemporary Art, San Diego, California
sixtyslippers, L.A. Louver, Venice, California
1996 *allarms*, L.A. Louver, Venice, California
mereubu, L.A. Louver, Venice, California
1995 *clearcannonbottles*, L.A. Louver, Venice, California
handbonesandthingsicanthrow, L.A. Louver, Venice, California
Peter Shelton, Gian Enzo Sperone, Rome
1994 *bottlesbonesandthingsgetwet*, Los Angeles County Museum of Art, Los Angeles
1993 *thingsgetwet: a work in progress*, Louver Gallery, New York
1992 *Peter Shelton*, Allen Memorial Art Museum, Oberlin College, Oberlin, Ohio
Peter Shelton, Faith and Charity in Hope Gallery, Hope, Idaho
Peter Shelton: Drawings and Sculptures, Arts Club of Chicago, Chicago
clearcuttubesandpipes, Gian Enzo Sperone, Rome
1991 *monstermawbaggutheaderhead* and *shirts*, L.A. Louver, Venice, California
Peter Shelton: Sculpture, Louver Gallery, New York
1990 *floatinghouse, DEADMAN*, Louver Gallery, New York
Peter Shelton: Drawings, L.A. Louver, Venice, California
1989 *bag BOX TUB tubes and pipes. Peter Shelton Installation and Related Works*, Fine Arts Gallery, University of California, Irvine, California
floatinghouse, DEADMAN, Herron Gallery, Herron School of Art, Indianapolis, Indiana
Peter Shelton: Castings, L.A. Louver, Venice, California
1988 *BLACKVAULT falloffstone: Sculpture Inside Outside*, The Walker Art Center, Minneapolis
Peter Shelton: Waxworks, La Jolla Museum of Contemporary Art, La Jolla, California. Traveled to San Jose Museum of Art, San Jose, California; and Des Moines Art Center, Des Moines, Iowa
STRETCH Spread, Lannan Museum, Lake Worth, Florida
1987 *Elements: Five Installations*, Whitney Museum of American Art, New York
floatinghouse, DEADMAN, Wight Art Gallery, University of California, Los Angeles
1986 *floatinghouse, DEADMAN*, University of Massachusetts, Amherst, Massachusetts
Peter Shelton: Recent Sculptures, L.A. Louver, Venice, California
1985 *lightman, BLACKMAN*, Permanent commission for State of California, Exposition Park, Los Angeles
1984 *pipegut, waterseat and STANDSTILL*, Portland Center for the Visual Arts, Portland, Oregon
1983 *MAJORJOINTS, hangers and squat*, Center of Contemporary Art, Seattle, Washington. Traveled to L.A. Louver and Malinda Wyatt Gallery, Los Angeles
1982 *SEATHOUSE and little principals* (150 element version), Santa Barbara Contemporary Arts Forum, Santa Barbara, California
trunknuts, WHITEHEAD, floater, Open Space Gallery, Victoria, British Columbia
white, round, HEAD, Artists Space, New York
1981 *NECKWALL, footscreen, sleeper*, Malinda Wyatt Gallery, Los Angeles
1980 *BIRDHOUSE, holecan*, Chapman College, Orange, California, in conjunction with L.A. Institute of Contemporary Art *Architectural Sculpture* exhibition
BROWNROOMS 1977–78, Los Angeles Contemporary Exhibitions, Los Angeles
HEADROOM, footspace, Artpark, Lewiston, New York
1979 *SWEATHOUSE and little principals* (111 element version), Wight Gallery, University of California at Los Angeles, Los Angeles

selected group exhibitions

1997 *20/20: CAP Looks Forward and Back*, Santa Barbara Contemporary Arts Forum, Santa Barbara, California
1996 *Art on Paper*, Weatherspoon Art Gallery, The University of North Carolina at Greensboro, Greensboro, North Carolina
Continuity and Contradiction, Museum of Contemporary Art, San Diego, California
Drawn from L.A., The Armory Center for the Arts, Pasadena, California
The Empowered Object, Hunsaker/Schlesinger Gallery, Los Angeles
The Panza di Biumo Collection: some artists from the 80s and 90s, Museo d'Arte Moderna e Contemporanea di Trento e Rovereto, Trento, Italy
Recent Past, The Museum of Contemporary Art, Los Angeles
Selections from the Nisenson Collection, Los Angeles County Museum of Art, Los Angeles
Shirts and Skins, The Contemporary Museum, Honolulu, Hawaii
Six Projects: Colson, Moses, Shelton, Therrien, Bobbie Greenfield Gallery, Los Angeles

1995 *Body, Mind and Spirit: Eight Sculptors*, The Ruth Chandler Williamson Gallery, Scripps
College, Claremont, California
California: In Three Dimensions, California Center for the Arts Museum, Escondido,
California
Group Exhibition, L.A. Louver, Los Angeles
1994 *Basic Black & White*, Herbert Palmer Gallery, Los Angeles
1993 *Elegant, Irreverent & Obsessive: Drawing in Southern California*, Main Art Gallery,
California State University at Fullerton, Fullerton, California
Mol, Nash, Shelton, Louver Gallery, New York
Prospect 93, Frankfurter Kunstverein, Frankfurt
1992 *Contemporary Works from the Collection*, The Museum of Modern Art, New York
LAX: The Los Angeles Exhibition, Los Angeles Municipal Art Gallery, Los Angeles
Panza di Biumo: The Eighties and the Nineties from the Collection, Museo Cantonale
d'Arte, Lugano, Switzerland
Recent Acquisitions, The Museum of Contemporary Art, Los Angeles
Selections from the Collection of Contemporary Painting and Sculpture, The Museum
of Modern Art, New York
1991 *The Artist's Hand: Drawings from the Bank of America Art Collection*, San Diego
Museum of Contemporary Art, La Jolla, California
Individual Realities in the California Art Scene, Sezon Museum of Art, Tokyo
Selections from the Permanent Collection, San Diego Museum of Contemporary Art,
La Jolla, California
1990 *Sculptors' Drawings*, L.A. Louver, Venice, California
Spirit of Our Time, Santa Barbara Contemporary Arts Forum, Santa Barbara,
California. Traveled to Louver Gallery, New York
Territory of Desire, Louver Gallery, New York
1989 *Art in the Public Eye—Selected Developments*, Security Pacific Gallery, South Metro
Center, Costa Mesa, California
Constructing a History: A Focus on the Permanent Collection, The Museum of
Contemporary Art, Los Angeles
1988 *Models: Handheld Ideas*, Main Art Gallery, California State University at Fullerton,
Fullerton, California
Sculpture Inside Outside, Walker Art Center, Minneapolis, Minnesota. Traveled to
Museum of Fine Arts, Houston
Sculture da Camera, Chamber Sculptures, Fisher Gallery, University of Southern
California, Los Angeles
Striking Distance, The Museum of Contemporary Art, Los Angeles. Traveled to Fresno
Art Museum, Fresno, California; Triton Museum of Art, Santa Clara, California; and
University Gallery, Sonoma State University, Rohnert Park, California
1987 *Abstract Expressions: Recent Sculpture*, Lannan Museum, Lake Worth, Florida
Avant-Garde in the Eighties, Los Angeles County Museum of Art, Los Angeles
California Figurative Sculpture, Palm Springs Desert Museum, Palm Springs,
California
Elements: Five Installations, Whitney Museum of American Art at Phillip Morris,
New York
1986 *American/European Painting and Sculpture. Part II*, L.A. Louver, Venice, California
Sculpture and Drawings by Sculptors, L.A. Louver,, Venice, California
1985 *American/European Painting and Sculpture. Part I*, L.A. Louver, Venice, California
Anniottanta, Galleria Comunale d'Arte Moderna, Bologna, Italy
1984 *Aperto '84*, The Venice Biennale, Venice
Constructed Metal: Modern Sculpture, College of Creative Studies, University of
California at Santa Barbara, Santa Barbara, California
1983 *Public Comments*, Center on Contemporary Art, Seattle, Washington
1982 *Une éxperience museographique: Echange entre artistes 1931–1982 Pologne-U.S.A.*,
Musée d'Art Moderne de la Ville de Paris and Ulster Museum, Belfast, Ireland
Forgotten Dimensions, Fresno Arts Center and Museum, Fresno, California
1981 *Divola, Picot, Shelton*, Libra Gallery, Claremont Graduate School of Fine Arts,
Claremont, California
1980 *Architectural Sculpture—History and Documents*, Los Angeles Institute of Contemporary
Art, Los Angeles
Maquettes and Models—Art with Architectural Concerns, Los Angeles Municipal Art
Gallery, Los Angeles
Sculpture 1980, Maryland Institute, College of Art, Baltimore
With More than One Sense, Los Angeles County Museum of Art, Los Angeles
1977 *Art in Public Places*, Cheney Cowles Memorial Museum, Spokane, Washington

selected bibliography

Anderson, Michael. "Peter Shelton." *L.A. Weekly* (27 February 1987): 121.
Art on Paper. Exh. cat. Greensboro, North Carolina: Weatherspoon Art Gallery, University of
North Carolina, 1996. Essay by David Dreishpoon.
Artner, Alan G. "What's New in Art? 20 Insiders Tell Who's Hot—and Why." *Chicago Tribune*
(29 June 1986): 13, 26, 29.
Baker, Kenneth. "Seductive Sculpture in San Jose." *San Francisco Chronicle* (16 March 1989): E5.
Ballatore, Sandy. "The Body Architecture of Peter Shelton." *Artspace* 13, no. 4
(September/October 1989): 52–57.
Barrie, Lita. "On the Scene: Los Angeles." *Artspace* 16, no. 3 (May/June 1992): 82.
Beamont, Mary Rose. "New Directions in International Sculpture." In *New Art: An
International Survey*, edited by Andreas Papadakis, Claire Farrow, and Nicola Hodges.
New York: Rizzoli International Publications, Inc., 1991.
Becker, Shizuoy. "bottlesbonesandthingsgetwet," *Bijutsu Techo* (Japan) 46, no. 690 (July 1994).
Bijvoet, Marga. "Engaging the Viewer/Participant." *Artweek* 18, no. 8 (28 February 1987): 1.
Blaine, Michael. "Formalist Shelter." *Artweek* 12, no. 18 (16 May 1981): 6.
Bodino, Maristella di. "I Dopotutto." *Epoca* (Milan) (19 July 1985): 42–51.
Body, Mind and Spirit: Eight Sculptors. Exh. cat. Claremont, California: The Ruth Chandler
Williamson Gallery, Scripps College, 1995. Essay by Mary Davis MacNaughton.
Bourdon, David. "Peter Shelton at Louver." *Art in America* 81, no. 9 (September 1993):
112–13.
Brenson, Michael. "A Transient Art Form with Staying Power." *The New York Times*
(10 January 1988): 33, 36.
———. "Art: From Robert Morris." *The New York Times* (15 January 1988): C23.
———. "Fossilization Evolves into a Modern Metaphor." *The New York Times* (31 January 1988):
31, 33.
———. "Coming to Grips with Contemporary Sculpture." *The New York Times* (19 June 1988): B33.
———. "Peter Shelton." *The New York Times* (1 March 1991): C25.
Britton, Donald. "Peter Shelton." *Art issues*, no. 6 (September/October 1989): 26.
Brodhead, Wendy. "Protection and Entrapment." *Artweek* 11, no. 39 (22 November 1980): 4.
Brougher, Nora Halpern. "Peter Shelton: L.A. Louver." *Flash Art* 25, no. 164 (May/June
1992): 117.
Burkhart, Dorothy. "San Jose Museum Strikes a Balance." *San Jose Mercury News*
(24 February 1989): E12.
Cabutti, Lucio. "Uno sguardo sugli anni ottanta—Bologna e altre città." *Arte* 15, no. 154
(July–August 1985): 26.
California in Three Dimensions. Exh cat. Escondido, California: California Center for the Arts
Museum, 1995.
Clothier, Peter. "Peter Shelton: Dwellings in the Abstract." *ARTnews* 86, no. 7 (September
1987): 83–84.
———. "L.A. Outward Bound." *ARTnews* 88, no. 10 (December 1989): 126–131.
Curtis, Cathy. "Peter Shelton's Eccentric Shapes at La Jolla." *Los Angeles Times* (4 May
1989): F12.
———. "Venice: The Galleries." *Los Angeles Times* (2 June 1989): F16.
———. "Simple Sculpture Exhibit Fills Austere Surroundings with Bold Presence." *Los Angeles
Times* (20 November 1989): F3.
Decter, Joshua. "Peter Shelton." *Arts Magazine* 65, no. 9 (May 1991): 103.
Deragon, Rick. "Equivocal, Provocative Forms." *Artweek* 20, no. 10 (11 March 1989): 4.
DiMichele, David. "Stiff Competition: LA-area sculpture exhibitions." *Artweek* 25, no. 6
(24 March 1994): 25.
Drohojowska[-Philp], Hunter. "Pick Of The Week: Peter Shelton." *L.A. Weekly* (1–7 May
1981): 62.
———. "The prize: $3,000 and a place in LACMA's permanent collection." *Los Angeles Herald
Examiner* (25 June 1985): C3.
———. "A Welder of Metal and Fervid Imaginings." *Los Angeles Times* (30 November 1997):
62, 65.
The Essential Gesture. Exh. cat. Newport Beach, California: Newport Harbor Art Museum,
1994. Essay by Bruce Guenther.
Facets of the Gas Company Collection. Exh. cat. Los Angeles: Southern California Gas Company,
1992. Essay by Josine Ianco-Starrels.
Fahr, Barry. "Enigmatic Architecture." *Artweek* 11, no. 23 (21 June 1980): 5.
Frank, Peter. "Pablo Picasso, Peter Shelton." *L.A. Weekly* 16, no. 22 (April–May 1994).
Friedman, Martin. "Growing the Garden." *Design Quarterly,* no. 141 (Winter 1988): 41.

Gardner, Colin. "Peter Shelton at L.A. Louver and Malinda Wyatt Galleries." *Images and Issues* 5, no. 1 (July/August 1984): 41.

——. "Peter Shelton: UCLA Wight Art Gallery." *Artforum* 25, no. 9 (May 1987): 158.

Gendel, Milton, "Report from Venice: Cultured Pearls at the Biennale." *Art in America* 72, no. 8 (September 1984): 45–53.

Glowen, Ron. "Morphology and Material." *Artweek* 15, no. 21 (26 May 1984): 5.

Groot, Paul. "Closed Qutoes." *Artforum* 23, no. 1 (September 1984): 107.

Hammond, Pamela. "Peter Shelton: L.A. Louver." *ARTnews* 89, no. 9 (November 1990): 178–180.

Harwig, Michael R. "Peter Shelton." In *The List*. 6th ed. New York: Independent Curators Incorporated, 1982.

Heartney, Eleanor. "New York." *Contemporanea* 3, no. 5 (May 1990): 54–55.

Hicks, Mary. "Peter Shelton." *Images and Issues* 3, no. 5 (March/April 1983): 63–64.

Jarrell, Joe. "Los Angeles, California." *Sculpture* 13, no. 4 (July–August 1994): 51.

Johnson, Ken. "Peter Shelton at Louver." *Art in America* 78, no. 3 (March 1990): 196–97.

Kachur, Lewis. "New York: Revivals and Survivals." *Art International,* no. 11 (Summer 1990): 69–72.

Kalina, Richard. "Peter Shelton—Louver Gallery." *Tema Celeste,* no. 25 (April/June 1990): 68–69.

Kandel, Susan. "L.A. in Review." *Arts Magazine* 66, no. 7 (March 1992): 88–90.

Knight, Christopher. "Your place or Shelton's." *Los Angeles Herald Examiner* (10 May 1981): E3.

——. "'DEADMAN' exhibit exudes life: Peter Shelton's huge sculpture reveals unique talent." *Los Angeles Herald Examiner* (26 February 1987): B7.

——. "Contemporary art concerns: Spatial imbalance strikes a blow at county museum." *Los Angeles Herald Examiner* (3 April 1988): F4.

——. "Shelton's sculptural delights: He gets physical in 'Waxworks.'" *Los Angeles Herald Examiner* (23 April 1989): E2.

Kosenko, Peter. "Peter Shelton." *Artweek* 22, no. 44 (26 December 1991): 13–14.

Larson, Kay. "Is There a Crimp in the Beauty Parlor?" *The Village Voice* (10–16 September 1980): 77.

Levin, Kim. "Artwalk." *The Village Voice* (5 January 1988): 84.

——. "Peter Shelton, Louver Gallery." *Village Voice* (30 January 1990): 93.

——. "Voice Choices: Art." *Village Voice* (15 June 1993): 71.

Lewinson, David. "Nebulae of Color." *Artweek* 12, no. 37 (7 November 1981): 6.

The Louis Comfort Tiffany Foundation: Awards in Painting, Sculpture, Printmaking, and Craft Media. Exh. cat. New York: The Louis Comfort Tiffany Foundation, 1988.

Lucie-Smith, Edward. *Art Today*. London: Phaidon Press, 1995.

Mahoney, Robert. "PeterShelton." *Arts Magazine* 64, no. 8 (April 1990): 109.

Mallinson, Constance. "Peter Shelton at L.A. Louver." *Art in America* 75, no. 2 (February 1987): 154–55.

Martin, Mary Abbe. "Walker's Sculpture Show Provocative, Grand in Scale." *Star Tribune* (Minneapolis) (27 May 1988): 2E

McKenna, Kristine. "A 'Contemporary Assemblage' of Politics, Desires." *Los Angeles Times* (21 August 1990): F4, F5.

Melrod, George. "Peter Shelton: Louver Gallery New York." *Contemporanea* 3, no. 5 (May 1990): 98.

——. "Peter Shelton, Louver." *ARTnews* 90, no. 5 (May 1991): 149–50.

Morgan, Stuart. "Past Present Future: Count Giuseppe Panza di Biumo interviewed by Morgan Stuart." *Artscribe,* no. 76 (Summer 1989): 53–59.

Muchnic, Suzanne. "Sprawling Sculptures." *Los Angeles Times* (2 November 1980): 90.

——. "Exploring a House that Floats." *Los Angeles Times* (2 March 1987): F1, 3.

——. "The Way We Are, Figuratively." *Los Angeles Times* (3 March 1987): 1, 4.

——. "MOCA gets Major Gift—Works by 10 Local Artists." *Los Angeles Times* (26 October 1994): F1.

Pagel, David. "Art Reviews: Shelton in Wonderland." *Los Angeles Times* (26 December 1991): F15.

Panza di Biumo, Giuseppe. "La Biennale." *Domus,* no. 652 (July–August 1984): 72.

The Panza di Biumo Collection: some artists from the 80s and 90s. Exh. cat. Trento, Italy: Museo d'Arte Moderna e Contemporanea di Trento e Rovereto, 1996. Essays by Gabriella Belli and Giuseppe Panza di Biumo; entries and biographies.

Peter Shelton: bottlesbonesandthingsgetwet. Exh. cat. Los Angeles: Los Angeles County Museum of Art, 1994. Essay by Carol S. Eliel; biography, exhibition history, and selected bibliography.

Pincus, Robert L. "Peter Shelton." *Los Angeles Times* (1 May 1981): F7, 8.

——. "Peter Shelton." *Los Angeles Times* (23 March 1984): F14.

——. "In 'Waxworks' Body Parts Make a Whole Exhibit." *San Diego Union* (23 April 1989): E1, E4.

——. "1989: The State of the Arts." *San Diego Union* (28 December 1989): E5.

——. "Shelton works are inspired playfulness." *The San Diego Union-Tribune* (10 April 1994): Section E.

Princenthal, Nancy. "The Body in Question." *Sculpture* 8, no. 5 (September/October 1989): 24–29.

Rico, Diana. "Young Talent Gets Award, Showing from Museum." *Daily News* (Los Angeles) (24 June 1985): 21.

——. "How to Dance Like Buddha." *ARTnews* 93, no. 8 (October 1994): 170–173.

Riddle, Mason. "A Modernist museum without walls." *New Art Examiner* 16, no. 5 (January 1989): 36–37.

Shelton, Peter. "kettlehouseIRONHOUSEicehouse." *ZYZZYVA* 6, no. 3 (Fall 1990): 66–67.

Smith, Roberta. "Fresh, Hot and Headed for Fame: These Are the Faces to Watch." *The New York Times* (5 January 1990): C21.

Snow, Shauna. "The Scene: Peter Shelton Drawings at L.A. Louver." *Los Angeles Times* (12 August 1990): 102.

Stephens, Richard. "Peter Shelton." *New Art Examiner* 16, no. 11 (Summer 1989): 48.

Tedeschi, Pierparide. "Private Collection: The Panza di Biumo Collection," *Contemporanea* 2, no. 6 (September 1989): 48–55.

Timberman, Marcy. "Peter Shelton: The Power of the Ordinary." *Artweek* 13, no. 40 (27 November 1982): 1, 16.

Turner, Jonathan. "The Berlingieris: A Nun, an Eskimo, and Elvis." *ARTnews* 92, no. 5 (May 1993): 83–84, 86.

Wilson, Raymond L. "Small Metaphors." *Artweek* 13, no. 17 (1 May 1982): 4.

Wilson, William. "meettheaccomplishedpetershelton." *Los Angeles Times* (9 March 1994): F1.

Wortz, Melinda. "A tropical sleeper." *ARTnews* 80, no. 8 (October 1981): 189.

——. "Peter Shelton: Contemporary Arts Forum, Santa Barbara." *ARTnews* 82, no. 5 (May 1983): 133–35.

Wright, Patricia. "Forum: Museums and Galleries." *Domus,* no. 627 (April 1982): 77.

ANTONI **tàpies**

born in Barcelona, 1923
lives and works in Barcelona
education Studied law at the University of Barcelona, 1943–46
Studied drawing at the Acadèmia Valls in the Carrer de Jonqueres, Barcelona, 1944

selected exhibition history

1999   *Antoni Tàpies*, Caja de Burgos and Sala Pelaires, Palma de Mallorca, Spain
1998   *Tàpies El Tatuatge I El Cos: Papers, cartons and collages,* Fundació Antoni Tàpies, Barcelona
  Antoni Tàpies, Pinacoteca Communale Casa Rusca, Locarno, Switzerland
1997   *Antoni Tàpies: Paintings, Sculpture, Drawings 1981–1997*, Kestner Gesellschaft, Hannover, Germany
  Inaugural Exhibition Ace Gallery, Ace Gallery, Mexico
1996   *Antoni Tàpies*, Marugame Genichiro Inokuma Museum of Contemporary Art, Kagawa, Japan
  Gaudi to Tàpies: Catalan Artists, Michael C. Carlos Museum, Emory University, Atlanta
1995   *Tàpies*, Solomon R. Guggenheim Museum SoHo, New York
  Antoni Tàpies, the 90s, Musée d'Art Moderne, Céret, France
  Antoni Tàpies: New Paintings, PaceWildenstein, New York
1994   *Antoni Tàpies: Paintings and Drawings 1955 to 1975*, Bellas Artes, Santa Fe, New Mexico
  Antoni Tàpies, Galerie nationale du Jeu de Paume, Paris
  Kounellis, Serra, Tàpies, Turrell, Galería Joan Prats, Barcelona
1993   *Antoni Tàpies: Prints and Illustrated Books*, Carpenter Center for Visual Arts, Harvard University, Cambridge, Massachusetts
  Antoni Tàpies, XLV Biennale de Venezia, Spanish Pavilion, Venice

Tàpies: Celebració de la mel, Fundació Antoni Tàpies, Barcelona
La Collection Maeght 1909–1993: Une Collection au XXème siècle, Espace Lyonnais d'Art Contemporain, Lyon, France
Sculptures: Bourgeois, Chillida, Derain, Gonzalez, Kirkeby, Lüpertz, Miró, Penck, Tàpies, Galerie Lelong, Zurich
1992 *Antoni Tàpies: Comunicació sobre el Mur,* Fundació Antoni Tàpies, Barcelona
Antoni Tàpies in Print, The Museum of Modern Art, New York
Arte en España: 1920–1990, Palau de la Virreina, Barcelona
1991 *Antoni Tàpies,* Galeria Carles Taché, Barcelona
L'ansietat de les influències. Tàpies vist per Llena, Fundació Antoni Tàpies, Barcelona
Tàpies in Print, Centro Cultural Arte Contemporáneo, A.C., Mexico City
Tàpies. Celebració de la mel, Centro Atlántico de Arte Moderno, Canary Islands, Spain
Del Surrealismo al Informalismo. Arte de los años 50 en Madrid, Sala de Exposiciones de la Comunidad de Madrid, Madrid
1990 *Contemporary Illustrated Books: Word and Image, 1967–1988,* Nelson-Atkins Museum of Art, Kansas City, Missouri
1989 *Antoni Tàpies,* The Elkon Gallery, New York
1988 *Antoni Tàpies—Figuren und Zeichen,* Galerie Brusberg, Berlin
Tàpies: els anys 80, Saló del Tinell, Barcelona
Antoni Tàpies. Graphic Work 1947–1987, Baxter Gallery, Portland School of Art, Portland, Maine
Les Tàpies de Tàpies, Musée Cantini, Marseille, France
Aspects of Collage, Assemblage and the Found Object in Twentieth-Century Art, Solomon R. Guggenheim Museum, New York
1987 *Le Siècle de Picasso,* Musée d'Art Moderne de la Ville de Paris, Paris
1986 *Antoni Tàpies. 31 Gemälde und 4 Skulpturen,* Gesellschaft bildender Künstler Österreichs and Künstlerhaus Wien, Vienna
Antoni Tàpies. New Paintings, Galerie Maeght Lelong, New York
Tàpies. Obres 1956–1986, Galeria Theo and Galeria Joan Prats, Barcelona
Pintar con papel, Círculo de Bellas Artes, Madrid
1985 *Tàpies,* Musée d'Art Moderne, Brussels
Tàpies. Peintures 1965–1980, Galerie Adrien Maeght, Paris
1984 *Antoni Tàpies. Neue Bilder und Blätter,* Galerie Brusberg, Berlin
La Grande Parade, Stedelijk Museum, Amsterdam
1983 *Tàpies íntim,* Städtische Galerie im Prinz-Max-Palais, Karlsruhe, Germany
Aspects of Postwar Painting in Europe, Solomon R. Guggenheim, Museum, New York
Expressive Malerei nach Picasso, Galerie Beyeler, Basel, Switzerland
Written Imagery Unleashed in the 20th Century, Fine Arts Museum of Long Island, Hempstead, New York
1982 *Antoni Tàpies, 1973–1980,* Palacio de la Lonja, Saragossa, Spain
Tàpies. Opere dal 1946 al 1982, Scuola di San Giovanni Evangelista, Venice
1981 *Paris-Paris. Créations en France, 1937–1957,* Centre Georges Pompidou, Paris
1980 *Antoni Tàpies. Exposición retrospectiva,* Museo Español de Arte Contemporáneo, Madrid
Antoni Tàpies, Stedelijk Museum, Amsterdam
1979 *Antoni Tàpies. Bilder und Objekte, 1948 bis 1978,* Badischer Kunstverein, Karlsruhe, Germany
1978 *Antoni Tàpies. Selected Work 1975–1977. Paintings, Works on Cardboard & Paper,* Martha Jackson Gallery, New York
Tàpies. Oeuvres sur papier, 1952–1977, Musée de l'Abbaye Sainte-Croix, Les Sables-d'Olonne, France
Tàpies. Obra 1945–1954, Galeria Artema, Barcelona
1977 *Antoni Tàpies. Thirty-three Years of His Work,* Albright-Knox Art Gallery, Buffalo, New York
Antoni Tàpies. Handzeichnungen Aquarelle, Gouachen, Collagen 1944–1976, Kunsthalle Bremen, Bremen, Germany
1976 *Antoni Tàpies (Obra 1956–1976),* Fundació Joan Miró, Barcelona
1975 *Tàpies. Obra recent,* Galeria Maeght, Barcelona
Tàpies 1957–1963, Galerie Jeanne Castel, Paris
Antoni Tàpies. Werke von 1954 bis 1974, Galerie Beyeler, Basel, Switzerland
Tàpies. Selected New Work, 1973–1974. Paintings, Objects, Works on Cardboard and Paper, Martha Jackson Gallery, New York
1974 *Antoni Tàpies,* Louisiana Museum of Modern Art, Humlebaek, Denmark
Antoni Tàpies. Retrospektive 1946–1973. Bilder, Objekte und Zeichnungen, Nationalgalerie, Berlin

Antoni Tàpies, Hayward Gallery, London
L'Homme et son empreinte, Château de Sainte-Suzanne, Mayenne, France
1973 *Antoni Tàpies. Exposition rétrospective, 1946–1973,* Musée d'Art Moderne de la Ville de Paris, Paris
Tàpies. Works 1962–1972, Martha Jackson Gallery, New York
1972 *Concept & Content—Cage, Thompson, Tàpies,* Martha Jackson Gallery, New York
1971 *Antoni Tàpies, Opere 1946–1970,* Il Collezionista d'Arte Contemporanea, Rome
Antoni Tàpies, Malningar, Collages, Grafik, 1959–71, Gallerie Börjeson, Malmö, Sweden
1970 *Tàpies,* Galleria dell'Ariete, Milan
Antoni Tàpies. Painting & Collages, 1969–1970, Martha Jackson Gallery, New York
1969 *A. Tàpies. Pintura. tapís, obra gràfica, "Fregoli,"* Sala Gaspar, Barcelona
1968 *Antoni Tàpies,* Kunstverein, Hamburg
Antoni Tàpies, Martha Jackson Gallery, New York
Menschenbilder, Kunsthalle Darmstadt, Darmstadt, Germany
Peintres Européens d'aujourd'hui/European Painters Today, Musée des Arts Décoratifs, Paris
1967 *Antoni Tàpies. Recent Paintings,* Martha Jackson Gallery, New York
1967 Pittsburgh International Exhibition of Contemporary Painting and Sculpture, Museum of Art, Carnegie Institute, Pittsburgh
Spanische Kunst der Gegenwart, Kunsthalle, Nuremberg, Germany
1966 *Tàpies,* Galerie Stadler, Paris
1965 *Antonio Tàpies. Bilder 1948–1964,* Galerie Rudolf Zwirner, Cologne, Germany
Antoni Tàpies. Paintings 1945–1965, Institute of Contemporary Arts, London
40 Key Artists of the mid-20th Century, Detroit Institute of Arts, Detroit, Michigan
1964 *Collagen und Zeichnungen von Antonio Tàpies,* Galerie Rudolf Zwirner, Cologne, Germany
Tàpies, Galerie Stadler, Paris
Tàpies, Gallery Moos, Ltd., Toronto
Documenta III. Internationale Ausstellung, Kassel, Germany
The 1964 Pittsburgh International, Carnegie Institute, Pittsburgh
1963 *Antoni Tàpies,* Martha Jackson Gallery, New York
1962 *Antonio Tàpies,* Kestner-Gesellschaft, Hannover, Germany
Antoni Tàpies, Solomon R. Guggenheim Museum, New York
Antonio Tàpies, Kunsthaus Zürich, Zurich
Antoni Tàpies, Museo de Bellas Artes, Caracas, Venezuela
1961 *Tàpies,* Martha Jackson Gallery, New York
Tàpies, Galerie Stadler, Paris
Arte e contemplazione, Palazzo Grassi, Venice
1960 *Ten Lithographs by Antonio Tàpies,* Martha Jackson Gallery, New York
New Spanish Painting and Sculpture, The Museum of Modern Art, New York
Before Picasso, After Miró, Solomon R. Guggenheim Museum, New York
Neue Malerei. Form, Struktur, Bedeutung, Städtische Galerie, Munich
1959 *Tàpies,* Galerie Stadler, Paris
Saura—Tàpies. Ölbilder, Galerie van de Loo, Munich
II. Documenta '59, Kunst nach 1945, Internationale Ausstellung, Kassel, Germany
Kunstsammler an Rhein und Ruhr. Malerei 1900–1959, Städtisches Museum, Schloss Morsbroich, Leverkusen, Germany
1958 *Neue Malerei in Frankreich,* Städtische Kunstsammlungen, Soest, Germany
XXIX Biennale Internazionale d'Arte, Venice
L'art du XXème siècle, Palais des Expositions, Charleroi, Belgium
The 1958 Pittsburgh Bicentennial International Exhibition of Contemporary Painting and Sculpture, Department of Fine Arts, Carnegie Institute, Pittsburgh
1957 *Antonio Tàpies, Recent Paintings,* Martha Jackson Gallery, New York
Tàpies, Galerie Stadler, Paris
Antonio Tàpies, Galerie Schmela, Düsseldorf, Germany
IV Bienal do Museo de Arte Moderna de São Paulo, São Paulo, Brazil
1955 *Pinturas de Antonio Tàpies,* Sur, Galería de Arte, Santander, Spain
Inaugural Exhibition, Galerie Stadler, Paris
The 1955 Pittsburgh International Exhibition of Contemporary Painting, Carnegie Institute, Pittsburgh
III Bienal Hispanoamericana de Arte, Palacio Municipal de Exposiciones, Barcelona
1953 *Antoni Tàpies,* Museo Municipal, Mataró, Spain
Antonio Puig Tàpies, Marshall Field & Company, Chicago
Antonio Tàpies, Martha Jackson Gallery, New York
1952 *Exposición Tàpies,* Galerías Layetanas, Barcelona

I Bienal Hispanoamericana de Arte, Exposición antológica, Museu d'Art
    Contemporani, Barcelona
  XXVI Biennale di Venezia, Venice
  The 1952 Pittsburgh International Exhibition of Contemporary Painting, Carnegie
    Institute, Pittsburgh
1951 *Tàpies,* Casino de Ripoll, Ripoll, Spain
1950 *Exposició Antoni Tàpies,* Galerias Layetanas, Barcelona
  Tàpies-Cuixart-Ponç, Galerías Sapi, Palma de Mallorca, Spain
  Séptimo Salón de los Once, Galería Biosca, Madrid
  The Pittsburgh International Exhibition of Paintings, Carnegie Institute, Pittsburgh
1949 *20 Salón de Octubre,* Galerías Layetanas, Barcelona
1948 *1st Salón de Octubre,* Galerías Layetanas, Barcelona
1950 Galerieas Layetanas, Barcelona

selected bibliography

After Picasso. Tàpies, Gordillo, Guerrero. Exh. cat. New York: DiLaurenti Gallery, 1987. Essay
    by Manuel J. Borja-Villel.
Agustí, Anna, *Tàpies. Obra Completa.* Barcelona: Fundació Antoni Tàpies and Ediciones
    Polígrafa SA, 1988 (vol. 1), 1990 (vol. 2) and 1992 (vol. 3).
Ainaud I Escudero, Joan-Francesc. *Introduccío a l'estètica d'Antoni Tàpies.* Barcelona:
    Edicions 62, 1986.
Alberola, Miquel. "Tàpies, l'amo dels signes." *El Temps* 7, no. 308 (14–20 May 1990): 46–49.
Antoni Tàpies. Exh. cat. New York: Martha Jackson Gallery, 1953. Essay by Gordon
    B. Washburn.
Antoni Tàpies. Exh. cat. New York: Solomon R. Guggenheim Museum, 1962. Essay by
    Lawrence Alloway.
Antoni Tàpies. 31 Gemälde und 4 Skulpturen. Exh. cat. Vienna: Künstlerhaus, 1986. Essay by
    Rudi H. Fuchs.
Antoni Tàpies. Arbeiten 1947–1988. Exh. cat. Bayreuth, Germany: Kunstverein, 1990. Essay by
    Marie-Therese Suermann.
Antoni Tàpies. Exposición retrospectiva. Exh. cat. Madrid: Museo Español de Arte
    Contemporáneo, 1980. Essays by Lluís Permanyer and José María Valverde.
Antoni Tàpies. Exposition Rétrospective 1946/1973. Exh. cat. Paris: Musée d'Art Moderne de
    la Ville de Paris, 1973. Essay by Jacques Lassaigne.
Antoni Tàpies. Graphic Work 1947–1987. Exh. cat. Portland, Maine: Baxter Gallery, Portland
    School of Art, 1988. Essay by Steven S. High.
Antoni Tàpies. Handzeichnungen, Aquarelle, Gouachen, Collagen 1944–1976. Exh. cat.
    Bremen, Germany: Kunsthalle Bremen, 1977. Essay by Werner Schnackenburg.
Antoni Tàpies. Mixed Media. Works on Paper. Exh. cat. Coral Gables, Florida: Metropolitan
    Museum and Art Center, 1987. Essay by Marvin Ross Friedman.
Antoni Tàpies (Obras 1956–1976). Exh. cat. Barcelona: Fundació Joan Miró, CEAC, 1976.
    Essay by Tomàs Llorens.
Antoni Tàpies. Opere 1946–1970. Exh. cat. Rome: Il Collezionista d'Arte Contemporanea,
    1971. Essays by Giuseppe Gatt and Nello Ponente.
Antoni Tàpies. Paintings 1945–1965. Exh. cat. London: Institute of Contemporary Arts, 1965.
    Essay by Roland Penrose.
Antoni Tàpies, Paintings, Collages, and Works on Paper, 1966/1968. Exh. cat. New York:
    Martha Jackson Gallery, 1968. Preface by Edward Albee.
Antoni Tàpies, papiers et cartons. Exh. cat. Paris: Galerie Berggruen, 1962. Essay by J. Dupin.
Antoni Tàpies. Recent Paintings. Exh. cat. New York: Martha Jackson Gallery, 1967. Essay by
    Dan Evans.
Antoni Tàpies. Retrospektive 1946–1973. Bilder, Objekte und Zeichnungen. Exh. cat. Berlin:
    Nationalgalerie, 1974. Essay by Werner Haftmann.
Antoni Tàpies. Thirty-three Years of His Work. Buffalo, New York: Albright-Knox Art Gallery,
    1977. Essay by José Luis Barrio-Garay.
Archer, Michael. "Antoni Tàpies: Waddington Galleries Ltd." *Artforum* (February 1992):
    131–132.
Ashton, Dore. "Antoni Tàpies." *Art International* 5, nos. 5–6 (June–August 1961).
Bärmann, Matthias. "Irritation und Spiel. Erfahrungen mit der Kunst von Antoni Tàpies." *Das
    Nachtcafé* 11, no. 24 (Spring 1985): 38–46.
Barrio-Garay, José Luís. "Antoni Tàpies." *Artscanada* 35, no. 1 (February–March 1978): 69–70.
Bass, Ruth. "Antoni Tàpies." *ARTnews* 81, no. 8 (October 1982): 155, 158.
Benincasa, Carmine. "Antoni Tàpies." *Flash Art* 36, no. 111 (January 1983): 8–14.
Berliner, R.K. "El homenaje a Picasso deTàpies." *Artes Plàsticas* 56 (1983): 39–40.

Bonet, Blai. *Tàpies.* Barcelona: Ediciones Polígrafa SA, 1964.
Bonet, Juan Manuel. "Tàpies. Pintor de la materia." *La Calle* 116 (10–16 June 1980): 44–47.
Borja-Villel, Manuel J. "A Note on Tàpies." *Artforum* 24, no. 2 (October 1985): 113.
——. "Antoni Tàpies in Print: An Interview." *The Print Collector's Newsletter* 23, no. 2
    (May/June 1992): 46–48.
——. *Fundació Antoni Tàpies.* Barcelona: Fundació Antoni Tàpies, 1990.
de Bure, Gilles. "Qui sont les têtes de l'art." *Beaux Arts* (October 1995): 21–27.
Cembalest, Robin. "Master of Matter." *ARTnews* 89, no. 6 (Summer 1990): 142–147.
Chamorro, Eduardo. "Tàpies." *Cambio* 16, no. 785 (15 December 1986): 164–170.
Cirici, Alexandre. *Tàpies 1954–1964.* Barcelona: Editorial Gustavo Gili, 1964.
Cirlot, Juan Eduardo. *Tàpies.* Barcelona: Edicions Omega, 1960.
——. "La peinture de Tàpies." *Quadrum* 11 (1961): 79–94.
——. *Significación de la pintura de Tàpies.* Barcelona: Editorial Seix Barral, 1962.
Clot, Manel. "Tàpies années 80." *Art Press* (November 1988).
Combalia Dexeus, Victòria. *Tàpies.* Barcelona: Ediciones Polígrafa SA, 1984.
——. "Dues converses amb Antoni Tàpies 1980–1988." in *Tapies: els ans 80.* Barcelona:
    Regidoria d'Edicions I Publicacions, Ajuntament de Barcelona, 1988.
——. "Antoni Tàpies, the Artist as Shaman." *View* (February–March 1989): 67–68.
Connors, Thomas. "Dossier: Barcelona, Spain." *Sculpture* (May/June 1992): 18–19.
Exposicion Antoni Tàpies. Exh. cat. Barcelona: Galerias Layetanas, 1950. Essay by
    Juan-Eduardo Cirlot.
Euclaire, Sally. "Antoni Tàpies/Bellas Artes." *ARTnews* (22 November 1994): 164–165.
Febrés, Xavier. *Diàlegs a Barcelona. Antoni Tàpies-Isidre Molas.* Barcelona: Ajuntament de
    Barcelona, 1988.
Fernández-Braso, Miguel. *Conversaciones con Tàpies.* Madrid: Ediciones Rayuela, 1981.
Franzke, Andreas. "Aspekte der Wirklichkeitswiedergabe im Werk von Antoni Tàpies." *Pantheon*
    38 (January–March 1979): 69–75.
——. *Tàpies.* Barcelona: Ediciones Polígrafa, SA; and Munich: Prestel-Verlag, 1992.
Franzke, Andreas, and Schwarz, Michael. *Antoni Tàpies. Werk und Zeit.* Stuttgart, Germany:
    Verlag Gerd Hatje, 1979.
Frank, Peter. "Art Picks of the Week: Hans Burkhardt, Antoni Tàpies." *L.A. Weekly* (18–24
    December 1998).
Frémon, Jean. "Autoritratti. Antoni Tàpies." *Tema Celeste* 6, no. 15 (March–May 1988): 20–22.
Galfetti, Mariuccia. *Tàpies. Obra gráfica 1947–1972.* Barcelona: Editorial Gustavo Gili, 1973.
Gasch, Sebastià. *Tàpies.* Madrid: Dirección General de Bellas Artes, 1971.
Gatt, Giuseppe. *Antoni Tàpies.* Bologna: Cappelli Editore, 1967.
Genauer, Emily. "Exhibition of Works by Tàpies Presented by the Guggenheim." *New York
    Herald Tribune* (22 March 1962).
Gimferrer, Pere. *Antoni Tàpies I l'esperit català.* Barcelona: Ediciones Polígrafa SA, 1974.
Habasque, Guy. "Au-delà de l'informel." *L'Oeil* 59 (November 1959): 62–71, 75.
Heartney, Eleanor. "Report from Barcelona: The Museum: Lights On, Nobody Home?" *Art in
    America* (September 1995): 39–43.
Jeffet, William. "Tàpies, Surrealism and Miró." *Apollo* 128, no. 319 (September 1988): 191–192.
Judd, Donald. "In the Galleries—Antonio Tàpies." *Arts Magazine* (December 1963).
Kramer, Hilton. "Tàpies's Gifted Yet Easy Victories." *The New York Times* (23 April 1978).
——. "American Chauvinism? Never! Exhibit: Tàpies." *The New York Observer* (1 June 1992): 1.
Kuspit, Donald. "Antoni Tàpies." *Artforum* 21, no. 2 (October 1982): 73.
——. "Antoni Tàpies at Maeght Lelong." *Art in America* 74, no. 9 September 1986): 73.
L'ansietat de les influències. Tàpies vist per Llena. Exh. cat. Barcelona: Fundació Antoni
    Tàpies, 1991. Essay by Antoni Llena.
Lascault, Gilbert. "Penser avec Tàpies." *Cimaise* 35, no. 193 (April-May 1988): 5–16.
Linhartová, Vera. *Tàpies.* Stuttgart, Germany: Verlag Gerd Hatje, 1972.
Lebovici, Elisabeth. "Antoni Tàpies." *Beaux Arts Magazine,* no. 29 (November 1985): 38–43.
Les Tàpies de Tàpies. Exh. cat. Marseille: Musée Cantini, 1989. Essay by Georges Raillard.
Marín-Medina, José. *Tàpies/Meditaciones/1976.* Madrid: Ediciones Rayuela, 1976.
Miller, John. "Antoni Tàpies. Marta Cervera Gallery." *Artforum* 28, no. 7 (March 1990): 163.
Millet, Catherine. "Antoni Tàpies, récit." *Art Press,* no. 49 (June 1981): 18–20.
Miralles, Francesc. *Antoni Tàpies. Tapissos.* Barcelona: Escola Massana, 1986.
Moreno Galván, José María. "L'obra d'Antoni Tàpies." *Questions d'Art* 26 (1973): 23–30.
Naves, Mario. "Serious Matter." *The New Criterion* (April 1995): 35–37.
Penrose, Roland. *Tàpies.* Barcelona: Ediciones Polígrafa SA, 1977.
——. "The Magic of Tàpies." *The Connoisseur* 208, no. 836 (October 1981): 150–152.
Peppiat, Michael. "Artist's Dialogue: Antoni Tàpies. An Art of Constant Renewal." *Architectural
    Digest* (August 1987): 40–47.
——. "Antoni Tàpies: Fields of Energy." *Art International* (Summer 1988): 36–42.

——. "The Soul Revealed by the Hand." *Art International* 13 (Winter 1990): 34–40.

Permanyer, Lluís. "Entrevista con Antonio Tàpies." *Playboy* 15 (January 1980) 23–30.

——. *Tàpies i la nova cultura*. Barcelona: Ediciones Polígrafa SA, 1986.

Pincus-Witten, Robert. "Entries: Tàpies Revised." *Arts Magazine* (October 1990): 64–67.

Politi, Giancarlo. "Domande per Antoni Tàpies." *Flash Art* 82–83 (May–June 1978): 42–44.

Preston, Stuart. "Art: Fifty Paintings by Antoni Tàpies." *The New York Times* (22 March 1962).

Raillard, Georges. *Tàpies*. Paris: Maeght Editeur, 1976.

Riding, Alan. "Antoni Tàpies." *Atelier* (June 1992): 70–72.

Rohrer, Judith. "A Theme for Reflection. The Recent Work of Antoni Tàpies." *Arts Magazine* (December 1975).

Russell, John. "Art: Recent Tàpies Work Keeps Old Spirit." *The New York Times* (15 November 1975).

Salinas, Florinda. "Antoni Tàpies. El arte exige ojos nuevos." *Telva* 576 (June 1988): 36–40.

Schmalenbach, Werner. *Antoni Tàpies. Zeichen und Strukturen*. Berlin: Propyläen Verlag, 1974.

——. *Drei Reden über Antoni Tàpies*. St. Gallen: Erker-Presse, 1977.

Serrano, María Dolores. "El misterio de Antoni Tàpies." *Gaceta Illustrada* 962 (16 March 1975): 39–62.

Smith, Roberta. "In Narrow Focus, a Painter of Wide Ingenuity." *The New York Times* (27 January 1995): C25.

Michel. *Antonio Tàpies et l'oeuvre complète*. Barcelona: Dau al Set, 1956.

——. *Antonio Tàpies*. Barcelona: Editorial RM, 1959.

——. *Antonio Tàpies*. Milan: Fratelli Fabbri, 1969.

Tàpies. Exh. cat. Barcelona: Galeria Maeght, 1978. Essay by Julio Cortázar.

Tàpies. Exh. cat. Brussels: Musée d'Art Moderne, 1985. Essay by José-Miguel Ullán.

Tàpies. Exh. cat. New York: Solomon R. Guggenheim Museum, 1995. Essay by Dore Ashton.

Tàpies. Exh. cat. Paris: Galerie Stadler, 1956. Essay by Michel Tapié.

Tàpies. Celebració de la mel. Exh. cat. Barcelona: Fundació Antoni Tàpies, 1991. Essays by Manuel J. Borja-Villel, Rudi Fuchs, Donald Kuspit, Georges Raillard, and Antoni Tàpies.

Tàpies Communicació sobre el mur. Exh. cat. Barcelona: Fundació Antoni Tàpies, 1992. Essays by Manuel J. Borja-Villel and Serge Guilbaut.

Tàpies. Die achtziger Jahre. Bilder, Skulpturen, Zeichnungen. Exh. cat. Düsseldorf: Kunstsammlung Nordrhein-Westfalen, 1989. Essay by Barbara Catoir.

Tàpies. Oeuvres sur papier, 1952–1977. Les Sables-d'Olonne, France: Musée de l'Abbaye Sainte-Croix, 1978. Essay by Jean Frémon.

Tàpies. Peintures 1965–1980. Exh. cat. Paris: Galerie Adrien Maeght, 1985. Essay by Bernard Lamarche-Vadel.

Teixidor, Joan. *Antonio Tàpies. Fustes, papers, cartons I collages*. Barcelona: Sala Gaspar, 1964.

Tharrats, Joan-Josep. *Antoni Tàpies o el Dau modern de Versailles*. Barcelona: Dau al Set, 1950.

Vallès Rivira, Josep. *Tàpies empremta (art-vida)*. Barcelona: Edicions Robrenyo, 1983.

Vicens, Francesc et al. *Antoni Tàpies o l'escarnidor de diademes*. Barcelona: Ediciones Polígrafa SA, 1967.

Vrinat, Robert. "Tàpies: 'Assassins.'" *Les Cahiers de la Peinture* 12 (July 1974): 16–17.

Watts, Harriett. *Antoni Tàpies. Die Bildzeichen und das Buch*. Wolfenbüttel, Germany: Hezog August Bibliothek, 1988.

ROBERT **therrien**

born in Chicago, 1947
lives and works in Los Angeles
education M.F.A., University of Southern California, Los Angeles, 1973
B.F.A., Brooks Institute, Santa Barbara, California, 1970

selected one-person exhibitions

2000　*Robert Therrien*, Los Angeles County Museum of Art, Los Angeles. Travels to SITE Santa Fe, Santa Fe, New Mexico; Contemporary Arts Museum, Houston; and Kemper Museum of Contemporary Art, Kansas City, Missouri

1998　Gallery Paule Anglim, San Francisco

1997　*Drawings*, Leo Castelli Gallery, New York

　　　Robert Therrien. Large-scale Sculpture, The Eli Broad Family Foundation, Los Angeles

　　　Sculpture by Robert Therrien. Under the Table, The Contemporary Arts Center, Cincinnati, Ohio

1996　Leo Castelli Gallery, New York

　　　Saidye Bronfman Centre for the Arts, Montreal, Canada. Traveled to The Art Gallery of York University, Toronto; Illingworth Kerr Gallery, Albert College of Art & Design, Calgary, Canada

1995　Galerij Micheline Szwajcer, Antwerp, Belgium

1994　The Eli Broad Family Foundation, Santa Monica, California

1993　Leo Castelli Gallery, New York

1992　Angles Gallery, Santa Monica, California

1991　Centro de Arte Reina Sofía, Madrid. Traveled to Haags Gemeentemuseum, The Hague, The Netherlands

　　　Leo Castelli, 65 Thompson Street, New York

1990　Konrad Fischer Gallery, Düsseldorf, Germany

　　　Leo Castelli Gallery, New York

1988　Leo Castelli Gallery, New York

1987　Konrad Fischer Gallery, Düsseldorf, Germany

1986　Leo Castelli Gallery, New York

　　　Leo Castelli Gallery, New York

1984　The Museum of Contemporary Art, Los Angeles

1982　Ace Gallery, Los Angeles

1979　Los Angeles Institute of Contemporary Art, Los Angeles

1977　Ruth S. Schaffner Gallery, Los Angeles

selected group exhibitions

2000　*The Anderson Collection; Selected Works*, San Francisco Museum of Modern Art, San Francisco

1999　*Culbutes dans le millénaire (Head over Heels into the Millenium)*, Musée d'Art Contemporain de Montréal, Montreal, Canada

　　　The Eclectic Eye: Selections from the Frederick R. Weisman Collections, California Center for the Arts, Escondido, California

　　　Multiplicity, Group Exhibition of Prints and Multiples, Angles Gallery, Los Angeles

　　　Summer Group Exhibition, Leo Castelli Gallery, New York

1998　*Densité ou le musée inimaginable (density or the unimaginable museum)*, Domaine de Kerguéhennec Centre d'Art Contemporain, Bignan, France

　　　PhotoImage: Printmaking 60s to 90s, Museum of Fine Arts, Boston. Traveled to Baltimore Museum of Art, Baltimore, Maryland; and Des Moines Art Center, Des Moines, Iowa

　　　Works from the Collection II, Magasin 3, Stockholm Konsthall, Stockholm

1997　*5th Anniversary Celebration: Contemporary Art from the Frederick R. Weisman Collections*, Frederick R. Weisman Museum of Art, Pepperdine University, Malibu, California

　　　The Artists of Castelli Gallery 1957–1997. Forty Years of Exploration and Innovation. Part Two, Leo Castelli Gallery, New York

　　　Book Obsession, Tel Aviv Museum of Art, Tel Aviv

　　　A Decade of Collecting: Selected Recent Acquisitions in Contemporary Drawing, The Museum of Modern Art, New York

　　　Magasin 3 Stockholm Kunsthalle at Arken. Selections from the Collection, Arken Museum for Moderne Kunst, Copenhagen

　　　Objects of Desire: The Modern Still Life, The Museum of Modern Art, New York. Traveled to Hayward Gallery, London

　　　Selections from the Collection, The Museum of Modern Art, New York

　　　Summer Group Exhibition, Gagosian Gallery, Los Angeles

　　　Sunshine & Noir. Art in LA 1960–1997, Louisiana Museum of Modern Art, Humlebaek, Denmark; Kunstmuseum Wolfsburg, Wolfsburg, Germany; Museo d'Arte Contemporanea, Castello di Rivoli, Rivoli, Italy; and Armand Hammer Museum of Art at the University of Los Angeles, Los Angeles

1996　*Avant première d'un musée—Le Musée d'Art Contemporain de Gand*, The Institut Néerlandais, Paris

　　　From Figure to Object: A Century of Sculptors' Drawings, Karsten Schubert, London

　　　The Human Body in Contemporary American Sculpture, Gagosian Gallery, New York

Leo Castelli: An Exhibition in Honor of His Gallery and Artists, Gagosian Gallery, Los Angeles

New Grounds Prints and Multiples, Contemporary Art Museum, Graphicstudio, University of South Florida, Tampa, Florida

The Panza di Biumo Collection: some artists from the 80s and 90s, Museo d'Arte Moderna e Contemporanea di Trento e Rovereto, Trento, Italy

Still Life, University Gallery, University of Massachusetts at Amherst, Amherst, Massachusetts

Twentieth-Century Sculpture at the White House, Washington, D.C.

1995 *Micromegas*, The American Center, Paris. Traveled to The Israel Museum, Jerusalem

Richard Artschwager, Edward Ruscha, Robert Therrien: Selected Works, Leo Castelli Gallery, New York

1994 *inSITE 94*, San Diego, California, and Tijuana, Mexico

1993 *From the Hand to the Head, the Theoretical Object*, Domaine de Kerguéhennec, Bignan, France

Galerij Micheline Szwajcer, Antwerp, Belgium

Le Jardin de la Vierge, Espace 251 Nord, Brussels

Mariusz Kruk, John McCracken, Robert Therrien, Galerie Froment & Putnam, Paris

1992 *Documenta IX*, Kassel, Germany

Guy Mees, Harald Klingelhöller, Richard Prince, Robert Therrien, Galerij Micheline Szwajcer, Antwerp, Belgium

Panza di Biumo, The Eighties and the Nineties from the Collection, Museo Cantonale d'Arte, Lugano, Switzerland

Surface to Surface, Barbara Krakow Gallery, Boston

1991 *Lafrenz Collection, Hamburg*, Neues Museum Weserburg, Bremen, Germany. Traveled to The Irish Museum of Modern Art, Dublin

Minimalism and Post-Minimalism: Drawing Distinctions, Hood Museum of Art, Dartmouth College, Hanover, New Hampshire. Traveled to The Parrish Art Museum, Southampton, New York

Summer Group Show, Leo Castelli Gallery, New York

1990 *Objects of Potential, Five American Sculptors from the Anderson Collection*, Wiegand Gallery, College of Notre Dame, Belmont, California

1989 *I Triennal de Dibuix Joan Miró*, Fundació Joan Miró, Barcelona

Art in Place: Fifteen Years of Acquisitions, Whitney Museum of American Art, New York

Dreams and Other Works on Paper, Leo Castelli Gallery, New York

Sculpture 1960s–1980s, Greenberg Gallery, St. Louis, Missouri

1988 *Lynda Benglis, John Chamberlain, Joel Fisher, Mel Kendrick, Robert Therrien*, Magasin 3, Stockholm Konsthall, Stockholm

Sculpture Inside Outside, Walker Art Center, Minneapolis. Traveled to Museum of Fine Arts, Houston

Skulptur. Material & Abstraktion: 2 x 5 Positionen. Aargauer Kunsthaus Aarau, Aarau, Switzerland. Traveled to Musée Cantonal des Beaux-Arts, Lausanne, Switzerland; and City Gallery, New York

Vital Signs, Whitney Museum of American Art, New York

1987 *Abstract Expressions Recent Sculpture*, Lannan Museum, Lake Worth, Florida

Leo Castelli y sus Artistas, Centro Cultural Arte Contemporaneo, Polanco, Mexico

small scale sculpture LARGE SCALE SCULPTURE, Atlanta College of Art, Atlanta

1986 *Abstraction*, Hans Strelow Gallery, Düsseldorf, Germany

A Collecting Partnership: Highlights of California Art Since 1945, Newport Harbor Art Museum, Newport Beach, California

Major Acquisitions since 1980: Selected Paintings and Sculpture, Whitney Museum of American Art, New York

New Work by Kosuth, Morris, Oldenburg, Serra, Stella, Therrien. Selected History of Contemporary Art, 1945–86, Leo Castelli Gallery, New York

Pasadena Collects: The Art of Our Time, Art Center College of Design, Pasadena, California

Structure to Resemblance: Work by Eight American Sculptors, Albright-Knox Art Gallery, Buffalo, New York

1985 *8 Artists: The Minimal Image*, John C. Stoller & Co., Minneapolis

Biennial Exhibition, Whitney Museum of American Art, New York

1984 *Awards in the Visual Arts—3*. San Antonio Museum of Art, San Antonio, Texas. Traveled to Loch Haven Art Center, Orlando, Florida; Cranbrook Academy of Art, Bloomfield Hills, Michigan

La Biennale di Venezia, XLI Esposizione Internazionale d'Arte. Aperto '84, Venice

Four Sculptors, Ace Gallery, Los Angeles

1982 *Quiet Commitment*, Fisher Gallery, University of Southern California, Los Angeles

1980 *Sculpture in California, 1975–80*, San Diego Museum of Art, San Diego, California

1977 *Four Californians. Visual Incantations*, La Jolla Museum of Contemporary Art, La Jolla, California

Los Angeles Contemporary Exhibitions, Los Angeles

1975 *Nine Artists*, Occidental College, Los Angeles

1974 *Young California*, Ruth S. Schaffner Gallery, Los Angeles

selected bibliography

XLI Esposizione Internazionale d'Arte. Exh. cat. Venice: La Biennale di Venezia, 1984. Essay by Suzanne Muchnic.

Abstract Expressions: Recent Sculpture. Exh. cat. Lake Worth, Florida: Lannan Museum, 1987. Essay by Bonnie Clearwater.

Acquisitions. Exh. cat. New York: Whitney Museum of American Art, 1989.

Art in Place, Fifteen Years of Acquisitions. Exh. cat. New York: Whitney Museum of American Art, 1989. Essays by Tom Armstrong and Susan Larson.

Awards in the Visual Arts-3. Exh. cat. San Antonio, Texas: San Antonio Museum of Art, 1984. Essay by John Yau.

Baker, Kenneth. "Prime Displays of Anti-Minimalist Art on Peninsula." *San Francisco Chronicle* (21 March 1990): E3.

Biennial Exhibition. Exh. cat. New York: Whitney Museum of American Art, 1985. Essay by Vivien Raynor.

Brenson, Michael. "Coming to Grips with Content." *The New York Times* (19 June 1988): B33.

Carnegie International 1995. Exh. cat. Pittsburgh: Carnegie Museum of Art, 1995. Essay by Richard Armstrong.

Delgado, Michael. "Pick of the Week: 'In Context.'" *L.A. Weekly* (23–29 March 1984): 100.

Documenta IX. Exh. cat. Kassel, Germany: Museum Fridericianum Kassel, 1992. Essay by David Pagel.

Doove, Edith. "Robert Therrien." *Metropolis M,* no. 2 (1995).

Drohojowska, Hunter, "Pick of the Week: Robert Therrien." *L.A. Weekly* (12–18 March 1982): 101.

——. "One Person Shows 'In Context.'" *Los Angeles Herald Examiner* (23 March 1984): 27.

——. "Therrien at Flow Ace." *L.A. Weekly* (8–14 March 1985): 47.

Four Californians. Exh. cat. La Jolla, California: La Jolla Museum of Contemporary Art, 1977. Essay by Richard Armstrong.

From Figure to Object: A Century of Sculptors' Drawings. Exh. cat. London: Karsten Schubert, 1996. Essay by Richard Shone.

Glueck, Grace. "Review." *The New York Observer* (13 March 1995): 18.

Hicks, Emily. "To Discourage Preconceptions." *Artweek* 13, no. 12 (27 March 1982): 7.

Huici, Fernando. "El eco de la imagen." *El Pais* (16 December 1991): 36.

——. "Robert Therrien, en el Centro de Arte Reina Sofía, Minimal Romántico." *El Pais* (13 December 1991): 9.

Iannaccone, Carmine. "Robert Therrien." *art issues,* no. 26 (January/February 1993): 40.

Individuals: A Selected History of Contemporary Art, 1945–86. Exh. cat. Los Angeles: The Museum of Contemporary Art, 1986. Essay by Kathleen Shields.

Johnson, Ken. "Robert Therrien at Angles." *Art in America* 81, no. 1 (January 1993): 108–109.

Keefe, Jeffrey. "Los Angeles, Robert Therrien, Ruth S. Schaffner Gallery." *Artforum* 16, no. 5 (January 1978): 75–76.

Kimmelman, Michael. "Robert Therrien." *The New York Times* (20 May 1988): C24.

Knight, Christopher. "MOCA's second show reveals a museum in search of a future." *Los Angeles Herald Examiner* (25 March 1984): E1, E9.

——. "New Border Customs." *Los Angeles Times* (1 October 1994).

Lambrecht, Luk. "Interessante tentoonstellingen in de Antwerpse galerijs." *De Morgen* (10 March 1995).

Leo Castelli y sus Artistas, XXX Años De Promocion del Arte Contemporáneo. Exh. cat. Polanco, Mexico: Centro Cultural Arte Contemporáneo, A.C, 1987. Essay by Lisa Tuttle.

Lynda Benglis, John Chamberlain, Joel Fisher, Mel Kendrick, Robert Therrien. Exh. cat. Stockholm: Magasin 3, Stockholm Konsthall, 1988. Essay by Carter Ratcliff.

Mallinson, Constance. "Robert Therrien at The Museum of Contemporary Art." *Art in America* 72, no. 9 (October 1984): 211, 213.

Marmer, Nancy. "Robert Therrien." *Los Angeles Times* (21 October 1977): Part IV, 10.

Menzies, Neal. "Beautiful Mysterious Objects." *Artweek* 15, no. 18 (5 May 1984): 3.

Morgan, Robert C. "American Sculpture and the Search for a Referent." *Arts Magazine* 62, no.

3 (November 1987): 20–23.

Morgan, Stuart. "Past Present Future, Count Giuseppe Panza di Biumo interviewed by Morgan Stuart." *Artscribe International,* no, 76 (Summer 1989): 53–59.

Muchnic, Suzanne. "Robert Therrien." *Artweek* 6, no. 44 (20 December 1975): 7.

——. "Four Abstractionists—Krebs, Spence, Therrien, Georgesco." *Artweek* 8, no. 28 (27 August 1977): 8.

——. "Robert Therrien." *Artweek* 8, no. 37 (5 November 1977): 16.

——. "Le Va, Therrien, Two Extremes." *Los Angeles Times* (9 April 1980): Part IV, 4.

——. "Bigger Is Better at Contemporary Museum." *Los Angeles Times* (15 March 1984): F1,11.

New Grounds Prints and Multiples. Exh. cat. Tampa, Florida: Contemporary Art Museum, University of South Florida, 1997. Essays by Hank Hine and Margaret Miller.

Objects of Desire: The Modern Still Life. Exh. cat. New York: The Museum of Modern Art, 1997. Essay by Margit Rowell.

Olejarz, Harold. "Robert Therrien." *Arts Magazine* 53, no. 4 (December 1978): 32–33.

Pagel, David. "Looking at Ourselves." *Los Angeles Times* (22 October 1992): F9-F10.

Painting and Sculpture Acquisitions, 1973-86. Exh. cat. New York: Whitney Museum of American Art, 1986. Essay by Kathleen Shields.

The Panza di Biumo Collection: some artists from the 80s and 90s. Exh. cat. Trento, Italy: Museo d'Arte Moderna e Contemporanea di Trento e Rovereto, 1996. Essays by Gabriella Belli and Giuseppe Panza di Biumo; entries and biographies.

Panza di Biumo, Giuseppe. "La Biennale." *Domus,* no. 652 (July–August 1984): 72.

Panza di Biumo, The Eighties and the Nineties from the Collection. Exh. cat. Lugano, Switzerland: Museo Cantonale d'Arte, 1992. Essay by Giuseppe Panza di Biumo.

Peterson, William. "Robert Therrien: With Responses by Robert Creeley." *Artspace* 13, no. 2 (May/June 1989): 58–63.

PhotoImage: Printmaking 60s to 90s. Exh. cat. Boston: Museum of Fine Arts, 1998. Essay by Clifford S. Ackley, 1998.

Pincus, Robert L. "Sense of Dimension: InSITE 94 Has Imaginations Big Enough for Depot's Space." *The San Diego Union-Tribune* (27 September 1994).

Plagens, Peter. "Nine Biennial Notes." *Art in America* 73, no. 7 (July 1985): 115–118.

Raynor, Vivien. "Art: Robert Therrien Is Showing 28 Works." *The New York Times* (6 June 1986): C26.

Robert Therrien. Exh. cat. Los Angeles: The Museum of Contemporary Art, 1984. Essay by Julia Brown.

Robert Therrien. Exh. cat. Madrid: Museo Nacional, Centro de Arte Reina Sofía, 1991. Essays by Margit Rowell; biography and bibliography.

Rowell, Margit. "Ordinaire-extraordinaire: l'oeuvre de Robert Therrien." *Art Press,* no. 164 (December 1991): 40–44.

Russell, John. "Art: Whitney Presents its Biennial Exhibition." *The New York Times* (22 March 1985): C23.

Salzman, Gregory. "Robert Therrien: Brood Nest." *Parachute* (April–June 1997): 14–17.

Saunders, Wade. "Talking Objects: Interviews with Ten Younger Sculptors." *Art in America* 73, no. 11 (November 1985): 136–137.

Sculpture in California, 1975–80. Exh. cat. San Diego, California: San Diego Museum of Art, 1980. Essay by Richard Armstrong.

Sculpture Inside Outside. Exh. cat. Minneapolis: Walker Art Center, 1988. Essays by Martin Friedman and Peter Boswell.

Seldis, Henry. "Robert Therrien at Ruth S. Schaffner." *Los Angeles Times* (19 December 1975): Part IV, 10.

Skulptur/Sculpture. Material und Abstraktion 2 x 5 Positionen. Exh. cat. Geneva: Black Cat Productions, 1988. Essays by Corinne Diserens, Lars Muller, Beat Wismer, and Stephan Kunz.

small scale sculpture LARGE SCALE SCULPTURE. Exh. cat. Atlanta: Atlanta College of Art, 1987. Essay by Lisa Tuttle.

Smith, Roberta. "Robert Therrien." *The New York Times* (21 June 1991): C20.

Solana, Almudena. "Madrid's Triangle of Art." *Rhonda Iberia* (February 1992): 60–72.

——. "An unclassificable sculptor." *Ronda Iberia* (February 1992): 11.

Southern California: The Conceptual Landscape. Exh. cat. Madison, Wisconsin: Madison Art Center, 1994. Essay by Peter Frank.

Stapen, Nancy. "The new art objects and ideas." *The Boston Globe* (4 April 1991).

Structure to Resemblance, Work by Eight American Sculptors. Exh. cat. Buffalo, New York: Albright-Knox Art Gallery, 1987. Essay by Michael Auping.

Sunshine and Noir. Art in Los Angeles 1960–97. Exh. cat. Humlebaek, Denmark: Louisiana Museum of Modern Art, 1997. Essay by William R. Hackman.

Tanner, Marcia. "Vistas into Shared Terrain." *Artweek* 21, no. 9 (8 March 1990): 1.

I Triennal de Dibuix Joan Miró. Exh. cat. Barcelona: Fundació Joan Miró, 1989. Essays by Margit Rowell and Rosa Queralt.

Upshaw, Reagan. "Robert Therrien at Leo Castelli." *Art in America,* no. 5 (May 1994): 108.

Valenzuela, Regina." El escultor Robert Therrien expone por primera vez en España." *El Pais* (28 November 1991): 39.

Vital Signs. Exh. cat. New York: Whitney Museum of American Art, 1988. Essay by Lisa Phillips.

Wilson, William. "Young California." *Los Angeles Times* (22 March 1974): Part IV, 11.

——. "'In Context' The Subtext Is Religion." *Los Angeles Times* (22 April 1984): 85–86.

ROY **thurston**

born in Huntington, New York, 1949
lives and works in Los Angeles
education M.F.A., Claremont Graduate School, Claremont, California, 1974
B.A., Colorado College, Colorado Springs, Colorado, 1971

one-person exhibitions

1996 Charlotte Jackson Fine Art, Santa Fe, New Mexico
1995 Thomas Solomon's Garage, Los Angeles
1991 Kiyo Higashi Gallery, Los Angeles
1989 Kiyo Higashi, Gallery, Los Angeles
1985 Todd Madigan Gallery, California State College, Bakersfield, California

selected group exhibitions

1998 Hunsaker/Schlesinger Gallery, Santa Monica, California
Patricia Sweetow Gallery, San Francisco
1997 *5 Easy Pieces, 5th Annual Invitational Exhibition,* Nevada Institute of Contemporary Art, Las Vegas
Selections from the Panza Acquisition, organized by Museo Cantonale d'Arte Lugano, Sa Llonja, Palma di Mallorca, Spain
1995 *The Panza di Biumo Donation: European and American Art '83–'93,* Museo Cantonale d'Arte, Lugano, Switzerland
1994 *Plane/Structures,* Otis College of Art and Design, Los Angeles
1992 *Panza di Biumo: The Eighties and Nineties from the Collection,* Museo Cantonale d'Arte, Lugano, Switzerland
1990 *Minimal 1960–1990,* Cirrus Gallery, Los Angeles
1989 *Quiet,* Oakland Museum, Oakland, California
1987 Burnett Miller Gallery, Los Angeles
1986 Angles Gallery, Santa Monica, California
1975 *Selected West Coast Painters,* Miami-Dade University, Miami, Florida

selected bibliography

Bensley, Lis. "Roy Thurston Unlocks a Translucent Realm." *The Santa Fe New Mexican* (13 September 1996).

Colpitt, Frances. "Roy Thurston: Palpable Surface/Elusive Depth." *Artspace* 15, nos. 4 & 5 (Summer 1991): 57.

Crockett, Tobey. "Roy Thurston at Thomas Solomon's Garage." *Art in America* 83, no. 6 (June 1995): 110–111.

Kornblau, Gary. "Roy Thurston at Kiyo Higashi." *Art issues,* no. 10 (March/April 1990): 24.

McKenna, Christine. "Cirrus Offers Minimalism with a West Coast Slant." *Los Angeles Times* (12 December 1990): F7.

Pagel, David. "Roy Thurston at Thomas Solomon's Garage." *Art issues,* no. 37 (March/April 1995): 44.

"A Text by Roy Thurston." *Spazio Humano* (February 1987).

The copyright information below applies for each work reproduced by the following artists:

© Carl Andre/Licensed by VAGA, New York, NY
Jean Fautrier: © 1999 Artists Rights Society (ARS), New York/ADAGP, Paris
© 1999 Robert Irwin/Artists Rights Society (ARS), New York
© 1999 Sol LeWitt/Artists Rights Society (ARS), New York
Robert Rauschenberg: © Untitled Press, Inc./Licensed by VAGA, New York, NY
© James Rosenquist/Licensed by VAGA, New York, NY
Mark Rothko: © 1998 Kate Rothko Prizel & Christopher Rothko/Artists Rights Society (ARS), New York
© George Segal/Licensed by VAGA, New York, NY
© 1999 Richard Serra/Artists Rights Society (ARS), New York
Antoni Tàpies: © 1999 Artists Rights Society (ARS), New York/ADAGP, Paris
Robert Therrien: © 1999 Artists Rights Society (ARS), New York/ADAGP, Paris
© Andy Warhol Foundation for the Visual Arts/Artists Rights Society (ARS), New York

All photographs appear courtesy of the artists and/or owners of the works. The following list, keyed to page numbers, applies to photographs for which a separate acknowledgement is due:

© Archivio Ugo Mulas, pp. 2, 10, 16 both; Photo by Paula Goldman, pp. 22, 89, 91, 131; Photograph © 1999 The Museum of Modern Art, New York, pp. 24 top; Getty Research Institute, Research Library 940004. Photo by Giuseppe Panza di Biumo, p. 32; Squidds & Nunns, pp. 36 left, 51, 55, 57, 60 bottom, 61, 62, 63, 64 top, 65, 68, 69, 70, 72, 74 both, 75 right, 76, 78, 80 bottom, 82, 86, 87, 88, 93, 94, 95, 96, 97, 98, 100, 101, 102, 103, 112, 115, 117, 118 bottom, 119, 120, 121, 122, 123, 124, 125, 126, 127, 135 left; Photo by Ivan Dalla Tana, p. 40; © The Solomon R. Guggenheim Foundation, New York, pp. 42 (Photograph by David Heald, FN 54.1387), 132 (Photograph by Sally Ritts, FN 91.3699), 135 right (FN 91.3867 a,b); Photo by Valerie Walker, Los Angeles, pp. 50, 52, 54, 105, 106, 107, 111; Fredrik Nilsen, p. 53; © Douglas M. Parker Studio, Los Angeles, pp. 75 left, 79 both, 73, 77, 80 top, 81, 176, 177, 207, 209; Brian Forrest, pp. 59, 60 top, 64 bottom, 66, 67, 83, 92, 108, 109, 110, 113, 147, 151 both, 153, 166, 167, 169, 172, 204 both, 205, 211, 213 left, 214 right, 215 both; © William Nettles, Los Angeles, p. 134; © Giorgio Colombo, Milan, pp. 136, 148; Photo by D. James Dee, pp. 139, 196, 197, 198; Courtesy L.A. Louver Gallery, Venice, California, pp. 195, 197, 198, 200, 201; and Photo © Dorothy Zeidman, p. 206.